ELLIOTT COUES

ELLIOTT COUES

NATURALIST AND FRONTIER HISTORIAN

PAUL RUSSELL CUTRIGHT
and
MICHAEL J. BRODHEAD

UNIVERSITY OF ILLINOIS PRESS
Urbana   Chicago   London

Publication of this work was made possible in part by a grant from the Board of Regents of the University of Nevada

Frontispiece: Elliott Coues, about fifty years old
(From Coues' edition of the Henry-Thompson journals, 1897)

LIBRARY OF CONGRESS CATALOGING IN PUBLICATION DATA

Cutright, Paul Russell, 1897–
    Elliott Coues: naturalist and frontier historian.
    Bibliography: p.
    Includes index.
    1. Coues, Elliott, 1842–1899. 2. Ornitholo-
gists—United States—Biography. 3. Historians—
United States—Biography. I. Brodhead, Michael J.,
joint author.
QL31.C74C87   598.092'4 [B]   80-12424
ISBN 0-252-00802-2

For
RICHARD AND ELIZABETH BRODHEAD
WITH LOVE AND GRATITUDE FROM
THEIR SON, MICHAEL J. BRODHEAD
and for
CHALMERS AND LORETTA PEAIRS,
A PERENNIAL SOURCE OF PRIDE AND JOY
TO THEIR UNCLE,
PAUL RUSSELL CUTRIGHT

CONTENTS

FOREWORD

DEAN AMADON

Lamont Curator Emeritus of Ornithology
American Museum of Natural History
New York City

Elliott Coues, a gifted scientist and brilliant stylist, will always retain his rank as one of the greatest of ornithologists. This was reflected anew in 1972 when the American Ornithologists' Union established a citation of merit for innovative work in that science to be called the Coues Award.

Three works in particular brought Coues eminence in ornithology: *Birds of the Northwest*, *Birds of the Colorado Valley*, and *Key to North American Birds*. The last went through six editions; the fifth and sixth were illustrated by the great Louis Agassiz Fuertes, whose genius Coues had at once recognized and fostered. The *Field Ornithology*, a companion piece to the *Key*, will always be treasured for its pithy advice to field men, in whatever branch of science.

Coues' erudition would suggest the cloistered scholar, but for years he was an Army surgeon at lonely outposts on the western frontier. Back east, he would be found at his desk writing "as though his life depended on it," to quote one visitor. In spare moments he compiled and saw through the press the four parts of his voluminous, scholarly, and valuable "Ornithological Bibliography."

Thus it comes as no surprise to learn that the ornithologist, indeed anyone with an interest in birds, still treasures the writings of Elliott Coues, not only as science but also as literature.

PREFACE

At the close of the nineteenth century Elliott Coues was one of the best-known figures in the scientific world, not alone in America but abroad as well. Since his death in 1899, however, there has been very little published mention of him, and it is therefore not surprising that today Coues is virtually unknown except to scientists—and to some historians—and known even to them as little more than a frequently recurring name in technical literature.

It is our purpose in this work to make more available to the general reader and the professional scientist and historian alike the life story of this colorful and influential American scientist.

Elliott Coues (pronounced "Cows") was born in Portsmouth, New Hampshire, his mother having been a Strawberry Banke Yankee and his father of Channel Islands stock. He lived in Washington, D.C., from an early age and was educated there, both formally, at Columbian College (now George Washington University), and less formally through much time spent in the then young Smithsonian Institution. After taking a medical degree, he joined the Army as a surgeon, spending a good many years during and after the Civil War at various border and frontier posts in the American West. Long before he completed his Army service, a period lasting twenty years, he had established himself as one of America's foremost ornithologists and systematic zoologists.

Apart from the tale of Coues' erratic and intense personal life, the chief interest in his biography must lie in his prodigious output as a scientific writer and taxonomist, in numerous collateral areas as well as in his primary field of ornithological nomenclature, and as an editor, lexicographer, historian, and general scientific gadfly.

We hope that the story we have depicted of Elliott Coues, drawn from the enormous volume of material resulting from his work, and from his dealings with his professional colleagues, friends, and foes, may repay the attention of the general reader as well as of scientists who follow, *ceteris paribus*, in Coues' wide-ranging footsteps.

For information and advice we are indebted to many historians, scientists, archivists, and librarians, and to the several institutions they represent:

ACADEMY OF NATURAL SCIENCES OF PHILADELPHIA
    Susan Klimley, head librarian
    Mary Trout, assistant in ornithology
AMERICAN MUSEUM OF NATURAL HISTORY, New York City
    Mrs. W. Alston Flagg, associate, department of ornithology
AMERICAN ORNITHOLOGISTS' UNION, Washington, D.C.
    George E. Watson, secretary
    Dorothea Curcio, assistant to the secretary
AMERICAN PHILOSOPHICAL SOCIETY, Philadelphia
    Murphy Smith, associate librarian
ARIZONA HISTORICAL SOCIETY, Tucson
    C. L. Sonnichsen, director of publications
    A. Tracy Row, assistant editor
BEAVER COLLEGE, Glenside, Pa.
    Josephine Charles, assistant librarian
    Mary Sturgeon, associate professor emerita of English
GEORGE WASHINGTON UNIVERSITY, Washington, D.C.
    Frederick R. Houser, registrar
    Elmer Louis Kayser, university historian
    Sabina Jacobson, reference librarian
GONZAGA COLLEGE HIGH SCHOOL, Washington, D.C.
    Clement J. Petrik, dean of studies
IDAHO STATE HISTORICAL SOCIETY, Boise
    Judith Austin, research historian
KANSAS STATE HISTORICAL SOCIETY, Topeka
    Nyle Miller, director
    Joseph W. Snell, director
LIBRARY OF CONGRESS, Washington, D.C.
    Elizabeth H. Auman, reference librarian, music division
McGILL UNIVERSITY, Montreal, Canada
    Mrs. Thomas Alison, librarian
MINNESOTA HISTORICAL SOCIETY, St. Paul
    Ruby J. Shields, chief of reference, manuscripts department
    Roger Barr, reference associate
MONTANA HISTORICAL SOCIETY, Helena
    Harriet C. Meloy, librarian
    Rex C. Myers, reference librarian
MUSEUM OF NEW MEXICO, Santa Fe
    Stephany Eger, librarian

NEVADA STATE LIBRARY, Carson City
  Joseph Anderson, state librarian
NEW MEXICO STATE LIBRARY, Santa Fe
  Norma R. Lee, assistant southwest librarian
PEABODY MUSEUM, Salem, Mass.
  Sarah F. Ingalls, curator of natural history
PENNSYLVANIA HISTORICAL AND MUSEUM COMMISSION, Harrisburg
  Carol W. Tallman, librarian
SMITHSONIAN INSTITUTION ARCHIVES, Washington, D.C.
  Richard H. Lytle, archivist
  William A. Deiss, associate archivist
  James A. Steed, assistant archivist
  Theodore S. Bober, museum specialist, division of birds
SOUTH DAKOTA DEPARTMENT OF EDUCATION AND CULTURAL AFFAIRS, Pierre
  Janice Fleming, librarian
STATE HISTORICAL SOCIETY OF IOWA, Iowa City
  Rolene Britson, reference librarian
  Karen Laughlin, librarian
STATE HISTORICAL SOCIETY OF WISCONSIN, Madison
  James L. Hansen, genealogy/reference librarian
UNIVERSITY OF CHICAGO
  Robert W. Allison, assistant curator for manuscripts
UNIVERSITY OF KANSAS LIBRARIES, Lawrence
  Alexandra Mason, Spencer librarian, Kenneth Spencer research library
UNIVERSITY OF NEVADA LIBRARY, Reno
  Harold G. Morehouse, director
UNIVERSITY OF OKLAHOMA, Norman
  George Miksch Sutton, George Lynn Cross research professor of zoology emeritus
UNIVERSITY OF WYOMING, Laramie
  Gene Gressley, director, western history research center

We wish to thank the following institutions for permission to use letters in their files written by Elliott Coues: Academy of Natural Sciences of Philadelphia, American Museum of Natural History, American Philosophical Society, Arizona Historical Society, McLennan Library of McGill University, Minnesota Historical Society, Smithsonian Institution Archives, University of Kansas Libraries, University of California (Berkeley and Davis), and Beinecke Library of Yale University.

For permission to reprint portions of our own previously published books and magazine articles, we express our gratitude to: Arizona Historical Society, *Io*, *New England Quarterly*, *Colorado Maga-*

zine, and University of Oklahoma Press. Also, we are grateful to the American Ornithologists' Union for permission to use previously unpublished material in their files.

It is a pleasure, as well as a duty, to acknowledge the encouragement and assistance of the following:

Anne Amaral	James C. Malin
Robert Armstrong	Helen Mitchell
Walter J. Breckenridge	Linda P. Newman
Maurice G. Brooks	Mary Nichols
Mrs. William A. Buell, Jr.	Richard M. Palcanis
Nicholas M. Cady	Mr. and Mrs. M. E. Phillips
E. W. Calderone	Robert Poor
Kenneth J. Carpenter	Sharon Prengaman
Joan L. Chambers	William S. Reese
John Davis	John N. Ritenhouse
Ralph W. Dexter	Terry E. Rowe
Pamela Dyer	Fred A. Ryser
Catherine S. Fowler	John T. Sharp
Noreen S. Gilb	Karen J. Shilts
Ellen M. Guerricagoitia	Keir B. Sterling
Naoma M. Hainey	Margaret Supancheck
E. Raymond Hall	Edward H. Taylor
Yoshi Hendricks	Roseline Tollefson
Fred R. Heryer	Carrie Townley
Kenneth L. Irby	Thomas B. Turner
Donna Jackson	Dorothy M. Vaughan
Lenore Kosso	James W. Wier
Keith Lummis	Roy G. Williams

University of Nevada (Reno) History Faculty

We extend our very great thanks to Donald Jackson, Colorado Springs, Colo., for steering our thoughts toward Elliott Coues; to William P. Coues, Boston, Mass., and Prouts Neck, Me., who, we are certain, cannot possibly realize the importance to us of the unpublished manuscripts of Elliott Coues he magnanimously made available for our use; to C. A. Peairs, Jr., Westboro, Mass., for introducing us to William P. Coues; to Marjorie Darling, dean emerita of admissions, Beaver College, for bettering our syntax; and to Dean Amadon, Lamont curator emeritus of ornithology, American Museum of Natural History, New York City, who gratuitously read our entire manuscript and, in instances where we had strayed ornithologically, set our course aright.

Finally, our full and enduring appreciation to our wives, Hwa-di Chang Brodhead and Gladys Pennington Cutright (deceased), for their understanding, guidance, and encouragement.

ELLIOTT COUES

CHAPTER I

On the Coast of Labrador

On June 23, 1860, the schooner *Charmer* left its berth at Newburyport, Massachusetts, and set sail for Labrador. In addition to its crew, the vessel carried sixteen passengers, one of whom was Elliott Coues, then a young man of just seventeen years who in due course would take his place among the foremost of American ornithologists of all time.

On the eve of his departure Coues, whose home was in the nation's capital, addressed a letter to his sponsor and mentor, Spencer F. Baird,[1] assistant secretary of the Smithsonian Institution, Washington, D.C.:

> Schr. Charmer, Newburyport
> Saturday, June 23
>
> Dear Sir,
>
> You no doubt are surprised at receiving another letter from me after the news I gave in my last. As soon as I received the summons I went immediately to Boston and bought the shot and alcohol—got my boxes delivered at Newburyport and went down there the same afternoon. There was a violent storm all day and night, a heavy sea over the "bar" and adverse winds prevented our sailing; yesterday Mr. Dodge received intelligence of another passenger, who has just arrived this morning, and I believe that now there is no obstacle to our starting *in a few hours.* . . .
>
> I am very much afraid that it is getting too late for the "run" of [bird] eggs, but I will do my very best. I have ever since I came away been having a pleasant time, and were I not in these peculiar circumstances, I should be perfectly contented—but as it is, the thought of *three weeks gone already* and the season so late, gives me great anxiety. But I assure you, nothing shall deter me from doing *my very best*, if we ever arrive at the "hunting grounds."
>
> Most respectfully,
> Elliott Coues[2]

Coues had made the trip from Washington by train, arriving in Boston on June 1. From other letters he wrote to Baird while waiting for the *Charmer* to sail, we learn that the train trip had taken "just 25½ hours" and that he had experienced not "the slightest difficulty or delay over the whole route." Coues reported, too, that his expenses thus far had been $15.68 and he would, of course, "keep them as low as possible."

Coues soon called on a fellow ornithologist, Dr. Thomas Brewer,[3] who dissuaded him from making a trip to Martha's Vineyard. Instead he went to Portsmouth, New Hampshire (his birthplace), where he divided his time between visiting relatives and "ransacking the woods" for birds. Before leaving Portsmouth he advised Baird that, because of the *Charmer's* delay in sailing, his funds were "really low," and that his heaviest expense had been the purchase of boots and an India rubber coat, which Mr. Dodge had told him were indispensable.

The "Mr. Dodge" alluded to by Coues was the master of the *Charmer*, John W. Dodge of Hampton Falls, New Hampshire. A few years earlier Dodge had begun expanding a profitable trading business started by his father. Each summer he had chartered a boat to carry trade goods to Labrador, where he exchanged them, at a substantial profit, for furs and other valuable commodities.

In looking ahead to the 1860 cruise, Dodge came up with an idea which, if successful, would yield additional revenue. The public learned of it from circulars which Dodge soon had printed and distributed. These read in part: "Excursion to the north [for a] . . . limited number of passengers . . . who may wish to supply their cabinets with interesting collections in Natural History, to invigorate their health, or to enjoy the pleasure of hunting and fishing, in a region abounding in game."[4] Another incentive, for those interested, would be a side trip to Cape Chidley, northernmost tip of Labrador where, on July 18, they could witness a total eclipse of the sun.

The response to Dodge's notice exceeded his most sanguine expectations. So many individuals requested passage on the *Charmer* that, to accommodate all of them, he chartered a companion vessel, the *Nautilus*. He may have been surprised, too, that the majority of those responding proved to be college students, primarily from New England schools such as Harvard, Bowdoin, and Williams. Among these students, Coues was something of an outsider; he was from Columbian College (now George Washington University) in Washington, D.C., where he had just completed his junior year of study.

At least three of the collegians aboard the *Charmer* that summer kept journals, and these three in years ahead distinguished themselves as naturalists: Alpheus S. Packard, Jr.,[5] of Bowdoin, Charles Hallock of Williams,[6] and Elliott Coues.

To the history of any expedition multiple accounts have special worth. Each journalist, with a different set of eyes, sees and reports incidents overlooked by others. And so it proved to be with this 1860 expedition to Labrador. As becomes evident further along in this chapter, Packard's and Hallock's journals provide us with useful information entirely missing from Coues', and vice versa. It may be mentioned here, too, that in future years the paths of Packard, Hallock, and Coues often crossed, as is so often the case when men have interests in common.

2

In the days ahead the *Charmer* skirted the coasts of Maine and Nova Scotia and on June 29 arrived at the Gut of Canso, the narrow channel separating Nova Scotia and Cape Breton Island. Here the passengers could leave letters for a southward-bound boat, and Coues reported again to Baird:

> I have just a moment here to spare before the pilot takes our letters. . . . We made Cape Sable [southern tip of Nova Scotia] day before yesterday morning; since then have kept Nova Scotia in view just on the horizon; and at the moment are just entering the Gut of Canso. I got over my [sea]sickness entirely the third day out, but it was *awful* while it lasted. . . .
>
> The birds I have seen already, though of course I could not get at them, are plenty of *Thalass. Wilsonii*,[7] several *Puffinus Anglorum*,[8] I believe, and some gulls. . . . I don't know when I shall commence collecting, but I hope it is not far out.

Once through the Gut of Canso, the *Charmer* entered the Gulf of St. Lawrence and then bore north-northeast to Sloop Harbor, an inlet on the southern coast of Labrador. Here, on July 3, ten days out of Newburyport, the *Charmer* made its first stop. Coues placed Sloop Harbor "a few miles south of Little Meccatina,"[9] one of the many small islands crowding the southern coastline of Labrador off the mouth of the St. Augustin River.[10] After a layover of three days at Sloop Harbor, in which time Coues seems to have collected more bird eggs than during the entire remaining weeks of the cruise, the *Charmer* left the harbor and, "passing the Murre Rocks, where the *Uria lomvia* [thick-billed murre] was breeding in immense numbers, proceeded directly to Esquimaux Bay."[11]

Esquimaux Bay (shown on some maps as Bonne Esperance Bay) is about seventy-five miles northeast of Sloop Harbor and at the western entrance to the Strait of Belle Isle, the channel which separates Labrador from Newfoundland. It was in the vicinity of Esquimaux Bay that the *Nautilus* caught up with the *Charmer* and, after a brief rendezvous, proceeded to Cape Chidley with those passengers bent on witnessing the total eclipse of the sun. Coues elected to stay with the *Charmer*.

Coues' travels in Labrador

From Esquimaux Bay, the *Charmer* sailed through the Strait of Belle Isle to Henley Harbor, at the Atlantic entrance to the strait. Here it arrived on July 7. Leaving Henley Harbor the next day, it moved north along the eastern coast of Labrador, making stops of from one to four days at such points as Square Island Harbor, Snug Harbor, Seal Island Harbor, Dumpling Harbor, Tub Harbor, Grosswater Bay, Tucker Island Harbor, Indian Harbor, and Flatwater River. On August 2 it dropped anchor at Rigolet, a Hudson's Bay Company post on Hamilton Inlet, where it remained for a week. This was the northernmost point attained by the *Charmer*. On August 10 it left Rigolet, turned south, and, after a number of brief stops at places visited going north, arrived back at Henley Harbor nine days later. Here it lay for fourteen days until September 2, when it sailed directly to Newburyport, tying up there on September 16.[12]

3

Coastal Labrador, even in mid-summer, could present a forbidding face. Coues gave his literary bent full rein: "Fogs hang low and heavy over rock-girdled Labrador. Angry waves, palled with rage, exhaust themselves to encroach upon the stern shores, and baffled, sink back howling into the depths. Winds shriek as they course from crag to crag in mid-career, till the humble mosses that clothe the rocks crouch lower still in fear. Overhead the Sea Gulls scream as they winnow, and the Murres, all silent, ply eager oars to escape the blast."[13]

Though an austere coast, it was in summer a lively one. Wrote Charles Hallock: "Little idea has the world of the populous community to be found on the Labrador coast from the first of June to the end of September." As far up as latitude 36°, "every little harbor is filled with vessels, mostly Canadian but many United States, engaged in catching cod, hunting seals and bartering for peltries."[14]

The 1860 boreal scene, as Hallock, Coues, and others aboard the *Charmer* discovered, was further enlivened as schools of porpoises and grampuses arched gracefully through the icy waters, as bowfin, right, and other species of whales "spouted" and displayed giant caudal fins, and as multitudes of birds filled the air or overspread island surfaces like huge, animated, particolored counterpanes. Alpheus Packard, reporter from Bowdoin, was impressed with the "strange commingling of life forms in the Strait of Belle Isle; the flora and fauna of the boreal regions struggling, as it were, to displace the arctic forms established on these shore lines since the ice period."[15]

Coues' specific assignment, given him by Baird, was to collect "specimens of the birds to be found there, together with their nests and eggs, and to study their habits during the breeding season."[16] The task was an altogether pleasing one to him, the more so because most of the birds, the mergansers, murres, plovers, gannets, puffins, and many other species, were unfamiliar to him. Indeed, his enthusiasm was so great that not even the hordes of black flies and mosquitoes, ubiquitously present, seem to have dampened it. Of these unrelenting tormentors, fellow-sufferer Packard wrote: "No wonder that these entomological pests are a perfect barrier to inland travel; that few people live during the summer away from the sweep of the high winds."[17]

A few months later Coues published an article about his summer of 1860 in Labrador. In it he voiced just one complaint, and that entirely unrelated to any physical hardship: "To my great disappointment, I was not permitted to land and examine the islands and their inhabitants; our captain . . . paying no regards to the wishes of the passengers . . . not for an hour, even, would he delay, to enable us to notice the birds or to obtain specimens."[18] Not strictly true, of course, since Coues, when the *Charmer* was in port, did visit nearby islands as well as the mainland.

Coues' article, "Notes on the Ornithology of Labrador," was largely technical. At about the time it appeared, Hallock brought out another, "Three Months in Labrador." It was in a popular vein and often amusing, especially in its allusions to Coues, who, to Hallock, was always "The Professor."

If we accept Hallock's comments as true, then Coues, in his pursuit of specimens, displayed extraordinary ardor, and quickly became the subject of many a wry remark. At Sloop Harbor, for example, "the Professor was in ecstacies. He gathered pecks of eggs of every size and hue." At another station: "The Professor is skinning birds at one table, with profuse use of arsenic and gypsum. Flayed carcasses hang from a rafter above, like poultry in a meat market." At yet another Labrador spot, "The Professor was the first on shore, and, with a shout, instantly plunged into the forest in search of 'specimens'." And at Rigolet: "After pipe, the weary guests retired to sleeping quarters that had been assigned to them, but not before the Professor, in the zeal of his vocation, had innocently brought his gun to bear upon a tame raven which sat in the dusk upon the roof of an adjacent building."[19]

If Hallock's mildly derisive remarks ever came to Coues' attention, his pique, if any, was short-lived. In years ahead the two men became friends. Coues would be lavish in his praise of Hallock's editorship of the magazine *Forest and Stream* and of his lifetime labors on behalf of the preservation and propagation of wildlife.[20] And Hallock, with sense of humor undiminished, would write kindly of Coues. On one occasion, recalling the latter's breathless fervor in collecting Labrador specimens: "This was Coues' initial trip afield and he did well, stuffed birds like a Christmas cook. He was then 17 years old."[21]

Elliott Coues was not the first ornithologist to have experienced the inhospitable mutabilities of Labrador's southern coastline. Twenty-seven years earlier John James Audubon, for one, had established a base several miles southwest of Esquimaux Bay. Here he painted birds brought to him by companions, often arising at two o'clock in the morning, for, as he wrote, "We scarcely have any darkness now."[22] During this stay Audubon kept a journal (later published), and Coues, as an important preliminary to his Labrador experience, had read it carefully. Just how well he mastered it becomes evident when we read Coues' "Notes on the Ornithology of Labrador," pertinent excerpts from which we provide in succeeding pages.

Coues kept a journal of *his* trip to Labrador, but unfortunately it has been lost. That he did keep one is manifest from statements found in his "Notes on the Ornithology of Labrador," such as, "Let a short abstract from my journal describe our approach. . . ." The loss of this journal is regrettable, primarily because his published article, limited almost entirely to technical data about birds, contains virtually nothing about his personal day-to-day experiences and reflections. If available, these would almost certainly provide us with much additional information of interest and value and, at the same time, would enrich our knowledge of Coues himself as the budding young naturalist.

Sometime before Coues left Washington, he made a list of the things he, as a collector, would need for a full summer's work in the field. The list, in Coues' own handwriting, is to be found on a sheet of paper preserved by the Smithsonian Archives. It includes some thirty items in all, in three major categories: weapons and ammunition, implements and articles for making birdskins, and instruments for blowing eggs.

In category one we find listed a double-barrelled shotgun, powder, shot of different sizes (15 lbs. of no. 10, 25 lbs. of no. 6, and so on), 1,000 waterproof caps, 2,000 wads, and extra nipples and mainsprings. Under the second heading Coues listed knives and scissors (for dissecting), cotton batting (for stuffing the bird's internal cavity left by removal of all parts except the skull and long bones), arsenic (a preservative), and wrapping paper (for covering and protecting the completed birdskin). And under the third, for blowing eggs, he listed drills and blowpipes. Coues listed other items, too, such as alcohol, mouse traps, a collecting chest, and boxes to contain eggs and nests.

Once a bird had fallen to Coues' gun, his most time-consuming job as a collector, and the one requiring the greatest amount of skill, was the preparation of the conventional birdskin.[23] Initially, Coues may have learned the requisite techniques simply by following written instructions; but, if so, he later refined them by watching an experienced hand, such as Baird. The steps necessary are several, as many as twenty-five according to one ornithologist.[24] As a novice, Coues probably spent as much as an hour or more preparing a skin, and was even then dissatisfied with the end product. As he became more expert, he could complete as many as eight or ten satisfactory skins in the same length of time.

By comparison, blowing eggs was simple, though, as Coues himself once remarked, "[It] is a rather fatiguing process, more so than it might seem; the cheek muscles soon tire, and the operator actually becomes 'blown' himself."[25]

4

Coues' "Notes on the Ornithology of Labrador," written when he was only eighteen years of age, bears the marks of a naturalist of maturer years. It reveals, in one so young, a surprising knowledge of birds (including an unusual command of ornithological terminology), an ability to express himself in language both effective and appropriate, and a remarkable observational competence. The article discloses, too, that Coues possessed a marked sense of humor and a goodly measure of self-confidence. He exposed his self-confidence when taking exception to certain of the observations and conclusions Audubon had expressed in his Labrador journal. In no instance, however, did Coues do so discourteously, such was his evident admiration and respect for the eminent artist and naturalist.

A few excerpts from "Notes on the Ornithology of Labrador" will substantiate, we believe, all that we have said in commendation of the youthful Coues.

We find a good illustration of Coues' observational abilities in a paragraph he wrote about Bonaparte's gull (*Larus philadelphia*):[26] "Many of these beautiful little Gulls . . . would often hover and sport around the stern of the vessel, so close that I could plainly see the dark spot behind the eye which characterizes the immature bird of this species . . . [and] I noticed that, while flying, individuals would scratch the head and neck with their claws, which operation, however, did not seem to impede their flight in the least."

Some of Coues' remarks about the common puffin (*Fratercula arctica*) well demonstrate his engaging and vigorous style of writing at this stage of his life. In general, his writing was reportorial, without embellishment or any conscious straining for words. In later years, as we shall have abundant opportunity to see, he became a master of the felicitous phrase, a talent somewhat unexpected in a man so highly disciplined in the sciences. Of the common puffin he wrote:

> The habit of collecting in immense numbers at particular localities during the breeding season, so charactristic of the whole family of *Alcidae*

[*viz.*, auks, murres, and puffins], is a trait exhibited in the highest degree by the species now under consideration. . . . When standing on a rock or at the entrance to their burrows, they present a peculiarly grotesque appearance, such as is afforded by no other bird. Their short thick bodies, big heads, enormous brightly colored bills and red legs, give them a comical appearance, which is enhanced by their upright position and the odd nature of their movements, as they twist the head and jerk the body in various directions. . . . We could never quite restrain a laugh when we saw one "attitudinizing" on the edge of a rock.[27]

In writing of the Eskimo curlew (*Numenius borealis*), a bird of more than passing interest today because it is close to extinction, Coues provided an example of his readiness to take issue with Audubon: "His observations [on the Eskimo curlew], however, differ much from mine, in reference to the time of the arrival and departure of these birds. He states that they made their first appearance on the 29th of July, and had all left by the 12th of August; whereas, I saw none until about the latter date, and none were to be seen on the first of September."[28]

By 1860 the ornithological world had begun to think that the great auk (*Pinguinus impennis*) was no longer of this earth, that it had suffered the fate of the dodo.[29] However, the possibility existed that a few of these birds might still be found inhabiting little-known islands in the Gulf of St. Lawrence or, more likely, other islands skirting the coasts of Newfoundland or Labrador. As a consequence Baird, before Coues left Washington, had instructed him to make inquiries among the residents of Labrador trading posts about this bird. In his "Notes on the Ornithology of Labrador," Coues reported his findings: "Concerning this most extraordinary bird . . . I made most diligent inquiry of every one who might be expected to have any knowledge of it. . . . Though none of the natives of Labrador whom I interrogated had any knowledge of it, the fishermen knew immediately to what I referred when I spoke of 'Penguins'—as they are called—and all with singular unanimity agreed in designating the Funks, an island off the north-west coast of Newfoundland, as the only place where the birds were to be found. Yet I could never find a person who had actually *seen* one of the birds."[30] It is now believed that the great auk was even then extinct. According to the most authoritative ornithological source: "Last certain record of a living bird, two taken June 3, 1844, on Eldet, Iceland."[31]

In his Labrador article Coues named eighty-three species of birds he had identified while with the *Charmer*, and the list, as he said, would have been longer if the captain of the boat had been a more agreeable

man and, in the interests of science, had allowed him to visit more of
the islands.

Coues' article was well received by ornithologists. For example,
one of the foremost journals then devoted to birds said that it contained
"very interesting notes on many of the species. The most important
discoveries were *Turdus Aliciae*[32] [gray-cheeked thrush], 'breeding a-
bundantly'; *Saxicola oenanthe*[33] [wheat-ear] of Europe, 'one example';
and *Aegiothus fuscescens,* a new red-poll, 'abundant along the coast of
Labrador.'"[34]

5

With the cruise of the *Charmer* over and Coues again back in
Washington, he was able to present a sizable collection of specimens to
the Smithsonian. Accession records of that institution state that the
collection consisted of 185 birdskins and nine sets of eggs.[35]

An interesting paper to be found in the Smithsonian Archives
bears information as follows:[36]

Smithsonian Institution
Washington, D.C., Oct. 31, 1860
STATEMENT OF COST OF COUES EXPEDITION

One gun. I Krider	30.00
Powder etc.	10.72
May 31. Cash for expenses SFB[37]	50.00
Sept. 20 ” ” ” ” SFB	20.00
	110.72
Mr. Dodge's bill	108.00
	218.72

If the above statement is to be credited, the entire expense of
Coues' 1860 summer excursion to Labrador amounted to $218.72, a
relatively small outlay, it seems to us, even in those days. The sum paid,
too, for intangibles, such as Coues' continuing education. He greatly
increased his knowledge of birds; he improved his skills in all aspects of
collecting and preparing specimens; and he sharpened his eyes and
other special senses so necessary in observational competence.

By the time of his return to Washington, if not before, Elliott
Coues (who had attained his eighteenth birthday on September 9) had
determined on his life's career: he would follow in the steps of
Alexander Wilson, John James Audubon, and Spencer F. Baird.

NOTES

1. Spencer Fullerton Baird (1823-87), prominent American naturalist. As assistant secretary of the Smithsonian (1850-78) and secretary (1878-87), he was a most important influence in Elliott Coues' life. We shall have much more to say about him in succeeding chapters.

2. This and other letters from Coues to Baird used in this work are to be found in the Smithsonian Institution Archives. For those written while Baird was assistant secretary, see Record Unit 52, Assistant Secretary, Incoming Correspondence, 1850-77.

3. Thomas Mayo Brewer (1814-80), naturalist and oologist, was born in Boston, Mass., and in 1835 graduated from Harvard Medical School. He was the author of *North American Oology* (1857) and, in collaboration with Spencer F. Baird and Robert Ridgway, *A History of North American Birds* (1874).

4. Graustein, "Collegians to Labrador and Greenland" (1970), 184-85.

5. Alpheus Spring Packard, Jr. (1839-1905), naturalist, was born in Brunswick, Me., graduated from Bowdoin College (1861) and Maine Medical School (1864). He was state entomologist of Massachusetts (1871-73) and for many years, beginning in 1878, professor of zoology and geology at Brown University. He was the author of such books as *Our Common Insects* (1873) and *The Labrador Coast, a Journal of Two Summer Cruises in That Region* (1891). For a time he was also editor of the *American Naturalist*.

6. Charles Hallock (1834-1917), editor and naturalist, was a graduate of Williams College and, afterward, long-time editor of *Forest and Stream* and the author of *Sportsman's Gazette*. For more about Hallock, see Coues, "Charles Hallock" (1899), 117-18.

7. Presumably Wilson's storm petrel (*Oceanites oceanicus*), at earlier date *Thalassidroma Wilsonii*.

8. The Manx shearwater (now *Puffinus puffinus*).

9. Coues, "Notes on the Ornithology of Labrador" (1861), 215.

10. Disputes between Canadian provinces over the Labrador boundary persisted for many years. At the time of Coues' visit (1860), Sloop Harbor and the Meccatina Islands were considered to be parts of Labrador. Today they are parts of Quebec.

11. Coues, "Notes on the Ornithology of Labrador," 215.

12. This itinerary is from "Book of Dates in the Life of Elliott Coues," a small notebook in which Coues in 1896 recorded most of the more important events in his life. This book, which has been of great value to us, is currently the property of Coues' great-nephew, William P. Coues, of Boston, Mass., and Prouts Neck, Me. Hereinafter, we shall refer to it as Coues' "Book of Dates."

    On p. 215 of Coues' "Notes on the Ornithology of Labrador" occurs the statement: "On the 6th of July, the vessel left Sloop Harbor, and . . . proceeded directly to Esquimaux Bay, where the greater part of the summer was spent." The statement is at variance with the itinerary from Coues' "Book of Dates," for Coues definitely made the trip to Rigolet from Esquimaux Bay, and that portion of the overall cruise consumed two-thirds of the summer. We have been unable to resolve the discrepancy in the two statements.

13. Coues, *Birds of the Northwest* (1874), 483.

14. Hallock, "Three Months in Labrador" (1861), 594.

15. Packard, *The Labrador Coast* (1891), 62.

16. Coues, "Notes on the Ornithology of Labrador," 215.

17. Packard, *The Labrador Coast*, 75.

18. Coues, "Notes on the Ornithology of Labrador," 257.

19. Hallock, "Three Months in Labrador," 586, 746, 748, 754.

20. Coues, "Charles Hallock," 117-18.

21. McAtee, "Elliott Coues" (1954), 432.

22. Maria Audubon, ed., *Audubon and His Journals,* 2 vols. (New York: Dover, 1960), I, 371.

23. The birdskin as used by the ornithologist was prepared for study by removing most internal parts and replacing them with cotton batting or the like. One great auk skin, Dean Amadon has informed us, was stuffed with German newspapers.

24. Chapman, *Handbook of Birds of Eastern North America* (1906), 24-27.

25. Coues, *Key to North American Birds*, 5th ed. (1903), I, 40.

26. For scientific nomenclature of birds we have relied, throughout this work, on the American Ornithologists' Union's *Check-List of North American Birds*, 5th ed. (1957).

27. Coues, "Notes on the Ornithology of Labrador," 247, 251-54.

28. *Ibid.,* 236. Though the Eskimo curlew is now listed among the endangered species of birds, in 1860 Coues, while at Cape Henley, found it in "immense numbers, flying very swiftly in flocks of great extent." He wrote, too, that "they are most delicious eating, being tender, juicy, and finely flavored" (*ibid.,* 215-16).

29. The dodo (*Didus ineptus*) was a large, heavy, flightless bird found originally on the island of Mauritius. It became extinct late in the seventeenth century.

30. Coues, "Notes on the Ornithology of Labrador," 249.

31. A.O.U., *Check-List,* 245.

32. *Hylocichla minima* (Lafresnaye) of A.O.U., *Check-List.*

33. *Oenanthe oenanthe* (Linnaeus) of A.O.U., *Check-List.*

34. *Ibis,* IV (1862), 85-86. Coues' new redpoll ("*Aegiothus fuscescens* Coues, nov. sp.—Dusky Red Poll") had a short life. He himself soon admitted: "I am now inclined to the opinion that my *Aeg. fuscescens*, originally described from Labrador as a distinct species . . . will finally prove to have been based merely upon the midsummer plumage of ordinary [*Aegiothus*] *linaria*" Coues, *Birds of the Northwest,* 115). Today Coues' "Nov. sp." is *Acanthis flammea;* see W. E. Clyde Todd, *Birds of the Labrador Peninsula and Adjacent Areas* (Toronto: University of Toronto Press, 1963), 655-57.

35. Letter of Feb. 23, 1973, to authors from Theodore S. Bober, museum specialist, Division of Birds, Smithsonian Institution. Mr. Bober adds: "However, through the years at least 82 skin specimens [of Coues' Labrador collection] were sent to various collectors and museums. Therefore, although I have not checked our collections, it is safe to assume that some of these skins are still in our possession."

36. Smithsonian Archives, Record Unit 7002, Spencer F. Baird Papers, 1833-89.

37. "SFB" is, of course, the initials of Spencer F. Baird, who had approved the expenditures.

CHAPTER II

Young Naturalist on the Piscataqua

Once, in a rare genealogical moment, Elliott Coues wrote that his name was Norman-French, and that it was "still not infrequently found in the north of France, pronounced in two syllables, with the grave accent on the last: Coue-ès—Coo-ays." He went on to say that his antecedents had moved from France to the Isle of Wight, where the pronunciation had been anglicized to *Cows*, though the original spelling, except for occasional changes to *Cowes*, had been retained by the family. He had, he said, no knowledge of the derivation of the word.[1]

The first of the Coues line to come to the United States was Peter Coues, the great-grandfather of Elliott. Most biographical accounts of the family state that Peter Coues was born on the Isle of Jersey (largest of the Channel Islands) and that, about 1735, he emigrated to Portsmouth, New Hampshire. These accounts leave unmentioned the Isle of Wight but, by that omission, do not rule out the possibility that Peter Coues, after leaving the Isle of Jersey[2] and before embarking for America, resided for a time on the Isle of Wight.

Interestingly, on the northern coast of the Isle of Wight is the city of Cowes, a well-known watering place. This city, furthermore, is just across the Spithead, the narrow channel, from Portsmouth, Hampshire, England. From these circumstances one wonders if the city of Cowes had derived its name from some progenitor of Peter Coues. But apparently that was not the case. The origin of the city's name, if we can believe one explanation, goes back to the sixteenth century when Henry VIII ordered forts to be built on each side of the Medina, the river that divides the island into East Wight and West Wight. These forts were called East Cow and West Cow, because they were believed "to give such an outward display of strength they would 'cow' any invader at sight."[3]

Peter Coues, soon after he had arrived in Portsmouth, New Hampshire, met and married Mary Long, a young woman who had been born in Plymouth, England. They had two children, both sons: Peter, Jr., and George. We know little more of Peter Coues, Sr., except that he spent his remaining years in Portsmouth and died at an advanced age, about 1782.

Peter Coues, Jr., the grandfather of Elliott Coues, was born on July 30, 1736. In family records he is almost always referred to as Captain Peter Coues and thus, because of that title, is easily recognizable in records from his father. Before the American Revolution Captain Peter had spent several years at sea and, for a time, had served as an officer in the British Navy. According to one source: "It is a family tradition that one time he was sailing master of the famous *Royal George* which [later], in August 1782, capsized and sank in the roadstead at Spithead, England."[4]

Captain Peter Coues married three times. His third wife,[5] the paternal grandmother of Elliott Coues, was Rebecca Elliott—hence the recurrence of the baptismal name of Elliott in succeeding generations. Peter and Rebecca Coues had eight children, six of whom died in infancy or when quite young. The two who survived to maturity were a daughter[6] and the last-born son, Samuel Elliott Coues.

In his later years Captain Peter resided in a house on the southwest corner of State and Atkinson Streets, Portsmouth, and in this same house operated a store which sold groceries, general merchandise, and ship chandlery. He also became much involved in community affairs; for instance, he was one of the founders of the Universalist Church of Portsmouth. He died on November 29, 1818, aged eighty-two. Obituary notices in the Portsmouth newspapers agreed that he had attained a good standing among his fellows.

Samuel Elliott Coues, father of Elliott Coues, was born on June 13, 1797, presumably in the old family dwelling at State and Atkinson Streets. He received a good education before entering business as a Portsmouth merchant, and for many years was the senior partner in the firm of Coues & Goodwin; the junior partner was Ichabod Goodwin, who later served as governor of New Hampshire. According to the Portsmouth *City Directory* for 1839-40, the firm had its offices in Coues' home at 2 Livermore Street. Engaged primarily in the "foreign carrying-trade," this partnership met with substantial success. As evidence, in 1839 (if not in other years) Coues & Goodwin were sole or partial owners of at least five ships: *Isaac Newton, Marion, Mary & Susan, Sarah Parker,* and *Susannah Cumming.*[7]

While Elliott Coues' father had thus early gained prominence as a

Franklin Pierce. In a letter to Pierce, following the latter's
in 1852 as the nineteenth president of the United States,
n in his criticism of Pierce's participation in the Mexican
d *not* like your going to Mexico, but all must be allowed to
themselves. . . . Receive this as the expression of an old and
iend. . . . Remember I can wield a pen but not a sword, and
n, I would do; and more."[12]

nuel Elliott Coues was married twice, first to Clara Sargent
.[13] His second wife was Charlotte Haven Ladd, a daughter of
nder Ladd and Maria Tufton Haven Ladd. Charlotte was born
eptember 29, 1813, at 2 Livermore Street, Portsmouth, in the
se then owned by her father. On the day of her marriage to Samuel
ott Coues, her father presented the Livermore dwelling to her and
r husband as a wedding gift. Later all five of their children were
rn there: Haven Ladd, on July 10, 1834; Maria Tufton Ladd, on
March 26, 1837;[14] Elliott, on September 9, 1842; Louis Dwight, on May
5, 1845; and Grace Darling,[15] on September 4, 1847.[16]

"The Livermore House," as it is called today, still stands. It is a
spacious, white, frame colonial, of a type found in many of the older
New England towns. Built in 1735, when Portsmouth was already into
its heyday, the Livermore home, with its gambrel roof, two large
chimneys, and notably gracious entrance, including a six-paneled door
and a rounded pediment over the carved cornice, is listed among the
prized historical sites of the old seaport.

From all accounts, Elliott Coues' mother was a remarkable woman.
She came of good pioneer stock, could trace her ancestry back, on
different lines, "to John Mason, the original grantee of New Hampshire,
to the Appletons and Havens of Massachusetts, and to other distinguished New England families."[17] There would be little additional
information about Charlotte Coues if it were not for three unpublished
documents currently the property of William P. Coues, great-nephew
of Elliott Coues.[18]

It was a particularly auspicious day for us when, on May 19, 1973,
we had lunch with Mr. and Mrs. William P. Coues in their summer
home on Prouts Neck, Maine, and afterward were shown the three
unpublished documents about which we had no foreknowledge. It took
only a few minutes to sense something of the value of these documents,
but it was not until later, after a much lengthier examination, that we
determined their true worth to biographers of Elliott Coues. The fuller
examination was made possible through Mr. Coues' generous proposal

New England merchant, he ?
distinction as a politician, .
As a politician, he served ter.
lecturer, he had the ability to
"Theories of the Tides," giver.
commented: "Mr. Coues has a h.
abstract ideas intelligible to the con.
sive reading on scientific subjects, his
of language, make him a very agreeab.

Samuel Elliott Coues, in his writh.
sciences, and published three books in that
System of Mechanical Philosophy (Boston, 1851)
the Elements of the Orbit of the Moon (Washington.
of the Earth, an Essay on the Figure and Surface-L
Geological and Meteorological Phenomena, and Its
(Washington, D.C., 1860). He was the author, to
unpublished works, among them a novel: "Light from
or, Modern Love Stories."[9]

Elliott Coues' father's excursions into science m
criticism than acclaim. For instance, in appraising *Outlines*
Mechanical Philosophy, one writer said: "Under this plain and
ising title, we were surprised to find ourselves very speedily abs
the perusal of an ingenious and elaborate attempt to overthr
doctrine of gravitation. A refutation of Moses seems much less sta
in the present day than a refutation of Newton; nothing less, howe\
is here attempted." The reviewer concluded that the book's novel
"will inspire interest, and its independent tone will command respect,
even if the arguments fail to produce conviction."[10]

Samuel Elliott Coues was better known, and certainly on safer
ground, as a humanitarian. For many years he was an extremely active
member of the American Peace Society and served as its president
from 1841 to 1846. In May, 1842, just four months before the birth of
Elliott Coues, he had traveled to Boston, where he addressed the
society on the topic "War and Christianity." In a later address, this one
at a "General Peace Meeting" held in Portsmouth, he revealed his
intense hatred of war by offering a resolution that "all international
war is in direct opposition to the spirit of Christianity."[11] This resolution
had been prompted and given impetus by the war with Mexico and the
earlier one against the Seminole Indians.

Elliott Coues' father had many prominent and influential friends, that we take the documents home with us where they could be studied at leisure.

In Chapter I we alluded to one of these documents, the "Book of Dates in the Life of Elliott Coues." The others are "Commonplace and Scrap Book of Charlotte Haven (Ladd) Coues, 1835-1853" and "Miscellaneous Mementoes of the Coues' Family, 1784-1896." These three works are filled with original material and are, as indicated, of tremendous value, each in its own way. The "Book of Dates," compiled by Elliott Coues himself, provides a chronological listing of practically every important event in the fifty-seven years of his highly active and productive life and, here and there, meaningful commentary.

The book of mementoes contains a miscellany of items: poems of Charlotte Coues, newspaper clippings about talks given by Samuel Elliott Coues, a small photograph of him, family letters, and an admixture of other papers and mementoes. It contains, too, the beginning of a diary by Charlotte Coues. Her initial entry, dated September 10, 1835, suggests a busy and dutiful housewife and mother who, nevertheless, is determined to improve her usefulness: "I have begun this past week to be more orderly & methodical in the management of my family & in the division of my time—believing *system* to be of great assistance in my employment. I have also resolved to keep a *very* exact & thorough account of my family expenses. So I have put my resolution on record— to the end, that if I become remiss & slack as before, I may look in this book, be ashamed, and do better."

In the early 1850s Charlotte Coues contributed articles regularly to such local papers as the *New Hampshire Gazette* and the *Portsmouth Journal of Literature and Politics*. These articles, of which there are a score or more in the "Commonplace and Scrap Book," are mainly about lectures delivered at the Portsmouth Lyceum by such prominent figures as Wendell Phillips and Oliver Wendell Holmes. Apparently Phillips, who was celebrated for his oratory, was in top form when Charlotte heard him: "[This address] was in every respect among the best and most interesting of the season." Holmes, however, disappointed her: "There was much pleasantry, some humor, but hardly a scintillation of real wit. . . . The lecture was not a bad one, decidedly, for nobody went to sleep, but nobody was tired out by attempting to comprehend what was beyond the scope of his ability."

For the further reading pleasure of Portsmouth residents, Charlotte Coues also wrote at least three essays on nature: "Spring Flowers," "Spring Birds," and "The Trees of Plymouth." This trio of essays immediately catches, and holds, our attention—the main reason being, of course, that Elliott Coues' mother loved birds, flowers, and trees, and wished to convey something of that love to her neighbors in Portsmouth. Excerpts from these essays testify to the depth of her passion for animate objects and to her ability to write about them invitingly and convincingly. In "Spring Flowers," which appeared in the *New Hampshire Gazette* of May 3, 1853,[19] she wrote in part: ". . . We love flowers—some of them. Not the stiff, high-colored flaunting things which autumn gives us, but, more than all others, the gentle, fragrant, modest blossoms of spring, with their delicate tints, their graceful tender forms, their refreshing perfumes. Our woods are now full of them. The flora of Portsmouth is uncommonly rich and varied. . . . "

Charlotte Coues' "Spring Birds," which appeared in the *New Hampshire Gazette* of May 24, 1853, may have pleased readers of that paper even more than her earlier charming tribute to the spring flowers. Mrs. Coues began it by expressing pity for "those who are confined all the bright Springtime to a crowded city; who therefore necessarily lose the two purest sources of pleasure that the young year can bring—flowers and the songs of birds. Nowhere in New England is this last employment to be had in greater perfection than in old Portsmouth, owing very much to the large number of gardens through-out the town, many of them nearly a century old." Of the Portsmouth birds, Mrs. Coues had her favorites:

> The most brilliantly beautiful, and one of the earliest of our Spring birds, is the Golden Oriole, or Baltimore Robin[20] [*Icterus galbula*], as he is often called. He is also one of our very sweetest songsters. We know of no sound in nature so delicious as the notes of this bird as he sits, on a bright May morning, on the very topmost twig of some tall cherry-tree, and pours out his soul in a full gush of melody. . . . Last Autumn, when the frosts had stripped the trees of their foliage, we counted seventeen of their curious hanging nests on the lofty Elm trees in Pleasant Street alone. . . .
>
> The exquisite little Ruby-throated Humming-birds [*Archilochus colubris*], whose very name is suggestive of all that is most delightful in nature—bright sunshine, and flowers, and grace—are also very abundant with us . . . and build their tiny nests wherever they find shelter and flowers to suit them. . . . We once saw, incredible as the story may appear, several hundred of them at one time, darting around a cherry tree, then in full bloom, looking as if a shower of rubies and emeralds were falling there. . . .

Charlotte Coues wrote engagingly about other birds, even one she disliked, the robin. Ever since childhood, when she had watched robins pulling earthworms from the ground and devouring them, she had disliked them. Furthermore, to her, the robin was a sham. "He is nothing but a Brown Thrush, and has no claim to being called a robin; for he is no relation, not even a second cousin, to the good little English Robin-redbreast [*Erithacus rubecula*] that was so kind and pitying to the babes in the woods. Not he! He is too busy catching spiders and caterpillars and earthworms on his own account. . . . But we shall never be forgiven if we abuse the Robins any longer."

Close attention to the writings of any man or woman will not in itself elicit an exact template of the individual's personality and capabilities. However, as in the case of Mrs. Coues' reports and essays, we may, through attentive reading, gain visible outlines. By reading no more than an entry or two from her short-lived diary, we derive assurance that she was a young woman possessing the virtues of integrity, determination, and love of family. Her assessments of the Lyceum lectures indicate a superior intellect, keen apperception, spontaneous wit, discontent with mediocrity, and stiletto-like ability to deflate pretense. For instance, when the Reverend Mr. Anderson of Roxbury began his Lyceum address by expressing regret at his inability to do justice to his subject, Charlotte Coues snapped, "Why did he choose it then?"

From reading Charlotte's essays about spring birds and flowers, we learn that she was a discriminating woman, with strong likes and dislikes; that she had an eye for beauty and an ear for music; and that she was blessed with observational competence. We doubt if anyone else in Portsmouth in the year 1853 counted seventeen nests of the Baltimore (northern) oriole in elms on Pleasant Street or noted several hundred ruby-throated hummingbirds "at one time, darting around a cherry tree."

When Theodore Roosevelt was once asked how he had come by his love of nature, he replied: "I can no more explain why I like natural history than why I like California canned peaches."[21] If Elliott Coues had been asked the same question, we feel confident that he would have answered, unhesitatingly, that he had inherited his love of natural history from his mother.

2

Portsmouth, New Hampshire, where on September 9, 1842, Elliott Coues was born, had been founded in 1623. Situated at the mouth of the Piscataqua River, and within sight and sound of Atlantic waters,

Portsmouth soon became a major shipbuilding port. By 1842 the city had a population of about 8,000 residents, and since then has witnessed steady growth until today (some 135 years later) its population exceeds 25,000. Shipbuilding and ship refitting continue as primary industries.

Residents of Portsmouth are justifiably proud of their city's history, and of its homes, churches, schools, streets, gardens, and parks. During Elliott Coues' boyhood Portsmouth must have been an even more attractive city than it is today, and some of its charm could be attributed to the abundance of large shade trees surrounding homes and lining both sides of winding streets. Charlotte Coues' essay, "The Trees of Portsmouth," which appeared in the *Portsmouth Gazette* of June 7, 1853, enhances our mental picture: "We have been walking through the town this balmiest of June mornings, looking with admiration at the many fine trees with which the streets are so delightfully shaded. . . . The Horse-chestnut trees are still loaded with their showy blossoms . . . and the Maples! State Street throughout its whole length is lined with them on either side. . . . The Linden is another noble tree of which we have many specimens. . . . There are some Butternuts, too . . . and plenty of the pretty Mountain Ash, white now with blossoms, to be succeeded in the autumn by its more beautiful scarlet berries."

But the most abundant tree in Portsmouth, and to Charlotte Coues the most beautiful, was the American elm: "Every tree has a character of its own, but our native American Elm seems to unite in itself, either in the different stages of its growth, or in some single noble specimen, all the distinguishing beauties of other trees, while it has some peculiar to itself. It combines the grandeur of the Oak, the stateliness of the Linden, the symmetry of the Maple with the delicate grace of a young Weeping Willow."

Portsmouth's early charm was further enhanced by its many attractive colonial homes, and also by its numerous flower gardens in which, in season, daffodils, tulips, pansies, roses, china asters, and other plants displayed their separate colors. The homes, whether frame or brick, generally stood close to the streets and presented deep-set windows, gambrel or mansard roofs, and handsome front doors. Some of the older doors still retained heavy carvings, such as figures of angels with extended wings or patterns of intertwined oak leaves and acorns.

Though a beautiful town, Portsmouth, like so many others scattered throughout the young nation, suffered from various worrisome problems. One of these, more serious because perennial and without known remedy, was the high rate of infant mortality. The parents of Elliott Coues, on the day of Elliott's birth, must have viewed his arrival with emotions fearfully tangled. Their first child, John, had died still-born; their second, Haven Ladd, had lived just nineteen months; and their third, Maria Tufton, had succumbed to a childhood disease when short of her third birthday. What, then, would be the fate of the infant Elliott, their fourth-born?

Additional cheerless thoughts tore at the memory of Charlotte and Samuel Coues. For instance, of four children born to Captain Peter Coues and his first wife all had died in infancy, and of thirteen born to Charlotte Coues' parents only four lived to a marriageable age. That Charlotte and Samuel Coues had survived such a succession of tragedies with minds unimpaired surely testifies to a strong belief in the doctrine of fatalism: that all events are predestined by fate and therefore unalterable by man.

It goes without saying that medicine as practiced in the 1840s was a far cry from its twentieth-century status. At that time, for instance, physicians were totally ignorant of the germ theory of disease (and would remain so until Louis Pasteur's monumental discoveries in the 1870s), and they carried in their medicine bags nothing even faintly resembling the efficacious sulfanilamides and antibiotics of today.[22]

3

The evidence seems conclusive that Elliott Coues, from an early age, demonstrated an interest in birds and other animals. According to one who later became Elliott's close friend: "As soon as he could exhibit a preference for any subject, his taste for ornithology was manifested . . . [and] no book nor story interested him unless animals were the subjects."[23]

We encounter support for this statement in Coues' "Book of Dates," in his mother's scrapbooks, and in his later writings where he often reminisced. He was definitely reminiscing when, as an adult, he wrote: "The first bird that ever arrested my attention, to the best of my recollection, was a Scarlet Tanager . . . which flamed through the green foliage like a vision. . . .The fiery trail of a meteor could not have left a more indelible impression than my mind received at that instant. I verily believe the sight of that Tanager determined to some extent the particular bent of my mind for ornithology rather than for any other branch of natural history." Coues then continued with this reflection: "When that Tanager brought the message to me, I was not different from other children, except that I was rather more delicate than a perfectly healthy child should be, and therefore more impressionable than an average child."[24] We cannot here quarel with Coues' assertion that he was frail as a child though we have no additional evidence to that effect.

Elsewhere (again as a grown man) Coues wrote that he had no recollection of learning to read and write, but had been told of learning his letters "from a circus and menagerie poster pasted on the wall of the nursery." From the same source we learn that his first scrapbook had been begun for him by his mother, and that it was filled "chiefly with newspaper clippings about animals."[25]

Even more convincing evidence of Elliott's childhood interest in animals is provided by three juvenile essays that he wrote and that his mother preserved in her "Commonplace and Scrap Book." His subjects were the bear, the cow, and the elephant, and, considering his age (he was no more than seven or eight), he did right well with them, especially with the one about the elephant:

> The elephant is the lagest and strongest animal that now lives upon the earth. It has a trunk which is very useful for with out it the animal would neather eat or drink. The animal is very strawn and is able to give so severe a blow as to kill horses and can lift a man with it.
>
> They live to be more than a hundred years old. When dearth approaches it is said they retire to some lonely spot where others of their race have wandered to die and there breath their last among the bones of their friends who have wandered there also.
>
> The elephant is a native of Africa and all of the southern country of Asia. They live entirely upon vegetable food but they are very fond of intoxicating licquors, and will drink it with great rapidity, and when they have drunk, they will lay the bottle down on the ground and bear[y] it.
>
> Elephants have so much sense that they can be taught to do most anything, even to taking care of little babes.

In Charlotte Coues' "Miscellaneous Mementoes" is another piece by young Elliott, one of somewhat different character, though it, too, had decided zoological overtones:

> Once upon a time, *Neptune, Pluto, & Genl. Boliver* set out together for *Athens* in the *Troy* a clipper ship of 500 tons burthen. When they were about 22 miles from land they got stuck fast on a *Coral* reef, from which they could not get off until the tide rose. When they got to the wharf at Athens, they were conveyed to a tavern by a merry looking horse striped like a *Tiger*. As it was 12 o'clock when they got to the tavern, they called for some dinner

which consisted of *Lions* flesh highly seasoned with *pepper*. At 9 o'clock they went to bed but were doomed to be disturbed; for just as they got to sleep a large *Swan* flew in the open window and bit of[f] Boliver's nose which made him roar so indiscriminately that he awoke every body in the house, for which he got a sound scolding by the landlord.

It is understandable that Elliott's mother treasured these essays and kept them, thus making it possible for us to read them today.

Further attesting to his interest in animals, Elliott Coues had his own museum of natural history. In later years he wrote of finding, when quite young, a dead snake with a partially swallowed frog (also dead) in its mouth, and of preserving this unique specimen in alcohol "as the chief treasure of a boyhood museum."[26]

No one of the above bits of information in itself provides conclusive proof that Elliott Coues had been born with an intrinsic, deep-seated love for birds and other animals. Taken collectively, however, they argue convincingly in that direction.

Entries in Coues' "Book of Dates" supply information about Elliott's Portsmouth boyhood unrelated to natural history. One of these, for the year 1849, states: "I remember sitting on the lap of Nathaniel Hawthorne, in our house on Livermore st., Portsmouth, N.H."

Another entry, for 1852, was considerably longer and more informative. It was an election year, with Franklin Pierce winning the presidential race against General Winfield Scott. Before the election tempers flared and fists flew. Wrote young Elliott, "A boy who was for Scott licked me."

Elliott devoted the greater portion of this entry to his Portsmouth schooling, naming both teachers and location of schools:

> I was then [1852] at school in Portsmouth to Israel P. Kimball—I think on High Street. . . . Before that I had gone to a school for a year or so at the public school on South st. under a Mr. Hoyt. Before that I had gone to a private school kept by a Miss Sheafe (a relative) on Court St. opposite the Courthouse and near the Stone Unitarian Church. I vaguely remember going to school to her before that at a little house I think on State St. Before or after going to school to Mr. Kimball on High St., I was at school to him in the Portsmouth Lyceum (Cameneum) building, and also in a house on corner of State and Islington Sts. . . . I studied Latin and learned the Greek alphabet under Mr. Kimball.

It seems obvious that Elliott Coues' parents tried to give him the best elementary school education possible. Latin and Greek, at that time considered to be of such importance that they were taught to children of grade-school level, would later (after continued study in college) prove to be of tremendous value to Coues, particularly in coining the scientific names (generic, specific, and so on) he would bestow on birds and other animals of his discovery new to science.

4

Elliott Coues' residence in Portsmouth ended in 1854, a few months short of his twelfth birthday. In the spring of that year his father, after accepting a position with the federal government, moved his family to Washington, D.C.

Strictly on the basis of evidence at hand, it would be a mistake to conclude that Elliott Coues, as a boy in Portsmouth, was a particularly energetic young naturalist. The evidence, already noted, is meager, and may be quickly summarized. He had written a few juvenile essays about animals; he had filled pages of a scrapbook with stories of animals clipped from newspapers; he had started a museum which included a dead snake with a frog in its mouth; he had read extensively in the field of natural history; and he had been deeply moved at the sight of his first scarlet tanager.

In later years, as already mentioned, Coues was forever reminiscing; but nowhere in his writings have we found, as would be expected if he had been an ardent, persistent juvenile student of nature, any allusion to boyhood notebooks crammed with ornithological and other data, any recollections of excursions to woods, fields, or seashores in the vicinity of Portsmouth, or any additional references to his boyhood museum. And, perhaps more significantly, he mentioned no companions, either youthful or adult, who might have shared his interest in animals and accompanied him on collecting trips.

Though seemingly a random and fitful student of animals during his Portsmouth years, Elliott Coues did possess, deeply implanted, a latent germ of interest in birds, mammals, and other animate creatures. To make the germ grow, it needed a proper catalyst—and that would soon be forthcoming.

NOTES

1. Coues, *Check List of North American Birds*, 2d ed. (1882), 101.
2. In his "Book of Dates" Coues wrote: "Peter Coues, Sr. came from Brittany via the Isle of Jersey. . . . Name *Coues* extant and well known in Brittany, the original Peter was probably *Pierre* Coues." Another source says: "Peter Coues . . . so far as we know, was born in St. Peter's Parish on the Isle of

Jersey about 1705, and was in all probability, originally known as Pierre Le Caux" (James A. Spalding, *Dr. Lyman Spalding* (Boston: W. M. Leonard, 1916), 79).

3. *Saturday Review*, July 27, 1968, 38.

4. Allen, "Biographical Memoir of Elliott Coues" (1909), 397. The *Royal George* was a British man-of-war of 108 guns. While being refitted at Spithead on Aug. 29, 1782, she suddenly, under strain caused by the shifting of her guns, keeled over, filled, and went down with her commander and nearly 1,000 others, most of whom were lost.

5. Captain Coues' first wife was Mary Jackson, his second Elizabeth Jackson. The latter gave birth to one child, Elizabeth Coues (1799-1838), who married Dr. Lyman Spalding (1775-1821), founder in 1820 of the U.S. *Pharmacopoeia*.

6. This daughter was Anne Coues, born in Aug. 20, 1795, died Oct. 17, 1845. She was Elliott Coues' "Aunt Nancy."

7. *Portsmouth Directory of 1839-1840*, which contains "List of Shipping Belonging to the District of Portsmouth." The "List" also states that the *Isaac Newton* was owned by Coues, Goodwin, and William A. Rice, was a ship of 600 tons, and had been built in Portsmouth in 1836.

8. From a newspaper clipping in Charlotte Haven (Ladd) Coues, "Commonplace and Scrap Book, 1835-1853." This book, like Elliott Coues' "Book of Dates," is presently the property of William P. Coues.

9. For this information see auction catalog, *The Private Library of the late Elliott Coues, to be sold at auction Monday and Tuesday, December 3 and 4, 1906. The Anderson Auction Co., 5 West 29th Street, New York*. This seventy-five-page catalog listed for sale more than 800 items formerly the property of Coues. The copy we consulted belongs to the library of the Academy of Natural Sciences of Philadelphia.

10. A clipping from the *Westminster Review* (London) (Jan., 1852) in Charlotte Coues' "Commonplace and Scrap Book."

11. Newspaper clipping in "Miscellaneous Mementoes of the Coues' Family," property of William P. Coues.

12. *Presidential Papers* (microfilm), Franklin Pierce Papers, Series 3, Reel 4, Library of Congress.

13. From this union were born Clara E. Coues, who died in infancy, and Samuel Franklin Coues. The latter, a half-brother of Elliott Coues and grandfather of William P. Coues, studied medicine and later held the rank of medical director in the U.S. Navy.

14. Both Haven and Maria died before the birth of Elliott, Haven on Feb. 2, 1836, and Maria on Nov. 6, 1839.

15. In all probability she was named after the British heroine Grace Darling, who, with her father in 1838, bravely rescued men from the *Forfarshire*, which had struck on the Farne Islands off Northumberland.

16. There was also an adopted daughter, Lucinda Parsons Nash, whose name, after adoption, was changed to Lucy Louisa Coues. She married James M. Flower and the two made their home first in Milwaukee, Wis., and later in Chicago.

17. Allen, "Biographical Memoir," 398.

18. William Pearce ("Peter") Coues (1908-   ) is president and treasurer of Wm. Pearce Company, Inc., Back Bay Annex, Boston, Mass. He married Mildred Davidson and to them were born two children: Pamela Coues and William Pearce Coues, Jr. The former married Renwick de Groat Dimond and they have two children: Renwick Dimond, Jr., and Ashley Dimond. The latter married Phoebe Dewing and they have two daughters, Phoebe and Amanda, and one son, Benjamin Pearce. We have listed all the members of this family because there are no others in the United States who now (1980) bear the name of Coues.

19. In Coues' "Book of Dates" (1852) we find: "This year and next mother was writing regularly for the New Hampshire Gazette. I have her scrapbook [i.e., "Commonplace and Scrap Book"] of her published articles."

20. In 1974 the American Ornithologists' Union changed the vernacular of *Icterus galbula* from Baltimore oriole to northern oriole.

21. *Memorial Edition of the Works of Theodore Roosevelt*, 24 vols. (New York: Charles Scribner's Sons, 1923), VI, 443.

22. Owing largely to the high rate of infant mortality, the average lifespan in the 1840s was about forty. Today, in the 1980s, it is seventy or slightly above.

23. Elliot, "In Memoriam: Elliott Coues" (1901), 21.

24. Rood and Coues, eds., *Papers Presented to the World's Congress on Ornithology* (1896), 26-27.

25. Coues' "Book of Dates" (1852).

26. Coues, "A 'Stand-off' between Snake and Frog" (1877), 123.

CHAPTER III

Beside the Potomac

Elliott Coues' "Book of Dates" for the year 1853 asserts: "Apr., May, June and July father was in Washington, securing his position in the U.S. Patent Office." The following year the same source informs us: "April 19th—father had taken house No. 397 12th st., Washington, D.C., and mother brought us children (Elliott, Louis, Grace and adopted sister Lucy) to this city to live. We occupied that house till father, May 3, 1866, lost his position and returned with mother to Portsmouth."[1]

What prompted Samuel Elliott Coues to surrender his station as a successful Portsmouth merchant and to make the decision to move to the nation's capital? One thing seems obvious: since the publication of his *Outlines of a System of Mechanical Philosophy*, he had fancied himself increasingly as a writer, and less and less as a businessman. For another, he seems to have been persuaded by his friend Franklin Pierce, by now president, that if he came to Washington, Pierce would obtain for him an acceptable government position. One source has it that he "expected to be made librarian of Congress."[2]

Whatever the motivation or expectation, Samuel Elliott Coues in the spring of 1854 did take up residence with his family in Washington, D.C. The Coues' first impressions of that city could hardly have been favorable. At that date, according to a contemporary writer, Washington was "a rather shabby Southern village scattered over a grandiose plan. . . . The improved streets were too wide to be improved from the tax receipts of an only moderately well-to-do population. . . . The abundant trees of the present had not been planted, though there were a few elms on 'The Avenue.' . . . The less frequented streets afforded an abundant grass, which was utilized by wandering domestic animals. It was all primitive, village-like, and yet not without charm."[3]

To young Elliott Coues, newly arrived from the beauty of Portsmouth's streets and gardens, the "charm" of the nation's capital was hidden. The city was a "mud-puddle in winter, a dust heap in summer, a cow-pen and pigsty the year round." It had for him, the budding ornithologist, just two redeeming features: "Good snipe-shooting within the city limits,"[4] and "shitepokes [green herons, *Butorides virescens*] bred there."[5]

Regardless of primitive conditions then existing in Washington, it was a circumstance of rare good fortune that brought Elliott Coues to that city. His new residence favored him with ready access to the zoological collections of the Smithsonian Institution and made possible his acquaintance with prominent Smithsonian naturalists, one of whom would shortly serve as the catalyst needed to bring fully alive Elliott's heretofore somewhat somnolent interest in animals. That man was Spencer Fullerton Baird, whom we introduced in Chapter I. As one scientist later wrote, it was Baird who befriended Coues and supplied "incentive and opportunities which he early and enthusiastically embraced."[6]

We may presume that young Elliott, after becoming settled in his new home on 12th Street, soon found his way to the Smithsonian. In the year 1854 the building was incomplete, construction of it having been started only a few years earlier. It was situated in that southern part of Washington called the Island, because it was then separated from the main part of the city by the James Creek Canal, an odoriferous sewage ditch. According to one writer, the Smithsonian of the 1850s "was approached by paths and driveways sparsely sprinkled with gravel and were ankle deep in mud on rainy days. The Washington Monument was a mere stump, and the Capitol, to the east, far from being that stately building of the present. It was not a pleasant undertaking then to reach the Smithsonian building on a slushy winter day."[7]

For close to thirty years, from about 1854 when Elliott Coues probably first met Baird, until the mid-1880s, Baird served as Coues' mentor, friend, and confidant and in those years, far more than any other individual, influenced and shaped his career. One of Baird's first acts in shaping Coues' life was, we will recall, to place him aboard the *Charmer* bound for Labrador.

Because of the close, long-continued relationship between Coues and Baird, it is important to increase at once our knowledge of the latter. Born on February 3, 1823, in Reading, Pennsylvania, Spencer Fullerton Baird, after public schools, entered Dickinson College in Carlisle, Pennsylvania. He graduated from Dickinson in 1840 and five years later returned to that college, at an annual salary of $400, as full professor and chairman of the department of natural history. Baird continued at

Dickinson until 1850 when, at the age of twenty-seven, he was elected assistant secretary of the Smithsonian, at a salary of $1,500.

During the five-year interval between his graduation from and return to Dickinson, Baird had devoted most of his time to amassing a huge collection of animal and plant specimens. He had, too, through visits to New York, Philadelphia, and other cities (and their museums), met and formed lasting friendships with many of America's leading naturalists, among them George N. Lawrence,[8] John Torrey,[9] John Cassin,[10] Thomas M. Brewer, John L. LeConte,[11] James D. Dana,[12] Louis Agassiz,[13] and John James Audubon.

Baird's friendship with Audubon was one of the more rewarding highlights of his long, exceptional career. It began as early as 1838, with an exchange of letters. Soon, after the two men met, Audubon instructed Baird in the fundamentals of painting birds. Somewhat later, as Audubon began laying plans for a trip up the Missouri River—an undertaking that materialized in 1843—he invited Baird to accompany him. Though enthusiastic at this prospect, he was bitterly disappointed when, at the last minute, illness forced him to decline.

The Smithsonian Institution was rounding out its fourth year of existence when Baird, in July, 1850, came to Washington to serve as its assistant secretary. He had been chosen for that post by Joseph Henry (1797-1878), the Smithsonian's first secretary, and a man of such scientific talent and attainment that it was said of him as he began his labors at the Smithsonian: "On the shoulders of young Henry has fallen the mantle of Franklin."[14]

Baird's immediate duties at the Smithsonian included supervision of its embryonic museum and assistance to Henry with its publications. In no way did Baird disappoint Henry. To the contrary, just three years after taking his new post, he was able to report that in this brief period the museum collection, under his guidance, had grown "from nothing to the front rank among American cabinets. . . . Nor had effort been confined merely to the acquisition of specimens, but to their concentration in mass, so as to supply all working naturalists with the materials of research."[15] Baird, a man of extreme modesty, said nothing in this report about his own contribution to the Smithsonian collection, namely, his personal museum, one of such size that it required two freight cars to convey it from Carlisle to Washington and was the nucleus of the original Smithsonian natural history collection.[16]

But Baird brought something to the Smithsonian of even greater importance than the treasures of his personal collection; and that, as one writer has emphasized, was his "tremendous influence in inspiring and training men to enter the field of natural history."[17] Among those who caught fire from Baird's magnetism and contagious enthusiasm, and who later contributed significantly to the advancement of science in America, were: William Stimpson,[18] Robert Kennicott,[19] Edward D. Cope,[20] A. E. Verrill,[21] Fielding Meek,[22] F. V. Hayden,[23] Theodore N. Gill,[24] James G. Cooper,[25] and, of course, Elliott Coues.

The majority of these men had been drawn to the Smithsonian through reports of Baird's personal interest in aspiring young naturalists. Once there, they stayed on, having been properly inoculated with the Bairdian fever to continue studying under him. Baird took care of them to the extent of providing free lodging in one or another of the Smithsonian towers, requiring only that they supply their own bedding and furniture and obtain their meals at nearby boarding houses.

Before long a number of the "tower" students, to reduce further their expenses, rented a cottage and organized themselves into a group which became known as the Megatherium Club. They engaged a black woman, affectionately called Aunty, to cook their meals. In time, to cut living costs still further, they acquired a flock of chickens, and when, as occasionally happened, there was a surplus of eggs, they "concocted a bowl of eggnog and indulged in vocal music in the evenings. . . . Rumors spread, and multiplied as they spread, of awful doings in the Megatherium Club."[26] Coues, though ineligible to join the Megatherium Club—he lived at home—may well have on occasion met with its members and contributed to their nocturnal songfests.

From various sources we learn that Baird and his wife "maintained a kindly supervision over the youngsters," and almost every Sunday invited them (Coues included) into their home where they met "men already distinguished in science" who related their experiences gained from travels in the Far West or other parts of the western hemisphere.[27] Baird, as we shall shortly learn, achieved great success in placing these young scientists with government-sponsored expeditions which, in the early years of the Smithsonian, explored remote areas of the West and, by amassing large collections, became markedly responsible for the rapid growth of the Smithsonian museum.

Baird continued as assistant secretary of the Smithsonian until 1878, when, on the death of Joseph Henry, he was named secretary. He held that position until his own death in 1887. He thus served the Smithsonian for thirty-seven years, a period in which both the institution and Baird grew conspiciously in scientific stature.

Among Baird's more significant accomplishments while at the

Smithsonian (other than those already mentioned) were: (1) his role in organizing the system of international exchange of publications, (2) his leadership in creating the United States Fish Commission, and (3) his authorship of numerous books and monographs on a wide variety of zoological topics. However, as one writer has stressed, "His work in ornithology was, perhaps, the most extensive and that which contributed more than any other to his reputation."[28]

Baird's first outstanding ornithological work was *Birds*, the ninth volume of *Reports* of the Pacific Railroad survey. Published in 1858 in collaboration with John Cassin and George N. Lawrence, this work, as Coues later wrote, "exerted an influence perhaps stronger and more widely felt than that of any of its predecessors, Audubon's and Wilson's not excepted, and marked an epoch in the history of American ornithology."[29] Coues wrote, too, that with its publication began the "Bairdian Period" in American ornithology.[30] Another important work was *History of North American Birds* (1874-84), a five-volume production (*Land Birds*, three volumes, and *Water Birds*, two volumes) which Baird wrote jointly with Thomas M. Brewer and Robert Ridgway.[31] Coues, too, had a hand in producing this multivolume work.[32]

Baird died on August 19, 1887, and was immediately, both at home and abroad, acclaimed as one of the world's foremost scientists, administrators, and producers of talented young naturalists. His death occurred at the Marine Biological Laboratory, Woods Hole, Massachusetts, an appropriate place, since Baird had been largely responsible for the founding of that laboratory, now world-famous.

2

Elliott Coues' education was resumed at Washington Seminary, a Jesuit school located on F Street between Ninth and Tenth. Washington Seminary, according to its catalog for the year 1854-55, offered two courses of study: a classical and a preparatory. We may presume that young Elliott chose the latter, since its announced object was to "qualify the pupils for the higher studies," and no one was allowed in it who could not read and write.

In sending Elliott to a Catholic school, his parents—who were Universalists—may have been influenced by its nearness to their home, by its annual tuition of only $24, or by the absence of a Protestant school which, in their opinion, afforded academic opportunities equal to those of the seminary. As one evidence of the seminary's good standing, it soon (1858) became Gonzaga College.[33]

In the fall of 1857, at the age of fifteen (and after two years at the

Jesuit school), Coues matriculated as a freshman at Columbian College (now George Washington University). Columbian was a small school for boys founded and largely sustained by the Baptist Church. Its 1859 catalog (the earliest available to us) listed a faculty of seven and a junior class of nine, one of them Elliott Coues. This catalog revealed other facts of interest. The admission fee was $10 and tuition $15. Also, under the heading "Disciplinary Regulations," the following admonitions were spelled out: "All immorality in word or deed and all ungentlemanly conduct are strictly forbidden. No student is allowed to attend the theatre or any such place; or to visit any bar-room or similar establishment; or to visit any hotel but for special and adequate reasons." We have no way of ascertaining whether Coues, not yet nineteen when he graduated from Columbian, scrupulously adhered to all of these college regulations.

Columbian prescribed all courses, though there was nothing unusual about that. At that time Harvard adhered to this traditional requirement, disallowing electives until 1869 when Charles W. Elliott assumed the presidency. Columbian, too, like other colleges of that day, placed great emphasis on Greek, Latin, and mathematics, which were required of all freshmen, sophomores, and juniors. Not until the second term of his junior year did Coues have the opportunity to supplement his knowledge of the biological sciences. In that year Columbian offered (and required) natural philosophy, natural history, botany, anatomy, and physiology. In the senior year the college required also physics, chemistry, geology, and astronomy.

Columbian catalogs issued during Coues' junior and senior years named just three science teachers: Nathan Smith Lincoln (professor of chemistry and natural history), George C. Schaeffer (professor of chemistry, physics, and natural history), and Theodore N. Gill (assistant professor of physics and natural history).[34]

Another fact about Columbian is pertinent to this study. It had a thriving two-year medical school called National Medical College (now, of course, the Medical School of George Washington University). Lincoln, Schaeffer, and Gill then taught courses in the medical school as well as in the undergraduate college. In years ahead Coues, too, would be on the teaching staff of National Medical College.

3

Soon after entering Columbian College, Coues met D. Webster Prentiss,[35] another member of the student body. They had a common interest in birds, quickly became friends, and thereafter were often together, especially on trips to such places in the district as Rock Creek, Woodley Park, and Anacostia marshes where they had gone to collect birds. On one occasion they visited Rock Creek south of the P Street bridge where, Coues wrote, they obtained "the raw flax which we use in mounting specimens."[36] Apparently Coues never became proficient in the art of mounting specimens, for in later life he wrote, "My own taxidermal art is of a low order, definitely not above average."[37]

On another occasion, at the height of the spring bird migration, Coues and Prentiss skipped classes to visit a glade bordering Rock Creek where they anticipated finding prairie warblers (*Dendroica discolor*). Subsequently Coues wrote: "The pretty little Prairie Warbler was one of my earliest acquaintances, and one I have always been fond of. . . . When we were shooting birds pretty much all the time . . . Prentiss and I knew just where to look for it, and it did not take long to get a few of the delicate birds, in their season. We were generally back in time for recitation, and even if that performance went lame in consequence, it did not seem much matter, comparatively. The inflection of the Prairie Warbler's notes was a much more agreeable theme than that of a Greek verb, and I am still uncertain whether it was not quite as profitable."[38]

At times Coues and Prentiss walked the streets of Washington at night and could clearly hear the sounds of birds in the sky above. Coues later wrote of one such incident: "Every night in early May, as we walk the streets, we can hear the mellow metallic clinking [of the bobolinks, *Dolichonyx oryzivorus*] coming down through the darkness, from birds passing high overhead, and sounding clearer in the stillness."[39]

Just how industriously did Coues collect birds while a student at Columbian? Years later he wrote to a friend: "I never had a private coll[ection], except a few hundred skins I made in my college days about this city before 1864, and some Smithsonian odds and ends Baird used to give me now and then, when I was a boy."[40]

For the youthful Elliott Coues the years 1854-59 and the first half of 1860 must have passed rapidly, and doubtless most pleasantly, with his schooling at Washington Seminary and Columbian, his sorties afield with Prentiss, and his occasional visits to the Smithsonian. We know little else about his activities in these years except that, in September, 1857, he began volume I of "Ornithological Notes," a book of some 200 pages devoted exclusively to observations on birds of the District of Columbia; in July, 1859, with volume I filled, he began volume II.[41]

We have proof, too, that "about 1859" Coues tried his hand as a bird artist, the evidence consisting of a page crowded with sketches of bird heads, beaks, and claws, and a full drawing of a secretary bird.[42] These ornithological activities may well have been prompted by Baird.

The image we have of Coues at this time, as he was growing from a boy of twelve to a young man approaching his eighteenth birthday, is fuzzy and imperfect, like a picture developed from an old discarded tintype. There can be no question, however, that he was a youth of serious mind and rare talent, and that he was increasingly enamored of birds. That his parents approved of his avocation and encouraged him in it, we have no doubt. That Baird, after only a brief acquaintance, foresaw in Coues great promise as an ornithologist became abundantly clear when in 1860, as we know, he put him aboard the *Charmer* bound for Labrador.

In our initial chapter we described Coues' experience and accomplishments in Labrador, and alluded to his resolve, when returned to Washington, of becoming a naturalist. Just how well Coues succeeded in his decision is the major theme of this study.

4

In the months immediately following his return from Labrador—those of his senior year at Columbian—Coues convincingly demonstrated a heightened interest in birds and a bolstered determination to emulate the deeds of such ornithological greats as Wilson, Audubon, and Baird. With memories fresh in mind of exciting moments among puffins, murres, gannets, and other boreal birds, and doubtless stimulated by words of commendation from Baird, Coues' increased enthusiasm, to those who knew him best, was something to be expected.

Specific evidences of Coues' enlarged interest in birds soon materialized. In his "Book of Dates" we read: "During the autumn and winter [of 1860-61] was writing Monographs of *Tringa* and *Aegiothus* and Notes on Labrador Birds." With this terse entry Coues was calling attention to the fact that, in his final year in college, he had written three articles about birds. In order of publication they were: "A Monograph of the *Tringeae* of North America," "Notes on the Ornithology of Labrador," and "A Monograph of the Genus *Aegiothus*, with Description of New Species."[43]

To young Elliott Coues, his paper on the Tringeae (sandpipers) was particularly special. For one thing, it was his very first, the first of hundreds of articles, reviews, and books he wrote and published about birds during his amazingly productive lifetime; for another, it appeared in the prestigious *Proceedings of the Academy of Natural Sciences of Philadelphia.*

At the beginning of his article on the sandpipers, Coues explained why he wrote it:

> In the latter part of 1860, during the examination at the Smithsonian Institution of an extensive and valuable collection of birds made by Messrs. Robert Kennicott and Bernard R. Ross[44] in the vicinity of Great Slave Lake and McKenzie's River, my attention was directed to a Sandpiper, nearly allied to *Actodromas maculata* and *Bonapartei*, but differing from both in many important features. Subsequent examination having proved it to be without doubt distinct from these or any other North American Sandpiper, I was authorized by the secretary of the Institution to describe and name it. To do so properly, necessarily involving a somewhat extended study of the North American Sandpipers, I was induced to make a monographic sketch of the section, as well as the particular genus to which the new species belonged.[45]

In this study, which provided detailed technical descriptions of one subfamily, seven genera, and eight species, Coues' primary focus, as indicated, was on the "new species." He named it "ACTODROMAS BAIRDII Coues—Baird's Sandpiper," and said of it: "In presenting to the scientific world this my *first* new species, I should do violence to my feelings, did I give it any other name than the one chosen. To SPENCER F. BAIRD, I dedicate it, as a slight testimonial of respect for scientific acquirements of the highest order, and in grateful remembrance of the unvarying kindness which has rendered my almost daily intercourse a source of so great pleasure, and of the friendly encouragement to which I shall ever feel indebted for whatever progress I may hereafter make in ornithology."[46]

Though this was Coues' maiden voyage in the choppy seas of taxonomy and binomial nomenclature, he had plied his oars with confidence and considerable skill—and also with deep satisfaction. He had not only paid liberal tribute to his benefactor but also, by attaching his own name to a binomial of his creation, had knowingly bestowed on himself a measure of immortality. In later years, it is true, the binomial was changed to *Erolia bairdii* (Coues);[47] nevertheless it still retains the names of both Baird and Coues.

Coues' article on the sandpipers won favorable notices in learned journals. *The Ibis*, leading British ornithological outlet, commented: "In the 'Proceedings' [of the Academy of Natural Sciences of Philadelphia] for last July we find 'A Monograph of the Tringeae of North America' by Mr. Elliott Coues—a new name to ornithologists, but not the less heartily welcome as that of a recruit to our ranks, who begins by fighting his first fight well, and against a very hard subject."[48]

J. A. Allen,[49] who later collaborated with Coues in the production of various publications, said of the monograph: "This was notable for the care and completeness with which the subject was treated, and would have been creditable to an author of greater experience. It fully foreshadowed the high charater of the subsequent work in systematic ornithology."[50]

We dealt earlier with Coues' "Notes on the Ornithology of Labrador." His "A Monograph of the Genus *Aegiothus*," the third of the three papers here under discussion, was a review of previous studies of redpolls, with special attention given to three species Coues described as new: *Aegiothus rostratus* Coues, *A. fuscescens* Coues, and *A. exilipes* Coues. In the hands of future systematists, these three species of Coues fared poorly,[51] and the article itself, therefore, lacks some of the importance attaching to the other two.

A book now difficult to locate—at least it was for us—is one by William D. Haley entitled *Philp's Washington Described, a Complete View of the American Capital, and the District of Columbia* (Washington, D.C., 1861). When we at last found this work, it proved of interest because it contains a four-page section by Elliott Coues on the ornithology of the district. In such short space Coues, of course, could do little more than generalize about the birds, numbering, he said, 236 species. He did commendably compress his material.

With the writing of this piece for *Philp's Washington Described*, Coues began to cash in on his knowledge of birds, though we do not know how much the publisher paid him. We do know that about this same time the Smithsonian gave him $100 for working up the birds collected (1857-61) and brought back by members of the Northwestern Boundary Survey.[52]

Already, at the relatively unseasoned age of nineteen, Coues had begun to make his way in the ornithological world, and among the naturalists who knew him best, there were those who spoke openly of him as a young prodigy.

5

The thirty-eighth commencement of Columbian College was held on June 26, 1861, in the E Street Baptist Church, Washington, D.C. On this academic occasion Elliott Coues was one of nine graduates to receive an A.B. degree. He received, too, the Davis Prize Medal for Elocution, awarded for the excellence of his rendition of "The Influence of Philosophical Theories upon National Literature and Character." It would appear, therefore, that Elliott, like his father before him, already possessed talent as a public speaker.

In his "Book of Dates" Coues recorded other events of 1861:

> Aug. 27, made Corresponding Member Academy of Natural Sciences of Philadelphia.
>
> Sept. 2, my Grandmother, Maria Tufton Haven Ladd, died at 397 12th St., Washn., D.C., aged 73. Daughter of Nathaniel Appleton Haven.
>
> Sept. 3, took mother with grandmother's body to New York. Sept. 4 and returned to Philada. Sept. 5, 6, at Phila. Sept. 7 home again.
>
> Sept. 9, nineteenth birthday.
>
> Oct. entered Medical Dep't. of Columbian College [*viz.*, National Medical College]; first lecture Oct. 28; assisted at first post mortem Nov. 1. First body snatching Dec. 14.

Of the above events recorded by Coues, three at least need comment. His election as corresponding member of the Academy of Natural Sciences of Philadelphia was apparently in recognition of his articles recently accepted for publication by the *Proceedings* of that institution. It was the first honor of that kind to come his way, but far from the last.

Soon thereafter Coues entered medical school, very probably at the recommendation of Baird. Medical education, such as that offered by National Medical College in 1861, did not amount to much. As one medical historian has written: "It consisted of two years of about four months each and the second year was largely a repetition of the first. During Civil War years, and for about 100 years before, there was nothing resembling science in medical schools today except anatomy. It was the molecular biology of the day. Descriptive anatomy and comparative anatomy were the things."[53]

The third event requiring comment, that of body snatching, catches our attention immediately, and if full details of Coues' role in his "first body snatching" were known, they would doubtless add measurably to the interest of this chapter.

The practice of body snatching had its origin soon after men—Leonardo da Vinci was one of the first—began seriously to study human anatomy; the practice increased as dissection of human cadavers became a recommended part of the training of medical students. In

time, the demand so exceeded the supply that bodies were often obtained
at almost any hazard, the commonest method being to dig them up as
soon as possible after burial. In Great Britain exhumations at first
caused no widespread concern, but as they increased and professional
grave robbers multiplied—in about 1825 there were an estimated 200
of them in London alone—the public began to clamor for legislation
which would abolish such a vicious practice. The clamor knew almost
no limits when, in 1828, the public learned that two Edinburgh men,
William Burke and William Hare, had resorted to murder to obtain
bodies for dissection. Burke and Hare, it was later revealed, had killed
a total of sixteen men and women whom they had then sold to Dr.
Robert Knox, anatomy teacher at the Edinburgh University school of
medicine.[54] In 1832, after Burke and Hare had been apprehended—
and Burke had been hanged[55]—Parliament passed the Anatomy Act,
which was designed to put an end in Great Britain to body snatching,
though, as one writer has said, "medical students still robbed a grave
now and then just for the fun of it."[56]

In the United States the practice of body snatching parallelled in
general that in Great Britain, though comparison is made difficult
because laws attempting to control the practice varied from state to
state. In 1883 Pennsylvania passed a law that served as an acceptable
model for similar laws in other states.[57] This legislation seems to have
been prompted, at least in part, by an event which occurred in Ohio in
1878. In May of that year Benjamin Harrison, who became president
ten years later, buried his father, and less than twenty-four hours
afterward found his father's body in the Ohio Medical School of
Cincinnati. News of this outrage, when published, shocked the nation
from coast to coast.

Before modern laws were passed in the United States, such as the
Pennsylvania one, the supply of cadavers to medical schools seems to
have been a hit-and-miss proposition, with students and professionals
alike participating. In general, bodies were obtained legally if they
could be and illegally if not. Medical students of those days probably
preferred illegal methods, since they were exciting and forbidden. No
schools required students to obtain cadavers—penalties were too high
for them to risk it if so inclined—though some of the schools were not
very well regulated and we have no certain way of knowing what
actually went on in them. In the National Medical College, as in the
others, the demand for cadavers exceeded the supply, so that Coues
may have found it necessary to snatch a body if he expected to learn his
anatomy through actual dissection. In any event, on December 14,

1861, according to his own admission, he did just that; he may have repeated the act later, since his declaration had stated, "*First* body snatching."

In the year ahead (1862) Coues involved himself in matters beyond his medical studies. He wrote more articles about birds, he pursued a course at Columbian leading to a master of arts degree, and he successfully passed examinations which resulted in his appointment as a medical cadet, U.S. Army. On May 8, 1862, the Army ordered him to report for duty at Mount Pleasant U.S. General Hospital, Washington, D.C.

In this year Coues, on his own, wrote and published four papers on birds and, jointly with D. Webster Prentiss, a fifth. Of the four he himself wrote, two were about loons and grebes, a third about gulls, and the fourth about terns.[58] That Coues' duties at Mount Pleasant interfered with his work on the article about terns is proved by a letter he wrote on May 29 to Baird: "I am *so* busy . . . the very day after I wrote requesting you to get some Terns ready for me, there was an accession of two or three hundred patients. I am fully employed the whole time, and I am sorry to say, that *Ternology* must languish for a while at least."

The joint effort of Coues and Prentiss resulted in "A List of Birds Ascertained to Inhabit the District of Columbia." This study, they wrote prefatorially, had been "suggested by S. F. Baird who gave us help and encouragement." They said, too, that while collecting material for the paper, they had been "constantly together, devoting all spare time which might not have been better employed, to the practical study of birds in the woods and fields."

In the body of their article Coues and Prentiss listed a total of 226 species of birds they had observed in the district over a period of five years. Some of their observations on the district birds may never again be duplicated in Washington and its environs and are, therefore, of more than passing interst. For instance, the golden eagle (*Aquila chrysaetos*) was then "apparently not rare," for Coues and Prentiss had observed or obtained individuals almost every winter, and two specimens had been given to the Smithsonian. The bald eagle (*Haliaeetus leucocephalus*) was "frequently seen sailing along the [Potomac] river and perched upon stumps and snags upon the 'flats.'" The hermit thrush (*Hylocichla guttata*) arrived "much the earliest [third week in March] of all the thrushes, and immediately becomes very abundant," and wild turkeys (*Meleagris gallopavo*) were "regularly seen in the markets all through the winter."[59]

As mentioned, in 1862 Coues was busy at Columbian working

toward his master's degree. In his "Book of Dates" we read: "June 25, received degree of A.M. at E st. Baptist Church, at 39th Commencement of Columbian College."

We have seen it stated that Coues' A.M. was an "honorary degree,"[60] but, as the Columbian catalog of 1861 makes clear, the degree was in no way honorary, certainly not in any gratuitous sense. Under the catalog heading "FOR THE DEGREE OF MASTER OF ARTS," we read: "Any student who shall attain, in all the studies for the degree of Bachelor of Arts, an average of 9 (the maximum being 10), not fall below 7 in any, and pass a satisfactory *review* examination upon all the studies in the several departments of the college at the end of his collegiate year, in the presence of the Faculty, and shall also attain the same average in all the studies of the Philosophical Course not required for the Degree of Bachelor of Arts, or upon such studies as the Faculty may deem as equivalent, shall be entitled to this degree."

We have been unable to obtain Coues' grades as an undergraduate at Columbian.[61] He must have been an outstanding student, however—at least by Columbian standards—else he would have been ineligible for the "review examination."

6

Mount Pleasant U.S. General Hospital, to which Medical Cadet Elliott Coues reported late in the spring of 1862, was located on 14th Street in a suburban area of Washington known as Mount Pleasant. This part of the city was three and a half miles north of the Capitol, just east of Rock Creek, and directly across from what is now the National Zoological Park. Situated on elevated ground, Mount Pleasant was regarded as perhaps the healthiest part of Washington.

Mount Pleasant Hospital had been built at the insistence of the U.S. Sanitary Commission and had opened its doors to patients in April, 1862, just one month before Coues assumed his duties there as medical cadet. Throughout the Civil War this hospital served chiefly as a receiving depot for the sick and wounded sent from the Army of the Potomac. The extent of Mount Pleasant Hospital's provision for patients may be understood from the fact that it had a capacity of 1,618 beds.[62]

From motives of economy, the builders of the hospital had been guilty of a number of construction mistakes. From a report submitted to superiors by Cadet Coues, we learn about one of them:

> The ten wards, with their accompanying rooms, are not entirely sep-

arated from each other, but all have communication with the general interior of the building. The partitions which form the sides of the main corridor and the passages leading into the wards, as well as the sides of the "isolating wards," scullery and bath-rooms, are only ten feet high, less than half the height of the ridge of the building. This partial separation affords a complete communication of the wards with each other through the main central portion. The only exception to this is the water-closets. The odor arising from them was found so offensive that it became necessary to continue the partitions between them and the rest of the building quite to the roof and add ventilators above and below. By these means the difficulty was entirely obviated.[63]

Coues' tour of duty at Mount Pleasant Hospital lasted for more than a year, from May, 1862, to mid-July, 1863. In that interval fighting between northern and southern forces, with the defeat on July 21, 1862, of Union troops at Bull Run, came perilously close to Washington (within thirty-five miles), and many of the soldiers wounded in that and succeeding battles, as well as those ill from disease, were rushed to Mount Pleasant. Existing records provide us with information about a few of the patients who received medical attention from Coues:

"Cadet Coues of Mt. Pleasant reports case of Maine private admitted to hospital after being wounded by minnie ball,[64] May 1863, at Chancellorsville."

"Coues reported amputation by an asst. surgeon of right arm of a N.Y. private wounded at Bull Run."

"Secondary amputation [by Coues] in the middle third of the shaft of the humerus of a New Hampshire private on May 3, 1863."[65]

During a part of Coues' stay at Mount Pleasant there occurred a high incidence of, and many deaths from, "Soldiers' Chronic Diarrhoea," the name Coues gave to this disorder. Of it, he wrote in part: " . . . there were treated during the last fall and winter months a very large number of cases of this disease, affording very favorable opportunities for its study. . . . The mortality was very great, the number of deaths from chronic diarrhoea during one month (December, 1862) equalling those from all other causes combined, gun-shot wounds alone excepted. The ratio of mortality is about twenty per cent; those occurring in December, twenty-one deaths in one hundred and six cases." Coues wrote of two cases in particular: Moses Burge, 49th Pennsylvania Volunteers, and O.S. Sheppard, 6th Vermont. Both died, in spite of such administered remedies as "tannin, opium, nitrate of silver and sulphate of copper."[66]

At this late date, a positive diagnosis of the "Soldiers' Chronic Diarrhoea" described by Coues is impossible. Physicians whom we have consulted incline to the belief that it was either bacillary or amoebic dysentery, or both.

On February 26, 1863, while still an "interne" at Mount Pleasant, Coues received his M.D. from National Medical College. The elapsed time between his matriculation and graduation at that school adds up to just seventeen months. That figure may mislead, however, for, if we subtract time expended on vacations, Coues probably spent no more than ten of the seventeen months in classroom and laboratory.

Important events quickly followed Coues' graduation from medical school, each contributing to a change in his medical status. On May 9 he applied for "position as Acting Asst. Surgeon, U.S.A."[67] Five days later his application was approved; however, since he was not yet of age—and would not be until September 9—he was ineligible for a commission. Two months later (mid-July) he was "detached from Mt. Pleasant Hospital for duty in the field, assigned to 57th Penna. Vols., 1st Brigade, Div. 3d Corps. . . . Was at Fredericksburg, Boonesboro, Harper's Ferry, &c."[68]

Concluding events of 1863, as Coues recorded them in his "Book of Dates," read as follows:

Nov. 18, to New York, attending Army Medical Board.
Nov. 25, finishing examination for Asst. Surgeon, U.S.A., in New York.
Nov. 26, Portsmouth, N.H.
Dec. 2-5, Boston and Cambridge.
Dec. 6, N.Y.
Dec. 7, Philada.
Dec. 8, Port Deposit, [Maryland]. Home in a day or two.
Dec. 21, elected Corresponding Member of the New York Lyceum of Natural History. Notified, Dec. 22.

Without doubt, Coues went to Portsmouth to visit relatives and friends. On his return to Washington, his stops in Boston, Cambridge, New York, and Philadelphia were unquestionably for the purposes of conferring with ornithologists and examining bird collections in the museums of those cities. Parenthetically, by 1856 the bird department of the Academy of Natural Sciences of Philadelphia had become the largest and richest in the world.[69]

Coues had reported three previous visits to Port Deposit, each with no explanation. Our best guess is that he had been drawn to that town by the charms of some Maryland belle. Coues' election on December 21 as corresponding member of another learned society, his second of this kind, presumably was a welcome Christmas present.

The year 1864 was not far advanced when tragedy struck the Coues family. In his "Book of Dates" for that year, Elliott's initial entry reads simply: "March 19 died my brother Louis Dwight Coues, at No. 397 12th St., Washn., D.C., aged 19 years. Buried in Mt. Olivet Cemetery, 21st." Louis was Elliott's only brother, and a figure clothed in relative obscurity. Some years later, in one of his books, Elliott wrote that on August 23, 1859, Louis had shot an albino bank swallow (*Riparia riparia*) and that the specimen was still preserved in the Smithsonian museum.[70] Surprisingly, in no other place, including all of Elliott's writings, have we found additional mention of events in the life of Louis Dwight Coues.

7

On March 30, 1864, Elliott Coues was "commissioned Asst. Surg., U.S.A.," a rank equivalent to that of first lieutenant, and on April 14 he received "Special Orders No. 147, for Dep't. New Mexico."[71]

"Special Orders No. 147," assigning Coues to an Army post in the Southwest, proved to be of far-reaching consequence to him. It led to other assignments in the West and they, in turn, to still others. Indeed, the original orders determined in large measure the pattern of Coues' life for the next twenty years and, to some degree, for the remainder of his life. From 1864, when Coues first went west, until his death in 1899, the majority of his published writings, whether zoological, medical, ethnological, topographical, or historical, were highly colored by his experiences and knowledge gained through travel and residence in the country west of the Mississippi.

Baird's influence was no doubt responsible for the Army orders dispatching Coues to a post in the Southwest. As early as 1850 Joseph Henry had advised Baird: "In behalf of the Smithsonian Institution, I authorize you to take charge of making collections in Natural History, intended for the Smithsonian Museum, and to request of officers of the Army and Navy of the United States and of other persons such assistance as you may think necessary for the accomplishment of the intended object."[72]

Construing Henry's instructions literally, Baird soon established a close and fruitful relationship with high-ranking federal officials whereby the latter cooperated with the Smithsonian in attaching zoologists, botanists, geologists, and other scientists to government-sponsored expeditions (primarily Army units) being dispatched to parts of the United States then relatively unknown to men of science.

A prominent scientist, later appraising Baird's successes in implementing Henry's instructions, declared that Baird "achieved wonders," as exploring expeditions to the West brought back "enormous collections" which filled Smithsonian cabinets.[73] Another writer said that Baird had "worked diligently to see that the [western] surveys were supplied with the proper scientific collectors. As might be expected, a number of his own protégés were appointed."[74]

Of Baird's protégés, Coues rated high; of that there can be no doubt. The 1860 summer trip to Labrador was an enviable scientific plum, one that other Smithsonian neophytes doubtless coveted, but Baird gave it to Coues. Also, we think that Baird, looking ahead, encouraged Coues to study medicine, and he definitely had a hand in placing him at Mount Pleasant Hospital. Writing to Baird soon after reporting for duty there, Coues said: "I have [here] as pleasant a situation as could be desired, for all of which I have to thank you in good measure." Then, after Coues had received his commission as an assistant surgeon, Baird arranged for him to join an Army unit bound for the Southwest, that appointment being another choice plum.

It was while Elliott Coues was still a student at National Medical College that he met D. G. Elliot,[75] a man of similar natural history leanings. They became good friends. Years later Elliot recalled that meeting: "It is now nearly forty years ago, when on a visit to Professor Baird in Washington one evening, in company with my old friend Dr. [Theodore N.] Gill, I first met Elliott Coues. He was then in his teens, a student of medicine, frank, simple, honest and confiding, with a boy's genuine impulses, and the glorious enthusiasm of the ornithologist manifest in speech and action."[76]

In this wise, from D. G. Elliot, we learn more of what Coues was like shortly before he began his journey to the American Southwest, where he would soon add substantially to his reputation as one of this country's most gifted young ornithologists.

NOTES

1. Edgar E. Hume, J. A. Allen, and others have stated in biographical sketches of Coues that the Coues family moved to Washington in 1853. That the actual year was 1854 is supported by the above entry from Coues' "Book of Dates" (1854).

2. Hume, *Ornithologists of the U.S. Army Medical Corps* (1942), 52.

3. Dall, *Spencer Fullerton Baird* (1915), 227-28.

4. Coues and Prentiss, "Avifauna Columbiana" (1883), 8.

5. Coues, ed., *History of the Expedition under the Command of Lewis and Clark* (1893), II, 729n. Hereafter cited as Coues-Biddle.

6. Allen, "Biographical Memoir," 398.

7. Dall, *Spencer Fullerton Baird*, 228-29.

8. George Newbold Lawrence (1806-95), ornithologist, was born in New York City and lived there throughout his life. He is perhaps best remembered as an authority on birds of tropical America and for his collaboration with Baird and Cassin in the authorship of *Birds* (1858), ninth volume of the *Reports of Explorations and Surveys for a Railroad Route from the Mississippi to the Pacific*.

9. John Torrey (1796-1873), botanist, was born in New York City. He became professor of botany at Princeton University and was the author of such books as *Flora of the State of New York* (1843) and *A Compendium of the Flora of the Northern and Middle States* (1826).

10. John Cassin (1813-69), ornithologist, was born in Delaware County, Pa. At the age of twenty-one he went to Philadelphia,where he soon became an active member of the Academy of Natural Sciences. He wrote many papers about birds and, with Baird and Lawrence, produced *Birds* (1858).

11. John Lawrence LeConte (1825-83), naturalist, was born in New York City and published widely on a variety of natural history subjects. One species of bird, LeConte's thrasher (*Toxostoma lecontei*), bears his name.

12. James Dwight Dana (1813-95), geologist, was born in Utica, N.Y. In the years 1838-42 he traveled with the Charles Wilkes expedition to the Pacific, and in 1849 was appointed professor of natural history at Yale.

13. Louis Agassiz (1807-73), celebrated naturalist, was born in Switzerland. After studies in various European universities he came to the United States, where in 1847 he was named professor of zoology at Harvard.

14. Goode, ed., *The Smithsonian Institution, 1846-1896* (1897), 122.

15. *Ibid.*, 315.

16. *Ibid.*, 167.

17. *Ibid.*, 157.

18. William Stimpson (1832-72), naturalist, was born in Roxbury, Mass. In 1852 he was appointed naturalist to the North Pacific Exploring Expedition and, on his return, made his headquarters at the Smithsonian. In 1865 he was named director of the Chicago Academy of Sciences. Six years later (1871) the great Chicago fire destroyed his lifetime collections. Stimpson never recovered from the shock and died the next year.

19. Robert Kennicott (1835-66), naturalist and explorer, was born in New Orleans. He came early to Washington and fell under the influence of Baird. In 1859-62 he made his first trip to Arctic America, where he assembled a huge collection of natural history specimens. In 1866, while on a second Arctic expedition, he succumbed to a heart attack.

20. Edward Drinker Cope (1840-97), distinguished paleontologist, was born in Philadelphia and served as curator of the Academy of Natural Sciences

(1865-73). In 1889 he was named professor of geology and paleontology at the University of Pennsylvania.

21. Addison Emery Verrill (1839-1926), zoologist, was born in Greenwood, Me., and in 1864 was appointed professor or zoology at Yale.

22. Fielding Bradford Meek (1817-76), paleontologist, was born in Madison, Ind. Largely self-taught, he became one of the country's outstanding paleontologists, contributing especially to knowledge of the fossils of Illinois and Missouri.

23. Ferdinand Vandeveer Hayden (1829-87), geologist, was born in Westfield, Mass. He served as professor of geology and mineralogy at the University of Pennsylvania (1865-72), and was the founder in 1867 of the U.S. Geological and Geographic Survey of the Territories and its director until it merged with the U.S. Geological Survey in 1878.

24. Theodore Nicholas Gill (1837-1914), naturalist, was born in New York City. He served as librarian of the Smithsonian (1863-66) and assistant librarian of the Library of Congress (1866-75). For many years he taught science at Columbian College. Among his published works are "Arrangement of the Families of Mollusca" (1871) and "Arrangement of the Families of Mammals" (1872).

25. James Graham Cooper (1830-1902), surgeon and naturalist, was born in New York City. He graduated from the College of Physicians (1851) and was with I. I. Stevens's Pacific Railroad survey expedition (1853-54). In 1870 he published a report on the birds of California, a work for which he is perhaps best known.

26. Dall, *Spencer Fullerton Baird*, 231-32.

27. *Ibid.*, 230.

28. Goode, *Smithsonian Institution*, 169.

29. Coues, *Birds of the Colorado Valley* (1878), 650.

30. Coues, *Key to North American Birds*, 2d ed. (1884), xxv.

31. Robert Ridgway (1850-1929), ornithologist, was born in Mount Carmel, Ill. In 1869 he joined the Smithsonian staff and in 1880 he was named curator of birds of the U.S. National Museum. With Baird and Brewer, he wrote *A History of North American Birds* (1874-84) and later, under his own name, *The Birds of North and Middle America* (1901-19).

32. For this work by Baird, Brewer, and Ridgway, Coues contributed the tables of orders and families (I, xv-xxviii) and the glossary (III, 535-60).

33. Today (1980) it is Gonzaga College High School, 19 Eye Street N.W., Washington, D.C.

34. We identified Gill earlier, but biographical data about Nathan Smith Lincoln and George C. Schaeffer have eluded us.

35. Daniel Webster Prentiss (1843-99), physician and ornithologist, was born in Washington, D.C. After graduating from Columbian College (in the same class with Elliott Coues), he studied medicine at the University of Pennsylvania and received his M.D. in 1864. He then served briefly (1864-65) with the U.S. Army as an acting assistant surgeon. From the end of the Civil War until his death he practiced medicine in Washington, D.C.

36. Coues and Prentiss, "Avifauna Columbiana," 24.

37. Coues, *Key to North American Birds*, 5th ed. (1903), I, 40.
38. Coues, *Birds of the Northwest* (1874), 63-64.
39. *Ibid.*, 178.
40. Coues to A. K. Fisher, Apr. 29, 1897, collection of Prof. Joseph Ewan, New Orleans, La. Fisher was an American naturalist.
41. Coues' "Book of Dates" (1857 and 1859).
42. In Coues' "Miscellaneous Mementoes." The secretary bird (*Sagittarius serpentarius*) is, as generally known, a large African bird of prey.
43. All three papers appeared in *Proceedings of the Academy of Natural Sciences of Philadelphia*, XIII (1861), the first in July, the second in August, and the third in November.
44. Bernard R. Ross (1827-74) was a factor of the Hudson's Bay Company. He shipped many specimens of birds and mammals to the Smithsonian. Ross's goose (*Chen rossii*) was so named in his honor by John Cassin.
45. Coues, "A Monograph of the *Tringeae* of North America" (1861), 170.
46. *Ibid.*, 194, 197.
47. A.O.U., *Check-List*, 196.
48. *Ibis*, IV (Jan., 1862), 84.
49. Joel Asaph Allen (1838-1921), naturalist and editor, was born in Springfield, Mass. He studied at Harvard under Louis Agassiz and in 1865 accompanied Agassiz to Brazil. In 1872 he was named assistant in ornithology to the Museum of Comparative Zoology, Cambridge, and, in 1885, curator of birds and mammals of the Musuem of Natural History, New York City. He edited the *Bulletin of the Nuttall Ornithological Club* (1876-83) and *The Auk* (1884-1912). Among his many published works was *Monographs of North American Rodentia* (1877), done jointly with Coues.
50. Allen, "Biographical Memoir," 400.
51. Owing to subsequent updatings, the genus *Aegiothus* has been supplanted by *Acanthis*. Of the three species regarded by Coues as new, *Aegiothus rostratus* Coues is now *Acanthis flammea rostrata* (Coues), a subspecies of the common redpoll; *A. exilipes* Coues has been changed to *Acanthis hornemanni exilipes* (Coues); and *A. fuscescens* Coues is now *Acanthis flammea flammea* (Linnaeus), the common redpoll.
52. Baker, "Survey of the Northwestern Boundary of the United States, 1857-1861" (1900), 62. See also Goetzmann, *Army Exploration in the American West* (1959), 428. Coues' ornithological report, for which he was paid $100, was never published.
53. Letter of Oct. 28, 1973, to authors from Roy G. Williams, Joseph Leidy Professor Emeritus of Anatomy, University of Pennsylvania School of Medicine.
54. Cohen, *The Body Snatchers* (1975), 61-77. Burke's body was later publicly dissected, its skin removed and tanned, and portions of the skin sold. Allegedly Charles Dickens obtained one of the pieces, which he used as a bookmark.
55. Hare turned state's evidence, was freed, and thus escaped a like fate.
56. Cohen, *Body Snatchers*, 77.
57. The Pennsylvania law stated, in effect, that persons buried at state expense

automatically became the property of the Anatomy Board, which would equitably distribute the bodies to various medical schools.

58. About loons and grebes: "Synopsis of the North American Forms of the *Colymbidae* and *Podicipidae*" and "Supplementary Note to a 'Synopsis of the North American Forms of the *Colymbidae* and *Podicepidae* [*sic*]"; about gulls: "Review of the Gulls of North America"; about terns: "A Review of the Terns of North America"; all in 1862.

59. Coues and Prentiss, "A List of Birds Ascertained to Inhabit the District of Columbia" (1862), 399-421.

60. Hume, *Ornithologists of the U.S. Army Medical Corps*, 52.

61. Writing us on Jan. 12, 1973, Frederick R. Houser, registrar of George Washington University, advised: "Concerning the academic record of Elliott Coues, there is no record available.

62. Smart, *Medical and Surgical History of the War of the Rebellion*, pt. III, vol. I, *Medical History* (1888), 917-20 and 960.

63. *Ibid.*, 920.

64. A kind of conical rifle bullet much used in the middle of the nineteenth century, named for its French inventor, Captain C. E. Minié.

65. Otis, *Medical and Surgical History of the War of the Rebellion*, pt. II, vol. II, *Surgical History* (1876), 580, 762, 785.

66. Coues, "Notes on the 'Soldiers' Chronic Diarrhoea'" (1863), 207.

67. Coues' "Book of Dates" (1863).

68. *Ibid.*

69. Stresemann, *Ornithology from Aristotle to the Present* (1975), 243.

70. Coues and Prentiss, "Avifauna Columbiana," 53.

71. Coues' "Book of Dates" (1864).

72. Dall, *Spencer Fullerton Baird*, 209-10.

73. Stresemann, *Ornithology from Aristotle to the Present*, 368.

74. Goetzmann, *Army Exploration in the American West*, 307.

75. Daniel Giraud Elliot (1835-1915), naturalist, was born in New York City and educated at Columbia University. In 1864 he began publication of his "Monograph of the *Tetraonidae*," the first of a series of sumptuous folio works with handcolored plates. In the years 1869-83 he lived in England. In 1894 he became curator of zoology at the Field Museum, Chicago. In 1915, in recognition of his interest in the American Museum of Natural History, he was made a trustee of that institution.

76. Elliot, "In Memoriam: Elliott Coues," 1.

CHAPTER IV

Trail to the Southwest

Beginning with the Lewis and Clark expedition, government exploring parties, such as those led by Zebulon Montgomery Pike, Stephen H. Long, and John C. Frémont, emphasized natural history, and their reports added much to the scientific knowledge of the West. So, too, did the collections and published observations of Prince Maximilian,[1] Thomas Nuttall,[2] John K. Townsend,[3] and other nongovernmental scientists. Prior to Coues' journey to the Southwest, much pioneering work on the natural history of the region had been done by C. B. R. Kennerly,[4] T. C. Henry,[5] S. W. Woodhouse,[6] and A. L. Heermann[7]—all of them Army surgeons who had received ornithological training from Baird.[8]

Yet much still remained to be done in 1864, and Arizona was almost virgin territory for a naturalist.

Coues was, of course, eager to exploit the opportunity. His mentors at the Smithsonian were likewise excited, and, fortunately, the Army was cooperative. Apparently Baird made arrangements with General James H. Carleton,[9] commander of the Department of New Mexico, to place Coues in a post within his jurisdiction that would be favorable for scientific collecting. It seems, too, that Coues and Baird assumed that the general could station Coues at Fort Garland, Colorado,[10] in the mistaken belief that the fort was within the limits of Carleton's command.

Coues left Washington for Columbus, Ohio, on April 23, traveling on the Baltimore and Ohio railroad.[11] For a reason that will be explained later, he spent the night there. On the following morning he boarded a train for Cleveland. Through a stroke of luck, as Coues reported to Baird in a letter of April 25, he had "got transportation over some of the roads as Special Army Correspondent [of the New York] Tribune!" From Cleveland, he went directly to Chicago, "passing the night of April 25 in the cars," and then to Madison, Wisconsin, where he visited for three days with his adopted sister, Lucy Coues Flowers.[12]

Even before his arrival in St. Louis (April 30) Coues had begun his scientific observations of the West. His excitement was particularly evident when he saw for the first time a yellow-headed blackbird (*Xanthocephalus xanthocephalus*). As he wrote to Baird on May 1: "On the cars between Madison & Chicago I had the first unequivocal evidence of getting into a new Avifauna. Standing on the platform of the cars,— a big *Xanthocephalus* flew up from the side of [the] road. I gave a *whoop* & such a jump that I nearly fell off and broke my neck." While riding through the suburbs of St. Louis with the distinguished botanist Dr. George Engelmann,[13] Coues noted the presence of lark sparrows (*Chondestes grammacus*).[14] Engelmann prevailed upon Coues to collect plants for him in the Southwest and, accordingly, had him elected a corresponding member of the Academy of Science of St. Louis.

Coues remained in St. Louis until May 6, awaiting the arrival of a Dr. Beers, who then accompanied him for much of the remainder of the journey westward.[15] Going up the Missouri River (May 6-13) on the steamer *Live Oak* to Kansas City, he "saw thousands of [bank swallows, *Riparia riparia*] along the banks, which were, in suitable places riddled with their holes."[16]

It was not until May 15, when he reached Fort Leavenworth, Kansas,[17] that his real western trek began. Up to that point he had been traveling on railroads and boats. Now he was to proceed to Santa Fe, his next destination, via mail coach. The journey would be "long and exceedingly toilsome . . . devoid (as all journeys beyond the precincts of steam must be) of every 'creature comfort,'" yet "exceedingly interesting and profitable to me in a scientific point of view."[18]

He might also have added that the trip was to be fraught with danger from hostile Indians. Even though he described himself as "a slender, pale-faced, lantern-jawed, girlish-looking youth, without a hair on lip or chin and hardly dry behind the ears,"[19] he was to prove himself brave enough to face the hazards of the inhospitable West.

Moving eastward over the Fort Leavenworth–Fort Riley military road, he reached the latter post[20] on May 22, where he was delayed for a week because of an Indian scare. "When we arrived here we learned that the Cheyennes, together with the Comanches and others, had made a 'raid' on the stage line, killed some of the drivers, and ran off with the stock on the road between here & Fort Larned." Meanwhile a detachment of soldiers from Fort Riley had galloped out to drive the hostiles from the trail.[21]

Coues "employed the time very profitably in observing and collecting birds along the Republican Fork of the Kansas River. The season . . .was propitious, and the place proved to be a famous one for birds."[22] His diary for May 22-27 tells of some thirty avian species that attracted his notice in the Fort Riley vicinity, though only a few were birds of the interior of North America, and consequently new to him, such as Bell's vireo (*Vireo bellii*), western meadowlark (*Sturnella neglecta*), clay-colored sparrow (*Spizella pallida*), and poor-will (*Phalaenoptilus nuttallii*).[23]

During his stay at the post he wrote to Baird on June 4 and sent him a "box of birds" he had shot in the area. While there he also collected mammalian specimens, including three western fox squirrels (*Sciurus niger*) on May 22 and a "wood hare" (possibly the cottontail, *Sylvilagus floridanus*) on May 25.[24]

2

Even though he was beginning to penetrate a portion of the country that was relatively unknown to ornithologists and was finding "further changes," the avifauna of the Fort Riley area was "still essentially eastern." Beyond Fort Riley, however, "the traveller at once comes upon the 'Great Prairie'—that vast level flower-bed which stretches without interruption along the Santa Fe road to the Arkansas River, and with but few breaks quite to the Raton Mountains. Here I immediately met with the true prairie-birds." As further evidence that he was approaching the High Plains country of the West, he also began seeing prairie-dog towns and the "inevitable" rattlesnakes (possibly the prairie rattlesnake, *Crotalus viridis viridis*).[25]

Coues arrived at Salina, Kansas, on May 29. Here the primitive conditions of western towns were all too apparent. According to his journal, Salina was "three houses and a pig stye."[26] A few years later he wrote of "a place called Salinas [*sic*], supposed by courtesy to be a town, although it consisted chiefly of a very dirty shed for a stable, and another smaller one, a shade cleaner, for a hotel." The yellow-headed blackbirds "were the most agreeable inhabitants of the place, and I whiled away some hours in watching them feeding in flocks about the stable yard."

Going out of Salina on the following day, he recorded that "we had prairie zoology in earnest; the Lark Bunting [*Calamospiza melanocorys*], Burrowing Owls [*Speotyto cunicularia*], Prairie Dogs and Buffalo [*Bison bison*]." He continued to notice the yellow-headed blackbirds, which "were seen almost every day while crossing the Plains. They would collect about camp in the evening, with flocks of Cowpen birds [brown-headed cowbirds, *Molothrus ater*], and ramble about for food among the mules and horses turned out to graze."[27]

Beyond Salina the coach turned to the southwest and began rumbling down the Santa Fe Trail. Passing the Great Bend of the Arkansas River, where he found nothing "except a miserable shack the stage company had built," his coach arrived on May 31 at Fort Larned, Kansas.[28] At this "mean place, built of adobe and logs," he found a "drunken officer in command; everybody half drunk already; and all were whole drunk by bed-time."[29]

During the revelry an "uproarious drinking song," Coues wrote, was "dinged into my startled ears," which "largely consisted of 'When Johnny comes marching home again, skewball! says I'; and 'We'll all drink stone blind, Johnny fill up the bowl!'"[30] Despite the distractions, Coues continued collecting specimens there, including a "Missouri barking squirrel" (black-tailed prairie dog, *Cynomys ludovicianus*).[31]

Leaving Larned the next day, his party camped on either Big or Little Coon Creek, "a puddlesome slough on the prairie," twenty-four miles from the fort. He remarked in the June 3 entry of his journal: "Our route since leaving Larned has been mostly along the north bank of the Arkansaw [*sic*]. Queer river that—a great ditch, chock full of grassy islets, stretching through the treeless prairie like a spotted snake, some seasons so dry you can't wet your foot in it for miles, and have to dig for a drink, sometimes a raging flood 200 yards wide."

Coues could not give his undivided attention to the natural features of the country because he learned that "the Cheyennes are on the rampage; Comanches and Kiowas too." On June 6 he passed an Indian camp, "a band of Arapahoes, at war with the Cheyennes."[32] The conflicts between these tribes and the local whites were soon to culminate in an infamous massacre. In November, 1864, Colorado volunteers surprised and needlessly slaughtered large numbers of Cheyennes and Arapahoes at Sand Creek, in southeastern Colorado.

Not long after crossing the border of Colorado Territory, Coues was perhaps heartened to reach Fort Lyon, "the first inhabited place on the Arkansas west of Larned."[33] Next, on June 7, his coach came to Bent's Old Fort. Although it had been destroyed in 1849, there remained in 1864 some chimneys and adobe walls.[34]

Up to that point for the young easterner the journey had been merely uncomfortable; now it became miserable. "Cold ride in the rain from 3 a.m. to 5 p.m., when we brought up at the fort. Here was our

crossing of the Arkansaw. Recent rains made the river unfordable; so
we had to ferry ourselves over the surging tide in a frail skiff—ticklish
business. However, we got safe across, with all our worldly goods—the
latter nothing to speak of, and stood shivering while the ramshackled
hack that met us on the other side was loaded and hitched up."

These unsettling incidents were only the prelude to "a series of
mishaps that reached to Fort Stanton [Fort Union?]^{35} in New Mexico,
and made the driver swear that 'the grace of God had petered out on
the other side of the Arkansaw.'" The coach struggled on to Iron
Springs, which was reached on June 8 ("road miry, pace snaily"), and
passed into New Mexico through the Raton Mountains.^{36} In the mountains Coues took particular note of the long-crested jay (a subspecies of
Steller's jay, *Cyanocitta stelleri*). The bird, although a "thief," "coward,"
and "bully," had "his good points, and I confess to a sneaking sort of
regard for him."^{37}

As given in the "Book of Dates," Coues' itinerary after crossing the
Arkansas included the following points: "June 8, Iron Springs. June 9,
foot of the Raton Mts., Purgatory River. June 10, Maxwell's Sta[tion].
June 11, Fort Union. June 12, via Las Vegas into Santa Fe."

3

At Santa Fe he stayed at the renowned western hostelry, La Fonda.
On June 14 he sent a long letter to Baird detailing more of the
difficulties encountered between Bent's Old Fort and the New Mexican
capital: ". . . we ran into the *mud* of three weeks' growth, and all
through the Raton mts., and to Fort Union, mud could only allow of 20
miles or so a day. Then the coach wheel broke down; we had nothing to
eat for 40 hours while dragging along. . . ." Yet it was not a total loss:
". . . . I have seen the buffaloes, the antelope, the *Cynomys* [prairie dog],
Athenes [*Athene*, the genus of burowing owls] & *Caudisona* [now *Crotalus*,
a genus of rattlesnakes]; and have arrived here in as good health and
spirits as could possibly be desired." Also, he had made "the fullest
notes on all the birds observed during the journey; place, date, numbers, habits etc. You may be sure I take these carefully."

Coues discovered at Santa Fe that he was to be stationed in Arizona
rather than Colorado: "Reported at Hdqrs. yesterday. General Carleton
was affable and courteous as possible: but he wondered how at Washington they could make such a mistake as to suppose that Ft. Garland
was in his domain. He says that he has no jurisdiction there. So Fort
Garland is *no go*." Coues and Carleton pored over the map of Arizona,

and the general suggested Fort Whipple "as the most eligible spot for collecting" because "it is an entirely unexplored region, and offers the finest opportunities." Carleton generously agreed to let Coues have an assignment elsewhere "if the place don't turn out well, or when I have used it up."

About Santa Fe, Coues wrote: ". . . a wretched place in my way of thinking. If here, I should either be sick with ennui,—or become dissipated & loaferish,—neither of which I propose to do. I've got a tangible, definite object in view big enough to claim all my time and energies and I intend to let it do so." Regarding the journey to his new post, Coues told Baird: "The train for Fort Whipple goes in four or five days. I am on duty with the command in my official position from the start. I am told that I must be very careful about wandering round the country; as it is full of hostile Apaches. However, that don't worry me at all." Coues also requested that more shot be sent to him from the Smithsonian. He wanted to know, too, if his recent monographs had been printed. Finally, he revealed a touch of loneliness when he begged Baird for a letter, because news from home meant much "to poor fellows in my fix." Before his departure from Santa Fe, Coues dispatched another box of specimens to the Smithsonian.

Coues was to accompany a column of troops going from Los Piños (some twenty miles south of Albuquerque) to Fort Whipple. The column was to follow the route laid out in 1853 by Lieutenant A. W. Whipple.[38] The unit, under the command of Captain Allen L. Anderson,[39] consisted of one company of infantry regulars and one troop each of California and New Mexico cavalry. Its responsibility was to escort a supply train for the provisioning of Fort Whipple. The column was to march across nearly 500 miles of uninviting terrain and dangerous Navajo and Apache country.

Certainly the supply train would have been a prize worthy of capture. It consisted of ". . . eighty wagons laden with commissary, quartermaster and ordnance stores, and twelve luggage wagons which carried the company and troop property, a herd of three hundred beef cattle and eight hundred head of sheep. To draw these niney-two wagons, and furnish mounts for wagon masters, herders and other train men, took five hundred and sixty mules. Add to these the one hundred sixty-three horses of the cavalry and officers. . . ."[40]

Coues was to serve as the column's medical officer. In addition, and more important to him, he carried an order from the Quartermaster General requiring Captain Anderson and Lieutenant Charles

A. Curtis,[41] the acting quartermaster of the column, to furnish transportation for shipping his collections eastward. As he explained to Curtis, he had been given his military assignment at the request of the Smithsonian so that he might "shoot up the country between the Rio Grande and the Rio Colorado."

Coues left Santa Fe on June 18 by stage and arrived at Los Piños on the following day. Curtis later recalled his first meeting with Coues at the officers' mess in Los Piños: "He was at that time still some months short of being twenty-two years old. . . . He was a man of good features and figure, a little above medium height, with light brown hair and no beard or mustache, and of a complexion bronzed in his calling of field ornithologist."[42]

During the few days in Los Piños, while the column was preparing for the march, Coues spent the time "busily in collecting."[43] Of particular interest to him was the "commonest and most characteristic" bird of the locality, the *burion*, as the Mexican-Americans called the house finch (*Carpodacus mexicanus*). Coues compared the finches with the human residents of the area, to the advantage of the former:

> In the Mexican towns they were as plentiful, fearless and familiar, as the English Sparrows [*Passer domesticus*] have become in many of our eastern cities, breeding in all sorts of nooks about the buildings, as well as in the forks of trees in the court-yards and streets. It is a pleasing feature in the dirty Mexican settlements which, with questionable taste, it selects as its abode, and where the air is vocal all the day long with its delightful melody. They are seldom molested by the worthless population, who have only energy enough to bask by day in the sun rolling cigarettes, and cheat each other at cards by night. . . .[44]

4

Sometime around June 23 the column began its march from Los Piños, on the Rio Grande, going westward across "a barren sandy waste of several days journey."[45] Near Puebla Laguna, Coues again observed his old friends the yellow-headed blackbirds: "A small stream spreads into a marsh, overgrown with reeds and tall rank weeds; a favorable spot, that thousands of the birds had selected as a nesting place, and were then busy with the duties of incubation."[46] The soldiers crossed the Rio Puerco on June 24. At Bero Springs (June 25-26) he obtained several specimens of that "most inoffensive and amiable of reptiles," the horned toad (*Phrynosoma douglassi*).[47]

As the party approached Fort Wingate[48] and the Zuni range of the

Sierra Madre on the western edge of New Mexico, the countryside
appeared more fertile and hospitable. After staying at Fort Wingate
from June 29 to July 1, they pressed on to the "Continental Backbone"
at Zuni Pass. First, however, Coues seized the chance, on July 3, to
climb a famous landmark thirty-five miles east of Zuni—Inscription
Rock: "It is a grand mass of Old Red Sandstone. I clambered to its top,
like [S. W.] Woodhouse, without my gun; and there in airy circles
round my head dashed the birds he called *Acanthylis saxatilis* [*Aeronautes
saxatilis*, white-throated swift]."[49]

By July 8 the column had reached the Arizona side—but not in
comfort, as Coues' journal entry for that day attested: "We read of the
delightful and equable climate of New Mexico; but we live and learn.
Last night we shivered under blankets, and blew our numb fingers this
morning. By ten o'clock it was hot; at eleven hotter; twelve, it was as hot
as—it could be. The cold nights stiffen our bones, and the hot days
blister our noses, crack our lips and bring our eyeballs to a stand-still.
To-day we have traversed a sandy desert; no water last night for our
worn-out animals, and very little grass."

Also "hard to bear" were the sand storms, "for the fine particles
cut like ground glass." Worse yet was the shortage of water. "For some
time it has been a long day's march from one spring or pool to another;
and occasionally more; and the liquid we find is nauseating, charged
with alkali, tepid, and so muddy that we cannot see the bottom of a tin
cup through it."

Coues made this entry while at Jacob's Well (in Apache County,
about twenty miles west of the New Mexico line), a "queer place" where
"in the Sibley tent[50] the heat is simply insupportable, and we are lying
curled up like rabbits in the slight shade we can find in the rain-washed
crevices of the 'Well.'" The well itself was:

> an undisguised blessing, and as such a curiosity. It is an enormous hole in
> the ground, right in the midst of a bare, flat plain; one might pass within a
> hundred yards and never suspect anything about it. The margin is nearly
> circular, and abruptly defined; the sides very steep—almost perpendicular
> in most places; but a path, evidently worn by men and animals, descends
> spirally, winding nearly half way around before reaching the bottom. It is,
> in fact a great funnel, a hundred yards wide at the brim and about half as
> deep; and at the bottom there is a puddle of green slimy water. Tradition
> goes, of course, that this is a bottomless pit; and as the water had not
> perceptably diminished after all our party and five hundred mules and
> cattle had had their fill, the story may go for what it is worth. The water is

bad enough—warm, and probably muddy, though the mud is not visible, owing to the rich green color of the dubious liquid. It contains, however, some suspicious looking creatures,[51] "four-legged fishes," said the man who caught several with hook and line.

Only a few birds—notably the ever-present yellow-headed black-bird—inhabited the area. "It is a scene of utter desolation; our bodily discomfort begets vague fears, and a sense of oppression weighs us down. The leaden minutes creep on wearily and noiselessly, unbroken even by the hum of an insect; two or three blackbirds, hopping listlessly about, as if they wished they were somewhere else but had not energy enough to go there, are the only signs of life that greet our faithful animals and ourselves."[52]

Throughout the march, according to Curtis, "Doctor Coues never ceased . . . making excursions along the flanks of the column and arriving in camp with many specimens. Clad in a corduroy suit of many pockets and having numerous sacks and pouches attached to his saddle, he regularly rode out of column every morning astride of his buckskin-colored mule, which he had named Jenny Lind on account of her musical bray. Rarely did we see him again until we had been some hours in the following camp but we heard the discharge of his double barreled shotgun far off the line of march."

The young surgeon's enthusiasm was catching, Curtis recollected: "He usually brought in all his pockets and pouches filled with the trophies of his search, and when he sat upon the ground and proceeded to skin, stuff and label his specimens, he was never without an interested group of officers and men about him. To anyone interested to learn the art of preparing specimens he became an earnest and painstaking instructor. In time pretty much every person in the command was contributing something to the Doctor's packing cases."

The enlisted men were not always so helpful. Coues, in addition to shooting birds, was also collecting other zoological specimens, including reptiles and batrachians (frogs and toads). These he preserved in a five-gallon keg of alcohol. Soldiers detailed to load the wagon where he stored the keg smelled only the preservative. The "chronic bibulants" began draining it off into their canteens, not knowing of the "snakes, lizards, horned toads," and other "creeping, crawling and wriggling things" therein. Curtis remembered that "some of them . . . did look decidedly pale about the gills when the head of the empty keg was smashed in and the pickled contents exposed to view."

Coues himself was not always a model soldier. As the column penetrated into the most hazardous Indian country, the men received orders not to discharge their weapons unnecessarily, and Coues was warned not to wander far from the main party. But when he spied a "beautiful and rare" bird overhead, he could not resist blasting it out of the skies. Hearing the shot, the soldiers rushed to the rear, whence it came. There stood their surgeon, holding his prize, explaining that he "really could not allow this bird to escape without causing a serious loss to science." The infuriated commander replied that he would "deprive science of any further collections for a week by placing you in arrest and taking possession of your gun and ammunition." By the next morning Allen had "slept off his vexation" and released Coues after delivering "a lecture on military science, with particular reference to service in an Indian country."

Despite this instance of disobedience, the young man proved himself a brave and capable member of the party. According to Curtis, Coues demonstrated that "he was possessed of true soldierly spirit" in three clashes between Indians and the column, when the Indians made attempts to stampede the animals.[53]

Beyond Jacob's Well the route had been: "[July] 9th Navajo Springs; 10th Lithodendron cr[eek]—11th, Colorado Chiquito [Little Colorado River], 12, 13, 14, 15 to crossing of the river. 16 stayed there. 17, 18 along the river. 19 left it. 20, Cosino Springs, San Francisco Mts. 21 dry camp. 22, by Antelope Springs to Volunteer Springs. 23 in camp. 24 'Willis' depot. 25 [on which day Coues secured an Abert's squirrel, *Sciurus aberti*],[54] past Bear Springs to dry camp. 26, across Rattlesnake Cañon to Hill Cañon. 27 to *old* Fort Whipple. 28 to Red Rocks."[55]

On the 29th the column completed its harrowing journey, having arrived at Fort Whipple, near Prescott, the capital of the infant territory. For the next several months Coues was to experience further dangers as well as thrills of scientific discovery.

NOTES

1. Alexander Philipp Maximilian, Prince of Wied-Neuwied (1782-1867), a prominent example of the many European savants who observed the natural history of North America during the early nineteenth century. He traveled up the Missouri River to the Rocky Mountains (1832-34). The published result of his journey was a two-volume work, *Reise in das innere Nordamerika* ... (1839-41).

2. Thomas Nuttall (1786-1859), English-American naturalist, was curator of

the botanical gardens at Harvard (1822-32) and author of *A Journal of Travels into the Arkansas Territory* (1821) and *A Manual of the Ornithology of the United States and of Canada* (1832-34).

3. John Kirk Townsend (1809-51), naturalist, traveled with Nuttall in 1834 and wrote *Narrative of a Journey across the Rocky Mountains to the Columbia River . . .* (1839).

4. Caleb Burwell Rowan Kennerly (1829-61) performed his most notable ornithological work while serving as surgeon and naturalist on the 35th parallel route of the Pacific Railroad surveys in the 1850s.

5. Thomas Charlton Henry (1825-77) served as post surgeon at various forts in New Mexico in the early 1850s and published some of the first ornithological studies of that territory.

6. Samuel Washington Woodhouse (1821-1904) served as surgeon and naturalist for Lieutenant Lorenzo Sitgreaves's expedition to the Zuni and Colorado rivers (1851-52).

7. Adolphus L. Heermann (c. 1818-65) collected ornithological specimens along the 32d parallel route of the Pacific Railroad surveys and in California.

8. Hume, *Ornithologists of the U.S. Army Medical Corps*, 1-2.

9. James Henry Carleton (1814-73) was commissioned a second lieutenant of dragoons in 1839 and served in the Mexican War. From 1862 to 1866 he commanded the Department of New Mexico. Throughout his long service in a number of southwestern posts he collected natural history specimens and sent them to the Smithsonian. Most of the biographical data on Coues' brother officers in this and subsequent chapters are taken from Heitman, *Historical Register and Dictionary of the United States Army* (1903).

10. Established in 1858, Fort Garland was located between Trinchera and Ute creeks in the San Luis Valley, near the present town of Fort Garland, Colo.; the post was abandoned in 1883.

11. Unless otherwise noted, Coues' itinerary is taken from his "Book of Dates."

12. Affidavit of Elliott Coues, Madison, Wis., Apr. 26, 1864, Coues Mss., Arizona Historical Society.

13. George Engelmann (1809-84), botanist, meteorologist, and physician, was born in Frankfort-on-the-Main. A year after receiving his medical degree in 1831, he immigrated to the United States, settling in St. Louis. He was instrumental in the founding of the Academy of Science of St. Louis.

14. Coues, *Birds of the Northwest* (1874), 160.

15. Coues to Baird, May 6, 1864. We have been unable to find any biographical data on Beers.

16. Coues, *Birds of the Northwest*, 90.

17. Established in 1827 as Cantonment Leavenworth, the name was changed to Fort Leavenworth in 1832. In Coues' time the post functioned as a general depot for supplying military installations in the Rocky Mountain area. Information on military posts in this and subsequent chapters has been taken from Frazer, *Forts of the West* (1965), and Prucha, *Guide to the Military Posts of the United States* (1964).

18. Coues, "Ornithology of a Prairie-Journey, and Notes on the Birds of Arizona" (1865), 157.

19. Coues, ed., *Forty Years a Fur Trader* (1898), II, 227n.
20. Situated between the Oregon and Santa Fe trails, Fort Riley (known as Camp Center durings its first month of existence) was established in 1853 and served in Coues' time primarily to protect travelers on both roads.
21. Coues to Baird, May 27, 1864.
22. Coues, *Birds of the Colorado Valley* (1878), 529.
23. Coues, "The Yellow-headed Blackbird" (1871), 197.
24. Coues and Allen, *Monographs of North American Rodentia* (1877), 336, 730.
25. Coues, "Ornithology of a Prairie-Journey," 158.
26. Coues, ed., *The Expeditions of Zebulon Montgomery Pike* (1895), II, 405n; Coues, "Yellow-headed Blackbird," 196.
27. Coues, "Yellow-headed Blackbird," 197-98.
28. Built in 1859, Fort Larned was located on the right bank of Pawnee Fork, eight miles from the Arkansas River, where it served to protect the Santa Fe trail. The post was closed in 1878.
29. Coues, ed., *Expeditions of Pike*, II, 426n.
30. Coues, ed., *Forty Years a Fur Trader*, II, 272n.
31. Coues and Allen, *Monographs of North American Rodentia*, 902.
32. Coues, ed., *Expeditions of Pike*, II, 435n.
33. *Ibid.*, 444n. Old Fort Lyon, established in 1860, was called Fort Wise until 1862. In 1867 it was relocated twenty miles up the Arkansas, two and one-half miles below the mouth of the Purgatoire River. This post, New Fort Lyon, was abandoned in 1889.
34. William and Charles Bent and their partner Ceran St. Vrain began constructing this justly famous trading post in 1828, completing their work in 1832. It was located in present-day Otero County, Colo., on the north bank of the Arkansas. In 1853 William Bent erected the much smaller Bent's New Fort thirty-eight miles downstream from the site of the original fort.
35. Fort Stanton, established in 1855, was situated on the Rio Bonita, twenty miles east of the Sierra Blanca range—too far into southern New Mexico for Coues to have passed through it. Perhaps he meant Fort Union, which was on the Santa Fe trail. Established in 1851, Fort Union served as a supply center for other military posts in the area until its abandonment in 1891.
36. Coues, ed., *Expeditions of Pike*, II, 447n.
37. Coues, "The Long-crested Jay" (1871), 771-74.
38. Amiel Weeks Whipple (1816-63) was born in Greenwich, Mass., and graduated from West Point in 1841. He was engaged in the survey of the northeastern boundary of the United States (1844-49) and in the survey of the boundary between the United States and Mexico (1849-53). He was killed at the battle of Chancellorsville and at the time of his death held the rank of major general of volunteers.
39. Allen L. Anderson graduated from West Point in 1859. In 1865 he became colonel of the 8th California Volunteers. He resigned from the Army in 1867 and died in 1910.
40. Curtis, "Coues at His First Army Post" (1902), 5.
41. Charles Albert Curtis, a native of Maine, was commissioned a second lieutenant in the 7th Infantry in 1862, was transferred to the 5th Infantry in

that same year, promoted to first lieutenant in 1864, breveted to captain in 1865, and resigned from the Army in 1870.

42. Curtis, "Coues at His First Army Post," 5-6.
43. Coues, "Ornithology of a Prairie-Journey," 159.
44. Coues, *Birds of the Northwest*, 108.
45. Coues, "Ornithology of a Prairie-Journey," 159.
46. Coues, "Yellow-headed Blackbird," 198.
47. Coues, "Synopsis of the Reptiles and Batrachians of Arizona" (1875), 591-92.
48. From its establishment in 1862 until 1866, Fort Wingate was located twenty miles south of Mount Taylor. In 1866 the post was moved sixty-five miles northwest, near the headwaters of the Puerco River, just east of present-day Gallup, N.Mex.
49. Coues to the editor, "Letters, Extracts from Correspondence, Notices, etc.," *Ibis*, 2d ser., I (Oct., 1865), 336. Woodhouse's discovery of the bird at Inscription Rock occurred sometime in early Sept., 1851.
50. The Sibley tent was widely used by the American Army in the nineteenth century. It was conically shaped, was erected on a tripod, and had a ventilating device at the top that allowed for fires to be built in the center.
51. The clouded tiger salamander (*Ambystoma tigrinum nebulosum*).
52. Coues, "Yellow-headed Blackbird," 199-200.
53. Curtis, "Coues at His First Army Post," 5-7.
54. Coues and Allen, *Monographs of North American Rodentia*, 738.
55. Coues' "Book of Dates" (1864).

CHAPTER V

"A Month's Journey
from Anywhere"

Before 1863 the area which was to become Arizona was the western half of New Mexico Territory. Early in the Civil War the South controlled much of the area, but by the summer of 1862 Carleton had broken the Confederate hold. In February of the following year President Lincoln signed an act to create the separate Territory of Arizona. It was not until January, 1864, that Governor John N. Goodwin (1824-87) and other territorial officials arrived at Fort Whipple. In the spring they laid out the town of Prescott. Fort Whipple was also only recently established, having been built in December, 1863. Its first location had been twenty-four miles from Prescott, but in May, 1864, the fort was relocated two miles from the capital.[1]

Almost immediately after his arrival, on August 1, Coues wrote again to Baird, describing the scientific results of his travels: "From Santa Fe here I have . . . collected everything that came in my way. Have some things; not much; for three fourths of the route is desert, with hardly a stray lizard to pickle." The yield in the mountains was better:

> Have young of [the] year *Cyanura* [now *Cyanocitta*, Steller's jay], *Gymno-kitta* [now *Gymnorhinus*, piñon jay]; a *Dendroica* [genus of wood warblers] I don't know but presume it is one of the western sp[ecies] I *always was* unfamiliar with. Have a keg full of Rattlesnakes, Phrynosomas [*Phrynosoma*, genus of horned lizards] and small saurians of all sorts. . . .Regarding the lizards[,] have all the *evanescent* colors carefully described. The herbarium Dr. Engelmann gave me is crammed full of spec[imens]; with notes of soil, altitude, etc. mostly procured by Capt. Anderson; who continues to be all I could wish for in a com'd'g officer.

Coues promised to send other specimens, including the fishes he had collected for Theodore N. Gill: "My Gill-ology is confined to a single pug-nosed fish found in the Zuni river; except some four-legged affairs, with gills and tadpoloid tails. . . .Genus *Siredon* [larval salamanders] are they not?"

He also outlined to Baird the zoological possibilities of his new station, which were enhanced by the fort's remoteness: "Fort Whiple is situated in a mountain valley three days journey W. of Bill Williams mt. A pretty place; and so far as I can judge, *good* for any amount of jays, tomtits, Sittas [*Sitta*, genus to which nuthatches belong], *Tyranni* [king-birds], Grouse, etc." Yet there were drawbacks: "*No water whatever*; and ornithologizing will require much wind and muscle. The Apaches are so hostile and daring that considerable *caution* will have to tinge my collecting enthusiasm, if I want to save my scalp."

Clearly Coues considered his military duties to be secondary to his "ornithologizing," telling Baird that "I have just arrived here and assumed charge of the Hospital and am at present busy getting official matters in running order,—which will occupy me a few days. I shall then get settled in my tent,—we have nothing else to live in,—and shall try to prosecute Nat. Hist. with the same animus with which I left Washington for this country."

Coues was not entirely uninterested in his medical duties, however, for he offered his services to the civilian population of Prescott, an-nouncing through the local newspaper that his specialty was surgery. He also entreated the citizens of Prescott to bring him "curious specimens of insects, reptiles, birds and plants. . . ."[2] He received his assignment as post surgeon on August 1 and had the hospital in working order by the 10th.

His attention to the political life of the territory was minimal: "'Prescott' the capital, is a mile from here; a few log huts grouped round a liberty-pole. The Governor and his whole *posse* are here."[3]

2

By November Coues had collected around 600 ornithological speci-mens.[4] Yet during the first several weeks in Arizona, he busied himself also in a matter related neither to science nor to military routine. He was extricating himself from a sticky personal situation that had originated in 1863. In March of that year he met Sarah A. Richardson in Washington and they soon became "illegally intimate." By June both Coues and Sarah became fearful "that the natural consequences of such intimacy would ensue," and Coues agreed to marry the girl should their appre-hension prove justified. When it was ascertained that she was pregnant,

Coues arranged for a marriage to be performed on September 9. On September 1 Sarah had a "natural miscarriage" in Baltimore. Since only Coues, Sarah, and an "intimate relation" of hers knew of the pregnancy and its aftermath, Coues assumed that his obligation had ended and "that the union would be productive only of unhappiness to both parties," and he "urged that he be released from his engagement." Sarah refused.

In January, 1864, the matter came to the attention of her brother and guardian, Colonel W. P. Richardson,[5] who began corresponding with Coues. Although he conceded that Coues "was not in duty bound" to marry his sister, he went on to demand the marriage and threatened "an appeal to Military Jurisdiction in the event of a refusal."[6]

By February Richardson had relented somewhat. In a letter from Camp Chase, Ohio (a Union prisoner-of-war camp of which he was commandant), he acknowledged that it was "a case of mutual guilt." Yet he insisted that his sister "must not be compelled to bear the penalty of guilt" of both parties. Therefore he proposed that Coues marry Sarah, live with her briefly, return to his military duties, "and when you have resided apart a sufficient length of time you can by mutual consent obtain a legal separation on grounds dishonorable to neither." Richardson recognized that "you do not love her, and cannot live with her" and therefore did "not desire to force you into a connection with my family, nor to thrust into your arms a wife you cannot love." The brother further offered to support Sarah after the separation. Coues, in a letter of April 6 from Washington, accepted the terms.[7]

Later he and Sarah agreed that the marriage ceremony was to take place in Columbus, Ohio, in April, while Coues was en route to the Southwest. It was further agreed that the union "was never to be ratified by a marriage bed."

This then explains why Coues spent the night of April 24 in Columbus during his journey to the Southwest. That evening he and Sarah were married at the American House by a "Rev. Mr. Hoyt." Witnessing the event were Colonel Richardson and Coues' friend (later his brother-in-law), Charles A. Page. Following the ceremony, Coues and Page retired, *sans* Sarah, to room 18 of the hotel. At 4:00 A.M. the following day Coues rose and boarded the train to Cleveland. Thus he could later offer proof that the union had never been consummated.[8] At various points throughout the trip westward he obtained notarized statements proving that he was traveling without his wife.

Upon his arrival in Arizona he wrote to Baird on August 1 of his determination to "leave no stone unturned" in settling "that *legal affair*" and begged his mentor not to mention his difficulty to others. Armed with affidavits, the notarized documents, and extracts from his correspondence with Colonel Richardson, he presented a memorial and petition to the territorial legislature, then in its first session. An act "For the Benefit of Elliott Coues," which "annulled and absolutely dissolved" the marriage of Elliott and Sarah Coues, passed easily. The act became effective on October 24, 1864, when it received the governor's signature.[9]

News of the end of the marriage was slow to reach poor Sarah. On November 11 she wrote to Baird regarding "my anxiety to learn my husband's present address," because she believed a letter to her from her "husband" had been lost in the mails.[10]

Perhaps here is an appropriate place to speak of an event in Elliott Coues' life which occurred on December 6, 1862, just four months before the indiscretion resulting in Sarah's pregnancy. We read in Coues' "Book of Dates" that on that date he made his "first visit to a house of ill fame." We call the reader's attention to this incident not because Coues visited a house of ill repute—too many other young men dallied with doxies in bordellos for us to single out this event for particular mention—but because it was father to other similar visits in succeeding years, as we shall have occasion to see. We may note, too, that Coues recorded this event in his "Book of Dates" seemingly unconcerned by the fact that others would read it.

3

Although free of the perils of marriage, he, along with his comrades, still faced the dangers presented by the Apaches. Yet not even his considerable involvement in Indian warfare, which we will discuss later, prevented him from seizing the scientific opportunities offered by the Southwest. And the scientific community both in the eastern United States and abroad took an interest in his activities in isolated Arizona.

The January, 1865, issue of the British ornithological journal *The Ibis* noted that "Dr. Elliott Coues, whose discriminating papers on several groups of North American birds are well known to many of our readers, has been recently stationed by his Government at Fort Whipple in Arizona—'a month's journey from anywhere.' We trust that the sojourn in the wilderness of this pains-taking naturalist may be productive of very great good to ornithology. He writes to us full of enthusiasm on account of the grand field of research that lies around him. He tells us of a new species of *Spizella* [a genus of sparrows]. . . ."[11]

After four months at Fort Whipple Coues submitted an article to *The Ibis* which recounted his "Prairie-Journey" and told of birds which, although rare in the East, were abundant in Arizona.[12] He later reported to *The Ibis* that ". . . my enthusiasm runs so high, that sometimes as I stand alone in the wilderness, thousands of miles from home and friends, hot, tired, dirty, breathless with pursuit, but holding in my hand and gloating over some new and rare bird, I feel a sort of charitable pity for the rest of the poor world, who are not ornithologists and have not the chance of pursuing the science in Arizona."[13]

Although the opportunity of studying the bird life of the region was a source of joy to Coues, parts of the region itself disturbed, even repelled him. As a product of the forested, humid, eastern seaboard, Coues found that the arid, treeless plains and deserts of the Southwest held few charms for him. He saw it as "a great sterile tract," "the Sahara of the West," "a land of desolation, a waste of shifting sand, here and there covered with salty efflorescence, like snow in place of verdure, given up to the dry gray wormwood, the thorny mimosa and bristling cactus."[14] Among the many dangers were rivers "in whose dry sandy beds the traveller may perish from thirst."[15] Just as treacherous were the frequent cloudbursts: "[A] six-mule team and driver were swept away and drowned by the torrent of water which flooded what had a few minutes before been the dry bed of a coulée, used for years as a road."[16]

Yet Arizona's terrain had redeeming features. The country had its "anomalies and contrasts," because "embossed in the wildest mountains are lovely valleys, moist, green and fertile."[17] Among the more pleasant areas he visited in Arizona was the headwaters of the Rio Verde, which he reached "in November, just before winter fairly set in, although frosts had already touched the foliage and dressed every tree and bush in gorgeous colors."[18]

Fortunately for Coues, he enjoyed also the high, forested, relatively well-watered vicinity of Fort Whipple. More importantly, the variation in climate, altitude, landscape, and vegetation made it ideal for gathering specimens. Since their habitat was situated between the Rocky Mountains and the Pacific Coast, the birds of Arizona, Coues observed, partook of the characteristics of the avifauna of both areas, as well as of northern Mexico. Yet in some ways the birds here were unique because the desert, particularly in southern Arizona, caused a "light, dull, apparently faded condition of plumage . . . forming true local races or varieties."[19]

While roaming the fort's environs, Coues collected an immense number of birds during his sixteen months' residence. Some of them were new to science and Coues received credit for their discovery. For example, there was the warbler he first found at Whipple Pass, near Fort Wingate, on July 2, 1864. Baird, at Coues' request, named it Grace's warbler (*Dendroica graciae*) in honor of his beloved sister, Grace Darling Coues.[20]

Perhaps even more thrilling was his discovery of the least greenlet (*Vireo bellii pusillus* Coues), a subspecies of Bell's vireo, on June 6, 1865, at Date Creek: "We were traveling hastily and uncomfortably on one of the raids upon Apaches . . . when the loud and melodious song . . . attracted my attention, and I lost no time in securing the interesting bird." Although naturalists elsewhere had found specimens of the same bird, Coues, in 1866, was the first to publish a scientific description. Receiving official credit for its discovery "seemed like a feverish dream" because it was a vireo, a bird family that had fascinated him since his boyhood reading of Audubon.[21]

On at least one occasion Coues mistakenly thought that he was the original discoverer of a species. This was the case with Lucy's warbler (*Vermivora luciae*), which he shot "one pleasant April morning along the little stream that flows past Fort Whipple." His joy no doubt turned to disappointment when he learned that Dr. James G. Cooper had previously described the "dainty bird" and had named it for Baird's daughter.[22]

Collecting involved more than the cold-blooded processes of pursuing, killing, and labeling. Bird-life was a source of many aesthetic and emotional experiences for Coues. He recalled that he and others at the post "were almost daily gratified with the sight of the 'Bullock's Oriole'" (a subspecies of the northern oriole, *Icterus galbula*) "gleaming through the sombre foliage like tiny meteors."[23]

The plumbeous bushtits (a subspecies of the common bushtit, *Psaltriparus minimus*) were "droll folk, quite innocent of dignity, superior to the trammels of decorum. . . . When fretted with the friction of garrison-life, I have often sought their society and amused myself like Gulliver among the Lilliputians." More disconcerting was the cañon wren (*Catherpes mexicanus*), in whose notes he "detected a shade of derision, as if, secure in its own rocky fastnesses, the bird was disposed to mock the discomforts and anxieties of a journey through hostile deserts."

Observing the bustling of the pigmy nuthatch (*Sitta pygmaea*) led him to ponder the ways of birds and men: "If I hurried breathless through the woods, in eager pursuit of some feathered prize that seemed likely to escape me, how did my haste in quest of a coveted thing differ from the bustling activity and restless energy they displayed in their search for what seemed good to them!"

Coues was positive that it was the song of the elusive Phainopepla (*Phainopepla nitens*) that had contributed to a grim ceremony—the burial of "the charred and dismembered body of a comrade, who had been killed and burned a few days before on that very spot, where the wolves had afterward fought for the remains. The bird of omen, for good or bad, appeared in sombre cerements, and sang such a requiem as touched every heart; the camp grew more quiet than usual, and went to bed early."

His wounding of a female plumbeus greenlet (*Vireo solitarius plumbeus* Coues, a subspecies of the solitary vireo) was the occasion of a "touching spectacle": "Her mate in a few moments came flying to her assistance. He alighted by her side, caressed her tenderly with his beak, and seemed to beseech her, in low, sympathetic accents to fly the fatal spot. She gathered herself for the effort, but only fluttered fainting to the ground, where she lay extended in the agonies of death, with her bowels trailing in the dust; but her brave mate, heedless of my presence, never left her side, nor ceased his fond attentions, till he shared her fate."[24]

It was not always necessary for Coues to obtain specimens with his shotgun. While attending to a dying fellow-naturalist, Dr. G. C. Leib, in his home in Prescott, Coues found a dead northern shrike (*Lanius excubitor*) which had sought refuge behind a piece of furniture during a storm.[25] He captured alive several "Oregon Juncos" (now the dark-eyed junco, *Junco hyemalis*) by spreading bread crumbs in a small "A-tent" and pulling a string attached to the flap.[26]

The habits and movements of a bird unique to the Southwest, the roadrunner or "Ground Cuckoo" (*Geococcyx californianus*), amused and fascinated him. "The ground cuckoo is a remarkable bird—a very distinguished character in his way, with more individuality, more crotchets and peculiarities than fall to the lot of many birds." As for the "famous pedestrian's" reputation for killing rattlesnakes, Coues conjectured that the roadrunner encircled the sleeping serpent with cactus burrs, aroused it by noisy flapping of the wings, and waited until the enraged, writhing rattler killed itself on the thorns.[27]

Even the more commonplace birds took on curious ways in the desert. Coues was struck by the fact that in Arizona the gentle mourning dove (*Zenaidura macroura marginella*) sometimes built its nest among the murderous thorns of the cacti.[28]

Searching for avian curiosities could result in finding equally curious human specimens. Once Coues and a companion rode twenty miles to call upon a colorful frontiersman named "Tennessee Bill," who, they had been told, had tamed three Cooper's hawks (*Accipiter cooperii*). Bill "tendered such hospitality as his log-cabin afforded—of that kind that, however varied in substance, is always much the same 'in spirit.'" He then whistled for his "pets," shot a sparrow, and fed it to the boldest of the three hawks. "This was the first time," wrote Coues, "I ever saw a Hawk at liberty come at a call, and take food from its master's hands. It was worth the ride."[29]

4

Coues' observations and collections of quadrupeds, although not as extensive and important as those of birds, made some noteworthy contributions to the natural history of the Southwest. White men had not made many inroads there, "and so savage and unreclaimed is its condition, that [the quadrupeds] are there to be seen in what is truly a state of nature."[30]

His killing of four-legged animals was usually incidental to his hunting of birds, and on one occasion, entirely unanticipated. While he was tracking a covey of quail near the fort, a wolf leaped from its grassy hiding place a few feet away. Both man and wolf were surprised at each other's presence. Fortunately, Coues recovered first and emptied both barrels of his shotgun into the animal. "With nothing but mustard-seed in my gun, I hardly expected to more than frighten the beast, but he was so near that he rolled over quite handsomely, his hind-quarters paralyzed with a charge that took effect in the small of his back."

The wolves could be as annoying as they were frightening. At night, after the hawks, vultures, ravens, and dogs had feasted on the offal in the fort's slaughtering area, the wolves, "emboldened by hunger and shielded by darkness," came for their share: "There they fed, and fought, and caroused, yelping like things possessed, til daylight surprised them and forced them to slink away. . . ." He and others killed many of the wolves "partly for the sake of their pelage, . . . partly in revenge for the disturbance their perpetual orgies occasioned."[31]

Nor did he find pleasure in the "famous polyglot serenades" of the coyote (*Canis latrans*): "One must have spent an hour or two vainly trying to sleep, before he is in a condition to appreciate the full force of the annoyance."[32]

Among the larger mammalian specimens he acquired was the grizzly bear (*Ursus horribilis*). A party to which he was attached killed several on nearby Bill Williams Mountain.[33] Although there were no buffalo in Arizona at that time, Coues claimed there was evidence that they had once been plentiful there.[34]

Of equal interest to Coues were the smaller mammals, especially the rodents. The scientific community gave him credit for discovering the Arizona gray squirrel (*Sciurus arizonensis* Coues). His specimen, acquired at Fort Whipple in 1865, remained the only one known to science for many years.[35]

Throughout his stay in Arizona he never saw the "strictly nocturnal" valley pocket gopher ("Red Sand-rat," *Thomomys bottae*) in its natural state. The little creatures exasperated Coues and his comrades "by their digging around, and partially undermining our tents, causing the canvas flooring to slump in when trodden upon. Pouring water in their holes or plugging them up with sticks, seemed to take effect mainly as a provocation to them to dig others." He found another local rat more useful: "The Bush Rat's [Mexican wood rat, *Neotoma mexicana*] food is as cleanly as that of a hare or squirrel, and there is no reason why its flesh should not be as good, as in truth I can assert it to be, having eaten it myself."[36]

Other four-legged species that Coues investigated in Arizona included the pallid bat (*Antrozous pallidus*); several varieties of shrews; cougar (*Felis concolor*); jaguar (*Felis onca*); long-tailed weasel (*Mustela frenata*); rock squirrel (*Citellus variegatus*); prairie dog; beaver (*Castor canadensis*), which the Indians call "'little brother' . . . in recognition of [its] sagacity, or instinct, or reason"; Ord kangaroo rat *(Dipodomys ordii);* muskrat (*Ondatra zibethica*), the skins of which the Indians used for quivers; "Jackass Hare" (antelope jackrabbit, *Lepus alleni*); black-tailed or mule deer (*Odocoileus hemionus*), which furnished "no small share of the food and clothing both of the Indians and white settlers" and was therefore diminishing in numbers; pronghorn (antelope, *Antilocapra americana*), "the swiftest animal of America"; and bighorn sheep (*Ovis canadensis*), which "stands in bold relief upon the edge of some abyss,— his massive horns, and towering form, and sinewy limbs clearly delineated,—the centre-piece of a great picture whose background may be a mountain or the sky itself."[37]

A friend and colleague, J. A. Allen, later wrote that Coues' mammalogical contributions, although "somewhat voluminous, were far less important than his ornithological writings, and relate to a field with which he was far less familiar."[38] The same assessment applies even more to his ventures into herpetology. Yet once again, because the region was relatively untouched by naturalists, collections by Coues in this line could not fail to make contributions.

Among his prize finds was a southwestern speckled rattlesnake (*Crotalus mitchelli pyrrhus*) obtained at Cañon Prieto "under the untoward circumstances of a hasty retreat from hostile Indians." In later years he told another naturalist that, while fleeing on horseback from the pursuing Indians, he removed the snake's skin and wrapped it around the barrel of his gun.[39] It was "regarded as a curiosity by the numerous persons who came to see a 'red rattlesnake.'"[40] He found only two "Harlequin snakes" (Arizona coral snake, *Micruroides euryxanthus*), one at Whipple and the other at Date Creek.[41]

He also continued to acquire as many specimens as he could of toads, frogs, and turtles. Specimens of the latter were captured along the Little Colorado River in July, 1864, and, with hook and line, at the headwaters of the San Francisco River in January, 1865.[42] Many lizards came into his hands and some of them he tried to keep alive, but his collection of collared lizards (*Crotaphytus collaris*) refused to eat, "apparently from pure chagrin, and all died within a few days."[43]

His single specimen of the famed gila monster (*Heloderma suspectum*) led him to make further caustic comments about the local Mexicans, who believed "it has the power of spirting its supposed venom." "The females of the same ignorant people have a superstitious belief in the influence that this and some other Saurians may exercise over certain periodical functions of their sex. I am informed by Dr. H. C. Yarrow that in some localities they attribute to *Amblystoma* [*Ambystoma*, genus of the tiger salamander] a miraculous power of causing contraception—a form of superstition doubtless found convenient at times, expecially if shared by their male relatives."[44] Coues' antipathy to Mexican-Americans continued at least up to 1883, when, in a review attributed to him, he warned against granting statehood to New Mexico.[45]

His disdain for the Spanish-speaking population of the Southwest was but one small factor in his growing desire to leave the area. As we shall see, Indian warfare, frontier military life, the diminishing returns in scientific discovery, and feelings of isolation led to a sustained, almost frantic effort to return to the East.

Coues' travels in the Southwest

NOTES

1. The name was changed to Whipple Barracks in 1879. The post was discontinued in 1898, regarrisoned in 1902, and discontinued again in 1913. Since 1922 it has been a federal hospital, at first operated by the Public Health Service and now by the Veterans Administration. Fort Whipple was named in honor of Major General A. W. Whipple.

2. *Arizona Miner* (Prescott), Aug. 24, 1864.

3. Coues to Baird, Aug. 1, 1864.

4. Coues, "Ornithology of a Prairie-Journey" (1865), 161.

5. At the outbreak of the Civil War William Pitt Richardson was commissioned a major in the 25th Ohio Infantry. At the close of the conflict he was a brevet brigadier general, and he died in 1886.

6. "Memorial to accompany the *Petition* of *Elliott Coues* to the *Legislative Assembly* of *Arizona* setting forth the reasons why, and the grounds upon which he

married *Sarah A. Richardson*; thereby rendering apparent the justice of his petition for divorce" (dated Prescott, A. T., Sept. 28, 1864), Coues Mss., Arizona Historical Society.

7. "Extract from letter of W. P. Richardson, dated 'Camp Chase, near Columbus, Ohio, Feb. 26, 1864' stating the terms of marriage, which were accepted"; "Extract from letter of Elliott Coues, dated Washington, D.C. April 6, 1864, accepting the terms of marriage as proposed by W. P. Richardson," Coues Mss., Arizona Historical Society.

8. Notarized statement by Charles A. Page, Washington, D.C., Apr. 27, 1864, Coues Mss., Arizona Historical Society.

9. *Acts, Resolutions and Memorials, Adopted by the First Legislative Assembly of the Territory of Arizona . . .* (Prescott: Office of the Arizona Miner, 1865), 20.

10. This letter is in the Smithsonian Archives, Record Unit 52, Incoming Correspondence, 1850-77.

11. "Letters, Extracts from Correspondence, Notices, etc.," *Ibis*, 2d ser., I (Jan., 1865), 117-18.

12. Coues, "Ornithology of a Prairie-Journey," 161.

13. "Letters, Extracts from Correspondence, Notices, etc.," *Ibis*, 2d ser., I (Oct., 1865), 536.

14. [Coues], "Of Doves and Thorns" (1869).

15. Coues, "Field Notes on *Lophortyx gambeli*" (1866), 46.

16. Coues-Biddle (1893), II, 395n.

17. Coues, "Field Notes on *Lophortyx gambeli*," 46.

18. Coues, *Birds of the Northwest* (1874), 569.

19. Coues, "List of the Birds of Fort Whipple" (1866), 40.

20. Coues, *Birds of the Colorado Valley* (1878), 293-94.

21. *Ibid.*, 532.

22. *Ibid.*, 220.

23. Coues, "Bullock's Oriole" (1871), 680.

24. Coues, *Birds of the Colorado Valley*, 128, 166, 141, 476, 517.

25. *Ibid.*, 560. We have been unable to find biographical data on Leib other than Coues' comment on this same page: "His name will be remembered by ornithologists in connection with his papers in the Journal of the Philadelphia Academy [1841] on *Fuligula 'grisea'* and on the nest and eggs of the Coot and blue-winged Teal."

26. Coues, *Birds of the Northwest*, 143.

27. [Coues], "Of a 'Fast' Bird" (1869).

28. [Coues], "Of Doves and Thorns."

29. Coues, *Birds of the Northwest*, 336-37.

30. Coues, "Quadrupeds of Arizona" (1867), 281.

31. Coues, *Birds of the Northwest*, 439, 382.

32. Coues, "Quadrupeds of Arizona," 289.

33. Coues and Yarrow, "Report upon the Collections of Mammals Made in Portions of Nevada, Utah, California, Colorado, New Mexico, and Arizona" (1875), 65.

34. Coues, "Quadrupeds of Arizona," 540. When other scientists expressed doubts over Coues' belief that the buffalo had resided in Arizona in

historic times, he backed off somewhat, telling J. A. Allen in 1875 "that he finds himself now unable to substantiate the statement," even though he remembered "being satisfied *at the time* of what I said" (Allen, "History of the American Bison" (1877), 540). Long before the coming of the white man to North America the buffalo's range did extend to Arizona.

35. Coues and Yarrow, "Report upon the Collections of Mammals," 116. Coues' letter of Dec. 21, 1884, to his Arizona friend Willard Rice sheds further light on this rare squirrel: "I am glad to hear from you and thank you for the strange squirrel, which has a stranger history. Do you remember shooting a squirrel for me at Prescott in 1865? Well, that was a species new to science, which I named *Sciurus arizonensis*, and published in 1867. From that day to this I never got another one like it, and I think only two or three specimens are known to naturalists besides these two of yours" (quoted in Mearns, "Mammals of the Mexican Boundary of the United States" (1907), 275).

36. Coues, "Quadrupeds of Arizona," 395, 400.

37. *Ibid.*, 363, 400, 535, 537, 540.

38. Allen, "Biographical Memoir," 416.

39. Theodore D. A. Cockerell, *Zoology of Colorado* (Boulder: University of Colorado, 1927), 102.

40. Coues, "Synopsis of the Reptiles and Batrachians of Arizona," 609.

41. *Ibid.*, 611.

42. *Ibid.*, 589.

43. *Ibid.*, 598-99.

44. *Ibid.*, 602. Henry Crècy Yarrow (1840-1929), surgeon and naturalist, was born in Philadelphia, and in 1861 graduated from the University of Pennsylvania Medical School. In July, 1861, he was appointed surgeon to the 5th Pennsylvania Cavalry, and served in various posts. After the war he was stationed at such places as Fort McHenry and Fort Macon. He and Coues became friends and later collaborated in the publication of a number of papers.

45. The anonymous review of James W. Steele's *Frontier Army Sketches* in *Nation*, XXXVI (Jan. 11, 1883), 43, was attributed to Coues by McAtee, *Elliott Coues as Represented in "The Nation"* (1955), 5.

CHAPTER VI

From the Desert to the Sea

The clashes between Indians and whites in Arizona during the 1860s aroused an odd reaction from Fort Whipple's surgeon. It was neither abject fear nor hatred, but frustration. The bloodshed, raids, counter-raids, and scouting expeditions obstructed his collecting of specimens. He wrote to Baird on March 31, 1865, that "we are fighting the Apaches *continually*. Killing a few only seems to stir up the rest to renewed atrocities. They kill & steal within gunshot of our houses; so that it is as much as a man's life is worth to go behind the nearest bush or rock alone."

In later years Coues described "a large patch of oaks" behind the fort which was particularly suitable for observing the plain titmouse (*Parus inornatus*): "This scrubby hillside . . . was a favorite resort of mine, not so much for what I expected to find there in the ornithological line, as for what I sincerely hoped not to find in the way of aborigines—for it was in full view of the fort, and much safer than the ravines on either side, where I have gone more than once to bring in the naked and still bleeding bodies of men killed by the Apaches. . . .[P]ractical ornithology in Arizona was a very precarious matter, always liable to sudden interruption, and altogether too spicy for comfort."[1]

His ventures outside the Whipple area were fraught with even more danger. While duck hunting along the banks of the Rio Verde (a tributary of the Gila River, to the east of Fort Whipple), he and three companions beheld a disturbing sight—several Apaches, all quite dead: ". . . from arrows sticking in them we judged, afterwards, that they had been killed by a stray band of Navajos."[2]

The prevalent Apaches in the Whipple-Prescott area "were known or supposed to be those of the Tonto basin, commonly called Tontos (Pinal coyoteros)." They "lurked behind every rock, and hid in every bush; or, failing that, under cover of every three blades of grass—a trick they did to perfection and reddened with blood every trail that led to the capital or the post. People were killed and stock was run off within a few hundred paces of both these places, and more than one pitched battle came off within ear-shot."

Despite all this, he came to realize the "other side of the picture": ". . . that the Apache has never committed an atrocity that we have not exchanged in kind, with the sole exception that we have probably never put a prisoner to death by slow torture, as was the Apache custom; that the Apache has not broken faith with us oftener than we are proud to say we have with him, and has not robbed us of more than we would like to take from him, if he had anything left to steal and we had the opportunity. The secrets of Indian agencies, like those of the Roman confessional, only leak out under great pressure."[3]

Coues also believed it unwise for the white authorities to interfere in wars between the Indians: "War is the necessary and natural state of affairs among savages; it is the main business of their lives, and the principal if not the only means of attaining all that is dearest to their hearts; and it is better for all parties to proceed on that understanding in a straightforward, businesslike way than to bushwhack for surreptitious scalps."[4]

Years later he gratefully recalled "a particular friend of mine," Willard Rice of Prescott, "who saved my life on a very ticklish occasion, when we were on a deerhunt together without other companions, and who . . . is to be credited with at least 20 'good' (dead) Apaches—none of the score women or children, either."[5] On the other hand, he had no use for the notorious King Woolsey: "I knew him in Prescott in 1864-1865, when his reputation as an Indian fighter was great, especially after his infamous 'Pinole treaty' [1864], in which many [Tonto Apache] Indians, invited unarmed to a feast and council, were treacherously butchered in cold blood."[6]

Coues' own participation in the wanton slaughtering of Indians gnawed at his conscience over the years and, writing in 1895, he confessed: "In January, 1865, it was my misfortune, which I shall never cease to regret, to be concerned in a cruel massacre—for I cannot call it a fight—in which about 30 Hualapais [Walapais] were killed, in the Juniper mts." Shortly after the shooting began, the commander of the expedition, Captain John Thompson of the 1st New Mexico Cavalry, shouted a warning to Coues, who then turned to see the chief a few feet away "and seeming to my imagination fully ten feet tall. He was drawing his bow at me. I raised my gun, but it snapt, and it would have been all over with me, had not Captain Thompson shot the Indian dead through the heart."[7]

The frequency and extent of hostile engagements between the men of Fort Whipple and the Indians are attested to by Coues' "Book of Dates" for January through August, 1865:

Jan. 8, started on scout for Indians from Ft. Whipple.—9th, Mint Valley.—10, Williamson's Valley and Burkes Holes.—11, remained.—12, moved on a hot trail in Juniper Hills, surprised and attacked a rancheria. Killed about 30 men, women and children, and retreated; no casualties on our side. Murdered a prisoner whom we captured. 13th, to breakfast at Burkes Holes, dinner at Williamson's Valley and about 5 miles further. 14th, noon Fort Whipple. This makes nearly 50 Indians we have killed in less than a month.

March 15-17 to Skull Valley to set a man's jaw. May 1-4th to Skull Valley and return, attending Pauline Weaver,[8] &c. May 5th-6th to Lynx Creek and return, attending Jerome Calkins.[9]

June 3, started on a scout from Whipple to Skull Valley; 4th to Date Creek; 5th in camp; 6 to People's [Peeples] Ranch; 7th to [word illegible] Creek; 8th, 9th, 10 trailing Indians over Bradshaw Mts. to Agua Fria Creek; 11, 12, 13, up this creek past Black Canon to Woolsey's Ranch; 14th to Fort Whipple.

July 10-17 on an Indian scout from Fort Whipple to the Rio Verde and return. Capt. Kendall,[10] Lieut. C. A. Curtis, Lieut. Darling[11] and myself; Willard Rice and Pauline Weaver, guides. Saw no Indians. Fifty soldiers on this trip.

July 20, there was a fight at Red Rocks, 6 miles from the fort. Next day we scouted through them. No Indians found.

Aug. 2-12 from Whipple via Kirkland's [Valley], People's. Antelope Mt., and Weaver to Wickenburg and return.

Such "desultory operations," he contended, "seemed to make little difference; it required [General George] Crook's systematic campaigns, on a large scale, to render the country inhabitable."[12] Moreover, as Coues complained to Baird on June 24, he could only observe, not collect birds while on these sporadic forays.

Although he was outraged by the white traders who overcharged and swindled the Indians, Coues observed that the Indians "had a way of getting even with the most unprincipled trader, sometimes of beating him at his own game."[13] In a similar vein, he half-seriously asserted that Indian paganism was superior to Christianity (especially Catholicism) because the Christian prayed for rain while the Indian danced for it— and danced till he got it, "if he had to dance all summer."[14]

In later life, at least, Coues had some sympathy and understanding for the people who had shot arrows at him with deadly intent and had killed not a few of his comrades. Shortly after leaving Arizona, he pondered the meaning of the passing of the buffalo and the Indian: "The nature and needs of both are diametrically opposed to the spirit of the white man's progress; and in the inevitable conflict,—with them for bare existence, with us for supremacy,—they cannot hold their own."[15]

In 1879 he published an article in which he expressed his thoughts on the orignal Americans. After detailing what he believed were the defects and virtues of the Indian's character and the evils that red and white men had visited upon each other, he concluded that "the Indian is neither a foreign power to be treated with, nor a wild beast to be hunted down, but a fellow-man to be reclaimed. Let us begin by calling him, that in the end we may make him, a brother."[16]

Toward the end of his life, when he had become thoroughly disgusted at white America's treatment of the Indians, he made a touching plea for tolerance: "Granting that Indians have all the defects of their qualities, and that some of these are peculiar to this remarkably picturesque race of men, it does not follow that there is not as much human nature in an Indian as in any other person. No professional secret is violated in saying that to treat an Indian as if he were a human being is to encourage him to return the compliment."[17]

2

Coues, according to another Army surgeon, was not entirely suited by personality for the military practice of medicine.[18] Nor was he, by his own admission, enthusiastic about camp life in the West. Yet he appears to have fitted easily into the rude social life of a western post. He recalled the many evenings when he and his brother officers would "settle down in earnest for the night's poker." He looked with good-natured tolerance upon the heavy drinking of the enlisted men, and he joked that it was "well known that officers never drink."[19] The fact that the enlisted men eagerly sought to help him in his scientific pursuits and to learn the art of preparing birdskins indicates a relaxed relationship with them.

He was fully aware of the value of noncommissioned officers: "Shoulder straps and chevrons understand each other well, and the latter may be heard to advantage with the former."[20] One enlisted man, however, was found wanting. "[M]y Hospital Steward," Coues informed Baird on November 24, 1864, "is a wretched stick, and a good deal of a rascal, in a small way, to boot, who wouldn't if he could, and couldn't if he would, help me in the least."

Although Coues formed friendships at the fort and in the vicinity of

Prescott, he longed for contact with the outside world, as illustrated by his March 3, 1865, letter to Baird: "The last mail we received from the East was Dec. 23.—the last from California only two weeks later. Our freshest 'news'-paper is the alta *Californian* [i.e., the *Daily Alta California* (San Francisco)] of Jany. 7!" He elaborated upon this theme in a communication to *The Ibis*, dated May 29, 1865:

> The most disagreeable part of my life here is the mails, or rather the want of them. How completely isolated I am can be imagined from the fact that I have received letters from London, Paris, Washington, and Santa Fé at the same time, and all written the same day! . . . Civilized mails come to grief sometimes by running off the track; our mails in a different way. Thus the last one, due a week ago, came in yesterday in a fragmentary condition. A hundred Apachés had attacked it in a cañon about twenty miles from here, killed one of the men, wounded the other badly, and stampeded the donkeys.[21]

Poor mail service was only one element in his growing unhappiness. He also complained that the lack of books and museum specimens hindered his work. While snowed in at Whipple he wrote to Baird on March 4, 1865, that he had requested a transfer to the East and begging him to use his influence with the Surgeon General to expedite the matter: ". . . *I want to come back.*" Among other things he complained that the "shiftless[,] loaferish life that an officer must spend on the frontier is fast making me forget what little of anything I ever did know and completely unfitting me for study or mental application of any sort." Also, he explained that the recent death of his brother, Louis Dwight Coues, caused him to worry over his father's health. Finally, Coues asserted that a year of collecting left little in the way of natural history for him at Fort Whipple. He summed up all of his anguish at the close of the letter. "Don't let me spend another fall or winter here, if you can help it! Please."

3

Later that summer, while his application for a transfer was being processed, Coues received (or wangled) an invitation from the commander of the District of Arizona, Brigadier General John S. Mason,[22] to journey to Fort Mojave[23] on the Colorado River. Traveling with others, he set out on September 5. He found little variation in the terrain throughout the 161 miles between Whipple and Mojave. At Beale's Springs, midway between, however, he saw changes in the avifauna: "*Pipilo aberti* [Abert's towhee] and *P. mesoleucus* [subspecies, *P. fuscus*

mesoleucus, of the brown towhee, *Pipilo fuscus*], two species abundant in
the Colorado valley, but never noticed at Fort Whipple."[24] Also at
Beale's Springs, on September 8, he killed a rabbit and, on the back of
the label he attached to it, he expressed his puzzlement over its identity:
"The common 'cotton-tail' of the Territory—new species??—*artemisia?*"
Years later his friend J. A. Allen determined that it was a desert
subspecies of the cottontail and called it *Lepus sylvaticus* var. *arizonae*.[25]
Today it is known by the trinomial *Sylvilagus audubonii arizonae* (J. A.
Allen).

After the party came through Union Pass, a point some fifteen miles
from the Colorado, Coues had the good fortune to have his first
encounter with LeConte's thrasher (*Toxostoma lecontei*). Although fatigued
from the long march, he "started on what came near being a wild-goose
chase" through the "sterile, cactus-ridden plain." He succeeded in killing
the bird, and after he had "smoothed its disordered plumage, and
strolled back to camp, I felt the old-time glow which those who are in the
secret know was not entirely due to the exercise I had taken."[26]

It was perhaps on this trek through Union Pass that Coues was
horrified by "the scene of at least one Indian ambuscade and attack upon
passing whites; and I have painful recollections of the atrocious cruelties
inflicted upon the cattle of a wagon train I met near the summit."[27]

After his arrival at Fort Mojave, Coues gladly agreed to General
Mason's request "to accompany him on a *pasear* down the Colorado
river, as far as Fort Yuma." This gave Coues precisely the opportunity he
had wanted of adding to his list "the many water-birds to be found in the
Colorado basin." Thus much of September "was consumed in passing
down the river to the point where the Gila mingles its waters with those
of the larger stream. . . ." Of added interest to Coues was the fact that the
commander of "the little steamer 'Cocopah'" (or *Cocopa*) upon which
they traveled was Captain D. C. ("Old Rob") Robinson, "the man who
twelve years before had piloted Lieutenant J. C. Ives and his party in the
'Explorer,' the first steamboat that ever passed over the shoals and
rapids of this difficult river."[28]

Coues and his group spent a few days at Fort Yuma,[29] a "flourishing
post, well built on a bluff. . . ." The heat was well-nigh unbearable,
sending "the mercury over 100°, sometimes to 120°." He was told "three
stock stories" about Fort Yuma: "of the dog that ran howling on three
legs across the parade ground because it burnt its paws, of the soldier
who died and went to hell, but who came back for blankets, and of the
hens that laid hard-boiled eggs."[30]

In another work he described his successful quest for several specimens of the "Wood Ibis" (wood stork, *Mycteria americana*) in the torrid environs of Fort Yuma.[31] Mammals, too, continued to gain his attention. In those parts the pallid bat made itself irksomely noticeable to Coues: "Numbers take up their abode in the chinks and crannies of the officers' quarters; and the proximity of these retreats actually becomes offensive from the multitudes crowded together. During the daytime, a continual scratching and squeaking, as of so many mice, is heard in their snuggeries; and, at night, they are even more annoying, fluttering by scores about the rooms."[32]

Coues returned to Fort Mojave on September 29 and to Fort Whipple on October 5. A letter to Baird, written on October 15, explained that his recall orders were on their way to him and that he would travel to San Francisco and sail to the East Coast via Panama. His itinerary provided for a stopover at Drum Barracks, near San Pedro Bay, in southern California. There he was to visit James G. Cooper, the pioneer ornithologist of the West Coast.

The long-awaited orders came on the 17th. On October 23 Coues left Fort Whipple in a party with the governor of the territory, John N. Goodwin, who had recently been elected Arizona's territorial delegate to Congress; Coues' friend, Lieutenant Curtis; "two servants, one of them my Mexican boy José . . . and the other Curtis' striker; and two teamsters, one of the 4-mule ambulance in which we rode, the other of the 6-mule wagon for our baggage and rations."[33] Arriving on the 28th at Fort Mojave, they ferried across the Colorado, where "before us to the westward lies the Colorado desert."[34]

Coues and the others "went 3 miles to some water called Beaver Lake; whence it was 22 miles to Piute springs, the first usual camp out from the fort. The road was fair, though mostly up and down hill, and either sandy or rocky." Spending the night at the springs, they traveled twenty miles to Rock Springs. Finding no water there, the party "went two miles further to water at what were called Government holes in those days." The next destination was the Sink of the Mojave River (Soda Lake). On their way there they "nooned at Marl springs, Nov. 1, went 15 miles further to a dry camp, and made the sink in 20 miles next day":[35] "A night at Soda Lake . . . was one of the strangest, as well as the most uncomfortable, I ever passed. . . . Along the road just traversed were strewn bleached skeletons of beasts that had fallen in their tracks beneath the scorching rays of the sun. At the foot of some cliffs near by lay whitening the heads and horns of the argali (*Ovis montana*) [bighorn sheep], shot by previous travelers. The bare bones looked of double size and fantastic shape in the uncertain moonlight." Then came "a blood-thirsty swarm of mosquitoes": "We were bitten on every exposed point; for days afterward our hands and faces were sore and swollen, inflamed by the tiny drops of poison instilled into each wound."[36]

Continuing along the Mojave River, they took their next rest at "the Caves" on November 3, "a usual stopping place in going up the Mojave from Soda Lake." Sixteen miles from the Caves was a squalid little post, Camp Cady, which they reached on November 4. Coues recorded his decidedly unfavorable impressions in his journal: "Half a day's pull through heavy sandy and gravelly washes brought us to this God-forsaken Botany Bay of a place, the meanest I ever saw yet for a military station, where four officers and a handful of men manage to exist in some unexplained way in mud and brush hovels."[37] No doubt happy to leave, the party pushed toward Grapevine, approximately twenty-five miles from Camp Cady, and arrived there on the 6th. They traveled on through Point of Rocks, Lane's Crossing of the Mojave River, Cajon Pass in the San Bernardino Mountains ("a narrow, deep, and tortuous cañon, the roughest I have ever traversed on wheels"), and Martin's Ranch.[38] Between the mountains and the coast he found "about eighty-five miles of plain, open and flat, though by no means desert and sterile, the continuity of which is hardly interrupted."[39]

Throughout his journey Coues recorded everything noteworthy in the way of feathered specimens. But his arrival at San Gabriel on November 14 was the beginning of what appears to have excited him most: the chance to observe water birds (something of a specialty of his in those days) on the Pacific and the opportunity to meet Cooper, then serving as a surgeon at Drum Barracks.[40] Although in time Coues' ornithological reputation would surpass Cooper's, Cooper was then more experienced and more widely known; Coues eagerly exploited his vast knowledge of the birds of California. Coues accompanied his new friend on a sail through San Pedro Bay where the elder scientist gave him valuable lessons and where they were pleased to find a variety of water birds.[41]

While on the beach of the bay, Coues became too enthusiastic. Believing that the "snow-white little beauties dallying so fearlessly with the huge waves" were snowy plovers (*Charadrius alexandrinus*), he ran "at full speed through the heavy soft sand." Without taking aim, he blasted away with his gun. Dipping his cap into the water to recover his supposed prizes, he found it full of common sanderlings (*Crocethia alba*): "I fancy my chagrin and disgust must have partaken a little of the sublime. . . . Dr. Cooper's cachinations nowise tended to smooth my ruffled mental image."[42]

From the stern of a steamer "anchored in the quiet, transparent water of the harbor of San Pedro," Coues watched pacific loons (a subspecies of the Arctic loon or black diver, *Gavia arctica*) diving for fish. He observed that their motion was not that of swimming or "walking," as was often supposed, but actually *flying* through the water.[43]

While at Cooper's quarters at Drum Barracks, Coues turned his sights once again on land birds. A prairie falcon (*Falco mexicanus*) "dashed past, returned in an instant, and alighted on the roof of the house, while Dr. Cooper and I were standing on the porch. . . . I went into the house for my gun, and loaded for its especial benefit. The bird watched the whole proceedings, eyeing me audaciously, and never stirred from its perch until I made an irresistible appeal."[44]

4

Coues lingered at Drum Barracks until November 29. On the 30th at San Pedro he boarded a north-bound vessel of the California Steam Navigation Company, the *Orizabo*, which sailed to San Francisco. The Pacific Mail Steamship Company's *Colorado* departed San Francisco on December 9, and according to the passenger list in that day's *Alta California*, "E. Cones" was on board. The *Colorado* (which had been armed for protection against the Confederate cruiser *Shenandoah*) landed at Panama on December 22, where the Panama Railroad Company transported Coues and the other passengers across the isthmus on the same day to Aspinwall (now Colón), where one of the North Atlantic Steamship Company's vessels, the *Atlantic*, carried them to New York.[45] On December 31 Coues wrote to Baird that he had arrived that morning.

Although eager to see his mentor, Coues informed him that he intended to go to Boston for a few days, hoping that "headquarters may not know of it," before going to Washington. In his trunk were only his smaller bird specimens; the larger items had been shipped from the West by Wells Fargo to the Smithsonian.[46]

In addition to these were the many avian specimens previously sent to the Smithsonian, along with specimens of plants, mammals, reptiles, insects, frogs, and toads. Coues and other naturalists used these collections for ground-breaking monographs in the various branches of natural science soon after they were deposited. The few specimens of southwestern fishes he had acquired were "unfortunately destroyed *in transitu.*"[47] By 1867 Coues had presented the remainder of his collections to the Smithsonian.[48]

The Arizona sojourn of Elliott Coues was the first and, from the standpoint of building his reputation, the most important of his western experiences. It also set a pattern for his subsequent military tours of duty beyond the boundaries of the District of Columbia: brilliant scientific exploitation of the area followed by a mental malaise once he had exhausted the challenges and opportunities. His persistent efforts throughout 1864-65 to get back to the East and the facilities of the Smithsonian make him appear to be a most restless and petulant young man.

To drop a naturalist of Coues' talents and enthusiasm for several months into the Southwest where, in 1864-65, the birds and other animals were largely unknown to him, and in considerable measure to science, was an almost sure-fire invitation to success. As it turned out, Coues so far succeeded that we experience difficulty in summarizing his accomplishments in small compass.

While at Fort Whipple and other points in the Southwest, Coues distinguished himself on three counts in particular: the size and quality of his collection, the discovery and description of animals new to science, and the volume of his resultant publications.

From the moment Coues hit the High Plains until, some eighteen months later, when he left the Bay of San Pedro to return east, he collected diligently and almost without interruption. Shortly before leaving Fort Whipple for California he was able to tell Lieutenant Curtis that he was taking with him "over two hundred and fifty species of birds."[49] But that could not have been the full number of different species of birds he had collected up to that time for, as we know, he had earlier, from Fort Riley, Los Piños, and Fort Whipple, shipped boxes to Baird containing other species. Also, while in California he obtained still others.

The total number of specimens, as opposed to species, collected by Coues, cannot even be estimated, for it was not unusual for him to kill a score or more of birds of a particular species, especially when the species was rare. He did so in order that he might provide the Smithsonian with an adequate series for study. Also, like other naturalists of the day when in little-known parts of the country, Coues collected mammals, reptiles, amphibians, fish, insects, and plants. We know, for instance, that he collected Coleoptera for Henry Ulke,[50] fish for Theodore N. Gill, and plants for George Engelmann.

The American Ornithologists' Union's *Check-List of North American Birds* (5th ed., 1957) credits Coues with the discovery and description at Fort Whipple of one species and five subspecies of birds new to science. The species was *Vireo vicinior* Coues, the gray vireo.[51] The five subspecies were: *Contopus sordidulus veliei* Coues, the western wood peewee;[52] *Vireo bellii pusillus* Coues, the least greenlet, a subspecies of Bell's vireo;[53] *Vireo solitarius plumbeus* Coues, the plumbeous greenlet, a subspecies of the solitary vireo;[54] *Spizella atrogularis evura* Coues, the Arizona black-chinned sparrow;[55] and *Spizella atrogularis cana*, the California black-chinned sparrow.[56]

The A.O.U. *Check-List* recognizes, too, *Asyndesmus* Coues[57] and *Micrathene* Coues,[58] new generic names for two previously described western birds, Lewis's woodpecker and the elf owl.[59]

More impressive in some respects than Coues' collections and descriptions were his literary contributions to the fauna of the Southwest resulting from his residence there. Beginning in 1865 and continuing for a number of years thereafter, Coues wrote more than a dozen important articles, the majority about birds. Some of these, about the yellow-headed blackbird, Gambel's quail, Bullock's oriole, and long-crested jay, were the first of numerous bird biographies Coues wrote during his lifetime. Of greater importance were two other articles, "Notes on Various Birds Observed at Fort Whipple," which was published in *The Ibis*, and "List of the Birds of Fort Whipple," which appeared in the *Proceedings of the Academy of Natural Sciences of Philadelphia*. The remaining articles were about mammals and on medical topics.

But these articles did not conclude Coues' writings about the Southwest. Throughout the remainder of his life he was forever recalling previously unreported events and observations of the Fort Whipple years and inserting them in such books as *Birds of the Northwest* and *Birds of the Colorado Valley*. Even during his last years, when editing the journals of early western explorers, he liberally footnoted those works with additional recollections of his months in the Southwest. Thus, to obtain anything like a full bibliography of Coues' literary contributions to the zoology of the Southwest as it was in Civil War days, one must become familiar with a considerable number of Coues' articles and books.

Needless to say, Coues' accomplishments during this period of residence, once they had been reported, quickly brought him to the fore as one of America's most promising young naturalists. It should not be overlooked that Coues, as he left Fort Whipple to return to Washington, had just passed his twenty-third birthday.

NOTES

1. Coues, *Birds of the Colorado Valley* (1878), 115.
2. Coues, *Birds of the Northwest* (1874), 570.
3. Coues, ed., *The Expeditions of Zebulon Montgomery Pike* (1895), II, 747-48n.
4. *Ibid.*, I, 257n.
5. *Ibid.*, II, 747-48n. Willard Rice was born in 1839 in Vermont and moved to Arizona in 1863. There he worked as a carpenter and miner, but is chiefly known for his activities as a guide at Fort Whipple and other posts in the territory. He died at Prescott in 1899.
6. Coues, ed. and trans., *On the Trail of a Spanish Pioneer: The Diary and Itinerary of Francisco Garcés*(1900), I, 118-19n. Tennessee-born King Woolsey (1832-79) was perhaps Arizona's most renowned Indian fighter of this period. Throughout his career there, and earlier in California, he worked as a miner, freighter, farmer, government contractor, and scout.
7. Coues, ed., *Expeditions of Pike*, II, 736n; Coues, "Adventures of Government Explorers" (1897). A brief account of the massacre, written by Indian agent John C. Dunn of Prescott, is found in *Walapai Papers*, Sen. Doc. no. 273, 74th Cong., 2d sess., 33-34. The few known facts of Thompson's life may be found in Stephen C. Jett, ed., "The Destruction of Navajo Orchards in 1864; Captain John Thompson's Report," *Arizona and the West*, XVII (Winter, 1974), 367-68.
8. Part-Indian Pauline Weaver (1800-1867) was a mountain man, Army scout, immigrant guide, and miner in Arizona, as well as a founder of Prescott.
9. Jerome Calkins was at this time sheriff of Yavapai County. Although we have been unable to ascertain his birth and death dates, the *Arizona Census, 1864,* 3d Dist., p. 106, lists him as a native of New York and thirty-four years of age.
10. Captain George D. Kendall was the commander of I Company, 7th California Infantry; see Richard H. Orton, comp., *Records of California Men in the War of the Rebellion, 1861 to 1867* (Sacramento: State Office, 1890), 790.
11. Lieutenant Edwin Darling was also an officer of I Company, 7th California Infantry; see *ibid.*
12. Coues, ed., *Expeditions of Pike*, II, 748n. George Crook (1829-90) graduated from West Point in 1852 and served with distinction during the Civil War. After the war he began his notable career as a pacifier of Indians, achieving his greatest success against Geronimo's Chiricahua Apaches in the early 1880s.
13. Coues, ed., *Expeditions of Pike*, I, 275n.
14. Coues, ed., *On the Trail of a Spanish Pioneer*, II, 449n.
15. Coues, "The Quadrupeds of Arizona" (1867), 540-41.
16. Coues, "The Western Sphynx" (1879), 193.
17. Coues-Biddle (1893), I, lxxxi.
18. Yarrow, "Personal Recollections of Old Medical Officers: Major Elliott Coues" (1927), 589.
19. Coues, ed., *Expeditions of Pike*, I, 72n, 41n.
20. Coues-Biddle, I, cii.

21. Coues, [Notes on various birds observed at Fort Whipple, Ariz.] (1865), 536.

22. John S. Mason (1824-97) graduated from West Point in 1847 and served in the Mexican War. His appointment as commander of the District of Arizona came in Nov., 1863. After the Civil War he served in various western commands and retired in 1890.

23. Fort Mojave was established in 1859 for the purpose of controlling the Mojave and Paiute Indians in the vicinity of the 38th parallel. The post was abandoned in 1890.

24. Coues, "From Arizona to the Pacific" (1866), 259.

25. Coues and Allen, *Monographs of North American Rodentia* (1877), 332.

26. Coues, *Birds of the Colorado Valley*, 72.

27. Coues, ed., *On the Trail of a Spanish Pioneer*, II, 315-16n.

28. Coues, "From Arizona to the Pacific," 260, 261. Joseph Christmas Ives (1828-68) graduated from West Point in 1852. In 1853-54 he assisted A. W. Whipple in the Pacific Railroad survey, and during 1857-58 he commanded his own expedition up the Colorado River. His report is considered a classic narrative of military exploration.

29. Fort Yuma was established in Nov., 1850, at the confluence of the Gila and Colorado rivers, on the California side. Abandoned in 1851, it was reoccupied in 1852. It was permanently abandoned in 1883.

30. Coues, ed., *On the Trail of a Spanish Pioneer*, I, 148n.

31. Coues, *Birds of the Northwest*, 514-15.

32. Coues and Yarrow, "Report upon the Collections of Mammals" (1875), 85.

33. Coues, ed., *On the Trail of a Spanish Pioneer*, I, 232n.

34. Coues, "From Arizona to the Pacific," 264.

35. Coues, ed., *On the Trail of a Spanish Pioneer*, I, 235-36n, 258n.

36. Coues, *Birds of the Northwest*, 537.

37. Coues, ed., *On the Trail of a Spanish Pioneer*, I, 239n, 242n. Camp Cady was established on the north bank of the Mojave River in 1865 to protect wagon trails in the area. It was abandoned in 1871.

38. *Ibid.*, 245n.

39. Coues, "From Arizona to the Pacific," 266.

40. Drum Barracks, built in 1862, was located one mile from Wilmington. The post was abandoned in 1871.

41. Coues, "From Arizona to the Pacific," 269.

42. *Ibid.*, 274.

43. Coues, "Birds Walking under Water" (1873), 149-50.

44. Coues, *Birds of the Northwest*, 340.

45. Eric Heyl, *Early American Steamers*, 6 vols. (Buffalo: N.p., 1953), I, 39-40, 93-94, 327-28.

46. Coues to Baird, Oct. 18, 1865.

47. Coues, "Notes on a Collection of Mammals from Arizona" (1867), 133.

48. *Annual Report of the Board of Regents of the Smithsonian Institution . . . 1867* (Washington, D.C.: Government Printing Office, 1872), 44-45.

49. Curtis, "Coues at His First Army Post," 5-9.

50. Henry Ulke (1821-1910), entomologist and portrait painter, was born in Frankenstein, Silesia, and came to the United States about 1845. He lived in

Washington, D.C., made friends at the Smithsonian, and amassed a large collection of insects. He opened a portrait studio in Washington and in time became known as "The Painter of Presidents."

51. For the original description, see Coues, "List of the Birds of Fort Whipple" (1866), 75; see also A.O.U., *Check-List,* 470.

52. Coues, "List of the Birds of Fort Whipple," 61; A.O.U., *Check-List,* 348.

53. Coues, "List of the Birds of Fort Whipple," 76; A.O.U., *Check-List,* 470.

54. Coues, "List of the Birds of Fort Whipple," 74; A.O.U., *Check-List,* 472.

55. Coues, "List of the Birds of Fort Whipple," 87; A.O.U., *Check-List,* 617.

56. Coues, "List of the Birds of Fort Whipple," 88; A.O.U., *Check-List,* 618.

57. Coues, "List of the Birds of Fort Whipple," 55; A.O.U., *Check-List,* 320.

58. Coues, "List of the Birds of Fort Whipple," 51; A.O.U., *Check-List,* 282.

59. For a complete list of birds described by Coues, see Appendix A. Coues described at least one mammalian subspecies collected at Fort Whipple, the Arizona gray squirrel; see Coues, "Quadrupends of Arizona," 357, for this description. Coues' collection of over fifty species of southwestern reptiles, frogs, and toads was described in Cope, "On the Reptilia and Batrachia of the Sonoran Province of the Nearctic Region" (1866), 300-314.

CHAPTER VII

Post Surgeon in Columbia

The *Atlantic* dropped anchor in New York on December 31, 1865. Less than two weeks later Elliott Coues received orders from the Adjutant General's Office "to report to Prof. Henry at the Smithsonian till May 1st."[1] Under the peacetime conditions then existing—the Civil War had ended in April of the preceding year—Army officers facing reassignment would ordinarily have been transferred to one or another of the numerous military posts scattered throughout the United States. Instead Coues was ordered to the Smithsonian, an assignment that may have been unique in the annals of the U.S. Army.

The Adjutant General's order, as we see it, admits of only one ready explanation. It had been issued at the behest of Baird, and on the grounds that Coues' untiring industry in the Southwest had enriched the Smithsonian museum to the extent of hundreds of valuable specimens, that his collection demanded close study forthwith, and that Coues, because of his familiarity with it, was the best possible choice for that job.

When Coues reported to the Smithsonian, Baird gave him an office of his own, probably in one of the Smithsonian towers. Here, free of medical duties for the time being, he was able to devote most of his working hours to the task of identifying, cataloging, and otherwise working up the specimens of his collection. It was a diversified collection, consisting not only of birds but also mammals, reptiles, amphibians, fish, insects, and plants. Since Coues' areas of specialization were limited to ornithology and mammalogy, he obtained the help of George Engelmann to do the plants, Theodore N. Gill the fish, Edward D. Cope the reptiles and amphibians, and Henry Ulke the insects.

Coues' scientific accomplishment during this Smithsonian interlude, one lasting just five months, went beyond working up the southwestern specimens. He found time to publish five articles, four of them ornithological and the other medical. One of his ornithological papers dealt with the birds of Arizona,[2] while the others continued his studies of the Procellariidae,[3] resulting in parts III, IV, and V. His medical piece described arrow wounds suffered by men in his Arizona outfit.[4]

During these Smithsonian months two events interrupted Coues' work, each time for several days. In February his father, owing to declining health, gave up his position with the Patent Office and he and Mrs. Coues moved back to Portsmouth. Elliott accompanied his parents. The second interruption began soon after his return to Washington from Portsmouth. On May 18 he "started back to Chelsea [Massachusetts] Naval Hospital and remained there about three weeks."[5] In no place have we been able to find an explanation of Coues' visit to this hospital, not even so much as a hint.

In June Coues was assigned by the Adjutant General's Office to new military duties in Columbia, South Carolina. Then, as now, Columbia was the state's capital, situated on the Congaree River one hundred or so miles northwest of Charleston. In 1866 it was a city of about 10,000 inhabitants. Coues arrived there on June 21. He was immediately attached to a military unit already in residence, one of many such units strategically positioned throughout the southern states during the period of reconstruction. Columbia was then rebuilding from the fire of February 19, 1865, which had reduced much of it to ashes, the result of General Sherman's march through the city.[6]

For information about Coues' stay in Columbia, where he spent the next two and a half years, we are dependent almost entirely on letters he wrote from the Army post there to Baird. In his first, dated June 27, he said in part:

> I am settled here in excellent quarters, as Post Surgeon, and am altogether as comfortably fixed as I could be anywhere, outside of home and the Smithsonian. . . . I have ample time to study, write or collect. As soon as it gets a little cooler I will go into the fields again, and perhaps pick up something nice. Just now it is too hot to stir out in the day time.
>
> Will you give me a letter of introduction to Dr. Gibbes?[7] And also one to the Lecontes, though I don't know exactly which ones are here.[8] Our quarters are in the buildings of S.C. University, and are as beautiful as Lafayette Square in Washington.
>
> I wish I had seen Dr. Bachman[9] in Charleston. Can't you give me also a letter to him, and I will then write myself.
>
> And please keep me posted on everything new that turns up in our department. What is the matter with [Theodore] Gill, that he don't write? Better address me: "Surg., 6th infantry Post, Col., S.C."[10]

So, as this letter to Baird informs, Post Surgeon Coues was attached to the 6th Infantry, and comfortably billeted in one of the University of South Carolina buildings, which had escaped the ravages of the 1865 fire.

We have no figures on the size of the Army unit in Columbia during Coues' stay there, but in 1879, the year after Coues left, the unit consisted of nine officers and 171 enlisted men.[11] The post was situated on the left bank of the Congaree, near the southern boundary of the city, and close to a large swamp. Except for malaria, Columbia was "remarkably healthful,"[12] and Coues' duties as a medical officer were rarely burdensome.

After Coues received from Baird the requested letters of introduction, he replied: "I am now fairly established here, have my newly opened hospital in working order, and plenty of time to do anything I choose." In succeeding letters to Baird he said that Professor LeConte (whether John or Joseph we cannot be certain) had called on him and that he was "on the most cordial and pleasant terms with Prof. LeConte and family." On the contrary, Dr. Gibbes had shown "most emphatically, that he can't 'go' my army connections."

No omniscience is required to understand Dr. Gibbes's coolness toward Coues. In the recent fire—which he resolutely attributed to Sherman and his Yankee minions—he had lost a museum-sized collection of birds, shells, minerals, fossils, and other natural history specimens, the work of a lifetime.

Somewhat later that year Coues received a welcome bit of news. The Adjutant General's Office notified him that, "for faithful and meritorious services during the late war," he had been promoted to brevet captain.[13] Actually, this promotion had been made while Coues was still in Arizona, though, for reasons unknown, he did not receive official notification until now. The rank of brevet then in vogue, but since discontinued, was often granted by the Army and Marine Corps to honor an officer without, at the same time, increasing his pay, rank, or authority.

2

Writing to Baird on September 18, 1866, Coues revealed a potentially ugly matter:

Yours of the 12th has just reached me enclosing Dr. Palmer's[14] of July 13th. I hardly know whether to be most amused or most angry at the letter.

Perhaps as you say I ought to have written him; but he has certainly jumped
at some very strange conclusions, and evidently is of [the] opinion that I
intend or have already defrauded him of the credit due him for some
portions of our collections. But you know of course that his idea is entirely
groundless. In sending the plants to Dr. Engelmann, and in giving the insects
to Dr. Ulke, I was particularly careful to tell both these gentlemen that Dr.
P[almer] was to have equal credit with myself for the collection. . . . The
Doctor seems to have the impression that I am using all his specimens to
prepare a report; and I will with pleasure, as you suggest, disabuse him of his
erroneous belief; though at the same time I shall find it hard to forget his
unjust suspicions, or to forgive his shabby conduct in sending to you so much
immeasured personal abuse of myself. He might at least have written to me to
enquire into the truth of what he has so readily taken for granted. It is
annoying to the last degree to me [to] have such things said of me, even
though they be as in this case wholly false.

In Dr. Palmer's own words: "Dr. Engelmann told me Dr. Coues
presented the collection to him without the least mention of my name in
connection [with] it. . . . It is humiliating to make collections under the
hardships and risks that had to be endured in Arizona and then have the
credit stolen."[15]

To better understand this sorry affair, we must go back to July 26,
1865, the day on which Dr. Palmer, after the long stagecoach ride from
Kansas City, arrived at Fort Whipple. Here he was welcomed by Coues,
who had in his first year there collected a number of plants for Dr.
Engelmann.

According to Palmer's biographer: "It may never be known what
arrangements the two men made, but evidently they collected together
during the summer. . . . When in early autumn [October 23] Coues left
Fort Whipple to return to the East, he was entrusted [by Palmer] with the
joint plant collections on condition that he submit them to the proper
authorities for determination. . . . When, some months after his departure from Arizona, he turned the plants over to Engelmann, he
minimized or entirely neglected to mention Palmer's part in their
collection. From Coues' negligence developed a situation about which
Palmer was extremely resentful."[16]

That Coues spiritedly denied Palmer's charge of wrongdoing is
evident from his above letter to Baird. He had, he said, been "particularly careful" to tell Engelmann that Palmer should receive "equal credit"
with himself. Equally evident, or so it seems, was Palmer's conviction that
Coues, when transmitting the plants in question to Engelmann, had
intentionally refrained from mentioning that many of the plants had

been collected by Palmer. The precise truth of the matter will probably never be known, though we are inclined to believe that Coues was innocent of any *willful* misconduct. One reason for thinking so is that in all of his published writings when drawing on others for information, he sems to have leaned over backward to give credit where credit was due.

If Coues' letter to Palmer—the one he told Baird he would write—were extant, it would possibly make good reading. As we shall have abundant opportunity to observe in later chapters of this study, in any argument or controversy Coues' best weapons were words. As he became more practiced in their use, he wielded them with increased vigor, finesse, and effectiveness. Few of his adversaries left the field of combat unmarked.

3

The year 1866 was nearing its end when Coues obtained a fifteen-day leave. He spent the greater part of it in Portsmouth with his mother and ailing father. After leaving them he stopped briefly at the Essex Institute in Salem, Massachusetts. Of this visit he wrote Baird: ". . . I saw Prof. Morse,[17] & Dr. Hyatt,[18] as well as Mr. Putnam.[19] Dr. Packard [of Labrador memory] was also there; and together they made a strong anti-Agassizian conclave, needing only H. J. Clark[20] to complete its belligerent aspect."[21] Apparently Coues' main purpose in visiting the institute was to examine its cabinet of birds. In any event, he soon afterward published a paper about that collection.[22]

Coues' sister Grace accompanied him on his return to South Carolina. She spent the winter there with him, much to his delight, for he held her in deep affection. In letters to Baird that winter, Coues occasionally ended them with such remarks as, "Gracie of *Dendroica* fame sends her regards." Presumably Baird was pleased, for, as we remember, he had earlier paid tribute to Grace by naming a warbler new to science Grace's warbler (*Dendroica graciae*).

The year 1867 had advanced only a few weeks when Coues informed Baird, "I am working on the high road to getting married." Details of the nuptials, which soon followed, are to be found in Coues' "Book of Dates": "May 3, married Miss Jeannie A[ugusta] McKinney[23] of Rushford, N.Y., at 8 P.M., at Trinity Church in Columbia, S.C., Rev. Dr. Shand, reception at Col. Moore's to 1 A.M., 4th; no wedding journey."

A few days later Coues wrote Baird: "The lady was Miss McKinney of New York, which fact may account for her fancying a Yankee; and of course I can state in reply to your question, that I considered her both 'conducive and nice.' Neither of us having much fancy for a wedding *tour*, we are quietly living in my quarters here. Although a stranger to you, she wishes me to give you her regards, as she seems almost to know you, I have spoken of you to her so often."

Outside of the fact that Jeannie came from Rushford, a small town in the western part of New York state and that her father was Owen McKinney, we know nothing more about her before she became Mrs. Elliott Coues. We may presume that Coues first met her in Columbia, perhaps while she was visiting local friends or relatives. Since Baird was aware of all the untoward circumstances attending Coues' first marriage, his question to him as to whether Jeannie was "conducive and nice" could hardly have been rhetorical.

4

Shortly before his marriage Coues had learned from Baird of an opportunity which, if seized, might advance him professionally. This chance arose soon after the United States, on March 30, 1867, acquired Alaska Territory ("Seward's Folly") from Russia. Baird wrote Coues immediately inquiring if he would be interested in transferring to the newly obtained territory. Coues replied on April 18:

> I have been away for three days, and only recd. yours of the 12th & 13th yesterday. I telegraphed at once that I would go; if you think best. The only thing that makes me hesitate, is that I expect to be married very shortly, and so of course feel disinclined to go unless she can go too—as she is very willing to do, provided it is practicable. Your letters are a little indefinite . . . I want particularly to know clearly if I go up on an exploring or other sort of an expedition, for next summer only; or whether I am to go as Asst. Surg., U.S.A., and be stationed there indefinitely. Of course I should like the former best; indeed would hardly like the latter at all, unless I was pretty sure of getting back to civilization when I got tired of Russian Am[erica]. Please write me fully on all points concerned and particularly your opinion concerning facilities for taking a prospective wife. . . . There is no part of our country I would prefer to visit [more] than the one contemplated.

This "part of our country" was then so new that the word Alaska apparently had yet to enter Coues' vocabulary; as noted, he called it "Russian America." At once, after Secretary of State William H. Seward had signed the treaty of transfer, and the United States had dispatched personnel, including troops, to take possession of the territory, Baird saw the opportunity to send a naturalist there with one of the Army units.

The Alaska matter hung fire for several months, with Baird and Coues continuing an exchange of letters expressing viewpoints both for and against. At one time it appeared that Coues had altogether lost the chance of going. Then, on March 23, 1868—practically a year after the proposition first presented itself—Coues wrote to Baird: "So Sitka is 'up' again! Well! I'm heartily sick of So. Ca. [South Carolina] and glad to go anywhere for a change. Recommend me for the place! But I want to know the following: Is it to be a permanent stationing, or a trip there and back? Can my wife & baby [his first child, Edith Louise Coues, had been born on January 31] go too in the former event?"

Possibly Baird's answers failed to satisfy Coues. In any event, just a few days later the matter was settled once and for all. That becomes clear when we read an entry in Coues' "Book of Dates" for March 25, 1868: "Letter from Surgeon General's Office offers orders to Alaska, if desired by me; declined." So neither then nor afterward, having refused the Alaska post, did Coues work up a "furor scientificus"—to use the words he employed in another connection—about the avian and other faunal delights of that territory.

Meanwhile the possibility of another job for Coues had arisen. Writing to Baird in mid-summer 1867, he said: "I have a contingent chance for the chair of Nat[ural] Sci[ence] in the University of Wisconsin, over which I am meditating a little. Greatly doubt my ability, particularly as to Chemistry, and [am] also somewhat disinclined to quit the definite lasting position of indolent ease at 2000 a year, with all my time my own, for anything involving work, and uncertainty of duration, and only $1500 p. ann. [per annum]. What do you think?"

When Baird wrote negatively, Coues replied: "I shall take good heed of your caution about resigning for the Wisconsin University. I do not much like the idea myself." Coues thereafter dropped any further consideration of Wisconsin and continued his Army sinecure in Columbia.

A somberly worded 1867 entry in Coues' "Book of Dates" reads: "July 3, died Samuel Elliott Coues, my father, at Portsmouth, N.H., at 9 A.M. Buried July 5 in family lot, Auburn St. cemetery." Immediately following this unhappy event, Coues wrote Baird: "I have just received intelligence, not the less sad because for some time anticipated, of the death of my father . . . I have applied for a leave of 30 days to go on to Portsmouth, and I will probably receive it. If so I shall possibly be in W[ashington] very soon, with Mrs. C[oues]. . . . Please let me know your intended movements for the summer."

Delayed by the illness of his wife, Coues did not leave Columbia until August, and then alone. It was August 19, from Portsmouth, that he next wrote to Baird:

> I was much disappointed not to meet you in Washn. when I came through. . . . I stay here a few days with mother & sister—Gracie will marry Mr. [Charles A.] Page, whom you know, now Consul at Zurich, in October—and then meander slowly back to Columbia. I am studying *Alcidae* [auks, murres, and puffins] this trip, and shall examine all the specimens in Boston, N.Y., & Phila. on the way. . . . Can I not have all the Smith[sonian] Auks sent to me at Columbia? . . . I expect to be several days with Mr. [John] Cassin in Phila. and one or two with Mr. [George N.] Lawrence & [D. G.] Elliot in N.Y. . . . Is there any likelihood we shall meet by the way anywhere? I have no time to come to Carlisle, [Pennsylvania], otherwise I certainly would. I should much like to see the scenes of your early exploits.

Some ten days later, again from Portsmouth, Coues advised Baird:

> I received your pleasant letter today. Much obliged for the proffered Auks, & still more for your kind invitation. I will try to come to Carlisle to see you and the place. I should like to be in the vicinity of the "Vale of Tempe"— for the associations which are indissolubly connected in my mind with the inception of my studies ornithological, and my "Alma pater," as I love to call you. . . . I go tomorrow to Salem, to see the Essex Institute men. By the way, they had a large "field meeting" here [in Portsmouth] the other day, at which I figured in an ex tempore lecture on Apaches, which "took" very well. . . . Things are changed very much at home—with the death of my father, and the preparations for sister's marriage. Mother will probably accompany her to Zurich, and we shall have no "family" left together anywhere. *Dendroica graciae* sends you her regards.

Coues was denied a requested extension of leave and so did not get to Carlisle, either then or later; however, as he wrote Baird: "I had a very pleasant & profitable time in Phila. Have full descr[iption]s etc., of all the Acad[emy] spec[imen]s, states of plumage, etc. which may not be in the S.I. coll[ections]; and also complete mss. copies of the articles relating to the subject in hand from all the authors needed to be consulted or quoted during investigation. Upon receipt of the S.I. specs. I think I shall be fully in possession of book and spec[imen] data for the proposed paper [on the Alcidae]."

5

In his letters to Baird from Columbia, Coues periodically deplored his inability to accomplish much in a scientific way, in spite of "ample time to study, write or collect." For instance, he early complained of his "lazy, apathetic state of mind" induced by his style of living. Later he wrote: "I have been an entire nonentity, ornithologically speaking." And still later, "I am just now vigorously engaged in doing nothing."

Coues was far from being as apathetic and unproductive as his letters to Baird had indicated. During his stay in South Carolina, more than two years, he published at least a dozen papers and, on leaving, had others in progress. In this period, too, Coues began to demonstrate some of the versatility which so markedly colored all of his later years. Until now his published works had been almost exclusively about birds, but at Columbia he blossomed as a mammalogist—writing two papers about the quadrupeds of Arizona[24]—and as anatomist. He even tried his hand as an artist.

Coues' anatomical studies dealt with the opossum (*Didelphis virginiana*). Early in 1867 he advised Baird: "I have made arrangements for getting a parcel of possums and will go into them. At this season I may find mating males, or pregnant females, and so may light upon some interesting points." Somewhat later, writing to Baird again, he said: "I am working hard 'On the structure of the Opossum' and am much interested in the strange beast's anatomy." He then confessed: "I have been practicing lately and find that I can *draw* bones & muscle much better than I had any idea was in my power. So I propose to have a lot of figures for the monogr[aph]. . . . I enclose a sample—thigh bone of Possum. Please return it, telling me frankly whether or not you think such drawings will pass muster."

When Coues' article about the opossum appeared in print, readers found that it contained excellent descriptions of the bones and muscles of that marsupial and that it was illustrated with thirty-five sketches, each done by Coues' own hand.[25] It is worthy of note that these drawings represented Coues' first *serious* efforts as an artist. In due course, as we shall see, he became an even more ambitious draftsman.

Only those scientists most familiar with Coues' education know what a commanding knowledge of anatomy he possessed, acquired through dissection of human cadavers—snatched or otherwise—while a student at National Medical College. In later life this knowledge enabled Coues to contribute brilliantly to an extended comprehension of the anatomy of birds.

While stationed at Columbia, Coues published several articles about birds, two of them of particular interest to ornithologists. One was about the Alcidae,[26] of which he had been writing Baird, and the other about the birds of South Carolina.[27] The former, revisionary and technical, ran to eighty pages. The latter, prepared at Baird's suggestion, listed 249 species that Coues regarded as eligible for his list. Coues asked J. A. Allen: "Did I tell you that I am bringing out a Synopsis of the So. Ca[rolina] birds? We shall then want only a careful list of Floridan birds to render perfect the chain of local lists along the Atlantic states, from Calais, Me., southward—Verrill's, Boardman's,[28] yours, Lawrence's, Coues & Prentiss', and mine. These lists, carefully compared, present some very valuable and decisive data. I am rather an enthusiast, as you may have surmised, on the subject of 'local lists'!"[29]

On reading Coues' paper on the South Carolina birds, we were surprised at the meagerness of "valuable and decisive" data he provided about some of the birds. Of the Carolina paroquet (*Conuropsis carolinensis*), for example, he wrote only: "This species is given in Prof. Gibbes' list, and appears to have been in former times a common bird; but its occurrence has not been noted of late years. It is scarcely entitled to a place in the list."[30]

Thus this bird, which the English naturalist Mark Catesby (c. 1679-1749), on his visit to the Carolinas in 1722, described as arriving autumnally in the rice fields "in infinite swarms,"[31] had so diminished in the Carolinas by 1868, some 150 years later, that Coues thought it scarcely worthy of mention. In later years, after Coues' knowledge of the Carolina paroquet had grown, he wrote: ". . . it would seem that if the cruel and wanton slaughter to which the gentle creatures are subjected by idlers goes on, they must before long be exterminated."[32] The "gentle creatures," now extinct, formerly ranged from Florida and the Gulf states north to Maryland, the Great Lakes, and Iowa, and west to Colorado, Oklahoma, and Texas. According to the most reliable of sources, one was last reported in February, 1920, on Fort Drum Creek, Florida.[33]

As a concluding note on Coues' publications during his South Carolina residence, it may be remarked that by now his writings were increasingly in demand by editors of the various scientific journals of the day. Heretofore almost all of his published papers had appeared in either *The Ibis* or the *Proceedings of the Academy of Natural Sciences of Philadelphia*. While stationed at Columbia, however, Coues found other outlets for his articles, notably: *Communications of the Essex Institute, American Naturalist*, and *Proceedings of the Boston Society of Natural History*. Obviously, Coues' reputation as a talented writer and scientist had been steadily mounting.

6

One of the happier and more productive experiences of Coues' life was his close relationship with J. A. Allen. It began with a letter which Coues wrote to Allen from Columbia on January 15, 1868: "I have long known of you . . . through our mutual friends at Salem, and am happy of even merely this epistolary approach to a personal acquaintance and relation; which I trust may some day ripen into something more and better." The friendship between the two men did indeed ripen and, in time, became an extremely important factor in the shaping and advancement of American ornithology.

Other letters which Coues soon wrote to the Cambridge naturalist reveal the quality of the former's thinking on topics of mutual interest. For example, in a particularly striking paragraph Coues disclosed to Allen his interpretation of truth: 'Truth is ever itself—it is the pendulum at rest at the golden mean; it is the swaying of men's thoughts that point to *seeming* change & that unsettles current opinion. We are all mere proof readers of Nature's book . . . and we are apt to insert our commas according to our day's beliefs; but we cannot alter the true manuscript."

In his first letter to Allen, Coues also put into words his burgeoning convictions about species: "Since Linnaeus founded the binomial system, we all insensibly look upon the command of a generic and specific name as prima facie evidence of an author's belief that the bird to which the appellation is adapted is a 'species.' In truth it is not, or at least may not be, and in numberless cases the author of the binom[ial] himself does not think so. . . . The definition of the word species is so far arbitrary & artificial that the man using it usually, to me, confesses his inability to say outright what he means by it. 'Species,' as we employ it, is not a fact, but a man's judgment upon a probable or possible fact, and hence virtually a term *de convenance*."

In some respects the decade of the 1860s was unlike any other in the history of science. It followed hard on the heels of Darwin's *On the Origin of Species* and was marked by a dramatic revolution in thinking when men, notably the biologists, sought to rationalize their thoughts in a newly created climate that disallowed fixed species in favor of evolving species. To Coues, as to so many others, an important question needed answering: what constitutes a species?

7

Columbia, South Carolina, was a far distance from Fort Whipple, Arizona Territory. At the latter station when Coues went afield, as he did almost daily, he often returned to base with a bird new to him, and sometimes new to science; not so in South Carolina. The birds of that state had long since been identified and described by naturalists who had preceded him there. Months before he left Columbia he expressed himself to Baird and others as "heartily tired" of the place.

That Coues grew increasingly discontent with his existence in South Carolina was not due entirely to a native avifauna destitute of undescribed species. In a letter of October 28, 1868, to George N. Lawrence, he revealed another reason:

> The state of society here is extremely unfavorable to study of any sort. We are in a continual ferment, in anticipation of open trouble about elections—the military being distributed all over the state in readiness for an outbreak, and everybody is in a 'quid nunc' frame of mind. The indications are decidedly in favor of trouble—perhaps to amount to much bloodshed. You who live in the quiet and prosperous North can hardly realize the state of things here. The large number of troops in this garrison keeps me busy all the time—and when my hours are not actually taken up, they are so liable to interruption that it is difficult to accomplish anything in a scientific or literary way.[34]

Just three months to the day after writing the above to Lawrence, Coues received the welcome news that he was being transferred to Fort Macon, North Carolina.

NOTES

1. Coues' "Book of Dates" (1866).
2. Coues, "List of the Birds of Fort Whipple" (1866).
3. Coues' "Critical Review of the Family *Procellariidae*," pts. III, IV, V (1866). In his "Book of Dates" Coues recorded visiting Philadelphia for a week (Mar. 8-15) to study Procellariidae.
4. Coues, "Some Notes on Arrow-Wounds" (1866), 321-24.
5. Coues' "Book of Dates" (1866).
6. Controversy still exists over whether Sherman's men set fire to Columbia or whether residents of the city applied torches to bales of cotton to keep them from falling into Union hands, and thus unwittingly fired the city.
7. Robert Wilson Gibbes (1809-66), physician and naturalist, was born in Charleston, S.C., and graduated from South Carolina College, Columbia.
8. There were two LeContes, both scientists, then living in Columbia: John and

Joseph. John LeConte (1818-91), physician, teacher, and physicist, was born in Liberty County, Ga. He graduated from Franklin College (later the University of Georgia) and afterward from the College of Physicians and Surgeons, New York City (1841). In the years 1856-69 he was professor of physics at South Carolina College. He is not to be confused with his first cousin, John Lawrence LeConte (1825-83), of LeConte's thrasher (*Toxostoma lecontei*) fame. Joseph LeConte (1823-1901), geologist, was born in Liberty County, Ga., and in 1841 graduated from Franklin College. In 1844, in company with his cousin John Lawrence LeConte, he traveled to the headwaters of the Mississippi, and in 1845 he graduated from the College of Physicians and Surgeons, New York City. Meantime he had made the acquaintance of such prominent naturalists as Audubon and Baird. In 1857 he went to South Carolina College as professor of physics.

9. John Bachman (1790-1874), naturalist and clergyman, was born in Rhinebeck, N.Y., and from childhood showed a marked interest in natural history. In 1814 he was ordained a Lutheran minister, and the next year was called to a pulpit in Charleston, S.C. Following a visit by Audubon to Charleston in 1831, the two men became friends. As a naturalist, Bachman is best known for *The Viviparous Quadrupeds of North America* (1845-49), a three-volume work produced jointly with Audubon.

10. Letters to Baird from Coues used in this chapter are from the Smithsonian Archives, Record Unit 7002, Spencer F. Baird Papers, 1833-89.

11. Frantz, "Columbia, S.C." (1875), 128.

12. *Ibid.*, 126-27.

13. T. H. S. Hamersley, *Complete Register of the Army, 1779-1879* (Washington, D.C.: By the author, 1880), 376.

14. Edward Palmer (c. 1830-1911), botanist, was born in England and, at the age of eighteen, came to the United States. After attending lectures at Cleveland Homeopathic College (1856-57), he went to Kansas to practice medicine. Interested in botany from an early age, he spent most of his later years traveling and amassing a plant collection numbering some 100,000 specimens.

15. Palmer to Harvard botanist Asa Gray. This letter (undated) is the property of the American Philosophical Society, Philadelphia.

16. McVaugh, *Edward Palmer, Plant Explorer of the American West* (1956), 25-26.

17. Edward Sylvester Morse (1838-1925), zoologist, was born in Portland, Me., and studied under Louis Agassiz at Lawrence Scientific School, Harvard. He was later professor of zoology at Bowdoin College, and still later director of the Peabody Museum.

18. Alpheus Hyatt (1838-1902), zoologist, was born in Washington, D.C., and in 1858 went to Harvard to study under Agassiz. During the years 1867-88 he was professor of zoology and paleontology at Massachusetts Institute of Technology.

19. Frederick Ward Putnam (1839-1915), naturalist and museum administrator, was born in Salem, Mass. After studying under Agassiz, he served as curator of ichthyology at the Boston Society of Natural History (1859-68). He was also, for a time, superintendent of the museum of Essex Institute.

20. Henry James Clark (1826-73), biologist, was born in Easton, Mass. In 1857 Agassiz chose him as his private assistant, and he was assistant professor of zoology at Lawrence Scientific School (1860-65). In 1866, the year Coues met him at Essex Institute, he was named to the chair of zoology, botany, and geology at Pennsylvania State College.

21. Just seven years earlier (1859) Charles Darwin had published *On the Origin of Species,* and Darwinian evolution had become a subject of heated controversy. Louis Agassiz, among others, had vigorously opposed it, whereas, from what Coues said, the men at Essex Institute had apparently accepted it.

22. Coues, "Catalogue of the Birds of North America Contained in the Museum of the Essex Institute" (1868).

23. Apparently her baptismal name was Jane Augusta McKinney (not McKenney, as some writers have it). On a genealogical chart belonging to William P. Coues the name appears incorrectly as Jane Ann McKinney.

24. Coues, "Notes on a Collection of Mammals from Arizona" (1867) and "The Quadrupeds of Arizona" (1867).

25. Coues, "The Osteology and Myology of *Didelphys virginiana*" (1872).

26. Coues, "A Monograph of the *Alcidae*" (1868).

27. Coues, "Synopsis of the Birds of South Carolina" (1868).

28. George Augustus Boardman (1818-1901), naturalist and sportsman, was born in Newburyport, Mass., and in 1828 moved to Calais, Me. In 1862 he published "Catalogue of the Birds found in the Vicinity of Calais, Maine, and about the Islands at the Mouth of the Bay of Fundy," *Procs. Bost. Soc. Nat. Hist.,* IX, 122-32.

29. This and other letters from Coues to Allen used in this work are from the Department of Ornithology, American Museum of Natural History, New York City.

30. Coues, "Synopsis of the Birds of South Carolina," 119.

31. George Frederick Frick and Raymond Phineas Stearns, *Mark Catesby, the Colonial Audubon* (Urbana: University of Illinois Press, 1961), 63.

32. Coues, *Key to North American Birds,* 5th ed., (1903), II, 617.

33. A.O.U., *Check-List,* 267.

34. Letter in Miscellaneous Mss. Collections, Department of Special Collections, Kenneth Spencer Research Library, University of Kansas, Lawrence.

CHAPTER VIII

Fort Macon, North Carolina

At one time Elliott Coues wrote of "the eccentric course of military migration" that had stranded him in 1869 "on a sandbar on the North Carolina coast."[1] The sandbar was Bogue Island, a thread of land twenty-six miles in length and averaging less than one mile in width, which extended roughly east and west and was separated from the mainland by Bogue Sound. Fort Macon, begun in 1826 and completed in 1834, was situated at the eastern end of Bogue Island, about ten miles northeast of Beaufort, the nearest city of consequence on the mainland. On April 25, 1862, combined Union army and naval forces had captured Fort Macon from southern troops.

Coues spent the better part of two years at Fort Macon, from mid-February, 1869, to late November, 1870. At first he seemed pleased with his new station. Writing to Baird a few days after his arrival, he said in part:

> Ornith[ologically] speaking, this place is a decided improvement on Columbia. I want to do some collecting this spring, and will do so, if I can get the needful—none to be purchased about here. Can you send me, as on other occasions, say
>
> | | |
> |---|---|
> | *Mustard seed* shot | bag 1 |
> | Powder | lb. 4 |
> | Caps | no. 1000 |
> | Wads, no. 14 | no. 1000 |
> | Arsenic | lb. 2 |

If so, I will give S.I. [Smithsonian Institution] pretty much everything I collect, as before. Also, lots of labels, like, e.g.

Expl. Coast, North Carolina. Smithsonian Institution No. _____	
Fort Macon, N.C.	Dr. Elliott Coues, U.S.A.

Can you tell me anything about [John] Cassin's last days, sickness &c.? I have nothing but the bare news of his sad and untimely death [at the age of fifty-six]. Does it not seem strange and hard that such men should be taken when thousands of worthless hulks "burn to the socket?"[2]

Coues also informed Baird that his article on the bones and muscles of the opossum was nearly ready for the professor and that Jeffries Wyman[3] had promised to prepare an appendix on the brain for it.[4]

On this same day Coues wrote also to his old friend, Dr. James G. Cooper, whom he had last seen in 1865 when they had been together on the Pacific Coast:

> . . . Of course you heard the sad, sad news that John Cassin's labors are ended. The loss to science none of us can measure. . . . Since Audubon passed away [in 1851] from the scene of his usefulness, death has struck no such cruel blow to our beloved science. . . . The all-worthy, time-honored quartette has been rudely broken. Now only a triangle, Lawrence, Brewer and Baird, remains of the last generation of American ornithologists. Who shall lead opinion when they too are gathered to their fathers? A higher trust than we perhaps appreciate, is laid upon the few of us this later day who pay devotion to the beautiful study of ornithology. It is no less than the keeping bright and untarnished, and transmitting to our successors, the name and fame of the science that has absorbed such minds as those of Wilson, Nuttall, Audubon, Bonaparte,[5] and Cassin. May we prove worthy servitors, guarding with jealous care our trust, watchful that the vestal fires shall ever burn at the shrine where we worship with a clear and steady flame.[6]

As a consequence of the several notable contributions Coues had already made to his beloved science, and the praise heaped upon him by fellow-ornithologists at home and abroad, his assurance and self-esteem had grown accordingly—and measurably. It seems obvious from his above comments to Cooper that the twenty-six-year-old Coues regarded himself as a worthy successor to Cassin and a logical heir apparent to Lawrence, Brewer, and Baird. Of course, as future events would prove, his confidence was justified.

2

With the coming of spring Coues, until now unfamiliar with the southern Atlantic beaches, found Bogue Island to be an increasingly congenial and rewarding place. It afforded rare opportunities for the collecting naturalist and, as a result, we find him soon displaying an interest in all kinds of animals common to the North Carolina littoral. The several boxes of specimens he shortly dispatched to Baird contained not only the expected birdskins but also reptiles, fish, insects, crabs, shells, and "Radiates."[7]

After the birds began nesting, Coues turned oologist. In particular, he questioned the number of eggs certain species were said to lay. In mid-June, 1869, for instance, he asked Baird: "Do you believe that Terns always lay three eggs—I don't. I have two, half-hatched from one lot of S[*terna*] *antillarum* [least tern].[8] Do you pin your faith to the statement that Plovers, Sandpipers &c. lay 4 eggs? I don't, for I have before me a complement of 3 eggs of *Aegialites Wilsoni* [Wilson's plover],[9] half hatched." Reflecting his continued absorption in this oological matter, Coues soon wrote to Baird again, saying that he had found two additional nests of Wilson's plover, each with three eggs, and three more of the least tern, one with two eggs and the other with one. Almost triumphantly he concluded: "So much for the 'fact' according to tradition that Terns lay three eggs and Plovers four."

The above about tern and plover eggs provides evidence of Coues' ability to note minute details, always the mark of a keen observer. Another example may be cited, that of his close attention to the coming and going of the birds of Bogue Island. Writing Baird in early June, he remarked that royal terns (*Thalasseus maximus*) were then common, that the sharp-tailed sparrows (*Ammospiza caudacuta*) had already gone north, that the seaside sparrows (*Ammospiza maritima*) were breeding everywhere, and that the willets (*Catoptrophorus semipalmatus*) and the plovers were apparently the only shore birds then present.

At Fort Macon, as in Arizona, Coues collected not only for Baird but also for other scientists. He collected fish for Theodore N. Gill, insects (such as "1,100 Orthoptera") for Samuel H. Scudder,[10] and "Crustyshins" (i.e., Crustacea) for William Stimpson.

To aid in his collecting, Coues soon enlisted, probably without the sanction of his commanding officer, the services of his hospital steward, A. C. Beals. Judging from what he wrote to Baird in a letter of mid-July, 1869, it was a highly satisfactory arrangement:

> By the way, I shall probably send in the box a few skins prepared by my steward. On general principles he is a numbskull, but with streaks of intelligence here and there. After a dozen trials he learned to skin first rate, as you will see. I have innoculated him with a little of the divine afflatus, and he picks up a good many things. Now a prime trait with him is a highly laudable ambition. If you were to write him a letter of his own, with S.I. stamp on it in full vig[nette], saying they are very good, and bestowing a little of that which you know so well how to bestow, it would set him up wonderfully. Moreover, if you were to have some labels stricken off, the counterparts of mine with "Hosp. Stew. A. C. Beals, U.S.A." on them, in

place of mine, he would be a fair candidate for the Asylum for awhile, and after that you would probably have a good many labels come back to you. I shall not always be with him, and the labels will perpetually egg him on.

Writing of Coues years afterward, J. A. Allen said: ". . . the kindness of his nature led him on many occasions to tender a helping hand to younger ornithological aspirants."[11] Young Beals would seem to have been one of the aspirants. We think that Coues was genuinely fond of him, in spite of his sharp words, and that he quickly responded to Beals's eagerness and ambition to improve himself. At the same time Coues was, of course, not blind to the services rendered gratuitously by Beals. Whatever may have been Coues' prime motive in requesting of Baird a letter and labels, Baird responded affirmatively. And on receipt of the labels, Beals was "extra duly delighted."

3

Limitations of space disallow reproduction in their entirety of many other letters that Coues wrote to Baird from Fort Macon. We would be at fault, however, if we ignored certain passages.

June 9, 1869: "Very poor chance of my getting a whiff of [Smithsonian] document room zephyrs. I can't get away—have just had to refuse a kind invitation from Dr. Samson[12] to come on at Commencement [of Columbian College] to make a speech. He says the fac[ulty] are going to give me a Ph.D." Beyond question, Coues' alma mater regarded him as one of their most distinguished graduates. It had already given him an A.B., an A.M., and an M.D., all earned degrees; now (1869), in recognition of impressive postgraduate achievements, it would bestow on him an honorary Ph.D.

June 9, 1869: "Isn't there *any* chance of my being able to get a Washington station as soon as I have squeezed Macon a little drier? I do want it so badly!" By "Washington station" Coues certainly meant a position at the Smithsonian, where he would have the satisfaction and benefits of working more closely with Baird. Indeed, as evidence supplied later strongly indicates, he coveted a Smithsonian post above all others. This craving may or may not have entered into his refusal that year of an offer to teach zoology and comparative anatomy at Norwich University in Vermont.

June 23, 1869: "You know I never *could* find [bird] nests. It is my great deficiency as an ornithologist." This is possibly an exaggeration, but even if true, the flaw seems to have interposed no great drawback to his success as a birdman.

July 28, 1869: "I envy your summer trips. Do you recollect, that in all these years, you and I never have once gone out to have a look at *live* birds together? I fancy I should relish a collecting-day with you!" Beyond question, an expression by Coues of profound regret.

October 15, 1869: "As my other letter shows, I am just getting off a box of birds, representing Beals' & my collections during Aug.-Sept. Nothing but birds this time, and most of them Beals'; please give him a good acknowledgement." Obviously Coues' (and Baird's) encouragement of Beals was paying dividends.

November 15, 1869: "I don't know of any line of work that takes so much time & hard study, as original dissection for a paper. I commenced 'possum [study] three years ago, and only got the ms. off my hands just now. But I work con amore at such things and so I shall probably recant, and go into it again." Coues did not recant; never again did he undertake an anatomical study that demanded such prolonged dissection.

December 31, 1869: "Allow me to wish you a happy new year, and many returns, to you & yours. . . . Have just had a small windfall. Struck a bargain with Ed[itor] of leading N.Y. Med[ical] Journ. for a series of articles on 'transcendental anatomy' at $3.00 a page, & 25 extra copies. Between us, who's the greener of the two—I to dare write, or he to dare publish, such inane abstruseness?"[13] Coues had another literary windfall this same year. According to his "Book of Dates," "During 1869 I wrote much for *Liberal Christian*" (eleven articles all told; see Bibliography).

May 14, 1870: "Packard & Morse arrived a few days ago, and we are just now dredging and collecting generally in Invertebrates. Morse has found *Lingulas*[14] already, and we have many other interesting things. They both desire to be kindly remembered to you." Coues was here referring to his friends Alpheus S. Packard and E. S. Morse, both last seen at Essex Institute. Presumably they had come to Fort Macon on Coues' invitation and on his assurance that Bogue Island was fertile ground for collectors.

May 25, 1870: "Packard and Morse left yesterday, escorting Mrs. C[oues] north. . . . You see I am left quite alone, but I hope for release soon. I can profitably put in a month or so in botany, and in finishing up some ms. on the general natural history of the place."[15] Never before, or after, did Coues exhibit such an interest in plant life.

4

During his stay at Fort Macon, Coues continued his correspondence with J. A. Allen, writing almost as often to him as to Baird. When advising Allen of his transfer to the North Carolina post, he pointedly remarked: "The only immutable thing in the Army, you know, is the certainty of mutability!"

On learning that Allen had recently returned from an ornithological visit to Florida, Coues expressed delight: "Now, I suppose, we shall soon have what I called attention to in my birds of South Carolina— as a desideratum—a good list of Floridan birds. We *must* have it. . . . With this acquisition we shall have a series of [local] lists from almost all adjoining localities from the extremity of Maine to the end of Florida."

In a letter of May 17, 1869, Coues urged Allen, when the latter began writing about Florida, to include in his paper[16] any or all observations on bird migration made while in the Everglade State. He then commented: "I have paid great attention to this particular branch of our study; and as a result I disbelieve considerably more than half that passes current among ornithologists, regarding what are called *resident* species of a locality. The more I learn, the fewer species present themselves to me as bona fide residents."

Writing somewhat later to Allen, Coues asked, "What do you think of [Thomas] Huxley's[17] new classification? . . . For myself, I am not prepared to 'go it whole'." Huxley's classification, based on the cranial bones of birds, was then a subject of much discussion among ornithologists. On learning that Allen agreed with him, Coues replied on January 6, 1870, that in a forthcoming paper[18] he proposed "to administer the needed rebuke ungloved. . . . We cannot afford to allow any meteor, however brilliantly flashing athwart the sky, to dim the luster of fixed stars. . . . Prof. Huxley's essay is only equalled in brilliancy by its unsoundness."[19] It should be remarked here that Coues had studied closely other classifications of birds, not only Huxley's but also those of such other ornithologists as Charles Lucien Bonaparte, Nicholas Vigors,[20] and Wilhelm Lilljeborg.[21]

In his letter to Allen of January 6 Coues again brought up the subject of species: "It is a part of my creed, at the present moment, both that I do not know what a species is in the least, and that no one else is much better off in this respect than I am." Coues then made an extraordinary proposition to his friend:

> Now about our several ideas touching species. . . . You know we don't agree exactly, each having closed-hugged theories that each of us may be able to defend with more or less success. Supposing now . . . I were to write you a formal "letter," with reference to its being printed, in which I would discuss some of the points involved . . . would you like to meet me on that

field in the shape of comments upon the letter; to follow it directly? I think it might be interesting and instructive so to do, to ourselves and others. We are both young naturalists, standing perhaps at opposite poles of a subject than which none is more important. A good square fight—on the basis of course of utmost personal friendliness & courtesy—might be a good stirring thing! What do you say? I've no doubt our numerous friends would willingly form a ring and stand interested spectators of the encounter.

Allen replied on January 12: "I like the frankness with which you speak of our differences of opinion on certain points, and most cordially accept your proposition for a public decision. . . . I only suggest a delay of it till after the appearance of my Florida paper." The "public decision," for reasons unknown, never materialized. The possibility exists, of course, that Allen, after completing his paper, had second thoughts about "a good square fight."

The evidence is strong by now that Coues' thoughts on biological topics were pitched increasingly on loftier planes. Writing to Allen in September, 1870, he said: "I shall be very glad to see your Florida work, having no doubt it will be of high value and interest. As Baird said to me, on reading over the ms. of my 'Water-birds,' we stand in far more need of *discussion, suggestion,* and papers dealing with *principles,* than of narrative descriptive ones presenting sure *facts.* . . . Facts are self-asserting; principles require assertion, and [word illegible] brighten the more they are rubbed."

5

At an undetermined date Coues began work on a book about the birds of Arizona. The first reference to it we have found is in a letter from Coues to Baird dated July 5, 1866: "I must get to work again on the Arizona ms."

The story of this manuscript, its sporadic growth, its misadventures, and its ultimate fate, constitutes one of the more moving and unhappy chapters in the life of Elliott Coues. For most of the details we have Coues' own words as they appeared in his letters to Baird.

When Coues next mentioned the work to Baird, six months later, he said: "I am writing vigorously on my 'Birds of Arizona.' Wonder if I can find a publisher for it." After another six-month interval, he reported, "I have nearly half-finished my Arizona book." A few weeks later, on March 13, 1868, he wrote: "I can turn over my [Arizona] ms. to a publisher within a month, if need be. I have taken the first steps toward publication by writing Dr. [Thomas M.] Brewer, as you suggest, explaining nature of work to him, and asking him to endeavor to secure the desideratum, as he can 'put the case' in Boston perhaps better than any one else. Will you do anything in the matter?" Apparently Brewer was unable, or unwilling, to "put the case"; at least Coues, in succeeding letters to Baird, did not again allude to Brewer.

Coues soon enlarged the scope of the Arizona work. He told Baird that he was including appendices on mammals, reptiles, insects, and, perhaps, fish, that he himself would do the one on mammals, but that Edward D. Cope, Joseph LeConte, Theodore N. Gill, and George Engelmann would write the others.

On April 27 Coues advised Baird: "Hope to work B.A.T. [*viz.*, Birds of Arizona Territory] off my hands shortly. Think I shall apply first to [the Boston publishing house of] Hurd & Houghton." Then, a few days later, "I have very encouraging word from Hurd & Houghton. They are favorably entertaining the proposition, and write for details about the work."

The Boston publishers, however, after studying the "details" of the manuscript, seem to have lost some of their original optimism. On July 12 Coues told Baird: "Hurd & Houghton, with apparently the best wishes toward me, decline the book unless I will make it a joint stock enterprise, paying $1,125, and dividing profits. They are evidently afraid they'll burn their fingers with it. Perhaps they're right. I could raise $100,000 as easily as $1,000, and consequently must give up hope in that quarter. But I'm going to try elsewhere. I've worked too long over the confounded book to be willing to let it drop."

Before leaving Columbia for Fort Macon, Coues alluded, in letters to Baird, at least once more to the Arizona book. In late October, 1868, he wrote: "My book still lies quietly in Mss., and may do so for an indefinite period. The older I grow the less things of my own seem to me. If it isn't printed soon, I should begin to rejoice that 2500 pages of 'stuff' didn't get before the public!"

It is understandable that Coues, at this point, should reveal a touch of bitterness. He had labored long, had completed a manuscript of huge size and probably of much worth, and had then utterly failed to interest a publisher.

Arrived at Fort Macon, where he faced a new environment and different interests, Coues seems to have put out of mind, for the better part of a year, any further thought of the Arizona work. It was not until January 1, 1870, that he again wrote Baird about it and provided him with unexpected news:

I am going to trouble you once more about the old thing—my Arizona book. I have an offer from a party to *give me outright* $1,100—the sum Hurd & Houghton to whom I first applied said they sh'd require on my part to print the volume. So I can now go ahead, and get the cord of Mss. in type as soon as I please! Having reached this point, I begin to feel an uneasy sensation about the pit of my stomach, lest the book may not be all that would be desirable, that even tho' fair now, young as I am, it would not remain such a good standing advertisement as I should care to have laid at my door say ten years from now. I'm half afraid there's enough nonsense in it to make it soon become a standing rebuke to youthful presumption. Now I'm not fishing you understand. Please say to me one word—*print, or not?*

Baird encouraged Coues to go ahead and print. That seems certain from the wording of Coues' reply: "Thanks for your kindly appreciation. . . . Shall look over this Ms., revise it thoroughly, make it smaller in all probability, and then, if I think it creditable, will publish; but have no certainty of so doing."

Almost eight months elapsed before we learn anything more about Coues' Arizona book—and then the news was astounding. Writing on August 31, 1870, to George N. Lawrence, Coues revealed: "[The Arizona manuscript] got altogether too big and unwieldy, so I destroyed it, to have it off my mind." Just that, and nothing more!

Our astonishment increases when we find that Coues did not tell Baird of his act until November 7, more than two months after he had informed Lawrence. In his letter to Baird, he was at least more explicit: "Did I tell you that my poor Arizona is dead? A short shrift it had, and is buried forever. You see it grew out of handling proportions. I had lost hope of finding a publisher, and saw it draining my time, as I was continually hammering over it; so to settle the matter, I burned the 3,000 pp. [of] Mss. It cut me to the quick, as there's much matter lost irrevocably; and even if three quarters of the book was mere writing, the other quarter was good. But, being in bad company, it had to be treated accordingly."

The explanation Coues gave Baird could hardly have satisfied the latter. In time, he doubtless learned more particulars, though what appears to be the whole story was not made public until after both Baird and Coues had died. Writing in 1901, D. G. Elliot provided the explanation:

> While a keen and just critic himself, he [Coues] was very sensitive regarding the opinion of others toward his own productions, and sought but approbation of those who were bound closely to him either by earthly ties or

an intimate friendship, or whose knowledge of the subject under consideration caused their opinion to be of special value. This extreme sensitiveness is
best illustrated by an act committed in his youthful days, when after having
labored for several years upon a work on Arizona, on reading his manuscript
to one, who, if not competent to judge of the importance of his labors, he had
the right to expect would exhibit sympathy for his efforts, and who must at
least have been impressed with its thoroughness and beauty of diction, yet,
was only able to consider its value as a commercial asset and therefore
commented upon it so unfavorably and with such strength of expression, that,
utterly disheartened at the want of appreciation for that which had been so
long a labor of love and of which he was so proud of his ability to produce, on
the impulse of the moment he cast the "copy" into the fire where it was
consumed, and then suffered a severe attack of illness in consequence of his
loss by his hasty action.[22]

The wound caused by Coues' impulsive act seems, in time, to have
healed, but it left a permanent scar. In years ahead he kept referring to
his misdeed, as though haunted by it. On one occasion, for example, he
deplored ". . . the destruction of my old Arizona manuscript, as a spirit
that would not be laid."[23] And he recalled the act as late as 1897, two
years short of his death: "Wrote a large work on Birds of Arizona which
[in 1870] I destroyed."[24]

At this late date it seems doubtful that we shall ever learn the name
of Coues' "angel," namely the individual who was willing to subsidize
Coues' Arizona work to the tune of $1,100. And it is highly unlikely that
we shall ever be able to identify the character whose undisciplined
judgment was responsible for Coues' consignment of his manuscript to
the flames.

6

As the months went by at Fort Macon Coues grew increasingly
discontent. For one thing, he and one of his commanding officers did
not see eye to eye. An entry in his "Book of Dates" (1869) stated simply,
"July and August trouble with Major G. M. Brayton."[25] He soon afterward wrote to Baird: ". . . we have such a curious set of officers here just
now (particularly the Commandant) that I'm afraid my Natural History
must be carried on clandestinely, if at all. I feel very indignant at times—
the more so, that I don't dare show it."

One surmises that Major Brayton—who may not have known the
difference between a partridge and a pear tree—thought that Coues was
spending entirely too much time collecting specimens and thereby

neglecting his duties as surgeon, as Coues may actually have been doing on occasion. The situation may have been aggravated by Coues' enlistment of the services of young Beals as a collector, if, as seems likely, he had taken that step without consulting Major Brayton.

Coues disliked Fort Macon for other reasons. Writing to George N. Lawrence in June, 1869, he explained: "It is a good place for field natural history, but exceedingly uncomfortable and disagreeable in other respects. Plentiful lack of all creature comforts."

Coues wrote an article about Fort Macon in which he detailed the discomforts, disadvantages, and primitive conditions under which he labored at this Army post. After describing at some length the geography and natural history of his surroundings (with which he found no fault), he deprecated, in turn, the weather, the fort itself, and the hospital building.

The most objectionable feature of the weather was the humidity which, in most seasons, was so high that "articles of dress, books, the solid extracts, &c." rapidly gathered mold. Coues complained, too, about "the shifting winds" which, in summer, "wafted malaria from the swamps of the mainland."[26]

As to the fort, there were no actual barracks, only casemates,[27] and in these some 125 enlisted men lived, but so crowded that in case of an epidemic "it would probably be necessary to evacuate the fort." Coues reported, too: "There are no bath or wash rooms—the men wash under a shed in the ditch at the postern gate . . . [and] there are no water-closets." The married soldiers (Coues, of course, among them) were separately quartered in six small wooden buildings. These were "of the most wretched description . . . and are now going to pieces; they all leak, and afford but little protection from the weather."

Equally shameful was the condition of the hospital building. It was, Coues wrote, "a disgrace to the service . . . the foundations have given way in all directions, and the building has settled unevenly in the sand; the floor presents a rolling surface, gaping here and there. . . . No possible repairs will fit the building for hospital purposes. The absolute and pressing necessity for a new hospital is obvious." Coues went on: "All slops and garbage [of the hospital] are twice daily removed by the prisoners, in barrels, and thrown far out upon the beach, where they are partly devoured by birds and crabs, and partly washed away with this tide; the most wholesome regulations in this regard have always been enforced since I have been at the post."

Under the sanitary conditions then prevailing at Fort Macon, the

health of the garrison seems to have been as good as could have been
expected. Coues reported: "Phthisis [tuberculosis] makes rapid progress
when fairly established, while common colds and coughs are apt to prove
tedious and troublesome. . . . Pneumonia requires close attention." He
thought the humidity and sudden changes of temperature exacerbated
pulmonary complaints. Of other diseases Coues wrote: "A moderate
amount of malarial fever occurs in summer; it is of a mild form. . . .
Nearly all the bowel diseases, of which there is a moderate amount . . .
have proven of a transient character, yielding readily; though occasionally cases of dysentery, dependent upon or associated with malarial
conditions, have been found intractable. Considering the atmospheric
influences there is a remarkable freedom from rheumatism. Venereal
disease is at a minimum."[28]

Obviously Coues had sound reasons for his growing unhappiness at
Fort Macon, but nothing he wrote more pointedly phrased his dislike
than a chance remark about prairie warblers: "They were the only
Warblers that showed bad taste enough to come voluntarily about Fort
Macon in any considerable numbers."[29]

In August, 1869, through George N. Lawrence, Coues learned of
steps being taken to form what would become the American Museum of
Natural History in New York City, and that this embryonic institution—
referred to initially by Lawrence as the "Park Association"—would
probably soon be looking for a prominent scientist to serve as its curator
of animals and plants. Being increasingly discontent at Fort Macon,
Coues at once became excited at the prospect of obtaining this post, even
though it would mean resignation from the Army.

Knowing only the little that Lawrence had told him but keen to
learn more, Coues wrote a letter to Lawrence that may have astounded
that gentleman. Dated September 23, 1869, it read in part:

> . . . I want to talk to you, frankly and honestly, about a certain matter, of
> truly *vital* interest to me. Please consider what is to follow as entirely between
> you and I [*sic*]. . . .
>
> Your mention of the Park Association, now apparently forming a
> zoological collection, emboldens me to open upon a subject I have had at
> heart for years. You can hardly imagine how I detest the Army, how utterly
> distasteful the military practice of my profession is to me. True, it has
> given me the time and means to study somewhat our favorite science and do
> a little something in that way. But it is not much, and I never can do much, so
> long as I am . . . packed in out of the way corners, severed from the
> intercourse with gentlemen of similar tastes & pursuits. . . . The years
> already passed since I entered manhood seem frittered away. . . .

Now you speak of this Association. . . . Do they want a naturalist? Would they give a place to a working naturalist, who would come and devote himself soul and body to scientific work with them for a compensation that would just keep soul and body together for himself and family? Could I get such a place? . . . [If so], I would resign the Army (how gladly), give up my profession, and enter heart and soul into the work.

. . . Can you, first, and will you, second, do anything for me in this regard? . . . I scarcely see a limit to this Association. There seems to be no reason why it should not be our American Regents Park or Jardin des Plantes. . . .

It is rarely, dear friend Lawrence, that I lay open my inmost feelings thus to anyone, but my heart is overflowing. . . . I shall await your reply so impatiently. . . .

Perhaps stirred by the seeming depth of Coues' miseries, Lawrence replied immediately. He was sorry to report, he said, that the job of naturalist at the fledgling museum had been tentatively filled by A. S. Bickmore,[30] that he himself really had little influence with any of the founders of the Park Association, and that Coues might wish to ask Baird about the likelihood of a position with the Boston Society of Natural History.

When answering the above from Lawrence, Coues expressed his bitter disappointment. Any prospect of his obtaining the post at the New York museum seemingly had vanished. The following March, however, Lawrence again wrote Coues: "Yesterday I had an interview with one of the trustees of the new Museum. . . . Your case was brought up, with the inquiry as to how distant you were, and whether it would be possible for you to come on at once, that they might have a personal interview, and judge as to your possible engagement at some future time. . . . My opinion is that . . . they begin to see the necessity of a resident naturalist. . . . I told him it was quite doubtful whether you could get leave of absence."

Lawrence was right about the leave. Coues replied: "I am sorry to say that it can't be obtained at present; it is too soon after the last one, for my application to be entertained." In months immediately ahead he did keep trying for a leave, though, as his letters to Lawrence attest, he failed.

Coues might well have continued indefinitely trying to get his leave, but in November he received news that he would soon be transferred to a more eligible post. As he wrote Baird: "It seems that 'they' remember a poor fellow who has been over four years under a cloud of southern exile, and indications are that I shall very shortly be established at Fort

McHenry, Baltimore. Isn't that nice? Quite as near the official lion's den as it is entirely convenient for an officer to be, and almost as near a certain 'institution' as I should desire to be. . . . I never ought to have been ordered to this detestable place at all, as long as there were contract doctors in the dept.; have always felt it a sort of vague disgrace, and been in a chronic state of disgust about it."

Having received this news, Coues at once lost interest in devoting himself "soul and body" to the future American Jardin des Plantes. To Lawrence, he confessed:

> I am afraid that you will have to throw me overboard altogether; for since my hopes in the direction of Central Park became dim, I devoted myself to getting something better than I had in the Army, and with such success that I could not now resign except under *much* more favorable conditions than I should then have been glad to accept. Besides now having one of the best posts in the gift of the army, with prospects for keeping it some years, the pay of our corps has been so largely raised by late Act of Congress that, with the other allowances, as house, fuel & forage, it represents an equivalent of $4,000 per annum for one in civil life. So I think that you will agree with me, that I had best let well enough alone.

It surely has become evident that Coues tended to paint his pictures in black or white, and a case in point was that of the Army. At the outset of his correspondence with Lawrence the Army to him was a depraved branch of the service that had severed him from "intercourse with gentlemen of similar tastes" and had reduced him to "a mere dabbler in science." As long as he remained with the Army, his life "would not be worth living." "How gladly," he had exclaimed, would he resign from the Army if offered the post then shaping up in New York City.

How different was Coues' picture of the Army after his transfer to Fort McHenry. The Army had dealt him "one of the best posts" at its command, had given him reason to believe he could remain there "some years," and had upped his pay from $2,500 (his income at Fort Macon)[31] to a figure approximating $4,000. What else could he say to Lawrence except, "I think I had best let well enough alone"!

NOTES

1. Coues, *Birds of the Northwest* (1874), 64.
2. From Wordsworth's lines: "The good die first / And they whose hearts are dry as summer's dust / Burn to the socket."
3. Jeffries Wyman (1814-74), anatomist, was born in Chelmsford, Mass. In

1833 he graduated from Harvard and in 1837 received an M.D. from Massachusetts General Hospital. In 1847 he was given the Hersey Professorship of Anatomy at Harvard and in 1866 became curator of archaeology and ethnology at the Peabody Museum.

4. Coues, it will be recalled, had begun this anatomical study of the opossum while still stationed in South Carolina.

5. Charles Lucien Bonaparte (1803-57), French ornithologist and nephew of Napoleon Bonaparte, was born in Paris and educated in Italy and came to the United States in 1822. He published many articles on American birds. In 1854, after returning to France, he became director of the Jardin des Plantes.

6. Letter in the Bancroft Library, University of California, Berkeley.

7. These "Radiates" were echinoderms, such as starfish, sea urchins, and sand dollars, all invertebrates with radial symmetry.

8. Modern ornithological texts state that the least tern of the East Coast (*Sterna albifrons antillarum*) lays from one to four eggs.

9. Today's binomial for Wilson's plover is *Charadrius wilsonia*. This bird, according to modern texts, lays three eggs. Coues' oological studies at Fort Macon on the least tern and Wilson's plover led to his publication of "Seaside Homes" (1869).

10. Samuel Hubbard Scudder (1837-1911), entomologist, was born in Boston, Mass. He graduated in 1857 from Williams College and in 1862 from Harvard. From about 1862 until 1872 he served as custodian of the Boston Society of Natural History. Among his published works were *Nomenclator Zoologicus* (1882-84) and *The Butterflies of the Eastern United States and Canada* (1888-89).

11. Allen, "Biographical Memoir," 424.

12. George Whitefield Samson (1819-96), Baptist clergyman and president of Columbian College (1859-71).

13. See Coues, "Antero-posterior Symmetry" (1868).

14. *Lingula* is a genus of the phylum Brachiopoda. Today's *Lingulas* are much as they were in the Ordovician, 400 million years ago, and perhaps constitute the oldest living genus of animals.

15. See Coues, "Notes on the Natural History of Fort Macon" (1871).

16. Allen, "On the Mammals and Water Birds of Eastern Florida" (1871).

17. Thomas Henry Huxley (1825-95), P.R.S., eminent English biologist, collected marine life in the Pacific from H.M.S. *Rattlesnake* (1846-50). A supporter of Darwin, he wrote on evolution, and also on anatomy, physiology, and other fields; two of his works are *Philosophical Transactions* (1851) and *Elementary Physiology* (1861).

18. Coues, "On the Classifiction of Water Birds" (1869).

19. Coues was a bit hard on Huxley. The latter's *palatal* basis for classification, while not entirely correct, still underlies part of the main classification of birds.

20. Nicholas Aylward Vigors (1785-1840), British naturalist.

21. Wilhelm Lilljeborg (1816-1908), European naturalist.

22. Elliot, "In Memoriam: Elliott Coues," 7-8.

23. Coues, *Birds of the Northwest,* 363.

24. Coues' "Book of Dates" (1897).

25. George Mitchell Brayton, Army officer, was born in Massachusetts. For gallant and meritorious service at the battle of Missionary Ridge he was made a brevet major (1865), the rank he held at Fort Macon (1869-70).

26. Coues, "Fort Macon, North Carolina" (1870), 87-88. The role of the mosquito (*Anopheles*) in transmitting malaria was then, of course, unknown.

27. Casemates were chambers, usually of masonry, in which cannon could be placed, to be fired through embrasures. Such chambers were primarily magazines, but could be used, as at Fort Macon, for quartering troops.

28. Coues, "Fort Macon, North Carolina," 88-90.

29. Coues, *Birds of the Northwest,* 64.

30. Albert Smith Bickmore (1839-1914), naturalist, was born in Tenant's Harbor, Me. In 1860 he graduated from Dartmouth College, after which he studied for a time under Louis Agassiz at Harvard. He traveled and collected (1865-67) in the Malay Archipelago and Dutch East Indies. On his return he was instrumental in influencing such prominent citizens of New York City as Theodore Roosevelt (father of "T.R."), Levi P. Morton, and J. P. Morgan to form what is now the American Museum of Natural History. Bickmore served as the museum's first superintendent (1869-84). Today he is sometimes called "Father of the American Museum."

31. From Fort Macon on Feb. 11, 1870, Coues wrote Baird: "This place . . . is worth about $2500 a year to me, all perquisites included."

CHAPTER IX

Fort McHenry, Baltimore

Throughout his stay at Fort McHenry "Elliott Coues, M.A., M.D., Ph.D., Captain and Assistant Surgeon, U.S. Army"—to employ Coues' preferred, full signature of that period—appears to have enjoyed relative peace of mind. In his numerous letters to Baird he expressed none of the discontent he had revealed in those written at Fort Macon. Not once did he allude to any clashes between himself and his commanding officer or to any form of Army restraint impeding his ornithological or other scientific labors. From the time of his arrival in November, 1870, until his departure in October, 1872, Coues complained only about the weather, which on certain dog days was intolerably hot, with temperatures crowding 100°F.

A number of things at Fort McHenry contributed to Coues' serenity. One was the attractive location of the fort, on Whetstone Point, a peninsula formed by the junction of the northwest branch of the Patapsco with the main river. The fort, too, was just three miles southeast of the center of Baltimore and only a short train ride to and from Washington and the Smithsonian.[1] Another thing pleasing to Coues was the fact that the men's barracks, officers' quarters, and hospital buildings were of sturdy construction, well heated and well ventilated. In short, Fort McHenry provided Coues and his family with the "body comforts" which had been lacking at Fort Macon.

Also, as at previous posts, Coues' duties as surgeon occupied only a fraction of his time. The garrison, consisting of only ten to twelve officers and some 170 enlisted men,[2] was small in comparison with that of many other forts; as a result, the hospital was never crowded. For the most part, too, the disorders were minor, such as bronchitis, rheumatism, catarrh, and remittent and intermittent fevers.[3] From first to last Coues was able to devote most of his time to his writing and research.

The nearness of Fort McHenry to Baltimore enabled Coues to

associate "with gentlemen of similar tastes & pursuits," an advantage which he had sorely missed at Forts Whipple and Macon. Of particular satisfaction and benefit to Coues was Baltimore's Maryland Academy of Science, to which he was elected a member on September 18, 1871; two months later he was invited to give a talk there.[4] We may question Coues' regular attendance at meetings of the academy; his unceasing labors with birds and mammals (about which much more later in this chapter) would probably have disallowed it.

Fort McHenry, to Coues, was a "crack station," and as such he would always remember it with warm regard. He would remember it, too, for events that brought him much gratification and happiness. Paramount among these was the birth of his first son. To Baird, on January 16, 1872, he wrote, "I am almost hourly expecting a domestic episode." Then, four days later: "The 'episode' put in an appearance yesterday, and may thus be diagnosticated: '♂, hornotinus, calvus, rubecundus, edentatus, lus similissimus.'" Freely translated, Coues' Latin reads: "Male, this year's model, bald, ruddy, toothless, pug-nosed, sleepless, bawling, and otherwise like most other menikin."

In an ensuing letter to Baird, Coues said: "I forgot to tell you that the 'episode' is named Elliott Baird [Coues]. I wanted Spencer Baird but wife had set her heart on Elliott, so we compromised as above." Thus, with the birth of Elliott Baird Coues, the father was pleased on two counts: he now had a son, and that son bore the name of his revered mentor. No doubt Baird was pleased too.

Throughout his stay at Fort McHenry Coues wrote more often to Baird than before, and the overall tenor of his letters tends to confirm our belief that the relationship between the two men was perhaps closer than it had ever been. In one communication to Baird, Coues wrote, "I need not say how much I feel your kindness. . . . It is the sort of thing I don't forget." And in others: "Thank you very much for your very acceptable notice—how do you always manage to say exactly what one most wants to hear? I wish I were big enough to [do] something for you occasionally. Perhaps I may show my appreciation best by in turn trying to do likewise to those who may come after."

In yet other letters Coues kept Baird *au courant* with whatever was uppermost on his mind at the moment of writing. In one, for example, we learn of his recently formed friendship with Dr. Yarrow: "My successor at Fort Macon, Dr. H. C. Yarrow, U.S.A., is a highly cultivated gentleman of scientific proclivities. He appears to have gone into science there [*viz.*, Fort Macon], as he writes me he is collecting busily for the

Philada. Acad." Soon afterward: "I have turned over to Dr. Yarrow all my *fish* & *insect* items, and he supplements my lists of shells, radiates & snakes with many additional names. Between us, and with the results of Packard's and Morse's doings there last summer, the Nat. Hist. of the place is getting pretty thoroughly overhauled."

As a result of the friendship thus formed, Coues and Yarrow would later collaborate in the publication of a number of important natural history articles. Years afterward, probably in the late 1870s, Yarrow recalled climbing to the top of the tallest tower of the Smithsonian and entering a small room where he found Coues seated at his desk in his shirtsleeves "writing away as if his life depended upon his work."[5]

In a broad, general way, Coues' life *was* dependent on his writing. His motto might well have been: Publish or Perish. At Fort McHenry, as well as at other stations before and after, Coues' overruling wellspring of contentment was his almost daily bout with pen and paper, as he endeavored to put into words the fruits of his labors as a collector of facts on a multitude of topics. Deprived of this absorption, Coues' life might well have become nearly intolerable to him.

At Fort McHenry Coues gave a demonstration of literary industry exceeding that at any of his previous Army posts. As proof, we hereby list his major publications, the majority about birds, a lesser number about mammals. Those about mammals included "Former Eastward Range of the Buffalo" (1871), "On the Myology of the *Ornithorhynchus* [the duckbill]" (1871),[6] "Geographical Distribution of *Bassaris astuta* [the cacomistle, a relative of the racoon]" (1872), "The Osteology and Myology of *Didelphys virginiana* [the opossum]" (1872), and "Notes on the Natural History of Fort Macon, N.C." (1872). This last paper included commentary not only on mammals but also, as earlier indicated, on birds, reptiles, and a wealth of marine invertebrates.

Of Coues' articles about birds written at Fort McHenry, several were life histories, of such species as the yellow-headed blackbird (*Xanthocephalus xanthocephalus*),[7] Bullock's oriole (*Icterus galbula bullockii*),[8] long-crested jay (*Cyanocitta stelleri macrolopha*, a variety of Steller's jay),[9] Clark's nutcracker (*Nucifraga columbiana*),[10] blue crow (piñon jay, *Gymnorhinus cyanocephalus*),[11] crissal thrasher (*Toxostoma dorsale*),[12] and ferruginous owl (*Glaucidium brasilianus*).[13] On other ornithological topics Coues published "Progress of American Ornithology" (1871), "Mechanism of Flexion and Extension in Birds' Wings" (1871), "Material for a Monograph of the *Spheniscidae* [the penguins]" (1872), and "Studies of the *Tyrannidae* [the tyrant flycatchers]" (1872).

Far and away the most important work Coues published while stationed at Fort McHenry was *Key to North American Birds*; indeed, it proved to be the most outstanding publication of his entire life. Later in this chapter we shall provide a detailed description of the *Key*, as well as notices of the recognition it received.

The above list of works published by Coues while at Fort McHenry, as we have already indicated, is incomplete. It does not include, for instance, a number of book reviews and several lesser papers. And the listing, quite naturally, provides not even a hint of significant work Coues had in progress at the fort but did not publish until later.

In his letters to Baird, Coues said little or nothing about most of the above titles. The letters did include, however, abundant commentary on two subjects, one of which, a study of rats and mice (Muridae), he did not begin until after he had reported for duty at Fort McHenry. The other subject was his *Key to North American Birds*. Since both projects proved to be significant contributions to science, we will discuss in the remainder of this chapter, first, Coues' studies of rats and mice and, second, the provenance, growth, and maturation of the *Key*.

2

It was at Fort McHenry, at the spot made immortal in 1814 by Francis Scott Key, that Coues for the first time threw himself vigorously into a study of mammals, an ambitious undertaking involving the structure and taxonomy of all known species of North American rats and mice. These rodents comprised a large, difficult, and little understood group of American mammals. It is understandable, therefore, that they appealed to Coues' scientific proclivity to bring order out of confusion. The fact that the animals were small, unattractive, and generally repellent was of no concern to him whatsoever.

Coues' first reference to his preoccupation with this branch of the Rodentia—at least the first we have found—was in a letter of May 18, 1871, to Baird:

> I have nothing special on hand at present except treadmill work in correcting proof sheets of book [*viz.*, sheets of the *Key*] & Opossum memoir, and lest Satan may "find some mischief still for idle hands to do," I want some matter to wreak myself on. Now can I have the *Arvicolas* [meadow mice of the genus *Arvicola*]?[14] I am very anxious to do up some such group of our mammals, and will undertake a thorough monograph of the N.A. sp[ecies] of this genus, if the S.I. will submit its material to me for the purpose. It would be, of course, desirable if not necessary to receive the entire "cord"

that you mentioned of specimens in skins, as well as any odd gallons of alcoholics there may be on hand.

At some earlier date Coues had evidently discussed this *Arvicola* project with Baird. Even if not, now that Coues had made known his intention, Baird seems to have been enthusiastic about the plan. In ensuing months the number of rat and mouse specimens, both skin and alcoholic, Baird shipped to Coues was more than enough to satisfy his needs. Coues continued to write regularly to Baird, often at length, advising him of the progress he had made in working up the Smithsonian material. Excerpts from these letters reveal Coues' unquestioned enthusiasm.

In early July he wrote: "Rejoice greatly, and be exceedingly glad, for the *Arvicolas* turn out in perfect order—not a hair gone, in the whole box. *Hesperomys, Reithrodon, Myodes* etc.,[15] will be good for comparative examination. The skulls are all in splendid shape, not a label displaced." Then, two weeks later: "I am warming up to the chase very nicely, and fully expect a good thing of it when I get through."

Several weeks went by, after which Coues was able to report to Baird: "The past summer I have worked up every inch of Mouse material; the subject has cooled down, and now I am ready to extend & correct or corroborate my present results with the rest of the material. I have been warmly interested in the subject; it is so nice, after dealing so long in genera of birds that are arbitrarily such, to pick out genera of mammals that actually have definite and tangible characters."

The year ended on a less sanguine note. Writing Baird on December 26, 1871, Coues said, "The last batch of skins has nearly been the death of me. These Arctic *Arvicolas* would puzzle old Nick himself!"

As the new year began, Coues' ardor, if ever lost, quickly returned. On January 16, 1872, he wrote: "These mice are a delightful study— such nice cranial & dental characters for the genera, and the species too. . . . I have got so that I can almost tell the faunal region of any specimen without looking at the label. . . . I believe I have got what I particularly wanted—a new species type of a new genus. It is from Labrador—a skull I picked up there in 1860."

Coues' remarks of this date interest us on two counts: (1) he had become so familiar by this time with the mouse material that he could "almost tell the faunal region of any specimen without looking at the label," and (2) in 1860 he had brought back from Labrador a mouse skull, a fact suggesting that he may have collected there additional mammalian material unknown to us.

To Baird again, early in February, Coues expressed further zeal: "Bring on your mice—who's afraid? If they be the death of me, my widow will call on the S.I. for funeral expenses; but I'm bound to see the thing through." And four days later: "There are eleven boxes of pickled mice in this room, safe & sound—not a bottle broken, nor a drop of alcohol spilled. I shall go at the lot at once; elaborate this fresh material, send you skulls to figure meanwhile, and can then submit to the S.I. about 400 pp. mss., which I shall be pleased to see out with reasonable expedition."

But much more remained to be done, and Coues, perhaps realizing for the first time the enormity of the task he had set for himself, soon began to evidence signs of weariness and diminishing fervor. In mid-March he admitted to Baird: "I hope never to see another U.S. murine"; shortly thereafter: "These *Muridae* are by far the most difficult investigation I ever undertook, and are taxing my powers to the utmost. I wish I could have the benefit of your mature experience." By the end of March Coues had reached an even lower state of mind: "Mice are below par—and I am in a slough of despond, as I always get at a certain stage of every investigation. Then I *drop it* for a little while, and cool off, and on reattacking the subject it straightens itself out. I won't be ousted by a confounded set of ratskins and pickles [namely, specimens 'pickled' in alcohol]."

Coues' common-sense approach in dealing with his "slough of despond" evidently paid off, for he could report to Baird in early May: "No doubt I can finish the Mice this summer; and if I go west with a load of Flycatchers[16] & Shrews,[17] my heart will be lighter." Thus, by this time, Coues had learned that he might soon be sent to a western post. Three weeks later Coues reiterated his determination to complete his work that summer on the Muridae if he did not, as a consequence, have to take to his bed or be committed to an insane asylum.

On July 7 Coues wrote Baird what may have been his final remarks on rodents while still at Fort McHenry: "Several days last week the mercury overtopped 100°F. in the shade, and mouse-work was wearisome indeed. The evaporating alcohol was almost intoxicating, but I didn't like the flavor, and, on the whole, should prefer to 'spree it,' if at all, with a different beverage."

One of Coues' correspondents at this time, as we know, was George N. Lawrence. In mid-summer Coues wrote Lawrence: "You may be glad to know, that instead of *new species* of *Muridae*, in the immense amount of material I am handling, I reduce the old species more than one-half. I have had *too many* species for the health of many a species of unblemished character hitherto!" Some biologists are prone to emphasize differences and hence to name or recognize numerous genera, species, or subspecies, as the case may be. Opposed to these "splitters" are the "lumpers," who think it is more important to emphasize that certain units are related to one another by combining them in the same species or genus. Throughout his career, Coues was a lumper.

While at Fort McHenry, Coues devoted more of his working hours to the Muridae than to any other group of animals. However, his publications stemming from that study did not begin to appear until 1874, and the more important ones, which included other mammals, not until 1877. It seems best, therefore, that we delay appraisal of Coues' contributions to mammalogy until a subsequent chapter.

By immersing himself so deeply in murine studies, Coues had not turned his back on birds. Indeed, in another of his letters to Baird from Fort McHenry he said: "Somehow, I work at mammals in cold blood, while birds are done con amore." How better to conclude this section, and to begin the next one—about birds?

Ornithologists seem to agree that Elliott Coues' *Key to North American Birds*, completed while he was stationed at Fort McHenry, was the cardinal achievement of his lustrous ornithological career. The original edition—there would be a total of six—came from the press early in October, 1872, shortly after Coues' thirtieth birthday.

3

Coues had begun work on the *Key* while still at Fort Macon. From that post on July 12, 1869, he broke the news to Baird:

> I have occupied myself at odd intervals lately, in getting up a short piece of manuscript that I think you will be both surprised & pleased to see some day. But to perfect it, I must spend a week or so in the S.I. with specimens at hand. It is an infallible artificial Key to N.A. birds, enabling any one, without the slightest knowledge of ornithology, to identify any specimen in a few seconds. It is really something quite curious, and so far as I know, unique in our science, though the botanists have corresponding tables—from which I took the hint. I have made my wife test it, in the case of all the birds I have shot here, and, without knowing a tarsus from a tail, hardly, she has in every instance given the scientific name of the specimen.

To our knowledge, Coues did not again mention the *Key* to Baird until November 7, 1870, the same date on which he had revealed to Baird the destruction of his Arizona manuscript. In a concluding paragraph of that letter, Coues wrote: "Losing that prodigious bantling [namely, the Arizona work], I have taken the 'Key' to my heart, and labored over it conscientiously. [Frederic Ward] Putnam has most of it in hand, is about printing the Introduction, & is cutting the pictures from my drawings. . . . He thinks it is going to be a success, even in a pecuniary way; and I shall put some money in it myself, going shares with the Peab. Acad. [Peabody Academy of Science, Salem, Massachusetts]."

The above paragraph illumines on at least five counts: (1) the *Key* had acted therapeutically following Coues' impulsive destruction of the Arizona work; (2) his work on the *Key* had been largely completed before he left Fort Macon; (3) he was providing the *Key* with illustrations of his own making; (4) he was digging into his own pockets to help finance publication of the *Key*; and (5) Putnam, then a director of the Peabody Academy of Science, had assumed editorship of the *Key*.[18]

Later that month (November, 1870) Coues reported for duty at Fort McHenry. In one of his letters to Baird from his new post, he wrote: "Putnam writes me that he would like to have the wood cuts as soon as convenient. I shall probably come over with the proofs of the 'Key' in a month or so." In succeeding letters Coues plead with Baird for cuts the latter had used in his books: "Please do your best for me, as the expense of the fig[ure]s, even for the very modest number & style I am restricting myself to, is, I fear, going to overrun the funds that are at the disposal of author and publisher combined."

By mid-April, 1871, the requested cuts not having reached Coues, he wrote Baird again, this time with a detectable note of insistence in his lines: "In reference to those [cuts] . . . I do hope you will be able to accommodate me. . . . I shall be quite at sea if I don't get them, as we have been all along confidently counting on them."

Baird finally delivered the cuts, and by early summer work on the *Key* was far advanced. Coues reported to Baird on June 22: "Putnam has decided on an edition of 2,000 copies of the bird book, and seems quite sanguine about its commercial success; but I wish I were *sure* of 2,000 purchasers. I shan't get it out with less than $1000 as my share of the interest. I never before *quite* comprehended what a *valuable* thing Science is!"

By November, five months later, portions of the *Key* were being printed. To Baird, on November 13, Coues wrote: "The 'Key' is in high feather; the introductory part, a sort of lecture on birds in general, being nearly through the press. Somehow Put[nam] & I have scratched up about 250 woodcuts, besides 3 steel plates, and we expect to put in a pretty good appearance."

In the months immediately ahead, for reasons unknown, the printing of the *Key* was delayed. It was April of the next year (1872) when Coues informed Baird: "Mr. Putnam tells me he is about ready to get out our prospectus, and advertise the book, so will you please send what you offered some time ago—a few lines in favor of the work that we can print. We expect a good deal from your name in this connection, and I hope that your real opinion of the probable merits of the work is not far behind what you might wish to say out of kindness to me. If you would also make a note of the announcement of the book, in the scientific column of Harper's, with a good word for it, it would be doing us a substantial favor likewise. . . . Prof. Marsh[19] has proposed to furnish a Synopsis of all the fossil birds of N.A. Won't that be a funny feature of a book? Quite a valuable item!"

In succeeding weeks, as the publication date drew nearer, Coues regularly informed Baird of each new development. On May 13: "I have requested Mr. Putnam to send you the book in signatures [sections] as you desired, and should be pleased to receive suggestions & criticisms." On June 26: "I am having a hard summer—fearfully overworked, as Putnam wants to finish the book before I go west." On July 1: "I am writing the last words of my book and probably the whole will be in type in less than a month." On September 12: "My book is all in type, and I am making the *Index*. Delightful occupation this, isn't it?"

The original edition of Coues' *Key to North American Birds* came from the press in October, 1872. It consisted, as Putnam had told Coues, of some 2,000 copies, each an imperial octavo of 361 pages, and it was illustrated with 238 woodcuts and six steel engravings. At the front of the book, on a page preceding the title page, appeared an extraordinary vignette, or decorative monogram. It was, we feel confident, a product of Coues' own particular artistic endeavor and whimsical sense of humor, and he thought well enough of it to use it in other books, including all five subsequent editions of the *Key*. The reader will note (see reproduction below) the conspicuous initials C and E, the bespectacled owl (universal symbol of wisdom) perched on the lower limb of the E, and the word "Key" prominent on the spine of the book held firmly by the owl.

Key to North American Birds was a remarkable composite. For a summary description of it, Coues' own is perhaps best:

> [It is] designed as a manual or text-book of the birds of N.A., and claims to be an exponent of late views of classification and nomenclature. The introductory part gives a general account of the structure, and more particularly, the external characters, of birds, with special reference to their classification, and an explanation of the technical terms usually employed in description. An artificial 'Key' or analysis of the North American genera follows, prepared upon a plan found practically useful in botany, but seldom applied to zoology, whereby a specimen may be readily referred to its proper place. The body of the work consists of brief diagnoses of the N.A. species, with reference to leading authorities; the families and higher groups being also characterized. The work introduces the first decided changes that were made in the nomenclature of the N.A. species since 1858, mainly by the recognition of geographical races of a great many previously accredited species. It also contains the first systematic account ever given of the fossil species, prepared under the revision of Prof. O. C. Marsh.[20]

The unique and most innovative feature of Coues' book, the one immediately catching the attention of amateur and professional ornithologists alike, was his artificial key—actually a series of keys, one patterned to enable the student to determine the taxonomic order to which a particular bird belonged, and the others to aid in finding the specific family, genus, and species. Elaborating at later date, Coues wrote: "These 'Keys' differ from natural analyses in being wholly arbitrary and artificial. They are an attempt to take the student by a 'short cut' to the name and position in the ornithological system of any specimen of a North American bird he may have in hand and desires to identify . . . but it must be remembered there *is no* 'royal road to learning.' . . . Nor must too much be expected of me here; I can take the student nowhere until he has learned the difference between the head and tail of a bird, at any rate."[21] The *Key* was an immediate success. J. A. Allen declared: "Its practicability was evident from the outset, and it proved to be the forerunner of almost numberless successors of 'Key' manuals in various departments of zoology."[22]

Another important feature of the *Key to North American Birds*, perhaps the most important of all, was Coues' introduction of a large number of those subspecies or geographical races which now are indicated by trinomials. Of this particular feature we shall have much more to say in chapters to follow.

Yet another aspect of Coues' *Key* attracting attention, and considerable comment, was the large number of illustrations (approximately 100 of the more than 200) done by Coues himself. The great majority of these sketches were of the head only, with no more than half a dozen of the entire bird.[23] Obviously Coues expended a tremendous amount of time and exacting labor in making these sketches, all in pen and ink. In the original edition Coues included nothing to indicate that he himself had done these drawings, but in all succeeding editions, below each figure, he appended the legend "Ad. nat. del. E.C.," his shorthand for "Delineated from nature by Elliott Coues." Presumably these drawings failed to elicit any spontaneous outburst of enthusiasm from contemporary ornithologists. In any event, when later commenting on them, Coues said: "The woodcuts, of miscellaneous character, are, with some exceptions, very poorly executed, adding little to the value, and detracting from the general appearance of the work."[24]

Did Coues unjustly deprecate his own artistic efforts? In an attempt to find out, we were fortunate enough to obtain the opinion of George M. Sutton,[25] who is regarded by some as our greatest living bird artist, and a worthy successor to Louis Agassiz Fuertes,[26] the greatest of them all. Dr. Sutton, with a copy of Coues' *Key* (5th ed.) before him, has written us as follows:

> When Coues made a direct-from-specimen drawing of a certain feature (*e.g.*, the Oystercatcher's bill on p. 787 of Vol. II), he did very well indeed. Here the proportions are as they should be and the absence of a major highlight does not disturb the viewer, for in a diagnostic, somewhat chartlike drawing of this sort what the viewer needs to see is clearly and accurately shown. It is good, if not excellent. On the other hand, such drawings as that of the Ruffed Grouse's head (Vol. II, p. 742), whether designed primarily to show proportions, markings, etc. or not, apparently were done in hopes of representing the living birds, and as such they are not only primitive but poor.
>
> For me the worst feature in the Ruffed Grouse drawing—and, alas, in virtually all of his drawings—is the schematic representation of the highlight in the eye. This odd little isosceles triangle of white, piercing both iris and pupil, was doubtless intended to give sparkle to the eye and lifelikeness to the whole; but for me what it does primarily is to prove that Coues could never have made the slightest effort to see for himself what a living (or freshly killed) bird's eye looked like. I suspect that he merely followed a tradition established by certain European delineators (Brehm[27] *et al.*). In some drawings, notably that of the Sandwich Tern (Vol. II, p. 1008), the eye is so poorly done and the general effect so bad that the representation becomes a kind of travesty, almost a caricature. Here the delineation of the bill is good,

but the great glaring eye with its pale iris, white lids, and stabbing highlight
does not look in the least like that of the living *Thalasseus sandvicensis*. In the
living bird the eye has a dull highlight unless it is struck directly by the sun's
rays, and the lids are so dark that they hardly show at all—even at close
range.

Coues' drawings of the whole bird were even less successful than those
of the head. In his drawing of the Blue-gray Gnatcatcher (Vol. I, p. 264) the
eye is very poor but the feet are poorer. Here no understanding whatever is
shown as to the way in which toes operate. The same must be said of the feet
of the Black-throated Green Warbler (Vol. I, p. 304). Pay special attention,
please, to the right foot in Coues' Black-capped Chickadee (Vol. I, p. 270).
Here the delineation of the toes is nothing short of dreadful. And the left
foot does not even have a hind toe. This was plain slovenliness on Coues'
part.

I suspect that Coues, a discriminating man surely, realized that his
drawings of the whole bird left much to be desired. He may even have
cringed when he looked at them. No wonder, no wonder at all, that he
[later] marvelled and "raved" over the talents of that unknown newcomer,
Louis Agassiz Fuertes.

Other twentieth-century bird portraitists agree with Sutton's appraisal. Walter J. Breckenridge, for one, has written: ". . . the eyes are
nearly all the same, with a standard highlight and a lid divided into tiny
segments in a very mechanical manner. I can imagine he did these all
alike regardless of the light in which he was viewing them."[28]

What did ornithologists of the 1870s think of Coues' *Key to North
American Birds*? One wrote: "[It] differed in one great respect from all
other works upon ornithology that had preceded it. It reached the
people. The great works of Audubon and Wilson were up to that time a
dream of all young American ornithologists, of which the 'Key' was the
realization. Its influence was both marvelous and good, and can hardly
be overestimated, for it became a living factor of the growing mind of the
coming generation of men of the time in which it appeared. It fell into
the hands of boys who could now, [by using its 'key'], 'find out the names'
of the birds which they saw and collected. It taught to classify, to observe,
to record, and as a result of all, to appreciate and admire."[29]

One young man to whom Coues' *Key* became a "living factor" was
Theodore Roosevelt. In an unpublished notebook titled "Remarks on
the Zoology of Oyster Bay," written in 1875, Roosevelt, then aged
sixteen, said: "In these notes I have adopted (with slight alterations) the
classification of Coues in his *Key to North American Birds*."[30] The following
year Roosevelt entered Harvard College with the declared intention of

becoming "a scientific man of the Audubon, or Wilson, or Baird, or Coues type."[31]

J. A. Allen was almost eulogistic in his praise of Coues' *Key*: "It has had above all others the most important influence on ornithology in our own land. It is a work that, in conception and masterly manner in which it is carried out in all its details, stands as one of the best, if not the best, bird book ever written."[32]

The British ornithologists were also enthusiastic, with one of them writing: "There is a freshness and boldness in the manner in which the facts are handled, which will be extremely acceptable to those who look upon ornithology as a branch of natural history rather than as an all-absorbing study of itself. . . . A key is appended for discovering the genera with facility, constructed on the same principle as those employed by the botanists."[33]

Almost all the reviewers emphasized the influence of Coues' *Key* on aspiring young ornithologists. To those of later decades of the nineteenth century it was their standby, just as Frank M. Chapman's *Handbook of Birds of Eastern North America* was the *vade mecum* of youthful bird students of the next generation. One naturalist—having in mind not only the original *Key* but also succeeding editions—went so far as to say that Coues' *Key* "was doubtless the most useful work in developing ornithological scientists that has ever been published."[34]

4

At Fort McHenry, as time went on, Coues wrote more often to Allen. Excerpts from his letters reveal thoughts uppermost in his mind, on a variety of subjects. On December 27, 1870, for instance, his subject was bird coloration as influenced by environment: "I think I know what of the *Raptores* give you the impression that Western types incline to be brighter & more ferruginous than the Eastern correspondents, but I hardly think any extensively applicable law can be deduced. . . . In the brief reflection I have given the subject, I do not find that the Western birds are brighter on the average. Those of the heavily wooded regions certainly are; but in the West there is plain & desert enough to counteract this, and reduce the average . . . and this brings me to your other hypothesis, that humidity deepens color; of which I think *there is no question.*"

Motivated by Darwin's *Origin*, ornithologists were then paying increased attention to the effects of environmental factors on the color and size of birds. Among Americans particularly active in these studies were Baird, Ridgway, Coues, and especially Allen. His "On the Mammals and Winter Birds of East Florida" (1871) provided much "evidence for the individual and geographic variation in size of all measurable exterior characteristics."[35]

Writing Allen on July 4, 1871, Coues continued on the environment-color subject: "If you are far enough south [on your trip], I wish you would keep in mind as a specialty, observing how far that curious rule of grayer color & longer tail of the birds will hold. *Icterus longicauda* [yellow-breasted chat] is a typical example of this, and there are very many other cases. Even the Chippies [namely, chipping sparrows, *Spizella passerina*] in Arizona[36] have longer tails than the Chippies here. I have been thinking of collating a list showing this . . . and meditate on a complete monograph of the species; though the thing is so heavy that I may have to be a long time pregnant before I can give birth."

Of all of Coues' letters to Allen from Fort McHenry, one, dated June 22, 1872, interests us most, for in it Coues described in detail a typical day's work:

> How perfectly I understand what you say about work! It is just the same with me. I do my duties & take an hour or two's writing in the forenoon, then write from lunch to dinner, play a game of billiards & settle to my desk again for the evening; but I find I can't get on as fast if I write past midnight as if I knock off at 11 or 12; for I'm not up to the mark next day. I have some warnings by noises in the head & confusion of ideas at times, so I know I must be careful. It is no use to stimulate—I can't write a word of sense if there's a drop of alcohol in me, and never could, and besides I'm afraid to try. If I'm alive next September the thing [the *Key*] will have been done, and I can take it easy.

Before reading the above, we had known something in general of Coues' working habits—his singleness of purpose and tremendous drive—but nothing, until now, quite so specific. We interpret the "duties" alluded to as his responsibilities to hospital patients. At the rate Coues described, he was at his desk with pen in hand at least nine to ten hours daily and possibly eleven or twelve. From this letter we learn, too, that his only form of exercise was a postprandial game of billiards, probably with another officer at the fort, and that, while actively writing, he never touched an alcoholic drink.

Coues' stay at Fort McHenry, approximately two years, must have passed rapidly. On September 29, 1872, just two days before boarding a train for "the wilderness,"[37] he wrote George Lawrence:

> I leave day after tomorrow for another period of exile—for how long,

the powers that be only know "and they won't tell." I do not mean however to let the geographic accident interrupt my studies in the least. I shall take a small museum with me, and shall set up my desk in the wilderness. My locale is altogether uncertain—somewhere in the Northwest—but the above address [care of Medical Director, Department of Dakota, St. Paul, Minnesota] will reach me always. I have had an overworked summer, and am suffering the physical and mental depression consequent, but have accomplished *much*. My book [the *Key*] is just in the throes of delivery; *Myiarchus* is out some time since;[38] *Spheniscidae* just issuing;[39] and probably you have noted constant writing in [*American*] *Naturalist*.

As Coues would soon learn, his uncertain destination would be Fort Randall, a post on the Missouri River in what is now South Dakota.

NOTES

1. Simpson and Bache, "Fort McHenry, Baltimore, Maryland" (1875), 40.
2. *Ibid.,* 43.
3. *Ibid.* Remittent and intermittent fevers were probably malarial. Some medical historians think that remittent fever was usually aestivo-autumnal malaria, characterized by chills and fevers every twenty-four hours or oftener, and intermittent fever either quartan or tertian malaria, the former characterized by chills and fever every seventy-two hours, and the latter every forty-eight hours.
4. Coues' "Book of Dates" (1871).
5. Yarrow, "Personal Recollections of Old Medical Officers," 588.
6. In his introduction to this article Coues wrote: "We are indebted to Prof. [Louis] Agassiz for the use of a specimen from the Museum of Comparative Zoology . . . an adult male, in good condition except that the head was severely shattered by a charge of small shot."
7. Coues, "The Yellow-headed Blackbird" (1871).
8. Coues, "Bullock's Oriole" (1871).
9. Coues, "The Long-crested Jay" (1871).
10. Coues, "Observations on *Picicorvus columbianus*" (1872).
11. Coues, "Contribution to the History of the Blue Crow of America" (1872).
12. Coues, "The Nest, Eggs, and Breeding Habits of *Harporhynchus crissalis*" (1872).
13. Coues, "A New Bird to the United States" (1872).
14. The meadow mice have been updated to the genus *Microtus*.
15. *Hesperomys*, genus of rice rats, has been supplanted by *Oryzomys*, and *Reithrodon*, genus of harvest mice, has been updated to *Reithrodontomys*. *Myodes*, genus of lemmings, has given way to *Lemmus*.
16. The full title of Coues' 1872 article on flycatchers is: "Studies of the *Tyrannidae*, Part I: Revision of the Species of *Myiarchus*." Though Coues planned Part II, he never got around to it.

17. Coues later wrote an article about shrews, "Precursory Notes on American Insectivorous Mammals" (1877).

18. Mrs. Sarah P. Ingalls, curator of natural history, Peabody Museum, Salem, Mass., wrote us on Feb. 20, 1974: "While Director of the Peabody Academy of Science, F. W. Putnam was also proprietor of a printing press known as the Salem Press. In 1867 he and the other members of the staff of the Peabody Academy of Science started to publish *The American Naturalist*, a popular monthly magazine. In 1869, the Naturalists' Agency was established and was really an outgrowth of *The American Naturalist.* . . . There was definitely a working relationship between the Peabody Academy and the Agency."

19. Othniel Charles Marsh (1831-99), paleontologist, was born in Lockport, N.Y. He was professor of paleontology at Yale (1866-99). His published works include "Monograph of the Extinct Toothed Birds of North America."

20. Coues, *Birds of the Colorado Valley* (1878), 690-91.

21. Coues, *Key to North American Birds,* 5th ed. (1903), I, 233.

22. Allen, *Auk,* XXI (Apr., 1904), 296.

23. Among these were the blue-gray gnatcatcher (*Polioptila caerulea*), black-capped chickadee (*Parus atricapillus*), sandwich tern (*Thalasseus sandvicensis),* and black-throated green warbler (*Dendroica virens*).

24. Coues, *Birds of the Colorado Valley,* 691.

25. George Miksch Sutton (1898–   ), bird artist, ornithologist, and author, was born in Lincoln, Nebr. He served as assistant curator of birds, Carnegie Museum, Pittsburgh (1919-24), and as curator of birds, Cornell University (1932-45). He is currently curator emeritus of birds and professor of zoology, Stovall Museum, University of Oklahoma, Norman. Among his published works are: *Mexican Birds* (1951), *Iceland Summer* (1961), and *Portraits of Mexican Birds* (1975).

26. Louis Agassiz Fuertes (1874-1927), bird artist and ornithologist, was born in Ithaca, N.Y. His paintings of birds have illustrated many books, among them *Citizen Bird* by Wright and Coues (1897), Coues' *Key to North American Birds* (5th and 6th eds., 1903 and 1927), and *Birds of New York State* by Forbush (1910).

27. Alfred Edmund Brehm (1829-84), German naturalist. Among his published works are *Das Leben der Vogel* (1860-61) and *Thierleben* (1863-69).

28. Breckenridge to authors, Apr. 12, 1974. Breckenridge is with the Museum of Natural History of Minnesota.

29. Shufeldt, "The Couesian Period" (1884), 323.

30. This and other unpublished notebooks by Theodore Roosevelt are today in the library of Harvard University.

31. Theodore Roosevelt, *An Autobiography* (New York: Charles Scribner's Sons, 1922), 23.

32. Allen, "Biographical Memoir," 402.

33. *Nature* (London), VIII (May 8, 1872), 22.

34. McAtee, "Elliott Coues," 431.

35. Stresemann, *Ornithology from Aristotle to the Present,* 245. See also Coues, "Progress of American Ornithology" (1871).

36. The Arizona "Chippie" referred to by Coues is today (1980) *Spizella passerina arizonae* Coues.

37. Coues' "Book of Dates" (1872).

38. A reference to Coues' "Studies of the *Tyrannidae.*"

39. Namely, "Material for a Monograph of the *Spheniscidae.*"

CHAPTER X

Fort Randall, Dakota Territory

As Coues left Fort McHenry for "another period of exile," he must have experienced mixed emotions. He was leaving a "crack" post for a destination somewhere in the vast expanse of the Northwest, and he would be separated from his family for an indeterminate period. On the other hand, the lure of the unknown, with its prospects for adventure and discovery, was still strong within him.

En route to St. Paul, his immediate destination, Coues stopped briefly in Chicago where he met, presumably by prearrangement, his first wife, Sarah Richardson, whom he had not seen since their marriage in Columbus, Ohio, eight years before. Why they met, what they talked about, and on what terms they parted, are questions to which we have no answers. If Coues had not entered in his "Book of Dates" (1872) the terse statement: "Oct. 2 or 3, Chicago, first met S.A.R. since our separation," we would know nothing whatever about this meeting.

After visiting his sister Lucy (now Mrs. James M. Flower) and her family in Madison, Wisconsin, Coues went on to St. Paul, arriving on October 8. It was only here that Coues learned that he was being sent to Fort Randall. To Baird, on the following day, Coues wrote: "I go to Fort Randall, Dakota Terr[itory]. Communication—all mail direct to Sioux City, then by steamer up the Missouri. . . . If you can get boxes to me, they will be as safe as anywhere else in the country. Randall is about the largest post in the Dep't." From Coues' "Book of Dates" we learn that he left St. Paul on October 14, arrived in Sioux City the same day, left Sioux City by boat on October 15, reached Fort Randall on the 18th, and assumed his duties as post surgeon the next day.

Situated on the north bank of the Missouri in what is now Charles Mix County, South Dakota, Fort Randall had served "as a base of supplies for the posts on the Upper Missouri, and as a protection to settlers against the Indians [Sioux, Ponca and others]" since its establishment in 1856.[1] The buildings, well constructed, stood about a half-mile from the river, which here was some 1,000 yards wide and navigable for light draft boats. In 1872-73, during Coues' stay there, the garrison consisted of 197 enlisted men and nine officers.[2]

Writing to Baird on October 28, Coues revealed a few of his first impressions of Fort Randall:

> You will be glad to learn that I am already settled and already itching to resume work. This Post is by far the most desirable in the Department, after St. Paul or Snelling,[3] both as regards accessibility & creature comforts. It promises *fairly*, but nothing extra, for collecting, being directly on the Missouri, with an unending strip of wooded river bottom running past. The drawback is the hostility of the Sioux, which will prevent any operations back of the river, though the immediate vicinity of the post is comparatively safe. *For the frontier*, I don't know where I could be less objectionably located. I have an assistant surgeon to do pretty much all the [medical] work, and so my time is all my own. Nothing but distance from books and specimens renders this less agreeable than my last station.

In a concluding paragraph Coues told Baird to use his own judgment—"tempered with mercy"—about sending him things, and that the distance to Sioux City was "about 275 miles, made in 2-5 days according to the time consumed sticking on sand bars."

On at least two counts, both important, Coues' above letter to Baird needs comment. The threat of hostile Sioux was real, and would continue in those parts even after Coues left Fort Randall. Almost every grade-school youngster knows what the Sioux, just four years later, did to General George Armstrong Custer and his troops in the valley of the Little Big Horn. Second, Coues' time was, indeed, all his own. Throughout his stay at Fort Randall Coues' medical duties were decidedly minimal. They would have been heavier, of course, if some disease in epidemic form had struck the garrison, but that did not happen; moreover, the great majority of the disorders afflicting the men were minor. According to an official medical report for 1872-73, there were thirteen cases of rheumatism, 137 of "other local diseases," sixty accidents and injuries, and only a few cases of more serious diseases, such as typhoid fever and consumption. The number of patients hospitalized *per diem* averaged five.[4]

Under these conditions, it is understandable that Coues could, with easy conscience, entrust most of the medical chores to his assistant, and did so, apparently, with no protest or rebuke from his commanding officer, as had been the case at Fort Macon.

It is all too evident what Coues' freedom from medical responsibilities meant to him: he could devote almost all of his time to his favorite pursuits, collecting and writing. Coues' contributions to science while at Fort Randall border on the incredible, particularly because of the relative brevity of his stay—just seven months—and because the winter, one of the worst on record, allowed only a minimum of field work. By late November Coues was reporting to Baird that the temperature had dropped to 5°F below zero. Later he wrote of much colder days, when the mercury fell to thirty, even forty, below,[5] and of an April snowstorm that almost buried the fort, the drifts being "level with the roofs."[6]

2

Now and then Coues, in his eagerness to obtain specimens of Dakota animals, traveled farther from the fort than prudence dictated. On one known occasion he ventured miles from the fort, to a lake[7] beside which he spent the night, hoping that in the morning he could collect specimens of wildfowl and hear the "booming" of the sharp-tailed grouse (*Pedioecetes phasianellus*). Of his experiences with the grouse, he later wrote:

> I shall never forget the first time their strange booming fell upon my ears—a new experience to me. . . . I was miles away from the fort or any other human habitation, whither I had gone into lonely bivouac the night before. . . . Awakened before it was light by the sonorous cries of the wild fowl making for the reedy lake where I had encamped, I arose . . . and pushed off into the expanse of reeds in a light canoe I had brought with me. . . . The sense of loneliness was oppressive in the stillness that preceded morning, broken only by the quack or plash of the Wild Duck, and the distant honking of a train of Wild Geese winnowing their sinuous way afar. . . . The light came on, the distant hills took shape and settled in firm gray outlines against the sky, and a breath of fresher, purer air, messenger of morning, passed over the lake . . . causing the reeds to sway in graceful salute to the coming sun. A Sparrow chirped from her perch with joy; a Field Lark rose from her bed in the grass. . . . The feathered orchestra sounds never so impressive as when it ushers in the day; never so fine and complete as when familiar voices sing the higher notes to the strange deep bass of the [sharp-tailed] Grouse. Heard for the first time, as it was on this occasion, the effect was indescribable. No one could say whence the sound proceeded, nor how many birds, if more than one, produced it; the hollow reverberations filled the air, more like the lessening echoes of some great instrument far away, than the voice of a bird close at hand. I listened to this grand concert, absorbed in the reflections it stirred within me, no longer alone, but in company I love, till the booming fell less frequently upon my ear, and then ceased.[8]

Because of the extremely cold weather, Coues, to observe the few birds that came about the fort during his stay that winter, ordinarily had to be content with watching them through the windows of his quarters. He was able to observe the pretty little snow bunting or snowflake (*Plectrophenax nivalis*) and thus to write engagingly about it:

> The Snowflake is extremely abundant in the Missouri River region in winter. They reached Fort Randall November 15, 1872, after a severe cold snap with a light snow-fall, and as I write (January, 1873), great numbers are swirling over the ground around, and in the fort. They keep pretty closely in flocks numbering from a dozen or so to several hundred, and, though they spread over the ground a great deal in running about after seeds, they fly compactly, and wheel all together. In their evolutions they present a pretty sight, and have a not displeasant stridulent sound, from mingling of the weak chirrups from so many throats. They are quite unsuspicious, trooping about our very doorsteps in search of food, unconscious of real dangers, but their natural timidity, as well as restlessness, is so great, that they seem to constantly take causeless alarm, scurrying off in an instant, perhaps, only to return to the same spot immediately.

Coues ended his depiction of this hardy northlands visitor with these words: "They do not appear to suffer with the cold, although the thermometer has been down to 30° below zero; those that I secured were in good condition, and proved excellent eating."[9]

A dastardly deed this, the shooting and eating of small birds like the snow bunting? As we view it today, in the latter years of the twentieth century, yes; but not so then. A hundred years ago a bird, if at all edible, was something to be shot down, just as a tree was something to be cut down. To provide another similar illustration, it is on record that the noted ornithologist Frank M. Chapman, on a memorable morning in the fall of 1878, shot two passenger pigeons, the only ones he ever saw in nature, and promptly ate both of them.[10] Of course it may have been that both Coues and Chapman shot the birds as specimens and then, incidentally, ate them. More recently, in various parts of the world, other naturalists have kept a stew pot on the fire into which they tossed the bodies of birds they had skinned out, even those down to warbler size.

John Burroughs once remarked that everyone sees the big things, but that the mark of a true observer is his ability to see the little things, to observe the presence of natural objects effortlessly, spontaneously, and without premeditation.[11] In that respect Coues, of course, had few equals. As an excellent illustration, we cite his recognition of a peculiarity of the western meadowlark (*Sturnella neglecta*), which, in the spring of 1873, came in large numbers to the grounds of Fort Randall:

> In April, before pairing, hundreds used to frequent daily the parade-ground of Fort Randall, where, as the grass was yet scarcely sprouted, good opportunity was offered of observing their characteristic habit—one not so generally known as it should be, since it is related to the peculiar shape of the bill. The birds may be seen scattered all over the ground, busily tugging at something, and on walking over the scene of their operations, the ground, newly softened by the spring thaw, is seen to be riddled with thousands of little holes, which the birds make in search of food. These holes are quite smooth—not a turning over of the surface of the ground, but a clean boring, like that made by sinking in the end of a light walking-stick; just as if the birds inserted the bill and then worked it about till the hole was of sufficient size. Whether they bored at random, or were guided by some sense in finding their prey, and what particular object they were searching for, I did not ascertain; but the habit was so fixed and so continually persevered in as to attract general attention.[12]

In spite of all handicaps, Coues nevertheless succeeded in making a sizable collection of natural history specimens while at Fort Randall. In late January he wrote Baird: "I have got for you . . . a nice lot of bird skins—nothing novel or even rare, but good fresh material." That he expected to do much better in the spring is proved by a circular he prepared and had distributed—with the consent and help of his superiors in St. Paul—to fellow officers in the Department of Dakota. Dated February 1, 1873, it read in part:

> Being engaged in preparing a report on the Ornithology of the North-west, to be published by the Department of the Interior, and forming one of the series issued by the U.S. Geological Survey of the Territories . . . the undersigned respectfully solicits the co-operations of those of his brother officers who may be interested in a certain portion of this work.
>
> With their friendly assistance, he hopes to largely increase, and render more precise, our present knowledge of the *Game Birds* inhabiting the region drained by the Missouri River and its tributaries. . . .
>
> The experience acquired by many officers in the pursuit of game birds represents a fund of interesting information, upon the habits and the traits of the species, which would form a valuable contribution to ornithology. Any such biological material would be extremely acceptable.[13]

Coues was successful at Fort Randall, too, in obtaining specimens of mammals, especially the large carnivores. He wrote to Baird on January 29: "I have got for you a splendid suite [series] of skulls of *Canis latrans* & *lupus* [i.e., coyote and gray wolf], skins of the former, and of *Vulpes velox*

[swift (kit) fox] and *macrourus* [*Vulpes fulva macroura*, great-tailed fox]. . . .
You will receive a large box of collections by me to the S.I. Having my
cabinet with me, I retain such as I want, so you need not reserve a suite
for me." Two weeks later he advised Baird:

> You will be glad to learn what a fine large series of Coyote skins & skulls I
> have for you. At present writing a dozen of each—half of the skins in good
> order for mounting. How many do you want? Twenty? Fifty? This material
> will cost you a trifle, as it has me. I can procure you any reasonable number of
> hunter's skins, not fit for mounting, but showing everything but the toes, at
> 50 to 75 cents. I have also got you some big wolves [*Canis lupus*] and a nice big
> stack of *Vulpes velox*. . . . I will put my specimen of *Vulpes macrourus* against
> any one extant! One of my *Canis lupus* skulls shows the rare anomaly of super-
> numerary & asymmetrical dentition—extra molar on one side of the lower
> jaw. There's positively nothing to be done on birds just now—only wait to
> spring!

3

At a later date Coues wrote of enjoying leisure hours at Fort Randall
with Captain John Hartley, who "was the best poker-player I ever
faced—for I never happened to play with General Custer."[14] Such hours
of diversion at the fort were probably infrequent. In bad weather, when
immured by intense cold and deep snow, Coues undoubtedly spent most
of his waking hours with pen in hand. His literary output, as at previous
other posts, defies the ability of the mind fully to comprehend. He wrote
book reviews for the *American Naturalist* and contributed several bird
articles to such periodicals as *Forest and Stream* and *American Sportsman*.
He produced an appendix, "Ornithology of the Prybilov Islands" (1873),
to a report done by Henry W. Elliott[15] on those islands. More important,
he completed one book, *Field Ornithology*, and did most of the work on
another, *Birds of the Northwest*[16] (about which much more later).

In mid-winter Coues quipped to Baird about his several scientific
activities then in progress or recently completed: "My taxidermy is all
gone to press, so I have nothing but this report, the *Tyrannidae*, the mice,
collecting, editorial work on [*American*] *Naturalist*, and a 'Key to North
American Mammals'[17] on hand—quite idle, you see!" In writing "My
taxidermy is all gone to press," Coues was alluding to his *Field Ornithology*,
or, to supply its full title, *Field Ornithology, Comprising a Manual of
Instruction for Procuring, Preparing and Preserving Birds, and a Check List of
North American Birds*. As this title indicates, *Field Ornithology* was actually
two works in one: a "Manual of Instruction" and a "Check List." In truth,
the latter had appeared separately, in pamphlet form, late in 1873,

whereas the two together did not come from the press until the following year.

Coues' "Manual of Instruction" differed appreciably from others of its kind. It had been written by a master of the art of exposition, by an author whose personality colored his work from beginning to end and consequently impressed itself upon the reader. In this manual we experience no problem in finding examples of his talents as a writer. For instance, who better than Coues could have informed the aspiring ornithologist, young or old, where to look for birds?

> Birds may be sought anywhere. . . . Some come about your doorstep to tell their stories unasked. Others spring up before you as you stroll in the field, like the flowers that enticed the feet of Proserpine. Birds flit by as you measure the tired roadside. . . . They disport overhead at hide-and-seek with the foliage as you loiter in the shade of the forest, and their music now answers the sigh of the tree-tops, now ripples an echo to the voice of the brook. But you will not always so pluck a thornless rose. Birds hedge themselves about with a bristling girdle of brier and bramble you cannot break; they build their tiny castles in the air surrounded by impossible moats, and the drawbridges are never down. They crown the mountain-top you may lose your breath to climb; they sprinkle the desert where your parched lips may find no cooling draught; they fleck the snow-wreath when the nipping blast may make you turn your back; they breathe unharmed the pestilent vapors of the swamps that mean disease, if not death, for you; they outride the storm at sea that sends strong men to their last account. Where now will you look for birds?[18]

Coues' "Manual of Instruction" touched all bases. It provided the reader with 116 pages of dependable and up-to-the-minute information on all aspects of procuring, preparing, and preserving birds and included much not ordinarily found in such works; and no one, of course, could legitimately question Coues' credentials. Though then just thirty years of age, he had already had more experience in the field than most of his contemporaries.

Back in the 1870s, more so than later, the success of a field ornithologist was measured by the size and quality of his collections and the skill and speed he demonstrated in preparing the conventional birdskin. How good was Coues at the latter? According to H. C. Yarrow, scientists often met in one of the Smithsonians offices to "talk over their triumphs past and to come." At one of these sessions the question arose as to which ornithologist then active was most proficient in preparing birdskins. The immediate consensus was that it had to be either H. W.

Henshaw[19] or Elliott Coues. Both men were then in Washington and arrangements were quickly made for them to meet on the following Sunday. "Accordingly, material having been prepared and supplied in the form of English Sparrows, they sat down side by side and commenced their work. Mr. Henshaw skinned his bird and prepared it for purposes of study in one minute and thirty-five seconds. Dr. Coues required one minute and forty seconds."[20]

How did Coues' "Manual of Instruction" fare in reviews by his fellow ornithologists? J. A. Allen, one of the most highly regarded, asserted: "This manual covered such subjects as collecting instruments, directions and suggestions for field work, registration and labeling of specimens, preparation of birdskins, determination of sex, etc. These, of course, based on many years of field experience of the author, and presented with a familiarity and charm of style that made even such dry details attractive."[21]

The manual here and there contained unexpected bits of important information. One of these provided further proof—if any more is needed—that Coues consistently kept journals on his trips. In a section on ornithological "bookkeeping," he wrote: "I use a strongly bound blank book, cap size, containing at least six or eight quires [twenty-four or twenty-five sheets] of good smooth paper."[22]

Prefatorially in *Field Ornithology* Coues wrote:

> The demand for a new CHECK LIST has become urgent. The last one published [1858], and only one now in use, expresses a former state of American ornithology. That great changes—presumably for the better—have lately been made, is shown by the fact that, in round numbers, fifty species have been since ascertained to inhabit North America, while one hundred and fifty have been removed from the former list as being extralimital, invalid or otherwise untenable.
>
> In the present state of our knowledge, and under a system of nomenclature that is proven inadequate and may before long become obsolete, recognition of numerous "varieties"—resultant modifications of species by physical conditions of environment—is imperative; and what are these varieties but the rills that flow into and help swell the mighty stream of descent with modification.[23]

That we may better understand Coues' references to "varieties," to a system of nomenclature "proven inadequate," and to his recognition of "the mighty stream of descent with modification," we should look back to Carolus Linnaeus (1707-78) and the beginnings of our modern system of classification (taxonomy) of plants and animals.

It was in 1735, at the age of twenty-seven, that Linnaeus left his native Sweden for the Netherlands to study medicine. With him in a knapsack he carried the outline of a new system of classification. Later that same year, in Leiden, he published the outline under the title of *Systema Naturae*.[24] This work was so favorably received that it ran through twelve editions, but it was the tenth edition (1758), wherein binomial nomenclature was first utilized, that biologists of the twentieth century recognize as the starting point of modern taxonomy. Binomial nomenclature—the practice of giving two Latin names, a generic and a specific, to each described plant or animal—soon won wide acceptance and "assured victory to Linnaeus' system and made his name immortal."[25]

In Linnaeus' day Latin was the accepted language of scholars; thus the first binomials coined by Linnaeus were in Latin, and scientists the world over, for the first time, found themselves in possession of a common language. Irrespective of country or tongue, the scientific name for man was *Homo sapiens*, that for the cardinal was *Richmondena cardinalis*, that for the painted trillium was *Trillium undulatum*, and so on. Globally there was now one name for each described species, and though of two latinized words, it was far preferable to the multiplicity of vernaculars with which naturalists previously had had to contend.

The Linnaean system at once stirred botanists and zoologists to explore further the earth's surface, its jungles, steppes, deserts, and grasslands. The incentive to discover the unknown and exotic, strong in pre-Linnaean years, was now tremendously magnified. The world was full of undisclosed and undescribed animals and plants, a million and more; Linneaus himself had described fewer than five thousand. More than that, the naturalist could now, by describing and naming a species new to science, achieve a measure of immortality. This was made possible through the practice, at once in effect, of attaching the name of the describer to the binomial of his choice. Thus it doubtless pleased Linnaeus to write *Homo sapiens* Linnaeus, the full scientific name for man, and it unquestionably gratified Elliott Coues, a century later, when he gave the world *Vireo vicinior* Coues, the accepted complete name of the gray vireo. For many botanists and zoologists "species tallying" became an almost full-time occupation, and the excitement attending the discovery and naming of a new species, though diminished, persists to this day.

A fact generally known, at least to biologists, is that Linnaeus believed in special creation, the theory asserting that all creatures large and small were created by the Almighty and continue immutable through all time. Until the publication in 1859 of Darwin's *On the Origin of Species*, this theory was almost universally accepted, but even before that date a small number of biologists had begun to question its validity. On the basis of their observations, they were impelled to believe that under certain environmental conditions some species, at least, did not forever continue immutable. In the forefront as challengers of special creation were ornithologists. Among them, before and immediately after Darwin's *Origin*, were such Americans as John Cassin, George Lawrence, Spencer Baird, J. A. Allen, Elliott Coues, and Robert Ridgway.

In the matter of obtaining evidence disputing special creation, Americans held a clear advantage over Europeans. North America was a much larger continent than Europe and the land surface more varied. In Europe, for example, there were no extensive grasslands or deserts, and the extremes of elevation, temperature, and moisture were less pronounced.

In due course, ornithologists established the fact that the range of various species of North American birds included the greater part of the continent, extending from the Atlantic to the Pacific. To emphasize the point that species inhabiting such large land areas are often conspicuously different in extremes of their range, one naturalist cited the song sparrow (*Melospiza melodia*) as an example, and then said of it:

> Every one at all conversant with North American birds knows that the Song Sparrow of the States east of the Mississippi River is very different from the Song Sparrow of the great elevated, arid plateau of the interior, and that this interior form is again very different from the forms found at different points along the Pacific coast. These various forms, in their extreme phases, are widely diverse, varying in size, color, and in the relative size of the bill, etc., and may be more readily separated from each other than can well-defined species be in some other groups of birds. Yet these very diverse forms of the Song Sparrow are found to intergrade at the points and over the areas where the physical conditions of these several climatic regions of the continent blend and in the same gradual manner. What occurs in the Song Sparrow occurs also in most species having the same vast extent of habitat.[26]

Ornithologists who early recognized the existence of "diverse forms" within a species, such as the song sparrow, promptly faced the problem of settling on a term for designating them. That they experienced difficulty is apparent from the variety of terms employed, among them "incipient species," "geographical races," "conspecies," "varieties," 'nascent species," "local forms," and "subspecies." In time, but only after extended reflection and discussion, "subspecies" emerged as the winner.

Somewhat concurrently another problem arose: how best to word the scientific name of a subspecies. As indicated, among the first subspecies to be recognized were those of the song sparrow. One of these was the gray (desert) song sparrow, an inhabitant of Utah, Nevada, Arizona, and portions of adjoining states. After some trial and error the scientific name of this subspecies appeared as *Melospiza melodia* var. *fallax*. Comprised of three Latin words, the name was now a trinomial (or "trinominal"), the true nature of which was but partially concealed by the intervention of the "var." This method of writing trinomials—with slight variations such as the use of "subsp." in place of "var."—continued in vogue for a few years, until it was simplified.

According to an authoritative source, "The father of modern trinominalism in ornithology was the famous Swedish ornithologist, Carl Sundevall, who in 1840 commenced to treat systematically the ill-defined species as geographical varieties, which he provided with a third name in addition to the specific appellation."[27] Sundevall was "closely followed by Hermann Schlegel, who, in 1844, applied the system to all the European birds in his 'Revue critique des oiseaux d'Europe.'"[28]

John Cassin seems to have been the first American ornithologist to employ trinomials. In his *Illustrations of the Birds of California, Texas, Oregon, and British and Russian America,* published in 1856, he used them somewhat freely, and in a manner strictly his own. For instance, he recognized four species of the great horned owl (*Bubo virginianus*):

Variety, *atlanticus* [native to eastern and northern parts of the U.S.]
Variety, *pacificus* [restricted to western states]
Variety, *arcticus* [Alaska along coast to California]
Variety, *magellanicus* [South America and probably southern North America][29]

Baird, Lawrence, and Ridgway, among other American ornithologists, soon followed Cassin's example in employing trinomials. J. A. Allen did so somewhat tardily; he "looked at the other side, pointed out the value of the species."[30] In his 1871 monograph "On the Mammals and Winter Birds of East Florida" he excluded trinomials altogether. Allen did, however, in that same paper, formulate a most important principle, a far-reaching practical rule: "Subspecies are distinguishable forms which intergrade, while species do not intergrade."[31]

As is evident, trinomialism in the United States was increasingly in the air—but we are getting ahead of our story.

A full century intervened between the tenth edition of *Systema Naturae* (1758) and Darwin's *On the Origin of Species* (1859). As that century neared its close, more and more biologists were challenging the Linnaean concept of fixity of species and nomenclature. To Elliott Coues, for one, Linnaean binomialism sufficed so long as "a thing was either square or else it was round—when species were held for fixed facts as separate creations; but now that we know a thing may be neither square nor round, but something between, it is lamentably defective."[32] Though Cassin and others were strong in their conviction that species, under certain conditions, were subject to change, they were uncertain about what caused the changes; such factors as humidity, mean annual rainfall, and a fuller measure of sunlight may have been responsible.

It was in the midst of these uncertainties and indecisions that Darwin published his classic work. Its theories were to invalidate special creation and, with its principle of natural selection, to offer a plausible explanation of the origin of species and subspecies. The essence of natural selection can be summarized briefly, as follows:

(1) *Variations* of all degrees are present in nature among individuals and species, and some of these are heritable.

(2) By the *geometric rate of increase* the numbers of every species tend to become enormously large.

(3) This involves a *struggle for existence*; individuals having variations unsuited to the particular conditions in nature are eliminated, whereas those whose variations are favorable will continue to exist.

(4) A process of *natural selection* therefore is operative.

(5) Such a process results in the *survival of the fittest*, or the preservation of favored races.[33]

Leading American biologists (Louis Agassiz was a notable exception) enthusiastically accepted natural selection. We know of Coues' endorsement from his description of "the mighty stream of descent with modification"; later he declared that ". . . the Darwinian Theory of Evolution . . . has become established."[34] "Darwinism" opened many doors heretofore closed, and in so doing provided great momentum to studies in practically all biological subjects, not the least of which was trinomialism. In later chapters we shall return to that subject.

Having digressed in order to provide the reader with a synopsis of taxonomic history from Linnaeus to Darwin, we may now, with clearer understanding, return to Coues' *Check List of North American Birds*.

4

The years 1872 and 1873 were marked by unusual nomenclatural activity by Elliott Coues. In 1872, as we know, he had published his *Key* and in 1873 his *Check List.* The arrangement and nomenclature of the latter were identical with the former, except for the inclusion of a few species and subspecies discovered and recognized since the *Key* had come from the press.

In introductory remarks to his *Check List*, Coues stressed the point that it differed from that in Baird's *Catalogue of North American Birds* in three respects: reduction in number of genera, addition of new species, and a decreased number of admitted species.[35]

Surprisingly, Coues left unmentioned a fourth difference, one of greater import to American ornithology than any of the three he did mention. In his *Check List* Coues included 147 subspecies,[36] a far greater number than in Baird's 1858 list. In so doing, Coues became the first ornithologist to apply trinomials "generally and systematically."[37] And he was not exaggerating, therefore, when he later wrote that he was "largely responsible for the growth and spread of trinomial nomenclature."[38]

As with many innovations, there was early opposition to subspecies and trinomials, more so in Great Britain (as we shall later see) than in the United States. Antagonism, however, was comparatively short-lived. Before many years had passed, most biologists agreed with a statement published by one of them: "Trinomials serve as convenient 'handles for facts,' in providing for the naming of forms which are known not to possess the requirements of true species, but which, it is equally evident, demand, in the interests of science, proper recognition. Without trinomials it would be necessary to either name such forms as species, and thus convey an idea of their rank which the person bestowing the name knows to be false, or else ignore them altogether, which would be plainly a dereliction of duty and a positive impediment to the progress of the science."[39]

Nevertheless, to some individuals the increased recognition of subspecies was so much falderol. One such was John Burroughs, the idolized "Sage of Slabsides."[40] Writing to fellow naturalist Eugene P. Bicknell,[41] he made it clear that he in no way agreed with the multiple fission of species as practiced by Coues and others:

> I regret to see that you have been re-baptizing some of our familiar birds in that muddy fount of scientific nomenclature, or else following the lead of someone who has—perhaps the feather-splitter, Dr. Coues. . . . I do not

sympathize at all with this practice. It is worse than useless. Doubtless if every specimen of wood thrush were examined minutely enough, no two could be found exactly alike; hence every individual should have a name of its own. The aim of science should be to simplify things, to show us unity under diversity, but ornithology of late years seems bent on making the surface confusion worse confounded. The common names of birds are alone permanent and reliable, the so-called scientific are in perpetual tilt and mutation.[42]

As is certainly true, a man may be critical of a specific human deed without necessarily harboring a dislike for the individual responsible. According to Burroughs' biographer, a high point in Burroughs' life was his receipt of a letter from Coues praising *Wake-Robin*, perhaps Burroughs' most celebrated contribution to the literature of nature. In this letter, dated February 5, 1874, Coues wrote that *Wake-Robin* had been to him "a green spot in the wilderness, where I have lingered with rare pleasure." He had learned through reading the book that the golden-crowned thrush (ovenbird, *Seiurus aurocapillus*) never "sang to me as he sang to you ... I never read thrush-music entirely aright before, nor had the least idea where the Canadian Warbler [*Wilsonia canadensis*] built its nest." In a final sentence Coues declared: "Now you come to tell me things no longer strange or wonderful, indeed, but, like a friend, pointing out new beauties I missed before."[43] Coues' letter, so full of evident warmth and compliment, could hardly have failed to please the popular American poet-naturalist, and his pleasure was no doubt enhanced because the tribute had come from the author of the recently published *Key to North American Birds*, the most talked-about and acclaimed bird book in the United States at that time.

Before complaining to Bicknell about "feather-splitting," Burroughs had undoubtedly read Coues' *Check List* and must have noted Coues' recognition of six subspecies of the song sparrow. The latest (1957) edition of the American Ornithologists' Union *Check-List of North American Birds* would have pleased him even less; it lists a total of thirty-one subspecies of the sparrow.

5

During the latter months of Coues' stay at Fort Randall an unfortunate and needless altercation between Coues and Robert Ridgway began to develop. We first learn that something unpleasant between the two might be brewing when, on January 20, 1873, Coues wrote Allen: "If R.R. is writing about geog[raphical] variation in N.A. birds as an untilled field, somebody will have to go for him. No one can touch that subject without building on an Allen foundation."[44]

Ridgway had just published the first of two installments of an article titled "On the Relation between Color and Geographic Distribution in Birds, as Exhibited in Melanism and Hyperchromism." It was, as Ridgway said, a straightforward account of the "two chief modifications of color experienced in the several geographical, or climatic, regions of the North American continent, by certain species of birds which are resident over a very extended area." He defined melanism as an increase in the intensity or extent of the black parts of the plumage, and hyperchromism as a greater brightness, or increased prevalence, of the primary colors, red, blue, and yellow.

Ridgway provided several illustrations of both melanism and hyperchromism. One of the former concerned the lesser goldfinch (*Chrysomitris psaltria*, now *Spinus psaltria*), then known to range along the Pacific coast from the 40th parallel through California south to Panama. In the more northern parts of its habitat the entire dorsal region of the bird was olive-green; in New Mexico and Arizona the olive-green was mixed with black; in Mexico black entirely replaced the olive-green; and in Costa Rica and Panama the black was appreciably more intense and lustrous. As a result of these obvious color variations, Ridgway recognized three subspecies: in Arizona and New Mexico, *Chrysomitris psaltria* var. *arizonae*; in Mexico, *C. p.* var. *mexicana*; and in Costa Rica and Panama, *C. p.* var. *columbiana*.[45]

Though we could cite other illustrations given by Ridgway, the above should suffice to make his general thesis clear. We hasten to add, however, that Ridgway's text alluded neither to Coues nor to Allen, both of whom had made earlier contributions on color variations. Coues resented the lack of acknowledgments.

After his letter of January 20 to Allen, Coues wrote others, each foreshadowing an article he ultimately published. On February 7 he told Allen: "By the way, somebody has got to give Mr. Robert Ridgway an overhauling. I'm going to write to him, and ask him what he has to say why sentence of death should not be passed upon him, and if he doesn't satisfy me, I'll go for him. His papers are splendid, but ... without allusions to you. Likewise, *every one* of his reductions are at second hand, so far as relates to N. Am. birds." Somewhat later Coues informed Allen that he had not yet heard from Ridgway. He then continued: "I wrote him a pretty pointed letter, and I am afraid it cut. He will show it to Baird, and perhaps Prof. will say I am not such a good boy as I used to be."

More time went by without any word from Ridgway, and on April 7

Coues told Allen that he had just sent an article about Ridgway to the *American Naturalist*. In this piece Coues quickly came to the points at issue:

> [Ridgway] writes as if his views were both novel and original, which is not the case. To speak plainly, the paper is based entirely upon Mr. Allen's view, without the slightest allusion to this author; and is illustrated chiefly by cases already published, yet without the proper references. . . . we will put the charge of appropriating Mr. Allen's work without acknowledgement into this shape: *a,* either Mr. Ridgway's views, here enunciated, are original, or, *b,* they are not. If *a,* we acquit him of scientific plagiarism, and accredit him with discovery, but accuse him of suppressing the fact, known to him, that the same discoveries had been already made by another person, and published about eighteen months previously. If *b,* the case speaks for itself too plainly to require further remarks.[46]

Of several instances cited by Coues of Ridgway's failure to acknowledge credit, Coues chose one in particular, and commented: "The leading illustration of the *melanistic* tendency selected is the remarkable case of *Chrysomitris psaltria* and its races; this we [namely, Coues himself] first worked out in 1866 (Proc. Phila. Acad., 81) exactly as it is here presented."[47]

Robert Ridgway at that time (1873) was just twenty-two years of age (Coues was thirty), and a young man of such demonstrated talent and promise as an ornithologist that he had already, through Baird's influence, been named to the Smithsonian staff. By nature shy, quiet-spoken, and unassuming, he nevertheless, on reading Coues' article, lost his composure. To be charged with what amounted to bald-faced plagiarism, and to have the accusation broadcast, was a matter so grave that he could not ignore it. He replied at once, carefully choosing his words: "To be charged with literary theft must be unpleasant even when it is merited; to be charged with 'scientific plagiarism' without any provocation, is an accusation which cannot be borne in silence. In this case, the charge bears with it so much arrogance, that a simple defense against it is not sufficient; and I should consider myself very unselfish and uncourteous, did I not make some return for the attention which I have received."[48]

As to having failed to give credit to Allen's contributions, Ridgway said that Allen should, indeed, receive all the credit due him, but one should not lose sight of the fact that "he is not the only one who has written upon the subject of climatic color-variation and geographical distribution." Baird, he declared, was "the pioneer in this case."[49]

At one point Ridgway defended his original article: "From the time when its preparation was first discussed in my mind to the time of its publication, the question never once occurred to me whether the laws which I endeavored to explain were my own discoveries, or whether their discovery was the property of others. I took it for granted, that the subject and its general principles were so familiar that a preliminary review of its literature would be a superfluous addition to a paper already overburdened with references."[50] This statement in Ridgway's defense had more bite and reason to it than any of his others, for, by and large, he had limited his paper to a close examination of several large series of birdskins (a total of 150 in one) in the Smithsonian collections. Hence we are inclined to believe him when he said that a preliminary review of the literature, which would necessarily have included recognition of the earlier pubished works of Allen, Coues, Baird, and others, would have been needless.

Whether or not Ridgway was guilty of a sin in ignoring the contributions of Allen and Coues to the subject is perhaps moot; but even if guilty, Coues surely committed a greater sin in the harshness of his criticism. No one else, not even Allen, felt impelled to accuse Ridgway of plagiarism.[51]

When and how did the altercation end? For the public, at least, it ended some three months later when the *American Naturalist* ran an editorial statement reading: "We are requested, by Dr. Coues and Mr. Ridgway, conjointly, to state that neither of these gentlemen 'desired to continue a controversy of no scientific consequence, and one which, furthermore, has lost its personal interest since a mutual misunderstanding in which it arose has been explained to their entire satisfaction.' Mr. Ridgway further desires us to state that 'he is willing to retract the implication of bad faith on the part of Dr. Coues.'"[52]

Several years later D. G. Elliot, who possibly understood Coues as well as any man did, attempted to explain Coues' several unduly severe criticisms of the published works of colleagues, such as that leveled in 1873 at Ridgway: "[Coues] set down 'naught in malice,' but employed a phraseology that he honestly believed was best suited to the case in hand, and after some severe article had been issued, he had spoken to me in the kindest way of the author of the work or act he had so criticised or condemned, apparently unconscious that it could ever possibly affect any friendly relations or be the means of any estrangement."[53]

On the surface Coues and Ridgway had seemingly patched up their differences; not so, as events described in later chapters will reveal. For the moment, at least, Coues did regret his ill-advised censure of Ridgway. Writing to Allen in November, 1873, he said, "Coues-Ridgway now happily squelched."

6

Early in 1873 Coues received news that his stay at Fort Randall might soon be terminated. To Baird, in mid-March, he wrote: "The matter of the Boundary Survey which you mention stands thus, so far as I know: Dr. [H. C.] Yarrow told me that Col. Farquhar,[54] commanding the Expedition, intended to apply for me as naturalist of the Survey. . . . This is what I want." The boundary survey was to be a joint undertaking of Great Britain and the United States, one that would survey the 49th parallel from Lake-of-the-Woods west to the Continental Divide.

With his appointment as naturalist to the survey soon confirmed, Coues revealed in a note to Allen on March 31: "Congratulate me! I have got my appointment as naturalist of the British Boundary Survey, and probably enter the field next May. Field operations till September, then back into Washington for winter quarters. Baird seems to have got it for me, as he does everything." To Baird himself, expressing his gratitude, Coues confessed: "You have laid me under a load of obligation from which I see no possible escape except by systematic ingratitude—and that would come harder to me than to stay in debt. I have got used to this, in the course of years!"

About this same time Allen wrote Coues a letter in which he seemingly questioned Baird's integrity. Coues immediately replied: "I cannot believe that Baird would take a single item to himself not his own. The Record looks somewhat unfavorable, but then see how freely—even generously—he has set you up on every occasion. What do you think his last dodge is? He offers me, for my Report, the use of all the cuts I want from his forthcoming work. I can't get over such a thing, and he has been doing such things for me for ten years. . . . B[aird] can have anything I've got; [he is] the only man in the U.S. who can write what he pleases [about] birds without my criticism." That Coues unhesitatingly rushed to defend Baird surprises us not at all. The relationship existing then between the two men was probably closer than at any other time in their lives.

NOTES

1. Weeds and Kimball, "Fort Randall, Dakota Territory" (1875), 418. Fort Randall was first built on the right bank of the Missouri about one-quarter of a mile from the river and just north of the point where the river crosses the Nebraska line. In 1870-72, just before Coues arrived, the post had been rebuilt about a quarter of a mile farther from the river. Fort Randall was abandoned in 1892.

2. *Ibid.*, 421.

3. Fort Snelling, established in 1819, was located at the confluence of the Minnesota and Mississippi rivers and was named for Colonel Joshua Snelling.   *Josiah*

4. Weeds and Kimball, "Fort Randall, Dakota Territory," 421.

5. Coues, *Birds of the Northwest* (1874), 158.

6. Coues, ed., *Forty Years a Fur Trader* (1898), II, 156n.

7. Almost certainly Lake Andes. A footnotes in Coues-Biddle (1893), I, 122n, mentions finding, on some maps, a Lake Andes which was "sort of a slough, and used to be our resort for duckshooting."

8. Coues, *Birds of the Northwest*, 412-13.

9. *Ibid.*, 118.

10. Chapman, *Autobiography of a Bird-Lover* (1933), 23.

11. John Burroughs, *Camping and Tramping with Roosevelt* (Boston: Houghton Mifflin, 1906), 102-3.

12. Coues, *Birds of the Northwest*, 192.

13. For a copy of this circular, see Baird-Coues correspondence, Smithsonian Institution Archives.

14. Coues, ed., *Forty Years a Fur Trader*, II, 356n.

15. Henry Wood Elliott (1846-1930), artist and naturalist, was born in Cleveland, Ohio. He served as private secretary to Joseph Henry (1862-78), as artist to the U.S. Geological Survey (1869-71), and as special commissioner for investigation of the Seal Islands (1872-74).

16. This was the "report" on the ornithology of the Northwest Coues had referred to in his 1873 circular to fellow officers.

17. Coues' "Key to North American Mammals," apparently begun at Fort Randall, was never completed.

18. Coues, *Field Ornithology* (1874), 21-22.

19. Henry Wetherbee Henshaw (1850-1930), naturalist, was born in Cambridge, Mass. He served with the Wheeler survey (1872-79), with the Bureau of Ethnology (1879-93), and with the U.S. Biological Survey (1905-16), of which he became head in 1910.

20. Yarrow, "Personal Recollections of Old Medical Officers," 588-89.

21. Allen, "Biographical Memoir," 406.

22. Coues, *Field Ornithology*, 45-46. To our knowledge, not even one of Coues' journals is now extant.

23. *Ibid.*, 1-3.

24. Stresemann, *Ornithology from Aristotle to the Present*, 50.

25. *Ibid.*, 54.

26. J. A. Allen, *Auk,* I (Jan., 1884), 102-3.

27. Stejneger, "On the Use of Trinominals in American Ornithology" (1884), 70. Carl Sundevall (1801-75), European naturalist, became in 1838 head of the vertebrate section of the Royal Museum, Stockholm, Sweden.

28. *Ibid.*, 71. Hermann Schlegel (1804-84), eminent German ornithologist, was born in Saxony and studied zoology in Vienna. In 1828 he was made conservator of the Leiden Museum, and in 1858 its director.

29. Cassin, *Illustrations of the Birds of California, Texas, Oregon, and British and Russian America* (1856), 178.

30. Stejneger, "On the Use of Trinominals in American Ornithology," 75.

31. *Ibid.*

32. Coues, "Progress of American Ornithology" (1871), 373.

33. Modified from Tracy I. Storer and Robert L. Usinger, *General Zoology,* 3d ed. (New York: McGraw-Hill, 1957), 220.

34. Coues, "On the Application of Trinomial Nomenclature to Zoology" (1884), 242.

35. Coues, *Field Ornithology,* 2-3.

36. Coues listed 138 in the text of his *Check List* and nine more in an appendix containing additions and corrections.

37. Stejneger, "On the Use of Trinominals in American Ornithology," 76.

38. Coues, "On the Application of Trinomial Nomenclature to Zoology," 244.

39. Stejneger, "On the Use of Trinominals in American Ornithology," 78-79.

40. John Burroughs (1837-1921), American naturalist and writer, was born in Roxbury, N.Y. In addition to *Wake-Robin* (1871), his other well-known works include *Locusts and Wild Honey* (1879) and *Whitman, a Study* (1896).

41. Eugene Pintard Bicknell (1859-1925), American botanist and internationally known banker, was an authority on the flora of New York state, a member of the Linnaean Society, and one of the founders of the American Ornithologists' Union.

42. Barrus, *Life and Letters of John Burroughs* (1925), I, 274-75. Common names of birds are not always as permanent as Burroughs declared. For instance, the vernacular of *Icterus galbula* was recently changed from Baltimore oriole to northern oriole, and that of *Junco hyemalis* from slate-colored junco to dark-eyed junco. At a considerably earlier date *Anthus spragueii* had a charming common name, Missouri skylark, but no longer. In modern bird books it is Sprague's pipit.

43. *Ibid.*, 146.

44. A reference to Allen's "On the Mammals and Winter Birds of East Florida."

45. Ridgway, "On the Relation between Color and Geographic Distribution in Birds, as Exhibited in Melanism and Hyperchromism" (1872), 454-55.

46. Coues, "Color-Variation in Birds Dependent upon Climatic Influences" (1873), 416.

47. *Ibid.*, 417. Ridgway belittled Coues' published statement on *Chrysomitris:* "Dr. Coues does not even note the progressive increase of black from *psaltris* to *Columbiana*—much less does he appear to consider the manifestations of any climatic law affecting color as applicable in this case."

48. Ridgway, "The Relation between the Color and the Geographical Distribution of Birds" (1873), 555.

49. *Ibid.*, 548-49.

50. *Ibid.*, 554.

51. Allen did, belatedly, write an article mildly critical of Ridgway's: "Laws of Geographical Variation in North American Mammals and Birds," *Amer. Naturalist*, VIII (Apr., 1874), 227-29.

52. *Amer. Naturalist*, VII (Dec., 1873), 760-61.

53. Elliot, "In Memoriam: Elliott Coues," 7.

54. Francis U. Farquhar (d. 1883) graduated from West Point in 1857 and in 1872 was appointed chief astronomer to the Northern Boundary Survey. In 1873 he was replaced by Major William J. Twining.

CHAPTER XI

Along the 49th Parallel

A minor ripple in the nation's foreign relations provided Coues with the opportunity for studying the fauna of the Upper Missouri Valley. Shortly before he went to Fort Randall, it was discovered that the boundary between Canada and the United States was, as Coues put it, "not exactly where it had been supposed to be."[1] In 1872 the governments of Britain and the United States created a joint commission to re-survey the 49th parallel from the Lake-of-the-Woods to the crest of the Rocky Mountains. Heading the American group was Archibald Campbell;[2] Captain Donald Cameron[3] was his British counterpart.

Surveyors, astronomers, axemen, teamsters, cooks, wheelwrights, blacksmiths, and soldiers—infantry, cavalry, and sappers—were sent out by both nations to work with the joint commission. In keeping with the practice of attaching naturalists to such enterprises, the British appointed George M. Dawson,[4] whose primary interest was geology, to accompany the survey; the U.S. Army designated Elliott Coues to serve as naturalist and medical officer for the American commission.

It is apparent by now that Coues, wherever he had been stationed, had collected not only birds but also mammals, reptiles, fishes, and, on occasion, even insects and plants. Thus his appointment to the commission enhanced the scientific significance of the survey. Other naturalists, such as F. V. Hayden, James G. Cooper, and J. A. Allen, had recently made observations in parts of the Northwest, and Audubon had visited the Upper Missouri in the 1840s, as did Prince Maximilian zu Wied-Neuwied in 1833. But the natural history of the area was far from complete and Coues was enthusiastic over the chance to extend it.

In October, 1872, before he received his assignment, the commission accomplished its first task; relocating the Northwest Angle of the Lake-of-the-Woods. Coues was not relieved of his duties at Fort Randall until March 31 of the following year, when he was ordered by the War Department to go to St. Paul, Minnesota, where other members of the American commission had gathered after wintering in Detroit.[5] The orders did not reach him until April 9. He left Randall on May 11 and reported for duty at St. Paul on May 15, 1873.[6] Later he recollected a pleasant stay at Fort Snelling, in the environs of St. Paul.[7]

Traveling with Major William J. Twining,[8] chief astronomer for the American party, Coues and other officials of the commission sailed down the Red River of the North from Moorhead, Minnesota, on James J. Hill's steamboat, the *Selkirk*. They arrived on June 1 at Fort Pembina ("our headquarters before taking the field westward"), located on the Dakota-Manitoba border.[9]

A few days later Major Marcus A. Reno of the 7th Cavalry, leader of the American military contigent, appeared. Poor Reno was immediately beset by two difficulties. The first was the surgeon assigned to his command, Dr. F. O. Nash, a drunkard. The second was Coues, who obtained from the commander at Fort Pembina an order allowing passes to enlisted men, when not on duty, to leave the garrison and help him collect specimens.[10]

Life for Coues was not all that free from annoyance, either. A colony of cliff swallows (*Petrochelidon pyrrhonota*) settled "beneath the low portico of the soldiers' barracks,"[11] and "their incessant twittering was considered a bore, while the litter they brought and their droppings resulted in a sad breach of military decorum."[12] Even more vexing were the mosquitoes: "My first lesson in mosquitoes was learned in Labrador in 1860; it was retaught me in 1873 on the Red River of the North— where horses, cattle, and caribou are sometimes killed by breathing mosquitoes till their nasal passages are plugged solid—where, in walking across a piece of prairie, colored gray with a veil of the insects settled on the herbage, one leaves a trail of bright green grass, over which a gray cloud hangs in the air."[13] After "repeated trials of the use of 'Persian Insect Powders' as a defense against mosquitoes," Coues could only report "a perfect failure."[14]

Coues was eager to get on with more pleasing studies of the area's fauna. Searching for the nests of some yellow-headed blackbirds, he spent most of the day wading in a prairie slough "sometimes up to my waist and in some spots considerably deeper."[15] Later in the month he succeeded in collecting some eastern chipmunks (*Tamias striatus*), northern flying squirrels (*Glaucomys sabrinus*), and Franklin's ground squirrels (*Citellus franklinii*).[16]

In a letter written on July 2 to J. A. Allen, he reported that despite the presence of mosquitoes, the absence of capable assistants, and the possibility of meeting hostile Indians in the field, he had done well already in his collecting: ". . . some 550 skins, nests and eggs. . . . Besides I have perhaps 1500 insects in alcohol, other alcoholics, and an herbarium." In tones of mock despair he complained, "The only thing that troubles me is the cruelly stringent orders I am under. The commissioner directed me to 'get what I want, go where I please, & do what I like.' Too bad, isn't it?"

2

The various British and American surveying parties began moving westward out of the Pembina area during June, on their way to the next observation point, Turtle Mountain—a distance of about 115 miles. Coues remained at Pembina until July 10. Riding a buckboard, he moved through the Pembina Mountains (July 11-13), crossed Long River (July 15), and joined the bulk of the American group at Turtle Mountain on July 18. Along the way he made observations that supported the assertions of J. A. Allen and Robert Ridgway, regarding geographical variations among North American birds: "The general *facies* of the birds of this region may be summed in a word. They are characterized by a *pallor* of plumage, the direct result of the low annual rain-fall."[17]

On the route between Pembina and Turtle Mountain he found Baird's sparrow (*Ammodramus bairdii*) to be "the most abundant and characteristic species," even though it was little known elsewhere in North America. The "Missouri Skylark" (Sprague's pipit, *Anthus spragueii*), also common here, was "another example of the curious fact that a very abundant bird, and one inhabiting no inaccessible region, may by mere accident remain for years almost unknown."[18]

The sounds of the poor-will heard along the 49th parallel conjured up strange imagery: ". . . in places where the birds are numerous the wailing chorus is enough to excite vague apprehensions on the part of the lonely traveler, as he lies down to rest by his camp-fire, or to break his sleep with fitful dreams, in which lost spirits appear to bemoan their fate and implore his intercession."[19] The sounds of the quadrupeds of the area likewise affected his imagination. The "shrill, sonorous whistle" of the elk (*Cervus canadensis*), "heard in the wilds of the West, in the stillness of the early dawn, before the first breath of day stirs, has always reminded me of a giant Aeolian harp played upon by a storm."[20]

Coues' troubles with humans no doubt disturbed his concentrations on nature. Major Reno finally packed the bibulous Dr. Nash off to

Fort Snelling. While waiting for a new surgeon, Reno requested that Coues attend to the medical needs of the soldiers. Although technically still an Army surgeon, Coues refused, informing the major that he worked only for the boundary commission. The Surgeon General's Office later issued a reprimand for his cavalier attitude.[21]

Coues was among those who irritated Commissioner Campbell. According to the diary of Secretary James E. Bangs[22] of the American commission, Campbell "takes the day to 'interview' me (the Dr. being out shooting). Long conversation in which Cameron, [Francis U.] Farquhar [Twining's predecessor as chief astronomer], Twining, Coues and everybody generally gets a good scoring."[23] The naturalist did make some friends, among them Captain Myles W. Keogh,[24] who was killed a few years later with Custer at Little Big Horn.

With the main party in early July, at "the isolated butte known as Turtle Mountain," Coues wrote to a fellow naturalist concerning the ruddy ducks (*Oxyura jamaicensis*) then breeding in the ponds of the mountain: "I obtained many newly hatched young; eggs were laid in June. This is the only breeding place of this species, of which I am aware by personal investigation."[25] He also "took several specimens in perfect plumage" of the eared grebe *(Podiceps caspicus)*— "under circumstances which left no doubt of their breeding at this point."[26] Even the summertime habits of the lowly cowbird (*Molothrus ater*) captured his attention: ". . . they appear to have no comprehension of danger whatever, and are occasionally punished with a crack from the 'black snake' of some facetious teamster,—and unlike a mule, they are never of any use afterward."[27]

He captured some birds alive. Here in northern Dakota he kept in captivity a young ill-tempered Swainson's hawk *(Buteo swainsoni)*.[28] Coues had better luck with a pair of great horned owls (*Bubo virginianus*) with which he traveled all summer. Affection and care made them good pets. Later the male, Solomon, suffered fatal burns from a grass fire; Sappho, the female, survived the return trip to St. Paul.[29]

Coues shot some game birds for food and recreation. Confessing that he had used "most methods, excepting slaughtering from a floating battery with a small cannon," for shooting ducks, he found that hunting them on horseback was "rare sport." The pintails (*Anas acuta*) he bagged were devoured at the officers' mess.[30] For himself, he preferred the American green-winged teal (*Anas carolinensis*), "a favorite bird . . . for shooting for the table, where I always thought it looked better than it did in my collecting chest. 'Two and a half teal, broiled, on toast,' became my well-known limit for supper; but I never succeeded in 'preserving' the third bird without mutilation."[31]

Along the northern border of Dakota Coues sought evidence of the former range of the buffalo: "I saw no signs whatever until the vicinity of Turtle Mountain, where an occasional weather-worn skull or limb-bone may be observed."[32]

3

In early August, after several days of geodetic and astronomical observations at the mountain, the various parties of the commission resumed their westward trek. Coues recorded that he made the first crossing of the Mouse (Souris) River on August 10. Along the way he was pleased to discover a flock of LeConte's sparrows (*Passerherbulus caudacutus*), hitherto little known to science, and secured five specimens.[33]

Here also the calls of the birds disturbed and delighted him. "Often as we lay encamped on the Mouse River, the stillness of midnight would be broken by the hoarse, rattling croaks of [sandhill] cranes [*Grus canadensis*] coming overhead, the noise finally dying in the distance, to be succeeded by the shrill pipe of numberless waders, the honking of geese, and the whistling of the pinions of myriads of wild fowl that shot past, sounding to sleepy ears like the rushing sound of a far away locomotive."[34]

Between Turtle Mountain and Mouse River, Coues began finding more evidence of the buffalo's recent inhabitation of the Dakota plains: ". . . the bony remains multiply with each day's journey, until they become common objects; still, no horn, hoof, or patch of hide."[35] Among the mammals still living in the area was the mink (*Mustela vison*). Using steel traps and deadfalls, a "friend with me procured a large number . . . without difficulty." Examination of the minks confirmed the notion that the entrapped animals did indeed gnaw their feet in attempting to free themselves.[36]

Although not so concerned with reptiles and amphibians as with birds and mammals, Coues did collect several species of snakes, lizards, frogs, toads, and turtles, including what he believed to be a new subspecies of the plains garter snake. He named it "Twining's Garter Snake" in recognition of the chief astronomer's "cordial cooperation in the scientific interests of the Boundary Commission, and in expression of our personal consideration."[37]

For the next several days after the first crossing of the Mouse

River, the route was as follows: "Aug 11 to North Antler Cr., 12th to South Antler Cr., 13th to second crossing of Mouse R.; in camp Terry to Sept. 4.—Sept. 5, 35 m. W. to St. Peter's Wells; 6th 18m. to Long Coteau Creek; in camp to 11th. Sept. 12, to La Riviere [des] Lac[s]."

In these areas Coues noted even more evidence of the buffalo's past residence, including "skulls still showing horns, nose-gristle, or hair, and portions of skeletons still ligamentously attached." At La Rivière des Lacs "there was a grand battue a few years since, as evidenced by numbers of buffalo bones, the innumerable deserted badger-holes, and the circles of stones denoting where Indian lodges stood."[38]

In mid-September most members of the expedition reached the Coteau of the Missouri. The Coteau was a long plateau astride the parallel, almost 300 miles from Pembina, rising some 2,000 feet, and was the divide between the watersheds of the Missouri and Red rivers.

Throughout the remainder of the month and for much of October, the surveying continued until cold weather set in. Coues apparently did not accompany the main party to the final observation point of the survey for this season, because he stated that he got only as far as "nearly to the Coteau de Missouri" and that he left La Rivière des Lacs on September 13, doubling back about ten miles east to the second crossing of the Mouse River (Camp Terry). He recalled staying there "till Oct. 7 *or later*." About that time most of the members of the American commission returned to Camp Terry, and it appears that he journeyed with the main party to St. Paul. According to his own account, he "started with Commissioner Campbell, of whose outfit I had charge all summer," going down "an easy wagon road" to Fort Stevenson.[39] He then "continued down Missouri R. on buckboard to Bismarck . . . and by rail to St. Paul immediately." There he remained for a few days, detained by "vexatious official business." He was able to report that it had been a "very successful" summer of collecting.[40]

4

Rather than wintering with the other Americans at Detroit, Coues returned to Washington and joined his family. Ensconcing himself in an office in the South Tower of the Smithsonian, he began writing up the scientific results of his first season with the boundary survey. Curiously, in light of the sharp exchanges between the two men in 1873, Coues shared the office with Robert Ridgway. The only recorded instance of testiness (which Ridgway later found amusing) that resulted from their joint tenancy of the quarters was when Coues reproached Ridgway for his habitual whistling.[41]

Coues' major accomplishment of the winter of 1873-74 was the completion of his *Birds of the Northwest*. A book of genuine scientific merit is generally several years in the making, and that was definitely true of *Birds of the Northwest*. Coues began it in 1862 at the Smithsonian; he resumed work on it in 1867 when stationed at Columbia, South Carolina; he virtually completed it in 1872-73 while at Fort Randall; and at the Smithsonian in 1873-74 he added the finishing touches. Thus twelve years elapsed between its provenance and completion, and three widely separated places served as locales for its production.

In 1878, four years later, Coues published *Birds of the Colorado Valley*. In most respects this volume was a continuation, a companion piece, to *Birds of the Northwest*. For that reason we deem it advisable to delay an appraisal of Coues' bird biographies, which are legion in both volumes, until a later chapter.

Also during that busy winter of 1873-74 Coues wrote many small pieces for professional journals and sportsmen's magazines. One of the latter, *Forest and Stream*, announced in its October 2, 1873, issue that Coues had become one of the periodical's "corps of paid associates, with a pecuniary interest in the concern."

In January, 1874, his third child, Haven Ladd Coues, was born. The little fellow survived for less than two years, dying in November, 1875.

5

In the spring of 1874 the British and American commissions began regrouping for their second season in the field. This time they would complete the survey by traveling across nearly all the northern boundary of Montana. Coues left Washington on May 29 and reached Chicago on the following day. The cryptic entry in his journal for May 31—"Grand Pacific Hotel, met S. A. R."—proves that he again met his former wife, Sarah A. Richardson, and this time surely not by chance.

On the next morning he arrived at St. Paul and stayed at the Merchant's Hotel until June 4. He proceeded to Bismarck on June 5 and on that day had "difficulty with Marcus A. Reno." On June 6 he challenged the major to a duel!

Although the duel apparently did not take place, the act of issuing such a challenge was by 1874 almost an anachronism. The practice had flourished in antebellum America, particularly in the South. The only guesses that can be offered here as to why Coues demanded satisfaction on the "field of honor" (other than his usual low boiling-point) are that he spent his childhood in a state that never had a law against dueling, that he was reared in a more-or-less southern city, Washington, D.C., and that he had spent a number of his adult years serving in southern military installations.

Later on the day of June 6 Coues and the other members of the American commission boarded the steamer *Fontanelle*, which deposited them at Fort Buford, Dakota Territory, on June 13. The fort, a "great place" according to Coues, was situated on the Missouri River near the mouth of the Yellowstone River, just east of the Montana line.[42] Nearby were the ruins of Fort Union, "formerly a somewhat noted locality, now a mere heap of rubbish."[43] From their winter quarters at Dufferin, Manitoba, members of the British commission reached the same vicinity.

Departing from Buford on June 21, the American column, in a train of 110 wagons, set out westward along the north bank of the Missouri: "21st, 6:30 a.m. to Little Muddy R. 22nd to Big Muddy R. 23. 24 stayed ('Poker Flat'). 25 Frenchman's Point. 26 Quaking Ash R. 27 Wolf R. 28 Little Porcupine R. 29 Big Porcupine R. 30 Buggy cr." After journeying over a hundred miles from Fort Buford, they arrived at the Milk River on July 1. Near here, at a trading post called Tom Campbell's Houses, an astronomical party which Coues accompanied struck northward while the main column continued up the Milk River.[44]

Coues and his companions crossed Little Rocky Creek and continued in a northwesterly direction to another trading post, Fort M. J. Turnay, which Coues pronounced "a very disagreeable place."[45] From there they resumed their march toward the international boundary (Coues riding in a buckboard), following Frenchman's Creek.[46] Along the way he collected, among other fauna, specimens of the "Sage Hare" (Nuttall's cottontail, *Sylvilagus nuttallii*) and the "Prairie Hare" (whitetail jackrabbit, *Lepus townsendi*).[47]

Upon reaching the parallel on July 5, Coues discovered what turned out to be a new species of crustacean which "occurred in myriads in several small prairie pools from a hundred yards to a half mile or so wide, exactly on the Boundary line."[48]

Moving along the boundary, the party reached the East Fork of the Milk River on July 15 and, one week later, Milk River Lake. Coues and his group joined the British and American main parties at the Sweet Grass Hills (the Three Buttes) on July 27. While there Coues paid more attention to obtaining mammals, such as the porcupine *(Erethizon dorsatum)* and "gopher" (Richardson's ground squirrel, *Citellus richardsoni),* than to searching for birds.[49] Of the numerous gophers, he commented that "their name is legion. If Dakota and Montana were the garden of the world (which they are not, however), either the gophers or the gardeners would have to quit."[50]

Coues' interest in bighorn sheep was as much culinary as it was scientific. He sent one of the party's hunters out to shoot a bighorn and lent him a mule for bringing it back. While the hunter was loading the carcass on the mule, "the latter objected strenuously, broke away, and ran to camp." When the hunter returned on foot, Coues offered him another mule. The unfortunate man replied: "Oh, no, doctor! I know how bad that mule can be, and am taking no chances on any other one."[51]

Having completed the surveying at the Sweet Grass Hills on August 5, the column resumed its march toward the Rockies. As they moved along the Milk River route, Coues directed his attention to the hawks of the region, particularly Swainson's hawk, which "occurs in great numbers over large areas of almost unbroken, arid and cactus-ridden prairie, where, even along the water-courses, there may be no trees or bushes for many miles."[52]

Also observed here were the ferruginous hawk *(Buteo regalis)* and the peregrine falcon *(Falco peregrinus).* Spying the seldom-seen nest of the latter on a river bank, Coues lowered a man down with a rope to collect it. He discovered another "on the bare face of a perpendicular embankment" and tried to lasso the three young falcons in it. Although the father "kept at a respectable distance," he found it necessary to shoot the mother, which "menaced me at close range." Failing to secure the young falcons, who eluded his noose, he "left the family to the care of the father, who, it is to be hoped, has since done more for his family than he did on the occasion just mentioned."[53]

Among the birds common to the Milk River watershed were the cliff swallow, "Arkansas Flycatcher" (western kingbird, *Tyrannus verticalis),* mountain plover *(Charadrius montanus),* horned lark *(Eremophila alpestris),* chestnut-collared and McCown's longspurs *(Calcarius ornatus* and *Rhynchophanes mccownii),* and the vesper sparrow *(Pooecetes gramineus).* Water birds seen nesting along the boundary included "mallards, widgeons, shovellers, teals, pintails, scaups, buffle-heads and wild [Canada] geese." Two "very elegant and interesting" wading birds, Wilson's phalarope *(Steganopus tricolor)* and the avocet *(Recurvirostra*

americana), used the "numberless alkaline pools or small lakes with
which portions of Dakota and Montana are cursed" as their "favorite
breeding resorts." Long-billed curlews (*Numenius americanus*) were
noticed almost daily along the route; at night "their piercing and
lugubrious cries resounded to the howling of the wolves."[54]

6

As the "tedious march through the monotonous country of the
Milk River" progressed, Coues found fewer ornithological surprises
and looked forward to discovering new or different specimens in the
mountains.[55] Perhaps it was the lack of avian novelties that caused him,
while still on the plains, to take careful notice of mammalian forms
such as the "Prairie Hare."[56]

In the previous season in Dakota he had noted only vestiges of the
buffalo's former presence along the 49th parallel. This season, however, he came upon the northern or "Yellowstone" herd shortly after
leaving Frenchman's Creek. He continued to observe them each day up
to the Sweet Grass Hills. Beyond, he found only their trails but was
convinced that they still roamed the area between the Sweet Grass Hills
and the Rockies.[57] Throughout the Milk River basin he and his comrades "traveled for weeks with no other fuel" than buffalo chips.[58] "As
an agent in the progress of civilization . . . the buffalo chip rises to the
plane of the steam-engine and the electric telegraph, and acquires all
the dignity which is supposed to enshroud questions of national importance or matters of political economy."[59]

As the Rocky Mountains began to loom before them, he was happy
to be leaving "the eternal sameness of flat, dusty, treeless prairie, where
the ground and the water and the air are loaded with Glauber's salts
[sodium sulfate, then widely used as a physic] and other vile saline
compounds." Entering the base of the mountains, he could now
"breathe a pure air, tread a clean ground, may loiter if we wish, in the
shade of evergreen trees, and drink iced water from brawling mountain
torrents and deep placid lakes." There stood the peaks, rearing
"their proud cold heads thousands of feet above us." "If not exactly
heaven, it is more like [it than] that paradise just left, which is not seldom
compared, in the energetic language of the West, to that other place
which also commences with 'h'."[60]

The final destination of the surveyors—and Coues' last major
collecting point—was Chief Mountain (Waterton) Lake, near the base of
Chief Mountain, which they reached on August 18. The water there was

"an angler's paradise." To catch the larger trout, the men of the survey used kettle handles for hooks, tent ropes for line, and salt pork for bait.[61]

In the ornithological field Coues was "particularly desirous of finding the Dipper [or water ouzel, *Cinclus mexicanus*],—a bird that in former years had given me the slip. . . . Nor was I disappointed."[62] Broods of harlequin ducks (*Histrionicus histrionicus*) caught his eye, but the "most interesting single result" of his investigations was learning that the Bohemian waxwing (*Bombycilla garrula*) "breeds on or very near the boundary of the United States."[63] Among other mammals, Coues encountered the golden-mantled squirrel *(Citellus lateralis),* the least chipmunk *(Eutamias minimus),* the pika *(Ochotona princeps),*[64] and two long-tailed weasels *(Mustela frenata)*—one of the weasels having been "killed up a tree with a stick."[65]

7

With the completion of their work on August 27, the joint commission returned to the West Butte of the Sweet Grass Hills, where they camped from September 1 to 3. From there the Americans turned southward, going along Marias River toward Fort Benton, on the Missouri. Their scout, George Boyd, filled the party's ears with "bloody stories" of Indian wars. Boyd, despite "being web-fingered in both

Coues' travels along the 49th parallel

hands, and having both feet sadly clubbed," was, Coues recalled, "very quick on the trigger, and could run a footrace with the best of us."

The scout's knowledge of Indians gave Coues and the others "immense relief" once when it looked as if a band of Indians was preparing to attack them along the river. Boyd spread a blanket—the sign of friendship—and the crisis passed.[66] Coues remembered lying on his blanket one night and overhearing a conversation between Boyd and Major Twining: "'George,' said the major, 'what'll happen if the Sioux jump us to-night?' 'Happen!' said George; 'they'll whale h—l out of us!' With which comforting assurance I rolled over and went to sleep."[67]

Coues and the majority of the Americans reached Fort Benton on September 8.[68] On September 12, in six Mackinaw boats, they began their voyage of 835 miles down the Missouri to Bismarck. Coues remembered the boat in which he sailed as "safe and commodious" and "not too heavy to be shoved off a sand-bar when we ran aground, if we all jumped overboard—an incident that no day passed without."[69] After shooting Dauphin Rapids, they reached Fort Peck, Montana.[70] Beyond, at Fort Berthold, Dakota, he ran his boat "snug under the bluff."[71]

Although traveling by boat cut short his collecting, Coues was ever the alert observer. He saw numerous beaver along the way as well as bighorn sheep and buffalo.[72] The latter "were seen almost daily during that part of the voyage which embraced the rapid portion of the river flowing between the bluffs of the Bad Lands."[73] At one point they provided a deathly spectacle:

> A herd of several hundred took the alarm at our approach, and rushed headlong up the bank. They got on very well for some distance—for the buffalo can climb steeper places than one would suppose from their ungainly and unwieldy form; but as they proceeded the way grew worse. Still those that were in the rear pressed so hard on the leaders of this climb that the latter could neither turn nor even stop; several of them lost their footing, rolled down, end over end, in a cloud of dust, and then tumbled off the cliff to be dashed to pieces on the rocks below.[74]

Upon arrival at Bismarck on September 30, the members of the American commission boarded a special train for St. Paul. From there Coues went to Chicago, where he spent the night of October 7; then, traveling by way of Buffalo, he arrived in Washington on the 13th. Later in the month he appeared in New York and passed an examination for promotion to captain.[75]

8

The Army then allowed Coues to settle in Washington to work as a "Resident Collaborator in Mammalogy and Ornithology" at the Smithsonian, where he deposited his sizable collections from the northern boundary. At the same time he was still attached to the boundary commission. In both capacities he set about writing articles and monographs on his recent findings.[76] They appeared in *American Naturalist, Bulletin of the Nuttall Ornithological Club, Forest and Stream, American Sportsman, Rod and Gun,* and the publications of the Academy of Natural Sciences of Philadelphia, the Essex Institute, and the Hayden, Powell, and Wheeler federal surveys of the West.

His writings on the Northwest dealt principally with birds and mammals and, to a much lesser extent, reptiles. The collections he made in other areas of natural history were turned over to appropriate specialists. David Starr Jordan[77] examined the fishes. Coues' relative ignorance of and indifference to this branch of science are reflected in his skimpy ichthyological field notes (which included such entries as "Lot of small fish, Mouse River, Dak., Aug. 17, 1873") and in the fact that he lost one-third of the fishes he did collect. Still, the remaining batch contained "some novelties, rarities, and other specimens of sufficient interest," and Jordan discovered among them a new genus which he named *Couesius.*[78]

Three other naturalists, Cyrus Thomas,[79] P. R. Uhler,[80] and W. H. Edwards,[81] wrote articles on his small but significant collection of insects. Of particular interest to Thomas were the grasshoppers, which, in the summer of 1874, had devastated crops on the northern plains. Coues himself believed that the sharp-tailed grouse (*Pedioecetes phasianellus*) was "in the very front rank of all the natural grasshopper-staying agencies" and that its protection from hunters would help prevent another such plague.[82] The plants gathered by Coues and George Dawson were turned over to J. W. Chickering, whose article on them provided "a fair idea of the flora of the belt of country surveyed by the Boundary Commission."[83]

Among the important results of Coues' sojourn with the commission—and a demonstration of his characteristic alertness—was the recognition of three distinct faunal communities along the line between Pembina and Waterton Lake. He designated them the Red River region, the Missouri River region (west of the Coteau), and the Rocky Mountain region. Each was sharply distinguishable from the others zoologically, botanically, and topographically. In describing them, he devoted most of his space to birds, much less to mammals, plants, and physical features.[84]

Coues spent the summer of 1873 in the Red River region, where in the eastern part (Red River valley) the birds were almost entirely eastern: robin, catbird, redstart, goldfinch, Baltimore (northern) oriole, and so on. To the west, in the more arid, treeless country, such as that drained by the Mouse River, Coues found strictly western species, such as Sprague's pipit, chestnut-collared longspur, Baird's sparrow, and the western horned lark (*Eremophila alpestris leucolaema*). Of mammals in the Red River region, Coues mentioned an abundance of rodents, such as ground squirrels and badgers. Of more interest, he found in 1873 only a few antelope and no buffalo at all.

In the Missouri River region, where Coues spent the early part of the summer of 1874, the terrain was vastly different from that east of the Coteau (Red River region), being treeless except along water courses, more arid, and generally level save for scattered areas of badlands. Also changed were the fauna and flora. Here the most characteristic birds were the lark bunting *(Calamospiza melanocorys)*, western kingbird, McCown's longspur, black-billed magpie (*Pica pica*), and sage grouse (*Centrocercus urophasianus*). Among the most characteristic mammals were the prairie dog, antelope, kit fox (*Vulpes velox*), long-tailed weasel, and, in the Sweet Grass Hills, bighorn sheep.

Farther west, in the Rocky Mountain region, there were different birds, such as the dipper, Bohemian waxwing, and harlequin duck, and different mammals, among them the pika, pack rat *(Neotoma cinerea),* and yellow-bellied marmot (*Marmota flaviventris*).

Another contribution—at the time a mere by-product of his work for the commission—took on far greater significance in his later years. His travels had taken him along much of the route of the Lewis and Clark expedition, and Coues prepared a bibliographical article on the various editions of their published journals as an aid in correlating his scientific investigations with those of the intrepid explorers.[85] The article, published in 1876, seems to have been overlooked by many students, yet it was the first of consequence *written about* Lewis and Clark, the earliest attempt to list all the published literature about the expedition, and the first to appraise in any manner the technical results of the journey. Thus Coues was an innovator—a forerunner—much in advance of a host of others who have since contributed so voluminously to an increased knowledge of this great American venture.

NOTES

1. Coues, ed., *New Light on the Early History of the Greater Northwest: The Manuscript Journals of Alexander Henry . . . and of David Thompson . . .*(1897), I, 25n. Hereinafter cited as *Henry-Thompson Journals*.

2. Archibald Campbell (1813-87) graduated from West Point in 1835 and resigned his commission a year later. After working as a civil engineer, he became in 1844 the secretary to the Secretary of War. Two years later he was appointed chief clerk of the War Department and served as the American commissioner for the U.S.-British Northwestern Boundary Commission (1857-61). His service as the American commissioner for the Northern Boundary Survey of 1872-76 was his last official post.

3. Donald Roderick Cameron (1834-1921) was commissioned into the British Army in 1856. In the later 1860s he participated in the suppression of the Red River uprising in Canada. After completing his duties with the boundary commission, he served on the British-Alaskan Boundary Commission in the 1880s. He retired from the Army in 1887 with the rank of major-general.

4. Upon finishing his work with the boundary commission, George Mercer Dawson (1849-1901) joined the Canadian Geological Survey, becoming its assistant director in 1883 and the director in 1895. He is chiefly remembered for his geological studies of the Yukon. Dawson City, Yukon Territory, is named in his honor.

5. Hume, *Ornithologists of the U.S. Army Medical Corps*, 76.

6. Unless otherwise noted, we have used Coues' "Book of Dates" for the dates and localities of his itinerary.

7. Coues, ed., *The Expeditions of Zebulon Montgomery Pike* (1895), I, 82n.

8. William Johnson Twining (1839-82) graduated from West Point in 1863, saw service in the Civil War, taught military engineering at his alma mater, and in 1867 was made chief engineer of the Department of Dakota. At the time of his death he was a member of the Board of District Commissioners at Washington, D.C.

9. Coues, ed., *Henry-Thompson Journals*, I, 80n. Fort Pembina was established in July, 1870, and abandoned in Sept., 1895.

10. Terrell and Walton, *Faint the Trumpet Sounds* (1966), 86.

11. Coues, "The Eave, Cliff, or Crescent Swallow (*Petrochelidon lunifrons*)" (1878), 109.

12. Coues, "Field-Notes on Birds Observed in Dakota and Montana" (1878), 571-72.

13. Coues-Biddle (1893), II, 431n.

14. Parsons, *West on the 49th Parallel* (1963), 62.

15. Coues, "Field-Notes on Birds Observed in Dakota and Montana," 602.

16. Coues and Allen, *Monographs of North American Rodentia* (1877), 664, 789, 885.

17. Coues, *Birds of the Northwest* (1874), x-xi.

18. Coues, "Notes on Two Little-known Birds of the United States" (1873), 697.

19. Coues, *Birds of the Northwest*, 261-62. This bird was discovered by Lewis and Clark on Oct. 17, 1804, just below the mouth of the Cannonball River in North Dakota, but was not technically described until Audubon, ascending the Missouri River in 1843, "rediscovered" it. The binomial Audubon gave it, *Phalaenoptilus nuttallii,* has stood up ever since.

20. Coues, "Musical Mice" (1876), 81.

21. Terrell and Walton, *Faint the Trumpet Sounds,* 86-87.

22. We have been unable to find any biographical information on Bangs.

23. Parsons, *West on the 49th Parallel,* 69.

24. Coues-Biddle, III, 1160n. Irish-born Miles Walter Keogh (1840-76) is chiefly remembered as the rider of Comanche, the horse who was the 7th Cavalry's sole survivor at Little Big Horn.

25. Ruthven Deane, "The Ruddy Duck," *Amer. Naturalist,* VIII (July, 1874), 434.

26. Coues, "Range of the Eared Grebe" (1873), 745.

27. Coues, "Field-Notes on Birds Observed in Dakota and Montana," 601.

28. Coues, "Habits and Characteristics of Swainson's Buzzard" (1874), 285.

29. Coues, "Pet Owls" (1874), 354.

30. Coues, "Duck Shooting *à Cheval*" (1875), 49.

31. Coues, "Field-Notes on Birds Observed in Dakota and Montana," 651.

32. Allen, "History of the American Bison," 539.

33. Coues, "Notice of a Rare Bird" (1873).

34. Coues, "The Cranes of America" (1874), 20.

35. Allen, "History of the American Bison," 539-40.

36. Coues, *Fur-Bearing Animals: A Monograph of North American Mustelidae* (1877), 175-76.

37. Coues and Yarrow, "Notes on the Herpetology of Dakota and Montana" (1878), 279. Twining's garter snake (originally *Eutaenia radix twiningi* Coues and Yarrow) is now apparently the western plains garter snake (*Thamnophis radix haydeni* Kennicott); see Karl P. Schmidt, *A Check List of North American Amphibians and Reptiles* (Chicago: American Society of Ichthyologists and Herpetologists, 1953), 172.

38. Allen, "History of the American Bison," 540. A battue is a mass hunt in which the animals are driven to the hunters.

39. Coues-Biddle, I, 262n. Fort Stevenson (McLean County, N.Dak.) was built in June, 1867, as part of a chain of posts guarding the routes to Montana. Abandoned in 1883, it is now inundated by the Garrison Reservoir.

40. *Forest and Stream,* Oct. 2, 1873, 120.

41. Harris, "Robert Ridgway" (1928), 32.

42. Coues, ed., *Forty Years a Fur Trader* (1898), I, 61n. Fort Buford was founded in 1866 and abandoned in 1895.

43. Coues, "The Prairie Gopher" (1875), 150n. For several years after being erected in 1828, Fort Union was the main trading post of the American Fur Company. The Army purchased it in 1866 and used its materials for buiding Fort Buford.

44. Parsons, *West on the 49th Parallel,* 101-2.

45. Coues-Biddle, I, 301n.

46. Alpheus S. Packard, "New Phyllopod Crustaceans," *Amer. Naturalist*, IX (May, 1875), 311.

47. Coues and Allen, *Monographs of North American Rodentia*, 302-3, 338.

48. Packard, "New Phyllopod Crustaceans," 311-12.

49. Parsons, *West on the 49th Parallel*, 111.

50. Coues, "The Prairie Gopher," 149-51.

51. Coues, ed., *On the Trail of a Spanish Pioneer* (1900), II, 383n.

52. Coues, "On the Nesting of Certain Hawks" (1874), 597.

53. *Ibid.*, 598.

54. *Ibid.*, 599-602.

55. Coues, "Field-Notes on Birds Observed in Dakota and Montana," 522.

56. Coues, "Synonymy, Description, History, Distribution and Habits of the Prairie Hare (*Lepus campestris*)" (1875), 74.

57. Allen, "History of the American Bison," 540.

58. Coues-Biddle, II, 424n.

59. Allen, "History of the American Bison," 540.

60. Coues, "From the Headwaters of the Saskatchewan" (1874), 193.

61. Jordan, "Report on the Collection of Fishes made by Dr. Elliott Coues, U.S.A., in Dakota and Montana" (1878), 793.

62. Coues, "Field-Notes on Birds Observed in Dakota and Montana," 552.

63. Parsons, *West on the 49th Parallel*, 120.

64. Coues and Allen, *Monographs of North American Rodentia*, 410, 805, 818.

65. Coues, *Fur-Bearing Animals*, 137-38.

66. Coues-Biddle, I, 319n; II, 479n; III, 1105n.

67. Coues, "Adventures of Government Explorers" (1897).

68. Founded in 1846 by the American Fur Company, Fort Benton, located about forty miles below the Great Falls of the Missouri River, became an important transportation center in 1859 when the first steamboat arrived on the Upper Missouri. It became a military post in 1869 and was abandoned in 1881.

69. Coues-Biddle, I, 4n.

70. Coues, ed., *Forty Years a Fur Trader*, II, 341n. Fort Peck, founded in 1867, was originally located near the present-day Fort Peck dam site. In 1871 the post was converted to an Indian agency. Six years later the agency was moved to Poplar, Mont.

71. *Ibid.*, 336-37n, 388n. The original Fort Berthold was a stockade established in 1845 by the American Fur Company. A rival firm built nearby Fort Atkinson in 1859. The American Fur Company acquired the latter in 1862 and changed the name to Fort Berthold, since the original Fort Berthold had been burned down that year by the Sioux. The newer post was largely destroyed by fire in Oct., 1874, within a month after Coues had traveled past it.

72. Coues, "Rodentia" (1884), V, 120.

73. Allen, "History of the American Bison," 541.

74. Coues-Biddle, III, 1109-10n.

75. Coues' rank is a puzzle. An act of Congress, July 28, 1866 (*U.S. Statutes at Large*, chap. 299, sec. 17), entitled assistant surgeons who had served three

years to the rank, pay, and emoluments of a captain of cavalry. Therefore the examination for promotion in 1874 is a source of confusion. Further bewilderment comes from the fact that in 1877 President Hayes submitted to the Senate a list of assistant surgeons whom he was nominating for promotion to captain, in accordance with the act of 1866. Included on the list is Coues' name, followed by the words "to rank from March 30, 1867," i.e., three years after his appointment as an assistant surgeon. The list was referred to a committee and apparently no further action was taken that session. See *Journal of the Executive Proceedings of the Senate . . . from March 5, 1877, to March 3, 1879, inclusive* (New York: Johnson Reprint Corp., 1969), XXI, 487-88. In 1879 Hayes again submitted a list of assistant surgeons to the Senate, nominating them for promotion to captain. Again Coues' name was on the list. The Senate responded with a resolution that the nominations be returned to the president "with the statement that, in the opinion of the Senate, no such offices exist by law as those named in the nominations" (*Ibid.*, XXII, 9, 11, 55, 75). Nevertheless, beginning with *Birds of the Northwest*, the title pages of many of Coues' works identify the author as "captain and assistant surgeon." William H. Powell's *List of Officers of the Army of the United States . . .* (New York: L. R. Hamersly, 1900), 259, identifies Coues as a captain as of Mar. 30, 1867; Heitman's *Historical Register*, I, 329, lists him only as assistant surgeon and brevet (as of 1865) captain.

76. *Annual Report of the Board of Regents of the Smithsonian Institution . . . 1874* (Washington, D.C.: Government Printing Office, 1875), 6, 30, 33, 43-44, 53.

77. David Starr Jordan (1851-1931) is largely remembered as a distinguished president of Stanford University, yet his contributions to biological knowledge, especially ichthyology, are still of value.

78. Jordan, "Report on the Collection of Fishes," 777, 785.

79. Thomas, "On the *Orthoptera* Collected by Dr. Elliott Coues" (1878). Thomas (1825-1910) served with the Hayden survey from 1869 until 1875, when he became state entomologist of Illinois. His later years were largely spent in ethnological studies.

80. Uhler, "On the *Hemiptera* Collected by Dr. Elliott Coues" (1878). Philip Reese Uhler (1835-1913), a protégé of Louis Aggasiz, served for many years as librarian for the Peabody Institute. In 1876 he became an associate in natural sciences at Johns Hopkins University, specializing in geology and zoology.

81. Edwards, "On the *Lepidoptera* Collected by Dr. Elliott Coues" (1878). William Henry Edwards (1822-1909) was perhaps the leading authority on the Lepidoptera in his time. His classic monograph on North American butterflies was published in installments from 1868 to 1897.

82. Alpheus S. Packard, "Report on the Rocky Mountain Locust and Other Insects Now Injuring or Likely to Injure Field and Garden Crops in the Western States and Territories," *Ninth Annual Report of the U.S. Geol. and Geogr. Surv. Terrs.* (Washington, D.C.: Government Printing Office, 1877), 658-59.

83. Chickering, "Catalogue of Phaenogamous and Vascular Cryptogamous

Plants" (1878), 801. John White Chickering (1831-1913) was for many years professor of natural science at Gallaudet College, Washington, D.C.

84. Coues, "Field-Notes on Birds Observed in Dakota and Montana," 545-46.

85. Coues, "An Account of the Various Publications Relating to the Travels of Lewis and Clarke [*sic*]" (1876).

CHAPTER XII

Life Histories and Bibliography

Elliott Coues' brilliant writing uniquely qualified him to write life histories, or species accounts, of birds. He published the first of these in the 1860s in *The Ibis,* the *American Naturalist,* and other leading scientific outlets of the day, and we have already inserted excerpts from some of them in earlier chapters. The great majority of these avian life histories appeared, however, in two volumes, *Birds of the Northwest* (1874) and *Birds of the Colorado Valley* (1878).[1] Herein he described American birds, primarily those of the West, with a fullness of detail and felicity of style that give the volumes permanent scientific and literary value.

These two large volumes consisted of reports by Coues on ornithological material collected and brought to the Smithsonian by F. V. Hayden and Major John Wesley Powell,[2] who had accompanied expeditions sent out by the federal government to explore watersheds of such trans-Mississippi rivers as the Platte, Missouri, Yellowstone, and Colorado.[3] To these reports Coues contributed a substantial body of information about birds that he had himself acquired. In a letter to Hayden from Fort Randall, Coues alluded to this material: "Do you know that all my biographical matter (a very large amount) gained in Arizona has not been published?[4] I will devote it all to this report, as far as it relates to birds common to the two regions."

At about this same time Coues explained the actual origin of *Birds of the Northwest* in a letter to Allen:

> . . . you haven't heard of my biggest job. In 1862 I wrote a Gov't. report of Hayden's Exploration in the Missouri region, and had actually forgotten all about it. Suddenly he [Hayden] writes me he wants to print it at once. I have had the original mss. sent to me, and am now furiously bringing it from status of '62 to that of '73. Fancy the job! I get off 15-20 pp. daily, but it is a fearful task on my head. It is going to be a "bigger" work than the *Key.* . . . Moreover, Hayden wants me to put in all birds of the region he *didn't.* I need not tell you that from Kansas to Yellowstone

and Fort Union to Denver takes in about five-sixths perhaps of all land birds. This big thing was sprung on me without warning.

During January, February, and March, 1873, Coues wrote often to Hayden. In each of his letters he expressed supreme confidence in his ability to produce a volume pleasing to Hayden in every respect. In one of them, for instance, he said: "I will promise to bring up the report to date, and to make it one you will be satisfied to stand godfather to"; in another: "Just give me room to 'swing myself' and if I don't make a '*Report*' take my head for a football. I am going to make of this a lasting monument to American ornithology—a legacy to the next generation of ornithologists."

Coues tried to sell Hayden on the desirability of illustrating *Birds of the Northwest*: "If we could get a lot of pictures in, it would wonderfully 'raise' the work with the public. . . . Think over this proposition. I *tell you*, we've got a big thing on hand." Though he persisted in his efforts to get pictures into the book, he failed; Hayden decided against them because of the added expense. Coues did better in regard to illustrations for *Birds of the Colorado Valley*. That work contained upward of seventy.

Coues also corresponded with Major Powell during his stay at Fort Randall. In one of his letters we learn that Powell had suggested the inclusion of mammals, as well as birds, in the volume. Coues dissented: "How we are to run in the mammals, too, bothers me a little. . . . I have rather taken a notion of letting this bird-book stand by itself as Vol. I of a 'Natural History' of the Colorado Basin. This would open the way for a series, the remaining vols. to be filled by others perhaps, in different departments."[5]

Coues satisfied Powell (and Hayden) that the volume in preparation should be devoted exclusively to birds, though his contemplated series, with additional volumes treating mammals, reptiles, and other vertebrates, failed to materialize.

2

Birds of the Northwest and *Birds of the Colorado Valley*, each consisting largely of life histories of western birds, are legitimate companion pieces and, as such, may logically be appraised together.

Distinguished books in science, like those in history, linguistics, and other fields, quickly gain formal recognition and praise, and that was true of *Birds of the Northwest* and *Birds of the Colorado Valley*. One reason was the sheer volume of material, running to more than 1,300 pages exclusive of indexes. Another was the diversity of the material, ranging from synonymy, bibliography and geographical distribution to anatomy, plumage, migration, behavior, associations, parasitism, courtship, food habits, nests, eggs, and songs.

The extent of Coues' synonymy[6] and bibliography impressed even the most learned ornithologists. Coues did not exaggerate when he wrote: "Nothing like this amount of bibliographical matter has before been presented in any work upon American Ornithology." Emphasizing the enormity of his task in assembling his synonymy and bibliography, Coues further declared: "The labor of such compilation does not appear upon the surface, and is only mentioned in the sincere hope that, once accomplished, the weary drudgery of future workers in the same vein may be materially lightened."[7]

To illustrate the depth of Coues' "drudgery," we submit his synonymy and bibliography for Clark's nutcracker (*Nucifraga columbiana*):

> *Corvus columbianus* WILS.,[8] Am. Orn. iii, 1811, 29, pl. 20, f 2. BP., Obs. Wils. 1825, No. 38; Syn. 1828, 57. Man. Orn., 1, 1832, 211.
>
> *Nucifraga columbiana*, AUD., Orn. Biog. iv, 1838, 459, pl. 362; Syn. 1839, 156; B. Am. iv, 1842, 127, pl. 235.—BP., List, 1838, 28. NUTT., Man. i, 1840, 251.
>
> *Nucifraga* (*Picicorvus*) *columbiana*, GRAY, Hand-list, ii, 1870, 9, No. 6165.
>
> *Picicorvus columbianus*, BP, Consp. i, 1850, 384.—NEWB., P.R.R. Rep. vi, 1857, pt. iv, 83. BD., B.N.A., 1858, 573, 925.—KENN., P.R.R. Rep. x, 1859, pt. iv, 32.—COOP & SUCK., N.H. Wash. Ter., 1860, 212.— HAYD., Rep. 1862, 171 (to Fort Laramie).—COUES, Pr. Phila. Acad., 1866, 91.—LORD, Pr. Roy. arty. Inst. iv, 121 (British Columbia); Nat. in Vancouver (Breeding near Fort Colville).—DALL & BANN., Tr. Chic. Acad. i, 1869, 286 (Sitka).—COOP., B. Cal. i, 1870, 289.—STEV., U.S. Geol. Surv. Ter., 1870, 465.—COUES, Ibis, 1872, 53 (biography).— ALLEN, Bull. M.C.Z., iii, 1872, 178.—HOLD.-AIKEN., Bost. Soc., 1872, 203 (Wyoming).—COUES, Key, 1872, 102, fig. 104.—B.B.&R., N.A.B. ii, 1874, 255, pl. 38, f. 4.
>
> "*Corvus megonyx*, WAGL."—(Gray).[9]

Since Coues introduced each species—some 400 all told—with a synonymy and bibliography similar to that above, the magnitude of that task alone is all too evident.

Yet another reason for the praise accorded *Birds of the Northwest* and *Birds of the Colorado Valley* was the revelation throughout of Coues' seeming familiarity with the published observations of practically every ornithologist in the country, living or dead, professional or amateur. He disclosed this fact through his frequent use of quotations and recurrent acknowledgments. In this manner we learn of his acquaintance not only with such notables as Alexander Wilson, Charles Lucien Bonaparte, and Thomas Nuttall but also with a veritable host of lesser lights. There was, for instance, Mr. George Bannston of Michipicoton on Lake Superior.

A final and more important reason behind the commendation bestowed upon these volumes stemmed from the distinctive quality of Coues' prose. Just as *Key to North American Birds* contributed signally to Coues' stature as an ornithologist, so did *Birds of the Northwest* and *Birds of the Colorado Valley* establish him as a writer of fresh, vigorous, and distinguished prose.

We have already produced a number of excerpts from the two volumes now under discussion. For the most part these selections—such as those about the pigmy nuthatch and the poor-will—have been brief and thus inadequately reveal Coues' literary strengths: his command of vocabulary, his fertile imagination, his ability to weave into delightfully worded sentences the results of his unusual observational competence, and his capacity to regale the reader with unexpected flashes of humor. We would now like to reproduce a few lengthier and, to us, more finished passages from *Birds of the Northwest* and *Birds of the Colorado Valley*.

Our first selection is from Coues' life history of the long-crested jay (*Cyanocitta stelleri macrolopha*), a subspecies of Steller's jay. In this account, written by Coues during his first stay at Fort Whipple, he succeeded, in our opinion, in effectively portraying with charm and humor the characteristic habits of this lively bird.

> All jays make their share of noise in the world; they fret and scold about trifles, quarrel over anything, and keep everything in a ferment when they are about. The particular kind we are now talking about is nowise behind his fellows in these respects—a stranger to modesty and forbearance, and the many gentle qualities that charm us in some little birds and endear them to us; he is a regular filibuster, ready for any sort of adventure that promises sport or spoil, even if spiced with danger. Sometimes he prowls about alone, but oftener has a band of choice spirits with him, who keep each other in countenance (for our Jay is a coward at heart, like other bullies) and share the plunder on the usual terms in such cases, of each one taking all he can get. Once I had a chance of seeing a band of these guerrillas on a raid; they went at it in good style, but came off very badly indeed. A vagabond troop made a descent upon a bush-clump, where, probably, they expected to find eggs to suck, or at any rate a chance for mischief and amusement. To their intense

joy, they surprised a little Owl quietly digesting his grasshoppers, with both eyes shut. Here was a lark! and a chance to wipe out a part of the score that the Jays keep against Owls for injuries received time out of mind. In the tumult that ensued, the little birds scurried off, the Woodpeckers overhead stopped tapping to look on, and a snake that was basking in a sunny spot concluded to crawl into his hole. The Jays lunged furiously at their enemy, who sat helpless, bewildered by the sudden onslaught, trying to look as big as possible, with his wings set for bucklers and his bill snapping; meanwhile twisting his head till I thought he would wring it off, trying to look all ways at once. The Jays emboldened by partial success, grew more impudent, till their victim made a break through their ranks and flapped into the heart of a neighboring juniper, hoping to be protected by the tough thick foliage. The Jays went trooping after, and I hardly know how the fight would have ended had I not thought it time to take a hand in the game myself. . . . The collector has no better chance to enrich his cabinet than when the birds are quarreling, and so it has been with the third party in a difficulty, ever since the monkey divided cheese for the two cats.[10]

Our next selection, about the cañon wren (*Catherpes mexicanus*), reveals the dimensions of Coues' talent in describing a bird song. In this instance the bird was singing in its favorite habitat, a canyon of the Southwest:

We remember the "rift within the lute"; in the Cañon Wren we have the lute within the rift—a curious little animated music-box, utterly insignificant in size and appearance, yet fit to make the welkin ring with glee. This bird-note is one of the most characteristic sounds in nature; nothing matches it exactly; and its power to impress the hearer increases when, as usually happens, the volume of the sound is strengthened by reverberation through the deep and sinuous cañon, echoed from side to side of the massive perpendicular walls till it gradually dies away in the distance. No technical description would be likely to express the character of these notes, nor explain the indelible impression they make upon the one who hears them for the first time amid the wild and desolate scenes to which they are a fit accompaniment. The song is perfectly simple; it is merely a succession of single whistling notes, each separate and distinct, beginning as high in the scale as the bird can reach, and regularly descending the gamut as long as the bird's breath holds out, or until it reaches the lowest note the bird is capable of striking. These notes are loud, clear, and of a peculiarly resonant quality; they are uttered with startling emphasis.[11]

As a final selection we have chosen Coues' description of another bird song, that of the Missouri skylark (Sprague's pipit, *Anthus spragueii*). He heard it commonly when crossing the extensive grasslands of northern Dakota Territory while aiding in the survey of the 49th parallel:

The ordinary straightforward flight of the bird is performed with a regular rising and falling, like that of the Titlark;[12] but its course, when startled from the ground, is exceedingly rapid and wayward; at such times, after the first alarm, they are wont to hover around in a desultory manner for a considerable time, and then pitch suddenly to the ground, often near where they rose. Under these circumstances they have a lisping, querulous note. But these common traits have nothing to do with the wonderful soaring action, and the inimitable matchless song of the birds during the breeding season—it is no wonder Audubon[13] grew enthusiastic in describing it. Rising from its nest, or from its grassy bed, this plain-looking little bird, clad in the simplest colors, and making but a speck in the boundless expanse, mounts straight up, on tremulous wings, till lost to view in the blue ether, and then sends back to earth a song of gladness that seems to come from the sky itself, to cheer the weary, give hope to the disheartened, and turn the most indifferent, for the moment at least, from sordid thoughts. No other bird-music heard in our land compares with the wonderful strains of this songster; there is something not of earth in its melody, coming from above, yet from no visible source. They are simply indescribable; but once heard they can never be forgotten. Their volume and penetration are truly wonderful; they are neither loud nor strong, yet the whole air seems filled with the tender strains, and delightful melody continues long unbroken.[14]

Parenthetically, it surely is of some interest that a president of the United States, Theodore Roosevelt, was equally entranced with the song of the Missouri skylark. He became familiar with it when he lived in the Dakota badlands and described it in these words:

Overhead a skylark was singing, soaring up above me so high that I could not make out its form in the gray morning light. I listened for some time, and the music never ceased for a moment, coming down clear, sweet and tender from the air above. Soon the strains of another answered from a long distance off, and the two kept singing and soaring as long as I stayed to listen, and when I walked away I could still hear their notes behind me. In some ways the skylark is the sweetest singer we have, only certain of the thrushes rival it, but though the songs of the latter have perhaps even more melody, they are far from being so interrupted and well sustained, being rather a succession of broken bursts of music.[15]

Coues' contemporaries thought well of *Birds of the Northwest* and *Birds of the Colorado Valley*. For example, writing of the latter, J. A. Allen said that it "was a marked event in the literature of North American ornithology" and that it "will ever remain a classic in ornithological literature."[16]

In later years well-known American writers have published anthologies of what they regarded as the best in natural history prose. We are acquainted with four: one by John Kieran, a second by Roger Tory Peterson, another by Donald Culross Peattie, and a fourth by Joseph Wood Krutch and Paul S. Eriksson. All of these contain passages from either *Birds of the Northwest* or *Birds of the Colorado Valley* or both.

Kieran chose Coues' biography of the burrowing owl (*Speotyto cunicularia*), remarking prefatorially that the describer of this odd bird "was something of an odd bird himself."[17] Peterson's choice was the scarlet tanager (*Piranga olivacea*),[18] a portion of which we quoted in an earlier chapter. Krutch and Eriksson chose the house wren (*Troglodytes aedon*)[19] and the catbird (*Dumetella carolinensis*).[20] Peattie, seemingly more enamored of Coues' literary gifts than any of the others, included four of the accounts in his anthology: the cowbird *(Molothrus ater)*,[21] plumbeous bushtit (*Psaltriparus minimus plumbeus*),[22] cliff swallow (*Petrochelidon pyrrhonota*),[23] and, like Kieran, the burrowing owl.[24]

In these anthologies Coues' passages were in good company, being alongside those of such other illustrious writers of natural history as W. H. Hudson,[25] Gilbert White,[26] Alfred Russel Wallace,[27] Sir Edward Grey,[28] and John Muir.[29]

It was Coues' perennial contention that an article about a bird or other animal "may be a contribution to literature as well as to science."[30] D. G. Elliot, for one, heartily agreed. Coues, he wrote, "possessed a command of language gained by few, and the beauty of his style and his felicity of expression have created numerous pen pictures of the habits and appearances of our wild creatures that have never been equalled . . . of none can it be more appropriately said, '*Nihil tetigit quod non ornavit.*'" That is, "He touched nothing which he did not adorn."[31]

3

While still at Fort McHenry, on March 27, 1871, Coues had written Allen: "To come to the point at once, are you open to a proposition touching our joint authorship in an article upon the complete bibliography of North American birds? I have been pregnant with the idea for a long time, and of late the scheme has taken definite shape in my mind; in fact, I have the whole plan and scope of the work elaborated pretty distinctly, and have even taken some steps toward it."

More than four years went by before we learn anything more about Coues' proposed complete bibliography of North American birds. On August 7, 1875, Coues advised Baird: "You may be surprised to learn how much I have done for a beginning of my bibliography. I have some

4000 titles, complete, *with comment,* & some 10,000 quotations of N. Am. birds alone. As a beginning, this is a success." Long before this, it seems obvious, Allen had made it clear to Coues that he had no particular interest in the proposed bibliographical collaboration.

Some six months later Coues informed the editor of *Forest and Stream*—his friend of Labrador days Charles Hallock—that he had in preparation "a complete digest of ornithological literature from Aristotle to 1874." He then went on to stress the point that he entertained no notions of immediate publication: "If I live long enough and have good luck, I may go to press with it in the course of ten or fifteen years, or at any rate shall be able to leave the plan of my work to my children as a family heirloom."[32] In these letters Coues was alluding to work already done on far and away the most ambitious project of his life, namely, a "Universal Bibliography of Ornithology." Originally he had planned to limit the work to North American birds, but in time he set his sights to include birds of all parts of the world.

Coues never finished the project; it was too much even for his durable body and stubborn determination. However, before laying down his pen, he had devoted to this work the larger part of at least five years, had exhibited a doggedness rarely equaled, and had seen to completion and publication four installments. Three of these represented the ornithological literature known to him about the birds of the western hemisphere, and the fourth that about the birds of Great Britain. Looked at in any way, these installments constituted an extraordinary accomplishment.

According to Coues himself, the requisite qualifications for success in preparing a bibliography included: "more zeal than discretion, youth, health, strength, staying power, unlimited time at command, and access to the foci of ornithological literature in some large eastern city."[33]

Coues' first installment appeared in 1878 as an appendix to *Birds of the Colorado Valley.* Titled "List of Faunal Publications Relating to North American Ornithology," it filled 218 pages and included almost 1,000 titles. The titles listed, as Coues explained, were limited to general publications, such as his own *Key* and *Field Ornithology.* He excluded all works dealing with specific families, genera, and species, leaving them for a later "systematic" installment (the third).

Describing his method of procedure, Coues wrote, "There is little to be said of the way in which the work has been done. . . . It should be stated, however, that the compiler has habitually regarded THE TITLE as a thing no more to be mutilated than a man's name; and that he has taken the utmost pains to secure transcription of title *verbatim, literatim, et punctuatim.*"[34] Coues further said that, in spite of his efforts to be accurate, he felt the weight of Stevens'[35] satire: "If you are troubled with a pride of accuracy, and would have it completely taken out of you, print a catalogue."[36]

The second installment appeared one year after the first, in 1879, and was published in *Bulletin of the U.S. Geological and Geographical Survey of the Territories* (vol. V, 1879, pp. 239-330). In his preface Coues wrote: "The present article may be considered to continue the subject, as it gives the titles of 'Faunal Publications' relating to the Ornithology of the rest of America [namely, Central and South America and the West Indies]. . . . Though of course much less extensive, containing only about 700 titles, it is scarcely less complete, and no less accurate, than the North American portion."[37]

Coues' third installment was published simultaneously with the second, in the same year and in the same journal. The labor required to complete it truly demanded "health, strength, staying power and un-limited time." In its published form it ran to 531 pages and contained an estimated 14,000 titles. It consisted of "all publications treating of particular species, genera, or families of birds, systematically arranged by *Families*, in chronological order under each family, with alphabetiza-tion of authors' names under each date. . . . The three installments together represent a near complete Bibliography of Ornithology so far as *America* is concerned."[38]

The tremendous volume of material in this third installment is not apparent until one notes and examines the abundant commentary, all of which is in very small type (six point). Examination reveals, too, that the commentary accorded certain titles is prodigious. For example, that given to John Gould's "A Monograph of the Trochilidae" stretched to four pages and contained more than 3,000 words.[39]

Scattered throughout the third installment are, of course, the titles of Coues' own publications, 157 of them if our count is accurate. By including the fifty-seven others listed in the first installment we reach a total of more than two hundred. All of these had been published from 1861 to 1878, a period of just seventeen years, and Coues excluded numerous titles of papers he regarded as unworthy of inclusion in such a prestigious compilation.

Coues' fourth and final bibliographical installment was a list of faunal publications relating to British birds. Briefer than the others, filling just 123 pages, it appeared in *Proceedings of the U.S. National Museum* (May 31,

1880, pp. 359-482). Of it, Coues wrote: "This present, *fourth* instalment of the work is of the same character as the first two, that is, it relates to 'regional' or 'faunal' as distinguished from 'systematic' ornithology; and it undertakes to do for British birds what the first two did for American."[40]

Having seen to completion these four installments, Coues went no further with his original grand design for a "Universal Bibliography of Ornithology." To have finished it would have required similar lists for the birds of Africa, Asia, Australia, and continental Europe.

Coues' achievement, so charged with erudition and scholarship, did not go unnoticed. In May, 1879 (when only the first installment had appeared), there came to him what was perhaps the most flattering professional recognition he ever received: a memorial[41] signed by thirty-eight members of Britain's scientific elite praising his ornithological bibliography. The memorial appealed to the War Department to grant Coues a leave of absence in order that he might travel to Europe to make use of its libraries and museums in completing his "Universal Bibliography."[42]

There can be little doubt that Coues, on reading the names of signers of the memorial, experienced much personal gratification. Among the signers were Charles Darwin, Thomas Huxley, Alfred Russel Wallace, Philip L. Sclater,[43] Alfred Newton,[44] Osbert Salvin,[45] John Gould, and R. Bowdler Sharpe.[46] Coues' friends and colleagues within the American scientific community were also impressed. In general they agreed that the memorial was "one of the highest compliments paid in years to American science."[47]

Writing to J. A. Allen on January 9, 1879, Coues quoted parts of a letter just received from Alfred Newton: "I must beg you to accept my *most hearty congratulations* on your bibliographical results. To say that they far surpass any previous attempt, whenever, wherever by whomsoever made, is to say only what you yourself must well know—but what I would have you know is that . . . you have distanced all other competitors in the same field. . . . Indeed its excellence makes one despair, for who is there to do the like for the literature of other countries?"

In later years, after all of Coues' bibliographical installments had been published, he received additional high praise. For example, Allen wrote that the work had "established a grade of efficiency never before attained, and set a model for the emulation of all future natural history bibliographers."[48] Another writer, even more enthusiastic, declared: "[Coues was] certainly the greatest of ornithological bibliographers . . . the author of some thousand pages of the most enlightened bibliography devoted to his field. . . . [This was] religiously executed, erudite, and perceptive bibliography, which was both literature and as masterly as was then imaginable."[49]

How Coues, in his extremely busy career, found time and stamina— particularly the latter—for the exacting labors necessary to produce such a comprehensive, three-dimensional bibliography almost defies explanation. Yet Coues provided one himself. Writing to Allen on February 8, 1881, he said: "I have found that it is only by firm purpose to leap over the moon that you can get over the bibliographical hedge!" Coues supplied an answer, too, to the question why, after completing the fourth installment, he had discontinued his bibliographical labors: his own "machinery for doing the work broke down."[50] The answer is credible, for in December, 1880, he stayed two to three weeks in the U.S. Naval Hospital in Brooklyn.[51] At this time, too, he was deeply immersed in marital problems, and the Army, much against his will, had ordered him to return to Fort Whipple.

In his letters to Allen and other friends Coues often alluded to the drudgery involved in finding and employing the extensive citations from literature required for the bibliographical installments. Drudgery this work doubtless was, and is, but it can also become a pleasurable addiction, and did so for Coues. If not, it is inconceivable that he would have pursued the work so energetically, and for such a length of time.

Just two years short of his death Coues reminisced about his earlier labors in the bibliographical vineyard:

> I found myself [in 1880] amidst the debris of the great plan I had projected or partially accomplished, with many thousand manuscript titles on hand and no prospect of their ever seeing the light. . . . I think I never did anything else in my life which brought me such hearty praise "in mouths of wisest censure"—immediate and almost universal recognition, at home and abroad. . . . It takes a sort of an inspired idiot to be a good bibliographer, and his inspiration is as dangerous a gift as the appetite of the gambler or dipsomaniac—it grows with what it feeds upon, and finally possesses its victim like any other invincible vice. It is lucky for me that I was forcibly divorced from my bibliographical mania; at any rate, years have cured me of the habit. . . . But my own care need not and will not deter others from trying bibliography for themselves. . . . After all these years, during which the vast accumulation of unpublished titles slept on my hands, and during which I abandoned all hope of their utilization, I have just sent to a gentleman everything I own in manuscript relating to British birds, for the preparation of a new and up-to-date edition of that portion of my published bibliography. . . . This raises another question, which may be put in this way: Where is the

man who will undertake to bring my North American Bibliography up-to-date?[52]

Thus Coues, in 1897, made a determined effort to interest other ornithologists in bringing up to date both his British and North American bibliographical installments. The man in England to whom he sent his unpublished material was W. Ruskin Butterfield.[53] In 1908 Butterfeld reported:

> In 1897 the late Dr. Coues entrusted to me the task of completing up-to-date the portions of his bibliography relating to our native birds, and placed in my hands the additional material he had collected; moreover, he procured from Professor [Alfred] Newton, of Cambridge, the consent of the latter to assist me with advice, a favour of which I took full advantage. But I speedily found that I had embarked upon a task of no small magnitude. It was easy enough to deal with the books in my possession, but when those were finished it became necessary to visit the great libraries in London, and at length, from various circumstances, I found it difficult to continue.[54]

At about the same time Coues forwarded his unpublished material to Butterfield, Witmer Stone,[55] ornithologist with the Academy of Natural Sciences of Philadelphia, chanced to read Coues' question: "Where is the man who will undertake to bring my North American bibliography up-to-date?" As it happened, Stone had been busy for some time with "a sort of index to ornithological papers," and he wrote to Coues at once "regarding this work and its relation to the bibliography that he was advocating." Coues promptly replied: "You are the very man, I should judge, to take up and complete the work. Why not? . . . If I could practically complete my bibliog. down to 1879, you should have little difficulty in bringing it down to date." Needing only this encouragement, Stone began work and eventually, by writing some 3,000 titles, brought the work down to 1900; at that point he, like Butterfield before him, foundered on the rocks of disincentive and irresolution.[56]

A quarter of a century now elapsed before anyone again seriously raised the matter of completing Coues' "Universal Bibliography." In 1928 *The Auk* ran an article by Casey A. Wood titled "A Plea for the Continuation of Elliott Coues' Ornithological Bibliography." Wood began his paper with these words: "No one can consult any of the installments of Coues' Bibliography without a mental doffing of the hat to a truly great man. The years of patient drudgery involved in that tremendous undertaking seem to dissolve in the amazement excited by the universal exhibit of the author-compiler's scholarship and erudition." Wood concluded by asking, "Are there no Americans who can or will assume the labor of completing the Instalments?"[57]

His appeal has gone unheeded. Since the years of Coues and Stone, ornithological literature has swelled so tremendously as to make completion of such a bibliography quite out of the question, unless perhaps through some form of computerization.

NOTES

1. On the title page of *Birds of the Colorado Valley* (1878) we find: "Part First, *Passeres* to *Laniidae*." Thus this volume was the first of a projected series, never completed.

2. John Wesley Powell (1834-1902), geologist and ethnologist, is noted for his explorations of the Southwest. In 1869, while making a survey of the Colorado River, he led a party by boat through the Grand Canyon. He was instrumental in founding the U.S. Geological Survey, and served as its director (1881-94). He published *Explorations of the Colorado River of the West and Its Tributaries* (1875) and *Reports on the Lands of the Arid Regions of the United States* (1878).

3. In 1856-57 Hayden served as naturalist in explorations of regions of the Upper Missouri, Platte, and Yellowstone rivers under the command of Lieutenant (later General) G. K. Warren, U.S. Engineers. In 1862 Hayden was naturalist to the expedition under Captain (later General) W. F. Raynolds which explored the Upper Missouri.

4. This is yet another oblique reference by Coues to the manuscript on Arizona animals which he, in a moment of despondency, had burned in 1870 at Fort Macon.

5. Coues' letters to Hayden and Powell are in the National Archives, Washington, D.C.

6. The synonymy of a plant or animal consists of a listing of the various scientific names which have been applied to a specific form at one time or another by its describer or later authors.

7. Coues, *Birds of the Northwest* (1874), vii.

8. Now *Nucifraga columbiana* (Wilson).

9. Coues, *Birds of the Northwest*, 207.

10. *Ibid.*, 217.

11. Coues, *Birds of the Colorado Valley*, 166. The words "rift within the lute" are from Tennyson's *Idylls of the King*.

12. Coues' "Titlark" is the related bird now called water pipit (*Anthus spinoletta*).

13. Audubon ascended the Missouri River in 1843. In his journal of that trip, under dates of June 19, 22, and 24, he alluded to the Missouri skylark.

14. Coues, *Birds of the Northwest*, 43.

15. Theodore Roosevelt, *The Hunting Trips of a Ranchman* (New York: G. P. Putnam's Sons, 1886), 225.

16. Allen, "Biographical Memoir," 410.

17. Kieran, ed., *Treasury of Great Nature Writing* (1957), 219-23, quoting from Coues, *Birds of the Northwest*, 321-27.

18. Peterson, ed., *The Bird Watcher's Anthology* (1957), 26-28, quoting from Coues, *Birds of the Colorado Valley*, 352.

19. Krutch and Eriksson, eds., *A Treasury of Birdlore* (1962), 112, quoting from Coues, *Birds of the Colorado Valley*, 74-76.

20. *Ibid.*, 152, quoting from Coues, *Birds of the Colorado Valley*, 57-60.

21. Peattie, *A Gathering of Birds* (1939), 277-81, quoting from *Birds of the Northwest*, 181-86.

22. *Ibid.*, 273-76, quoting from Coues, *Birds of the Colorado Valley*, 125-29.

23. *Ibid.*, 277-81, quoting from Coues, *Birds of the Colorado Valley*, 426-35.

24. *Ibid.*, 286-90.

25. William Henry Hudson (1841-1922), naturalist and writer, was born near Buenos Aires, Argentina. In 1874 he went to England, where he lived the rest of his life and wrote many books, among them *Green Mansions* (1904), *Far Away and Long Ago* (1918), and *Birds of La Plata* (1920).

26. Gilbert White (1720-93), English curate and naturalist, was born in Selborne, and is widely known for his *Natural History and Antiquities of Selborne* (1789).

27. Alfred Russel Wallace (1823-1913), English naturalist, first came to prominence with publication of his *Travels on the Amazon and Rio Negro* (1853). Later, after travels in the East Indies, he wrote *The Malay Archipelago* (1869), a classic among books of biological exploration. Among biologists he is well known for his ideas on natural selection, which closely paralleled those held by Darwin.

28. Sir Edward Grey (1862-1933), British statesman and naturalist, served as Britain's Foreign Secretary (1905-16), and was the author of *The Charm of Birds* (1927) and other ornithological works.

29. John Muir (1838-1914), naturalist and writer, was born in Scotland. After coming to the United States he became celebrated as a conservationist and the author of such books as *Our National Parks* (1901) and *The Yosemite* (1912).

30. Coues, "Langdon's Revised List of Cincinnati Birds" (1879), 112-13.

31. Coues, *Key to North American Birds*, 5th ed. (1903), I, xii.

32. *Forest and Stream*, Feb. 24, 1876, 36.

33. *Osprey*, II (Nov., 1897), 39-40.

34. Coues, *Birds of the Colorado Valley*, 568.

35. Henry Stevens (1819-66), American bibliographer.

36. Coues, *Birds of the Colorado Valley*, 569.

37. Coues, "Second Instalment of American Ornithological Bibliography" (1879), 239.

38. Coues, "Third Instalment of American Ornithological Bibliography" (1879), 521-22.

39. *Ibid.*, 670-74. John Gould (1804-81) was an English artist and ornithologist. With the help of other artists, including his wife, Gould brought out such illustrated works as *Monograph of the Trochilidae* (1849-61) and *Birds of Great Britain* (1862-73).

40. Coues, "Fourth Instalment of Ornithological Bibliography" (1880), 359.

41. The word "memorial," as used here, is a statement of fact or petition usually addressed to a government or some branch of it.

42. *Bull. Nutt. Orn. Club*, IV (July, 1879), 176-78.

43. Philip Lutley Sclater (1829-1913), English naturalist, was secretary of the Zoological Society of London (1859-1902), and the author of such works as *The Book of Antelopes* (1894-1900) and *Report on the Birds Collected during the Voyage of H.M.S. Challenger in the Years 1873-1876* (1880-95).

44. Alfred Newton (1829-1907), English zoologist, was elected traveling Fellow of Magdalen College, Cambridge, in 1854 and in 1866 became the first professor of zoology and comparative anatomy at Cambridge, a post he held until his death. Among his published works were *Zoology* (1872) and *A Dictionary of Birds* (1893-96). In the years 1865-70 he edited *The Ibis*.

45. Osbert Salvin (1835-1909), British naturalist, was the author of several important ornithological works and curator of birds at Cambridge University (1874-82).

46. Richard Bowdler Sharpe (1847-1909), English ornithologist, was the author of such valuable works as *The Birds of Great Britain*, 4 vols. (1894-97).

47. *Nation*, XXVIII (June 12, 1879), 404-5.

48. Allen, "Biographical Memoir," 411.

49. Mengel, "Bibliography and the Ornithologist" (1966), 121.

50. *Osprey*, II (Nov., 1897), 39-40.

51. Coues' "Book of Dates" (1880).

52. *Osprey*, II (Nov., 1897), 39-40.

53. Biographical data on W. Ruskin Butterfield have eluded us.

54. Wood, "A Plea for the Continuation of Elliott Coues' Ornithological Bibliography" (1928), 150.

55. Witmer Stone (1856-1939), naturalist, was assistant curator of the Academy of Natural Sciences of Philadelphia (1891-1908), curator (1908-24), and director of the museum (1925-28). He edited *The Auk* (1912-36) and wrote such books as *Birds of New Jersey* (1909) and *Birds of Old Cape May* (1917).

56. Wood, "Plea for the Continuation of Elliott Coues' Ornithological Bibliography," 153-54.

57. *Ibid.*, 148, 150.

Coues at twenty-one, in his uniform as assistant surgeon, U.S.
Army

Sketches made by Coues in about 1859, when he was sixteen or seventeen. *"Gymnophorenus Serpentarius"* is the secretary bird of Africa.
(From Coues' "Miscellaneous Mementoes," unpublished)

Sketches made by Coues for his *Key to North American Birds* (1872)
(From Hume, *Ornithologists of the U.S. Army Medical Corps,* 1942)

Upper left—Derby Flycatcher.   Upper right—Marsh Hawk.

Lower left—Ruffed Grouse.   Lower right—Cardinal Grosbeak.

Lower center—Helmet Quail.

J. A. Allen, June, 1885

Spencer Fullerton Baird, about 1850

H. C. Yarrow
(From U.S. Army Medical Library)

William Brewster (left) and Robert Ridgway

D. G. Elliot
(From *The Auk*, XXXIV (Jan., 1917), 1)

Theodore N. Gill
(From *The Auk*, XXXII (Oct., 1915), 391)

Thomas M. Brewer
(From *The Condor,* XXX (Sept.-Oct.,
1928), 270)

D. Webster Prentiss, sometime
during the Civil War
(From U.S. Army Medical Library)

U.S. Boundary Commission. *Seated left to right:* Gregory, Coues, Campbell,
Twining, Bryant. *Standing left to right:* Bangs, Boss, Greene, Ames, Doolittle,
Wilson, McGillycuddy

Jeannie Augusta McKinney Coues,
second wife of Elliott Coues
(From O'Shaughnessy, *A Diplomat's
Wife in Mexico,* 1916)

Pages from Coues' "Book of Dates." Note particularly "August, 1872,
Orig. Ed. Key N.A. Birds published."

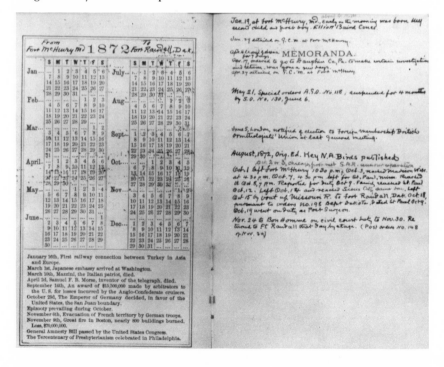

A wash drawing of Harris's sparrow (*Zonotrichia querula*) by Louis Agassiz
Fuertes (Courtesy of George M. Sutton, who owns the original presented to him by
Mrs. Louis Agassiz Fuertes)

Louis Agassiz Fuertes

Left to right: A. C. Vroman, Manuel Chaves, Elliott Coues, Amado Chaves, Frederick Webb Hodge, George Winship Parker, 1899 (just a few months before Coues' death) (From Mahood, *Photographer of the Southwest,* 1961)

CHAPTER XIII

The Years with Hayden

On July 3, 1876, good news reached Elliott Coues. The Adjutant General's Office relieved him of his duties with the Northern Boundary Commission and directed him to report to the Secretary of the Interior, Zachariah Chandler, for a new and most desirable position as secretary and naturalist of F. V. Hayden's U.S. Geological Survey of the Territories.[1]

The transfer of Coues to the Hayden survey was a logical move. In 1873 the survey had listed him as one of its collaborators.[2] His *Birds of the Northwest* had been issued as the survey's "Miscellaneous Publication No. 3," and he had also contributed articles to the *Bulletin*, another series in Hayden's ambitious publication program.

Other (and often competing) federal surveys of the West had also printed monographs authored or co-authored by Coues. His "Abstract of Results of a Study of the Genera *Geomys* and *Thomomys*" appeared in John Wesley Powell's report on *Exploration of the Colorado River of the West* (1875). Volume V of the reports of George M. Wheeler's[3] Geological Surveys West of the One Hundredth Meridian (also 1875) contained Coues' "Synopsis of the Reptiles and Batrachians of Arizona" and (co-authored by H. C. Yarrow) the "Report on Collections of Mammals." Coues also contributed a series of ornithological sections in J. H. Kidder's report on the natural history collections of the transit-of-Venus expedition.[4]

Because of the energetic and diversified labors of such scientists as Coues, and the broad scope of the federal agencies for which they worked, Washington became an increasingly important center for the sciences during this period. It can be argued that by the 1870s the nation's capital surpassed Philadelphia in this regard.

Not only was the new assignment a fitting one for Coues, it was also no surprise. He and Hayden had persuaded the Secretary of the Interior to apply to the Secretary of War for Coues' services. All went well until Coues' superiors in the Office of the Surgeon General balked. Coues then had, with Colonel Charles Henry Crane, assistant surgeon general, "my *first* square frank talk, the gist of which was the recognition by him of the fact, that I *had* claims upon the Surgeon General's Office, in view of my scientific career, upon which special consideration in the matter of details might be based." Such blunt talk, so characteristic of Coues, along with the intervention of his friend Senator John A. Logan of Illinois, brought about the desired result. Logan, a powerful congressional supporter of the Hayden survey, had made a "personal request" that the transfer be made.[5] It was agreed that Coues was to receive "his pay proper from the Army, the survey paying his commutation for quarters and fuel."[6]

For Coues the new assignment promised to be a splendid opportunity. Now he felt certain of being able to remain "for two or three years longer" in Washington, with its great museums and library facilities.[7] Just as welcome was the continued freedom from military life and discipline. His associates in scientific circles believed it was "a matter of congratulation that Dr. Coues' time will as heretofore be devoted to zoological pursuits."[8]

Since 1873 the Hayden survey had concerned itself mainly with the topographical and geological mapping of Colorado and had de-emphasized its previous attention to the natural history of the West. Scientists and sportsmen rejoiced that, with the appointment of Coues, the survey would once again show proper concern for zoology.

Immediately after accepting his new duty, and perhaps at his own request, Coues was directed by Hayden to organize a natural history party for the purpose of exploring any portion of the Colorado Rockies he wished. His group was designated as "the fourth or zoological party."[9]

One major consideration bothered Coues as he made his preparations for taking to the field. In 1875 Indians had attacked a Hayden party in the Sierra la Sal country of eastern Utah. Even more sobering for Coues were the events of June 25, 1876, at Little Big Horn. He had become acquainted with many officers and men of the 7th Cavalry when a contingent of that regiment had served as an escort for the boundary commission's field work. He expressed his anxiety, as light-heartedly as possible, in a letter to the editors of *Rod and Gun*, dated July 31: "Some graceless wag has taken an atrocious liberty with my name, and the joke is current here. He said that Hayden wisely takes Coues along this year to pacify Sitting Bull! To which I modestly but firmly reply, that as I value my scalp, S. B. shall do no carving, if I can help it."[10]

The main object of his Colorado trip was the observation of the mammals of the area; the study of birds was to be secondary. Two men were selected to assist Coues in the field: L. M. Cuthbert of Washington, D.C., and W. W. Karr of Memphis.[11] It is not known how many persons accompanied Coues, Cuthbert, and Karr into the West, though the party appears to have been small.

2

Sometime in early August Coues and his associates traveled by rail to Cheyenne, Wyoming.[12] They stayed for a few days at nearby Fort D. A. Russell and Camp Carlin.[13] At the latter place Coues was the guest of Captain James S. Gilliss.[14] The captain's wife, Julia, maintained a yard full of tame black-tailed prairie dogs. Coues was so fascinated by this feat of domestication that he persuaded Mrs. Gilliss to write an account of her pets. Her brief article on the "funny little creatures" soon appeared in *Rod and Gun*.[15]

From Camp Carlin the Coues party journeyed across the Laramie Plains, up the Big Laramie River, through the Medicine Bow Mountains, and into Colorado's North Park. Here they remained for three weeks and made the park their principal stopping place. Coues believed "this portion of Colorado [was] the one least frequented, and therefore likely to offer the greatest attractions to the naturalist and hunter."[16]

Abundant in North Park were large game animals which Coues collected and observed: antelope, American elk, mule deer, big-horn sheep,[17] grizzly bear, and black bear (*Ursus americanus*).[18] Coues commented that he had "nowhere else found antelope so abundant as they were in North Park during the summer of 1876. They were almost continually in view, and thousands must breed in that locality."[19]

A special treat was the sighting of a small herd of buffalo, in this case "the woodland buffalo, known to the hunters as 'mountain bison [*Bison bison athabascae*].'" This form, he explained, was only a variety of the more familiar plains buffalo (*Bison bison bison*) and not a separate species, even though the woodland buffalo was "decidedly darker and more uniformly colored" than the plains variety.[20] Also plentiful were smaller animals such as the long-tailed weasel, badger (*Taxidea taxus*),[21] porcupine, beaver, golden-mantled ground squirrel, and Abert's squirrel.[22]

In late September, near Rabbit-ears Mountain, Coues and his companions crossed the Continental Divide and entered Middle Park, staying there until early October. Going through Berthoud Pass on October 7, they soon made it to a point near Denver. They then pressed northward over the plains east of the Front Range. On October 10 they were opposite Long's Peak. Along this stretch Coues took particular note of the large number of striped skunks (*Mephitis mephitis*).[23]

On October 12 Coues and his men returned to Cheyenne. He was pleased when his friend and host, Captain Gilliss, led him to a place near the town inhabited by a group of dogs, formerly domesticated and now living in a wild state.[24] Coues was excited at the chance to observe them because he had been intrigued by the relationship of wolves, foxes, and coyotes to domestic dogs.[25]

By late October Coues was back in Washington. He deposited in the U.S. National Museum all of the Rocky Mountain faunal specimens he had collected except for the osteological items, which were given over to the Army Medical Museum.[26]

He had hoped to bag a black-footed ferret (*Mustela nigripes*) in Colorado, but had had no luck. Since 1874 he had advertised for a specimen of this animal.[27] Fortunately, the collection of stuffed animals of the Rockies prepared by Martha Ann Maxwell, a talented naturalist and taxidermist of Boulder, had been taken east as part of Colorado's exhibit for the nation's centennial exposition at Philadelphia. In the winter of 1876-77 this collection was displayed in Washington, and Coues was an appreciative visitor. Not only did Mrs. Maxwell have specimens of the elusive ferret, but she was also able to pass on to Coues much information about its habits.[28] Coues was so delighted with Mrs. Maxwell's exhibit that he gladly prepared a list of the mammals of the collection, with annotations based partly upon his own observations and partly upon information supplied him by the astute "lady naturalist." This brief (nine-page) appendix was the only work by Coues devoted exclusively to Rocky Mountain mammals.[29]

In 1878 Coues took a vacation in some of the same areas of the Rockies through which he had trekked two years earlier. This is note-worthy, for at last he had found a part of the West appealing to him. He had acquired a good deal of professional satisfaction in his tours of duty in Arizona, Dakota, and Montana, yet he had no fondness for these areas.

Coues left Washington on August 17, 1878, and arrived in Chicago on the 20th. There he picked up two of his nephews, E. C. and G. H. Flower (the sons of his sister Lucy). The boys and their uncle set out by rail for Cheyenne. From there they went to North Park, where they camped and roamed for most of September. Sometime around the beginning of October Coues arrived back in Washington.[30]

As Coues indicated in a letter written in later life, the collections made in the Rockies during 1876 and 1878 were his last significant ones in the West.[31] The journey of 1878, however, seems to have been mostly for pleasure. Few Americans working in the 1870s more richly deserved a vacation than Elliott Coues. If any period can be singled out as the most productive of Coues' career as a scientist, it is the time from 1872 to 1880, especially the years spent with the Hayden survey. The Rocky Mountain expedition of 1876 was simply the auspicious beginning of a most happy four years.

3

Coues served with the Hayden survey from July, 1876, until late in 1880. Most of this time was spent in Washington. His principal duties were certainly enough to keep anyone busy: editing all the publications of the survey, soliciting manuscripts for its *Reports* and *Bulletin*, and making several contributions of his own to these volumes.[32]

A good deal of his energy was taken up with goading, cajoling, and mollifying the employees of the Government Printing Office so that the survey's publications would appear on schedule. When J. A. Allen wanted to make substantial changes in one of his contributions, which the G.P.O. already had in galley proof, Coues informed him in a letter of October 9, 1879, that the delay *"did* make a row at the Printer's which it took quarts of my most refined fusel oil to quiet down."

A retrenchment-minded Congress, in Coues' view, had appropriated too little money for the survey's publishing program, causing even more anguish. In a letter of March 8, 1880, to Allen he exploded: ". . . curse a spigot-stopping policy, with the bung hole flowing, as it always is! The Legislative solons squirm and squeal over a few thousand dollars for science, and smile away millions 'between drinks.' The printing of their own unnecessary and ridiculous proceedings costs more than all they vote for science, and isn't worth as much as the clean paper was before it got inked over."

Coues and other officials in the Hayden, Powell, King, and Wheeler surveys also feared that Congress would soon consolidate these four agencies into a single federal survey. He expressed his concern in December, 1878, to Allen: "Great panic and row here anent the Surveys and Nat[ional] Acad[emy]—we are all like Turkeys hopping on a hot gridiron."

Occasionally he felt overwhelmed by the problems. In July, 1879, he told Allen: "It is hot and torrid here, and I am overworked & depressed. What a d— fraud life is anyhow!"

His most significant accomplishment of the first months of service with the survey was the publication of his two volumes on mammals: *Fur-Bearing Animals* and (with J. A. Allen) *Monographs of North American Rodentia*, both published by the survey in 1877. These works originated from Coues' ambitious plan for a large-scale "History of North American Mammals."[33]

Hayden and Coues decided to bring out *Fur-Bearing Animals* as a single volume, on the Mustelidae, in advance of the general "History" because many of the animals within this family were economically significant in America, as predators or as sources of valuable furs.[34] Since Coues hoped the volume would appeal to nonspecialists, he wrote it in a compact, popular style, with technical matter kept to a minimum.

Most of the specimens used for the study had been obtained by Hayden's field collectors and were housed in the U.S. National Museum.[35] Coues was also able to squeeze into the book some observations of western Mustelidae that he himself had made in his Rocky Mountain trip of 1876. Reprinted in the work, as a means of facilitating the writing of the complete "History," was a circular from the Surgeon General's Office requesting the Army's medical officers to send mammalian specimens to Coues.[36]

In the course of writing *Fur-Bearing Animals*, Coues found it necessary to consult the literature of the early American fur trade.[37] Although he could not have known it then, this was a valuable introduction to an area of scholarship which he would himself enrich in later years.

The collaboration with Allen on the Rodentia was a much weightier task. Coues. as we know, had been examining and arranging the collections of rodents at the National Museum since the early 1870s.[38] The partners divided the work as follows: Coues wrote the monographs on Muridae (the family of Old World rats and mice), Zapodidae (jumping mice), Saccomyidae (now called Heteromyidae, pocket mice, kangaroo mice, and kangaroo rats), Haplodontidae (*Aplodontia*, mountain beaver), and Geomyidae (pocket gophers). Allen handled the chapters on Leporidae (hares and rabbits), Hystricidae (*Erethizon*, porcupine), Lagomyidae (now Ochotonidae, pikas), Castoroididae (fossil beaver), Castoridae (beaver), and Sciuridae (squirrels).

The published volume turned out to be hefty (ten pounds, two ounces) and rich in technical detail. Writing after Coues' death, Allen conceded that the work did not have the lasting impact which the authors hoped it would have. Allen explained that the *Monographs* had been written "at the height of a wave of conservatism that engulfed

American mammalogists and ornithologists alike between the years 1872 and 1882, in respect to the 'species question.'" During this period it was assumed, particularly in the field of mammalogy, that virtually all of the various American species had been discovered, thoroughly studied, and properly classified.[39] After 1882 new field techniques, such as the use of the cyclone trap, made these assumptions—and the writing based on them—outdated.[40]

In 1894, years after publication of the *Monographs*, Coues expressed similar thoughts in a letter to his old collaborator: "I have been reading the *mammal* papers you & others have dropped into my mail. . . . It almost takes my breath away—Arabian Nights and Gulliver's Travels are less astonishing! There were evidently no prophets when a certain Monogr. N. A. Rodentia was being written. But who could have foreseen such a result in 1877?"

The *Monographs* is nevertheless far from worthless. As Allen noted, they "contain much of permanent value, especially in relation to the historical and bibliographical phases of the subject, and as a summary of previous knowledge of the groups treated."[41] Specifically, Appendix B, a bibliography of mammalogy prepared by Coues and Theodore Gill, is probably the most enduring contribution of the entire volume. Hayden's assessment of the effort was sound: "Though regarded by the authors as incomplete, it is nevertheless, by far the most extensive and elaborate exposition of the subject extant."[42]

Working with Gill tried Coues' limited patience, according to David Starr Jordan, then a promising young naturalist, who first met Coues in 1877. Gill was invariably behind on his part of the collaboration. Jordan also gave a clue concerning Coues' ability to write so much during his association with the Hayden survey. "On the walls of his den in the Survey," Jordan recalled, "he posted large placards, two of which read as follows":

I DREAD INTERRUPTION MORE THAN THE DEVIL
THE VERY FACT OF A DOOR HAS IN IT A SUGGESTION TO THE INQUIRING MIND.[43]

The Hayden survey was only one of the outlets for Coues' talents in the 1870s. In 1878 he became associate editor of the *American Naturalist*, taking charge of the magazine's departments of ornithology and mammalogy.[44] In 1879 he became the (unpaid) curator of mammalogy at the National Museum.[45] Between 1876 and 1883 he was listed as an associate editor of the *Bulletin of the Nuttall Ornithological Club*. According to the club's historian, Coues' position was purely nominal and his name was used on the title page only to enhance the prestige of the publication. In fact, the same authority wrote that there was fear among the club's members that Coues would seize actual editorial control in 1881 when the health of the editor, J. A. Allen, broke: ". . . the Bulletin belonged to the Club, not to any individual, and the members felt that Dr. Coues, with all his brilliancy, was not the type of man to maintain the standards the Club had set." The anxiety of the members disappeared with the recovery of Allen's health.[46]

In any case, Coues supplied a number of articles, notes, and reviews to the *Bulletin*. He successfully entreated Allen to publish in the *Bulletin* "a curious list of birds drawn up by my nephew [George Hughes Coues, son of Samuel Franklin Coues], being those actually seen & most shot in the grounds of the Naval Hospital of Brooklyn."[47]

Coues also published several items in the *American Naturalist*, the *Nation*, and the sportsmen's magazines, such as *Forest and Stream* and *Rod and Gun*.

In his "Book of Dates" Coues tells us that on May 3, 1879, there appeared the first issue of the *Washington World*, a weekly newspaper for which he was associate editor. Coues noted only that "it died soon."[48]

4

During his years with Hayden, the scientific world heaped numerous honors on Elliott Coues. Foremost of the laurels bestowed upon him was his election on April 17, 1877, to membership in a most elite group, the National Academy of Sciences. Coues, then thirty-four years of age, became the academy's youngest member.[49] Other learned societies which elected him to membership in this period included the Zoological Society of London (corresponding member, May 18, 1876); the American Association for the Advancement of Science (August, 1876); Davenport (Iowa) Academy of Sciences (April 27, 1877); Nuttall Ornithological Club (honorary member, February 4, 1878); American Philosophical Society (September 20, 1878); Anthropological Society of Washington (May 8, 1879); and the Society of American Taxidermists (first honorary member, May 7, 1880).

Since the fall of 1875 he had been a member of the Literary Society of Washington. He became the organization's vice-president for 1877-78 and its secretary for 1879-80. According to his "Book of Dates" he attended a meeting on May 19, 1875, at the Cooper Institute in New York City, "to organize International Association for the protection of game and fish." Despite the inclusion of such other worthies as Robert B.

Roosevelt,[50] Edward D. Cope, John L. LeConte, and Charles Hallock in the organization, Coues recorded that "it never came to anything."

No doubt Coues appreciated the honors awarded him and welcomed the closer association with the other great names of science which the honors brought. Still, they entailed little or no monetary reward, and Coues was then experiencing some extra expenses. In a letter to Hayden he asked ("demanded" might be a more accurate word) his chief's assistance in a financial matter: "I find it necessary to have a little money just now, in furnishing my house, and the bank will loan it to me, if you will endorse the enclosed draft. Please do so, and return without delay, as I am in quite a strait. The bank only requires your name on the back of the draft, and your initials in the lower left hand corner."[51]

Coues also sought to augment his income through writing. He received monetary compensation for the articles and reviews published not only in the popular and sportsmen's periodicals but also in the staid New York *Nation*. He informed Allen in a letter of January 6, 1879, that the latter journal paid "$7.50 a column, or 15 a page for reviews."

The need for money stemmed in part from the fact that his family continued to increase. A son, Charles Page Coues, was born in 1875, and another son, Beverly Drinkard Coues, in 1878.[52]

The desire for additional income seems to have been a consideration in his acceptance, in the spring of 1877, of a lectureship in anatomy at his alma mater, the National Medical College. He delivered his inaugural lecture on April 5.[53] On March 18, 1880, he gave an address ("Hygeia") to the college's graduating class, and that fall, on October 4, he delivered the opening address to the students for the new term.[54] In later years his part-time lectureship evolved, as we shall see, into a full-time professorship.

5

In September, 1879, Coues published a largely bibliographical article in the Hayden survey's *Bulletin* entitled "On the Present Status of *Passer domesticus* in America, with Special Reference to the Western States and Territories." At first glance it appears to be a minor exercise on a species, the English (house) sparrow, in which Coues was currently interested.

One needs only to read his introductory remarks and a few of the bibliographical entries to realize the absolute incorrectness of this assumption. The subject was far from being a matter of mere passing interest to the author. In fact, it was one of several articles and notes published by Coues on this bird over a number of years; these were among his most vitriolic writings. They form his contribution to the "Sparrow War," one of the most heated battles ever fought among men of science.[55]

The first, unsuccessful, attempt to bring the English sparrow into the United States occurred in Brooklyn in 1850, while Coues was still a child in New Hampshire. More ambitious efforts were made in Brooklyn in 1852 and in Portland, Maine, in 1854.[56]

The great importing mania swept the eastern seaboard in the 1860s. It was widely believed that English sparrows could rid the urban centers of caterpillars, cankerworms, and other pestiferous insect larvae. Also, many recent immigrants from Europe prized them as reminders of the homeland.[57] The birds were captured or purchased (usually in England or Germany), carefully transported across the Atlantic, and released by the thousands in New York (1860-64), Boston (1868), and Washington and Philadelphia (1869).[58]

At the same time, those introduced earlier were working their way westward and southward, until shortly after the turn of the century English sparrows ranged over the entire country. Their remarkable diffusion resulted in part from the solicitude shown to the earliest arrivals. Mostly, however, they prospered because of their hardiness, extraordinary fecundity, and freedom from the enemies which had checked their increase in Europe.[59] By the end of the century it was recognized that the importation of the sparrows had been a mistake, but the Americans had been a long time realizing it.

In the 1860s Coues was perhaps too busy launching his career to give much attention to the sparrow craze. His 1868 catalog of the birds of New England contained merely the dispassionate observation that the bird was "introduced, and at present only found in certain localities, though it will doubtless before long become generally distributed."[60] In a letter to J. A. Allen that year, on August 10, Coues expressed idle curiosity about the bird's introduction: "Can you give me the 'latest news' regarding the introduction of the Sparrows in *Boston?* I have positive information only regarding them at Portland, Me. & New York."

In the first edition of *Key to North American Birds* Coues voiced mild concern that the sparrows would soon interfere with the native species. On the other hand, the author believed that the bird was "highly beneficial" for its work against cankerworms. Coues later neglected to mention that he had once paid the bird a compliment.[61] Yet at the time the *Key* was in press, Coues wrote to Allen, on May 28, 1872, and gave his true feelings: "Do you share my apprehensions about that wretched ornithological bouleversement—*Passer domesticus*? I despise the sight of that bird in this country."

Meanwhile, misgivings and anger mounted, and by 1874 the great "Sparrow War" was on. The principal combatants were Coues and Thomas M. Brewer, Boston physician, journalist, ornithologist, and ardent champion of the English sparrow. Prior to the "war" relations between the two men had been cordial. In *Birds of the Northwest* Coues had thanked Brewer, his "kind friend," for supplying information on the prairie warbler.[62] Even after the stormiest phase of the controversy Coues referred to his antagonist, perhaps grudgingly, as "long the leading oölogist of the United States."[63]

But once the Sparrow War was under way in earnest, the notes and articles of the two men displayed an increasing bitterness toward each other. An exchange between them in 1877, through the pages of the *Washington Gazette*, illustrated how personal the argument had become. In the June 3 issue Brewer insinuated that Coues' stand against the sparrow was an example of "a lie well stuck to being as good as the truth." In the following month Brewer wrote to the editor apologizing for his remarks. The paper printed Coues' gracious acceptance of Brewer's denial of "intentional offensiveness."[64]

Friends of the sparrow gained a vocal ally in Henry Ward Beecher.[65] In 1878 the renowned clergyman denounced Coues' opposition to the birds as "treason" because he had "incited a riot" against the sparrows.[66] Coues dismissed Beecher's statements by remarking that "many uninformed and misinformed persons may agree with him."[67] And he could smile at the charge of Henry Bergh, founder of the American Society for the Prevention of Cruelty to Animals, that he was a "murderer."[68] Coues later sneered at Bergh's "ranting pseudo-zoophily."[69]

But he could not ignore Brewer, and the bitterness between the two men intensified in 1878. In January Brewer confronted Coues in his office in Washington. After they exchanged hot words over the sparrows, Coues proposed that the prestigious Nuttall Ornithological Club (a Boston-based organization of which Brewer was a member) undertake an objective investigation of the sparrow question. Brewer's reply, according to Coues, "was complimentary neither to the sincerity of my proposition nor to the ornithological ability of the Club." Disregarding the rebuff, Coues urged the group to begin the study. The club responded by calling an open meeting at which members, among them such luminaries as William Brewster,[70] H. W. Henshaw, and J. A. Allen, expressed their unanimous condemnation of the sparrow. "Dr. Brewer," Coues remarked, "for some reason did not attend the meeting." For his part, Brewer scoffed at "the three tailors of Toodle street, Boston, [who] have made their resolutions, committing the people of the United States to antagonism on the sparrow question."[71] When an anonymous article, similarly hostile to the Nuttall group, appeared in a Boston newspaper, Coues asked Brewer if he were the author. Despite a denial, Coues suggested later that Brewer had lied.[72]

Coues considered his own major contribution to the sparrow question to be an article published later in 1878, entitled "The Ineligibility of the European House Sparrow in America." An offended reader of his strong remarks commented that Coues had divided the bird's friends into five categories, four of them composed of "idiots" and the fifth of the "weak-minded."[73]

In a letter to Allen of May 19, 1879, Coues privately abused Brewer in verse:

> There was an old person of Beacon-street,
> Of whom History Itself doth Repeat—
>   That he stood on his head,
>   Till the Sparrows all said,
> "It is quite an anonymous feat!"

Coues' attacks should have subsided after 1880, when Brewer—the only reputable ornithologist to befriend the sparrow consistently—died. Yet Coues spared neither Brewer's memory nor the sparrows. To Allen on March 28, 1880, Coues wrote: "We both know that Brewer was a cantankerous old ass at the time he had the good taste to fall asleep in Jesus." In a steady barrage of notes and articles he continued to announce the latest outrages by the obnoxious bird.[74]

Yet by 1883 Coues began to show signs of weariness and acknowledged the uselessness of waging the "war." "I am almost as tired of writing against the sparrows as I am of the sparrows themselves."[75] Finally he gave up: "I led the 'sparrow war' for twenty years and only surrendered to the inevitable. You may do what you please, shoot or poison as many as you can, more will come to the funeral, and nothing you can do will make any appreciable difference. The case is hopeless."[76]

Even after acknowledging defeat, Coues neither forgave nor forgot the sparrows and those who defended them. For the remainder of his life he seldom missed an opportunity to blast them both. Shortly before his death Coues revived the sparrow question in the ornithological journals. Feeling slighted because a recent Department of Agriculture bulletin on the sparrows[77] failed to give sufficient credit to his earlier crusade, he took the occasion to review the battles of the 1870s. He wrote that the late Dr. Brewer had been "a narrow-minded, prejudiced, and tactless person"[78] who had "made a fool of himself about the Sparrows for years."[79]

A letter to the editors of another ornithological journal complained of the questionable taste of Coues' diatribe against his fallen opponent.[80] Coues responded with fresh outbursts against Brewer, whose death did not absolve him of wrong-doing: "The harm he did was incalculable, and his name deserves to be stigmatized as long as there is a Sparrow left in the United States to shriek 'Brewer! Brewer! Brewer!'" "Dying," he wrote, "makes a great difference to the person chiefly concerned, but has no retroactive effect upon the events of his life, and only sentimentalists allow it to influence their estimate of personal character." Coues then blasted the correspondent who had criticized him—a gentleman who had the added misfortune to live in Brewer, Maine—for his "silly" remarks.[81]

Shortly after this last round of the Sparrow War, Coues died in the sure knowlege that he had been correct in his denunciation of the sparrow. Yet his energy and dedication (as well as occasional below-the-belt punches) were futile. As he put it: "I had proven my case to the satisfaction of the public, and the Sparrow had proven *his* case—which was, that he had come to stay. I could whip all my featherless foes, but the Sparrows proved too much for me."[82]

6

On February 5, 1874, Coues wrote a letter to John Burroughs lauding Burroughs's triumph of nature writing, *Wake-Robin*: "My normal state has been for some years that of a 'wader' through books about birds, till I have come to regard ornithological literature as just so much shop-work. . . . Your book has been to me a green spot in the wilderness, where I have lingered with rare pleasure, enjoying the birds as nowhere else excepting in the woods and fields—where you carry me straightway."[83] Coues' congratulatory prose contains perhaps a touch of envy. Despite his own considerable literary abilities, it is obvious that he believed that ornithological writing—his own included—should be something more than "shop-work."

As usual, Coues was not slow in acting on his beliefs. During his busiest months with the Hayden survey he began experimenting with poetry as a means of expressing ornithological—and human—concerns. His first known published effort in this line was an article written in poetic prose. Coues called it an "imaginative piece," and as such it was printed originally in the *Chicago Field* of January 6, 1877.[84] Entitled "To the Swallow," it deals largely with the swallow's evocation of memories of childhood. Coues concluded it on a somewhat more profound note:

> But tell me, swallow!—bird of flight swift as the lapse of years—is it naught but memory that thou lendest wings? Doth not thy constant life foreshadow things that may hereafter come to pass? Even now, as I tread the busy thoroughfare, jostled and jostling in the eager crowd which surges onward to their fancied goal, I sometimes see thee still, and know thy life is still linked with man's. So may it ever be; though we may change, thou art always the same, and thy teaching is—be brave, be true, be steadfast!

On January 23, 1877, Coues prevailed upon Baird for what seemed to be a routine favor: "I have a short bird-article I want to send to Harper's [*Harper's New Monthly Magazine*]. As tending to insure favorable consideration could you give me a line of introduction to those publishers, who probably never heard of me?" Baird, of course, readily complied; when Coues thanked him a few days later, he confessed that his "bird-article" was actually "a poetical effusion." The poem, a free-verse offering which *Harper's* published in the spring, was indeed an effusion. Entitled "The Song That the Bluebird Sings," it begins with the questions

> *Have you listened to the carol of the bluebird in the spring?*
> *Has her gush of molten melody been not poured forth in vain?*

and concludes with the belief that

> *All is not lost if the message that the bluebird bears be heeded,*
> *For her mission is to tell us "God is love!"*[85]

According to the "Book of Dates" three more poems were written in February, 1877. The first was a "Poem with music by J. P. Caulfield."[86] This romantic ballad, entitled "O Breathe It under Thy Breath Love!" was published in July, 1877, by Oliver Ditson & Company, Boston. A copy of the sheet music is in the Library of Congress. The second poem, "In the Toils," was never published. The third poetic effort, "The Cigarette," according to one bibliography of Coues' works, was published in the April, 1879, issue of a periodical called *Town and Country*.[87] Our efforts to locate copies of the latter two poems have been unsuccessful.

Although Coues was no rival to Walt Whitman or, for that matter, to a host of lesser poetical lights of the nineteenth century, it is regrettable that some of his poems have disappeared. Quite possibly they would have revealed other unique thoughts and emotions of this many-sided man.

The question of the nature of the poem on cigarettes is especially intriguing in light of the fact that Coues was a chain-smoker. Two of the best physical descriptions of Coues for this period of his life make cigarette-smoking an almost integral part of his person. H. C. Yarrow remembered him as "a handsome man of less than forty, with bushy, brown hair and brown beard, only ceasing his work [of writing] occasionally to roll a cigarette, the tobacco for which he took from a calvarium on the table before him."[88] Frank Chapman told a story which revealed much about Coues' personality, as well as his tobacco intake:

> Coues was the focal point of every meeting that he attended, and could always be counted to do something that defied tradition. "Laws, gentlemen," I once heard him say, "were made to break," and he never hesitated to uphold this precept.
>
> He was an inveterate smoker of cigarettes, and his fingers were deeply stained from their use. He "rolled his own," carrying papers in his right-hand vest pocket and loose flake tobacco in his coat-tails. It was a day when there were still places where smoking was prohibited, and I recall his saying in the restaurant of the National Museum, "I wonder if we can smoke here?" Then adding, "I guess the best way to learn is to try." Whereupon a paper was produced, tobacco sprinkled in it and, after a practiced twirl, he was soon inhaling calmly.[89]

Coues himself discussed his love for tobacco with obvious relish in *Field Ornithology*: "I have had so much experience in the use of tobacco as a mild stimulant that I am probably no impartial judge of its merits: I will simply say that I do not use it in the field, because it indisposes to muscular activity, and favors reflection when observation is required; and temporary abstinence provokes the morbid appetite and renders the weed more grateful afterward."[90]

In a paper read before the Literary Society of Washington on March 17, 1877, Coues indirectly explained his sudden compulsion to express himself poetically. In his paper, entitled "Imagination," Coues announced that he had acquired "a great and growing contempt" for mere facts. Furthermore, he let it be known that he was not one of those scientists who dismissed poetry as "sensuous caterwauling." He agreed with a writer who had said that "poetry is the first and last of all knowledge—it is immortal as the heart of man." The best scientists and the best artists had much in common, said Coues, since both employed the gift of imagination. "The microscopic eye which peers too long and too intently upon the motes of facts which play in the sunbeam, will be blinded to the truths which both the motes and the beam conspire to announce."[91]

Coues saw no contradiction, then, between scientific endeavors and the "higher faculty" of imagination.[92] It is also clear that he felt a need to think beyond his immediate calling as a scientist and seek greater intellectual fulfillment.

If any of his scientific colleagues disapproved of or scoffed at Coues' delving into poetry, we have found no record of such a reaction. The nineteenth century was a time when people of virtually all walks of life freely and frequently expressed themselves through poetry, either by quoting it or by trying their own hands at versifying. There was nothing peculiar about a man of Coues' mental attainments using poetry as a vehicle for expressing ideas and emotions.

7

Coues' poetical flings appear to have been confined largely to the winter of 1877. Yet other poems occasionally were to come from his pen in later years. Among them was one mentioned cryptically in the May 15, 1879, entry of his "Book of Dates": ". . . last poem to Mrs. Cameron written." This is no doubt the same woman mentioned in the following entries for the year 1876:

> June or July[,] excursion of a few days down the Potomac to Norfolk and Fortress Monroe [Virginia], with Mrs. Senator Cameron, &c.
> July 4, picnic with Mrs. Cameron, Senator Logan, etc.

Two questions arise. First, there is the matter of identity, since there were four "Mrs. Senator Camerons" in the 1870s. Margaret Brua Cameron, wife of Senator Simon Cameron of Pennsylvania, cannot be the woman in question since she died in 1874. Simon's son, J. Donald Cameron, succeeded his father to the Senate in March, 1877, and his first wife can be ruled out because she too died in 1874. His second wife did not become "Mrs. Senator Cameron" until 1879. If the wives of the Pennsylvania Camerons can be eliminated, this leaves Mary Baker Cameron (1835-1907), wife of Angus Cameron, senator from Wisconsin from 1875 to 1885. According to an obituary, Mary Cameron possessed considerable charm and had "entered heartily into the social life of the city and was a social leader in Washington during Senator Cameron's long term as United States senator."[93]

The second question is whether Coues was having an affair with the woman. The question presents itself not simply because Coues wrote poems to her but, rather, because he was apparently having affairs with other women in these years. On September 3, 1877, Coues wrote to Baird from Oakland, Maryland, saying that he was "taking a little vacation, much needed." Likewise, in a letter to Hayden from Oakland, Coues told his chief that he was "taking my sorely needed rest for awhile."[94] No doubt he deserved some respite from his labors with the survey, but the "Book of Dates" tells a different story: "Spent latter part of this summer [1877] with Miss F. F. at Oakland, Md." Perhaps he was a bit more candid about his stay at Oakland in a letter to John Wesley Powell: "This is a famous place for work, as my time is absolutely my own, with no distraction & *no questions asked*."[95]

The "Book of Dates" also informs us that in August, 1879, Coues spent "about a month . . . at Atlantic City, N.J. (Had not then met Mrs. S. O. A.) Our relations must have begun this fall, about the time of [the] opening of the [National Medical] College—say Oct., 1879." Very likely Mrs. S. O. A. was S. Olivia Weston-Aiken, who will be discussed in a later chapter.

The identity of Miss F. F. is still unknown. We cannot know with certainty that Coues was having affairs with either of these women, or Mrs. Cameron. Yet these entries in his own journal suggest extramarital activity.

We were unable to learn anything about Mrs. Coues' role in or reaction to all this womanizing. In the next chapter we can only conjecture that her husband's activities led her to work for his banishment from Washington.

NOTES

1. Coues' "Book of Dates" (1876).
2. *Bull. U.S. Geol. and Geogr. Surv. Terrs.*, I (Washington, D.C.: Government Printing Office, 1875), 4.
3. George Montague Wheeler (1842-1905) headed the Army's western geological survey from 1871 to 1879. He retired, with the rank of major, in 1888.
4. Coues, ed., "Contributions to the Natural History of Kerguelen Island" (1875); Kidder and Coues, "Oology, etc." and "A Study of *Chionis minor*" (1876). Jerome Henry Kidder (1842-89), naval surgeon, served as the

medical officer of the transit-of-Venus expedition, 1874-75. He is remembered as the founder of the Naval Museum of Hygiene.

5. Coues to Baird, July 11, 1876.

6. "Geological and Geographical Surveys," House Exec. Doc. 81, 45th Cong., 2d sess., 5.

7. Coues to Baird, July 11, 1876.

8. "Scientific News," *Amer. Naturalist*, X (Aug., 1876), 504.

9. Coues, "Au Revoir (?)" (1876), 299.

10. *Ibid.* Despite his generally sympathetic view of the American Indian, Coues had no use for Sitting Bull: "In the course of his long career of professional scoundrelism and criminality, he probably made more mischief, and did more damage than any other contemporary Indian" (Coues, ed., *Forty Years a Fur Trader* (1898), II, 430n).

11. No biographical data on these men have been found. At the conclusion of the expedition Coues expressed his gratitude for their "zealous and efficient services" ("Dr. Coues' Colorado Expedition," *Forest and Stream*, Nov. 2, 1876, 200).

12. Unless otherwise noted, we have used the "Book of Dates" for the dates and localities of Coues' itinerary. For fuller details of this journey, see Brodhead, "A Naturalist in the Colorado Rockies" (1975).

13. Fort D. A. Russell was established in 1867 to protect workers constructing the Union Pacific railroad. Camp Carlin, officially known as Cheyenne Depot, was created later in the same year and dismantled in 1890. Fort D. A. Russell was renamed Fort Francis E. Warren in 1930 and later became Francis E. Warren Air Base.

14. A year before his death in 1898 Gilliss was elevated to the position of Assistant Quartermaster General, with the rank of colonel.

15. Julia S. Gilliss, "Prairie Dogs as Pets," *Rod and Gun*, Sept. 2, 1876, 362 (introduction by Coues).

16. "Dr. Coues' Colorado Expedition," 200.

17. *Ibid.*

18. Coues, "Notice of Mrs. Maxwell's Exhibit of Colorado Mammals" (1879), 221-22.

19. *Ibid.*, 221.

20. *Ibid.;* "Dr. Coues' Colorado Expedition," 200.

21. Coues, *Fur-Bearing Animals* (1877), 141, 285.

22. Coues and Allen, *Monographs of North American Rodentia* (1877), 384, 446, 735n, 816.

23. *Ibid.*, 218-20; Coues, "Notice of Mrs. Maxwell's Exhibit of Colorado Mammals," 220.

24. Coues, "Reversion of the Dog to the Feral State" (1876).

25. Coues, "The Prairie Wolf, or Coyoté: *Canis latrans*" (1873), 385, 388.

26. *Annual Report of the Board of Regents of the Smithsonian Institution . . .1876* (Washington, D.C.: Government Printing Office, 1877), 57.

27. Coues, "Wanted!" (1874), 129.

28. Coues, *Fur-Bearing Animals*, 151. Martha Ann Dartt Maxwell (1831-81) kept the collection in Boulder for many years. Later in her life she removed it to

Denver. Shortly after Mrs. Maxwell's death, her daughter asked Coues for advice on how to deposit the collection in the Smithsonian or some other worthy museum; see Mabel Maxwell to Coues, July 26, 1881, J. A. Allen Mss., American Museum of Natural History. We do not know Coues' response, if any. Sadly, Mrs. Maxwell's life work was sold to persons who allowed the specimens to deteriorate and disappear; see Junius T. Henderson, "A Pioneer Venture in Habitat Grouping," *Procs. Amer. Assn. Museums*, IX (1911), 90-91.

29. Coues' "Book of Dates" (1878).

31. Coues to A. K. Fisher, Apr. 29, 1897. A copy of this letter was sent to the authors on Dec. 3, 1976, by Joseph Ewan, professor of botany, Tulane University.

32. For a full listing of the publications of the Hayden survey, see L. F. Schmeckebier, "Catalogue and Index of the Publications of the Hayden, King, Powell, and Wheeler Surveys . . .," *Bull. U.S. Geol. Surv.*, no. 222 (1904), 9-37.

33. Coues, *Fur-Bearing Animals*, iii.

34. *Ibid.*

35. *Ibid.*, iv.

36. *Ibid.*, vi-viii.

37. *Ibid.*, 2.

38. *Annual Report of the Board of Regents of the Smithsonian Institution . . .1875* (Washington, D.C.: Government Printing Office, 1876), 50; *Annual Report . . . 1877*, 45.

39. Allen, "Biographical Memoir," 419-20.

40. Sterling, *Last of the Naturalists: The Career of C. Hart Merriam* (1974), 199-205.

41. Allen, "Biographical Memoir," 420.

42. Coues and Allen, *Monographs of North American Rodentia*, v.

43. Jordan, *Days of a Man* (1922), I, 159, 177-78.

44. *Amer. Naturalist*, XII (Feb., 1878), 123n.

45. *Annual Report of the Board of Regents of the Smithsonian Institution . . . 1879* (Washington, D.C.: Government Printing Office, 1880), 69.

46. Batchelder, "An Account of the Nuttall Ornithological Club, 1873 to 1919" (1937), 30, 32-33.

47. Coues to Allen, Dec. 3, 1878.

48. The *Washington World and Citizen-Soldier* ceased publication on Feb. 9, 1884, and had by that date published nine volumes. From May to Oct., 1880, it was known as the *National Citizen-Soldier*. After Nov. 19, 1881, it was called the *Washington Weekly World and Citizen-Soldier*.

49. Hume, *Ornithologists of the U.S. Army Medical Corps*, 80.

50. Robert Barnwell Roosevelt (1829-1906), lawyer, political figure, and nature writer of New York City. His concern with reform and conservation considerably influenced his nephew, Theodore Roosevelt.

51. Coues to Hayden, Nov. 6, 1878 (transcription), J. V. Howell Collection, Box 20, Archive of Contemporary History, University of Wyoming.

52. Charles Page Coues lived only to 1879.

53. Coues, "Our Washington Letter. Zoology and Comparative Anatomy" (1877).

54. Coues' "Book of Dates" (1880). In his letter to Allen on Mar. 22 Coues reported, "My oration was a great success."

55. For more details of Coues' participation in the controversy, see Brodhead, "Elliott Coues and the Sparrow War" (1971).

56. J. O. Skinner, "The House Sparrow," *Annual Report of the Board of Regents of the Smithsonian Institution . . .1904* (Washington, D.C.: Government Printing Office, 1905), 424.

57. *Ibid.,* 426.

58. Thomas G. Gentry, *The House Sparrow at Home and Abroad . . .* (Philadelphia: Claxton, Remsen, & Haffelfinger, 1878), 33-35.

59. Skinner, "House Sparrow," 424.

60. Coues, "Catalogue of the Birds of North America Contained in the Museum of the Essex Institute" (1868), 283-84.

61. Coues, *Key to North American Birds (1872)*, 146.

62. Coues, *Birds of the Northwest* (1874), 64.

63. Coues, *Check List of North American Birds*, 2d ed. (1882), 57.

64. Coues, "On the Present Status of *Passer domesticus*," 182-83.

65. Beecher (1813-87), from his pulpit at the Plymouth Church of Brooklyn, became the best-known preacher of his day. He was famous for accepting the concept of evolution and for rejecting the concept of hell.

66. Beecher, "Star Paper," *Christian Union*, XVI (Aug., 1877), 103.

67. Coues, "On the Present Status of *Passer domesticus*," 184.

68. "Dr. Coues' Column," *Osprey*, I (May, 1897), 124. Bergh (1823-1888), an American writer, diplomat, and philanthropist, founded the ASPCA in 1866.

69. Coues, "The Sparrow Pest in Australia" (1882), 140-41.

70. William Brewster (1851-1919), New England ornithologist, was the author of several important studies, including *The Birds of the Cambridge Region of Massachusetts* (1906). He was a founder of the Nuttall Ornithological Club and the American Ornithologists' Union and served as president of both.

71. Coues, "On the Present Status of *Passer domesticus*," 184-91.

72. *Ibid.,* 185.

73. *Ibid.,* 191.

74. For example, Coues, "Habits of the English Sparrow" (1882).

75. *New York Times,* July 18, 1883, 3.

76. Skinner, "House Sparrow," 427.

77. Walter B. Barrows, *The English Sparrow (Passer domesticus) in North America, Especially in Its Relations to Agriculture,* U.S. Department of Agriculture, Division of Econ. Orn. and Mamm., Bull. no. 1 (1889).

78. "Dr. Coues' Column," *Osprey*, I (Apr., 1897), 113.

79. Coues, "The Documents in the Bendire Business" (1897), 23.

80. "Correspondence," *Nidologist,* IV (May, 1897), 106-7.

81. Coues, "Documents in the Bendire Business," 22-23.

82. "Dr. Coues' Column," *Osprey*, I (May, 1897), 124. We wonder what Coues' reactions would have been had he known that the A.O.U. presented the Elliott Coues Award for 1975 to Richard Johnston and Robert K. Selander for their study of the evolution of the English sparrow in North America.

83. Barrus, *Life and Letters of John Burroughs,* I, 146-47.
84. Coues, "Third Instalment of American Ornithological Bibliography" (1880), 527. The piece also appeared in *Rod and Gun,* Feb. 3, 1877, 277.
85. In his "Third Instalment of American Ornithological Bibliography" Coues states (p. 544) that the poem was "Reprinted in *The Country,* Dec. 1, 1877, and elsewhere."
86. We have been unable to find any information on Caulfield.
87. Ballou, "Bibliographical Manual of American Naturalists" (1880), 221.
88. Yarrow, "Personal Recollections of Old Medical Officers," 588.
89. Chapman, *Autobiography of a Bird-Lover,* 74.
90. Coues, *Field Ornithology* (1874), 42.
91. Coues, "Imagination" (1877), 455, 457-59.
92. *Ibid.,* 459.
93. *La Crosse* (Wis.) *Chronicle,* Oct. 10, 1907.
94. Coues to Hayden, Aug. 7, 1877 (transcription), Howell Collection.
95. Coues to Powell, Aug. 24, 1877, "Letters Received by John Wesley Powell, Director of the Geographical and Geological Survey of the Rocky Mountain Region, 1869-79," Microcopy no. 156, Roll 3, National Archives Microfilm Publications.

CHAPTER XIV

Agony in Arizona

In a lifetime of receiving accolades, it is difficult to guess which one, in Coues' mind, was the greatest. There is, however, no difficulty in designating the lowest point of his career. The Adjutant General's Office, through Special Orders no. 251, paragraph 4, dated November 26, 1880, directed him to report for duty as a medical officer at Whipple Barracks, Arizona Territory.[1] Sixteen years earlier the same assignment had helped to launch his career as a naturalist. By 1880 he was America's best-known ornithologist. Sending him back to Arizona was, at best, an insult.

Nevertheless Coues followed orders and left Washington on December 3, going first to the naval hospital at Brooklyn, New York, where his half-brother, naval surgeon Samuel F. Coues, was stationed.[2] Since Coues' letters of this period frequently emphasized, as we shall see, that he was acutely ill, it is likely that he called on his half-brother for professional treatment. While at the hospital, he was temporarily cheered by a visit from his friend, J. A. Allen.[3]

After a few weeks at Brooklyn, Coues boarded a train for the West and, according to his "Book of Dates," followed this itinerary: "Went to Fort Whipple [renamed Whipple Barracks in 1879] by railroad via Sacramento, Cal., to Maricopa, Arizona [about 100 miles southeast of Prescott], thence by stage Dec. 28; arrived probably Dec. 29; reported for military duty to Medical Director A. K. Smith[4] and General O. B. Willcox[5]; S. N. Benjamin, Asst. Adj. Gen'l."[6]

Early in January, 1881, he wrote to Allen in an optimistic mood:

> You will be glad to hear of my safe arrival, and that my lines have fallen in a pleasant place—where I laid a cornerstone for myself in '64 & '65. Every stick and stone is familiar, but a grand military establishment, with all modern improvements has replaced the stockade and the Apache. It is perhaps the most isolated place in the U.S. except Alaska—travelled over 4000 m. by rail, and 150 by stage. I have received every consideration, shall

have no professional duty, am attached to Hdqrs. and going on a combined inspecting and shooting tour in a few days. Though not fully recovered, the change of scene and the bracing air of these 6000 feet mts. are doing wonders for me. . . .

Despite the almost cheerful tone of this letter, Coues' second tour of duty in Arizona, which lasted for nearly nine months, was utterly miserable.

Why did the Army suddenly treat its distinguished naturalist as just another assistant surgeon, suited for nothing better than service as a medical officer on the remote frontier? One interpretation of Special Orders no. 251 is that the military establishment was too stupid or short-sighted to appreciate Coues' scientific reputation. Coues himself, in his published works, blamed the War Department for the "annoyance" and "outrage"[7] of being forced back into "tent-life in unbookish Arizona,"[8] and lashed out at "the obstacles in the way of good scientific work which the Army delights to furnish,"[9] thus lending support to the notion that the whole affair was the result of Army pig-headedness.

This view is clearly unacceptable. Throughout Coues' many years of Army service his superiors had been more than generous to him. Again and again he was allowed ample time and facilities to carry out his scientific objectives. Ever since 1873, when he had been attached to the Northern Boundary Survey, he had been an Army surgeon in name only. Obviously more complex—or darker—forces were behind Coues' virtual banishment.

As usual, Coues turned immediately to Baird for help. In a series of letters from Whipple Barracks Coues poured out a bewildering variety of explanations for his predicament—some of them contradictory—accompanied by pleas for Baird to use his influence in getting Coues back to Washington.

At first Coues wrote, March 21, 1881, that he had himself obtained the assignment in the West because of his "break-down in health," which had been "more serious than many of my friends were aware—so much so, that the enforced idleness resulting from the army order I secured was considered necessary to save my life." Later, in another letter that same day, he maintained that he merely accepted the order for reasons of health and wailed that the order had been "secretly procured by my worst enemy, in a very unusual manner." Still later, on March 27, 1881, he revealed the identity of his "worst enemy"—his wife, Jeannie Augusta McKinney Coues: ". . . my whole career is at present blocked, in the deadlock brought about by the most devilish malignity and ingenuity of

my infamous wife, whose subtle antagonism has been manifested for
years in every possible endeavor to thwart and hamper and degrade
me. . . . I have been utterly helpless; and so sure did a long matured plot
succeed, that thus far I can see no way out of my overwhelming troubles.
She is in full possession, has my name, house, children, and money. . . ."

Coues insisted that he was "as unjustly, cruelly, and terribly
WRONGED a man as you ever knew." In his letters to Baird in the spring of
1881 Coues repeated these and other frantic denunciations of his wife's
machinations and the protestations of his own innocence. His tone is so
desperate that the reader might well wonder if Coues' breakdown was
more mental than physical. For example, he told Baird on March 27: "I
should have destroyed myself last fall, when my wife fired her infernal
train, so terrible were the effects upon my mind, had not a determination to defeat her evil purposes come to my aid as a fixed and controlling
power."

With Coues supplying such a variety of explanations, it is impossible
to know the true facts behind his exile in Arizona. Despite his denials of
wrong-doing, Coues, in his correspondence with Baird, let slip a few
hints that his wife's "malignity" had been triggered by his relationships
with other women. He told Baird on March 21 that the order sending
him to Arizona came about

> . . . when I had carelessly allowed appearances to falsely tell against me
> so heavily that any attempt at self-justification or self defense seemed
> hopeless, even had I not been too sick to make the attempt. I went away
> quietly as the best if not the only thing to be done, all things considered, and
> still believe this course was the wisest, though it left me unheard under
> seriously compromising imputations, and in fact looked more like confes-
> sion than justification. I am paying the penalty of a *blunder*, not of a crime,
> being absolutely innocent excepting in a disregard of conventionalities,
> which was partly my pride, and partly my absorption in work, and chiefly my
> carelessness. But after all, the motive that chiefly influenced me in accepting
> the order was my health—for there is no question that the end would have
> come soon had I not brought up with round turn, the way over-work and
> domestic unhappiness had been wearing me for years.

"Supposing," he wrote later in March, "that all such as brought
against me be true—it should not be—it would not be enough to justify
the snuffing out of a life of so much past accomplishment and future
promise as mine." He asked Baird, ". . . have you not confidence enough
in me to believe there may be another and truer side of the story than the
slander which has doubtless reached you? And does not my character

and position warrant my friends in giving me a chance to retrieve myself, even supposing the worst allygations [*sic*] have any basis in fact?"

The possibility that Coues' predicament was the result of his philandering is supported by some remarks made by William Brewster in a letter to Allen of December 10, 1880: "I am sorry to hear a scandalous report from Washington affecting Dr. Coues. I trust it is untrue, or at least much exaggerated."

In a letter to Allen of January 3, 1881, Coues suggested that the damage to his health was linked to the damage to his reputation:

> The fact is, Allen, I could not have *lived* long the way I was going on— You saw [at Brooklyn] how shattered I was—and it was better to break up temporarily at any sacrifice than break down permanently. I have but a dim and confused recollection of my last two weeks in W[ashington]—but it is over, and let the past be past. I feel as if I had awakened from a terrible nightmare—and though the cost to my good name can hardly be estimated, I can stand that, to be free, and recover my powers of mind and body.

Throughout his unhappy months in Arizona he corresponded regularly with Allen. In the letters he made frequent, often impassioned protestations of friendship. Certainly he needed a person such as Allen for a friend during this time of troubles. Perhaps Coues hesitated to pour out his heart to his Washington associates who would know more of the facts of the case and therefore be unsympathetic. Allen, in addition to his kindly nature, was, by virtue of his residence in Cambridge, geographically removed from the scene of Coues' sorry plight.

Assuming that Mrs. Coues was instrumental in getting her husband shunted off to the frontier, the question arises as to how she accomplished it. Again we have only Coues' version, which is largely a series of accusations that his wife had influence with the War Department and the higher reaches of the administration. Coues told Baird on March 27 that she had "the ear of the Kitchen Cabinet." He exonerated the Surgeon General's Office ("I am positive of the friendliness of the S. G. O.") and stated that "I do not think I have an active enemy in Washington except my wife and two or three women in a certain clique, who are her cronies and dupes." To another correspondent Coues complained: "I find myself cut off in my career by a senseless, useless and atrociously unjust military order, which was procured by a clique of enemies from the War Dept., over the heads of my immediate superiors in the Surgeon General's Office."[10]

Whatever the reason and whoever the persons behind the Arizona assignment, Coues was justified in believing that, for him, a return to

Washington was not only "personally the *gravest possible* matter" but "also
a matter of interest to science."[11] So, for the sake of his own mental well-
being and of science, Coues begged Baird in April to seek every means to
get him back to Washington. "For God's sake, Professor, help me out of
this ditch, where I have been left to lie after being butchered in as foul a
plot as was ever gotten up to destroy an innocent if unwary man; and
discuss the merits of the case if need be, when I am on my feet again."

As he had done in the past, Baird responded by trying to help his
protégé. First he suggested a transfer to a station at Point Barrow,
Alaska. Although Alaska could hardly have been an improvement over
Arizona for Coues, the duty was to be only for one season. After this
brief stint, Baird explained, Coues could come back to Washington. In
any event, Coues at first declined, stating "that my health would scarcely
be equal to the demands necessarily made upon physical endurance of
the exposure incident to such a position; besides which I have already in
hand so many scientific interests, still held in abeyance by the protracted
result of my long sickness last fall, that I should hesitate to accept any
new reponsibilities, favorable as would be the circumstances of the
proffered engagement for the prosecution of my favorite studies."[12]

Baird evidently had discussed the Alaskan possibility with the
Surgeon General's Office and Coues had written to Assistant Surgeon
General Crane. Coues further informed Baird in the letter of March 21
that he would prefer either a "return exactly to my former status" or "the
position now vacant in the Army Medical Museum."[13]

Yet within a week after rejecting the Point Barrow proposition,
Coues reconsidered, writing to Baird on March 27 that he would indeed
go to Alaska if it were only for a single season "and especially if, as I now
think probable, it *might lead up* to my return to W[ashington] quietly and
naturally." Then, with all-too-obvious craftiness, he added: "In arranging any preliminaries of my possible going to Alaska, would it not be
proper or necessary for me to confer with you and other authorities in
person? It seems to me that *that* might be a short and easy first step."[14]

Also, in a letter of May 23 to Joseph Leidy,[15] Coues made the claim
"that an act of Congress, (ordering a work of which I am the author, on
which thousands of dollars have already been expended, and which
cannot be completed unless I have access to a library and museum,) has
been arbitrarily set aside by military order." He pursued the same
argument in his March 27 letter to Baird: ". . . work of mine ordered by
the Government ought to be official enough reason for recall."[16]

Coues sought help from Leidy as well as Baird: from a letter of April

6—"I beg to engage your friendly attention, and if necessary your influence, with reference to securing a position in some college as professor of human or comparative anatomy, having already had as you know, several years experience in teaching that branch of the medical course of study." Leidy apparently responded with the suggestion that Coues look into a vacancy at Princeton College, because Coues replied on May 23 that he was "under the impression that the Chair of Biology at Princeton has already been filled."

It will be noted that the job possibilities about which he and Leidy were corresponding were civilian posts. Even while trying to secure a more favorable military assignment Coues was inclining toward resignation of his commission. He told Leidy on May 23 that he was "at the age of 40 [actually 39], and unfitted by long absorption in other things for the practice of medicine." To Baird he wrote on March 27 that he was "unfitted for the professional duties of a medical officer, and have in fact nothing more to hope for in life if my scientific career is closed."

He summed up his relationship to the military (or at least his interpretation of the relationship) with this statement:

> I know the Surgeon General's Office to be entirely friendly, and in fact that the settlement of my case as I suggest would relieve great embarrassment. It is perfectly understood there that I am by taste and training unfitted for routine medical practice in the army, and it is felt that "reduction to the ranks" is hardly compatible with my scientific record & position. I accepted my recent orders because I was too sick to raise hand or voice in protest. I have entirely recovered, and am as sound and strong in body & mind, as ever. My present position is one of the utmost embarrassment & humiliation; it is simply out of the question for me to setle down to Army life, after what I have been and that I still am; and if there be no other escape, I shall be compelled to resign.[17]

2

While Coues was committing himself to thoughts of getting out of Arizona—and the Army—his superiors in the Department of Arizona were certainly showing every indication that they considered distinguished ornithologist Elliott Coues to be nothing more than Assistant Surgeon Coues. Not only did he perform medical chores at Whipple Barracks, but, as entries from the "Book of Dates" show, he was also assigned temporarily to other posts within the department. Orders of January 3, 1881, directed him to Fort Verde,[18] where he remained a few days on a tour of inspection. On February 24 he was ordered to Fort

Mohave to serve as a temporary post surgeon. He left Whipple Barracks that day by stage and stayed at Mohave from March 1 to 11. By mid-March he was back at Whipple. On March 28 and on May 2 he served on two boards of survey. During the latter half of May he was again at Fort Verde.

On May 30 he received orders relieving him of his duties at Verde and assigning him as medical officer for a military expedition led by Lieutenant Colonel William R. Price,[19] of the 6th Cavalry, to the Grand Canyon country of northwestern Arizona. The purpose of the expedition was to learn more of the condition of the Havasupai and Walapai Indians. In a work published almost twenty years later Coues gave many details of that reconnaissance:

> We went from Fort Verde, on the river of that name, to Fort Whipple and Prescott, and thence through Williamson's and Chino valleys, in which latter we camped at Roger's ranch, June 4. Next day we flanked the west base of the Picacho and followed an Indian trail to Cullen's well, as it was called, near the base of Mt. Floyd. The proper name of this tinaja or tank is Kerlin's—so called from Beale's[20] clerk of 1857-58, F. E. Kerlin, whose name is cut in the rocks. It is on the Beale road, but hard to find, at the head of a ravine, and is not living water. On the 6th we sought unsuccessfully for Kisaha tank, and returned to Kerlin's. On the 7th, with a detour eastward along the Beale road, and then a turn northward past that other elevation [Pineveta Peak] which is 6 miles due N. of Mt. Floyd and about 7,000 feet high, we kept on north with some westing to what was known in those days as Black tank, but is now lettered Wagathile tank of the U.S.G.S. maps. This was a stretch of some 30 miles, not halfway to the rancheria [Indian village] of which we were in quest, and the last water hence to Cataract cañon. Black tank was a nasty hole in the rocks, containing perhaps 5,000 gallons of dead water and filth, in which lurked an enormous number of the repulsive "fishes with legs," or axolotls, also called guaholotes—a species of *Amblystoma*.[21] Here we rested on the 8th, and next day made a straight break due north, along a dim Indian trail, over good ground partly wooded, to a dry camp.[22]

On June 10, after a ten-mile march, the party arrived at its first main destination, Cataract Canyon, the home of the Havasupais. They came "abruptly to the brink of the precipice—a sharp-edged jump-off of perhaps a thousand feet."[23] Next, a small group of soldiers led by Lieutenant H. P. Kingsbury[24] began the harrowing process of reaching the Havasupai village at the canyon's bottom. Coues, Lieutenant Carl F. Palfrey[25] of the Corps of Engineers, and "an old Arizonian scout" accompanied the Kingsbury contingent. Coues later wrote that the experience "was enough to make my head swim":

There was no side cañon here for gradual descent—the firm level ground gave no hint of the break before us till we were actually upon the verge, and when the soldiers lined up to look down an involuntary murmer of astonishment ran through the ranks. Dismounting and going in single file, each man leading his horse, we took the dizzy trail—a narrow footpath, in many parts of which a misstep would have been destruction to man or beast. The way zigzagged at first for some distance, on the "switchback" principle by which railroads sometimes make grades otherwise impracticable; the face of the precipice was so steep that, as we filed along, those of us at the head of the procession looked up to see the other sections of the train almost overhead—certainly a fall of any man there would have been right on top of us. Then the trail took a long lurch to the left with little descent, hugging the face of the cliff, and we looked like a row of ants on a wall. This brought us at length to the head of a great talus, down which the trail zigzagged—the incline was too steep for straight descent, probably at an angle of 45°. This fetched us into the bed of Cataract cañon. . . .[26]

While in the canyon, Coues gave the other members of the party even more anxiety when, as was his habit, he strayed from the column in search of birds and became lost. "Indian scouts were sent out upon his trail. They, expecting to find him dead from thirst, planned a division of his clothing and equipments, and were sorely disppointed at finding him at one of [the] small 'seep' springs, in the wall of Cataract Creek, serenely lunching upon roasted mountain sheep."[27]

Coues tells us little about the meeting with the Indians other than that "the Havasupai chief, who had been advised of our coming, was there to meet us with some of his men, all mounted; and he took us up the cañon about five miles to a place where there was a scanty aguage [i.e., water supply], not sufficing for the wants of the whole party."[28] Although his memory of the purpose and details of the meeting with the Indians was slight, he later produced a full word-picture of their canyon home:

The bed of the main cañon sometimes runs water from near its head downward; but is ordinarily dry almost down to the Havasupai settlement. When I traversed it, the bed was dry as tinder, sandy, rocky, and choked with cactus; only here and there was some seepage through the walls, either trickling idly away and soon evaporating, or, if stronger, collecting in some little rocky tank. The scene changes as if by magic at the point said, where Cataract creek bursts out of the ground at a beautiful spring. . . . The water is of a deep blue color, and so heavily charged with lime that it forms stalactites wherever it drips, and incrusts everything upon which it dries. . . . The arable land, including that rendered available by artificial irrigation, is probably not over 400 acres; on this little farm stretched along the creek the Indians raised their corn, beans, melons, squashes, peaches, apricots, and sunflower-seeds. They lived in brush lodges scattered over their secluded demesne, except some whom I found occupying caves in the rocky sides of the cañon which they had walled up, quite like the prehistoric cliff-dwellers. These hermits seemed quite content with their half-underground lot, and only anxious to be let alone.[29]

He likewise recorded the party's journey down the canyon on June 11 to the village of the Havasupais: ". . . we retraced our steps down the cañon and kept on in its bed till we reached the wonderful blue spring above described and the rancheria of the Indians—a distance from last night's camp of about 25 miles, as we had struck the cañon some 20 miles above the living water."[30]

The party remained in the village until the following day, and by June 15 they had returned to Black Tank, where they stayed until the 16th.[31] On the 18th they reached Peach Springs, about sixty miles southwest of the Havasupai village, whence Coues and Lieutenant Palfrey pushed down into the Grand Canyon of the Colorado River:

> The trail was plain, and though then unimproved, we made the descent on horseback, only finding it convenient to dismount once or twice at some little jump-off or awkward twist of the path, and noting how readily a carriage road could be worked through even the worst places. . . . This Peach Springs or New Creek cañon which we descended was dry as a bone till it ran into Diamond Creek cañon, nearly at a right angle; it is only a collateral cañon of the latter. The junction is about a mile and a half from the main river. Turning sharp to the left at this point, we followed down Diamond creek till we stood on the brink of the vast current of the Colorado which rushes into the abyss.[32]

Although Coues acknowledged that the "sensation at the sight was satisfactory," he went on to contradict the impressions of millions of tourists from his own day to the present: ". . . the view was decidedly disappointing in spectacular effect. There is nothing specially inspiring in blank walls of rock, such as shut out every prospect except that of a patch of sky directly overhead; and this is all that is visible at the depth of some six thousand feet, where Diamond creek makes its modest contribution to the mighty flood."[33]

Coues and Palfrey spread their saddle blankets over some "scrawny bushes," crept underneath to escape the heat, and ate lunch. Coues decided upon a bath in the river, "more for the name of the thing," he wrote, "than because I needed it." Then he and Palfrey began their journey back to the main party. "The round trip [from Peach Springs to the Grand Canyon and back] was thus easily made between an early breakfast and a late supper, and I have never regretted the 32-mile ride."[34]

After he and Palfrey had returned to the main body of the expedition, the soldiers had the following itinerary for the next week: "[June] 20, 21, to and at Milkweed; 22 to edge of Grand Canon; 23, 24, at Milkweed; 25 to Hackberry; 26 to Willows; 27 to Oaks and Willows."[35] The purpose of the reconnaissance of this area was to gather information on the condition of the Walapai Indians. Because of the intrusion of railroad interests and settlers, the Walapais were deprived of much of their former hunting grounds and water supply. Their desperate situation was duly and sympathetically reported later by Colonel Price. Curiously, most of the Walapai Indians remained peaceable. Only one of their leaders, a subchief named Little Captain, threatened trouble.[36] By July, 1881, Little Captain had been taken prisoner, and it was perhaps the Price party which had arrested him, because Coues, in writing later about the expedition, stated that "a threatened outbreak [of theWalapais] was averted by putting the chief in irons."[37]

It was apparently this threat that prompted the Price expedition to reactivate temporarily the abandoned Camp Hualpai, which the soldiers renamed Camp Price.[38] This they did on June 28 on the return march to Whipple Barracks. On the next day they passed again through Williamson's Valley and, on the 30th, reached Whipple Barracks.[39]

The main result of the expedition was Price's recommendation that a new reservation be provided for the destitute Walapais. On January 4, 1883, President Arthur ordered the creation of a reservation with exactly the boundaries suggested by Price.[40]

The march to the Grand Canyon revived Coues' health and spirits, at least temporarily. On July 1, after his return, he informed Allen:

> Have been out scouting with troops for a month—and it would make your heart glad to see the rugged, browned "stalwart" I have become—do you remember me at Brooklyn? How I wish you could have been with me. It would have done *you* as much good too. The trip was a hard one—terrible country to get over, great suffering from want of water, heat, & fatigue—and in one case imminent peril—but I seemed to imbibe new strength from dear old Mother Earth every time I lay in her stron[g] but kindly arms, under the stars. . . . There is good in everything, even in such apparently unmixed misfortune as mine—and with the regained flush of physical vigor comes the *balance* as well as the strength of mind.

3

For Coues the expedition was the one memorable adventure of an otherwise maddening year. Although he told Allen in his letter of July 1 that he had not taken a gun along and had been "fully occupied in professional duties & in taking care of my body—so did no science," he had been able to make some scientific observations along the way. At Black Tank, June 7, he took particular notice of a pair of "White-bellied Wrens" (Bewick's wren, *Thryomanes bewickii*). On the second visit to this spot a week later, finding that the wrens had deserted the area, he collected their nest and later published a full description of it in a note for the *Bulletin of the Nuttall Ornithological Club*. In the same note he turned his comments on the "Carolina" (mourning) doves in the area into a condemnation of Arizona:

> These latter birds are extremely abundant all over Arizona and in the dry season they are often at such straits for water as to congregate in immense flocks at the water-holes, few and far between, which alone render it possible to traverse some parts of the unblest Territory. On the morning of which I write, reveille was sounded by the clapping and whistling of a thousand eager wings, now venturing near, then frightened from the coveted water where men and animals were crowding. In other times, the Dove brought tidings of dry land; in Arizona now, where everything goes by contraries, river-sites are many, but the sight of a Dove is a surer sign of water.[41]

While in the Grand Canyon with Palfrey, Coues had been surprised to find certain birds, namely Gambel's quail and the black phoebe (*Sayornis nigricans*), "so far below the surface of the earth."[42]

Earlier in the year, on February 20, 1881, Coues had obtained a hybrid (later turned over to the National Museum) of the yellow-shafted and red-shafted flickers.[43] Thus he would probably not have been dismayed by the A.O.U.'s action of 1973 lumping the two forms, along with the gilded flicker, into one species, the common flicker (*Colaptes auratus*). It was also in February that Coues wrote another of his ornithological poems, "Moriturus" or the "Song of the dying swan." The poem appeared in the second (1884) and subsequent editions of the *Key to North American Birds*.[44]

Sometime during his stay at Whipple Barracks he renewed his acquaintance with Willard Rice, the old Indian fighter, whom Coues described as "an amateur naturalist of excellent powers of observation." On the basis of Rice's testimony, Coues reaffirmed his earlier belief that the king vulture (*Sarcoramphus papa*) of Mexico occasionally entered Arizona.[45]

He passed on to Allen some information that supported his friend's well-known views on geographical variation among animals: "I find that all the mice are darkest in wet places, palest in dry places, almost bleached in the desert, exactly as in the birds. I find also the diminution in size of peripheral parts, like feet & ears in cold countries, and their enlargement in warm ones; and finally a great difference in the furring of the feet, ears and tail, according to temperature—none of which will be new to you!"[46]

Other than the minor writings that resulted from his Arizona observations of 1881, Coues was able to do some work on a couple of his more important projects. He read and corrected the proof sheets for the second edition of his *Check List*[47] and for the first of the two volumes of *New England Bird Life*. Technically, the latter work was written by Winfrid A. Stearns and merely edited by Coues. Actually, the prose was largely Coues' own. To Allen he confided on February 8, 1881, that he regretted having shouldered the responsbility for what he called "the Crazy book": "I wish the whole thing were in the bottomless pit. I was foolish to undertake it, just for the asking—but wanted to help the poor incompetent fellow out." In a letter of November 15, 1881, he again disparaged the nominal author: "The more I hear of Stearns, the less I fancy co-authorship." When the work was published, knowledgeable reviewers were aware that it was mostly written by Coues.[48]

He also made two modest contributions to the ethnology of Arizona. In a letter datelined "'Suppai Settlement,' Arizona, June 20, 1881," to the editor of the *Nation*, he discussed the origin of the word "Yavasupai."[49] And in the vicinity of Fort Verde, Coues observed "a cliff-house on Beaver Creek at its junction with the Rio Verde, 40 miles from Fort Whipple."[50]

4

Whatever his scientific and literary output in Arizona during 1880-81, it was meager compared to any other period in his career. No one was more furiously and acutely aware of this than Coues himself. The Army's actions continued to enrage and frustrate him. On July 14, 1881, he sent a "request and protest" to Surgeon General Joseph K. Barnes, probably about a transfer. Despite Coues' earlier assurances to Baird that the Surgeon General's Office was not to be blamed for sending him to Arizona, his request was turned down on August 1. In the meantime Coues was sent to Camp Hualpai as post surgeon for most of July and part of August.[51]

During the summer of 1881 his relations with his wife became even worse. He ceased to send money to her, which prompted Jeannie Coues to retain a lawyer, probably, Coues believed, to initiate divorce proceedings.[52] By early July he was complaining that the attorney was "hounding after" him.[53]

He confided to Allen on July 13 that he was prepared to resign his commission as a means of extricating himself from his difficulties: "All that is wanted is my money—all that is attempted is to keep me *here* to earn it. Supposing I decline to sacrifice myself for the benefit of another who has treated me so shamefully?" Concern for his children, he wrote, prevented him from taking any drastic steps, at least for the time being.

The situation was becoming intolerable. On August 23 Coues did manage to wring from the Department of Arizona one concession, Special Orders no. 97, granting him a month's leave of absence, to take effect upon the arrival of a surgeon to relieve him, and further granting permission to apply for an extension of three months. Coues was, of course, determined to use the leave as an opportunity to change his fortunes. He was ready to begin his journey to Washington on September 1 but had to wait until the 3rd for his actual departure, by stage, from Whipple Barracks.[54]

According to his "Book of Dates" he reached Maricopa on the 4th. From there, traveling by rail, his itinerary was: Deming, New Mexico, September 5; Kansas City, the 9th; Chicago, the 10th; and Baltimore, the 11th. Two days later he resumed his travels and went to "Clermont" (Claremont, Virginia?) on September 14. Going by way of Ridge, Maryland, he reached Washington the following day.

Once in the capital, he took his battle immediately to the War Department. On September 24 he applied for a three-month extension of his leave, "tendering resignation to take effect at its expiration if Arizona orders were not revoked."[55] That same day he gave Allen an assessment of the situation:

> . . . and here I shall "stay." It will probably cost me my commission, but I cannot help that. It is hard for any individual to fight a Department, especially the "Force Department," with that cantankerous old galoot [William T.] Sherman sticking his nose in everything. I have taken a terrible old bison by the horns in daring to reappear here at all—but having taken him, I am more afraid to let go than to hold on! Excepting the War Dept.,

everything is lovely: friends are rallying warmly and vigorously. All seem unaffectedly glad to see me, and hope I may win the dreadful fight. As for the "scandal" so-called, it has done its worst long ago, and now the streets could be placarded with it without further injury. I have nothing to lose, and everything to gain; the scare has all been scared out of me, and I am ready to take whatever comes next,—except exile. This is not *Russia!*

He gained a partial victory when on September 29 he was "authorized to delay returning to Arizona till further orders." Nevertheless, on the next day Coues wrote to Allen:

I shall very likely resign, but if so, it will be of my own free will without the slightest pressure. You see they know I have worked up the case carefully for Congress & the press, and *they* don't want the abominable way the order to Arizona was procured raked over. A paper I sent to the War Dept was regarded as *a threat*—and *it was so effective* that I was privately requested to withdraw it, and put in a milder one! I don't know that I will do so. Thus far, I have forced a stay of proceedings and my attitude is simply tentative & expectant, with open declaration that I will accept *no* orders that conflict with the dignity of my scientific position, or interfere with my scientific labors. Isn't all this a good deal to accomplish in a few days, without the slightest resort to "influence" or intrigue, just by boldly presenting the case on its own merits? I *knew* I had only to return to win!

On October 11 he turned in his unconditional resignation, "to take effect Dec. 31."[56] "I had to resign," he informed Allen on October 17. "I could get no consideration at the War Dept.—they said 'Arizona or your commission' and of course I had to wish them good morning."

But it soon became apparent that leaving the Army was no easy matter, lending credence to Coues' belief that his "enemies" had influence in high places. On November 3 President Arthur refused to accept the resignation, and Coues was ordered to return to Arizona. On November 5 he "requested leave of absence on Surgeon's certificate of disability." This, too, was refused, and on the 11th he submitted his resignation once again. This time he was successful; on November 17 the president accepted his resignation.[57]

A letter to Allen of November 19 reveals Coues' joy at being rid of the Army connection and something of the difficulties he experienced in doing so:

. . . you will rejoice with me now—the last possible move of the enemy has been met and foiled—I am free at last, and can speak out now. Fancy the cunning and malignity that had carried a man's family linen to *three* presidents of the United States, and washed it for nearly two years in the

War Department! The last move of the desperate game was the appearance of my wife & her friends before the President, between midnight and morning, to worry out of him the declination of my resignation, on statement that there were "charges" against me, in face of which I should not be permitted to resign. Then I *had* to speak out, and I sent such a paper to the War Dept. as never went there before, showing up the d——d pest—you know at what sacrifice of delicacy & even decency. The Sec'y of War [Robert T. Lincoln] took a firm, just stand, and the matter was for the first time brought fairly before the President, with all the papers in the case. *There were no charges*—nothing but gossip and slander. My resignation was accepted at once, and my record was left clean. Now I am *free*—and if there be any troubles to come they are of a strictly private nature, and I am in position to meet them.

He concluded with these cryptic words: "There is a deeper and darker mystery about the whole affair than any one has fathomed yet. *That* once cleared up, all would be as plain as day, and I, while not blameless, would be seen as the victim of a far greater wrong. But I can never divulge it— and I can only hope and pray that time may roll a wave of oblivion over the long dark tragedy and the crime that came of it. Truth is stranger than fiction—you have in this case one of those tragedies,—rare, thank God—which leaves one forever with the shadow of an unmentionable sorrow."

Even if Coues had remained in the Army and even if he had secured an assignment in the Washington area, his future as a government scientist would have been uncertain. The federal science establishment was at this time experiencing a considerable shaking-up. The bitter rivalries between the Hayden, King, Wheeler, and Powell surveys, along with congressional concern over duplication of the work of the surveys, resulted in 1879 in legislation that consolidated the four agencies into the new U.S. Geological Survey.

In the battle for the directorship of the U.S.G.S., Hayden lost out to Clarence King, former head of the 40th Parallel Survey. Hayden was allowed to remain as an employee of the new survey, but only for the purpose of clearing up the unfinished business of his old agency.[58] This consisted largely of the publishing of the last *Reports* and *Bulletins*. While in Arizona Coues had occasionally performed editorial tasks for Hayden, even though he was no longer the survey's editor.[59] Upon his return to Washington he continued to lend an unofficial editorial hand to Hayden.[60] By February, 1882, he was telling Allen that "the H[ayden] business has been galvinized [*sic*] longer than the condition of the corpse justifies, and B[aird] & others are strongly opposed to having any more of it."

Oddly enough, the combative Coues had managed to avoid the heated struggles between the surveys while he had been with the Hayden survey. In fact, as we have seen, he made published contributions to the Powell and Wheeler surveys, but *not* to King's. So Coues had no prior official connection with the new director. King, moreover, was a powerful force in the Cosmos Club, an organization of Washington's intellectual elite. According to the "Book of Dates," Coues had been elected to membership in the club on December 1, 1879, but he penned to this entry a terse addendum: "Dropped Sept. 1881." Also (and this is pure conjecture), since Coues and the brilliant, often erratic Clarence King were similar in temperament, it is possible that they were cool toward each other.

Although John Wesley Powell, with whom Coues was on good terms, took over the directorship of the U.S.G.S. in 1880, there was no place for a naturalist such as Coues because the new agency was devoted almost exclusively to geology and related sciences.

By 1881 service with the military would have allowed fewer opportunities for scientific studies. "Army science," such as represented by the Wheeler survey, had been attacked by civilian scientists throughout the 1870s, and by the end of that decade the Army was voluntarily disengaging itself from scientific endeavors.[61] In fact, the federal government generally was ceasing to be the great employer of naturalists it once had been. Instead, the nation's universities and larger museums were replacing the government as the centers of research and publication in the natural sciences.

A man of Coues' attainments had no need to worry about finding a suitable position in civilian life. Indeed, he found one quickly and soon was as busy and productive as he had been before his stay in Arizona. Yet in many respects he was, as a scientist, a different man after "that year of hell," as he later called it.[62] He was to continue to publish scientific works, but now they would be confined largely to books and articles for popular consumption or re-editions of earlier volumes. No longer would he produce technical monographs based largely on his own fresh researches and thinking, such as *Birds of the Northwest* or *Fur-Bearing Animals*. Nor would he write other volumes of *Birds of the Colorado Valley* or additional installments of the "Bibliography of Ornithology." The "History of North American Mammals" was never published. The major works of Elliott Coues during the 1880s and 1890s would for the most part relate only indirectly to natural history.

NOTES

1. Coues' "Book of Dates" (1880).
2. *Ibid.*
3. Coues to Allen, undated letter, ca. Dec. 20, 1880.
4. Andrew Kingsbury Smith entered the Army in 1853 as an assistant surgeon. He retired in 1890 with the rank of surgeon and colonel, and died in 1899.
5. Orlando Bolivar Willcox graduated from West Point in 1847. He had a commendable record in the Civil War and later on the frontier. In 1887 he retired with the rank of brigadier general and died in 1907.
6. Samuel Nicoll Benjamin graduated from West Point in 1861 and served there as an assistant professor of mathematics. He also served in the Civil War and in the West. Major Benjamin, a recipient of the Medal of Honor, died in 1886.
7. Coues, "Editor's Preface" to Stearns, *New England Bird Life* (1883), 5-6.
8. Coues, *Check List of North American Birds,* 2d ed. (1882), 77.
9. Coues, "Contributions to the Anatomy of Birds" (1883), 167.
10. Coues to Joseph Leidy, May 23, 1881. This and other letters from Coues to Leidy are in the Leidy Mss., Academy of Natural Sciences of Phildelphia.
11. *Ibid.*
12. Coues to Baird, Mar. 21, 1881 (first letter).
13. In a letter of Apr. 6, 1881, to Allen, he stated that "I was to have Dr. [George A.] Otis's place in the Army Medical Museum, when he died, but missed it."
14. To Allen on May 15, 1881, he wrote: "I made a proviso that I be allowed to come east to settle private affairs—and I fancy—indeed I hope that *blocks* it—for they know d——n well that if I ever set foot in W[ashington] I should not be likely [to] go away."
15. Joseph Leidy (1823-91) was a distinguished surgeon, naturalist, paleontologist, and parasitologist; professor of anatomy, University of Pennsylvania (1853-91); professor of natural history, Swarthmore College (1870-85); president of the Academy of Natural Sciences of Philadelphia (1881-91); and author of *The Ancient Fauna of Nebraska* (1854) and *Fresh Water Rhizopods of North America* (1879).
16. In a note printed in *Nation,* XXX (Apr. 29, 1880), 327, we find some notion of what Coues was talking about: "Congress has recently ordered the publication of vol. xiv of the quarto series of the Hayden Survey publications, being the 'Final Report on Zoology.' This consists of the 'History of North American Mammals,' upon which Dr. Elliott Coues has been engaged for several years. The edition ordered is 5,000 copies, with the necessary illustrations. The work will probably make a volume of some 1,000 pages, fully illustrated with wood engravings in the text and a series of chromolithographic plates. Much of the MS. is ready for the printer, and the appearance of the work will probably not be delayed longer than is required to execute

the illustrations, many of which are already at hand." The authorship of this note has been attributed to Coues himself by McAtee, *Elliott Coues as Represented in "The Nation,"* 327.

17. Coues to Baird, Apr. 7, 1881.

18. Established in 1864, Fort Verde (originally Camp Lincoln) was used advantageously by the Army in its campaign against the Apaches in the 1860s. It was abandoned in 1890. In later years Coues wrote: "I was post surgeon there in 1881, and know how important a military establishment this one had been" (Coues, ed., *On the Trail of a Spanish Pioneer* (1900), II, 462n).

19. William Redwood Price rose to the rank of brigadier general of volunteers in the Civil War. He remained in the regular Army after the war and served for several years with distinction on the frontier; he died in 1881.

20. Edward Fitzgerald Beale (1822-93) began his career as a naval officer and served in the Mexican War. As superintendent of Indian affairs for California (1852-65) and surveyor general of California and Nevada (1861-65), he conducted important surveying expeditions over much of the West. In 1857 he surveyed a wagon road route from Fort Defiance, N.Mex., to the Colorado River.

21. Axolotls are larval salamanders of the genus *Ambystoma.*

22. Coues, ed., *On the Trail of a Spanish Pioneer,* II, 342-43n.

23. *Ibid.,* 343n.

24. Following his graduation from West Point in 1871, Henry Peoble Kingsbury served on the frontier until 1890 and saw action in the Spanish-American War. He retired with the rank of colonel in 1914 and died in 1923.

25. Carl Follen Palfrey graduated from West Point in 1870 and retired with the rank of captain in 1895; he died in 1920.

26. Coues, ed., *On the Trail of a Spanish Pioneer,* II, 342n, 343n.

27. Mearns, "Mammals of the Mexican Boundary of the United States," 237.

28. Coues, ed., *On the Trail of a Spanish Pioneer,* II, 344n.

29. *Ibid.,* 341n. Since 1881 the Havasupais have suffered the loss of most of their traditional lands and have thus experienced severe economic dislocations. They now cling to a much diminished reservation in Cataract Canyon; tourism is their main hope for economic survival. In Coues' time their population was around 250; it sank to 166 early in the twentieth century and is now up to about 500. See Henry F. Dobyns and Robert C. Euler, *The Havasupai People* (Phoenix, Ariz.: Northland Press, 1971).

30. Coues, ed., *On the Trail of a Spanish Pioneer,* II, 344n.

31. Coues' "Books of Dates" (1881).

32. Coues, ed., *On the Trail of a Spanish Pioneer,* II, 327-28n.

33. *Ibid.,* 328n.

34. *Ibid.*

35. Coues' "Book of Dates" (1881).

36. *Walapai Papers,* Sen. Doc. 273, 74th Cong., 2d sess., 130-36.

37. Coues, ed., *The Expeditions of Zebulon Montgomery Pike* (1895), II, 736n.

38. Called Camp Toll Gate at the time of its establishment in 1869, Camp Hualpai, as it was renamed in 1870, was located forty miles northwest of Prescott. The War Department abandoned the post in 1873.

39. Coues' "Book of Dates" (1881).

40. *Walapai Papers*, 135, 146. About 700 Walapais currently occupy the tribe's reservation, which extends from Peach Springs to the Grand Canyon National Park. The reservation is relatively large, but the lack of water and arable land has meant that the economic mainstay of the tribe in recent years has been the sale of timber. See Bertha P. Dutton, *Indians of the American Southwest* (Englewood Cliffs, N.J.: Prentice-Hall, 1975), 195.

41. Coues, "Nesting of the White-bellied Wren *(Thryothorus bewicki leucogaster)"* (1882), 52-53.

42. Coues, ed., *On the Trail of a Spanish Pioneer*, II, 328n.

43. Coues, "A Curious *Colaptes*" (1881).

44. Coues' "Book of Dates" (1881).

45. Coues, "Probable Occurrence of *Sarcorhamphus papa* in Arizona" (1881).

46. Coues to Allen, undated letter from Whipple Barracks.

47. Coues to Robert Ridgway, Apr. 23, July 1, and July 23, 1881. McLennan Library, McGill University.

48. Brewster, "Stearns and Coues's 'New England Bird Life'" (1883), 164.

49. Coues, "Names of the 'Blue-Water' Indians" (1881), 73.

50. *Annual Report of the Board of Regents of the Smithsonian Institution . . . 1881* (Washington, D.C.: Government Printing Office, 1883), 681.

51. Coues' "Book of Dates" (1881).

52. Coues to Allen, July 1, 1881.

53. Coues to Allen, July 6, 1881.

54. Coues' "Book of Dates" (1881).

55. *Ibid.*

56. *Ibid.*

57. *Ibid.*

58. Goetzmann, *Exploration and Empire* (1972), 582-91.

59. Coues to Allen, Mar. 29, 1881.

60. Coues to Allen, Oct. 18, 1881.

61. A. Hunter Dupree, *Science and the Federal Government: A History of Policies and Activities to 1940* (Cambridge, Mass.: Harvard University Press, 1957), 184, 191.

62. Coues to Allen, Jan. 18, 1882.

CHAPTER XV

Army Surgeon to Civilian

For Elliott Coues, the transition from a vagabond Army surgeon to a plain, everyday civilian posed problems, all difficult to resolve immediately. One, of course, was marital, now that he and his wife had chosen to go their separate ways. Presumably Mrs. Coues continued to reside at 1617 K Street, where, before Coues' second tour of duty in Arizona, the entire family had lived. Coues himself, after his return to Washington, moved in with his mother and sister Grace at their home on the northwest corner of N Street and Vermont Avenue.[1] By arrangement—whether amicable or not we do not know—Mrs. Coues was allowed custody of their daughter, Edith Louise, and younger son, Beverly Drinkard.[2] The older son, Elliott Baird, went with his father.

The adjustment to civilian life, after some twenty years in the service, may have been extremely difficult for Coues, particularly as he tried to regain mental stability after the periods of near irrationality and depression which had beset him during his second stay at Fort Whipple. Some of Coues' acquaintances, after pondering a few of his later actions, may have felt that he never did completely succeed in recapturing his previous mental well-being.

Following his resignation from the Army Coues' sole sources of income, so far as we know, were royalties from previously published books and stipends from Winfrid A. Stearns for revising and editing Stearns's *New England Bird Life*.[3] Coues had anticipated economic difficulties. To Allen, shortly before resigning, Coues had written, "I shall be a beggar." To Allen again, soon after leaving the service: "There's a luxury in being your own master, even if free is to starve. My worldly goods are not as much as $500, and my income is $000." Though not quite as penniless as he had indicated, Coues did face the problem of quickly finding employment, and find it he did.

In his "Book of Dates" (1881) Coues wrote, "This fall resumed Profesorship of Anatomy, National Medical College, session of 1881-

2."[4] The income from this position, though it eased Coues' financial situation, was only a fraction of the pay he had received from the Army.[5] In order to remain solvent, it was imperative that he find additional sources of revenue. Presumably, therefore, it was with much gratification that in early May, 1882, he was invited by Robert E. Thompson,[6] editor of the American Supplement to the *Encyclopaedia Britannica*, to provide material about birds for the supplement. Replying on May 4, Coues wrote in part:

> The article "Birds" in the 9th ed. of the E[ncyclopaedia] B[ritannica] was written by a particular friend of mine [Alfred Newton] who is [a] very high authority, and is an admirable one, so that I could hardly see the necessity for anything further on the subject in the American Supplement.
>
> If, however, something more especially to the point for the American public be desired, I have no doubt I could furnish such an article.
>
> Will you, with reference to the probable arrangement between us to this end, please send me a sample page of the Supp[lement], and also inform me how *long* an article you would wish to have. Please also inform me whether the article would appear in my name or not.[7]

We are fortunate in having available to us at least a score of further letters from Coues to Thompson, covering a period of almost two years. In the earlier ones Coues makes it obvious that he is not only eager to contribute to the supplement but also perfectly willing to write articles about mammals too. In a letter of June 20, 1882, for example, he told Thompson: "I may like to touch upon mammals as well as birds, being equally familiar with that class, as represented in North America. But this would of course be at your option, as we have no understanding as yet to that effect."

Thompson appears to have been quite agreeable to Coues' proposal because on June 20 Coues wrote: "I think we understand each other perfectly, as to a more or less extensive lot of short articles on natural history, with special reference to the zoology of N. Amer. I will send you such as occur to me, on special subjects which I am competent to treat satisfactorily. . . . I cannot well comply with your request to send you a list of mammals I could write on. But I know, or think I do, about what your requirements would be in that line, and, as in the case of the birds, will try to fill the bill to your satisfaction." In this same letter it also appears that Coues was preparing for Thompson a piece on the anatomy of birds.

Soon afterward, with his foot now well anchored in the *Britannica* door, Coues assured Thompson of his ability to furnish articles for him about animals other than birds and mammals. On August 1 he wrote:

> I am satisfied that you cannot do better than to place Fishes in [Theodore N.] Gill's hands. . . . With the Fishes given over to Gill, I can easily manage the rest of the Vertebrates myself. If you have no specialists engaged upon Invertebrates, I will keep that part in mind also, and furnish short articles upon various of the prominent or more important groups. . . . If I may consider myself on the editorial staff of the Suppl., in the department of natural history, I shall be willing to devote a good deal of time to the work. I may say frankly, that the remuneration is enough to make it worth my while from a business point of view, while such writing is entirely congenial, and of a kind in which I have had a long practical experience. I may perhaps add, that I have acquired some facility of expression in giving clear concise definitions and descriptions in these departments of science I cultivate.

Coues here allowed his vanity to surface, and again even more so in his next letter to Thompson: "I see you insert some contemporary biography. If not too late, there is one name before the end of 'C,' the vanity of the owner of which suggests that half a column or so might not be entirely out of place, especially as you do not want to let some other Ency[clopedia] get ahead of you!!"

The correspondence between Coues and Thompson had begun with a request for a single article about birds. When the supplement finally appeared, it contained approximately one hundred pieces by Coues,[8] each with his by-line, about birds, mammals, and various invertebrate groups. Then, too, "before the end of 'C,'" there was a biographical sketch of Coues.[9] It followed one by Coues on the cotton rat, and occupied a full column. We find nothing to indicate that Coues did not write it himself.

Throughout the period of financial embarrassment Coues apparently turned down no offer of work that would fatten his pocketbook. In his "Book of Dates" (1882) we read: "Sept. 8, letter of T. S. Conrad, President Virginia Agric. and Mech. College,[10] Blacksburg, engaging services @ $500 for Mar. and April. '83." After accepting, Coues wrote Allen, "Too advantageous pecuniarily to forego—$20 a lecture." Elsewhere in his "Book of Dates" Coues noted that while in Blacksburg he lectured "thrice weekly, before faculty and students."

From a notice in an 1883 periodical we learn of another offer Coues received and accepted. The notice read: "S. E. Cassino & Co., Boston, announces a 'Standard Natural Library of Natural History,' or popular encyclopedia of the animal kingdom, of which the editorship will be in the competent hands of Dr. Elliott Coues and Mr. J. Kingsley."[11]

Actually Coues contributed just one article to this work, correctly titled *The Standard Natural History*, and Kingsley was the sole editor.[12]

2

The year 1883 was well advanced when Coues finally found a post that paid well enough to take care not only of his immediate needs but also, as it turned out, of those for several years to come. Writing Allen on July 5, 1883, Coues said: "I am dreadfully busy—the old story. Did I tell you I have undertaken the revision and correction of the zoological words in the 'Imperial Dictionary'[13] for the new 'Century Dictionary'?" And in Coues' "Book of Dates" (1883) we find: "May or June opened correspondence with the Century Dictionary of New York regarding Century Dictionary; made arrangements for the work; visited Prof. Whitney[14] at Yale College, New Haven, in company with the [Century] office editor, B. E. Smith[15] . . . began first hour's paid work on June 16."

Coues' labors with *The Century Dictionary* continued for more than eight years, until September 9, 1891.[16] He was one of thirty-one editorial contributors, each engaged to define words in the area of his particular specialization. Coues' specific areas, for instance, were zoology and comparative anatomy. Collaborating with him were such other outstanding men of science as Edward S. Dana,[17] physicist (Yale); Frank H. Knowlton,[18] botanist (U.S. National Museum); Theodore N. Gill, ichthyologist (Columbian); and Lester F. Ward,[19] paleontologist (U.S. National Museum).

During his years with the Century Company Coues supplied an estimated 40,000 definitions and for most, if not all, he provided derivations. Additionally, according to one writer, he was responsible for "hundreds of illustrations, largely original, drawn under his supervision by E. T. Seton."[20] When Seton wrote his autobiography several years later, he verified the fact that he had made illustrations for *The Century Dictionary*, some 1,000 altogether; he said nothing, however, about having done them under Coues' supervision.[21]

On occasion Coues found it expedient to consult other zoologists. He turned to L. O. Howard,[22] for instance, when having trouble with some of the entomological terms. Howard had first met Coues in 1878 when he went to the latter's office to consult with him on an anatomical matter. He found Coues in a bad mood, and was brusquely received. After Howard had explained the object of his visit and had shown Coues the thirty or so cards constituting his bibliography on the subject, Coues testily remarked: "Humph, do you call that a bibliography? Look here"—and he pointed to an array of card cases—"here are twenty thousand cards, forming my bibliography of North American birds."

Howard, much taken aback, left Coues' office as hurriedly as possible and did not encounter him again until about 1885, when Coues requested his help in defining entomological terms. Thereafter, as Howard later wrote: "I worked on the dictionary at odd times until it was completed, and my relations with Coues were extremely pleasant. He was a very extraordinary and very eccentric man. After he married his second [third] wife, he had a beautifully furnished home on N Street, between Seventeenth and Eighteenth, and no matter how late in the evening I called I found him at work in his study, with a coffee-pot and with innumerable cigarette butts scattered about."

But Howard's most vivid recollection of Coues occurred one day as their work on the dictionary was nearing its end. It was then, Howard wrote, that Coues "went through Scudder's 'Nomenclator Zoologicus' and discovered that the last word [in it] was entomological. In great glee he said to me, 'You are going to have the honor to define the last word in the English language.' I asked what it was and he told me that it was *Zyxomma.* . . . I told him that it was the name of a very obscure genus that had no business in the dictionary, and he said that did not make any difference. 'For the honor of zoology we must have the last word.'"[23] As a consequence, in the original (and later) editions of *The Century Dictionary* one finds at the bottom of the last page: "*Zyxomma*—A genus of Indian dragonflies, of the family *Libellulidae*, having the head large, the face narrow, the eyes of great size, and the first three abdominal segments vesicular."

Now and then, it appears, Theodore N. Gill also assisted Coues with definitions. According to one source, when Gill submitted to Coues "a definition of the family of giraffes Coues read it carefully and turning to Gill exclaimed, 'That isn't English, it is Choctaw.' 'No,' said Gill, 'it is an exact definition of the family *Giraffidae*,' and as such it was duly incorporated in the Dictionary."[24] Gill's definition of Giraffidae may be found on page 2519 of volume III of our edition of *The Century Dictionary*: "*Giraffidae*—A family of ruminant artiodactyl ungulate animals, having the placenta polycotyledonary and the stomach quadripartite with developed psalterium, the cervical vertebrae much elongated, the dorsolumbars declivous backwards, and horns present only as frontal apophyses covered with integument." Choctaw or English? It was, of course, sound, respectable technical English. Coues, the learned anatomist, had been chaffing Gill.

Throughout his years with the Century Company Coues continued to correspond regularly with Allen, and often referred to the dictionary and his definitional labors for it. On September 9, 1888 (coincidentally Coues' forty-sixth birthday), he wrote: "I am simply buried beneath the great dictionary . . . and it is only now and then I can steal an hour for anything else." On August 23, 1889, he reported: "As a matter of fact, I am simply absorbed & immersed in the Dictionary, and mostly live at my desk, just as you do at yours—though I turn loose now and then & 'stir up the animals' . . . with a lecture or something."

Still later (on March 6, 1891) he had even more to say to Allen about his work on the dictionary: "For seven years now I have been carrying the load, and at times it has almost staggered me. Actual penwork has averaged over 8 hours a day all the time, and I have come to feel that I can do positively nothing else 'till this cruel war (*lege* Dictionary) is over.' The net result seems incommensurate with the labor; but not even so experienced and hard-working a scientist as yourself has a realizing sense of what it means in the way of toil and tact to express the very essence of biology, zoology & anatomy in those curt paragraphs which make a dictionary. Were my work perfect, it would argue archangelic omniscience and infallibility vastly more than papal!"

Coues' contributions to *The Century Dictionary*, when that great lexicon was finally completed, came in for much praise. Allen declared: "The ornithological matter, both as regards text and cuts, forms a conspicuous feature of the work, which is thus practically an encyclopedia of ornithology. For those who know Dr. Coues' ability at giving the gist of a bird's history in a few happily worded sentences, it is unnecessary to say that a vast amount of information is compressed into the space of a few lines."[25]

L. O. Howard later declared that the work Coues did for *The Century Dictionary* "had a high educational value. Things that I learned then have been of service in many ways."[26]

Another writer who had taken a close look at Coues' definitions asserted: "The advanced strides of knowledge in these branches [of biology, zoology, and anatomy] during the past quarter of a century, with which Prof. Coues's own name is so closely identified, have resulted in the coinage of thousands of new technical words, and most of these already in use require to be defined. . . . For this vast work . . . Prof. Coues has shown himself peculiarly well fitted, not only by his profound erudition in his own departments, but [also] by his habit of painstaking precision in the minutest details of dry fact."[27]

Coues himself thought highly of *The Century Dictionary*. To Allen (on October 20, 1889) he wrote: "[It is] the greatest work ever undertaken by an American house, the greatest dictionary of our language ever issued since [Samuel] Johnson. . . . I think you will be pleased with the way general biology & zoology show up in it. For no dictionary thus far published has had a 'professional' zoologist on the staff." In another letter to Allen (on March 6, 1891) Coues forthrightly affirmed, "I regard my share of the C[*entury*] D[*ictionary*] as by far the most important and enduring work of my life thus far."

An incredible statement, but did Coues actually mean it? If so, he was then relegating to secondary importance earlier works, such as his *Key, Birds of the Colorado Valley*, and ornithological bibliography. We can't believe it.

Coues had written, we may recall, that the long-crested jay was "a stranger to modesty." Evidence continues to accumulate that Coues in that respect resembled the jay. Writing to Allen on January 26, 1891, after Allen had received an advance copy of the dictionary, Coues said: "By the way, if you want to do a friendly and gracious thing, which I think you can do with a good conscience, send Prof. B. E. Smith, Century Company, a swinging good complimentary and appreciative letter about the dictionary, especially its biological and in particular its zoological aspects, in which you are a competent judge & critic. Something he can use, you know—and he would value it the more as being thus spontaneous & unsolicited! Or you can write me a private note of admiration or exclamation, just because you couldn't help it, you know, yet with due regard to the fact that I *might* show it to him. Holy old virgins in literature like us have to be very chaste & severe you know." Earlier (December 16, 1879) Coues had written Allen, "I believe in a little 'embroidery' and horn-blowing. Modesty is a jewel, but not in commercial transactions."

3

How else did Elliott Coues occupy his time during this interval of transition? To a man of his talents and ambition, it was not enough simply to teach, to revise a book on New England birds, and to write articles and definitions for dictionaries. He also lectured to public audiences, continued to contribute to natural history magazines, helped to form a most important ornithological society, and brought out reissues of books he himself had published earlier.

Like his father before him, Elliott Coues was able to capture and hold the attention of audiences, and getting speaking engagements was made easier by the fact that by now he was widely recognized as one of America's foremost scientists.[28] Coues' "Book of Dates" provides proof that in 1882 and 1883 he lectured to such scientifically oriented organizations in Washington as the Unity Club, the Biological Society, and the Philosophical Society, and also to groups of high school students and church bodies. The same source informs us, too, that on October 2, 1882, he delivered the opening address of the National Medical College and that on March 1 of the following year, in Boston's Tremont Temple, he addressed an audience of 1,800.[29]

In this same two-year period Coues published a dozen or more magazine articles about birds, the majority in the *Bulletin of the Nuttall Ornithological Club*. This output was, of course, far below that of the late 1870s, when he averaged between thirty-five and forty articles per year, and was doubtless a reflection of his difficulties in adjusting to civilian life.

Two lines of endeavor begun in this period transcended all others and are of such importance as to require extended treatment in succeeding chapters: his role in the formation of the American Ornithologists' Union, and his reissues of *Key to North American Birds, Check List of North American Birds*, and, with D. Webster Prentiss, "List of Birds Ascertained to Inhabit the District of Columbia."

There is one other event of note in Coues' life at this time. In the fall of 1883 Coues and presumably his son Elliott Baird, moved from his mother's house to a house located at 1726 N Street. Except for periods of travel when he was away from Washington for various lengths of time, Coues resided at this address for the remainder of his life, a total of sixteen years.

NOTES

1. See Coues' "Book of Dates" (1881).
2. Beverly Drinkard Coues was the fifth child born to Elliott and Jeannie Augusta Coues. In his "Book of Dates," when listing his children, Coues wrote of him: "Beverly Drinkard, b. Washington, D.C., 14th St." Beyond doubt Coues named him Beverly Drinkard because of his admiration for Dr. William Beverly Drinkard, professor of anatomy (until his death in 1877) at National Medical College.
3. *New England Bird Life* appeared in two parts, part one in 1881 and part two in 1883. Both were published in Boston by Lee and Shepard and in New York by Charles T. Dillingham.
4. Information provided us in 1973 by the registrar of George Washington

University states that Coues served the National Medical College as "lecturer" (1878-82) and as "professor" (1882-87). In his "Book of Dates" (1877) Coues wrote that he had begun his stint as lecturer in 1877 (not 1878), and that he had been elected "in place of Dr. W[illiam] B[everly] Drinkard, who died Feby. 13. Inaugural lecture Apr. 5."

5. It may be recalled that in 1872 while at Fort McHenry, Coues informed George Lawrence that his Army pay was the "equivalent of $4000 per annum for one in civil life." Coues remained in the service nine more years, and it is likely that during that time the Army increased his pay; however, if so, we have found no record of it.

6. Robert Ellis Thompson (1844-1924), Irish-born educator and economist. Thompson came to Phildelphia in 1857 and graduated from the University of Pennsylvania in 1865. He later became editor of *Penn Monthly*, the first dean of the Wharton School of Finance and Economy, and one of the editors of the American Supplement to the *Encyclopaedia Britannica*.

7. This and other letters from Coues to Thompson are held by the library of the American Philosophical Society, Philadelphia.

8. In the American Supplement Coues is listed as a contributor to three of five volumes: I, II, and IV. If our count is correct, he wrote fifty-four articles for vol. I, thirty-seven for vol. II, and three for vol. IV. The full title of this work is *Supplement to Encyclopaedia Britannica, a Dictionary of Arts, Sciences, and General Literature* (1888-89). Hereinafter cited as *American Supplement*.

9. For this sketch see *American Supplement*, II, 16.

10. Now Virginia Polytechnic Institute and State University.

11. *Nation*, XXXVI (Mar. 8, 1883), 212. John Sterling Kingsley (1853-1929), American biologist, was born in Cincinnatus, N.Y., and graduated from Williams (A.B., 1875) and Princeton (Sc.D., 1885). He was editor of *The Standard Natural History* (1882-86) and professor of zoology, University of Illinois (1913-21).

12. Coues, "Rodentia" (1884).

13. An English dictionary published by Blackie & Son, London.

14. William Dwight Whitney (1827-94), American Sanskrit scholar and philologist, was born in Northhampton, Mass., and graduated from Williams College (1845). He was editor-in-chief of the original edition of *The Century Dictionary* published beginning in 1889.

15. Benjamin Eli Smith (1857-1913), editor, was born in Beirut, Syria. In 1877 he graduated from Amherst College and in 1882 joined the editorial staff of *The Century Dictionary*.

16. See Coues' "Book of Dates" (1891) wherein he wrote: "Sept. 9, [49th] birthday, finished last word of my work on the Century, begun June 16, 1883."

17. Edward Salisbury Dana (1849-1935), American mineralogist, was born in New Haven, Conn., graduated from Yale (1870), and served as curator of the mineral collection at Yale (1874-1922).

18. Frank Hall Knowlton (1860-1926), botanist, was born in Brandon, Vt. In the years 1887-96 Knowlton was professor of botany at Columbian, and he was the author of botanical terms for *The Century Dictionary*.

19. Lester Frank Ward (1841-1913), botanist and paleobotanist, was born in Joliet, Ill., and graduated from Columbian in 1869. In 1882 he was appointed geologist to the U.S. Geological Survey.

20. Hume, *Ornithologists of the U.S. Army Medical Corps*, 77. Ernest Thompson Seton (1860-1946), British-born artist-naturalist, after coming to the United States, wrote and illustrated many books on natural history, among them *Two Little Savages* (1903) and *Lives of Game Animals* (1925-28).

21. Seton, *Trail of an Artist-Naturalist* (1940), 280-81.

22. Leland Ossian Howard (1857-1950), entomologist, was born in Rockford, Ill., graduated from Cornell (1877), and was chief of the Bureau of Entomology, U.S. Department of Agriculture (1894-1927).

23. Howard, *Fighting the Insects* (1933), 79-80.

24. Palmer, "In Memoriam: Theodore Nicholas Gill" (1915), 398.

25. Allen, "The Ornithology of the Century Dictionary" (1891), 222-24.

26. Howard, *Fighting the Insects*, 81.

27. Lawton, "Elliott Coues, Scientist" (1891), 122.

28. Among examples of recognition in 1882-83 by fellow scientists were: election to honorary membership in Linnaean Society of New York, election as corresponding member of the Boston Zoological Society, and election as an original member of the Society of Naturalists of the Eastern United States.

29. At this meeting Coues was introduced by Boston's mayor. Coues' subject was "The Daemon of Darwin," about which more later.

CHAPTER XVI

Ornithological Exactitude

There is nothing extraordinary about a scientist publishing a work of such merit that it is later, after revision, reissued, sometimes several times. A classic example is Henry Gray's *Anatomy of the Human Body*, which by 1973 was in its twenty-ninth American edition. Not so often, however, does a scientist experience the good fortune of having two works reissued, and three reissues are even more rare. Yet it happened to Elliott Coues.

It will be recalled that in 1862 Coues and D. Webster Prentiss collaborated to produce "List of Birds Ascertained to Inhabit the District of Columbia," that in 1872 Coues published *Key to North American Birds*, and that in 1873 he brought out a *Check List* of North American birds. Early in the 1880s all three were reissued: the *Check List* in 1882, the list of D.C. birds in 1883, and the *Key* in 1884.

Once again we wonder at the diligence and durability of the man. At the same time Coues was reissuing these three works, he was also regularly teaching anatomy to Columbian medical students, contributing liberally to the *Encyclopaedia Britannica* Supplement, *The Standard Natural History*, and *The Century Dictionary*, and energetically collaborating with Allen and Brewster to form the American Ornithologists' Union.

The three reissues, greatly emended and enlarged, immediately attracted widespread attention, especially the *Key* and the *Check List*, and were instrumental in adding substantially to Coues' standing, already formidable, as an ornithologist. As a consequence, each reissue deserves separate and somewhat extended attention.

2

To Coues, there were sound and impelling reasons for a new and revised *Check List*. As he said, "The science of ornithology [since 1873] has progressed, and our knowledge of North American birds has increased, both in extent and precision, until the original list, faithful as it was at the time, fails now to answer the purpose of adequately reflecting the degree of perfection to which the subject has been brought. A new edition has therefore become necessary."[1]

This second *Check List* differed conspicuously from the first, not so much in the expected changes of names as in the addition of a mass of new and innovative material. In a prefatorial paragraph Coues gave his reasons for adding the new material:

> In revising the list for the main purpose of determining the ornithological *status* of every North American bird, the most conspicuous attention has been paid to the matter of nomenclature. . . . The more closely this matter was scrutinized, the more evidences of inconsistency, negligence or ignorance were discovered in our habitual use of names. It was therefore determined to submit the current catalogue of North American birds to a rigid examination, with reference to the spelling, pronunciation, and derivation of every name,—in short, to revise the list from a philological as well as an ornithological standpoint.

Coues explained further the philological portion of his *Check List*:

> It consists in a treatise on the etymology, orthography, and orthoepy [pronunciation] of all the scientific, and many of the vernacular, words employed in the nomenclature of North American birds. Nothing of the sort has been done before, to the same extent at any rate; and it is confidently expected that the information given here will prove useful to many who, however familiar they may be with the appearance of these names on paper, have comparatively little notion of the derivation, signification, and application of the words; and who unwittingly speak them as they usually hear them pronounced, that is to say, with glaring impropriety. No one who adds a degree of classical proficiency to his scientific acquirements, be the latter never so extensive, can fail to handle the tools of thought with an ease and precision so greatly enhanced, that the merit of ornithological exactitude may be adorned with the charm of scholarly elegance.[2]

For various reasons, it seems expedient that we reproduce in part Coues' exact words on etymology, orthography, and orthoepy. For one thing, an attempted paraphrase would no doubt fail to measure up to Coues' "scholarly elegance." For another, Coues was the first ornithologist to become so deeply immersed in the capricious waters of technical linguistics. For yet another, Coues' choice of words, not always prudent, would at once raise the hackles of some fellow ornithologists (they did not like, for instance, to be reminded of their "glaring improprieties"). And finally, Coues' "Remarks on the Use of Words," though not free of error, was a brilliant and important contribution to the science of ornithology.

Some conception of the enormity of Coues' task—prolonged, tedious, and exacting—may be gauged from the fact that publication of the revised *Check List* was delayed a full year because of the tardily added philological matter.

Because of the labor involved in determining the derivation of each scientific name (and some common ones), Coues experienced more difficulty in assembling his thoughts on etymology than on either orthography or orthoepy. As he said:

> The large majority of the scientific names of birds are Latin and Greek words, or modern compounds of such, derived comformably to the rules for the construction of classic terms. . . .
>
> Many pure Greek or Latin names of birds in classic times have been transferred to ornithology, in a wholly arbitrary manner, to totally different species. Thus the *Trochilus* of the ancients was the Egyptian Plover; in [today's] ornithological nomenclature, it is a genus of Humming-birds. So, also, many proper names, and many of the epithets which classic writers were so fond of bestowing, have been adopted as generic or specific names, with little reason or with none, except the will of the namer. . . .
>
> The remaining names, not classic in origin, are a miscellaneous lot not easy to characterize tersely. Many are modern geographical or personal names in Latin form, as *wilsoni*, genitive case of Alexander Wilson's name . . . not a few are wholly barbarous, as *Pyranga*,[3] *Guiraca*.[4] . . . Some are monstrous combinations, like *Embernagra*[5] and *Tanagra*,[6] or *Podilymbus*[7] from *Podiceps*[8] and *Colymbus*.[9] . . .
>
> The student who confidently expects to discover erudition, propriety, and pertinence in every technical name of a bird, will have his patience sorely tried in discovering what lack of learning, point, and taste many words imply. Besides the barbarisms, anomalies, and absurdities already indicated, he must be prepared to find names with as little regard for precision of meaning, almost, as those of Smith, Brown, and Jones. . . .[10]

In writing his section on orthography, Coues experienced fewer problems and consequently found less to quarrel about:

> The literation of the scientific names is fixed and exact in nearly all cases. Their derivation being known, and their form having crystallized in a language "dead" for centuries, the proportion of cases in which the orthography is unsettled is comparatively small. In general there is no alternative spelling of a Greek or Latin word. . . . In some instances, of course, two or more admissible forms of the same word occur: as *hyemalis* and *hiemalis*. But, in general, there remains only one right way of spelling, and that may be

easily determined. We say, there remains; for of course there were centuries when the classics were undergoing the incessant changes incidental to all spoken or living languages, just as our tongue is now. But having, in the usual process of evolution, reached that point which we mean when we use the term "classic," the Greek and Latin have come down to us in a certain form, so measurably fixed as to permit no decided ulterior modification. Our orthography, as far as possible, should reflect the purity and lucidity of such crystallization; and a little care will enable us to make such reflection clear.

In the case of actual Greek and Latin words employed as names of birds, there are probably not in the whole list a dozen instances of words which admit of defensible alternative spelling.[11]

Coues began his remarks on orthoepy by saying, "Correct pronunciation of Greek and Latin is a lost art":

The best we can do now is to follow the usage of those scholars who conform most nearly with what they show reason for supposing to have been the powers of letters as spoken by the Greeks and Romans. Unfortunately for the student, there are three reputable schools who pronounce certain letters, especially the vowels *a*, *e*, and *i*, so differently that their methods are irreconcilable.

1. *The English Method.* In England, and generally in America, excepting in the Jesuit colleges, the letters have nearly or exactly their English powers. This school teaches us "how not to do it," that is, to pronounce as the Greeks and Romans never did. If we imagine a dialogue between an English professor of Latin and the Nanes [ancestral spirits] of Cicero, we are bound to infer that they would not understand each other. . . .

2. *The Continental Method.* This is universal in Europe, excepting in England, and has gained much ground in America through the teaching of the Jesuits[12] and other learned scholars. It is also known as the Italian school. It may be defined, in brief, as a compromise between English Latin and Roman Latin. . . .

3. *The Roman Method.* This way of speaking Latin, if practicable, is obviously preferable; and it is believed that a close approximation to Latin orthoepy is feasible. . . .

Nevertheless, the practicability of introducing such radical reform among naturalists, to whom the writing and speaking of classical words is but an incident of their scientific studies, may be seriously doubted, however desirable it is to do so. We question whether ornithologists, of this generation at least, can be induced to say *Kikeronia, Kirke,* and *Pikikorwus* . . . for Ciceronia, Circe, and Picicorvus.

Upon such understanding, we offer, for pronouncing the Latin names of North American birds, a scheme which insists upon the Roman sounds of the vowels and diphthongs, but yields the point in the disputed cases of certain consonants; conceding, for example, that *c* may remain soft before *e*, *i*, and *y*, and that *v* need not be turned into *w*. . . . Much of the end we have in mind will be attained, if we can succeed in preventing those barbarisms and vulgarisms which constantly come from the lips of some persons of great accomplishment in the science of ornithology. Having ourselves heard *Onanth* and *Fully-gewler* for *Oenanthe* and *Fuligula,* we must not affect to conceal our belief that some ornithologists may profitably look a little further into the matter than they appear to have hitherto done.[13]

3

Having paid dutiful attention to Coues' philological convictions as revealed in his 1882 *Check List,* we may now turn to the *List* itself, namely, the enumeration of avian species and subspecies recognized by Coues as then inhabiting North America. But before going into the merits and demerits of the *List,* it seems advisable first to note some advancements that had been made in the use of trinomials—a third name to designate geographical subspecies (races)—by Coues and others between 1872-73, the dates of Coues' original *Key* and *Check List,* and 1882, the year he brought out his second *Check List.* In that ten-year period Coues, in his more important works like *Birds of the Northwest* and *Birds of the Colorado Valley,* had employed trinomials increasingly and, at the same time, had continued to advise biologists that trinomials were "the only fit instruments of expression of nice shades of zoological meaning."[14]

Trinomialism made further progress in the United States in 1874 when Baird, Brewer, and Ridgway published *A History of North American Birds.* In this three-volume classic its authors, as one scientist wrote, followed the practice set by Coues in his *Key* and 1873 *Check List* of describing "all stages between the extremes as 'subspecies or geographical races,' adding their names, prefixed by 'var.,' to the species name."[15]

With the ready acceptance of trinomialism by such prominent American ornithologists as Baird, Brewer, Ridgway, and Coues, it was no time until one scientist wrote: "The systematic application of trinomials to the whole North American ornis had simply become a necessity."[16] J. A. Allen was soon declaring: "To Dr. Coues . . . is due the credit of suggesting, if not indeed of actually advocating, the adoption of a trinomial system of nomenclature as necessary to a proper recognition of geographical races or incipient species."[17]

Leading American ornithologists, constituting what Europeans called "the American School of Trinomialism," continued until 1881 to write their trinomials with subspecific names preceded by "var." In that year Robert Ridgway published "Nomenclature of North American Birds,"[18] in which, through the simple expedient of dropping the "var.," he "took the decisive step toward true trinomial nomenclature."[19] For example, the trinomial for Swainson's thrush, previously written *Hylocichla ustulata* var. *Swainsoni*, appeared in Ridgway's "Nomenclature" as *Hylocichla ustulata Swainsoni*—and that is the way the name appears in bird books today except that *swainsoni*, as with all specific and subspecific names, is not capitalized.

Coues' second *Check List* came from the press in 1882 and agreed with Ridgway's "Nomenclature" in the use of "true trinomial nomenclature." It differed, however, in one conspicuous and significant respect: Coues provided the derivation of each scientific word in binomial or trinomial, indicated its proper spelling, and, by use of the conventional diacritical marks, revealed what he considered to be its correct pronunciation.

In both the original and the revised *Check Lists* Coues began his enumeration of species with the robin. A comparison of the two versions reveals that in the former he wasted no words, writing simply: "TURDUS MIGRATORIUS L. ROBIN." In the latter, however, he supplied a fuller treatment:

> *Turdus migratorius* L. Robin. B. 155, C. 1, R. 7.[20]
> *Tŭr-dŭs mĭ-grā-tō-rĭ-ŭs.* Lat. *turdus*, a thrush. Lat. *migro*, to move from one place to another; *migrator*, a wanderer, a migrant; *migratorius*, migratory.[21]

But what Coues had to say about the spelling, pronunciation, and derivation of *Turdus migratorius* was scant in comparison with what he said about many other birds, for example, Lewis's woodpecker:

> *Asyndesmus torquatus* (Wils.) Coues. Lewis's Woodpecker.[22]
> *Ă-sȳn-dĕs-mŭs tōr-quā-tŭs.* Gr. ά privative, σύν, together with δεσμός, a bond; in allusion to the loosened texture of the feathers of the under parts. —Lat. *torquatus*, collared; *torquis*, a necklace, collar; *torqueo*, I twist, twine around; *tortus*, twisted, distorted, contortion; so also torture, as of one wrenched or racked. The allusion is to the ashy collar on the neck of the bird. The English name is that of Merriwether [*sic*] Lewis, the explorer in company with Clark (Clark's Crow, *Picicorvus*).[23]

Coues' philological treatments encompassed a total of 878 avian species and subspecies. Only by reading all of them can one come close to appreciating the magnitude of his task.

In many instances Coues made side excursions into areas quite unrelated to philology. Of interest was his practice of consistently identifying the men and women whose names appear in avian binomials, trinomials, and vernaculars. To mention a few, which, we suspect, even some professional ornithologists might have difficulty in recognizing: Maxwell's screech owl (*Otus asio maxwelliae*), named for Mrs. Martha Ann Maxwell of Boulder, Colorado, who discovered it; Bullock's oriole (*Icterus galbula bullockii*), named for William Bullock, proprietor of a London museum and a onetime collector of birds in Mexico; Couch's tropical kingbird (*Tyrannus melancholicus couchii*), named for Lieutenant D. N. Couch, U.S. Army, who collected extensively in Texas and northern Mexico; Virginia's warbler (*Vermivora virginiae*), named for Mrs. Virginia Anderson, wife of Dr. W. W. Anderson, who discovered it; Virginia rail (*Rallus virginianus=R. limicola*), named for the state of Virginia, "mother of Presidents, and wet-nurse of Secession"[24] and western house wren (*Troglodytes aedon parkmanii*), named for Dr. George Parkman of Boston, murdered by Professor John W. Webster in 1849.

A number of Coues' contemporaries, while agreeing that his philological contributions possessed a measure of value, nevertheless found much in them to quarrel about, especially in respect to his fixed ideas on spelling and pronunciation of scientific names. David Starr Jordan, for example, after admitting the overall worth of the *Check List*, went on to say: "In it, however, so much learning and labor has been expended in the mending and remodeling of scientific names, as fairly to bring purism in that regard to *reductio ad absurdum*."[25]

A few examples of Coues' "mending and remodeling" follow: (1) *Chordeiles* (genus of nighthawks) was "an inadmissible contraction," even though the English naturalist William Swainson had written it that way. The word, Coues insisted, should be *Chordediles*. (2) *Sphyrapicus* (genus of sapsuckers) should be spelled *Sphyropicus*. Coues contended that the connecting vowel should be *o* in this case. (3) *Thyroideus*, as in *Sphyrapicus thyroideus* (Williamson's sapsucker) should be *thyroides*. Declared Coues, "It has always been wrongly thyroideus."[26]

Coues had his own personal convictions, too, about how to pronounce certain common names of birds. He insisted, for instance, that "Junco" should be pronounced as though it were spelled "Yoonco."[27]

Coues may have been taken aback—but not for long—when an article appeared critical of his *Check List* etymology. The author was Augustus C. Merriam,[28] uncle of C. Hart Merriam and a full-fledged philologist. Merriam began his article with these words: "The 'Coues Check List and Lexicon of N.A. Birds' (1882) deserves in one of its features some further consideration than appears yet to have been given it. This feature is its philological treatment of the nomenclature of ornithologists," which is "open to criticism in numerous particulars."[29] With that as a start, Merriam then proceeded to cite, in language both civil and temperate, several instances of Coues' usage of Latin and Greek which he regarded as faulty.

Coues lost no time in replying, in an article he called "Ornithophilologicalities." He began by saying: "Professor Merriam may imagine with what mixed amusement and consternation we find ourselves sent down to the foot of the class for missing our lesson and kept in after school to learn it. . . . Professor Merriam's review of the 'Coues Check List of North American Birds' is a piece of obvious hypercriticism from beginning to end. It is pitched upon a philological E-string instead of the natural A. Every scholar will recognize the skill with which this is done. . . . But it is a canon of criticism, which book-reviewers recognize, and which we suspect Professor Merriam has yet to learn, to hold in view always what the author undertook or intended to accomplish, not what the reviewer thinks the author might, could, would, or should have done."[30]

The remainder of Coues' article, in which he attempted to refute Merriam's censure, was equally flippant and supercilious. One individual, after having read both papers, felt impelled to say: "The predominant feeling is that if these literary amenities are essential to science, we must forego the science. . . . Where opinions are so radically opposed what gains can be expected? Has all the controversy hitherto been able to accomplish anything?"[31]

J. A. Allen, editor of *The Auk*—in which all three papers had appeared—now tried to answer this pertinent question. After a preliminary statement of consequential length, Allen asserted: "We are quite aware that a considerable number of our readers share the 'lay view' of the case, as presented by our correspondents, and we even sympathize with them in their disgust, but beg to assure them that it is just such discussions of the abstract and dry details of nomenclature that advance, in a certain necessary way, the *science* of ornithology; although nomenclature is not in itself science, but merely one of the indispensable tools of science."[32]

In this particular instance of verbal sparring Coues won no laurels for himself. Even his best friends must have winced as they read his reply to Merriam, a rejoinder needlessly disparaging a man of scholarly attainment and sound reputation.

Though Merriam and Jordan found fault with the philological

portion of Coues' revised *Check List*, it was nevertheless a work of much merit, one that the ornithologists of that period could no more ignore than they could Coues' *Key* and bibliographical installments. William Brewster, for one, was immediately enthusiastic: "The erudition and scholarly research involved in this undertaking must be apparent to the most casual reader. The practical value of the work is equally plain, and perhaps it is not too much to say that it calls for a fuller measure of gratitude on the part of ornithologists than anything which the versatile author has hitherto produced."[33] Brewster added later: "Its favorable reception can be a matter of no uncertainty, for it fills a field of usefulness peculiarly its own, and one which need in no way conflict with that so ably covered by Mr. Ridgway's recent 'Nomenclature.'"[34] Even Jordan admitted that his work was "in many respects most valuable,"[35] and Allen, commenting specifically on its philology, acknowledged that it was "a thing never done in this country before."[36]

Even though many of us no longer have a classical education, we still like to be informed about the meaning and origin of words—in this case the scientific and vernacular names of birds. But when, as with Coues, such studies were used as a basis for correcting, improving, and hence changing the scientific names applied to birds, confusion soon became rampant. Experts did not agree; as we have seen, almost as soon as his list was out, Coues was challenged by David Starr Jordan and others. As a result, the international committee later placed in charge of such matters decreed that scientific names as originally published are to be followed to the letter, no matter how "barbaric" they may be. The only exception is when an out-and-out typographical error or *lapsus calami* can be demonstrated. For example, if an author says he is naming a species after Coues and the name is printed *rouesii*, a correction to *couesii* is permitted. As a consequence, all the names Coues inveighed against, such as *Chordeiles*, *Sphyrapicus*, and *thyroideus*, are today found in their original form, as the latest A.O.U. *Check-List* (5th ed., 1957) attests.

A valuable feature of Coues' revised *Check List* not to be overlooked was an appendix: "Catalogue of the Author's Ornithological Publications, 1861-1881." In this "Catalogue" Coues listed exactly 300 titles he had published, a rather staggering total for a period of only twenty years. It becomes even more impressive when we remember that Coues had also published a considerable number of articles on anatomy, medicine, and mammalogy. In a letter of January 4, 1882, to Allen about the "Catalogue" Coues facetiously admitted: "I ain't proud, and there's nothin' mean about me!"

In years ahead, in the opinion of many of his contemporaries, Coues continued to pay undue attention, in both his writing and public utterances, to the spelling and pronunciation of ornithological names. He kept saying, for instance, "Common sense certainly tells us to spell correctly if we can."[37] And at the 1887 Boston meeting of the A.O.U. he outdid himself. Frank Chapman later described the scene: ". . . one of the members of the Union, Dr. J. A. Jeffries,[38] in placing a diagram on the blackboard, misspelled a word connected with it. At the conclusion of his remarks Coues arose impressively (everything he did was impressive) and in his clear, vibrant voice, with the slightest trace of sarcasm, said, 'Will the gentleman from Boston tell me what the orthography of the word —— is in Boston?' From anyone else it would have been foolish; from Coues it seemed to condemn the whole paper."[39] Obviously the remark, both needless and in poor taste, did not endear Coues to Chapman or to others of Coues' colleagues present at the meeting.

During the late 1870s and on into the 1880s there was much gossip circulating in Smithsonian offices and elsewhere about Coues' alleged extramarital affairs. In a letter to Allen dated March 21, 1881, Coues makes it clear that he was quite aware of the talk, and that there might soon be more of it:

> The Check-List is going through, if no other work of mine does. I suppose there will be a howl when it comes out, at my "shamelessness" in placing the name of my "mistress" on the title page with my own, and so "stamping the scandal." Curse the curs who have yelped at my heels—curse the Fauns and Satyrs who sit on my shoulders grinning at me in derision! A blameless woman, one of the purest and noblest creatures I ever knew, has been most cruelly slandered, and no less seriously compromised than myself. I will show all my enemies, and all the blind fools that no cowardly truckling to their slanderous tongues shall deprive her of her just credit in the work, or prevent my having the honor and the pleasure of associating her name with mine.

The woman's name was Mrs. S. Olivia Weston-Aiken, and in her relations with Coues she was apparently innocent of any misconduct. In his introduction to the *Check List*, Coues wrote highly of Mrs. Weston-Aiken's "scholarly attainments" and of her "invaluable assistance" to him and felt that it was "no less a duty than a pleasure to recognize the cooperation of this accomplished lady."[40]

All ornithologists worthy of the name, irrespective of their feelings toward Coues as a man, undoubtedly consulted his revised *Check List*. Since it came from the pen of one so distinguished in science, they could not afford to ignore it. Whether they lauded it, as Brewster did, or damned it with faint praise, as Jordan and others did, they had been exposed to a salutary lesson in "ornithological exactitude."

4

When Coues and Prentiss reissued their "List of Birds Ascertained to Inhabit the District of Columbia" in 1883, they agreed on a new title: "Avifauna Columbiana." We first learn of plans for the revision through a letter that Coues wrote to Baird in November, 1882: "On behalf of Dr. D. W. Prentiss and myself, I beg to submit the manuscript of our 'Avifauna Columbiana,' or list of the Birds of the District of Columbia, &c., with reference to its publication, if acceptable, in the Bulletin of the U.S. Nat. Mus., as one of the projected series of District monographs."

"Avifauna Columbiana," when published, consisted of 128 pages and was thus a more elaborate production than its twenty-two page antecedent. Coues and Prentiss had, as they said, "entirely recast the [original] article; embodied the additions to the list made meanwhile by others; extended their remarks on the habits of birds in many cases; included a more elaborate notice of the Topography of the district with reference to the local distribution of the Birds; and added the Game Laws now in force in the District."[41]

Further contributing to the worth and attractiveness of the revision were some 100 illustrations, many of them by Coues himself. The reissue listed 248 species, as opposed to 226 in the original. Since more than twenty years had elapsed since the appearance of the first list, the authors were not surprised at the increase. It must have come as something of a surprise to find, however, that since their student days at Columbian some species had noticeably declined in numbers. Among major factors responsible for the decreases, as they saw it, had been the expanding population of Washington—from 60,000 in 1862 to near 180,000 in 1882—and the arrival of the English sparrow, which had since multiplied exceedingly.

Among the district birds reduced in number by the English sparrow, Coues and Prentiss alluded specifically to the purple martin (*Progne subis*), the American goldfinch (*Spinus tristis*), and the warbling vireo (*Vireo gilvus*). Other birds had been decimated by hunters. Of the passenger pigeon, for example, the two authors wrote: "The last large flight we remember took place in the fall more than twenty years ago—we think about 1858 or 1859."[42]

To the average reader of today these facts about the English sparrow, goldfinch and other birds may provoke only slight interest. The same can hardly be true of what they had to say about certain birds which were commonly on sale, in season, in markets of the nation's capital and often served throughout the district at state and other dinners:

> Cedar waxwing (*Bombycilla cedrorum*): "In the fall, when they grow fat, they are frequently offered for sale in the markets."
> Bobolink or reedbird (*Dolichonyx oryzivorus*): "From the 20th of August until October, the restaurants are supplied with 'Reedbirds'—luscious morsels when genuine; but a great many Blackbirds and English Sparrows are devoured by accomplished gourmonds, who nevertheless do not know the difference when the bill of fare is printed correctly and the charges are sufficiently exorbitant."
> Pileated woodpecker (*Dryocopus pileatus*): ". . . regularly exposed for sale in the markets, being brought in from the surrounding country."
> Great horned owl (*Bubo virginianus*): "It is sometimes found in markets, having been taken in the vicinity, if not actually within the District."
> Marsh hawk *(Circus cyaneus):* "It is one of the species [of hawks] most frequently exposed for sale in the markets."[43]

Also on sale in Washington markets were, of course, the expected game birds: ducks, geese, pheasants, and wild turkeys. As a result, when seeking wildfowl for the table, the district housewife could register no just complaint about the lack of variety offered her. On occasion, perhaps, it was a toss-up whether she should serve baked great horned owl or broiled pileated woodpecker!

Of avian events in the nation's capital recorded by Coues and Prentiss, none seems to have impressed them more than the phenomenal influx of birds into the city during the spring migration of 1882:

> We had, in fact, a "tidal wave" of birds during the second and third weeks of May. It stormed for ten days up to about the middle of the month and before the cold rain ceased there was such a gathering of birds in the city as had never been witnessed by the "oldest inhabitants." Many thousands of birds filled the streets and parks; so great was the number and so brilliant the assemblage that the newspapers took it up and published their notes and queries. To account for the unwonted apparition, someone started the story that a vessel, just arrived at a wharf in Georgetown from the West Indies, had brought a cargo of tropical birds which had in some manner escaped! And no wonder, when the city was swarming with Scarlet Tanagers, Golden [Baltimore] Orioles, Rose-breasted Grosbeaks, Redstarts, Summer and other

Warblers, all as strange to the average Washingtonians as the most brilliant exotic birds could be. . . .

In the parks it was common to see a flock of six or eight Scarlet Tanagers in one tree. There were flocks of Rose-breasted Grosbeaks in the Smithsonian grounds. . . . The most remarkable sight we witnessed ourselves was a great troop of a hundred or more Orchard Orioles in the Smithsonian grounds, rambling with a few Baltimores over the new-mown grass like a flock of Blackbirds, while at the same moment, on turning the head, the black, white and rose-color of the beautiful Grosbeak was seen contrasted with the green overhead; Summer [yellow] Warblers, Black-and-Yellow [magnolia] Warblers, and Chestnut-sided Warblers were skipping together through the tender foliage; Hermit Thrushes were hiding in the evergreen shrubbery, and the ubiquitous Sparrows were chaffing and dickering on every hand.[44]

Even the most discriminating ornithologists took note of "Avifauna Columbiana," with one of them declaring: "In rewriting the list the authors, besides incorporating the additional species, have expanded their annotation four-fold, through fuller notices of the habits of the species, and in noting the changes in the bird-fauna resulting from the growth of a big city. The subject in general is treated not only with great fullness, but is very attractively set forth, and in general plan forms an excellent model of what a faunal list should be."[45]

5

Ornithologists familiar with the second edition of Coues' *Key to North American Birds* will doubtless concede that its publication in 1884 was probably the most important ornithological event of the year. In the months preceding its appearance, Coues had labored long and diligently revising the original issue and had made generous additions to it. Consequently the reissue was, as J. A. Allen observed, "so different from the first as to be essentially a new work."[46]

The second edition contained 863 pages, more than twice the number (361) in the first, and, through the consistent use of smaller type where called for, almost four times the amount of textual matter. The new *Key* consisted of four parts: (1) "Field Ornithology," a near duplication of his "Manual of Instruction" in the *Field Ornithology* of 1874; (2) "General Ornithology," a greatly extended version of the introductory part of the first edition; (3) "Systematic Synopsis of North American Birds," much enlarged from the original synopsis; and (4) "Systematic Synopsis of the Fossil Birds," an up-dated and fuller presentation of material on fossil birds than in the original edition.

Preceding all this was a "Historical Preface," a concise (twenty-page) history of North American ornithology from its beginnings, early in the seventeenth century, to the year 1884. Coues divided this account into epochs and periods and, with his customary clarity and vigor of characterization, delineated the ornithologists who in his opinion had figured most prominently in each. His epochs (six in all) and major ornithologists of each follow herewith:

The Archaic Epoch: to 1700—John Smith, Thomas Morton.

The Pre-Linnaean Epoch: 1700-1785—Mark Catesby, George Edwards.

The Post-Linnaean Epoch: 1785-1800—John Forster, Thomas Pennant, William Bartram.

The Wilsonian Epoch: 1800-1824—Louis J. P. Viellot, Alexander Wilson.

The Audubonian Epoch: 1824-1853—Charles L. Bonaparte, William Swainson, John Richardson, Thomas Nuttall, John James Audubon.

The Bairdian Epoch: 1853-18- —John Cassin, George N. Lawrence, Thomas M. Brewer, Spencer Fullerton Baird.

Ornithologists read the "Historical Preface" with lively interest, and discussed among themselves whose names might most correctly be attached to the next epoch and its periods. One of them soon wrote: "In my judgment, the time from 1872 to 1884, or that between the two editions of the 'Key,' may appropriately be termed the 'Couesian Period,' and I am sure that readers will with one accord endorse the propriety of my proposition."[47]

The revised *Key* differed from the original in yet other respects. It was more fully illustrated, and the portraits by Coues himself (roughly one hundred) now bore the legend: "Ad nat. del. E.C." Also, this second edition—unlike the first—was dedicated to Baird:

To
SPENCER FULLERTON BAIRD
Nestor of American Ornithologists
This work,
Bearing to Others the Torch Received from Him in Earlier Days
Is Dedicated

In yet another way Coues' reissued *Key* differed from the first. It had a greater influence in giving direction, inspiration, and enthusiasm to aspiring young ornithologists. At least two of America's most outstanding ornithologists, Ernest Thompson Seton and Frank M. Chapman, have left testimonials to that effect. Seton's affirmation reads as follows:

Into my life [in 1884 at the age of twenty-four] came another sweeping change. This landed me in the Northwest, and to learn the birds, and equipped for the first time, with a book—with nothing less than Coues' *Key*. What a sunrise that was for me! No man can overestimate the blessing that that book has been to all the world of bird folk in America. Faults it had in abundance, I now know; but it was the first successful effort to take exact bird knowledge from the museum, and give it to the multitude, to place it within reach of all the world of those who loved to hold our birds, not as skins, but as loving friends. Under its inspiring force, my collection of bird skins grew; and about me there also sprang up a group of younger boys who, like myself, were keen to know the birds, but who had hitherto been wholly without guide.[48]

Chapman's testimony makes it obvious that he, too, as a young man found Coues' *Key* of 1884 to be a "sunrise":

I saw [c. 1884] in the window of a [New York City] book store (I think it was Dodd, Mead & Co.) on the west side of Broadway at Eighth Street an opened volume showing a frontispiece in color of the anatomy of a pigeon facing a title-page which read, "*Key to North American Birds*, Revised Edition, by Elliott Coues." That was a memorable day. I acquired that book and for the first time learned that there were living students of birds, worthy successors of Wilson and Audubon. From that moment I was no longer handicapped for lack of tools. Here was a work which from preface to index offered an inexhaustible store of information, its technicalities so humanized by the genius of its author that they were made attractive and intelligible even to a novice. In my opinion there never has been a bird manual comparable to Coues' *Key*, the work of a great ornithologist and a master of the art of exposition. Its nomenclature and classification may now [1933] be out-of-date but one may still go to it for information that is not to be found elsewhere.[49]

As comes out later, Chapman in time developed a dislike for Coues, but his antipathy toward the man did not ever extend to his *Key*.

Even before young Chapman had discovered Coues' revised *Key* in a New York City bookstore, other, older ornithologists had already obtained the book and were writing highly favorable reviews of it. An English writer was struck particularly with the "General Ornithology" section: "[In this part] there is condensed into some 180 pages a more complete account of the structure and classification of birds, brought up to the present standard of our knowledge, than any other with which we are acquainted. . . . It ought to be in the hands of every ornithologist."[50] And another British scientist, writing somewhat later, declared: "The year 1884 was signalized by the appearance of Professor Elliott Coues's revised edition of the 'Key to North American Birds,' a work the author of which America may be proud to claim as one of her children. It is still the ornithologist's *vade-mecum*."[51]

So popular was the revised edition that on July 26, 1885—just one year after it came from the press—Coues wrote to Allen: "The 'new' *Key* is already about exhausted, and my publishers will be ready for the third edition probably before I am." In due course we shall take note of the third edition of Coues' *Key to North American Birds*, and then of the fourth, and the fifth, and the sixth.

Somewhat ironically, though the artificial key's aspect of the *Key* may have been important to Seton, Chapman, and others, it is today, according to an outstanding authority, "the least valuable part of the book."[52]

NOTES

1. Coues, *Check List of North American Birds*, 2d ed. (1882), 3.
2. *Ibid.*, 3-4.
3. Now *Piranga*, a genus of tanagers, including the scarlet, summer, and hepatic of North America. The word was coined by the French naturalist L. J. P. Vieillot (1748-1831).
4. A genus of grosbeaks; see *Guiraca caerulea* (L.), the blue grosbeak. The word was coined by the British naturalist William Swainson (1789-1855).
5. *Embernagra* has been supplanted by *Arremonops;* see A. *rufivirgata* (Lawr.), the olive (Texas) sparrow.
6. Genus of the family Thraupidae (tanagers). The U.S. tanagers belong to the genus *Piranga*.
7. Genus of pied-billed grebes. The word was originated by the French naturalist R. P. Lesson (1794-1849).
8. Genus of red-necked, horned, eared, and least grebes.
9. *Colymbus* has been supplanted by *Podiceps*.
10. Coues, *Check List*, 2d ed., 11-12.
11. *Ibid.*, 12-13.
12. Coues, of course, was well informed on Jesuit teaching, having attended Washington Seminary, a Jesuit school (1855-57).
13. Coues, *Check List*, 2d ed., 14-15.
14. Coues, *Birds of the Northwest* (1874), 227n.
15. Stresemann, *Ornithology from Aristotle to the Present*, 246.
16. Stejneger, "On the Use of Trinominals in North American Ornithology," 75-76.
17. J. A. Allen, "Belding and Ridgway's Birds of Central California," *Bull. Nutt. Orn. Club*, IV (July, 1879), 168.
18. Ridgway, "Nomenclature of North American Birds" (1881). This work was

essentially a revised edition, very materially modified, of Ridgway's "A Catalogue of the Birds of North America" (1880).

19. Stresemann, *Ornithology from Aristotle to the Present*, 246. Stresemann further said (p. 246): "Schlegel had already resorted to trinomial nomenclature, but his principles were fundamentally different. He adhered to the theory of fixity, regarding his 'conspecies' as stable variations from the 'type' of the species, without letting his judgment be affected by the geographic distribution of the forms that he had compared. The Americans, on the other hand, were disciples of the theory of evolution; for them the third name served to designate the species that were coming into being ('nascent species')."

20. The three capital letters, "B," "C," and "R," stand respectively for Baird's *Catalogue* (1858), Coues' *Check List* (1873), and Ridgway's "Nomenclature" (1881). The number following each letter is that which the bird alluded to bears in each of the lists.

21. Coues, *Check List*, 2d ed., 23.

22. Today Lewis's woodpecker carries the binomial *Asyndesmus lewis* (Gray), and hence both the scientific and vernacular names recall the leader of the Lewis and Clark expedition.

23. Coues, *Check List*, 2d ed., 79.

24. *Ibid.*, 109.

25. Jordan, "The A.O.U. Code and Check-List of North American Birds" (1886), 394.

26. Coues, *Check List*, 2d ed., 72, 78.

27. *Ibid.*, 55.

28. Augustus Chapman Merriam (1843-95), American philologist and archaeologist, was born in Lewis County, N.Y. He graduated from Columbia (1866), was named adjunct professor of Greek at Columbia (1880), and promoted by Columbia to the chair of archaeology (1890).

29. Merriam, "The Coues Lexicon of North American Birds" (1884), 36-37.

30. Coues, "Ornithophilologicalities" (1884), 49-50.

31. Hazard, "A Lay View of 'Ornithophilologicalities'" (1884), 300-302. Apparently the author of the article was Rowland Gibson Hazard (1801-88), American manufacturer and sometime philosopher.

32. *Auk*, I (July, 1884), 302-4.

33. *Bull. Nutt. Orn. Club*, VII (1882), 111.

34. *Ibid.*, 246.

35. Jordan, "The A.O.U. Code and Check-List of North American Birds," 394.

36. J. A. Allen, "Ridgway on the Nomenclature of North American Birds," *Bull. Nutt. Orn. Club*, V (July, 1880), 178.

37. Coues, "Corrections of Nomenclature in the Genus *Siurus*" (1877), 30n.

38. John Amory Jeffries (1859-92), naturalist and physician, was born in Milton, Mass. In 1881 Jeffries graduated from Harvard with an A.B. degree and in 1884 from the same school with an M.D. He was vice-president of the Nuttall Ornithological Club (1880-84).

39. Chapman, *Autobiography of a Bird-Lover*, 51.

40. Coues, *Check List*, 2d ed., 4.

41. Coues and Prentiss, "Avifauna Columbiana" (1883), 8. The title page of this work recognizes both authors as teachers in the National Medical College, the former as "Professor of Anatomy" and the latter as "Professor of Materia Medica and Therapeutics."

42. *Ibid.*, 91.

43. *Ibid.*, 53, 70, 81, 84, 86.

44. *Ibid.*, 31-32.

45. J. A. Allen, "Coues and Prentiss's Avifauna Columbiana," *Auk*, I (Oct., 1884), 336.

46. Allen, *Auk*, XXI (Apr., 1904), 293.

47. Shufeldt, "The Couesian Period" (1884), 323.

48. Seton, *Trail of an Artist-Naturalist,* 222.

49. Chapman, *Autobiography of a Bird-Lover,* 31-32.

50. *Ibis*, VII (1885), 100-101.

51. Sharpe, *A Review of Recent Attempts to Classify Birds* (1891), 22.

52. Dean Amadon to authors, Mar. 15, 1977.

CHAPTER XVII

Coues and the A.O.U.

"Since we sent out the last number of the *Bulletin* [of the *Nuttall Ornithological Club*], a great many of our feathered friends have called upon us to pass the compliments of the season." In this manner Coues began an article which appeared in the January, 1883, issue of the *Bulletin*.

The article possessed a measure of charm, for Coues had endowed his "feathered friends"—among them a redpoll and an owl—with the human attributes of memory, thought, and speech. As a result, they were able to converse intelligently with Coues on a variety of ornithological topics. For instance, the redpoll "was kind enough to assure us personally that he had forgotten all about the trouble we made in his family in 1860, when we visited him in Labrador, and afterward spoke so shabbily of his appearance." The owl, "polite and dignified, as usual," had heard that "we were about to publish a new edition of the 'Key' which he trusted would be much more handsomely illustrated than the former one."[1] Also, and more important to us at the moment, the owl entreated Coues "to suggest the propriety of calling a Congress of American ornithologists."[2]

This particular representative of the owl family was preternaturally astute and foreseeing. Coues was, indeed, giving serious thought to an organization of American ornithologists, as we can see from a letter he wrote to Allen soon after the January, 1883, issue of the *Bulletin of the Nuttall Ornithological Club* was made available to its readers:

> . . . I forgot to say in my other letter that one of the Western papers has already taken up the suggestion I let fall in the "Compliments of the Season" and is howling for a national association of ornithologists, to meet and decide nomenclature &., &., &. So you see it is "in the air," and there is no knowing how soon we may need to move with silence, sagacity and celerity to shape it as we want it. It *must not* be taken away from Cambridge, nor out of our hands. . . . Probably the "call" will have to be sounded in the July Bull. [i.e., the *Bulletin of the N.O.C.*] for a fall meeting, and I think doubtless best

by the editors[3] with perhaps the additional names that will occur to you.

I have asked the editor of the [western] paper to send you a marked copy. *Note it well,* as a sign of the times. It was a surprise to me. I have written Fitch[4] the editor, that the time is perhaps not quite right, suggesting much to be done before it can be successfully shapen &c.—in short, blandly suggesting to him to shut up his mouth for the present. We have got to be alive, and shoot the thing on the wing, or it will fly by into some other game-bag. *Nota bene.*

I have never opened my mouth on the subject since our conference.[5]

As is well known, the American Ornithologists' Union was the issue of Elliott Coues, J. A. Allen, and William Brewster. They constituted a self-designated three-man committee which conceived the organization, fathered it during its incubation period, and supervised its birth. At a later date Allen wrote that the A.O.U. was "to some extent an outgrowth" of the Nuttall Ornithological Club.[6] True enough if he had in mind, as we think he did, that he was then editor of the *Bulletin,* Coues an associate editor, and Brewster president of the club.

Both Allen and Brewster then lived in Cambridge, home of the Nuttall Ornithological Club, and Coues, of course, in Washington. In light of later events, it should be mentioned that in 1883 Allen was forty-four, and the senior member of the trio, while Coues was forty-one and Brewster thirty-two.

Of the three men, it may have been Brewster who first thought of a national ornithological association. During the winter of 1882-83 the future of the N.O.C. looked so bleak to him that he despaired of its survival. In February of that winter he expressed something of his pessimism in a letter to Charles F. Batchelder,[7] a fellow member of the club: "The home members, with the exception of Purdie[8] and Allen, don't seem to care a hang whether the Club and its organ live or die. . . . I often feel tempted to go to work on a plan I have had in mind for some time, one which includes the dissolution of the Club and the organization of a new association. . . . An American Ornithologists' Union . . . could, I think, be made up in such a way as to be a very strong institution."[9]

Regardless of who first conceived the idea, it seems obvious from Coues' above letter to Allen that the two of them (and presumably Brewster) had, by the winter of 1882-83, been giving serious thought to forming a national organization. Even though Coues, since his conference with Allen, had never opened his mouth about their discussion, he had opened that of the owl, with the result that Mr. Fitch, in an editorial, had recommended to readers of his paper the formation of a national ornithological club. So, the idea was "in the air" and, to Coues at least, he and Allen and Brewster should soon take steps "to shoot the thing on the wing."

2

When Coues next wrote Allen he was in Blacksburg, Virginia, where he had gone, we will recall, to give a series of lectures to students of the Virginia Agricultural and Mechanical College. From there on March 30 he wrote Allen at length:

... As to our plans for the A.O.U., they will doubtless shape themselves anon. It's a very important matter to us that the first steps be taken wisely. I hope W.B. [William Brewster] won't turn loose in a hurry, nor let anything off at half-cock. Yet I have misgivings, if he comes to Washington while I am off here in the woods. I hear nothing more from any point, and am satisfied the thing can sleep till midsummer. I am afraid I have got to stay out here till May.

As to place of meeting, my choice would be N.Y. City. The only two [other] points really concerned are Cambridge & Washington, and better not have it in either, to keep all local color or sectional considerations out of the question. I have no doubt that we could get the place [in New York] where the Linn[aean] Soc[iety] meets. . . . Mr. Lyman Foster,[10] one of the L.S. fellows who edited their 1st vol. Trans[actions] so handsomely, is a cousin of mine, and would no doubt engineer any thing of the sort I might ask him.

My notion of the "call" is to have it by the editors of the Bull. [of the N.O.C.], or perhaps by the N.O.C. impersonally; to keep it *secret* till it is sprung in the July No. and to call it, not for any specific single object, such as revision of the list of N.A. birds, but to found a A.O.U. like the B.O.U. [British Ornithologists' Union]. . . .

I think the response to the call would be spontaneous, immediate and extensive. The first meeting would be a great success if we could do the necessary *business,* and leave the ornithology alone.

I think the dues should be $5.00 nominally for expenses of the Bulletin . . . and incidentals of meetings. The $5.00 to of course be equivalent to subscribing to the Bull.; all those who are members and pay this sum to receive the Bull. free.

The point to be stressed would be who *to get in, not* whether we could get enough—no trouble about that! If we issue an open call, I suppose everybody would have the right to say he would like to come; anybody whoever came to the first meeting would be *ipso facto* one of the "founders," if he likes to go into the thing when he gets there. But I would strongly urge that no one who merely sends word should be a founder. Better by far *found* on 3 or

6 or a dozen, and then lay plans for increase by the process of election.

I suppose three or four *officers* would suffice. Pres., V.P., Sec., and Treas., or the two latter in one. These with perhaps some "standing committees," or "a [word illegible]" to be the minor wheel, and mainspring of operation. Three or four names will immediately present themselves to you. One of the present editors of the Bull. would obviously figure most appropriately in the roll of Honorary memberships.

The real gist and heart of the whole busines is the control and management of the publication. The rest may be taffy, or perfunctory, or what not. *N.B.*

These are some of my early blush reflections at this stage. Now suppose you and W.B. lay your heads together and draw up, 1st, a call, 2d, a plan of operation, 3d, a statement of the objects, purposes, & proposed methods of the A.O.U. I will do the same, and we will then exchange manuscripts, compare notes, and decide upon our comments.

Meanwhile, I am fully persuaded of the expediency, indeed, the great desirability, of keeping perfectly mum till we are ready to spring the thing. Too many cooks, etc.

A most interesting letter, in some respects extraordinary, for practically every suggestion advocated by Coues—meeting place, dues, membership, and officers—was later adopted. Even the secrecy he so strongly urged was maintained, right up to the time in September of the organizational meeting. Clearly, and characteristically, Coues was not dragging his feet, nor did he intend to play second fiddle.

Before leaving Blacksburg Coues wrote Allen at least two more letters, both brief. In one he said that his ideas about forming the A.O.U. had taken "pretty clear & definite shape" but that "no one knows exactly how a cat on a woodshed will jump." In the other he said, "I think we must without doubt get the call out in July, let it cook until Sept., stir it up again and have the meeting some time that month. . . . I shall certainly be back [in Washington] by the 20th inst."

Once again at his desk in the capital toward the end of May, Coues stepped up his output of letters to Allen and enlarged upon his "early blush reflections." Their plans for the organizational meeting should be agreed upon and completed as soon as possible.

Since New York City was conveniently located midway between Boston and Washington, Allen and Brewster concurred with Coues that the meeting should be held there. For reasons unknown, Lyman Foster was unable to obtain the hall (in the American Geographical Society) where the Linnaean Society regularly met. On learning this news, Coues advised Allen, "The Amer. Geog. Soc. is obviously a false step, but one easily retaken. . . . I will write to Mr. Bicknell at once."

On August 21 Coues wrote Allen: "I enclose copy of letter from E.P.B. [Eugene P. Bicknell] in which at my request he tendered thanks for the use of the lecture-room of the A.M.N.H. [American Museum of Natural History], so that is all right. . . . If you approve, I will ask Bicknell to please consider himself with Holder[11] a committee of arrangements. I don't know that there is anything for them to do, but it seems well on general principles to have somebody who is on the ground to assume that capacity—and be responsible." With that matter settled, Coues wrote Allen about the date: "September would suit me better than Oct., when I shall have just started in on my regular lectures [at Columbian], but I do not voice the point. If after Oct. 1, one day will suit me as well as any other." The date finally agreed upon was September 26-28.

Perhaps the most difficult problem to be solved by Coues, Allen, and Brewster was determining which ornithologists should be honored with invitations to attend the history-making convention. On June 4, after receiving from Allen a tentative list of invitees, Coues replied:

> The list of names you send is to me perfectly unobjectionable. There are several others that will probably be added. I have already suggested Chas. Aldrich[12] of Webster City, Iowa; would suggest also Prof. S. A. Forbes[13] of Illinois . . . Dr. R. W. Shufeldt,[14] Dr. J. C. Merrill,[15] Hon. Geo B. Sennett[16] (a first-rate fellow, moneyed, who would be pleased I am sure, and take hold of it well). Shall probably think of some others. How about [name illegible] of Portland, Me., F. C. Browne[17] of Framingham, Mass., Prof. H. A. Ward,[18] Rochester, N.Y. . . . I scarcely think that ½ we ask will come—it does not generally prove so. The point is chiefly who *not* to ask. There are several black sheep wot of, which few are the real occasion of making the call private after all [instead of public in the *Bulletin* as earlier considered]. I think the three signers[19] would spot everyone of them alike, and for the rest, supposing the signers agree here and now, to exclude anybody that *any two of them* may wish?
>
> This of course to be carefully avoided, the slightest appearance of cliquism or sectionalism, to which ends our invitations ought to be as catholic as possible, *geographically* speaking. The Western names are well, for this if for no other reason—and by the way, there is F. H. Snow,[20] the Kansas man, and J. G. Cooper, good for Cal[ifornia]—not likely either will come.
>
> I am of the policy of keeping the active membership small and select, both to make it something of an honor, and to keep it working smoothly. The temptation will be to increase, for $5. At the same time, we must have some definite theory of who are eligible and who are not, to avoid any imputation of personalities. . . .

I think we had better ask the whole body of present Honorary Members [of the N.O.C.], with view to making them active in the A.O.U., and
dropping the present Hon. Mem. list.

Our foreign members offer a matter of such delicacy that I think we
had better not touch them—but, as I said to W.B., transfer them *en bloc*
[from the N.O.C.] to the A.O.U. Tht will be the simplest and best way of
treating them handsomely and retaining them. . . . For all the little fishes
that fringe about the affair, we can provide enough with a fairly elastic list
of "corresponding members" to be elected by the founders subsequently.
So I wouldn't say anything about *that* in our invitation.

Somewhat later Coues provided Allen with a few last-minute
thoughts on invitees: "I suppose you and B. have agreed with me on
O.C.M. [Othniel Charles Marsh]—how about Geo. A.B. [George A.
Boardman]??"[21] To Allen again, on August 8:

Papers rec'd O.K.—I have already signed and addressed them [the invita-
tions], and the envelopes will be printed tomorrow. I have made the list of
course exactly as you sent it, adding E.D.C. [Edward Drinker Cope], at your
suggestion. One name on reflection, I am satisfied had better be omitted.
That is Montague C. [Montague Chamberlain][22] whose recent exploitations
show that we should find in him an inharmonious element. . . . Three other
names occur to me as proper to be included, J. B. Holder, especially as we
are looking to the Am. Mus. Nat. Hist. for a nidus. Another is A. E. Verrill, New Haven, by all means! T.G. [Theodore N. Gill] here I think would
feel hurt as a biologist . . . especially if E.D.C. goes. I submit the three additions and one subtraction. Will send the rest of the list at once—let me hear
at once about these changes.

On the very next day Coues advised Allen: "All the invitations go
out today (to you and Brewster for your signatures). I enclose Mr.
Chamberlain's, with reference to my remarks of yesterday, in which I
think you will agree with me, and I heartily advise you *not* to send it. For
Deane,[23] I have only 'Chicago' as address and it may not catch him. Have
you more explicit address? I should like if you agree to send a bid to Dr.
D. W. Prentiss, of Coues & Prentiss, who is just out now with me in a
considerable book,[24] and a lifelong friend." When Allen next replied, he
must have argued convincingly for the retention of Chamberlain's name
on the list. In any event, when Coues again wrote to Allen, he said, "All
right about M.C.—but he shouldn't cut up those kind of capers."

In his "Book of Dates" (1883) Coues wrote, "Aug. 1, call issued for
founding of American Ornithologists' Union by J. A. Allen, E. Coues &
W. Brewster." On July 9, three weeks earlier, Coues had urged Allen:
"Get up the call *very elegantly*, on a sheet of note paper, headed with mono-
grammatic 'A.O.U.' Better have it actually signed, not our names

printed. Call on me, of course, for my share of whatever expense—or if you like, I will have it printed here and call on you and W.B."

The invitations were dated August 1, though not mailed until a few days later. They went to the scientists, some fifty of them, finally agreed upon by Allen, Coues, and Brewster, and read as follows:

Cambridge and Washington
August 1, 1883

To ————
Dear Sir:

You are cordially invited to attend a Convention of *American Ornithologists*, to be held in New York City, beginning on September 26, 1883, for the purpose of founding an AMERICAN ORNITHOLOGISTS' UNION, upon a basis similar to that of the "British Ornithologists' Union." The place of meeting will be announded hereafter.

The object of the UNION will be the promotion of social and scientific intercourse between American ornithologists, and their co-operation in whatever may tend to the advancement of Ornithology in North America.

A special object, which it is expected will at once engage the attention of the UNION, will be revision of the current lists of North American Birds, to the end of adopting a uniform system of classification and nomenclature, based on the views of a majority of the UNION, and carrying the authority of the UNION. Other important matters will be doubtless presented for consideration at the first meeting.[25]

It is proposed to hold meetings at least once annually, at such times and places as may be hereafter determined, for the reading of papers, the discussion of such matters as may be brought before the UNION, and the transaction of the usual business of a scientific Society.

Those who attend the first meeting will be considered *ipso facto* Founders of the AMERICAN ORNITHOLOGISTS' UNION. Active and Corresponding Members may be elected in due course after organization of the UNION, under such rules as may be established for increase of membership. Details of organization will be considered at the first meeting.

Should you favor this proposition, and propose to attend the first meeting, please so signify to any one of the undersigned.

J. A. ALLEN, Cambridge, Mass.
Editor of the Nuttall Bulletin

ELLIOTT COUES, Washington, D.C.
Assoc. Editor of the Nuttall Bulletin

WILLIAM BREWSTER, Cambridge, Mass.
President of the Nuttall Club[26]

With the invitations in the mail, Coues, Allen, and Brewster discussed the future, if any, of the Nuttall Ornithological Club. Would it continue to exist if the A.O.U. was successfully launched? That the thorny problem was much on Coues' mind is evident from his several references to it in his letters to Allen. In one he said: "As to the business of the first meeting, it will be a great stroke of success if the N.O.C. commit harikari gracefully and successfully, [when] the A.O.U. is firmly started . . . and satisfactory provision made for the continuance of the Bull. [i.e., the N.O.C. *Bulletin*] under competent editorial management, with a regular publisher like E. & L. [Estes and Lauriat], and under the title of the Auk, or Phililoo-bird, or whatever we may conclude to call it." Shortly before the September convention Coues wrote again to Allen: "We should have a clear-cut notion of what is best to do, especially with reference to the N.O.C., the future of the Bull[etin of the] N.O.C. being so intimately related in all probability to the success of the A.O.U." The final resolution of the problem was a feature of the September meetings, of which more later.

Coues soon began receiving replies to the invitations and, as they arrived, he answered them. On August 17, for example, he replied to Baird, who had written saying that he could not attend:

> Many thanks for your kind and encouraging words on behalf of the new association. We shall look for your presence in "spirit" if not in person, and hope everything from your strong assistance. The thing will pretty surely succeed with your patronage, especially as this prevents any possible suspicion of any lack of perfect harmony in the ornithological family. I think that in time the A.O.U. will become a strong and important organization, devoted to the best interests of the science in this country, and we are willing to work hard to that end. We already have many cordial and encouraging replies to our circular, and the general feeling, so far as I can see, could hardly be better. Is there any objection to our use of your letter publicly? Or, if so, would you send us something of like tenor, which you might wish to express more formally? Such a paper would of course be of the greatest possible assistance in confirming and establishing finally the *status* we are anxious to secure for the new association.

Baird could not be present at the New York meetings, and as the date drew nearer, it seemed that Allen might not be able to attend either. Throughout the period of planning, indeed for several years before, Allen had suffered from a chronic ailment which at times reduced him to semi-invalidism. In a letter of September 8 Coues expressed his concern: "I do hope you feel strong enough to go to N.Y. We would take the best care of you possible, and keep actual work or friction off your hands. It would hardly do for one of the signers to be absent." As it turned out, his health failed to mend in time and Allen could not attend.

3

On September 26, 1883, the organizational meeting of the A.O.U. convened in the lecture room of the American Museum of Natural History. Twenty-one individuals[27] put in an appearance, and these automatically became founders of the American Ornithologists' Union. Two others, Allen and Baird (both unavoidably absent), were quickly named as founders.[28] The meeting was called to order by Brewster, and Coues was elected temporary chairman and Bicknell temporary secretary. It subsequently came out that Brewster had expected to be chosen temporary chairman and had prepared a detailed written agenda for the meetings. As a commentator later wrote, "His plans went awry [when] this honor was awarded to Coues. . . . On Brewster's original manuscript now in the archives of the Union [in Brewster's own handwriting] is the notation, 'exit, W.B.'"[29]

The meetings lasted for three days, and with Coues firmly ensconced in the chair, matters went pretty much as he, Allen, and Brewster had planned. A provisional constitution was read and, after considerable discussion, adopted. The leading provisions were: (1) members to be divided into four classes: active, foreign, corresponding, and associate; (2) dues to be $5.00 per year; (3) officers to consist of a president, two vice-presidents, a secretary-treasurer, and five councillors; (4) officers to be elected annually at stated meetings of the union; and (5) stated meetings to be held annually at such time and place as the union may determine.

Following adoption of the constitution, the founding members elected officers for the ensuing year: president, J. A. Allen; vice-presidents, Elliott Coues and Robert Ridgway; secretary-treasurer, C. Hart Merriam;[30] and councillors, Spencer F. Baird, George N. Lawrence, William Brewster, H. W. Henshaw, and Montague Chamberlain. To the list of active members, represented by the founders, they added twenty-four more,[31] thus raising the total to forty-seven.

With elections completed, the chair appointed various committees on classification and nomenclature of North American birds, migration of birds, avian anatomy, oology, eligibility or ineligibility of the European house sparrow in America, and faunal areas. Of these the committee on classification and nomenclature was by far the most important. It consisted of Coues as chairman, Allen, Brewster, Ridgway, and Henshaw.

During the convention the A.O.U. founders kept quiet about the Nuttall Ornithological Club and its *Bulletin*. The only action taken even remotely related to the N.O.C. was a provision of the constitution authorizing the council to issue publications. In the October, 1883, number of the *Bulletin*—its final issue—the editor provided a report summarizing actions taken at the inaugural meetings of the A.O.U. and results of a session of the council held immediately after adjournment of the convention. In this report we read that the council voted to establish a journal, to publish its first number in January, 1884, and that it had chosen Allen as its editor. The report then went on:

> It may be further announced . . . that upon this action being known, it became a question with the members of the Nuttall Ornithological Club whether the Nuttall Club should continue to publish an organ, which, under the new conditions, could only be a rival of that of the Union. The two organizations being virtually one in interest and purpose,—the later being to some extent an outgrowth of the earlier,—and necessarily identical in membership in so far as can be the case where a greater includes a lesser, the Nuttall Club, at a meeting held on October 1, voted to discontinue its Bulletin with the close of the present volume, and to offer to the American Ornithologists' Union its good will and subscription list,—to place the Bulletin in the hands of the Council of the Union with its traditions and prestige, with the tacit under-standing that the new serial of the Union shall be ostensibly a *second series* of the Nuttall Bulletin.[32]

But all was not so serene and harmonious between the N.O.C. and the fledgling A.O.U. as the above report implied. For one thing the N.O.C. editor's remark, "the later being to some extent an outgrowth of the earlier," was unfortunate in that it did not jibe with the facts as known to members of the N.O.C. And there were other regrettable events. These were publicly aired many years later when Charles F. Batchelder published "An Account of the Nuttall Ornithological Club, 1873-1933":

> I cannot let the opportunity pass of correcting a wide-spread error. It may never be known from whose misguided imagination first came the statement that the American Ornithologists' Union was in some fashion the offspring of our Club. With varying phraseology, the assertion has been made so often—always by writers who had no first-hand knowledge—that it has almost become an established tradition. It is fully time that the myth should be exploded. The fact is that the Club had nothing whatever to do with the inception of the plan of a national organization, or with the actual birth of the Union. Not only was it not consulted by the men who originated

the scheme, but the members as a whole were entirely unaware of it. The invitation to take part in the organization of the Union was signed by J. A. Allen, Elliott Coues and William Brewster, and but three or four members of the Club were among the ornithologists to whom it was sent.[33] Probably no one of these had known much, if anything, of what was being planned, and certainly to all the rest of the Club the proposed institution came as an entire surprise. Indeed the Club, in general, felt no great enthusiasm for the new-born Union, especially when it was asked . . . to give up publishing the Bulletin.[34]

If any one person was responsible for the ill feeling that developed among members of the N.O.C. toward the A.O.U., that person must have been Coues. From the beginning, as we know, he had insisted that the planning be kept as secret as possible, and neither Allen nor Brewster disagreed, so far as we know. Even if Allen had entertained doubts as to the wisdom of secrecy, he might not have expressed them. According to Batchelder, Allen "had no desire to be an autocrat," and his "extreme natural modesty" made him reluctant to differ with others. For instance, when N.O.C. members objected to the publication of certain pieces in the *Bulletin,* "Allen always accepted the verdict, a little surprised but unperturbed."[35]

During preceding years the names of Allen and Coues had been closely linked in a number of ventures, particularly in their joint publication of *Monographs of North American Rodentia.* That Allen had been able to collaborate amicably with Coues over such an extended period may well have been due to the former's even disposition and disinclination to argue points. We have noted, too, in the letters Coues wrote to Allen during the months they were planning the A.O.U., just one instance of Allen's differing with Coues, and that was over Coues' attempt to "blackball" Montague Chamberlain.

It was at a meeting of the A.O.U. council held in the U.S. National Museum on December 13, 1883, that the name for the new A.O.U. journal was agreed upon. According to the minutes of that meeting, the only names suggested were the *American Ornithologist* and *The Auk.* Initially the majority of the council favored the former name, but "after a long argument by Professor Baird, the question was put to a vote by Dr. Coues and the Council voted in favor of *The Auk.* The decision was in accordance with the precedent set by the British Ornithologists' Union, after which the A.O.U. was modeled, in naming its organ *The Ibis.*"[36]

Some ornithologists were quick to criticize the name chosen, and with such vehemence that Coues had to reply in the first number of *The*

Auk (January, 1884): "The outcry from all quarters excepting head-quarters of American ornithological science against the name of our new journal satisfies us that the best possible name is THE AUK...The editors beg to say that they have copyrighted, patented, and 'called in' the following pleasantries: That THE AUK is an awkward name ... That the Auk is already defunct, and THE AUK likely to follow suit (*Mortua alca impennis—in pennis ALCA rediviva!*). . . . That THE AUK apes 'The Ibis.' (Not at all. It is a great improvement on the Ibis. . . . We would like to 'ape' or otherwise resemble 'The Ibis' in vitality and longevity. May its shadow already 'sacred' be cast while pyramids stand; may THE AUK in due time be also known of men as an antient and honourable foule!)"[37]

On September 30, just two days after the New York A.O.U. congress had adjourned, Coues reported to Baird. He was clearly enthusiastic about the role he had played in the formation of the union, and optimistic about its future:

> I think you will be much pleased with the result of the Convention which founded the American Ornithologists' Union. Everything worked to a charm, and everybody seemed more than pleased with the successful result. The utmost harmony and good feeling prevailed, and I think that the formation of the Union has entirely done away with some differences which might otherwise have become inevitable. The original plan of the signers of the call has been carried out almost to the letter. It had been carefully considered and met with much approbation. At one time, before it was generally known what my own intentions were, the situation was uncertain. I see now that I could have carried the convention for the presidency; but I felt that the key to the situation was to decline to be a candidate in favor of Allen. There was a scheme laid by some outsiders to make trouble, if not break up the thing in its inception, but that was hastily met. Your letter was a great help.

In a concluding paragraph Coues told Baird of his being "called to the Chair" and, after the election of officers, of his continuing to preside, in Allen's absence, and of his committee appointments. He wrote, too, "Yourself and Mr. Allen were by special motion included among the Founders, on obvious grounds."

One ornithologist has written, "Indeed, to Doctor [J. A.] Allen might well be applied the title 'Father of the American Ornithologists' Union'."[38] With equal if not greater justice, the same title might be bestowed on Coues. As we have seen, he played a dominant part—and we suspect a dominating one at times—in founding the A.O.U. He served for ten years as the organization's vice-president, and for three more (1892-95) as its president. As chairman of the important Classification and Nomenclature Committee, he contributed as much as or more than any other member of that committee in drafting the original A.O.U. "Code of Nomenclature" and the first and second editions of the union's *Check-List of North American Birds* (more on this in a later chapter). He was also an associate editor of and frequent contributor to *The Auk* in its early years.

The American Ornithologists' Union is fast approaching its one hundredth anniversary. Starting with forty-seven active members, it is today (1980) the largest organization of its kind in the world, with more than 3,000 active members, and *The Auk* is, indeed, "an antient and honourable foule!"

Coues was eminently pleased with his role in founding the A.O.U. Writing to Allen on January 26, 1891, he said: "Everybody who had any hand in making it what it is has reason to be proud, if he never does anything else to speak of."

The formation of the A.O.U. is a good example of significant trends in the middle and late nineteenth century in scientific and professional circles: nationalization, professionalization, and specialization. The ornithologists were doing what doctors, lawyers, and historians were doing at about the same time. The American Medical Association was founded in 1847, the American Bar Association in 1878, and the American Historical Association in 1894. Other examples of the same tendency can be seen in the establishment of the Modern Language Association of America (1883), the American Economic Association (1885), and the American Mathematical Society (1888).

Earlier in the century scientific societies tended to be general (such as the American Association for the Advancement of Science, founded in 1848), local, or both (such as the Academy of Natural Sciences of Philadelphia, 1812). In addition to the founding of the A.O.U., the growth of specialized, national organizations within the sciences later in the century may be seen in the formation of the Geological Society of America (1886), the Entomological Society of America (1889), and the American Society of Zoologists (1890). The creation of the A.O.U. is an instructive chapter in the overall consolidation of America's economic, political, and professional life.

NOTES

1. Coues, it will be recalled, had earlier written disparagingly about the draw-ings he had made for the first edition of the *Key*.
2. Coues, "Compliments of the Season" (1883), 1, 5.
3. J. A. Allen was at that time editor of the *Bulletin*, and Baird and Coues were associate editors.
4. The identity of this man Fitch eludes us.
5. All letters from Coues to Allen used in this chapter are from McLennan Library, McGill University.
6. *Bull. Nutt. Orn. Club*, VIII (Oct., 1883), 226.
7. Charles Foster Batchelder (1856-1947), ornithologist and editor, was born in Cambridge, Mass., and graduated from Harvard in 1878. He was as-sociate editor of *The Auk* (1887-93) and editor of *Proceedings of the New England Zoological Club* (1899-1947). He was one of the founders of the A.O.U. and its president in 1905-8.
8. Henry Augustus Purdie (1840-1911), ornithologist and botanist, was born in Asia Minor. Purdie was an original member of the N.O.C. and the A.O.U.
9. Batchelder, "An Account of the Nuttall Ornithological Club," 46.
10. Lyman Spalding Foster (1843-1904), ornithologist and publisher, was born in Gloucester, Mass., but spent the greater part of his life in New York City as a stationer and dealer in natural history books. He was for some years treasurer of the Linnaean Society and publisher of *The Auk* (1886-1900). Actively interested in ornithology, he contributed papers on birds to *The Auk* and other publications. His principal contributon to ornithology was a bibliography of the ornithological writings of George N. Lawrence. Foster and Elliott Coues were cousins because Peter Coues (1736-1818) was their paternal grandfather.
11. Joseph Basset Holder (1834-1917), naturalist and physician, was born in Lynn, Mass. After graduating from medical school, he served as surgeon of the military prison, Fort Jefferson, Dry Tortugas Islands, Florida (1861-65). From 1870 until his death he was curator of invertebrate zoology, ichthyolo-gy, and herpetology in the American Museum of Natural History.
12. Charles Aldrich (1828-1908), naturalist, was born in Ellington, N.Y. In 1875 he was with the U.S. Geological Survey in the Rocky Mountains. He was, too, one of the founders of the A.O.U. Quite by coincidence we discovered holograph letters from Coues to Aldrich in the bound volumes of *Bull. Nutt. Orn. Club* and *The Auk* at the library of the University of California at Davis in 1970.
13. Stephen Alfred Forbes (1844-1930), scientist and administrator, was born in Silver Creek, Ill. He was educated at Rush Medical College and Indiana University and served as dean of the College of Science, University of Illinois (1885-1905).
14. Robert Wilson Shufeldt (1850-1934), ornithologist, surgeon, and anatomist, was born in New York City. He graduated from Cornell (1876) and the medical school of Columbia University (1878). He wrote *The Myology of the*

Raven (1890) and many ornithological and anatomical papers. Coues used Shufeldt's painting of the internal anatomy of the pigeon as a frontispiece for his second edition of *Key to North American Birds* (1884).

15. James Cushing Merrill (1853-1902), ornithologist and surgeon, was born in Cambridge, Mass., and graduated from the University of Pennsylvania Medical School (1874). He was an occasional contributor of articles about birds to American journals.

16. George Burritt Sennett (1840-1900), ornithologist, was born in Sinclairville, N.Y. By vocation a manufacturer of oil well machinery, he was also ornithologist to expeditions which took him to Minnesota (1867) and Texas (1877, 1878, and 1882). Sennett wrote "Notes on the Ornithology of the Lower Rio Grande, Texas" (1878) and other articles about birds.

17. Francis Charles Browne (1830-1900), naturalist, was born in Cambridge, Mass. He was a graduate of Harvard University (1851).

18. Henry Augustus Ward (1834-1906), was born in Rochester, N.Y. There he founded Ward's Natural History Establishment, a leading supplier, even today, of biological specimens and materials.

19. Namely, Allen, Coues, and Brewster.

20. Francis Huntington Snow (1840-1935), naturalist and teacher, was born in Fitchburg, Mass. He graduated from Williams College in 1862 and was professor of natural history (1870-99) and chancellor (1890-1901) of the University of Kansas.

21. Boardman was a close friend of Baird and Brewer and a frequent contributor to such journals as *American Naturalist* and *Forest and Stream*.

22. Montague Chamberlain (1844-1924), ornithologist, was born in St. John, New Brunswick. He served as secretary to the Lawrence Scientific School (1893-1906). He was a member of the N.O.C. and a founder of the A.O.U.

23. Ruthven Deane (1851-1934), ornithologist, was born in Cambridge, Mass., and educated in Cambridge schools. He later went to Illinois, where he was president of the Illinois Audubon Society (1898-1914) and a member of the Chicago Academy of Sciences. He was also an original member of the N.O.C.

24. This book was, of course, Coues and Prentiss's "Avifauna Columbiana."

25. Coues may well have been overruled when it came to the inclusion of this paragraph. In letters to Allen of earlier date he had favored, in the original meeting, only attention to organizational matters.

26. *Bull. Nutt. Orn. Club*, VIII (Oct., 1883), 221.

27. The twenty-one men were: Charles Aldrich, Iowa; H. B. Bailey, E. P. Bicknell, D. G. Elliot, A. K. Fisher, J. B. Holder, E. A. Mearns, and C. Hart Merriam, New York; C. F. Batchelder, William Brewster, C. B. Cory, and H. A. Purdie, Massachusetts; C. E. Bendire, Oregon; N. C. Brown, Maine; M. Chamberlain, New Brunswick; Elliott Coues, D. W. Prentiss, and Robert Ridgway, District of Columbia; T. McIlwraith, Canada; R. W. Shufeldt, Louisiana; J. M. Wheaton, Ohio.

28. Twenty-three is the number as reported in *Bull. Nutt. Orn. Club*, VIII (Oct., 1883), 222. Actually the full number was twenty-five. Inadvertently, or otherwise, the names of H. W. Henshaw and George N. Lawrence had been

excluded. All twenty-five were later shown in "A Photograph of Photographs" which appeared in Chapman and Palmer, eds., *Fifty Years' Progress of American Ornithology, 1883-1933* (1933).

29. Chapman and Palmer, eds., *Fifty Years' Progress of American Ornithology*, 7.

30. Clinton Hart Merriam (1858-1952), naturalist, was born in New York City. He was educated at Yale's Sheffield Scientific School (1874-77) and College of Physicians and Surgeons (1879). He was later chief of the U.S. Biological Survey (1885-1910).

31. As reported in *Bull. Nutt. Orn. Club.*, VIII (Oct., 1883), 233, the twenty-four added were: W. B. Barrows, G. B. Grinnell, and J. H. Sage, Connecticut; F. E. L. Beal, Iowa; L. Belding and J. G. Cooper, Caifornia; Ruthven Deane and S. A. Forbes, Illinois; N. S. Goss, Kansas; T. N. Gill, H. W. Henshaw, and J. H. Kidder, District of Columbia; F. W. Langdon, Ohio; G. N. Lawrence and N. T. Lawrence, New York.; J. A. Jeffries, Massachusetts; F. H. King, Wisconsin; J. C. Merrill, Montana; H. Nehrling, Missouri; E. W. Nelson, Colorado; T. S. Roberts, Minnesota; W. E. D. Scott, Arizona; G. B. Sennett, Pennsylvania; and W. E. Saunders, Canada.

32. *Bull. Nutt. Orn. Club*, VIII (Oct., 1883), 226. That the Nuttall Ornithological Club continues to this day was probably due to Charles F. Batchelder's interest and effort. It remained a rather small and select group which, for years, held its meetings in his home. At the time of his death in 1954, Batchelder, then in his ninety-eighth year, was the last surviving founder of the A.O.U. In recent years the Nuttall Ornithological Club has resumed publication by sponsoring an important series of ornithological monographs.

33. Members of the Nuttall Ornithological Club who received invitations (in addition to Allen and Brewster) appear to have been H. B. Bailey, C. F. Batchelder, H. W. Henshaw, and H. A. Purdie.

34. Batchelder, "An Account on the Nuttall Ornithological Club," 46-47.

35. *Ibid.*

36. Chapman and Palmer, eds., *Fifty Years' Progress of American Ornithology*, 14-16.

37. *Auk*, I (Jan., 1884), 105.

38. Frank M. Chapman, "Joel Asaph Allen," *Memoirs Nat. Acad. Scis.*, XXI (1926), 5.

CHAPTER XVIII

Welcomed in Europe

Coues had good reason, as we know by now, for feeling kindly toward British scientists. As early as 1863 *The Ibis* had begun to take note of Coues as a most promising young American naturalist and in the years immediately ahead had published several of his articles, notably "Ornithology of a Prairie-Journey," "Notes on Various Birds Observed at Fort Whipple," and "From Arizona to the Sea." In 1872 the British Ornithologists' Union, then the largest organization of its kind in the world, had elected him to foreign membership. In 1876 the prestigious Zoological Society of London had made him a corresponding member. And in 1879 British scientists had honored him even more significantly: by transmitting to him the memorial signed by Charles Darwin, Thomas Huxley, and others which extolled his superlative contributions to ornithological bibliography. During these years, too, British ornithologists had regularly corresponded with Coues, and their letters had often reflected the admiration they felt for his scholarly attainments. Among those who had written him most often were Philip L. Sclater and Alfred Newton, and from time to time they had urged him to visit England.

It was early in 1884 when Coues first gave serious consideration to accepting the invitations from his fellow scientists on the opposite side of the Atlantic. As he wrote to Baird on February 5: "I hope to be able to make a visit to England soon, for a few months, accepting a very flattering invitation formerly extended to me. . . . You might possibly have something to be attended to for you there, and I should, of course, be pleased to go in some representative capacity."

Coues did not leave for Europe until May 24, by which date he had completed his revision of *Key to North American Birds* and had convinced the Century Company people that his commitments to them would in no way suffer because of his trip abroad. Also, with the National Medical College then in recess until fall, he had no concern about his obligations to that institution. Everything considered, the time seemed propitious. That he considered making the trip at all—an expensive one—is the strongest evidence possible that by now, if not before, he had the requisite means.

Coues sailed from New York aboard the S.S. *Oregon,* and seven days later disembarked at Liverpool.[1] On June 4, from the Covent Garden Hotel in London, he wrote Baird:

> I reached here yesterday, and find myself in very good hands; indeed, as you may suppose, Dr. Sclater having kindly tendered his hospitality, and put me in the way of all I could desire, I shall probably be able to spend a month or more here very pleasantly and advantageously, before making my continental tour. Let me know of any specific object which I can accomplish for you, apart from the general purposes of the letter you gave me. I shall spend a few days with Prof. Newton in Cambridge next week, but otherwise have no definite programs outside of London, where friends seem to be easily found to help me to all sorts of agreeable things.[2]

From this letter we first learn that Coues anticipated traveling on the Continent after a few weeks in England. The letter, too, provides evidence that he was making the visit, as he had wished, as a representative of the Smithsonian.

The outstanding event of Coues' stay in London occurred on July 1, when he addressed a special meeting of British zoologists. This meeting was held in the lecture room of the Zoological Department of the British Museum, South Kensington, the result of a call worded as follows:

> Sir: Taking advantage of the presence in this country of the distinguished American Zoologist Dr. Elliott Coues (who represents the advanced opinion of American naturalists), it is proposed to hold a meeting of British Zoologists to consider the expediency of adopting certain changes, more especially in the direction of trinomial nomenclature.
>
> For the purpose of obtaining a discussion of the question a meeting will be held . . . on Tuesday, July 1st, at 3 P.M. (Professor Flower[3] in the chair). . . . As the question is one of great importance to Zoologists your attendance at this meeting is *earnestly requested*. Dr. Coues will be present.[4]

The call, carrying the date of June 24, was signed by R. Bowdler Sharpe, to whose initiative and industry the organization of the symposium seems to have been due. Since Coues by then had been in England more than three weeks, the timing and wording of the call suggest that the meeting had been hurriedly arranged.

Many years later a prominent German ornithologist had this to say of the July 1 meeting of zoologists: "In 1884 a spark flew over the ocean and kindled a fire in Europe; immediately a general alarm was sounded to preserve the venerable structure of Linnaean nomenclature and, if possible, to smother the conflagration entirely."[5] This writer made it clear that the "spark" was, in essence, trinomial nomenclature, that it had been conveyed across the Atlantic by Elliott Coues, and that European zoologists were much more receptive to Coues the man than to his ideas on trinomialism. Even though Sundevall (a Swede) and Schlegel (a German) had been first in using trinomials, European zoologists in general had lagged behind the Americans in accepting trinomials. That this was particularly true with the British becomes obvious when we consider what was said at the London meeting of July 1.

The meeting was called to order by Professor Flower, who at once read a letter from Thomas Huxley expressing regret that official business prevented his being present. After brief introductory remarks the chair then introduced in turn R. Bowdler Sharpe, Henry Seebohm,[6] and Elliott Coues, each of whom addressed the audience on the subject of trinomialism.

Sharpe, after speaking at some length, concluded that the system could be employed to advantage in certain instances. The greatest difficulty he foresaw was that "it would open the door to a multiplication of species, or races."[7]

Seebohm, "with an extraordinary display of acute logic and brilliant dialectic," expressed himself as ready to adopt the American system (in spite of dangers foreseen by Sharpe) if allowed a slight modification, namely, the engrafting on trinomials "a means of designating the connecting links between such forms."[8] He suggested, for example, that the trinomial for a local race of a dipper found in Asia Minor and Persia be written *Cinclus aquaticus melanogaster-cashmiriensis.*[9]

Coues, when called upon, began by saying that he "was much gratified with the interest shown in the subject of zoological nomenclature." As reported in the local press, he said that

> Nomenclature was a necessary evil, and the point was always to employ that method of naming of objects which should most often reflect not only the characters of the objects themselves, but [also] our ideas respecting these characters and the view we take of them. As to what constitutes a species, there has been an absolute revolution in the definition of a species since the time of Linnaeus, the opinion having been long held that every species was a distinct and individual creation. But that idea had passed out

of existence in the minds of most natural historians of the present day, who accepted a general theory of the evolution of species by a gradual modification. That being the case, it was idle to inquire "What is a species?" No such thing existing any more than a genus; and so intimately related were all forms of animal and vegetable life that, if they were all before us, no naming would be possible, for each would be found to be connected completely with another; therefore the possibility of naming any species was, as it were, the gauge and test of our ignorance. . . .

What of so-called species the connecting links between which are still before our eyes? In illustration of this he would cite some instances of connecting links which exist between certain forms. He then referred to the case of one of the best-known Woodpeckers in North America (*Picus villosus*) [hairy woodpecker, now *Dendrocopos villosus*] and discussed its climatal and geographical variations. He was of the opinion that all these geographical races were indistinctly separable forms, and he would indicate them by trinomial names, proceeding upon the definite principle of geographical variation according to conditions of environment, meaning by all this the external influences which modify the plastic organism.

After commenting briefly on certain of the external influences, such as moisture, heat, and latitude, Coues concluded by reading a paragraph from his new *Key to North American Birds* which contained the rule now in use by North American ornithologists for the employment of trinomials.[10]

With the addresses by Sharpe, Seebohm, and Coues completed, the chair asked if others present would care to comment. The response was immediate, from several sources, and generally opposed to trinomialism. The most common objections were inconvenience and the risk of increase in numbers of species named. When all had had their say, Coues was given the opportunity to reply. According to the press report:

. . . the system of trinomial nomenclature had nothing whatever to do with individual variations of specimens from one locality. It was not a question of naming varieties or hybrids, but there was a definite principle to proceed upon, namely, that of geographic and climatal variation. He was well aware that the use of three names to designate objects in zoology was no new thing;[11] but he believed that the restricted application of trinomialism to the particular class of cases he had discussed was virtually novel, and that his system would prove to be one of great practical utility. He thought that the application of the principle was a question which, after this discussion, and after further private discussions, might well be left to the discretion of authors.[12]

To the above Coues might have added a comment on the trinomial system he had made earlier elsewhere: "The purpose of the trinomial system is an obvious one, yet that system is so sharp a tool, that without great care in handling, one is apt to cut his fingers with it."[13] Many of the British zoologists present at the meeting would have generously applauded that appraisal.

Before adjourning the symposium, Chairman Flower courteously remarked: "I hope that Dr. Elliott Coues is satisfied with the manner with which his views have been received. Although there are some uncompromising binomialists present, many have pronounced themselves as what may be termed limited trinomialists, and some appear to go as far as Dr. Coues himself. . . . I must express the thanks of the meeting to Dr. Coues for having brought his views and those of his countrymen, of whom he is such a worthy representative, before us."[14]

Addressing Britain's foremost zoologists, many of whom were Fellows of either the Royal Society or the Linnaean Society, was unquestionably an exhilarating and memorable experience for Coues, and we are convinced that Coues, with his ready tongue, seasoned intellect, specialized knowledge, and forceful personality, favorably impressed his British colleagues and was a material factor in their ultimate acceptance of trinomialism.

Almost immediately following the symposium, Coues wrote Allen. His letter was surcharged with ebullience:

> [My visit thus far has been] a continued round of "dining and wining" and receptions through the height of the London "season." . . . Have seen *everybody*, and I doubt that any unofficial character could have received more attention, personal, social or scientific. . . .
>
> All this led the way up to the formal meeting of British zoologists, as per what I enclose, which I brought about by carefully refraining from seeming to do so. . . . The assault on the works of Brit. conservatism was carried at the first rush. . . . Trinomialism is established. (Seebohm is sending the *Auk* a brief note, in the nature of a dispatch. I send you a copy of the "invitation." Now *print this invitation* in the *Auk* as a footnote to Seebohm's letter. Then take the "Field" report of the Proceedings and print that editorially, or make up an editorial digest of it. There is to be a verbatim report of the meeting to run through several numbers of *Nature*. See that, too, and use it for *Auk* in any editorial way your judgment dictates.)
>
> Well it is all abroad!! In the air. I have made psychic commotion enough, and now let the fire run along the lines! A.O.U. stock is clear up in the skies, by patient diplomacy and then sudden audacity. Take advantage

of the boom and let it reverberate at the coming [A.O.U.] meeting. Sclater, Saunders, Seebohm and others will be there. Keep your grip firm on everything, so as to be sure everything goes exactly as we want it. As I said to Newton (a private crony of mine now) who asked me why I must be back at the next diaper-changing of our infant, you and I have swaddled it up so tight, that neither of us can open it without the other. *L'A.O.U. c'est nous,* and don't forget this, nor the fact that nobody in England now supposes it to be anything else! And it would be ludicrous if any mistakes of ours should result in anything else.

Coues' "Book of Dates" (1884) tells of other gala events in London: on June 16 *The Ibis* gave a banquet in his honor and on July 4 he dined with Thomas Huxley, P.R.S., who, since Darwin's death in 1882, had become the doyen of British zoologists.

2

Just before Coues left the United States for Europe, an American journalist had informed his readers that Coues was making his European trip "partly for research and partly for recreation."[15] On the basis of the meager information at hand, it would appear that his travels on the Continent were more for recreation than science.

Coues began his tour on July 12 and completed it some six weeks later, on August 24. In that time he visited Belgium, Germany, Switzerland, and France and stopped in several of the larger cities of each.

Leaving London at 7:30 A.M. on July 12, Coues traveled by way of Dover, Calais, and Brussels to Cologne. On the 14th he ascended the Rhine by boat to Mainz. On the 15th he went by rail to Heidelberg and on the 16th, again by rail, to Cham (a town in the canton of Zug), Switzerland.[16] He remained in Switzerland eight days and, like many tourists before and since, moved rapidly from place to place. His itinerary, as it appears in his "Book of Dates," reads as follows: "[July] 18, 19 at Cham; July 20, to Zug; boat on Lake Zug; up the Rigi by cog road. July 21, down the Rigi to Vitznau; boat on Lake Lucerne to Fluellen; carriage to Altdorf; rail to Goshenen; carriage by Furea to Rhone glacier. July 22 horseback over mt. to Grimsall and Imboden, passing Chute de L'Har, thence carriage to Meiringen. 23, carriage to Lucerne, rail back to Cham. July 24 at Cham. 25, via Lucerne, Basle, Mainz and Cologne to Elberfeld." During the next three weeks Coues divided his time between such German cities as Elberfeld, Düsseldorf, Würzburg, Bayreuth, Nuremberg, Stuttgart, and Cologne. On August 19 he left Elberfeld for Paris, where he stayed four days. He returned to London on the 24th, sailed from Liverpool on the 30th, and disembarked in New York City on September 10th.

It would make for a more comfortable feeling if we could report in more detail about Coues' activities while on the Continent, especially during the three weeks near the end of his visit when he was shuttling back and forth from one German city to another and in the four days he spent in Paris. We feel confident that Coues, in both countries, must have taken time to visit with fellow scientists and to examine museum collections, though we have found nothing whatever to support our confidence.

We would be happier, too, if we could report that while in England Coues had persuaded a British ornithologist to accompany him to the countryside to help him identify the English birds. Is it possible that he returned to the United States without having become acquainted with the nightingale, robin, blackbird, chaffinch, jackdaw, blackcap warbler, and other birds he had read so much about in English ballads, novels, and nursery stories? We think it unlikely, but, again, nowhere have we found anything to indicate that he did.

Coues did *not* visit the Isle of Jersey, where his great-grandfather Peter Coues had been born, nor did he make a side-trip to Normandy in an attempt to locate individuals bearing the name of Coues. He had earlier written, we will recall, that his name was "Norman-French, and is still not infrequently found in the north of France."

There were other things that Coues did not do while in Europe. He did not, for instance, climb either the Jungfrau or the Matterhorn; but he did attain heights, lofty personal ones, never before attained: *The Ibis* gave a banquet in his honor, the most eminent of British zoologists invited him to speak on the subject of trinomialism, and Thomas Huxley, renowned champion of Darwinism, asked to share a meal with him.

3

It would be to our advantage if we knew Coues' frame of mind while crossing the Atlantic on his return to the United States. Despite most pleasant recollections of the past three months, was he eminently happy and in high spirits? Unless we are sadly in error, not entirely.

Coues was returning to a broken home, to ambitions as yet unrealized, and to work which, though not distasteful, held no promise of advancement professionally. Before leaving for Europe, he had been happily engaged in fashioning the reissues of his *Key* and *Check List*.

Now, with those labors done, he had little to look forward to beyond the resumption of his lectures at the National Medical College, his definitional commitments to *The Century Dictionary,* and the writing of occasional articles for *The Auk* or other periodicals. Furthermore, by their very nature these jobs had almost completely divorced him from the out-of-doors and companionship with birds and other animals which, for so many years, had provided wholesome rewards in the form of relaxation, contentment, and the anticipation of discovery.

There was ample time during the Atlantic crossing for Coues to consider his future. There was time, too, to compare his present lot with those of British friends, such as Newton, Sharpe, and Flower, who held important posts at Cambridge University and the British Museum. If such thoughts did run through Coues' mind, as they may well have, then they were tinged with dissatisfaction if not bitterness. For several years Coues had wanted a position on the Smithsonian staff. As early as 1869, while at Fort Macon, he had written Baird, we may recall: "Isn't there *any* chance of my being able to get a Washington station as soon as I have squeezed Macon a little drier? I do want it so badly!"

Years passed and Baird seemingly never even considered appointing Coues to a station in Washington. He did find places for others. In 1880, for instance, he had made Robert Ridgway, younger than Coues by eight years, curator of birds at the U.S. National Museum, an appointment that did not go unnoticed, of course, by Coues.

At some point Coues' attitude toward his former mentor began to change, perhaps soon after his resignation from the Army, when it became apparent to him that Baird would probably never find a place for him at the Smithsonian. Evidence that his attitude did change, and that he did continue to covet a post at the Smithsonian, is to be found in a series of letters to which we now turn.

In October, 1884, about a month after Coues' return from Europe, he wrote Baird:

> I find my desk nearly clear of bird work, for the first time for many years, and am strongly desirous of completing the history of N.A. mammals,[17] which has been in the stocks so long. This can be done with your assistance, probably not without.... I have bushels of manuscripts, but none of it is in shape for printer's copy, and as I have nothing but my time to live upon I am obliged to make it the support of my family, by writing that which people will pay me to read. Consequently, the case is a very simple one: ... if you can give me, or procure for me, an official position which shall be to any reasonable extent commensurate with what I suppose

my standing as a naturalist to be, and which shall at the same time afford me a decent livelihood, I shall be glad to bend my energies in this direction. I think my proposed work is very much needed, there having been, as you know, no complete systematic treatise on N.A. M[ammals] since 1857,[18] and I know that I have both the material and the ability to make a creditable & valuable work. Let me add . . . it could easily be made a Smithsonian or National Museum publication, if you should wish it. . . .

There was nothing novel, of course, about Coues importuning Baird for favors; he had been doing that for more than twenty years, and from points as widely separated as Fort Macon, North Carolina, and Fort Whipple, Arizona Territory. To our knowledge, though, he had never before quite so forthrightly appealed to Baird for an "official position," by which he meant, beyond little doubt, one at either the Smithsonian or the U.S. National Museum.[19]

Two weeks and more went by without a reply from Baird, and Coues, seemingly unable to control his impatience longer, wrote him again: "Will you kindly let me know what to expect, with reference to my last letter on the matter of the History of Mammals? . . . I can do nothing in that direction without your countenance & cooperation . . . and I appeal to you to assist me in preventing the results of several years' labor from coming to nought."

On December 2, apparently still awaiting a reply from Baird, Coues addressed himself to J. A. Allen, in words making all too plain how far his previously close and harmonious relationship with Baird had deteriorated: "I am truly sorry to hear what you say in your last letter. . . . I have never thought you sufficiently appreciated, nor paid enough there [at the Museum of Comparative Zoology]. . . . You do not say what you expect, or where it is to be.[20] . . . I wish you could be here [at the Smithsonian]—is that possible? But it is B's [Baird's] settled policy never to have one of his peers or betters about him—so that this establishment is simply a hatching house of henchmen who make an honest living by doing what they are told to do. . . ."[21]

Coues had vented his spleen, as he had done before and would again, but this time, incredibly, against the one man in the world who had done more to advance him professionally than any other. His action, as we see it, admits of only one interpretation; he was nettled because Baird had failed to find a place for him at the Smithsonian. Looking at the other side of the coin, it seems plain enough that Baird, who knew Coues inside and out, foresaw more headaches than help if he added Coues to his staff.

Baird finally replied to Coues, and though we do not have his letter, by reading Coues' answer, written December 14, we can easily guess what Baird had told him:

Your letter is to hand, and very carefully considered, both in spirit and in letter. While it is of course, as you suggested, disappointing in particulars, it is even more unsatisfactory in a larger and more general sense, which I fear you do not rightly or fully appreciate. I thank you for your kind offer of assistance in my mammalogical work. There is not the slightest difficulty in getting *published* anything I write now;[22] the point is that I need the use and benefit of some small fraction of the money which you hold in trust and disburse for the increase and diffusion of knowledge. The special point at issue will be met if you will kindly provide me with the services of an amanuensis, a draughtsman and a messenger for the furtherance of such desirable scientific purposes as I have in view, and the result of which, I make bold to say, I have the knowledge, the ability and experience to make creditable to the Institution and to yourself. If there be, as you say, no fund for the endowment of scientific research, why not, among the multifarious lines of administration which you so ably and deservedly control, involving the disbursement of many hundred thousand dollars annually, make such change that scientific research may be, if not "endowed," at least more successfully prosecuted and in some respects more worthwhile represented than it has always been of late?

I am far from presuming to criticise, still less to appear to dictate in any detail of your administrative policy; but I have been for some years a silent, observant and reflective "looker on in Venice," and have come to certain settled conclusions which I think it is important for you, *for your own sake*, to know and weigh. The Secretary of the Smithsonian Institution has of course no lack of friends, but even Professor Baird may need to know who of those about him are such. I am no alarmist, and far as possible from meddling with what is not my own business; but I think you cannot be fully aware of a certain state of things about you which means not only difficulty to you, but [also] positive danger. A recent affair was but a little flash of explosive material which lurks in many an unsuspected corner of your great establishment. I speak advisedly; and your reputation for diplomacy and sagacity will be hard to maintain if your eyes continue closed with a sense of security which has little foundation in fact. I do not write more explicitly since it appears that my personal letters to you may come under the observation of some of your subordinates whose views and wishes, rather than your own judgment, have in at least one late instance dictated your reply—which, in my judgment, is not as it should be.

Many things may be said of the above letter, few of them flattering to its writer. For example, in spite of his disclaimers, Coues *was* critical, demanding, meddling, and by no means innocent of trying to dictate. Also, he was outrageously disrespectful, as when implying that subordinates "in at least one late instance" had dictated Baird's recent letter to Coues. We do not know what the "certain state of things" threatening Baird was, but Coues' remarks suggest an institution beset by intrigue, with enemies of Baird lurking in every corner.

Baird answered Coues at once, on December 16, and in this instance we do have his letter:

> In reply to your letter of December 14, I can only renew the assurance of the impossibility of doing what you ask in the way of furnishing you with the necessary assistance to carry on your scientific work, the value of which no one appreciates better than I do. The Institution has, on several occasions furnished to investigators whose work was considered desirable, the means for their researches, when not too expensive, this including material and apparatus, and to some extent books. It has never undertaken to supply parties with clerical or office aid. The Smithsonian always has on hand a larger number of publications which are offered freely to it, without any consideration or stipulation, than it can publish; and the rule was long ago established by Professor Henry and accepted by myself—the object being to present as large an amount of original matter as possible—that it is better to take the same money to print two memoirs furnished complete than it is to prepare and print one. Another important principle is that all expenditures connected with the preparation of material for publication must be for those that will in all probability be printed by the Institution itself; and this, of course, in view of the enormous magnitude of your undertaking and the amount of illustrations involved would be far beyond our means to compass.
>
> You speak of my having the control of the disbursement of many hundreds of thousands of dollars annually, and suggest that out of that I might make some arrangement for meeting your request. Even if this were abstractly proper, you do not consider how rigidly the accounts of all disbursements are scrutinized at the Treasury Department, and any expenditure not strictly germane to the words of the appropriations being promptly disallowed.

Manifestly, in replying, Baird had been firm and forthright, but also courteous. A man of lesser stature might have been curt and reproachful. Further to his credit, he utterly ignored Coues' veiled allusion to the "certain state of things" threatening his personal welfare and, by indirection, that of the entire institution.

No reply from Coues to the above has been found—quite possibly he made none—so we are unable to assess Coues' reactions to what

Baird had written. We can attest, however, to the immediate and long-range effects of this most unfortunate exchange of letters. Coues did not then or ever obtain the "official position" he had requested, and he had to abandon once and for all his hopes of completing the projected history of North American mammals. Even more deplorably, the once close relationship between the two men suffered irreparable damage. Coues would write to Baird again, infrequently, but not one of his succeeding letters ended, as had ones of earlier years, with strong expressions of gratitude and affection.

The story of the Coues-Baird relationship does not end quite yet. Baird died three years later, on August 19, 1887, and on August 25 Coues wrote Allen: "*Nestor* has departed—Well time flies, and some of the rest of us will be there before a great while. We have of course the proper action to take officially, and no doubt the great loss to science, & the A.O.U., should find appropriate expression next October. What shall we put in the Oct. *Auk*? Probably a black-edged page, with brief formal notice, & statement of further action to be taken at the coming Congress." These remarks, about the man who had once been Coues' "Almus pater," need no comment; they speak for themselves.

In days ahead, at Allen's request, Coues obtained printed copies of a Baird portrait to be used in *The Auk*, and officers of the A.O.U. discussed who should deliver the memorial address on Baird at the next A.O.U. congress. On hearing from Allen that Ridgway had been chosen for that honor, Coues replied immediately:

> I think likely, Ridgway's unexpected acceptance has been due to me, for I saw him and rather urged it upon him, that he should prepare something about Baird—not knowing, of course, that the matter was then to be made one of formal invitation—in which case, and it should be put upon ceremony or officiality or made a matter of honoring a person by giving him the chance—that of course belongs rightfully to me, and yet is not given me, and by your own admission, the most fit has been displaced for the next most so. As I am no intriguer and not good at complications I cannot enter the list of contestants for any favors, and simply withdraw from any participation in the memorial address or whatever the *Auk* may have to say—which can no doubt be perfectly well prepared by anyone else.

Now Coues knew full well that the prerogative to deliver the memorial address honoring Baird did not "rightfully" belong to him. Indeed, he admitted as much in his next letter to Allen: "Pardon my hasty letter [of September 8]. I had been irritated all that day by a series of disagreements, & just in the mood to jump at a wrong conclusion. I see at once that I was quite in the wrong, & hasten to say so. You are always good enough to take the trouble to explain my mistakes to me. . . . Everything is all right, thanks to your care, and I am agreeable to any way the programme may eventuate." It was to Coues' credit, of course, that he admitted his mistake, though we think the reason prompting it was his ever-present envy of Ridgway, not his irritation "by a series of disagreements."

Coues did not attend the 1887 A.O.U. congress, held in Boston that year. Instead, he honeymooned in Portsmouth, with his third wife (about whom more later). Perhaps it was just as well, for we doubt if he would have enjoyed listening to Ridgway's glowing tribute to Baird, and particularly to the part which said: "A very marked trait of Professor Baird's character was his aversion to personal controversy, which was so decided that under no circumstances would he be drawn into one. It was his invariable rule to answer his critics by a dignified silence, no matter how great the provocation to reply, or how strong a case his side presented."[23]

Irony may often unexpectedly insinuate itself into situations. In Coues' "Book of Dates" (1887) we find: "Nov. 17, elected Honorary Member of the Spencer F. Baird Naturalists Association of Reading, Pa."

4

The highlight of this general period for Coues was, of course, his trip to Europe and his meetings with British zoologists. He must also have been pleased with two events which happened at home, each an expression of affection and gratitude. He referred to one of these in his "Book of Dates" (1884): "Early this year or late in 1883 was published B. G. Lovejoy's Life of Lord Bacon,[24] dedicated to me." Lovejoy's dedication reads:

> To his earliest and latest friend,
> Professor ELLIOTT COUES, A.M., M.D., Ph.D., Etc.,
> Distinguished in two continents as a scientist,
> cherished by the few who know him best for
> his warm, unselfish heart and capacity
> for disinterested friendship,
> this volume
> is affectionately dedicated by
> the author

At about this same time (though unmentioned in Coues' "Book of

Dates"), J. Hibbert Langille dedicated to Coues his *Our Birds in Their Haunts*.[25] Langille's dedication read:

To Dr. Elliott Coues
Whose printed works, private correspondence
and
Great personal kindness
Have been of inestimable value to any success
possible for this book,
it is
gratefully and affectionately
dedicated by
the author

We have mentioned before, and shall do so again, how helpful Coues could be to new acquaintances, no matter what their age.

NOTES

1. See Coues' "Book of Dates" (1884).
2. On his way to London from Liverpool, Coues made stops at such places as Rowsley, Chatsworth, Coventry, Kenilworth, and Stratford-on-Avon. See his "Book of Dates."
3. Sir William Henry Flower, F.R.S. (1831-99), English zoologist, was born in Stratford-on-Avon, studied medicine at University College, London, and in 1884 was made director of the natural history department of the British Museum.
4. Allen, "Zoological Nomenclature" (1884), 338.
5. Stresemann, *Ornithology from Aristotle to the Present*, 250.
6. Henry Seebohm, F.L.S. (1832-95), British ornithologist, was the author of such books as *A History of British Birds* (1883-85) and *The Birds of Siberia* (1901).
7. Allen, "Zoological Nomenclature," 342.
8. Stresemann, *Ornithology from Aristotle to the Present*, 250.
9. Allen, "Zoological Nomenclature," 350.
10. *Nature* (London), July 17, 1884, 277.
11. In other words, Coues was familiar with Sundevall, Schlegel, and others who were forerunners in the use of trinomials.
12. *Nature* (London), July 17, 1884, 279.
13. Coues, "On the Application of Trinomial Nomenclature to Zoology" (1884), 246.
14. Allen, "Zoological Nomenclature," 349-50.
15. *Auk*, I (July, 1884), 306.
16. Coues' "Book of Dates" (1884).
17. See "Material for a Bibliography of North American Mammals," in Coues and Allen's *Monographs of North American Rodentia* (1877), 951-1081.

18. Coues was here referring to Baird's *Mammals of North America* (1857).

19. The U.S. National Museum is an outgrowth of, and under the direction of, the Smithsonian Institution.

20. Presumably the American Museum of Natural History, New York City, since Allen went there the following year (1885) as its curator of birds and mammals.

21. For this letter see Hellman, *Bankers, Bones and Beetles* (1969), 97-98.

22. On Nov. 10, 1884, Coues' sister Grace married the Boston publisher Dana Estes, of the firm of Estes and Lauriat. Coues, therefore, was sure of himself when telling Baird that he had "not the slightest difficulty in getting *published* anything I write now." In fact, Estes and Lauriat had already published Coues' *Check List* (1882) and the second edition of his *Key* (1884).

23. Ridgway, "Spencer Fullerton Baird" (1888), 10-11.

24. Benjamin G. Lovejoy (-1889), author of *A Fool's Paradise, a Story of Fashionable Life in Washington* (1884) and *Francis Bacon (Lord Verulam), a Critical Review of His Life and Character with Selections from His Writings* (1883). In his "Book of Dates" (1889) Coues wrote: "Nov. 21, 10:30 A.M. died Benj. G. Lovejoy, 902 12th St. Funeral 23d. One of the wisest and best friends I ever had; since 1854."

25. James Hibbert Langille (1841-1923), Baptist minister and ornithologist, was born in Nova Scotia, graduated from Oberlin College in 1867, and afterward prepared for the ministry. In 1885 he gave up his ministerial work and moved to Maryland, where he devoted much of his time to studying birds and contributing articles to *The Auk* and other periodicals. *Our Birds in Their Haunts, a Popular Treatise on the Birds of Eastern North America* was published in 1884.

CHAPTER XIX

Theosophy and Spiritualism

Coues' early life gives no hint of a commitment to religion. The Universalist-Congregationalist background of his family seems to have made no impression on him even during childhood. His association with a Catholic institution, Washington Seminary, had been one of educational convenience alone. In fact, the only consistent theme in matters of religion was a prolonged antipathy to Catholicism. In his later writings he seldom missed an opportunity to hurl gratuitous insults at the Church of Rome.[1]

The "Book of Dates" shows that in 1867 he became affiliated with a quasi-religious organization: "Richland Lodge, A[ssociated and] F[ree] M[asons] No. 39, Columbia, S.C., initiated Feb. 27, passed Apr. 18, and raised to 3d degree May 30." Membership in the Masons is mentioned in only two other entries, for 1889: "Apr. 23, Royal Arch Masonic Banquet, Temple, West 23d st., N.Y." and "June 5 is date of DIMIT of Richland Lodge No. 39, of Columbia, S.C., of which I was made a Master Mason [third degree] in 1867 or 1868."[2]

During the late 1860s science absorbed his mind and energies almost exclusively, and it is safe to assume that his involvement in Freemasonry was brief or superficial. Yet is is also likely that initiation into the mysteries of the order helped to prepare him for later delvings into even more esoteric matters.

Dissatisfaction with science for its own sake was expressed in his February 5, 1874, letter to John Burroughs (in which he complained of being involved in mere "shop-work"), in his paper on "Imagination" (1877), and in his poetic outbursts of the later 1870s.[3] It was apparent by that time that he wanted some answers which science alone could not provide.

The first emphatic break with orthodox science, so far as we know, did not come until May 6, 1882, when at a meeting of the Philosophical Society of Washington he delivered a paper entitled "On the Possibilities of Protoplasm." In his talk he announced his belief in the human soul, composed, in part, of a semi-material substance which he called "biogen." He defined biogen as "spirit in combination with the minimum of matter necessary to its manifestation. Biogen is simply soul-stuff, as contradistinguished from ordinary matter; it is the substance which composes the thing which a well-known and very frequently quoted writer calls the 'spiritual body.'"[4]

As Coues readily acknowledged, the concept was by no means a new one, but since he, a distinguished scientist, was endeavoring to give it scientific respectability, it is no wonder that members of the audience, notably Theodore Gill and John Wesley Powell, voiced polite but firm opposition to such a deviation from the accepted canons of science.[5]

This sort of opposition seems only to have steeled Coues' resolve to compound his "heresy." Later that year he had the paper published in pamphlet form, with the title *Biogen: A Speculation on the Origin and Nature of Life*. Although he failed to persuade the editors of the American Supplement to the *Encyclopaedia Britannica* to include an article on biogen,[6] nothing could stop him from incorporating a discussion of biogen and related matters into the later editions of his own *Key to North American Birds*.[7] If we interpret his meaning correctly in *Biogen* and later works, "biogen," "ghost," and "astral body" are virtually interchangeable terms.

This was simply the beginning of Coues' long search into "forbidden" areas. Next came a long, blank-verse poem entitled *The Daemon of Darwin*, which had been "originally prepared as a memorial address to be delivered from the Chair of Anatomy of the National Medical College at Washington, at the opening of the session, Oct. 2, 1882. . . ."[8] The poem concerns the death and burial of Charles Darwin and the evolution of his soul into the spirit world. The more important part of it is the dialogue between the spirits of Socrates and Darwin in which the truths of the philosophy of the ancients are reconciled with modern evolutionary science.

Taking *Biogen* and *The Daemon of Darwin* together, Coues was saying not only that he believed in the existence of the human soul but also that the soul, being at least semi-material, was subject to the process of evolution—that the soul evolved into the higher realms of the spirit world. In *The Daemon of Darwin* Socrates put it this way to Darwin:

The terms of Greek philosophy sound stronger with the meaning after-centuries have found, since mind has been applied so close to nature that the two seem one possessor of each other's mystery. Let me in turn select the phrases of a later day, to indicate the subtile chemistry by which that "duplicate substantial" thou has named, that spiritual body, is evolved by natural selection from the grosser states of matter which compose the earthly body, and thus fitted to survive. Such is the human soul, investiture of spirit, which configures spirit in the overworld as is itself configured by the body in the underworld. No thaumaturgy this, the growth of soul, but natural law, which operates to a defined result, yielding soul-substance in the process: matter still, but altered in the aggregation of the atoms and their modes of motion, sensed by the rational soul in terms of thought. So doth thy new philosophy confirm the old; so mayst thou, from thy lofty station with the stars, disseminate thy fruitful spirit everywhere, that earth-born man, his feet the solid ground of Nature treading, firmly may cross the threshold of the unseen world, to view eternal verities.[9]

Coues delivered the poem again later in the year, on November 14, "at Claybaugh Hall, 14th St., before Trinity Presbyterian Church." He gave a third reading of it in the following year, February 19, 1883, at the "High School Building."[10] Some of the leading intellectual lights of Boston, including Alpheus Hyatt, and the mayor, Albert Palmer, invited him to favor their city with a reading. Coues consented and delivered it at Boston's Tremont Temple on March 1, 1883. Nearly 2,000 people were present to hear Palmer give the speaker a warm introduction. For the most part Coues' listeners and the Boston press responded favorably to the lecture-poem.[11]

The attempt to reconcile science with religion, made poetically by Coues in *The Daemon of Darwin*, was enunciated in a prosaic and often confusing address before Washington's Unity Club on December 15, 1882. The talk (which was published as a pamphlet in 1883) was entitled "The Harmony of Scientific Knowledge and Religious Faith." In it he took the practitioners of both science and religion to task for creating an artificial antagonism between the two. He was especially hard on his fellow scientists for relying too much on mere reason. The scientist, Coues urged, should recognize that imagination is a higher faculty than reason, and that faith is the highest human attribute: "Faith is spiritual reason; it is the eye back of the eye. *Faith is the soul's self-knowledge.*"

I must take it for granted, then, that there is this "other world" around and about us—a world of light and life, teeming with veritable spiritual existences, and exhibiting an infinitude of immaterial phenomena, ranged in orderly inter-relationships under the "reign of law" as immutable as that which governs us; in short a REAL WORLD; of which according alike to the esoteric doctrines of Egyptian, Chaldean, Hindoo and Christian philosophy, this visible world of ours is but, as it were, a shadow. We are accustomed to call this the realm of the supernatural, and to designate its phenomena as spiritual; but I submit that the simple word "natural" covers all the ground. A spiritual thing is certainly not *un*natural, and if the other world be not a blind chaos (which is inconceivable), it is subject to conditioning as proper to itself—that is to say, as natural, as those known in the physical world.[12]

2

Thus far Coues' forays into unconventional (for a scientist) areas of thought appear not to have caused much comment among his scientific associates. But in 1884 his deviation from the conventional became, to his colleagues, even more embarrassingly public. That year, while in England, he met some of the leaders of the movement known as Theosophy, founded by Mme. Helena Blavatsky.

Coues' second edition to his *Check List* (1882) makes a passing reference to *Isis Unveiled* (an early work by Mme. Blavatsky, published in New York in 1876),[13] but his introduction to the Theosophists (including perhaps Mme. Blavatsky herself) in England apparently brought about a full commitment to the tenets of the group. Upon his return to the United States he became the founder and president of the Gnostic Theosophical Society of Washington.[14]

Neither Mme. Blavatsky nor Theosophy can be easily explained. Helena Petrovna Hahn-Hahn Blavatsky was born in 1831 in Russia. At the age of seventeen she married an elderly official, Nikifor Blavatsky, from whom she separated a few months later. According to her own, often vague testimony, she traveled in the United States, Mexico, Canada, and the Far East for the next several years. After her return to Russia in 1858 she became a well-known spiritualistic medium. She immigrated to the United States in 1873 and became a naturalized citizen. Along with some of her followers she founded the Theosophical Society in 1875 in New York. Long after her death in 1891 she remained the center of a controversy over the genuineness of her teachings and claims. Dismissing her as a fraud is not satisfactory. The influence of her writings continues in occult circles today.

Although Theosophy is, by the admission of its adherents, almost impossible to define, we can characterize it as a syncretistic cult which attempts to combine and synthesize mystical and occult teachings from all the major religious traditions, but actually leaning heavily on Buddhism and Hinduism. Coues himself wrote that Buddhism and Theosophy were "much the same thing."[15]

Between 1884 and 1889 Coues served the cause of Theosophy in America with his characteristic vitality. No doubt the Theosophists counted themselves fortunate to have such a famous and energetic person in their midst, and in short order he became a leader of the movement. At the July 4-5, 1885, meeting in Cincinnati of the American Board of Control of the Theosophical Society, he was made its president.[16]

At the same gathering Coues was also appointed "censor" of the recently established American Society for Psychical Research. In this capacity Coues was "to publicly review and criticise any and all of the Proceedings, Transactions, Bulletins, or other printed matter which the said Society may publish, at his judgment and discretion," and to explain, from a theosophical standpoint, any findings made by the society. Coues told J. A. Allen on July 26, 1885, that the office of censor was created because the Theosophical Society's offer to cooperate with the new organization had been met with a snub.[17] The announcement of the appointment drew an understandably outraged response from members of the A.S.P.R. One of them publicly charged that the Theosophists created the office out of fear that their "shadowy tenets" would be undermined by the researches of the A.S.P.R.[18]

Coues was re-elected to the presidency of the board of control at its next meeting, at Rochester on July 3, 1886.[19] By that year he was also a member of the "Executive Council of India."[20] On November 2, 1887, he was made an honorary member of the Arjuna Theosophical Society of St. Louis, and in the following year, April 22-23, he "presided over the annual Convention of Theos. Soc. at the Sherman House, Chicago."[21]

Coues did not confine his occult activities to Theosophy alone. While in England on June 30, 1884, he was elected to associate membership in the London Society for Psychical Research.[22] The possibility of psychical research was no mere academic question for Coues. He shocked many of his friends and colleagues by a letter to the editor of *Science* entitled "Can Ghosts be Investigated?" His answer was an emphatic "Yes."

Science refused to print his letter, but Coues succeeded in getting it published in the December 25, 1884, issue of the *Nation*. In the letter he stated that he had investigated ghosts by means of smell, sight, sound, and touch, and "by the physical, chemical, or microscopical examination of detached portions of them, as hair, nails, or pieces of any substance which may envelop them more or less completely." He even asserted that ghosts (or "veridical phantoms") could be weighed, even though he admitted that he had not yet employed this means of investigation.[23] Since Coues here claims that on numerous occasions he had conjured up ghosts and talked with them, we are disappointed that he never tells us *which* ghosts he encountered.

In another letter to the editor of the *Nation*, written on December 28, 1884, he sought to unite mental telepathy to his own pet theory by suggesting that the transference of "thought waves" from one person to another was accomplished by means of biogen.[24] His address to the 1885 graduating class of the National Medical College, entitled "The Meaning of the Human Body," was a recondite lecture which blended anatomy, Theosophy, and the biogen idea.[25]

On April 26, 1888, at the First Methodist Church of Chicago, he spoke on "The Signs of the Times: From the Standpoint of a Scientist." Although he was vague about almost all of the topics treated in the address, he discussed "The Woman Question," "The Naros or Cycle of 600 Years," "The International Congress of Women," "Evidence of the Truth of Spritualism," "Phenomenal Spritualism," "Animal Magnetism and Its Dangers," "The Biogen Theory," "The Astral Body," and "Natural Magic." The speech was printed in the *Religio-Philosophical Journal* of May 12, 1888, and sometime later in *Light* ("the leading English Spritualistic periodical"). So popular was it in occult circles that it was published in pamphlet form in 1889.[26] On January 14 of that year Coues reported to Allen that an edition of 3,000 copies was nearly sold out.

Coues almost single-handedly created a new outlet for the publication of works written by himself and other writers on theosophical and occult subjects: the Biogen Series. The series was launched in 1884 with a second edition of *Biogen*. In 1885, as number two in the series, came the first appearance in print of *The Daemon of Darwin*. Number three was *A Buddhist Catechism* (1885), by the most influential American Theosophist, Henry Steel Olcott,[27] with notes by Coues. The fourth number in the series was *Can Matter Think?* The author of this pamphlet simply identified himself as "F. T. S." (i.e., Fellow of the Theosophical Society). Coues edited and wrote a preface and the notes for the work. The preface contains a letter from F. T. S. stating that his own views were "not widely at variance from those to which you have given expression in 'Biogen.' . . ."[28]

Number five was entirely by Coues: *Kuthumi: The True and Complete Oeconomy of Human Life, Based on the System of Theosophical Ethics.* This work, published in 1886, is understandable only by the *cognoscenti.* In it and in his extensive notes to *A Buddhist Catechism* and *Can Matter Think?* Coues showed himself to be thoroughly steeped in oriental religious teachings.

The Biogen Series was something of a family enterprise: Coues was the general editor as well as its chief contributor, and his brother-in-law, Dana Estes,[29] was one of the partners of the Boston firm which published the series. Grace Darling Coues, whose first husband, Charles Page, had died in 1873, married Estes at Coues' Washington home on November 10, 1884.[30]

In 1885 Coues was given an additional editorial post in the cause of the occult: the associate editorship of *Die Sphinx,* a Leipzig, Germany, monthly devoted to mysticism.[31] Its subtitle was: *Monatschrift für Seelen und Geistesleben.* The first number appeared in 1886 and the journal continued to be published until 1896. We do not know how long Coues was associated with it, but assume that his editorial duties were light or nonexistent.

Coues' last activity in connection with organized Theosophy occurred on April 24, 1889, when he spoke to a "large assemblage" at Cartier Hall in New York City on the topic "Modern Miracles."[32] According to *Appleton's Annual Cyclopaedia,*

> He condemned the commercial kind of spiritualistic *seances,* but he maintained that the phenomena of spiritualism were so generally experienced that it no longer lay in the power of any one to deny the spiritual existence. The astral body could certainly make itself manifest to some beings—to such as were in sympathy allied to it; but only those who had been initiated could understand the mysteries of theosophy and enjoy its philosophy. To these there are no mysteries. In the astral existence, time and space do not embarrass as they do in the material existence, and the range of the astral intelligence is not limited by them. The number of those who sincerely desire to receive the light of theosophy and to believe is rapidly on the increase.[33]

3

In its story on the Cartier Hall speech the *New York Times* reported that Coues was soon to depart on a world tour that would take him to

London and Europe (where he would consult with Mme. Blavatsky and other leaders of Theosophy), Egypt, and India (where he would converse with "nature Princes").[34]

Not only did the trip never take place, but on June 22, 1889, Coues found himself expelled from the Theosophical Society!

Exactly what caused the break is not known. Yet even before 1889 there is evidence of a strained relationship between Coues and the theosophical movement. As early as 1886, in a communication to *Science*, Coues asked "to be allowed to use this occasion to protest against and to obviate the prevalent misconception that 'Blavatsky' and 'theosophy' are synonymous terms, or that either the manners or morals of any individual theosophist necessarily represent the methods, objects, and purposes of the theosophical society."[35] Here Coues was doubtless referring to the allegations of Mme. Blavatksy's immorality, which included accusations of bigamy. In a letter to the editor of the *Religio-Philosophical Journal* dated September 21, 1888, Coues emphasized: "Though I have allowed my name to become in some measure identified with the modern cult which is now widely known under the name of 'Theosophy,' and though I have acquired through this association some knowledge concerning which I think it inexpedient at present to take the public into my confidence, I am far from insisting upon the superiority of theosophical doctrines for all persons or all purposes."[36]

According to one biographical account of Coues, the break was precipitated by his failure to capture the presidency of the American branch of the movement.[37] His scientific associates believed that his stormy departure from theosophical circles resulted from his disenchantment with both the claims and the officials of the cult.[38] The latter view is reinforced by a long (full-page) interview with Coues reported in the *New York Sun*. Here he pulled out all stops—accusing Mme. Blavatsky of rampant sexual promiscuity, plagiarism, financial chicanery, and all manner of fraud and knavery. Her most prominent American disciples, Olcott and William Q. Judge,[39] were labeled as both dupes and willing accomplices. Coues even tried to convey the impression that he himself had never been a member of the cult:

> I confess to a natural irritation at the way I found my name associated in public opinion with her clap-trap, and the use made of it as a foil to the fraudulent schemes of a pack of scoundrelly vulgarians would be enough to excite any honest man's indignation. Besides, there was the more serious

consideration, that a great many reputable persons had been influenced more or less by the belief that I was a convert to theosophy, when in fact I was simply investigating for myself, as any scientist is bound to do in a matter of vital interest, both in its psychological and its ethical aspects.[40]

By this time Coues was a veteran of many a controversy, but heretofore (with the Sparrow War as a notable exception) they had been largely confined to private and professional circles. The clash with the Theosophists was quite public, quite nasty, and potentially embarrassing to all concerned. In airing the dispute in the newspapers, Coues was acting on some advice he had given J. A. Allen in August, 1886: *"While you are in a controversy*, no matter what are the merits of the case, or who is right—strike for the great dailies and weeklies."

Mme. Blavatsky reacted vigorously. First she prevailed upon one of her English followers, the fascinating Annie Besant, to go to America and investigate the "Coues conspiracy."[41] Next she and Judge filed libel suits against the *Sun* and Coues. Before these cases reached trial, however, Mme. Blavatsky died, on May 8, 1891.[42]

On September 26, 1892, the *Sun* printed a retraction of the Coues interview, claiming to have been "misled into admitting . . . an article by Dr. E. F. [*sic*] Coues . . . in which allegations were made against Mme. Blavatksy's character, and also against her followers, which appear to have been without solid foundation." The same issue carried an article on Mme. Blavatsky by Judge which the *Sun* contended "disposes of all questions relating to Mme. Blavatsky as represented by Dr. Coues, and we desire to say that his allegations respecting the Theosophical Society and Mr. Judge personally are not sustained by evidence, and should not have been printed."[43]

Coues' fellow scientists preferred to think that his departure from organized Theosophy meant that he was severing all ties with the occult. David Starr Jordan wrote that Coues had "suddenly developed an incongruous interest in theosophy, afterward abandoned as abruptly as it had been adopted," and that Coues defined his relationship with the cult in these words: "Not a damned theos!"[44]

L. O. Howard's memoirs give an even more curious interpretation: "He [Coues] pretended to be interested in Spiritualism and was a great friend of Madame Blavatsky. Before he died he told me that his Spiritualism was only a pose, and that he was really slyly investigating Spiritualism and Theosophy."[45] Either Howard's recollection of Coues' remarks was imperfect, or Coues had not been candid with him. Coues' involvement with the occult was so deep, long-lasting, public, and controversial that it is impossible to believe that it amounted to nothing more than a "pose."

Moreover, Coues *never* lost interest in the occult, especially spiritualism and psychical research. On September 16, 1891, he was made vice-chairman of the "Committee on a Psychical Science Congress to be held in connection with the World's Columbian Exposition of 1893" at Chicago.[46] John C. Bundy, editor of the *Religio-Philosophical Journal*, was the chairman.[47] In the *Nation* Coues announced the projected activities of the committee.[48]

William Q. Judge and other Theosophists submitted to the organizers of the exposition a request that they be allowed representation. The application was routed to the psychical science committee. Upon learning that Coues was an official of the committee, the Theosophists saw to it that the application was channeled instead to the committee on moral and social reform, unaware that this group was chaired by Coues' sister, Lucy Flower, another member of the family with a finger in the pie. The Theosophists escaped their predicament by arranging for their own separate conference at the exposition.[49]

From early March to late April of 1892, Coues was in Chicago attending to the details of the committee's work. In August Bundy died and Coues assumed the chairmanship. He returned to Chicago in October for the dedicatory exercises of the exposition and for a meeting of the committee. In the following year, August 21-26, at Chicago, he presided over the Psychical Science Congress, which was one of many groups belonging to the World's Congress Auxiliary of the Columbian Exposition.[50]

Two other examples of continued association with the occult were his election in 1892 to membership in the Esoteric Christian Union of London and, in the same year, to the Society for Psychical Research of Munich.[51]

He also made further written contributions to the study of the occult. In 1892 he published an article in which he claimed that Theosophy was an ancient and respectable doctrine that was not to be confused with "the set of wild notions now covered by the term 'theosophy,' as appropriated by Blavatsky and her agents."[52] Later that year another of his articles asked the question, "Can Ghosts Be Photographed?" Although he did not deny the possibility of spirit photography, he concluded that the examples with which he was acquainted were fraudulent.[53]

In his studies of spiritualism and related matters Coues could be maddeningly coy about his own experiments and experiences. Yet in an article printed in 1895 he not only outlined a "telekinetic theory of levitation," but he also described in considerable detail his witnessing of a table being moved about the sittingroom of his Washington home by a "phantom individual."[54]

The fullest account of his adventures in the spirit world is found in an interview printed in 1900:

> I have myself seen the ghosts of a good many dead persons.... I remember one occasion when I had just gone to bed, the light being turned out. I was composing myself to sleep, when I suddenly became aware of a presence in the room. The impression conveyed to my mind was that it was the presence of a certain person lately deceased, with whom I had been on very intimate terms; in fact, I felt an overpowering sense of the nearness of the individual in question. At about the same moment there arose slowly from the floor a nebulous mass of what looked like shining white vapor, which began to take shape, as did the smoke from the casket opened by the fishermen in the Arabian Nights tale. Gradually it assumed a more distinct outline, until it presented a radiant image of my friend. The lips appeared to move, and from them came an intelligible utterance—a message, in short, from the departed. I do not care to say what that message was, but I can assure you that the vision was no dream, and the nature of the message was such as to eliminate, to my own satisfaction, at all events, the theory of hallucination. What, then, was this shape of shining white vapor? Was it a human soul? It is a question pregnant with much interest.

> Every afternoon . . . at about five o'clock I lie down on the sofa in my library for a brief rest before dinner. Occasionally, while enjoying this repose, though perfectly awake, there comes upon me the peculiar sensation of the ghost chill, which I will presently speak of. I wait with much attention and interest to see what is going to happen, and presently I find my own consciousness [i.e., astral body] projected objectively, as it were, so that my conscious self stands out in the room and views my body lying on the lounge. About the latter is a bright light, which grows gradually until it has filled all the room, and my conscious self finds itself surrounded by phantoms, most of them persons who appear to be strangers to me, while others resemble acquaintances who have long been dead. They seem to walk about and converse in the ordinary way, though not audibly. All the time I am clearly aware of the situation and make useful mental note of whatever I observe, until after a few brief moments the spectacle vanishes and I feel myself on the sofa again. It is obvious, if ghosts exist at all, that they must be made of something. My belief is that they are in a sense substantial and possess a semi-material stucture.

Coues then explained the nature of the "semi-material structure" (i.e., biogen), and concluded by saying:

> My own experience is that the coming of an apparition is always preceded by that curious sensations [*sic*] which I called the "ghost chill." When this symptom arrives, the threshold of consciousness seems to be shifted to the extent of rendering possible a perception of something ordinarily invisible. The change is usually very brief, lasting only a few seconds, during which the manifestation occurs. The real spectre of a dead person shows few signs of life, resembling a magic lantern picture more than anything else, to which it is readily comparable. It appears by daylight as often as at night, but never with any purpose in its actions that is at all comprehensible. Occasionally it is self-luminous.

This article appeared just after Coues' death, indicating that his fascination with spiritualism remained to the end of his life. The writer of the article stated that Coues "had promised several of his friends that, if able to do so, he would appear to them after his own demise, and now they are waiting with no little interest to see if he will carry out the agreement."[55]

Another example of the retention of earlier beliefs was that the fifth edition of his *Key to North American Birds* (published posthumously in 1903) includes brief discussions of biogen.[56] At the time of his death Coues' library contained a great many works on religion, mysticism, and spiritualism.[57]

4

The assertion that his affiliation with the occultists was a joke is untenable for another reason: Coues was not the sort of person to subject himself to ridicule. And certainly a good deal of opposition to his views, much in the form of ridicule, came his way, from both the religious and secular presses.

Worse yet was the negative response from scientific circles. Josiah Royce concluded a blistering review of *Biogen*, which appeared in *Science*, by saying that Coues ". . . not only talks confusedly about his unintelligible biogen but he helps to disseminate the impression that a belief in a spiritual truth in the world depends upon a faith in the existence of some fluid so thin that you cannot say any thing definite about it. All this is rank paganism; for it is analogous to the views of those people whose gods are conceived after the fashion of smoke."[58] The tone of a review of the same work in the *Nation* by Asa Gray, Harvard's famous botanist, was more charitable than Royce's, yet Gray found *Biogen* "fairly effective in its destructive portion, and in its constructive portion neither illegitimate nor truly scientific."[59]

Sometimes Coues responded to his critics. He politely crossed swords with entomologist Samuel H. Scudder (who had called Coues "the well-known ghost-smeller") in the pages of *Science* over the question of mental telepathy.[60] He likewise twitted another detractor, Robert W. Shufeldt, for the latter's criticism of Theosophy.[61]

Some of the unkindest reactions of the scientists were not subject to rebuttal by Coues because they were expressed privately. For example, in 1886 Edward D. Cope wrote to his daughter: "I had some entertainment at a mtg. of a circle to discuss Theosophy and 'occult' science 5th day evg. Dr. E. Cowes [*sic*] made a speech, which for bare faced humbug in fine language was a masterpiece. His ingenuity in keeping up a pretense of knowledge by asserting that Theosophy is too deep to be told to ordinary people was rich."[62]

A series of letters from Coues to J. A. Allen in 1885-86 indicates that his friend had warned him that some other members of the A.O.U. considered Coues unfit to be elected to further offices of the organization because of his association with Theosophy. Coues replied on November 22, 1885, that his views on religion in no way diminished his worth as a scientist and that those who believed it did were narrow-minded.

More than that, he asserted in a letter of January 13, 1885, that his biogen theory was a landmark achievement in science: "I know that I have made a great discovery which conservative science will properly be slow to acknowledge. I also know that I can demonstrate the thing. Meanwhile, people may call me what they please, and I say proudly, with [Luigi] Galvani, 'they may call me the frog's dancing master—but I know that I have discovered one of the great forces of nature.' Galvinism [*sic*] is an accepted scientific fact: so will Biogen be in due time, and sooner perhaps than even I supose." In the same year on November 30 he also wrote: "I must be about right, people are so unanimous in calling me wrong. Always so, in case of any great large new true idea put forth. I stand about, in psychic research, where Darwin did in biological physics, in December, 1859 [when *The Origin of Species* was published]."

Finally, Coues made (in April, 1886) what in retrospect appears to be a questionable assessment: "As a matter of personal fact, I may say that today I am better known, more widely known, and wield more intellectual influence through the 'Biogen Series' than by means of all my other books taken together."

Nevertheless, Coues was sensitive to the attitudes of his brother scientists. When he broke with the Theosophists, he hastened to tell

Allen on October 14, 1886: ". . . I *can't* & *won't* be identified any longer with any of their irresponsible utterances & indescribable opinions. I only took it for a flyer to amuse myself with, and anybody who thinks I am 'off' in any way is sadly deluded. If you think advisable, spread this among the A.O.U.'s on any occasion." On a more cynical note, he wrote to Allen on November 25: "So I am now back in my immaculate scientific robes, humble devotee of materialism, agnosticism and other orthodox half-truths."

We may conclude that Coues' commitment to the occult was prolonged and sincere. Yet the question remains: Why did he make this commitment? Even if we cannot single out any conclusive explanation, a number of possible reasons can be mentioned.

In the first place, Coues was not alone. Many men and women in the late nineteenth century were similarly seeking solutions to the problem of reconciling science, especially evolutionary theories, with religion. Many intellectuals of his time, too, were fascinated with spiritualism. A list of men and women who were drawn to psychical research and related pursuits reads like a *Who's Who* of the western world's writers, thinkers, and artists. William James, Ambrose Bierce, Cesare Lombroso, George Bernard Shaw, William Butler Years, Yeats's friend George William Russell ("E. S. Russell"), Arthur Conan Doyle, and Alfred Russel Wallace are a few out of many names that might be mentioned in this regard.

Spiritualism was especially prevalent in America at this time because of the enormous death toll of the Civil War. Americans from all walks of life feverishly sought contact with loved ones who had fallen in the conflict. Among the spirits Coues evoked, or claimed to have evoked, were possibly those of men who had made the ultimate sacrifice between 1861 and 1865.

Finally, we must take into account Coues' own reasons. First, he believed that the so-called supernatural was knowable by means of conventional scientific methods. He objected to the unscientific attitudes of those who believed that only the material world was capable of being known scientifically. By the same token, he objected to the term "natural science." He put it bluntly in his address to the World's Congress on Ornithology at the Columbian Exposition: "I know of no unnatural science."[63]

No matter how distressing Coues' occult pursuits were to his colleagues, his delving into the spirit world did little if anything to diminish his historical standing as a scientist. Nor was it a bizarre aberration. His probing into the "other world" was just another example of a relentless search for knowledge by an adventurous mind. Some may think it is to his credit—others not—that he sought a higher truth than that held out by conventional science.

Developments in the twentieth century have done much to vindicate Coues' belief in the scientific respectability of psychic research. In 1969 the Parapsychological Association was admitted to membership in the American Association for the Advancement of Science. Several universities and research centers now regularly conduct serious experiments in psychic phenomena with, in the opinion of many persons, convincing results.

NOTES

1. For example, see Coues, ed., *The Expeditions of Zebulon Montgomery Pike* (1895), II, 599n.
2. A "dimit" (also spelled "demit"), in Masonic terms, is a document certifying that a member has resigned from a lodge honorably and in good standing.
3. See Chapter XIII.
4. Coues, *Biogen: A Speculation on the Origin and Nature of Life*, 2d ed. (1884), 55. For citing this work we use the second edition. The first edition was published in Washington by Judd and Detweiler in 1882.
5. *Ibid.*, 15-17.
6. Coues to Richard Ellis Thompson, Apr. 30, 1884, Misc. Mss. Coll., American Philosophical Society.
7. Coues, *Key to North American Birds*, 5th ed. (1903), I, 198.
8. Coues, *The Daemon of Darwin* (1885), 12n.
9. *Ibid.*, 63-64.
10. Coues' "Book of Dates" (1883).
11. Coues, *"A Woman in the Case,"* 2d ed. (1890), 36-37.
12. Coues, *The Harmony of Scientific Knowledge and Religious Faith* (1883), 22, 15.
13. Coues, *Check List*, 2d ed. (1882), 34.
14. Hume, *Ornithologists of the U.S. Army Medical Corps*, 79.
15. Coues, ed., *A Buddhist Catechism* (1885), 70n.
16. Coues' "Book of Dates" (1885).
17. Enclosed with the letter is a circular announcing Coues' appointment as censor.
18. C. S. Minot's letter to the editor, *Nation*, XLI (Aug. 6, 1885), 113.
19. Coues' "Book of Dates" (1886).
20. Coues, "The Collapse of the Theosophists" (1886), 102.
21. Coues' "Book of Dates"(1887, 1888).
22. *Ibid.* (1884).
23. Coues, "Can Ghosts Be Investigated?" (1884), 543.
24. Coues, "An Explanation of Telepathy" (1885), 54.
25. Coues, "The Meaning of the Human Body" (1885).

26. Coues, *The Signs of the Times* (1889).

27. Henry Steel Olcott (1832-1907), lawyer and journalist, was co-founder of the Theosophical Society and its first president.

28. Coues, ed., *Can Matter Think?* (1886), 7.

29. Dana Estes (1840-1909), publisher, began his financially successful partnership with Charles E. Lauriat in 1871. In later life he collected valuable archaeological artifacts in Africa.

30. Coues' "Book of Dates" (1884).

31. *Ibid.* (1885).

32. *New York Times*, Apr. 25, 1889, 3.

33. *Appleton's Annual Cyclopaedia and Register of Important Events of the Year 1893* . . . (New York: D. Appleton, 1894), 717.

34. *New York Times*, Apr. 21, 1889, 10; Apr. 25, 1889, 3.

35. Coues, "Collapse of the Theosophists," 102.

36. Coues, *Signs of the Times*, 46.

37. Hume, *Ornithologists of the U.S. Army Medical Corps*, 79.

38. Elliot, "In Memoriam: Elliott Coues," 6.

39. William Quan Judge (1851-96) was Olcott's law partner, a loyal follower of Mme. Blavatsky, and vice-president of the Theosophical Society.

40. *New York Sun*, July 20, 1890.

41. Arthur N. Nethercot, *The First Five Lives of Annie Besant* (Chicago: University of Chicago Press, 1960), 306. Annie Besant (1847-1933), socialist, feminist, and organizer of a movement for home rule for India, was also president of the Theosophical Society (1907-33).

42. Neff, comp., *Personal Memoirs of H. P. Blavatsky* (1967), 186. In his "Book of Dates" (1891) Coues noted that Mme. Blavatsky's death came at 2:25 P.M. By the end of her life she was the acknowledged head of an organization of close to 100,000 members, with journalistic organs in London, New York, and Madras.

43. Neff, comp., *Personal Memoirs of H. P. Blavatsky*, 186.

44. Jordan, *Days of a Man*, I, 177.

45. Howard, *Fighting the Insects*, 80.

46. Coues' "Book of Dates" (1891, 1892).

47. We have located no biographical data on Bundy.

48. Coues, "Psychical Science at the World's Fair in 1893" (1892), 282.

49. Nethercot, *First Five Lives of Annie Besant*, 390.

50. Coues' "Book of Dates" (1892, 1893).

51. *Ibid.* (1892).

52. Coues, "Theosophy: What It Is Not" (1892).

53. Coues, "Can Ghosts Be Photographed?" (1892).

54. Coues, "The Telekinetic Theory of Levitation" (1895).

55. "Coues's Ideas on Ghosts," *Current Literature*, XXVI (Mar., 1900), 246-47. The interview was originally published by the *Boston Transcript*.

56. Coues, *Key to North American Birds*, 5th ed., I, 180, 198.

57. *The Private Library of the Late Elliott Coues. To Be Sold at Auction Monday and Tuesday December 3 and 4, 1906. The Anderson Auction Co., 5 West 29th Street, New York* (n.p., n.d.).

58. Royce, "Coues's Biogen," *Science*, III (May 30, 1884), 661-65. Josiah Royce (1855-1916), philosopher, was a member of the Harvard faculty from 1881 until his death. He wrote *The World and the Individual* (1900), *The Religious Aspect of Philosophy* (1885), and *The Conception of God* (1897).

59. [Gray], review of *Biogen* in *Nation*, XXXIX (July 3, 1884), 20. Attributed to Gray by Daniel C. Haskell, comp., *The Nation . . . Indexes of Titles and Contributors*, 2 vols. (New York: New York Public Library, 1951), I, 148.

60. Coues, "Feline Telepathy" (1886).

61. Coues, "Is the Dodo an Extinct Bird?" (1886).

62. Henry Fairfield Osborn, *Cope: Master Naturalist* (Princeton, N.J.: Princeton University Press, 1931), 561.

63. Coues, "The Presidential Address" (1896), 27.

CHAPTER XX

A.O.U. Code and Check-List

J. A. Allen viewed Coues' occultist period as practically devoid of achievements in ornithology and mammalogy: ". . . he ceased to impress, to any considerable extent, his personality upon either of these two branches of investigation."[1] Coues was inclined to agree: "If my friends are to to believed, I had quite a reputation as a scientist at one time from some writings I published about Rupa [i.e., the material world]. I should be disinclined to admit that soft impeachment now."[2] Coues also pointed out that science was merely a "half-way house"[3] on the road to truth, and he was quick to denounce the "arrogance" of scientific claims of a monopoly on truth.[4]

In the sense of producing major zoological works based upon fresh thinking and original investigation, Coues, in the late 1880s and throughout the 1890s until his death, was certainly not the force he had been. Yet it is wrong to conclude that he divorced himself completely from the more conventional realms of science.

During this period Coues continued to fulfill his obligations to *The Century Dictionary* and the American Supplement of the *Encyclopaedia Britannica*. He made additional contributions (usually notes and reviews) to *The Auk, American Naturalist, Science,* and the *Nation*. He revised and published the third (1887) and fourth (1890) editions of *Key to North American Birds*, though these were only slightly revised and enlarged versions of the second (1884) edition. His London-published *Handbook of Field and General Ornithology* (1890) was also merely a reprint of portions of the fourth edition of the *Key*. Perhaps his most original scientific writings of this period were two articles dealing with human anatomy, one of which was co-authored by another professor of anatomy at the National Medical College.[5]

In these years Coues also vigorously engaged in affairs of the American Ornithologists' Union. As we have seen in Chapter XVII, he served for seven years (1883-90) as its vice-president and three (1892-

95) as its president. His role as chairman of the A.O.U. Committee on Classification and Nomenclature will receive full attention further along in this chapter.

For three years (1884-87) Coues was an associate editor of *The Auk*, and in 1887 he was made a member of the A.O.U.'s Publications Committee. In 1886 he was named chairman of the Committee on Avian Anatomy; the only other member was Robert W. Shufeldt. In delivering that committee's report for 1887 (one largely written by Shufeldt), Coues praised the younger man's work and, no doubt influenced by painful memories of his own similar predicament of a few years earlier, begged the A.O.U. "for its aid in behalf of securing Dr. Shufeldt's transfer from a frontier post [Fort Wingate, New Mexico] to one of the larger cities near the Atlantic seaboard, within reach of the libraries and museums so indispensable to his work."[6] At the union's congress of the following year Coues again read the report of the Committee on Avian Anatomy, as well as a paper of his own on "The Flight of Birds."[7]

Other concerns of the A.O.U. attracted Coues' attention and help. At its second (1884) meeting he expressed his "earnest support" of a motion to appoint a committee for the "protection of North American birds and their eggs against wanton and indiscriminate destruction."[8] At the 1888 meeting he was appointed a member of a committee created to investigate "some uniform method of measuring birds."[9]

In addition to his responsibilities with the Committee on a Psychical Congress at the Columbian Exposition, Coues had others as president of the exposition's World's Congress on Ornithology, which had been organized "to treat of birds from the standpoints of the scientist, the economist, and the humanitarian."[10] Coues' presidential address, on the "use and beauty of birds," emphasized the beneficial economic functions of American birds. Some birds, he pointed out, were not worthy of protection; the English sparrow was, of course, "beyond hope of redemption." Coues did not deliver the address in person, but in conveying his regrets to the group he stated, perhaps with an impish reference to his occult involvements, "I am with you in spirit."[11]

Frank Chapman first became acquainted with Coues at the 1886 A.O.U. congress and, after hearing him speak, recorded his impressions: "[He was] confident, assuming, slightly pompous, his faith in his own ability undoubted. Addresses the house in clear, assertive tone. Tall, full beard, long wavy hair brushed back from a good forehead, gold eyeglasses, fingers stained from cigarette smoking; not stylishly or shabbily dressed, but not well-dressed; pleasant spoken, unreserved and affable."[12]

After the 1888 convention Chapman provided further impressions of Coues:

> There was a vividness, a fire in this man's personality that made his presence felt even when he was silent. When he arose to speak the air was charged with possibilities. Every word in the dictionary seemed to be at his command, and one had the comfortable assurance that he would choose the right one. He was an eloquent, brilliant, finished speaker. Years later Walter Hines Page told me of walking into the smoking room of a St. Lawrence River steamer and finding all its occupants gathered about one man, whom he recognized as Elliott Coues. None of the other men knew him but they were drawn to him as bits of steel are attracted to a magnet.

At a reception held for A.O.U. members the young Chapman attempted with only partial success to strike up a conversation with Coues: "I had prepared myself for this event by bringing a message from Captain [Charles A.] Curtis of Gainesville [Florida]. Coues at once recalled him, and when this subject failed, I retired. Coues was not a man to talk unless you had something to say, or he considered you a worthy listener. I never became really well acquainted with him."[13]

That Coues in these years was elected to active or honorary membership in a wide variety of scientific societies is evidence that he was still looked upon by many as an esteemed man of science. Even though his attachment to the occult embarrassed and provoked old friends and colleagues, his achievements and personality still made him a commanding figure in ornithology.

2

We have already discussed the importance to ornithology of Coues' *Key*, his bibliographical installments, and his part in the formation of the American Ornithologists' Union. These events occurred in the years 1872-83. In the years that followed, Coues, as chairman of the powerful A.O.U. Committee on Classification and Nomenclature, made another significant contribution to ornithology.

This committee consisted of Coues, J. A. Allen, William Brewster, H. W. Henshaw, and Robert Ridgway, and its primary and immediate responsibility was to prepare and publish *The A.O.U. Code of Nomenclature and Check-List of North American Birds*. Though actually two works, a "Code" and a "Check-List," the two were published together. Comprised of five of the most illustrious names in the history of American ornithology, the committee expended much time and effort in producing these works. Nor were they the only men participating, for the committee on occasion invited Leonhardt Stejneger,[14] C. Hart Merriam, Theodore N. Gill, Robert W. Shufeldt, Howard Saunders,[15] Montague Chamberlain, and Charles B. Cory[16] to give it the benefit of their knowledge and experience.

The committee met on four different occasions over a period of more than a year, and held sessions on a total of twenty-one days.[17] Members of the committee also expended much time and labor between these four major meetings. Coues, for instance, investigated "the anatomy of the *Tanagridae*,[18] with special reference to their mutual relationship with *Fringillidae*[19] and *Mniotiltidae*."[20] The committee created a number of subcommittees, but two of them were more important than the others. In the minutes for December 19, 1883, we read: "Moved by Dr. Coues that the committee resolve itself into two subcommittees, to one of which shall be referred the whole subject of specific and subspecific determinations of North American birds, and the other of which be referred to the subject of formulation and codifying the nomenclatural results reached by the Committee; the former subcommittee to consist of Mr. Ridgway, Mr. Brewster and Mr. Henshaw; the latter to consist of Mr. Allen and Dr. Coues."[21]

Ridgway, Brewster, and Henshaw, as the minutes in time disclose, prepared what amounted to an initial draft of the A.O.U. "Check-List," while Allen and Coues put together a set of rules (canons) that ultimately grew into the A.O.U. "Code of Nomenclature." Before being discharged, these two subcommittees labored conscientiously, though intermittently, for more than a year. They fully realized the difficulties and importance of their tasks.

The A.O.U. Code of Nomenclature and Check-List of North American Birds came from the press in 1886. The "Check-List" differed conspicuously from earlier ones, such as those of Baird, Coues, and Ridgway. It began with the "lowest" or most specialized birds and ended with the "highest" or most generalized.[22] It included higher taxonomic groups (classes, orders, and families) where previous lists recognized only genera, species, and subspecies. It referred to published works wherein genera, species, and subspecies had been first named. It briefly stated the geographical range of each listed species and subspecies.[23] And it numbered species consecutively—and permanently. Then and now, for instance, the A.O.U. number for the cardinal (*Richmondena cardinalis*) is 593.

This first A.O.U. "Check-List" differed from earlier lists in some lesser respects, such as in the number of species and subspecies recognized,[24] in the subdivision of certain genera, in the elevation of subgenera to generic rank, and in the deletion of several subspecies. Of course, Coues had a hand in these changes. For example, at the meeting of December 18, 1883, he made a motion, which was seconded and passed, that the cormorants be subdivided into three or more subgenera.[25]

As earlier indicated, the "Code of Nomenclature" was largely the handiwork of Coues and Allen, though the full committee scrutinized closely each canon, altering some and leaving others unchanged. It consisted of a lengthy introduction and an even lengthier recitation of the canons, fifty-two in all. The introduction emphasized two features in particular: a résumé of taxonomic rules earlier formulated by scientific organizations and individual zoologists, and the committee's decision to appropriate the Stricklandian Code[26] as a starting point and basis of procedure for the A.O.U. "Code."

The Stricklandian Code was a set of nomenclatural rules that had been adopted in 1842 by the British Association for the Advancement of Science. With later emendations, it had done much "to bring zoological nomenclature from a loose and almost chaotic state to a fair degree of stability and orderly consistency."[27]

While utilizing the Stricklandian Code as "the natural and proper basis of any new code," Coues' committee disagreed with the wording of certain of its canons and rephrased three of them:

(1) The adoption of the date of the Xth edition of the "Systema Naturae," 1758, instead of that of the XIIth, 1766, as the starting point of the law of priority for names of whatever groups; because this date, 1758, is in fact that of the establishment of the binomial system of nomenclature in zoology, and of its first application to the whole animal kingdom.

(2) The rule that prior use of a name in Botany does not make that name unavailable in Zoology.

(3) The principle of Trinomials: namely, departure from strict binomiality to the extent of using three words as the name of those subspecific forms which are sufficiently distinct to require recognition by name, yet which are known to intergrade with one another; the name of such forms to consist of three terms—a generic, a specific, and a subspecific,—written consecutively and continuously, without the intervention of any mark or punctuation, any arbitrary character, or any other sign or form whatever.[28]

The A.O.U. "Code" differed from the Stricklandian Code in some other respects. It gave greater emphasis to the law of priority—namely, the taxonomic principle that the first published name of a species or genus takes precedence over any later published—and it introduced a new rule, Canon XL.

The first action we find in the committee minutes—all of which, incidentally, were recorded by Ridgway as secretary—with a specific bearing on Canon XL occurred on April 16, 1885, when "on motion of Mr. Allen it was ordered that the 'canons' be read, and that they be considered seriatim."[29]

Canon XL, which the committee considered in due course, read as follows:

> The original orthography of a name is to be rigidly preserved, unless a typographical error is evident. . . . In view of the fact that stability of names is one of the essential principles in nomenclature, and that the emendation, as shown by the recent history of zoological nomenclature, opens the door to a great evil,—being subject to great abuse on the part of purists and classicists, who look with disfavor upon anything nomenclatural which is in the least degree unclassical in form,—it seems best that correctness of structure, or philological propriety, be held as of minor importance, and yield place to the two cardinal principles of priority and fixity.[30]

According to the minutes, "Canon 40 [XL] was read without comment."[31] We find it near impossible to believe that Coues allowed the adoption of Canon XL "without comment." Who, among ornithologists of that time, was more of a "purist and classicist"? Who, to serve the purposes of correct spelling, favored more "the emendation of names"? Who, more than he, consistently preached "philological propriety"? Yet Canon XL was adopted, we suspect because by the time it came to a vote Coues knew that all the other members of the committee favored it. If silent then, he would not be for long. Writing to Allen just a few months later (on November 14, 1885), he unburdened himself on a number of scores:

> In my own Committee [on Classification and Nomenclature], where my chief interest centers, I have usually found myself in a minority of one or two, whence it is evident that my views are at variance with those of most of my colleagues; and as a majority, however poorly informed or incompetent, rules, it is obvious that I must look elsewhere than in the Union or the Committee for such support as my views and wishes are entitled to receive. . . .
>
> I noted the printing of our List with livelier concern & deeper regrets

than even you can be aware of. It is the *reductio ad absurdum* which I feared, and against which I raised my warning voice in the beginning. . . .

As Coues continued, he let it be known that he would not be attending the upcoming A.O.U. congress and that vexatious ripples of a different kind were stirring the already murky waters of his discontent:

> I should like to meet you and talk over bird-matters, but shall not be present at the coming meeting of the A.O.U. No doubt the Union can get along very well without me, and it is not necessary that my services in founding it should be remembered. It seems to be going on very well, and has my best wishes for its continued success. . . . If I do not mistake the present attitude of the Union towards me, it is unfriendly on the whole, through petty jealousies to which my nature is such a stranger, that I cannot condescend even to recognize such things, much less to combat them. Keenly as I feel the injustice and unkindness I have found in the Union after all the time and brains I have given to its service, I am not a man to give any sign of the hurt excepting a contemptuous indifference—say rather a haughty unconcern. . . . If the Union thinks it owes my anything, in any way, they will doubtless pay me. But I am not dunning for debts of honor, and not disposed to expose myself to snubs from those who ought to know better, but do not.

Coues could have attended the A.O.U. meetings of that year if he had been so inclined; he had no commitments preventing him. That some members of the union snubbed him we can well believe, and do not have to seek far for eligible reasons. For one thing, over the years Coues had often been high-handed, had needlessly thrown his weight around and, by so doing, had rubbed many of his associates the wrong way. There was also his persistent and unbending bond with purism and classicism in the use of scientific names, which, according to Allen, "was the cause of estrangement between himself and some of his (otherwise and formerly) most esteemed colleagues."[32]

In a letter to Allen of January 1, 1887, Coues alluded to an individual (without naming him) who had been "stupid enough to 'get off' on me about Theosophy." Through his espousal of spiritualism and the occult, Coues had left himself vulnerable to attacks from enemies who heretofore had concealed their true feelings about him because of the high regard in which he was held professionally. Now, with his Achilles tendon, his adversaries no longer felt such restraint and undertook, sometimes openly, to discredit him. The "present attitude" of certain A.O.U. members may well have stemmed from Coues' unfortunate affiance with the vagaries of Mme. Blavatsky's teachings.

In Coues' above letter to Allen he did not criticize specific A.O.U. members for their "injustice and unkindness" to him, so we cannot say who the individuals may have been. At the same time, we cannot ignore the possibility of three men in particular: Robert Ridgway, C. Hart Merriam, and Leonhardt Stejneger. Between Coues and these men there had been, was, and would continue to be mutual dislike, distrust, and enmity. It is from Coues' letters to Allen that we learn much of the strained relationships between Coues and this trio of distinguished ornithologists.

The animus that existed between Coues and Ridgway had its provenance in 1873 when, as we recall, Coues had accused Ridgway of plagiarism, apparently through sheer envy. Almost concurrently an article by Baird and Ridgway had appeared in a scientific journal,[33] and a book by Baird, Brewer, and Ridgway neared publication date.[34] At no time, then or thereafter, did Baird propose to Coues that the two of them might collaborate on a paper or book. In 1880 Coues' envy mounted when Baird named Ridgway curator of birds of the U.S. National Museum, and in 1883-85 the disaffection between the two increased when Ridgway, as a member of the A.O.U. Committee on Classification and Nomenclature, helped to jettison some of Coues' more cherished wishes.

Excerpts from Coues' letters to Allen reveal the extent of the breach between Coues and Ridgway. On September 10, 1880, for instance, Coues wrote, "R.R. is in the [Smithsonian] building, but perhaps the cad is too busy over the S.I. Checklist to mind his manners." Again, on October 16, 1885, he confided to Allen: "It must be well known to you, that our friend R. never yet went twice over any group of birds with the same result, and those that he studied longest are most like a game of hop-scotch to him." In yet another letter to Allen, dated February 20, 1897, Coues turned back the clock: "R. and S[tejneger] had their heads together getting up the 'Water Birds' [*A History of North American Birds: Water Birds* (1874-84)]—it was anything to beat the *Key*. I wrote the beginning and the end . . . and appear throughout almost as coauthor; [yet], in the two vols. of the 'Water Birds' I think my name hardly occurs, except to be criticized and minimized."

Beyond much doubt the hostility that for many years marred the relationship between Coues and C. Hart Merriam had its origin when Coues, in his article titled "Ornithophilologicalities," had ridiculed a paper written by Merriam's uncle, Augustus Merriam. A letter of

August 13, 1882, from Coues to Allen pretty well delineates the frosty relationship between Coues and C. Hart Merriam:

> I know perfectly well that C.H.M. is and has been an enemy of mine for years. . . . I know he has slandered and belittled me and done his best to injure me in *many* ways. Knowing which, do you suppose I forget or forgive? . . . I am of course solely responsible for what I say, and as one of the founders and editors of the *Auk* I may have some privileges in that journal that do not extend beyond the staff. My advantage in such a case is, that while C.H.M. can beat me in private malice & slander behind my back, he can't hold a candle to the way I am ready to talk & act in public & write for print, because he has got his petty little name & place in the world to nurse, & I haven't. Moreover, *many* persons hate his mixed bulldozing and intriguing and would rejoice to see him bowled over. I hate him for his cowardice and dishonesty on general principles.

Just when the feud between Coues and Stejneger began we cannot be certain, though possibly the date coincided with some disparaging remarks the latter made about Coues' "Historical Preface" (a feature of his 1884 *Key*), and about Shufeldt's suggestion of a "Couesian Period." To Allen on December 9, 1884, Coues expressed himself as follows: "Your reviews are just and fair, on the whole, and there was properly no occasion for you to even allude to Stejneger's hasty and jealous attempt to ride down my 'Historical Preface.' His opinion, that I am getting too much credit in our nomenclatural matters, and his obvious *motive* in penning his paper, are things I will attend to myself when the time comes." Again to Allen, two weeks later: "There, for instance, is poor Stejneger, who thought it proper and necessary to object to the Couesian Period. What if Coues should object to Stejneger? The difference is, that I have withstood so many shocks & assaults that I am become practically invulnerable, while I know that I can make him tingle and writhe with a stroke of my pen. So it turns out, that those who meditate anything against me had better take Punch's advice to those about marriage—'Don't.'"

In another letter to Allen (November 5, 1885), Coues alluded to Stejneger's "shysterism," and in still another (December 4, 1896) to the suffering he had endured "from Dr. S's animosities." In time Coues seems to have grown somewhat philosophical about Stejneger. In an undated letter to Allen he remarked: "This is a wicked world Bro. Allen—and the more Stejnegerization it gets the wickeder it grows."

In fairness, it must be said that we have uncovered no direct evidence anywhere linking Ridgway, Merriam, or Stejneger with the hurt or inequity that moved Coues to stay away from the 1885 A.O.U. congress. At the same time, we do recognize the possibility, even the likelihood, that one or more of them had a hand in the matter.

The Code of Nomenclature and Check-List of North American Birds came from the press in 1886, and at once won high praise from the majority of American ornithologists. As Coues himself put it: ". . . no sooner had the book appeared than it became the standard and indeed the only recognized Nomenclator in American ornithology. That which the Committee had stamped with the seal of the Union became the current coin of the realm, other than which our venerable fowl, *The Auk*, should know none."[35]

3

With the original A.O.U. "Code" and "Check-List" published, Coues no doubt felt that these obligations had ended. However, only a few years went by until the union reappointed the same Committee on Classification and Nomenclature (with the exception of Merriam for Henshaw) and instructed it to produce second editions of the "Code" and "Check-List." This time the A.O.U. published them separately, the former in 1892 and the latter in 1895.

The new *Check-List* proved to be similar in style and typography to the original. It differed mainly in providing increased information about the ranges of species and subspecies and many nomenclatural modifications.[36]

The committee made only a few changes in the new *Code*, and none at all in the wording of Canon XL. By now, however, Coues seems to have been more outspoken about the rule. He disliked in particular its opening sentence: "The original orthography of a name is to be rigidly preserved, unless a typographical error is evident." He soon gained a formidable ally in the person of D. G. Elliot, who privately and in published articles fully supported Coues' opposition to Canon XL. At the same time he uncovered a vigorous opponent in the editor of *The Auk*, J. A. Allen.

In one article Elliot wrote:

> To spell correctly is the first qualification of any one claiming to have received an education, and one who is unable to do this should not be encouraged to commit errors by the assurance of a committee of a scientific society that his faults should be made perpetual. . . . It is satisfactory to know that one at least of the Committee that assisted at the advent of its unlovely offspring, born out of due season, did not at the time, although an

accomplished accoucheur, regard with favor this result of combined efforts, and Dr. Coues of late both with tongue and pen has expressed his disapproval of this article [Canon XL] and advocated its suppression. Let it therefore be eliminated from the Code.[37]

Allen replied: "To charge the A.O.U. Committee with placing a premium on illiteracy through the adoption of Canon XL, as Mr. Elliot and Dr. Coues have done, is almost too absurd for serious consideration. . . . Nearly all modern codes of nomenclature agree that 'A name is only a name and need have no necessary significance.' . . . Mr. Elliot may prefer one 'spelling,' Dr. Coues another. The result would be endless emendation and constant confusion." Allen then raised the all-important question: ". . . which of two grave evils is the lesser,—namely, the emendation of thousands of names, some of them so radically [misspelled or wrongly constructed] that they retain little resemblance to their original forms, or the retention of a few gross and shocking verbal malformations against which their literacy instincts must ever revolt?"[38]

Elliot responded in a single article: "Dr. Allen thinks it 'too absurd for serious consideration,' the charge that this Canon XL places a premium upon illiteracy, and yet what are the facts? It provided for the retention of names no matter how ridiculous they may be, nor how grossly they may violate all rules of orthography and etymology, and then assures all those who may commit such blunders that they shall be perpetuated."[39]

Allen stuck to his guns. He at once reminded Elliot that "satire is not argument," and then continued: "Dr. Elliot refers to the fact that one member of the A.O.U. Committee agrees with him on the subject of Canon XL, and rather intimates that if we knew the whole truth in the case there might be others on his side. He can be assured that such is not the case; and if he had been present at a discussion of this matter at the last meeting of the A.O.U. he would have been much enlightened, and possibly surprised, by the unanimity with which Canon XL was sustained by the participants in the discussion, one only speaking in opposition."[40]

Elliot had brought up the point, too, that the British had no equivalent of Canon XL in their "Code," that the authors of their *Catalogue of Birds* "have throughout the long series of volumes already issued . . . completely ignored and repudiated this Canon XL."[41] Here Elliot may well have taken his cue from Coues, who a few months earlier had written: "It is needless to add that no British author follows our absurd rule of misspelling names, for no other reason than that they were spelled wrongly at first."[42]

All readers of *The Auk* followed the debate closely. Whether Elliot and Coues won converts to their side we do not know; Allen, of course, had the full support of Brewster, Merriam, and Ridgway and doubtless other A.O.U. members. As with any controversy so fully publicized, all pertinent facts became well known.

Not so well known, however, was Coues' persistent and often eloquent attempt at this time to persuade Allen to change his mind about Canon XL. He was warming up to this effort as early as January 2, 1897, when he wrote Allen: "You and I both had 'knock-out drops' administered in 1884-86, and it is high time we got over that dose." In his next letter, some three months later, he came directly to the point: "You know that our Code has no heartier supporter than myself, except in *one* or perhaps *two* canons, concerning which I am going to kick as hard as I know how, and try to get changed. Canon XL is a perpetual fly blister to me; and unluckily, I believe it is one you most strongly support. If we could compromise a little—just a little—to loosen up the strictness of that, I think we should never have another serious disagreement in the whole Code." The very next day (April 15)—after his admission that there *had been* serious disagreement between them about Canon XL—Coues wrote again: "I'm afraid you won't exactly like the way I take on about Canon XL. . . . You and I actually drafted the whole Code, and nothing could be more desirable than that we should *always* appear in print as one in the whole matter."

In his several replies to Coues Allen continued unbending in his attitude toward Canon XL. Nevertheless Coues kept trying to alter his friend's stand. Writing on June 2, he said, "I am proud of you, and don't despair of getting you *to spell things* right"; again, less than two weeks later: "By the way, about Canon XL, won't it be polite, to say the least, for you to withdraw your opposition; you don't want to show Spanish enough to maintain a surely indefensible position. . . . We [Elliot and I] are going to try to get the obnoxious canon cancelled next November [at the 1897 A.O.U. congress], & substitute something reasonable. Now don't you oppose it, but be found on the right side of the fence. You can find plenty of reason for change of base, if you only choose to."

If Coues and Elliot did attempt to get Canon XL changed at the November A.O.U. meetings, they failed. Writing again to Allen in December (after the congress), Coues said only, "I am slowly realizing how you feel on that XL subject." So far as we know, Coues did not again try to change Allen's convictions about the controversial canon.

What, if anything, did the A.O.U. do about Canon XL in ensuing years? Seemingly nothing until 1908, by which time Coues had been dead several years. In that year the union published a third (and final) edition of its "Code." The committee[43] delegated to produce the revision retained only its initial sentence, the one which had created all the dissent. Also, as though to banish forever any reminder of Canon XL, they attached the sentence to Canon XXXVII.

The A.O.U. "Code" was long ago superseded by the International Rules of Zoological Nomenclature (also called International Code or simply the Code). Even before the A.O.U. "Code" of 1908 appeared, it had become evident to most ornithologists that both zoological and botanical nomenclature was an international matter and could be handled only by an international set of rules. One scientist, writing in 1905, described the confusion then existing from multiple codes: "English systematists were following the Strickland Code; French systematists were following the International Code; German systematists were following the German Code; American systematists were divided between Stricklandian, the A.O.U., the Dall,[44] and the International Code; systematists in special groups were in some cases following special or even personal codes; and systematists of Italy, Russia, and some other countries were following either the International or some other code."[45]

It is surely clear by now that the system of binomial nomenclature introduced by Linnaeus—that species should have two names, a generic and a specific—made possible for the first time a consistent, international method of listing the then rapidly increasing known species of plants and animals. Nothing has been said, however, of certain problems which arose, some of which still cause difficulties.

One of the problems had to do with priority. When more than one author described the same species, the oldest name, it is now agreed, has priority. This sounds simple, but to this day old publications are being found containing earlier descriptions of species. Often the earlier ones are so vague or inconsistent that even specialists cannot agree on what species was meant.[46] Also, the sensible "fifty-year rule" (still opposed by some), that if a name has been used for that period it becomes established regardless of any earlier description that may turn up, creates disagreement.

A second problem concerned Linnaeus's practice of using Latin names (and even Latin descriptions, still used by botanists). Latin had the immense advantage that it is a dead language and chauvinism does not enter in. The problem arose from the stipulation, stated or implied, that if names were not Latin words they were to be latinized, and if the incorrect form had earlier been used it was to be corrected. Even so, such barbaric names as "urubu" and "mitu" (South American Indian names) began to be introduced almost from the start. Classical scholars such as Elliott Coues naturally attempted to "purify" scientific names by putting them in good Latin. But as we have seen from his controversy with Augustus C. Merriam, Allen, and others, even classical scholars do not always agree. The number of changes became overwhelming, and now, except for demonstrable mistakes (usually corrected in the same volume or paper), no changes in names are permitted.

Yet another problem is that of similar words. For example, are *Picus* (a genus of woodpeckers) and *Pica* (a genus of magpies) admissible or are they merely forms of the same word? They are now admitted, but for a long time there was no consensus on such cases.

All that remains to be said of Canon XL, and its initial sentence insisting that the original spelling of a word be maintained, is that the International Code put it into different words but left the original intent unchanged.

As we have seen, Elliott Coues was chairman of the A.O.U. committee that produced the first two editions of the union's *Code of Nomenclature and Check-List of North American Birds*. Though the A.O.U. "Code" is a thing of the past, having been supplanted by the International Code, the A.O.U. *Check-List* continues. It has run through five editions, the last three since Coues' committee was relieved of its duties.

During their existence—the "Code" for a relatively brief period and the *Check-List* for nearly a century—these works have served as Bibles for the American Ornithologists' Union, each a *vade mecum* to which its members turned for solutions of their multifarious taxonomic and other problems. Their importance can hardly be exaggerated. Clearly Coues helped make yet another most significant, and lasting, contribution to American ornithology.

NOTES

1. Allen, "Biographical Memoir," 420.
2. Coues, ed., *Can Matter Think?* (1886), 28.
3. Coues, ed., *Buddhist Catechism* (1885), 62n.
4. Coues, *The Harmony of Scientific Knowledge and Religious Faith* (1883), 14.

5. Coues, "Renumeration of the Spinal Nerves and Reconstruction of the Plexuses in the Human Subject" (1884); Coues and Shute, "Neuro-Myology" (1887).

6. "Fifth Meeting of the American Ornithologists' Union," *Auk*, V (Jan., 1888), 98.

7. "Sixth Congress of the American Ornithologists' Union," *Auk*, VI (Jan., 1889), 56-57.

8. "Second Meeting of the American Ornithologists' Union," *Auk*, I (Oct., 1884), 376.

9. "News and Notes," *Auk*, VI (Jan., 1889), 82.

10. *Ibid.*, X (Oct., 1893), 386-87.

11. Coues, "The Presidential Address" (1896), 22, 15.

12. Chapman, *Autobiography of a Bird-Lover*, 43-44.

13. *Ibid.*, 51. Captain Curtis was, of course, the "Lieutenant Curtis" of Coues' first (1864-65) stay at Fort Whipple.

14. Leonhardt Stejneger (1851-1913), Norwegian-born naturalist, came to the United States in 1881 and served as curator of birds in the U.S. National Museum (1881-89).

15. Howard Saunders (1835-1907), British ornithologist, came to the United States to attend the A.O.U. congress of 1884 and was thus able to sit in on meetings of Coues' committee.

16. Charles Barney Cory (1857-1921), American ornithologist, was educated in the Lawrence Scientific School of Harvard, and was one of the founders of the A.O.U. In later years he was curator of birds in the Field Museum of Natural History in Chicago.

17. "Proceedings of the Committee on Classification and Nomenclature of the American Ornithologists' Union," 1-118. Hereafter cited as "Minutes A.O.U. Committee." These minutes are presently in the files of the A.O.U., National Museum of Natural History, Washington, D.C.

18. The family Tanagridae (now Thraupidae) includes the tanagers: scarlet, summer, hepatic, and western.

19. The family Fringillidae includes grosbeaks, finches, sparrows, and buntings.

20. The family Mniotiltidae (now Parulidae) includes the wood warblers.

21. "Minutes A.O.U. Committee," 36-37.

22. This original A.O.U. "Check-List" began with diving birds (*Pygopodes*) and ended with perching birds (*Passeres*), pretty much the reverse of earlier check-lists.

23. See, for these differences, Allen, *Auk*, III (July, 1886), 397.

24. The first A.O.U. "Check-List" recognized 768 species and 183 subspecies, Ridgway (1880) had recognized 764 species and 160 subspecies, and Coues (1882) had recognized 776 species and 212 subspecies.

25. "Minutes A.O.U. Committee," 31. Many of these changes resulted "from the strict enforcement of the law of priority" (see *Auk*, III (July, 1886), 398).

26. So called because it was prepared by Hugh Edwin Strickland (1811-53), British naturalist.

27. *The A.O.U. Code of Nomenclature and Check-List of North American Birds* (1886), 5.

28. *Ibid.*, 5, 11.
29. "Minutes A.O.U. Committee," 64-65.
30. *A.O.U. Code of Nomenclature and Check-List*, 51.
31. "Minutes A.O.U. Committee," 71.
32. Allen, "Biographical Memoir," 424.
33. Baird and Ridgway, "On Some New Forms of American Birds" (1873).
34. Baird, Brewer, and Ridgway, *A History of North American Birds: Land Birds* (1874).
35. Coues, *Key to North American Birds*, 5th ed. (1903), I, viii.
36. The new *Check-List* included numerous additions and nomenclatural changes made in the several supplements to the *Check-List* since 1886. These supplements had appeared in 1889, 1890, 1891, 1892, 1893, and 1894. Assisting the committee from time to time, on request, had been Charles Bendire, Frank M. Chapman, Walter Faxon, A. K. Fisher, Gerrit S. Miller, Jr., and T. S. Palmer.
37. Elliot, "Canon XL, A.O.U. Code" (1898), 294-98.
38. Allen, "A Defense of Canon XL of the A.O.U. Code" (1898), 298-99.
39. Elliot, "Truth *versus* Error" (1899), 42.
40. Allen, "'Truth *versus* Error'" (1899), 47-48.
41. Elliot, "Truth *versus* Error," 39.
42. Coues review of *Catalogue of Birds in the British Museum* (1898), 63.
43. This committee consisted of J. A. Allen as chairman, Theodore Gill, H. W. Henshaw, Harry C. Oberholser, Wilfred H. Osgood, Charles W. Richmond, and Witmer Stone.
44. About 1875 the American Association for the Advancement of Science appointed William H. Dall as a committee of one to prepare, after consultation with leading American naturalists, a set of rules for deciding nomenclatural questions. The so-called "Dall Code" (1877) is still one of the best essays on zoological nomenclature.
45. Ernst Mayr, E. Gorton Linsley, and Robert L. Usinger, *Methods and Principles of Systematic Zoology* (New York: McGraw-Hill, 1953), 205.
46. Hence the later stipulation that a type specimen must be designated, which can be referred to if there is a later question about what species was decribed.

CHAPTER XXI

A New Wife and Women's Rights

One can only speculate whether Elliott or Jeannie Augusta Coues suffered more during the last estranged years of their marriage. In any case, on May 12, 1886, Jeannie filed a bill for divorce in the District Court of Washington, D.C.[1] On July 27 the judge granted the divorce, on the grounds of desertion. According to the decree, Jeannie was to receive fifty dollars a month from Coues and was to have custody of the children, except Elliott Baird, who was to stay with his father. According to a newspaper account, Coues was "not averse to the decree."[2] Coues' divorce came at about the time of J. A. Allen's wedding. To his old friend Coues wrote in August, 1886: "I hope . . . that you are happy in your new chains of love. I am happy as a bird in shaking off at last the old fetters of hate."

A few days after the granting of the divorce, Coues wrote to Baird about his domestic affairs. His letter raised more questions that it answered:

> I think it only right and proper to inform you that a very happy solution of the long difficulty under which I have labored for seven years had been reached by decree of divorce granted July 27. There was no evidence against me that would stand examination for a moment, and the decree was granted on the technical grounds of my non-appearance to defend the suit, and as best on the whole for both parties. You know that I have steadily refused, all these years, to vindicate or even defend myself at the expense of another person, preferring to take what might come to me like a man, rather than turn the weapons I held against a woman. I have followed that course to the end with the result above said. Now I trust that the whole affair may be buried out of sight forever, and I see no reason or excuse for its ever being brought up again. If the whole truth in this deplorable affair were known, my vindication would be complete. But since it never will be, I simply claim my right to entire immunity from any further adverse criticism or personal hostility that has been based upon my course of action throughout this protracted and serious matter. I accept the

situation, and am responsible for all my words and deeds; but I submit that I should no longer suffer, in my personal and scientific relations in Washington, any further injustice or other hardship which it may be in your power to prevent. While under the cloud, I took what came without complaint; and now that it has passed, I have no other favor to ask, than that my proper and rightful position among scientists be recognized and respected.

It was appropriate that Elliott Baird Coues remained with his father. Of the three Coues children, he seemed the most likely to follow a career in science. In October, 1886, Coues was pleased to inform Allen: "My boy, Elliott Baird C. [aged 14], now about as tall as I am is turned out an indefatigable ornithologist, always in the field & with a good collection already." The proud father went on: "I should be gratified extremely to have [him] elected an associate [member of the A.O.U., of which Allen was president] this fall; and as I scarcely ought to move in the matter, will you kindly see it through?" Allen apparently complied with the request, and young Coues was admitted to associate membership later that year.

Two years later the son prepared a brief, competent paper on "Nesting of the Prairie Warbler," which his father submitted to *The Auk* for publication, along with these words to editor Allen:

> I take pardonable pride and pleasure in sending you for the Auk my boy's *first fruits*, and I think you will agree with me that his paper is very creditable. Though in my ms. it is wholly his own effort. I did not assist him in the least in preparing it, and scarcely changing anything in copying— only a verbal touch here and there. He would be delighted to have a pleasant word from you—and you know how such things count *in the beginning*. He seems to be thoroughly in earnest, and I envy him the genuine pleasure that ornithology has in store for him, let us trust! As for us old stagers—well, you know, as I do, that "dew drops do not last all day."

Allen responded quickly, both in accepting the contribution for publication and in sending some complimentary remarks to the author. "Your praise of Elliott's paper," Coues told Allen, "makes me 'pleased as punch.' I think it *was* good for a 15-[actually sixteen] year older, and gives earnest of great work at maturity." The article appeared in the October, 1888, issue of *The Auk*.[3]

In August, 1889, a letter from Coues to Allen again displayed pride in his son's pursuits: "My boy has just come from Magdalen Bird Rocks [the Magdalen Islands, in the Gulf of St. Lawrence]—had a thrilling time, and I was glad to see him back with his life, to say nothing of his barrel of eggs & birds. He had been before in Florida & at Cobbs Island, Va. [Cobb Island, on the Atlantic side of Virginia's Eastern Shore], and I have seldom seen a more persistent and energetic young collector than this chip of my block."

In 1890, after attending Columbian University, he entered Harvard's Lawrence Scientific School. During his stay at Cambridge he became a member of the Nuttall Ornithological Club. Additional evidence of his continuing interest in ornithology is found in a letter of October, 1891, from his father to Allen, telling of the young man's intention of attending the 1891 meeting of the A.O.U. in New York.

He left Harvard after two years and in 1895 received an M.D. degree from Bellevue Hospital Medical College, New York.[4] After a few years of practicing his profession in New York and Haiti, young Coues' record becomes dim. In the writings of Edith, his sister, we find numerous references to his death on January 2, 1913, in Zürich, Switzerland. We do not know the nature of the illness, but Edith mentions his "days of physical and spiritual anguish."[5] A year after his death she recorded her emotions:

> I feel anew the sword of grief that pierced me in that gray, foggy dawn at Zürich, when I realized that I must get up and do something that was undoable. Countless millions know the complete revolt of humanity against the laying of one's own in the earth. The beautiful Mass at the *Liebfrauen Kirche* was strength to my soul. Pater Braun's handsome, earnest face, as he spoke Elliott's precious name in prayer and supplication, the light playing around the pulpit, and the beatitudes in mosaic against gold—all are graven on my heart. I could only read through tears *Beati qui esuriunt* [Blessed are they who hunger]—Elliott's life history. And that peaceful hour with him afterward, in the flower-filled room, when we felt that it was only his afternoon rest we were watching over! When they came to cover his face forever I was so uplifted that I could turn those screws myself, instead of leaving it to hirelings to shut the light away from those noble features.
>
> Oh, that loving heart, that crystal brain, with its power of original thought, that gift of industry! How far Elliott might have gone on the road of science! Others will discover and progress, but he, so fitted to lift the veil, has slipped behind it. Oh, my brother![6]

Edith, as the foregoing lines attest, was in one respect a truer heir to her father's literary talents than either of her brothers. She became a forceful and prolific writer. She received her education in Maryland at the Convent of Notre Dame and from private tutors. In 1901 she married Nelson O'Shaughnessy (1876-1932), a career diplomat. A son,

Elim, was born in 1907, and he too spent most of his adult life in the diplomatic corps.

Her first and best-known book, *A Diplomat's Wife in Mexico* (1916), is a classic account of the Mexican Revolution. Most of her other works are likewise based on observations made while residing in foreign lands with her well-traveled husband: *Diplomatic Days* (1917), *My Lorraine Journal* (1918), *Intimate Pages of Mexican History* (1920), *Alsace in Rust and Gold* (1920), *Viennese Medley* (1924), *Married Life* (1925), *Other Ways and Other Flesh* (1929), and *Marie Adelaide: Grand Duchess of Luxemburg, Duchess of Nassau* (1932). She died in New York in 1939.[7]

A noteworthy feature of Edith's writings was her intense preoccupation with Catholicism. Considering Elliott Coues' extreme aversion to that branch of Christianity, we wonder if she embraced it in spite of or because of her father. In her books are several indications that her mother and Elliott Baird Coues also became Roman Catholics.

Another characteristic of her writing was her frequent expression of love for both Elliott Baird and her mother. Conversely, she never mentioned her father. It is not difficult to assume that she disliked, even hated him. Writing sometime in the 1920s, Edith left a full word-picture of Jeannie Augusta Coues:

> My mother is very tall, her figure little or not at all bent by time, and her gait is of a peculiar rhythmic majesty. She generally wears capes of unique and beautiful cut. . . . Often too I picture her sitting at one end of the long white table of the white upper chamber, the light from the electric bulb in the paneled ceiling, cutting out her beautiful, high, straight nose, deepening her large-socketed, still blue eyes, tracing her delicate, so often smiling lips, and finding the gleam or sparkle of something around her un-ravaged throat. Over her face lies a great calm which has come after much combating with circumstance and many enforced or voluntary re-nunciations. . . . Under that light yesterday she was saying, for she is well taught of life and speaks often in general as well as in particular terms, "Love your griefs; they are your best friends. Looking back over these many years I see that the good and admirable things of life have indeed belonged to adversity rather than prosperity."[8]

Certainly the death of Elliott Baird Coues was one of the griefs to which she alluded. Was another the memory of Elliott Coues?

Jeannie Augusta Coues seems to have spent her last years traveling with Edith and her family. She died in January, 1925, in Rome.[9]

Of Coues' other son, Beverly Drinkard, we know almost nothing. J. A. Allen's memoir of Elliott Coues, published in 1909, stated that

Beverly was then living in Europe and was unmarried.[10] It is possible that he died sometime before his brother, for Edith's January 1, 1912, entry in her journal mentioned "that other dead one of our blood, lost to men but not to God. Was he sleeping quietly?"[11]

2

There can be little doubt that Coues' relations with other women contributed to the break-up of his marriage. The "Book of Dates" has entries for 1885 and 1886 indicating that before and after his divorce he had begun another round of womanizing:

> This summer [1885], in greatest part, spent at Oakland, Md., Mrs. Smith and Miss Alice W. Mitchell.
> Early this year [1886] met Mrs. J. W. Bates, 1814 Chestnut St., Philada.
> Mrs. J. W. B. Sailed for Europe.
> Part of this summer spent at Cape May, N. Jersey, with Mordecai Evan and Miss Mitchell.
> Mrs. J. W. B. returned from Europe.
> In Washn., before her return, Miss Marie Willcox.

We have been unable to identify Mrs. Smith, Alice W. Mitchell, and Marie Willcox, but there is no mystery about Mrs. J. W. Bates. She was the former Mary Emily Bennett, who was born August 26, 1835, into a well-connected New England family. Miss Bennett was taught by private tutors in Paris and London, receiving an education that was considerably better than that available to most women of her time. Much of her early life was spent in Europe—by 1887 she had crossed the Atlantic twenty-four times. In 1866 she married in Dresden a wealthy Philadelphia merchant, Joseph W. Bates. The union did not result in any children, and Bates died in March, 1886.

Thus the woman Coues met in 1886 was a highly intelligent, recently widowed, well-to-do matron. More than that, she was "an accomplished musician, an art critic, a linguist and brilliant society woman." The Bates mansion in Philadelphia "was noted for the elegance and lavishness of its hospitality, its wonderful dinners and one of the finest private collections of paintings in this country."[12]

Small wonder that Coues found Mary Emily Bates attractive. Evidently she was attracted in return, for on October 25, 1887, she became the third Mrs. Elliot Coues. The ceremony was performed in the parlors of the Hotel Vendome in Boston, at 1:00 P.M., with the noted divine, the Reverend Edward Everett Hale, officiating.[13] The bride was given away by Chicago banker Charles Henrotin.[14] Dana Estes served as best man, and Eliot Lord[15] and William A. Hayes[16] were the ushers. Following the wedding breakfast the couple journeyed to Coues' native city, Portsmouth, New Hampshire, where they stayed at the nearby Wentworth Hotel. About a month later they were in Washington.[17] The Coues residence at 1726 N Street was to be their home for the remainder of his life.

Coues seems to have found happiness in a marriage for the first time in this, his third attempt. Two months before the wedding Coues described Mary Emily Bates to J. A. Allen as one "who to my eyes & those of most persons, I believe, combines all the desirabilities in person & place in the world, and whose wealth is not an insuperable object." Her wealth may have proved a blessing to Coues, because a few months before the marriage he lost a major source of income: his position on the faculty of the National Medical College.

The loss of his professorship was the result of yet another controversy in his life. In this instance the embroglio was a product of idealism and high courage on Coues' part. On March 16, 1887, he delivered the commencement address for the medical college, at the Congregational Church on G Street. The address, entitled "A Woman in the Case," was a forthright oration on behalf of rights for women.[18]

In a sense his message was appropriate: on this occasion, the sixty-fifth annual commencement, the medical college was granting for the first time a degree to a woman, Clara Bliss Hinds. Since there were many respected men in all walks of life who supported equal rights for women, Coues' theme was not necessarily an explosive one. Nevertheless, his outspokenness managed to shock many of his listeners.

In his talk he listed "the three great stumbling-blocks" in woman's path to progress: "religious intolerance," "scientific insolence," and "social tyranny." The first of these evoked his strongest language. Both Protestantism and Catholicism came in for a thorough lambasting. In one-half of one paragraph he succeeded in abusing three major branches of Christianity:

> And where the hand of the Roman Church is heaviest, there the head of womanhood is bowed lowest down. The revolt from Catholic tyranny that was inevitable . . . was found in Protestantism. The mistress of Martin Luther inspired the Reformation when she fired the imagination and girded the loins of that sturdy protester. If one woman did that, no wonder that among the many nearest Henry the Eighth, one was found able to precipitate yet another rebellion by stiffening that magnificent brute into imposing upon the predominate race of men a placid and intensely re-

spectable Episcopacy,—that emasculate bastard of the scarlet woman of Rome.

By "scientific insolence" he meant the bigotry which had prevented women from seeking careers in the sciences. This was especially deplorable, he believed, because women would make better scientists than men: "The point is not that womanly minds are unscientific, for the greatest scientists who have ever lived have been men who possessed those peculiarly feminine powers of creative imagination and those intuitions which enabled them to divine truths they had afterward to support and defend with their slower masculine logic. I should rather say that such fine fibre and sheeny quality of mind are superscientific, reaching over and beyond, securing most precious acquisitions denied forever to duller understanding."

His third point, "social tyranny," dealt most with the enslavement of women by fashion:

> Everybody knows that nobody is anybody who is not in fashion. Every woman knows, I am informed, that the consciousness of being well dressed brings a peace of mind that religion cannot confer. And doubtless there are conquests to be made in other fields than those of science. What shall I say? I do not know. But there is something rotten in Washington, if there never was in Denmark, when to be well dressed is to be half-undressed, putting religion quite out of mind, and putting science to its trumps in trying to cure pneumonia. Dress reform, for one thing, cannot begin too soon for morals or for health, or stay too long for the benefit of society. . . .

His manuscript contained further remarks on the same theme, but he did not share them with his audience because it had "grown so scary and gaspy at this point." In a printed version of the speech he commented on the "present state of fashionable society, so cunningly contrived to stimulate sexual passion and punish its gratification." And— no doubt thinking of the whispers his own conduct had produced—he went on to condemn the gossip-mongers in Washington.[19]

Despite his decision not to read some of the more shocking statements in his manuscript, the damage had been done. Newspaper accounts of the event told of the "holy horror" produced by Coues' remarks.[20] "The Faculty," wrote a female reporter for the *Washington Post*, "grew nervous, and, while endeavoring to appear calm, felt something very like an earthquake beneath their feet, and could not keep from quaking."[21]

There seems to have been no censure of Coues by the college officials, nor a demand for his dismissal. Yet it was made clear to him through informal channels that his address had been not only inappropriate but also embarrassing to the institution as well. In particular, he was told that his treatment of religion was, in addition to being offensive, contrary to the college's charter, which had a clause "expressly forbidding any question of religion to be brought up by [the faculty]."[22]

Coues responded a few days later by offering to resign. At first the faculty declined to consider his resignation. On March 31 he sent a formal letter of resignation. The tone of the letter was remarkably polite and he expressed his great affection for his colleagues and the genuine regret he felt in leaving the school. He went on in the same gracious manner to let them know that his views on the matters discussed in the address were unchanged.[23] On April 16 the faculty accepted his resignation.[24]

3

Coues' sympathies for the rights of women, although not publicly articulated until his speech of 1887, must have developed much earlier. His own mother and sisters were capable, intelligent women. Throughout his career Coues encouraged, and sometimes collaborated with, a number of women in the natural sciences: Martha Ann Maxwell, Julia S. Gilliss, Olive Thorne Miller,[25] E. Irene Rood,[26] Florence Merriam Bailey,[27] Mabel Osgood Wright,[28] and Genevieve E. Jones.[29]

His attachment to Theosophy, although brief and stormy, seems also to have contributed to his high estimate of womankind. The founder of the cult, Mme. Blavatsky, was a woman of undoubted brilliance, and the central spiritual figure of Theosophy was the female deity Isis. In his commencement address of 1887 Coues struck a theosophical note when he said that once the fetters of Christianity were removed from women, "then will the woman-soul of the world have been enthroned again, even as it was before the tempter came and conquered. Then will have been regained in triumph that divine estate she lost so long ago. Then will the seed of her spirit have bruised the head of the serpent. And then shall the Veil of Isis be riven, and the naked truth be not ashamed. Then shall the seal set upon the lips of the Sphinx be broken, that man may know from whose lips to learn the secret of life, for the want of knowing which he now dies daily."[30] At least one of the newspaper reporters present at the commencement believed that Coues' remarks were theosophical in tone and content.[31]

His spiritualistic address at Chicago in 1888 ("The Signs of the Times") referred even more directly to the "Woman Question": ". . .

and the first among the Signs of the Times is the 'Woman Question.' That is, indeed, not only the first, but also last, and always." He went on to speak enthusiastically of his recent attendance at the International Congress of Women in Washington. After praising the good work, courage, and progress of the women's rights movement, Coues insisted that spiritualism and women's rights were inextricably linked in American history: "They grew up together, along parallel lines of evolution, though seldom did their faces turn to one another, so fixed were the eyes of each upon their respective goals. And as they thus grew side by side, the one never knocked louder at the gates of Congress than the other has knocked at the door of the understanding of millions of Americans, begging to be heard."[32]

A newspaper account of Coues' divorce from his second wife reported that Jeannie Augusta Coues had not shared Coues' beliefs in the occult,[33] nor had she seemingly earned his high regard for women in general. On the other hand, his third wife believed in psychic phenomena and was described as ". . . the secretary of the Women's National Liberal Union and a prominent member of various other organizations for the promotion of enlightened and progressive thoughts among women, though she has thus far shrunk from taking the position of a public writer or speaker. Her attitude is that of the extreme wing of radical reform now being agitated."[34] Coues dedicated the second edition of *"A Woman in the Case"* to "my dear wife . . . Love for whom inspired This Tribute to Ideal Womanhood."[35]

Several entries in the "Book of Dates" indicate the breadth and seriousness of the commitment of Elliott and Mary Emily Coues to the cause of women's rights:

Jan. 10 [1889], Sorosis[36] Banquet at Delmonico's, N.Y.

Jan. 25 [1889], address on Hygiene before Woman's Industrial and Educational Union, 516 Eleventh st., Washn., D.C.

Apr. 25 [1889], reception of N.Y. City Woman's Suffrage League, Park Ave. Hotel, N.Y.

Winter 1889-1890, or Spring of 1890, was founded at Washn. the Pro Re Nota (Woman's) Club. The constitution was drawn up by Mrs. Coues, Clara Barton,[37] Miss de Puys[38] & myself, at 1726 N st.

Feb. 24, 25 [1890], Woman's National Liberal Union Convention at Willard's Hall. My address Feb. 24, p.m.

Apr. 30 [1892], attended reception of Woman's Press Club, 126 E. 23d st., N.Y.

Aug. 25 [1893], reception by Chicago Woman's Club, Athenaeum Building.

Reception [by] Woman's Federation, Galt House [Louisville] May 27 [1897].

4

Coues' active participation in the fight for women's rights came to an end in the early 1890s—apparently not because of any dissaffection with the goals or leaders of the movement but because his energies became otherwise diverted.

In the late summer of 1891 he and Mrs. Coues began a lengthy tour of the West. In one respect this was curious: he had for years associated the western United States with his unhappy second tour of duty in Arizona. In 1882 he had expressed his feelings about the West in a letter to Robert E. Thomspon: "Though I had the misfortune to serve at times in Dakota and Arizona . . . my interest in those western regions has been wholly that of a naturalist."[39]

Why, then, by 1891 had he changed his attitudes sufficiently to travel into the land of such bitter personal memories? In the first place, he indicated that the trip was for reasons of health, his constitution having "utterly broken down."[40] Later Coues wrote that an attack of "La grippe" in 1891 had made him "an oldish man" and that he had "never been the same since."[41]

Also, he seems to have been experiencing a markedly common phenomenon of the Civil War generation. By the 1890s the "old soldiers" had mellow memories of the 1861-65 period. Veterans' organizations such as the Grand Army of the Repubic swelled in numbers partly because of the great wave of nostalgia felt by the veterans and their desire to relive and justify their youthful military adventures. We feel certain that Coues' 1891 journey westward was to some extent motivated by a desire to recapture the exciting and professionally productive days of his western sojourn of 1864-65.

The trip, via railroad, got under way from Washington on September 10, 1891.[42] Coues and his wife arrived in Chicago on the next day. There, until September 21, they stayed at the home of his sister Lucy. Leaving Chicago on the Rock Island line, they arrived in Denver on the 25th, spending the night at the Windsor Hotel. On the following afternoon they journeyed to Colorado Springs, where they remained until October 5.

On September 29 they went to the summit of nearby Pike's Peak by means of the recently completed cogwheel railroad. "By the latter mode of conveyance," he later wrote, "I have ascended the Rigi in

Switzerland, as well as Mt. Washington in my native state; but neither of these afforded the sensation I experienced upon the summit of Pike's Peak. . . ."[43]

The Coueses spent the night of October 5 in Pueblo and on the next day resumed their journey by rail through the Far West. On the 7th they were in Salt Lake City, where they remained for two days. On the 11th they arrived in San Francisco and registered at the Occidental Hotel. On October 14 he and Mrs. Coues traveled to and returned from Palo Alto.

One of the purposes in going to the Bay Area was to participate in the annual meeting of the American Library Association. On October 16 he attended the association's banquet at San Francisco's Palace Hotel and, according to his "Book of Dates," became a member of the A.L.A. at "about this date." The "Book of Dates" also gives us the itinerary for the remainder of their stay in California: "Oct. 17, 8:30 A.M. left for Santa Cruz with A.L.A. and arrived Oct. 17-Dec. 5 at Santa Cruz. 5th, 3:15 p.m. left for Watsonville. Dec. 6-8, Del Monte; left 1:15, arr. San Francisco 6 p.m. Dec. 8-28, San Francisco."

In the closing days of 1891 he and his wife reached the last and perhaps the main destination of the western tour: "[Dec. 28] left 5 p.m. for Arizona. Dec. 29 Mojave and Barstow. 30 Prescott Junction; 31st left at 11 a.m. and reached Prescott 3 p.m. ending the year."

Coues did not record whether the weeks they had spent in California were pleasant or not. On the other hand, there can be no doubt whatsoever that he was thrilled to be back in Prescott and that the citizens of Prescott were delighted to have him in their midst.

On February 8 the *Prescott Morning Courier* printed a letter from Coues in which he made an eloquent appeal for the formation of a local historical society. He emphasized that such an organization was needed to perpetuate the memory of those who had won the territory from the Apaches:

> Every one who now enjoys his home in peace and security, under the established laws of the land, has to thank the pioneers, the early settlers, the Indian fighters, for the possession of such a home. A sentiment of gratitude should quicken an interest in the history of Arizona, and make sure that the latter receives an enduring form. But this will never, never be done as well as it should be, if it be not done quickly. The present is a fitting time, just before the generation of men which gave birth to Arizona shall have passed off the stage of life, and before the new order of things effaces the memory of the old.

Of course he alluded to the Indian fighters whom he had known personally: "How many of us are left to recall Pauline Weaver and his associates? I could tell you who cut Apache arrow-heads out of that old pioneer, but who remembers the man who died of his wounds received in the fight that Weaver survived? How many men are left like Willard Rice, a type of the very brain, bone and sinew of the territory, who guided many a military scout to success, and whose own rifle-stock could be notched from breech-plate to heel-plate with the tally of good dead Indians?"

Coues' appeal fell upon receptive ears. In announcing a meeting to be held on February 25 for the purpose of organizing "a permanent historical society," the *Arizona Journal-Miner* of Prescott remarked that "Dr. Elliott Coues, who was stationed in this territory during its early history, has been active in getting up the society and will assist in making it a success."[44] The meeting took place at the courthouse. After being nominated as chairman by the mayor of Prescott and unanimously elected, Coues "then addressed the meeting in his usual interesting and happy manner, and was greeted with frequent bursts of applause. The speaker dwelt upon the necessity of such a society as the one proposed, and thought the need urgent and the occasion timely for its organization." After other orators had been heard from, Coues was elected the first honorary chairman of what was to be known as the Prescott Historical Society.[45]

In a small way Coues engaged in some ornithological activity while in Arizona. He supplied *The Auk* with notes on the canvasback[46] and the golden eagle[47] in the territory and investigated rumors of the occasional presence there of a certain Mexican parrot.[48]

Coues and his wife apparently began their return east a few days after this pleasant occasion. The March 16 issue of the *Courier* contained a letter from Coues, in which he stated: "I trust that I may be able to return soon, and do all in my power for the development and prosperity of my beloved Arizona; meanwhile I hope you will do what you can in your valuable paper to promote the interests of the historical society, which I have so much at heart." The *Courier* also quoted a story from the *Chicago News* concerning Coues' activities in Prescott: "The professor seems to have captured Prescott, whooped up the boys, waked the snakes and then jumped the town, he—if it was not his astral—appeared in Chicago a few days later." By April the Coueses were back in Washington.[49]

Coues' change of heart *vis-à-vis* the West—particularly his "beloved Arizona"—was nothing short of remarkable, and, as we shall see, he had committed himself, even before his travels of 1891-92, to a major project embracing the history of the West. Nevertheless, we can be certain that the enjoyment of the trip added to the zest with which he plunged into the last phrase of his varied career—as a historian of the American West.

NOTES

1. Coues' "Book of Dates" (1886).
2. *New York Times*, Aug. 3, 1886, 2; Dec. 27, 1899, 7.
3. Elliott Baird Coues, "Nesting of the Prairie Warbler (*Dendroica discolor*) in the Vicinity of Washington, D.C.," *Auk*, V (Oct., 1888), 405-8.
4. Palmer, "Elliott Baird Coues" (1943), 633.
5. O'Shaughnessy, *Diplomatic Days* (1917), 198.
6. O'Shaughnessy, *A Diplomat's Wife in Mexico* (1916), 128-29.
7. *New York Times*, Feb. 19, 1939, 39.
8. O'Shaughnessy, *Other Ways and Other Flesh* (1929), 81, 85, 86.
9. *New York Times*, Jan. 31, 1925, 13.
10. Allen, "Biographical Memoir," 425.
11. O'Shaughnessy, *Diplomatic Days*, 184.
12. Willard and Livermore, eds., *A Woman of the Century* (1893), 210-11.
13. Coues' "Book of Dates" (1887). Edward Everett Hale (1822-1909), Unitarian clergyman, chaplain of the U.S. Senate, and writer, is best remembered as the author of *The Man without a Country*.
14. In addition to his successful career as a financier, Charles Henrotin (1843-1914) served in consular posts in his native Belgium and in Turkey.
15. Boston journalist Eliot Lord (1851-1928) is best known for his classic account, *Comstock Mining and Miners* (1883).
16. We have been unable to find any biographical data on Hayes.
17. Coues' "Book of Dates" (1887).
18. Coues, "*A Woman in the Case*" (1887). The second edition (1890), which was no. 6 of the Biogen Series, will be cited in subsequent notes.
19. Coues, "*A Woman in the Case*," 12, 14-15, 18-19, 23-24n.
20. *Ibid.*, 54.
21. *Ibid.*, 31.
22. *Ibid.*, xiv.
23. *Ibid.*, xiii-xvi.
24. Coues' "Book of Dates" (1887).
25. Olive Thorne Miller (1831-1918), author of children's and nature books. See Coues' reviews of her works in *Nation:* LIV (May 26, 1892), 403-4; LVIII (May 10, 1894), 347; LXIII (July 23, 1896), 72-73; LXIV (Apr. 18, 1897), 271.
26. Other than the fact that E. Irene Rood collaborated with Coues in the

editing of *Papers Presented to the World's Congress on Ornithology* (1896), we are unable to identify her.

27. Florence Merriam Bailey (1863-1948), ornithologist and nature writer, was sister of C. Hart Merriam and wife of biologist Vernon Bailey. See Coues' reviews of her books in *Nation*: LXIII (Nov. 12, 1896), 374; LXVI (June 23, 1898), 483-84.

28. Mabel Osgood Wright (1859-1934), American writer, was born in New York City. She was the author of *Birdcraft* (1895), *Citizen Bird* (with Coues, 1897), *Dogtown* (1902), and other books.

29. Genevieve Estelle Jones (died 1879, age thirty-two) and her associates (mostly members of her family) produced the lovely *Illustrations of the Nests and Eggs of Birds of Ohio* (1886). Coues gave the highest praise to the various installments of the work in reviews in *Bull. Nutt. Orn. Club.* and *The Auk.* See his obituary of Miss Jones in *Bull. Nutt. Orn. Club*, IV (Oct., 1879), 228, and his letter of Oct. 22, 1879, to J. A. Allen.

30. Coues, "*A Woman in the Case*," 15-16.

31. *Ibid.*, 29-33.

32. Coues, *The Signs of the Times* (1889), 2, 7-8.

33. *New York Times*, Aug. 3, 1886, 2.

34. Willard and Livermore, eds., *A Woman of the Century*, 8.

35. Coues, "*A Woman in the Case*," v.

36. Sorosis, founded in New York in 1868, was the first women's club in the United States.

37. Clara Barton (1830-1912) first gained recognition for her hospital work during the Civil War. She later undertook similar humanitarian efforts during the Franco-Prussian War. In 1882 she became the first president of the American Red Cross, a post she held until 1904.

38. We have been unable to identify Miss de Puys.

39. Coues to Thompson, June 20, 1882, Misc. Mss. Coll., American Philosophical Society.

40. Coues' "Book of Dates" (1891).

41. Coues to Allen, Apr. 15, 1896.

42. The itinerary is given in the "Book of Dates" (1891-92).

43. Coues, ed., *The Explorations of Zebulon Montgomery Pike* (1895), II, 454-55n.

44. *Arizona Journal-Miner* (Prescott), Feb. 24, 1892, 3.

45. *Prescott Morning Courier*, Feb. 27, 1892, 4.

46. Coues, "Wintering of the Canvasback in Arizona" (1892).

47. Coues, "Nesting of the Golden Eagle in Arizona" (1892).

48. Coues to Allen, Apr. 7, 1892.

49. Coues' "Book of Dates" (1892).

CHAPTER XXII

Coues and Lewis and Clark

One of the more memorable events in American history occurred on September 23, 1806. On that day Captains Meriwether Lewis and William Clark, after having completed their amazingly successful twenty-eight-month transit of the continent, arrived back in St. Louis. Because of Lewis's tragic death three years later, publication of the original journals of the expedition was delayed until 1814. When they did come from the press they were in the form of a paraphrase done by Nicholas Biddle,[1] a brilliant young Philadelphia lawyer.

After publication of this 1814 edition, now often referred to as "the Biddle edition," no scholar came forward to study it critically, and thus to extend knowledge of the Lewis and Clark expedition, until 1893, almost eighty years later. In that year Elliott Coues, for the New York publisher Francis P. Harper,[2] edited a reissue of the Biddle edition, one that remains even today an essential reference work for all students of the Lewis and Clark expedition.

Harper first approached Coues in 1891, at which time the latter had almost finished his definitional labors for *The Century Dictionary* and was casting about for a new challenge. That he was immediately enthusiastic about Harper's proposal is evident from his reply, dated June 23, 1891:

> In regard to your proposition to publish "Lewis and Clarke"[3] under my editorial supervision:
> Some years ago I made a special study of the L. & C. literature,[4] and I could therefore undertake the desired work with confidence. It would also be congenial work.
> I will therefore do it with pleasure, if circumstances justify you in making me an offer that I could afford to accept. Literature is my profession; and other things being equal, I must choose the most remunerative. I have for several years been forced to decline all proffered engagements, owing to my absorption in the "Century Dictionary," now nearly finished,

and shall not be able to undertake anything else till some time next autumn.[5]

Soon afterward, his health impaired by his strenuous, prolonged lexicographic and other duties, Coues left for the West, where he planned to rest and regain his customary vigor. Before his departure he wrote Harper: "This reprint [of Lewis and Clark] I think you will agree with me should be verbatim et literatim et punctuatim after the original, even to copying typographical errors, and should indicate also the original pagination." In light of subsequent events we should remember this statement: Coues' thinking, like the plumage of his beloved birds, sometimes changed.

The project remained uncertain for almost a year while Coues slowly recovered his health. It was late June, 1892, when Harper wrote him again: "How about the Lewis and Clarke? We are anxious to have this matter under way, as I am informed that another publisher has under consideration the republishing of this work." Coues, by then back in Washington, replied that he would like very much to have his name connected "with a reissue of the memorable book." He presumed that his name would be on the title page and that Harper had in mind a new, critical, bibliographical preface as well as explanatory notes. "If you think we can come to terms," Coues concluded, "make your offer . . . and I will give you a final answer at once."

Harper responded that he could afford to pay $500 to $750 for a bibliography and "such explanatory and historical notes as would make the edition a valuable book for reference." Perhaps fearful that Coues might refuse his modest offer, Harper expressed his belief that extensive research would be unnecessary—because of Coues' wide experiences in and knowledge of the West—and further said that he desired his services as editor because he was "the best person living for such a work."

Coues accepted Harper's offer, and soon afterward transported himself and his "desk" to a summer home in Cranberry, North Carolina, a small place in the mountains near the Tennessee line, which afforded the seclusion and quiet his temperament desired. Here, approaching his fiftieth birthday, he began his labors editing the Biddle volume. Almost at once he was struck with the thought that "this History, which has held its own for nearly a century as a standard work of reference, has never . . . until now been subjected to searching and systematic criticism."[6]

Harper quickly learned that Coues was a demanding editor. In months ahead the letters coming to his desk from Coues averaged two to three a week, and in each Coues asked Harper for something. For instance, in one alone he requested Harper to (1) typewrite and return a manuscript, (2) have a portrait of Sergeant Patrick Gass[7] touched up, (3) look for portraits of Lewis and Clark, (4) copy from some encyclopedia a biographical sketch of Clark and forward it to him, (5) locate and send Jefferson's 1806 "Message to Congress,"[8] and (6) reproduce and reduce in size a cut of an animal picture he enclosed.

Coues wrote his publisher most often for needed reference works. Before the summer ended, Harper, at what must have been immoderate expense of time and effort, obtained, wrapped, and mailed many books, among them the 1814 Biddle edition of Lewis and Clark, Sergeant Gass's *Journal*, Washington Irving's *Astoria*, Zebulon M. Pike's *Expeditions*, Major Stephen H. Long's *Account of an Expedition from Pittsburgh to the Rocky Mountains*, the Reverend Samuel Parker's *Journal of an Exploring Tour beyond the Rocky Mountains*, and several of the apocryphal editions of Lewis and Clark. Unquestionably Coues was hampered by lack of library facilities at his Appalachian retreat, but he might well have anticipated his need for some of the above volumes and brought them with him from Washington.

Most important to Coues was, of course, the 1814 Biddle, or *editio princeps* as he sometimes called it. On receiving it, Coues promptly advised Harper that he proposed to go through it "line by line, make my marks and put in what notes I can here, where I am without any of the authorities." After preliminary study, he relayed additional comment:

> [It was] very badly edited from the rough field-notes of the explorers, after those notes, in a chaotic state, had had a precarious existence for seven to ten years & went through various hands after Capt. Lewis blew his brains out in 1806 or thereabouts.[9] The printer, Inskeep,[10] probably did the best he could with the copy furnished him, but it is wretchedly set up, the pointing in particular being terrific, the spelling often very funny, and the "parts of speech" dislocated in a thousand places. Who, for example, would know that the word printed "louservia" was meant for loup cervier [Canada lynx]? I think you will agree with me that it would *not* be desirable, even if it were possible, to "recast" or "rewrite" the book—for you must be able to assure your public that you are giving them the original genuine "Lewis and Clarke," without abridgment or alteration—yet I can in going over the book put in the necessary touches, to make "the nouns and verbs agree," etc., and thus insure some degree of literary excellence, without presuming to so much as recast a single sentence.

Thus Coues was already proposing to abandon "verbatim et literatim et punctuatim after the original." Also, he was overly critical of Biddle's punctuation, spelling, and parts of speech.

As the summer progressed, editor and publisher deliberated on what new material might profitably be incorporated into the reissue. They tossed back and forth opinions and suggestions about such likely addenda as illustrations, maps, memoirs of Clark and Gass, bibliography, index, and, of course, the character and quantity of annotations. Coues stressed "identification of places [along the Lewis and Clark route] as they were then with what they are now." He anticipated no problem with this task for in 1872-74, as he told Harper, he had traveled "nearly a thousand miles in the very tracks of L. & C." As to the quantity of notes, Harper thought about 200 pages (to go with some 1,000 pages of text) would be about right, while Coues believed something less than that would be adequate, somewhere between 100 and 200. If Harper had known then how high the figure would ultimately go, he might well have withdrawn from the project then and there.

Coues made commendable progress editing Biddle during his summer stay at Cranberry. Shortly before leaving for Washington he told Harper: "You will be surprised, and I think much pleased, to find how much more and of what kind I have put into the edition. It has interested me deeply; I have worked con amore, and done little else than this for a couple of months. Have already more than filled up my side of the work—I never stint work I once take up." He added that he had had "no idea of how much was required in the way of topography, ethnology and natural history."

Coues' interest soon mounted—and with good reason. "You will rejoice to hear," Coues exulted in a letter to Harper of September 29, "that I have found out all about [the location at the American Philosophical Society, Philadelphia, of] the original manuscripts [of Lewis and Clark] through Judge Craig Biddle (son of Nicholas Biddle). Also lots of letters of Clark, &c.—and the original copper plates of the ed. of 1814. I am also in correspondence with Clarke's *son* [Jefferson Kearny Clark]."

As Coues later wrote, "The acquisition of the [original] manuscripts was not foreseen."[11] When he and Harper began their collaboration, they had no information about them other than nebulous reports of their existence; one rumor was that they probably occupied some forgotten niche in one of the federal departments in Washington. Thus Harper wrote to Coues on July 7, 1892: "We would desire (if you can secure it) the unpublished portion in mss. owned by the government, that you thought you could get access to, as then we could start with additional matter never before published which might help along the sale of the book." Coues replied that on his return to Washington he would invade the archives of the Congressional Library and War and State Departments to search for any unpublished material. To this he added, "I do not know, first, that there is any; second, that if there be, whether I can get it; but will see."

Incredible as it may seem to us today, the truth is that no one then, except for a few informed members of the American Philosophical Society, appears to have had even the vaguest notion about the whereabouts of the original handwritten journals of Lewis and Clark. As Coues himself said when subsequently addressing that society, it was common knowledge that the manuscripts of the famous explorers did exist, but what they were and where they were kept, "few could have told."[12] Only a few knew that Nicholas Biddle in 1818, following publication of the Biddle edition, had deposited the original manuscripts at the American Philosophical Society.[13] And there they had remained, virtually unknown, unheralded, and untouched, for three-quarters of a century. Today, appraised by scholars as among the most priceless of American historical documents, they are guarded with the care traditionally afforded crown jewels. Their "discovery" by Coues, measured by most any yardstick, was an event of incalculable consequence to the further accounts of the Lewis and Clark expedition and to that of United States history.

Coues returned from Cranberry to Washington in early October. True to his word, he at once began visiting government agencies. On October 14 he wrote Harper: "Have examined all the War Department archives. Some nuggets, a few of which we shall print as historical curiosities." Again, a few days later: "Have discovered a lot more precious historical material, never published."[14] In days ahead he benefited from visits to the U.S. Bureau of Ethnology, the Smithsonian Institution, and the U.S. Geological Survey.

From his home in Washington Coues soon began sending copy to Harper. With it went his latest reflections on editing: "No *rule* can be laid down in the reprinting of historical works; but each case must be editorially decided on its own merits. . . . I have taken some liberties with the original text, and gone so far as I dared in capitalization, spelling, punctuation, etc., if we are to advertise 'a faithful reprint'. But we must not go too far in that direction; and in general, we must be scrupulously particular in the cases of all *proper* names, which, when 'wrong', must be left so in text, and explained in notes." So Coues was, indeed, taking liberties with the text, liberties that no reputable historian today would even consider. In due course these would lead to justified heavy-handed censure.

Early in November Coues advised Harper that he planned to visit Philadelphia to examine the original Lewis and Clark manuscripts there. Until he had done so, he felt "a little shaky about sending back proofs," for an inspection of these documents might "put quite a different aspect on our arrangements." Harper replied to this letter at once: "Let the Phila. original manuscripts go for the present. You have been so fortunate in finding so much important additional material that I think we have enough for the purpose."

Throughout this period of joint effort, editor and publisher understandably did not always see eye to eye. In a number of instances, as the correspondence attests, the former graciously deferred to the wishes of the latter. However, Coues was not about to forgo these important original manuscripts. As he wrote to Harper, "It would be inexcusable not to *consult* the original mss., in case it [*sic*] is accessible, and when such a work as ours is going through the press. To what extent, if any, we should then wish to utilize it, or work it up, is another question. I may not want to do *anything* with it. But the fact of being able to say that I had examined it, in our prospectus, would be an advertising point that I should think you would be quick to recognize the advantage of."

Before Coues had the opportunity of examining the manuscripts, he found himself faced with an unrelated matter demanding prompt attention: "I have discovered that the name printed Clarke throughout our book should be Clark. I have copies of the Clark genealogies from the family Bible back to 1724, and have lately examined many signatures of Mr. [William] Clark. There is no sign of an *e* anywhere. I have private letters from the son & grandson [Meriwether Lewis Clark], both now living, & they both sign Clark. So we must adopt the correct spelling in our edition." Oddly enough, Clark *is* spelled correctly on the title page and in the preface of the *editio princeps*. Throughout the text, however, Biddle had rendered it Clarke, despite his meetings with William Clark and the several letters he had received from him.

Delayed by illness, Coues did not get to Philadelphia until near mid-December. Once there, and armed with a requisition from Jefferson Kearny Clark, he petitioned the American Philosophical Society for permission to take the Lewis and Clark manuscripts with him to

Washington where he might examine them at leisure. The minutes of the society for December 16 include this terse entry: "Dr. Elliott Coues presented a request for the loan of the Lewis & Clark Mss. which was granted."

A day or two later, while still in Philadelphia, Coues advised Harper: "I go home tomorrow with all those Manuscripts of L. & C., voted to be loaned to me by the Philosophical Society. If your prospectus is not out say in it that I have possession of all the original field note books of L. & C., with which to check the History as published in 1814, and that much new matter of the utmost importance will be incorporated in my notes, as the Biddle narrative is very little like the originals."[15]

Back in Washington again, Coues informed Henry Phillips, then secretary of the American Philosophical Society, that he would "return the papers in better order" than he had obtained them and that, unless there was specific objection, he would remove the old brass clasps from the journals. "Most of them," he declared, "are broken off already, and I have taken away the stumps of them. They injure the covers, and are a nuisance. The loose papers I will furnish with covers." Presumably Phillips did not object; when one examines the journals today, he finds no trace of brass clasps on any of them.

A few days later Coues reported further to Harper:

> I have been working the mine opened in Phila., and now have all the Mss. in perfect order for reference and when necessary for citation by vol. and page. There are 18 bound note books, and 12 small parcels of other Mss., making in all 30 codices, and I think something like 2,000 written pages. Of course we shall not be idiotic enough to ever let the Mss. go out of our hands without keeping a copy. I have an expert copyist already at work, making an exact copy, word for word, letter for letter, and point for point. I do not know how the expense will come out; if you will authorize the expenditure of $150, I will make up the balance, whatever it will be, and the copy thus become[s] our joint property. I think most probably, *after* our present edition, if that turns out as well as you have every reason to expect, you will want to bring out another volume reproducing the orig. Mss. *verbatim*. It would be such a curiosity as the world has never yet seen and make a great sensation.

After additional study of the original journals, Coues was even more excited about them. To Harper he said, "You know the discovery and utilization of the Mss. put a new complexion on the whole enterprise. I regard it [*sic*] now as one of the greatest and most novel things in literature, sure to make a great sensation, and be the corner stone of a grand reputation for you as a publisher. . . ."

These letters Coues wrote to Harper reveal more than simply Coues' actions and attitudes as a historical editor. They contain not only the first descriptions of the original Lewis and Clark manuscripts at the American Philosophical Society (subsequently others would be discovered elsewhere) but also the first appraisals of their literary and historical worth. They state, too, Coues' recognition of the fact that the manuscripts should be published *verbatim* and his tacit admission that he would like a hand in that project.

What else Coues did with the manuscripts he shortly explained to Phillips:

> The 18 bound vols., as you know, are in perfect order. The loose Mss. (66 pieces) I have gone over with the utmost care, pressed and put in the best possible shape, interleaved with onion skin writing paper, and made up in twelve parcels in smooth stiff paper covers. I have paginated each book, and each parcel, and arranged the whole in a series of 30 "Codices" (Codex, A, B, etc.). The entire material is now in perfect permanent order, *citable* by codex and page like the vols. of a published work.
>
> In doing this work, I have elaborately indexed the contents of every bound book & Ms. parcel, and prepared for publication a short paper on the L. & C. manuscripts. Of course the A.P.S. should have the refusal of this; so will you please offer it for publication to the Society's *Proceedings*. On notification of acceptance, I will send it to you at once.[16]

Although Coues had in his hands "one of the greatest and most novel things in literature," he was unawed by it, as his cavalier actions amply testify. Nor did he say anything whatever to Phillips about his making a copy of the journals. Harper seems not to have questioned the propriety of this action. In his response to Coues he manifested concern only about the expense incurred: "If the work is really much different and would not conflict with our 1812 [1814] reprint, you can call on me for $150 for copying. I to own half interest in the Mss., then if our L. & C. is a success, we can talk about the publishing of this afterwards."

Coues immediately assured Harper that the amount of new material in the codices was large, that it differed appreciably from that in Biddle, and that it would in no way conflict with their work in progress. To this he added, "Meanwhile, however, let us simply possess ourselves of the copy, and we can talk about printing it later. . . . Better keep very dark about this." Whatever interpretation we may place on Coues' motives for covertly transcribing the manuscripts or the seemliness of his action, the fact remains that the documents belonged to the American Philosophical Society, and he had no license to copy them. From his advice to Harper advocating secrecy about his action, it is quite evident that he himself doubted its propriety.

From January right up to the moment in early fall when the reissue came from the press, Coues labored industriously. He neglected no phase of his editorial responsibility. As publication date crept ever nearer, he and Harper faced final decisions about maps, illustrations, and other possible inclusions. Constantly nibbling away at Coues' time and strength were frequent visits to federal agencies, consultations with Smithsonian and other scientists, and the inevitable nerve-biting surfeit of letters. In time he complained to Harper of feeling heavily the strain "in performing in less than four months an amount of labor probably greater than Mr. Biddle's in the original writing of the whole book." He went on to say, however, that he experienced a just pride in having brought to the work a full measure of his talent. "Nothing short of that," he declared, "would have enabled me to edit the text at such 'lightning express' speed, sift and digest the 3,056 pages of the manuscript of the codices, and hold in mind every one of the thousands of minutiae requisite for my commentary."

If Coues had had his way, he would have livened the reissue with numerous illustrations, regarding them as "almost essential" because "no previous edition had had any." To Harper he repeatedly expressed his desire for likenesses of Lewis, Clark, and Gass as well as pictures of plants, animals, and Indians. He wanted, too, a photograph of the monument erected on the site of Lewis's death and burial, and would have made the trip to Tennessee to obtain it if Harper had not withheld permission.[17] Locating satisfactory likenesses of the two captains proved to be difficult, in spite of the fact, as we now know, that there were at least a half-dozen portraits of Lewis then in existence and more than twice that number of Clark.[18] Coues did locate sketches of Lewis and Clark in one of the apocryphal editions, but they were "wretched blotches" he did not care to touch,[19] and Harper found, in an early periodical, the now well-known full-length crayon by Charles de Saint Mémin of Lewis dressed in Indian garb.[20] Coues thought they might use this crayon "simply as a historical curiosity," but not "as *our* protrait of Lewis." He objected to it on grounds that it was poorly executed and hardly a likeness of Lewis's face.

When the reissue finally appeared, it displayed just two portraits, engravings of Lewis and Clark prepared especially for it from the original paintings by Charles Willson Peale. As Coues told Harper, they were done in about 1807, were "the most 'historic' of all the likeness[es], and best for our purpose, as they show the men as they were just off the trip."[21] When Coues first learned of their whereabouts—in Independence Hall—he thought Harper would be fortunate to obtain copies because Philadelphians were notoriously "great sticklers for forms and precedents"—in spite of the fact that he had just profited from the laxity of the A.P.S.

As to maps, Coues was eager to reproduce what he referred to as "the famous Mandan map of 1804-5, even though it was geographically worthless—simply a precious historical relic." After receiving a proof of it, he told Harper of discovering so many names misspelled or omitted that he would have to "go over all of them with a magnifying glass, and make quite a number of corrections. It *must* be as nearly as possible a facsimile, to be of any account; and since that is now impossible, the next thing is to secure a literally accurate copy." So Coues did not hesitate to alter original maps as well as original text.

What Coues really needed was an up-to-date map on which he could trace, in red, the Lewis and Clark route. Through the good offices of men associated with the U.S. Geological Survey (expecially its director, John Wesley Powell), he finally obtained what he wanted. He wrote to Harper on April 25: "By the enclosed correspondence . . . you will see we have struck it rich, and you will be glad to accept Mr. Bien's[22] terms of $135 for the edition of 1000 copies. This map I selected as being almost the duplicate in size of our 1814 [of Biddle], and of showing detail enough to answer our purpose by marking the L. & C. trail. I will mark the red lines, and Mr. Bien will print these upon the map."

When the 1893 reissue appeared, it contained three large folding maps: the original 1814 of Biddle, the "Mandan" map, and the modern one obtained from Bien "to show what wasn't known beyond the Mandans in 1805." The reissue also contained the five small charts present in the original Biddle.[23]

According to Coues, "There ought to be a law against indexless books, with heavy penalty."[24] Since none of the earlier editions of Lewis and Clark (including those of Gass and the apocrypha) included an index, it was doubly imperative to Coues that his reissue should have one. As a letter to Harper proves, Coues' index, except for preliminary matter yet unpaged, was completed by July. When finally printed it was another first for Lewis and Clark literature—obviously thanks to Elliott Coues.

Coues prevailed upon Harper to publish autograph letters of both commanders. With a communication to Harper dated April 9, he enclosed one by Clark he had received from Judge Craig Biddle. It had been selected from about fifty "as being important and interesting in itself, a good specimen of Clark's handwriting, and a characteristic autograph." Clark had written this letter to Nicholas Biddle on January 27, 1818, instructing him to deposit the original manuscripts of the expedition, entrusted to him during his editorship, with the American Philosophical Society. The letter from Lewis chosen by Coues bore the date March 2, 1807, and was his resignation from the "1st U.S. Regt. Infantry" submitted to Henry Dearborn, Secretary of War.

Coues and Harper weighed carefully every change and supplement, even such relatively minor matters as pagination, wording of title page, dedication, and table of contents. Coues thought the table of contents should be limited to chapter titles, shorn of the "nonpareil synopses," since nobody ever read those synopses "except unhappy authors and editors & proofreaders." Coues also asked Harper what he thought of dedicating the reissue to Henry Villard, a journalist and financier who held a controlling interest in the Northern Pacific Railroad. Harper advanced another, more acceptable dedication: "To the People of the Great West."

While still rusticating in North Carolina, Coues had submitted his idea for the title page. It remained substantially the same as in Biddle except for an addition: "edited by Elliott Coues, A.M., M.D., and Ph.D.," and for the deletion of the word "Captains" preceding Meriwether Lewis and William Clark. He would excise this word, he told Harper, because "these men are in 1893 illustrious historical characters whose names eclipse all possible titles—it is only poor devils of authors and such that need to be tagged." However, perhaps to Coues' chagrin, someone blue-penciled his own personal tag of "A.M., M.D., and Ph.D."

From the beginning Harper was concerned about Coues' prolific output of notes. As early as December, 1892, on receiving the first batch of copy, he expressed himself firmly: "We contracted and figured on 50 to 150 pages of notes (that is at the most 205 additional matter) but at the rate we are starting out the notes would outrun the original text." After the discovery of the original manuscripts, he did agree to an increase but nevertheless continued pressing Coues to curb his annotative ardor. Throughout it all Coues remained impassive; after one such caveat, he replied: "You can sleep the sleep of the just about my notes. I know pretty well what I am about, and I expect to fetch you out the 300 pp. or so near it you will have nothing to say. I fully recognize the reasonable limitations of the case." In the end Coues' notes did come perilously close to outrunning the original text.

It was perfectly natural that Coues should wish to include a bibliographical introduction; he was an old hand at that sort of thing. As early as 1874 in *Birds of the Northwest* he had, as we know, contributed bibliography exceeding that in any previous work on American ornithology, and two years later he wrote "An Account of the Various Publications Relating to the Travels of Lewis and Clarke," the first time any writer had concentrated specifically on this subject. As he said in his letters to Harper, his attention to the apocryphal and other early editions of Lewis and Clark stemmed from an eagerness to add to his earlier bibliography. In July, 1892, for instance, he remarked to Harper on a rare and "worthless" apocryphal book just received, "the full title of which has never been given in any bibliography correctly."

As publication date neared, a wind blew in from the West kicking up waves on the Coues-Harper sea of serenity. One of the heirs of William Clark was unhappy that Harper had failed to reserve first copies of the limited, numbered edition of the reissue for members of the Clark family. As Coues wrote Harper:

> Item, about Mr. W. H. Clark [William Hancock Clark, grandson of William Clark], who has evidently got a fishbone crosswise in his throat. Of course we don't want to hurt his feelings, and could not afford to offend him. He must be pacified—if not for his own sake, then for the memory of his illustrious grandpa. It would never do to get the numerous and influential Clark family down on the book! They have no doubt got enough of old William's stuffing in them to raise hell, if they took a notion. I fancy Jeff C. [Jefferson Kearny Clark] in St. Louis when he discovered I had 18 codices to his one, got a little grumpy. Now you do this: write to W.H.C. the politest and most deferential letter you can concoct. Illuminate his grandfather, & let the reflected glory alight on his on head. Say how infinitely you value his genealogical charts, which you could hardly have got along without, and that you know your editor prizes them not less lightly. Say how very sorry you are you did not ascertain his wishes sooner regarding Nos. 1 and 2 of the large paper copies; but that No. 1 had been sold long before; but that the moment Dr. Coues heard of his wishes regarding early copies, he, Dr. Coues, "generously relinquished" Nos. 2 and 3 for himself and Jeff. C. which therefore you have the pleasure of placing at his disposal, etc., etc. In fact, unless No. 1 itself has "really and

truly" gone beyond your control, it might be worth while to recover it. I had supposed you preempted it for yourself! For myself, I don't care a rush what no. I receive. You may make mine No. 200 if you want to.

Unfortunately we do not know Harper's response to this typically Couesian letter.

History of the Expedition under the Command of Lewis and Clark came from the press in early fall of 1893.[25] Coues at once lauded Harper (and inferentially himself): "You have on hand a noble, enduring work, in stately and sumptuous form, on which you can safely build up your reputation as a publisher. I am as thoroughly pleased with the whole affair as you yourself can be. So everything is lovely."

"A noble, enduring work," yes, but not altogether "lovely." If we compare it with the original Biddle, we quickly find numerous instances of Coues' alterations and defacements. In the first three sentences alone we note six changes: the substitution (for no comprehensible reason) of the word "earnestly" for "early," the insertion of a comma where none had been, and capitalization of four uncapitalized words. Of course we do not need to be reminded of Coues' earlier declaration to Harper that the reissue should agree with the 1814 Biddle word for word, letter for letter, comma for comma, and typographical error for typographical error.

Reverting now to the original Lewis and Clark manuscripts Coues had on loan from the American Philosophical Society, we find that in July, having had them in his hands by then seven months, he wrote reassuringly to Henry Phillips (seemingly in response to a query):

> Lest you have any anxiety about the L. & C. mss. already longer in my hands than perhaps either of us expected they would be, I can assure you of their entire safety. On leaving home a month ago they were placed in the fireproof vaults of the Safe Deposit Company of Washington, where only besides myself my private secretary had access to them; and only one vol. at a time can be taken out, for the purpose of copying. The new edition will be *out* next month; I will then bring the mss. back to Phila. in person, upon my return from Chicago and a further west tour I shall make. They will be found in perfect order. You must not be surprised to learn that from them, and other sources of new information, I have added as much more new matter to the Biddle edition as there was in the original. . . . The work promises to be a great success; nearly the whole edition has been taken up by subscriptions before publication, showing a very widespread interest in our immortal explorers.

From Coues' casual reference to taking just one volume of the manuscripts at a time from the deposit box "for the purpose of copying," Phillips could not well have deduced that Coues was copying the original journals and other assorted documents *in toto*.

Coues continued trying to persuade Harper to reproduce the original manuscripts once the Biddle reissue was published and out of the way. For instance, at about the same time he wrote the above to Phillips, he told Harper of his pleasure at seeing a proof of the Bien map and then added: "It is *not*, however, the L. & C. map of the future which we shall want, and which I think I can get the [Geological] Survey to prepare expressly for us, on a large scale . . . with the route in minute detail, every camp located and dated, every locality lettered with the L. & C. name of it and the modern name, etc., which of course will be in order as soon as you work off the present one."

But Harper, for reasons unknown to us, vetoed the idea of publishing the original Lewis and Clark journals. Instead of putting Coues' obvious editorial talents to work annotating these documents, he engaged him to edit the journals of Zebulon Montgomery Pike, by comparison prosaic and less consequential. He thus left open the door to Reuben Gold Thwaites,[26] who a decade later performed the task so deeply coveted by Coues. We view Harper's decision with regret. With his extensive geographical and zoological knowledge of the West, his acquaintance with Smithsonian and other scientists, his years of editorial experience, and his familiarity with the original Lewis and Clark journals, Coues was far better prepared for the task than Thwaites. Coues would have brought to it, too, a greater enthusiasm, having been so recently the "discoverer" of the originals. And if Harper had backed him to the limit financially and had allowed him the same freedom of expression permitted with the Biddle reissue, we presumably would have today a much more richly annotated edition of the *Original Journals of the Lewis and Clark Expedition* than we do. Certainly current Lewis and Clark scholars familiar with the Thwaites version are unanimous in desiring a new edition.

Several months went by after Coues had announced that he was having the originals copied before he again brought up the subject. Writing Harper in mid-December, he said: "The copying of the L. & C. Mss. has been completed, and now we own the only cops. in existence after the original, made with great care & skill, and practically perfect. It is a very valuable piece of property! I shall in a few days, as soon as I can catch up with my correspondence, take the originals back to the Philos. Soc. and deliver them over. I want to time myself to catch a public meeting of the Society, and make a few remarks on the occasion." Minutes of the society for January 5, 1894, show that Coues did, indeed, return the manuscripts; that they "were correct in number and condition; that Dr. Coues had arranged them in a most-excellent and careful manner, so as to facilitate all further reference; in fact they were in a much better condition than when loaned by the Society."

Today's informed student of Lewis and Clark may find, with William Hancock Clark, "a fishbone crosswise in his throat." In one significant respect Coues did not return these priceless manuscripts in "a much better condition than when loaned." In truth, what he did to them is now regarded by historians as shocking, indefensible, and irresponsible. Instead of treating them with the scrupulous care and inviolability ordinarily accorded valuable documentry material by reputable scholars, he disregarded such precepts and handled them, as one historian has said, like "mere copy for the printer, which might be revised with impunity."[27]

An examination today of the Lewis and Clark codices reveals innumerable interlineations in Coues' characteristic handwriting. In Codex A alone (i.e., Clark's journal from May 13 through August 14, 1804), we have counted more than one hundred instances where he marred the original pages by scribbling in black ink words intended to improve the text.[28]

Members of the American Philosophical Society apparently failed to note the interlineations made by Coues after he had returned the manuscripts to them; they remained unnoticed until Thwaites began editing them ten years later. Beginning with Thwaites, historians have dealt harshly with Coues, and by emphasizing his editorial indiscretions, have thereby beclouded his significant, positive contributions to the Biddle reissue.

An objective, unhurried appraisal of Coues' editorship of Biddle reveals numerous benefactions to that work. In the first place he must, of course, be credited with rediscovery of the original journals of Lewis and Clark (if he had not unearthed them, it is anyone's guess how much longer they would have remained in obscurity). Second, he arranged the manuscripts in an orderly manner, thus facilitating their use by future students. In the third place he heightened the value of Biddle by attaching supplementary material in the form of memoirs, a twenty-five-page bibliographical introduction, a biological chapter derived from Lewis's Fort Clatsop diary, and a much-needed index.

Finally, and far more important, he expanded immeasurably the

value of the work by contributing extravagant commentary. This fo-
cused attention, for the first time, on the vast amount of unpublished
and unknown botanical, zoological, geographical, and ethnological data
in the original journals and, as a further consequence, on the two
commanders as important pioneering naturalists. Heretofore people
had regarded and portrayed Lewis and Clark only as explorers, woods-
men, and exemplary military leaders.

Coues amassed his abundant commentary in less than a year—a
triumph in itself. The feature which most enhanced its worth, and
attracted the immediate attention of all who read it, was the inclusion
(for the first time anywhere) of portions of the original journals in the
precise words of their authors.[29] Coues' phalanxed notes exemplified a
highly trained, inquisitive mind seemingly bent on wringing from the
fabric of recorded history each drop of pertinent knowledge. These
notes fall into four main categories: geography, botany, zoology, and
ethnology.

2

Coues produced a multitude of geographical notes, generally
about the rivers and creeks encounterd by the explorers. Quite early in
the journey, for instance, Clark announced the arrival of the party at
Little Manitou Creek, and Coues asserted in a footnote that this stream
was "the R. au Diable of D'Anville, 1752; the Petit Manitou of Perrin du
Lac, 1805 (whence *Little* Manitou of our text); Manitou creek of Nicollet,
1843; Manitoo of Brackenridge, 1814. . . ."[30] So we learn almost at
once that Coues had before him the maps of Jean Baptiste D'Anville,
Perrin du Lac, and Joseph N. Nicollet[31] and the published *Journal of a
Voyage up the Missouri in 1811* of Henry Marie Brackenridge.

Coues limited his commentary on other streams largely to such
topographic information as source, country traversed, and point of
embouchure. For example, he said that North Dakota's Cannonball
River originated "somewhat north of the Black Hills proper, and east
of the Little Missouri river; flows in a general east course, traversing
Hettinger and Morton counties, and falls into the Missouri in Morton
Co., on the boundary of Boreman, and opposite Emmons, eight miles
below the site of Fort Rice."[32] After one reads similar data about
numerous other affluents of the Missouri and Columbia, one is not at
all surprised with Coues' statement that ". . . if there is anything I do
know, it is exactly where Lewis and Clark were on every day, about
every hour, from start to finish of their famous expedition."[33]

On several occasions Coues employed his commentary as an opportunity for expressing personal convictions. For instance, he was openly critical of cartographers who had presumed to change names applied by Lewis and Clark: "Hundreds of names . . . should be restored, not only in equity, but [also] on the plainest principles of the law of priority, which geographers pretend to obey."[34] In at least one instance Coues turned denominator himself. Noting that the expedition's 1806 campsite on the Clearwater River near present-day Kamiah, Idaho, had no name, he called it Camp Chopunnish, an appellation now firmly fixed in Lewis and Clark literature.[35]

More than any other individual, Coues credited Alfred J. Hill of St. Paul, Minnesota, with helping him to accumulate his geographical commentary.[36] Several of his letters to Hill are extant, and a portion of one of them, dated November 20, 1892, explains the kind of information Coues obtained from Hill:

> . . . I have bent & shall bend all my energies to the determination: 1st of the modern or present names of every locality named by L. & C., and its accurate geographical identification, both old & new names; 2d to the etymology of all these old names, or their original significance. Some are French, some Indian, some English, some nobody knows what. . . . If you care to give me the benefit of your information on any or all such points I should be grateful, and would gladly make due public acknowledgments of such assistance in my preface and notes. I should like very much to have you send me a list of all L. & C.'s places in going up the Missouri, with the modern equivalents or any equivalent names from 1806 to the present day, which can be found in published works or maps, together with their etymological significance. Such a list would be invaluable. . . . [37]

A most significant feature of the expedition, one almost entirely unrecognized until Coues spotlighted it, was the gradual development of William Clark into a prime maker of maps. Clark was, Coues insisted, "one of the greatest geographical geniuses this country ever produced."[38]

Coues was the first writer even to intimate that Lewis and Clark might also legitimately have merited the credentials of the naturalist. In footnotes Coues credited them with the discovery (and original descriptions) of numerous animals new to science: cutthroat and steelhead trout among fishes, prairie rattler and horned toad among reptiles, blackbilled magpie, western tanager, mountain quail, Nuttall's poorwill, whistling swan, Clark's nutcracker, and Lewis's woodpecker among birds,[39] and coyote, prairie dog, pronghorn, mule deer, Oregon bobcat, pack rat, mountain goat, mountain beaver, and grizzly bear among mammals.

Again and again, as in the case of the ring-necked duck (*Aythya collaris*), Coues wrote, "L. & C. are again discoverers of a new species," or, as when making a note on the western grebe (*Aechmophorus occidentalis*), Lewis's word picture was "the original and an easily recognizable description of this bird."[40]

In determining identities of birds and mammals alluded to by Lewis and Clark, Coues relied largely on his own personal knowledge. In these areas he was equal or superior to most other naturalists of his day. In seeking accurate identifications of animals lower on the evolutionary ladder, he unhesitatingly turned to other scientists, such as B. W. Evermann[41] for fishes and L. O. Howard for insects, both Smithsonian experts.

When botanists read Coues' plant notes, they learned for the first time of Lewis and Clark's discovery of numerous western herbs, shrubs, and trees unknown to science before the expedition. Among them were bigleaf maple, Oregon grape, Mariposa lily, camas, mountain lady's slipper, Lewis's wild flax, Osage orange, Indian tobacco, Engelmann's spruce, ponderosa pine, golden currant, salmonberry, buffaloberry, bear grass, ragged robin (*Clarkia pulchella*), and bitterroot (*Lewisia rediviva*). Unfortunately Coues did not know when editing the Biddle reissue (nor, it seems, did anyone else) of the existence of more than 200 dried, pressed plant specimens collected by Lewis that then were stowed away in a forgotten niche at the American Philosophical Society.[42] Coues made no pretence to any special knowledge of plants. As a result he engaged another Smithsonian man, Frank H. Knowlton, to identify plants mentioned or described by Lewis and Clark.[43]

In a memorable footnote Coues explained why Nicholas Biddle passed over so much of the natural history of the codices:

> When about to bring out this work, after the death of Governor Lewis, General Clark made a contract with Benj. S. Barton,[44] of Philadelphia, by the terms of which the latter was to produce a formal work on the natural history of the Expedition. In consequence of which Mr. Biddle, of course, passed over such points in the codices. Dr. Barton soon died, having done nothing. . . . This is the simple explanation of the meagerness of the History in scientific matters with which the codices are replete—to the keenest regret of all naturalists, and the great loss of credit which was justly due these foremost explorers of a country whose almost every animal and plant was then unknown to science. My notes may in some measure throw back

upon them a reflection of what is their just due—but it can never be more than reflected glory, for in the meantime others have carried off the honors that belong by right to Lewis and Clark.[45]

Of necessity, Coues had to pull out most stops when composing his ethnological annotations. He faced a near herculean task in bringing a semblance of order to the mass of data in the codices about the American Indian. Along the endlessly meandering road from the Mississippi to the Pacific, a multiplicity of natives, of many tribes, mores, and tongues, had been encountered by Lewis and Clark. They were relative newcomers to ethnology—as a science—and, like other students of Indians at that time, they had no staffs to lean on, such as textbooks and manuals providing systems of classification. As a consequence they made no attempt to group western Indians in an orderly manner, beyond noting similarities of language and custom among various tribes.

Coues experienced no such problems, for he had at hand treatises on classifications, including the very latest, *Indian Linguistic Families of America North of Mexico* by John Wesley Powell. Though relying mainly on Powell, Coues took whatever he needed for his notes from the published works of such other Indian authorities as Henry Schoolcraft,[46] Albert Gallatin,[47] George Catlin,[48] and Maximilian. He also made abundant use of Meriwether Lewis's "Statistical View," first published in 1806 in Jefferson's "Message to Congress."[49]

A striking example of Coues' ethnological annotative ardor is the five pages he devoted to Siouan tribes alone. Here and elsewhere he lauded the two captains for their unending efforts to portray American aboriginals as they found them. He declared, for example, that Lewis's description of the Shoshoni "will be forever the best." Of Lewis and Clark's report that Eneeshur tribesmen immediately above Celilo Falls of the Columbia understood only a few words of the Echelutes residing below, he said: "[This] well illustrates the great attention paid by Lewis and Clark to ethnology, and the discernment they showed in discriminating similar appearing Indians who were nevertheless of distinct linguistic stocks, at a time when modern scientific classifications had no existence."[50]

Limitations of space disallow further examination of Coues' annotations. It may be said, however, that in comprehensive compass they provide yet another instance of the whole being greater than the sum of its parts.

As an appropriate postlude to Coues' industry as editor of the

1893 reissue of Lewis and Clark, we reproduce a footnote Coues later appended to another work:

> It would surprise most persons to realize how quickly a neglected core of fact gathers the mold of myth. Take the Lewis and Clark Expedition, for example. Never, perhaps, was a true story more minutely and completely told; to know all about it, we have only to read what the explorers themselves had to say, less than one hundred years ago. But the take-it-for-granters, the forsoothers, the forgetters, the prevaricators, the misquoters, the unreaders—the whole tribe of quidnunc impressionists—have meanwhile found out more things that never happened in this case than they ever learned about what did happen.[51]

It should be evident by now that Coues was profoundly impressed with the exploits of Lewis and Clark. It should not be surprising, therefore, that soon after his reissue of the Biddle edition came from the press he became enthusiastically involved in a project to erect a monument in memory of Sergeant Charles Floyd. We first learn of it through a letter he wrote to the editor of the *Sioux City* (Iowa) *Journal,* dated May 22, 1895:

> I hail with acclamation the proposition made in your paper of the 16th to erect a monument to the memory of Sergeant Charles Floyd, the first—and only—member of the Lewis and Clark expedition who lost his life in the long course of that ever to be remembered enterprise. As the editor of "The History of the Lewis and Clark Expedition," and the first to publish any account of it in the very words written from day to day by the immortal explorers, having all their original manuscript journals and field note books before me, I have the most vivid and keenest possible personal interest in everything that relates to the subject. I must confess that I am what my friends call me—"A Lewis and Clark enthusiast." But I do not think that anyone can read that "national epic of exploration" without sharing my enthusiasm. It is one of the grandest episodes in the history of our country. Every American can be proud of it. Every person in Missouri, Iowa, Kansas, Nebraska, South and North Dakota, Montana, Idaho, Oregon and Washington—for the expedition passed through all these states—has an interest in the immortal achievements of those dauntless pioneers. For every Iowan this interest focuses about the saddest incident of the whole journey—the death of Charles Floyd.
>
> Correspondence with Mitchell Vincent[52] has already informed me of what has thus far been accomplished, and I sincerely trust that the good work will go on to a speedy and successful issue. Nothing could be more appropriate than for all who are interested to assemble on the spot where Floyd was buried, August 20 next, on the ninety-first anniversary of his

death, and form a Floyd Monument association, for the purpose of carrying the project into effect, under the auspices and with the substantial cooperation of the state legislature.

Residents of Sergeant [Floyd] Bluffs and vicinity are better informed than myself of the exact nature of the ground at and near the original grave, and of the conditions under which a tract could be secured; but I can heartily indorse and warmly urge the proposition made by Mr. Vincent and others to purchase a tract of twenty or thirty acres to be set aside for a public park, upon the culminating point of which the monument is to stand.

It is now nearly twenty years since I have been in Sioux City, and there must have been great changes in its environment; but according to my recollection Sergeant Bluffs has natural advantages which could at moderate expense be artificially improved with striking effect.

It will give the greatest pleasure to forward the good work by every means in my power.[53]

Showing his good faith, Coues did attend the scheduled obsequies for Sergeant Floyd on August 20, gave a short talk, and that evening in the Y.M.C.A. delivered a lecture on Lewis and Clark.[54] At other times during his stay Coues met with prominent residents of Sioux City engaged in forming the Floyd Memorial Association and, in due course, was elected vice-president of it. He was also named to a committee on publication and was persuaded to prepare a report of the Floyd Memorial Association.

Coues prepared the report expeditiously and submitted it to the president of the organization on January 4, 1896. It was no small task, for, when printed, it ran to fifty-eight pages and contained, as he wrote in his letter of transmission, "1. All that is known of Floyd's antecedents, life and death. 2. All accounts of his reburial in 1857. 3. A full account of the origin, organization and proceedings of the Association before, during and after the memorial exercises of Aug. 20, 1895."[55]

The primary objectives of the association were to procure land for a Sergeant Floyd Park and to gain support and funds for an appropriate monument. Unfortunately Coues did not live to see these objectives realized. For instance, the monument, an obelisk of white stone 100 feet high, was completed and dedicated on May 30, 1901. Though Coues was not present, those in charge of the ceremony saluted his contribution in making the monument a reality.

NOTES

1. Nicholas Biddle (1786-1844), Philadelphia lawyer, writer, and financier. In 1823 he became president of the Bank of the United States.
2. Francis Perego Harper (1856-1932), a New York City book dealer and publisher of western books. He was a grandson of a brother of the three Harper brothers who founded the publishing firm of Harper & Brothers (now Harper & Row).
3. Though generally prepared for this undertaking, Coues had yet to learn much about Lewis and Clark, such as the correct spelling of Clark (without the terminal e).
4. Coues, "An Account of the Various Publications Relating to the Travels of Lewis and Clarke" (1876).
5. The Coues-Harper correspondence is the property of the Yale University Library.
6. Coues-Biddle (1893), I, vi.
7. Patrick Gass (1771-1870), one of four sergeants with Lewis and Clark, and one of the journalists of the expedition. He published his journal in 1807.
8. Thomas Jefferson, *Message from the President of the United States . . .* (Washington, D.C.: A. & G. Way. 1806).
9. The actual date of Lewis's death was Oct. 11, 1809. It occurred at a wayside place, Grinder's Inn, on the Natchez Trace, Tenn. The manner of his death continues controversial, though most current scholars of the expedition, as a result of new information recently unearthed by Donald Jackson, believe that Lewis died a victim of his own hand.
10. John Inskeep, of the Philadelphia firm of Bradford & Inskeep, publisher of the 1814 Biddle edition of Lewis and Clark.
11. Coues-Biddle, I, vi.
12. Coues, "Description of the Original Manuscript Journals and Field Notebooks of Lewis and Clark" (1893). This paper was read by Coues at a meeting of the American Philosophical Society held on Jan. 20, 1893.
13. See letter of transmission dated Apr. 6, 1818, American Philosophical Society Library.
14. This material included "much official correspondence" between Clark and Henry Dearborn, Secretary of War; see Coues-Biddle, I, lxxiv.
15. Coues did not discover *all* existing Lewis and Clark material. In a later report to the A.P.S. he said: "I do not find quite all of the Biddle deposit, as itemized in the receipt given him by the Society; for example, no [Indian] vocabularies and no maps" (see Coues, "Description of the Original Journals," 19). Neither then nor later did Coues learn of additional Lewis and Clark journals, papers, and maps then in the Clark family. It remained for Reuben Gold Thwaites to discover them, some ten years later, when he was editing *Original Journals of the Lewis and Clark Expedition, 1804-1806.*
16. The Coues-Phillips correspondence quoted here and below is in the American Philosophical Society Library. Coues must have labored day and night on the manuscripts after obtaining them, for he read the paper about them

at a meeting of the A.P.S. on Jan. 20 (see note 12 above), less than a month after bringing the originals to Washington.

17. Coues was disappointed at this rebuff. He wanted not only to obtain the photograph but also to collect information on the manner of Lewis's death. As he wrote Harper, "I am going to raise the whole question of murder vs. suicide." And this he did; see "Supplement to Jefferson's Memoir," Coues-Biddle, I, xliii-lxii.

18. See Paul Russell Cutright, "Lewis and Clark: Portraits and Portraitists," *Montana*, XIX, no. 2 (Apr., 1969), 41-53.

19. Apparently Coues found these sketches in the Dayton, Ohio, apocryphal edition (1840). Another set, equally "wretched," appeared in a Philadelphia apocryphal edition (1812) published by William Fisher.

20. This crayon, by Saint-Mémin (1770-1852), a French artist who came to the United States in the 1790s, was made probably on Lewis's second and last visit to Philadelphia (1807). The Indian costume, a robe of white weasel (long-tailed weasel, *Mustela frenata longicauda*) skins, had been presented to Lewis by the Shoshoni chief Cameahwait in 1805 near Lemhi Pass. The periodical in which Harper found the likeness was *Analectic Magazine and Naval Chronicle* (1816). The portrait herein was actually an engraving done by William Strickland, Philadelphia artist, from Saint-Mémin's original.

21. These engravings, at either Coues' or Harper's behest, were done by a London-born artist, Samuel Hollyer (1826-1919). The originals may still be found in Independence Hall National Historical Park Collections. Coues had the mistaken notion that Rembrandt Peale painted them. Charles Willson Peale made his portrait of Lewis in 1807, and that of Clark in 1810.

22. Julius Bien (1826-1909), for years chief lithographer of maps and illustrations for western surveys made by the U.S. government.

23. These five portrayed: (1) "Ancient Fortifications on the Missouri River," (2) "Great Falls of the Missouri," (3) "Great Shoot or Rapids of the Columbia River," (4) "Great Falls of the Columbia," and (5) "Mouth of the Columbia."

24. Coues-Biddle, I, cxxv.

25. On Sept. 9 Coues had written Harper, ". . . if quite convenient, I wish you would make the ostensible date of publication Sept. 9. That is my 51st birthday, and the sentiment of the date would please me." Unfortunately, Coues did not get his wish; the publication date was somewhat later that fall.

26. Reuben Gold Thwaites (1853-1913), distinguished historian and editor, was born in Dorchester (now a part of Boston), Mass., and educated at Wisconsin and Yale. Thwaites is best known for his editing of *Jesuit Relations and Allied Documents*, 73 vols. (completed in 1901), *Early Western Travels*, 32 vols. (1904-6), and *Original Journals of the Lewis and Clark Expedition*, 8 vols. (1904-6).

27. Thwaites, ed., *Original Journals of the Lewis and Clark Expedition*, I, xlix-l.

28. Interlineations occur also in red ink. These are attributed to Biddle.

29. Coues first quoted from the originals in a footnote, I, 31. On June 10, 1804, Clark wrote, "Passed the two rivers of Charletons which mouth together."

30. Coues-Biddle, I, 15n.

31. Coues' notes alluded to other maps he had consulted, such as those by Aaron Arrowsmith, G. K. Warren, Captain W. F. Raynolds, Governor I. I. Stevens,

Major W. J. Twining, Geological Survey, and Missouri River Commission. He relied, too, on books other than those he had received from Harper. Among them were LePage du Pratz's *History of Louisiana*, John Bradbury's *Travels in the Interior of America*, and the scholarly works of such naturalists as Frederick Pursh, Sir John Richardson, Alexander Wilson, George Ord, C. L. Bonaparte, Spencer F. Baird, and Maximilian (Prince of Wied).

32. Coues-Biddle, I, 171n.

33. Coues, "Notes on Mr. Thomas Meehan's Paper on the Plants of Lewis and Clark's Expedition" (1898), 291.

34. Coues-Biddle, I, 324.

35. *Ibid.*, III, 1010n.

36. Alfred James Hill (1833-95), geographer and historian, was a resident of St. Paul, Minn., and the author of several works (largely articles and maps) on the history, geography, and ethnology of the Upper Mississippi region.

37. Coues' letters to Hill are held by the Minnesota Historical Society.

38. Coues-Biddle, II, 421n.

39. Significantly, when Coues wrote *Birds of the Northwest* some thirty years earlier, he did not once allude to Lewis and Clark.

40. Coues-Biddle, III, 889n, 882n.

41. Barton Warren Evermann (1853-1932), ichthyologist, was born in Monroe County, Iowa. He is perhaps best known as the author (with David Starr Jordan) of *The Fishes of North and Middle America*, 4 vols. (1896-1900).

42. These plants were discovered there just three years later (1896) by Thomas Meehan, botanist at the Academy of Natural Sciences of Phildelphia. They comprise today the major portion of the Lewis and Clark Herbarium at the academy. The latest study of this collection revealed 216 herbarium sheets. See Cutright, *Lewis and Clark: Pioneering Naturalists* (1969), 367.

43. Coues, "Notes on Mr. Meehan's Paper," 291-92.

44. Benjamin Smith Barton (1766-1815), physician, naturalist, and professor of botany at the University of Pennsylvania, wrote *Elements of Botany* (1803), the first textbook of botany written in the United States.

45. Coues-Biddle, II, 400n.

46. Henry Rowe Schoolcraft (1793-1864), traveler and writer, was born at Guilderland, N.Y. He was the author of *Travels in the Central Portions of the Mississippi Valley* (1825).

47. Albert Gallatin (1761-1849), statesman, financier, and ethnographer, was also U.S. Secretary of the Treasury (1802-14) and author of *A Synopsis of the Indian Tribes in North America* (1836).

48. George Catlin (1796-1872), artist, traveler, and ethnologist, was born in Wilkes-Barre, Pa. He traveled extensively painting and studying Indians and wrote *The North American Indians*, 2 vols. (1913).

49. See also Thwaites, ed., *Original Journals of the Lewis and Clark Expedition*, VI, 80-120.

50. Coues-Biddle, I, 97-101n; II, 479n, 672n.

51. Coues, ed., *Forty Years a Fur Trader* (1898), I, xvi-xvii.

52. Mitchell Vincent was one of several Sioux City residents most active in promoting the objectives of the Floyd Memorial Association.

53. The editor of the *Sioux City Journal*, to whom Coues addressed this letter, was George D. Perkins. The letter itself is today the property of the Iowa State Historical Society, Iowa City.
54. Coues' "Book of Dates" (1895).
55. Coues, *In Memoriam, Sergeant Charles Floyd* (1897).

CHAPTER XXIII

Further Adventures in Historical Editing

After finishing his monumental task of editing the Lewis and Clark journals, Coues and his wife embarked in the summer of 1893 upon a tour of the Northwest. In part he was motivated by the same nostalgia that had beckoned him to the Southwest in 1891-92: he would be retracing some of the route of his travels with the Northern Boundary Survey in 1873-74. The fact that he would also be covering much of the trail of his heroes, Lewis and Clark, was an even greater inducement to revisit the region.

He and Mrs. Coues did not go directly to the Far West. On June 26 they left Washington and arrived the following day at his mountain retreat in Cranberry, North Carolina.[1] There they remained until August 14, when they left for Chicago, where, as we have already noted, he was present at a reception of the Chicago Women's Club (August 25) and participated in three activities connected with the Columbian Exposition: the Psychical Science Congress, the World's Congress on Zoology, and the Congress on Ornithology. On his birthday, September 9, he was no doubt delighted to receive from his publisher the "first copy of Lewis and Clark, just out."[2]

The next day the Coueses began their western trip in earnest, facilitated by free passes to travel the Northern Pacific Railroad (of which his friend Henry Villard was chairman of the board of directors) and the Great Northern Railroad (of which his friend James J. Hill was president).[3] According to his "Book of Dates" they visited the following points on or near the routes of Lewis and Clark and his own trails of 1873-74:

> Sept. 10 left Chicago. 11, Ryan House, St. Paul. 12 left via N[orthern] P[acific] R. R. Sept. 13, Bismarck, N. Dak., Glendive [Montana], Miles City.

14 stayed. 15 Pompey's Pillar[4] at 2 a.m. To Livingstone same day. 16 stayed. 17 rail to Cinnabar, coach to Mammoth Hot Springs, Yellowstone Park [Wyoming]. 19-25 tour of the Park. 26 to Livingstone. 27 Bozeman. 28 Helena, Mont.[5] 29 stayed. 30 G[reat] N[orthern] R. R. to Butte, and U[nion] P[acific] R. R. to Red Rock. Oct. 1 stage over Lemhi Pass [on the Idaho-Montana border] to Sunderlands.[6] 2. to Salmon City, Idaho and return. 3 to Red Rock. 4 by U. P. to Butte, by N. P. R. R. to Logan. 5 to Helena; lectured.[7] 6 to Great Falls. 7-9 stayed, lectured 7th. 10 by rail to Cascade. 11-13 wagon to top of Lewis & Clark Pass and return to Cascade. 13 rail to Great Falls. 14 rail to [Fort] Benton. 15 return. 16 to Helena. 17 to Butte. 18 to Missoula. 19 stayed. 20 to Fort Missoula.[8] 21 four mule ambulance up Bitter Root Valley to Victor. 22 to Darby. 23 to Sula and Waugh's house.[9] 24 on a mule to top of Gibbon's Pass and return to Waugh's, back to 1 mi. below Darby. 25 to Stevensville. 26 to Fort Missoula. 27 stayed to 2:40 p.m., took cars. 28 Tacoma [Washington] 3 p.m. Nov. 4, to Seattle, and left at Midnight on G. N. R. R. Nov. 8 passed Fort Buford [North Dakota]. Nov. 9 arr. St. Paul. Nov. 18 dinner given by Mr. A. W. Krech.[10] *About* Nov. 23 to Chicago for about 3 weeks, and then home to Washn. direct, Dec. 18th.

Because of this trip, Coues did not attend the A.O.U.'s annual meeting held that year in Cambridge on November 20-23, even though this was the first year of his presidency of the organization and the tenth anniversary of the group's original meeting (1883). Then there were just twenty-three active members; in 1893 there were forty-eight active members, twenty-two honorary, seventy-three corresponding, and 439 associate, for a total of 582. At the Cambridge meeting Coues was re-elected (*in absentia*) for a second term as president.[11]

2

From St. Paul Coues wrote to Harper on November 15, 1893, that despite "beastly weather in Tacoma" and "various accidents and delay," he had had a "grand tour" and had obtained "an immense amount of available material about L. & C. trail. Crossed the Continental Divide 15 times, and 7 different places, including *all* the Passes L. & C. made."

In the same letter he said that he had a "startling proposition" for Harper: that he prepare a new edition of the journals of Zebulon Montgomery Pike (published first in 1810). Since the Pike expeditions up the Mississippi River and into the Southwest (1805-7) were second in significance only to the travels of Lewis and Clark among the early explorations of the American West, a reissue of his journals, with notes by Elliott Coues, was a natural venture for the team of Coues and

Harper. Indeed, on September 25, 1892, while editing the Lewis and Clark journals, Coues had requested from Harper "a copy of Z. M. Pike's Travels. . . . There are some things in it I must examine."

Their correspondence during the winter of 1893-94 indicates that Harper had agreed to Coues' proposal for a reissue of Pike. By February, 1894, editor and publisher had come to terms on financial matters. A contract was signed in which it was agreed that Coues was to receive a $1,000 honorarium and a royalty of 10 percent of the retail price of each copy sold.[12]

Even before these arrangements were made, Coues had plunged into the work. In some respects his task was similar to the Lewis and Clark project: providing annotation for the original published journals, as well as such addenda as a preface, a biographical memoir of the explorer, allied documents, index, and maps. And once more he was bombarding Harper with requests for books and maps as well as with suggestions for publicizing the forthcoming volumes.

Yet there were differences between the two projects. Biddle's edition of Lewis and Clark was a smooth paraphrase; Pike's volume of 1810 was in his own inelegant prose. "The author," wrote Coues, "was quite innocent of literary strategy." Moreover, the original edition of Pike's narrative was ill-organized, badly edited, and wretchedly printed. Therefore Coues took even more liberties—some of them justifiable— with the reissue of Pike than he had taken with the *editio princeps* of Lewis and Clark. He reorganized Pike's account into what to him was a more logical order, and although he did "not think that any editor may feel free to re-write his author," he did feel free to make improvements on what he called "non-essentials," such as misprints, punctuation, and grammar.[13]

A major difference between the Pike project and the Lewis and Clark reissue was that this time Coues uncovered no significant manuscripts. Indeed, even though he searched the archives of the War and State departments for a specific batch of original materials—the papers and maps confiscated from Pike by Spanish authorities in Mexico during his incarceration there—he failed to find them.[14]

A few years after Coues' death the items in question were discovered in the Mexican archives and were returned at long last to the American government. They were used by Archer B. Hulbert and Stephen H. Hart for their volume (1932) on the southwestern leg of Pike's journeys.[15] These and other materials which come to light in the twentieth century were incorporated into the latest (1966) and fullest edition of the Pike journals, edited by Donald Jackson. The splendid Jackson edition supersedes the work of Coues and other earlier editors of Pike, yet Jackson has emphatically stated that Coues' edition continues to be "of immense value."[16]

When the three volumes of his edition of Pike's account were presented to the public by Harper in 1895, Coues was characteristically and justifiably proud of his second literary triumph in the field of western exploration. Yet he correctly assumed that the work on Pike "cannot be reasonably expected to make such a hit as L. & C. did."[17] Even in the midst of his editorial labors on Pike, his mind went back to the original Lewis and Clark manuscripts reposing in the American Philosophical Society and to thoughts of editing them. As he told Harper in April, 1894: "We must do it someday. I could make it a marvel of literature."[18]

3

Coues' dream of editing the Lewis and Clark manuscripts never materialized because Harper demurred. Fortunately, there were other narratives of exploration and travel to engage his energies. While preparing the reissue of Biddle, he became familiar with the careers of Alexander Henry the Younger,[19] a fur trader of the Northwest Company, and of David Thompson (1770-1857), who had served the Northwest Company as a geographer and explorer and whose travels had intersected the trails of Lewis and Clark.

It was therefore with considerable interest that he responded to an offer from the Reverend Edward D. Neill,[20] of St. Paul, to let him look at a manuscript copy of a journal kept by Henry, detailing the fur trader's visit to the Mandan country in 1806. After receiving the 186-page manuscript from Neill, Coues was excited. Although it was not in Henry's own hand, it contained valuable information on the Lewis and Clark expedition as well as much other important historical material which, as Coues said, had "never seen the light."[21]

Apparently Neill had planned to edit the journal and was seeking Coues' help in the enterprise. Coues thanked Neill for allowing him to look at it and commented, "Very likely the Henry mss. ought to be published, and I might possibly see my way to help you to that end, though I cannot promise."[22] Neill died a few months later, and Coues afterward wrote that Neill had "made [the journal] over to me unconditionally, a short time before his death."[23] By January, 1894, Coues and Harper had agreed that Henry's Mandan journal would become another editing venture which, according to Coues, "with my preface & notes, will make a nice little vol[ume], just what we want to come into our series after L. & C."[24]

Since it was a relatively compact, easy-to-read clerk's copy, and since Coues was thoroughly familiar with the historical and geographical background necessary for the editing of it, he could write to Harper on January 7, 1894, that he was "working on it already, and can send a copy for printers in a few days." On the 10th Coues acknowledged the receipt of $100 from Harper "for Henry manuscript, with introduction and notes & index by Dr. Elliott Coues, and seeing it through the press." He also told Harper, "I will let you know about the Pike mss. as soon as I get around to it. One thing at a time! Just now I am finishing up the Henry mss. Can send, all ready for printer, as soon as I can get hold of a Canadian map of the Assiniboine river region."

Within the next few months any thoughts of bringing the Henry manuscript into print before completing the Pike project evaporated. Evidently Coues learned that more Henry material, as well as some David Thompson manuscripts, might exist in Canada, and on June 26 he and his wife set off, traveling by way of New York City (where he doubtless visited Harper) and Niagara Falls.

Soon after their arrival in Toronto on July 7, Coues visited the spot where Pike had been killed during the War of 1812. More important, he examined the unpublished memoirs of David Thompson. The owner of the manuscripts, Charles Lindsey,[25] offered them for sale at $1,750. Coues, who had been authorized by Harper to offer up to $750, had to report on July 15 that the negotiations had totally broken down. As we shall see, Coues shortly discovered that there would be little cause for regret.

Next he journeyed to Ottawa, arriving there on July 11. At the Library of Parliament he struck the rich vein he had perhaps anticipated: 1,642 pages, with writing on both sides, of the journals of Alexander Henry for the years 1799-1814. It was not in Henry's own hand but, rather, in that of one George Coventry. Coues was convinced from internal evidence that Coventry had fully and faithfully copied Henry's original journals (which have never been located). He was also convinced that the plan for publishing Henry's Mandan journal needed to be expanded to encompass all of Henry's narrative.

The officials of the Library of Parliament, displaying more wisdom than those of the American Philosophical Society, told Coues that the Henry materials could be examined only in the library. Yet they were willing to let them be recopied on the premises. Coues engineered an agreement between Harper and the library whereby the publisher would pay a clerk fifteen cents per folio to prepare an authentic copy.[26] While negotiations were being completed, Coues received more good news: a large number of David Thompson manuscripts were housed in the archives of the Crown Lands Department of Ontario, at Toronto.

Rather than rush immediately back to Toronto, Coues (and presumably his wife) went to Montreal on July 17 and took a boat trip down the St. Lawrence River to Quebec, where he spent three days (July 19-21). Then he went up the Saguenay River to Tadoussac and Chicoutimi. On the return trip up the St. Lawrence, he spent July 23 and 24 at La Malbaie (Murray Bay) with his friend D. G. Elliot. On July 28 he reached Toronto. Working quickly, Coues located the Thompson manuscripts at the Crown Lands Department. He persuaded officials there to let him examine these documents in his hotel rooms, but only after he agreed to sign a bond for $2,000, with two sureties, for the safe return of the manuscripts.[27]

Coues spent the next few days going over the Thompson journals and concluded that they were far more valuable historically than those offered for sale by Lindsey. The latter were Thompson's recollections of his journeys in the early nineteenth century, written down at such an advanced age that Coues believed they betrayed signs of senility. On the other hand, the journals in the Crown Lands Department had been written by Thompson during his youthful travels.[28] And Coues became even more impressed by how closely Thompson's itinerary paralleled that of Henry, both geographically and chronologically.

4

Coues halted his Canadian labors for the time being to return to the United States and trace part of Pike's route in the Upper Mississippi River region. In fact he was determined to visit the headwaters of the Mississippi—a site which Pike had failed to find because he believed that the source of the river was Leech Lake.

Starting from Toronto August 2, Coues and Mrs. Coues traveled on the Canadian Pacific Railroad to Owen Sound, Ontario, where they boarded a vessel which took them through Georgian Bay to Sault Sainte Marie. From there, on August 8, they took a boat to Duluth, Minnesota. By rail they came to Deer River, which Coues later described:

> The hamlet of Deer River, Minn., consists largely of two rival saloons and some less reputable houses, where the lumberjacks live or resort when

not engaged in their arduous occupations. Liquor is sold openly to Indians in defiance of law, and it is the express boast of the place that no U.S. marshal dare show himself there. I remember seeing . . . a drunken Indian who had been swaggering and staggering about town till he had spent his last cent for whisky, groveling in a heap on the ground, hugging the knees of a man and begging piteously for "just one more drink" with the maudlin tears streaming down his cheeks. We do not seem to have improved the Ojibways much between Henry's time and ours.[29]

At Deer River he made preparations for a rugged trip in a birch-bark canoe to Lake Itasca—the true source of the Father of Waters. He hired a guide, Frank Lytle,[30] and on August 15 the two men began paddling up the river through a succession of lakes. The first two camps were made at Ball Club Lake (August 15) and Winnebigoshish Lake (August 16). On the 17th he met Jacob V. Brower, commissioner of Itasca State Park.[31] In Brower, an enthusiast for the history of the Upper Mississippi, he found a kindred spirit and a man who then and later provided valuable information for Coues' researches.

The "Book of Dates" gives the itinerary for the remainder of the journey to his main objective: "[August] 18 Cass Lake. 19 Bemidji & Irving Lakes. 20 up river. 24 to Searles [the house of a person by that name] and by wagon to Itasca."[32] At Lake Itasca Coues, by tracing the longest feeder of the lake, successfully sought what geographer Joseph N. Nicollet in 1836 had determined to be the ultimate source of the Mississippi. "I located the spot at which the Mississippi issues from the ground, a little trickling stream, perhaps not more than six inches wide and two deep. Along this streamlet I lay at full length, and drank out of the middle of the channel, so that I can say with exact truth that I have literally 'covered' the Mississippi River."[33]

Shortly after this bit of drama Coues and Lytle began their return trip. On August 29 they paddled through a body of water, measuring some 1,450 acres, which Henry Schoolcraft in 1855 had named Andrusia Lake. After Coues had returned to the East, he was pleased to receive a letter from Brower, written on September 15, stating that he had renamed the place "Lake Elliott Coues, as a slight recognition of your services to the public, and for the purposes of a more accurate and correct geographical description."[34] We count it regrettable that since Brower's time the Schoolcraft designation, Andrusia, has become the official name of the lake.[35]

The canoe voyage ended at Deer River on September 3. Perhaps it was here that Coues rejoined his wife. The next day he took a train to

Duluth. Before leaving Minnesota, there was one point of historic interest that he was determined to visit: the site of Pike's stockade at Little Falls. There on September 8 he, Mrs. Coues, and the mayor of Little Falls, Judge Nathan Richardson, examined the spot where Pike's men had erected the stockade in 1805. Since there were no vestiges of the original log structure, Coues and his companions built a cairn.[36]

On September 10 Coues and his wife were in St. Paul, where he addressed the Minnesota Historical Society. On the 12th they began their homeward trip, stopping in Chicago for about a week where they visited his mother and sister Lucy. The Coueses arrived at their Washington home on September 21, completing three rewarding and pleasurable months of travel and research. Later that fall, November 13-15, he attended the twelfth annual meeting of the A.O.U. and was elected to a third term as president. In the afternoon session of the first day he gave a paper entitled "Remarks on the Avifauna of the Source of the Mississippi River."[37]

The decade of the 1890s was for Coues primarily one of historical research and travels related to that research; his scientific papers were briefer and fewer in number compared to his output in earlier decades. Yet he was able to give these later contributions, as the title of his 1894 address to the A.O.U. attests, a new historical and geographical dimension. Over the next few years he would publish a number of articles and notes which combined his knowledge of western exploration with that of natural history.

Even though Coues continued to write ornithological pieces during a time when he was mainly occupied with history, one of his most significant contributions to zoology was, as we next see, the discovery of Louis Agassiz Fuertes.

5

While at Fort McHenry Coues had written Baird thanking him for recent favors and saying: "I wish I were big enough to [do] something for you occasionally. Perhaps I may show my appreciation best by in turn trying to do likewise to those who may come after." One who did come after, and for whom Coues did much in the way of favors, was Louis Agassiz Fuertes (1874-1927), who is today generally regarded as the most brilliant bird portraitist America has produced—just as Elliott Coues is now regarded by some as the most brilliant ornithologist our country has produced.

In genuine heartwarming appeal no chapter in Coues' entire life, as we view it, quite measures up to his relationship with Fuertes. It began in December, 1894, and ended with Coues' death five years later.

Fuertes was born in Ithaca, New York, on February 7, 1874; in 1894, when he first met Coues, he was a second-year student at Cornell University, where his Puerto Rican−born father, Esteban Antonio Fuertes, was professor of civil engineering. Even before young Fuertes entered Cornell, he had exhibited an intense interest and marked ability in drawing birds and, if he had had his way, would have pursued a course leading to a degree in art. Instead, having bowed to his father's wish, he was studying architecture, for which he had no appetite. Studying to be a bird artist, Fuertes's father insisted, would be a complete waste of time, for who ever heard of anyone able to make a living drawing pictures of owls, crows, hawks, sparrows, blue jays, and the like?

As future events proved, it was a rare bit of good fortune that Fuertes, on entering Cornell, had joined its Glee Club. During the Christmas holidays of 1894 the Glee Club toured the Middle Atlantic states giving concerts in Washington and other cities. A fellow member of the club, knowing of Fuertes's artistic talents and ornithological aspirations, told him that he had an uncle living in Washington who knew all about birds and might like to see some of the drawings of birds he had already made. The fellow member's name was Charles Henrotin,[38] and his uncle was Elliott Coues.

From that moment wild horses could not have kept the youthful Fuertes from making the concert tour, even though his father disapproved because "Louis was so young and unaware of the temptations of great cities."[39] Whether or not Fuertes owned a copy of *Key to North American Birds*—and he probably did—the name of its author was known to him, as it was to every aspiring young naturalist of that period.

Fuertes's meeting in Washington with Coues most likely took place in the latter's home at 1726 N Street. From the beginning they hit it off. Coues was impressed with Fuertes' drawings, immediately recognizing his potential. Just as important, perhaps, he liked Fuertes and, in turn, Fuertes liked Coues. After examing closely each of the bird portraits, Coues told Louis that, on his return to Ithaca, he must devote every spare moment to his talent and that Coues stood ready to help by introducing him and his work to other ornithologists, one or more of whom might be looking for an illustrator.

From that day forward, inspired by Coues, Louis Fuertes "never thought of adopting any other profession than that of bird portraiture."[40] But, as he told Coues on leaving, his father would do everything he could to discourage him. As a result, on December 31, 1894, Coues wrote Louis: "I will ask you to hand the enclosed [letter] to your father whose full name and address I do not know. Two of Audubon's granddaughters have been spending the afternoon here, and were very much pleased with your paintings. I will be glad to look over the rest of them, which you said you would send."[41]

Unfortunately this letter to Fuertes's father has been lost, so we can only speculate on its content. When situations warranted, Coues could be the most diplomatic of men, and in this instance he probably bent over backward in his effort to win the father's good will. Beyond doubt he stressed Louis's talent and what might be expected of that talent if properly abetted and channeled.

Of the close relationship thus established between Coues and Fuertes, and of Coues' role in sustaining it, a foremost American ornithologist has written: "Doubtless there was no one in the world who could have been of greater service to him [Fuertes]. It would be impossible to over estimate the stimulating effect that Coues' magnetic personality must have had on Fuertes' responsive, appreciative nature. Nor can we value too highly the influence which Coues exerted in developing Fuertes' talents and in shaping his career."[42]

In succeeding chapter we shall return to the Coues-Fuertes friendship and the good that came of it.

6

For Coues the year 1895 was largely taken up with further researches on the early history of the fur trade. The first half of the year found him particularly absorbed in the pursuit of data on Henry, Thompson, and their contemporaries.

Only occasionally did he participate in the social and professional affairs of Washington. On January 25, at a meeting of the National Geographic Society, held at the Cosmos Club, he gave a lecture on the source of the Mississippi. On April 1 he attended a reception for Clara Barton's Red Cross Society, and on the 16th he went to a reception, held at the Smithsonian, for the National Academy of Science.[43]

On April 20 Coues received from his publisher a prospectus announcing the forthcoming Pike volumes.[44] We may feel certain that Coues was now almost entirely free to work on Henry and Thompson. On June 22 he told Harper that the Henry and Thompson journals

"should be worked up together, for the light each throws on the other."
Since further work was needed on the Thompson manuscripts, Coues
abandoned plans for a tour of Mexico and headed for Toronto on July
16.

With some difficulty he persuaded the Crown Lands Department
to allow him to "examine at leisure" the Thompson manuscripts in his
rooms at the Queen's Hotel. From July 18 to August 11 he studied the
journals. He soon found the bulk of the data therein—for example, the
numerous meteorological tables—unbearably dull. Yet there was too
much valuable information in the journals to abandon them altogether.[45]
Therefore he copied only those pages, 176 folios out of about forty
volumes of around a hundred pages each, that pertained directly to
Thompson's travels from 1798 to 1812.[46]

After completing this task, Coues and his wife embarked upon
further western travels. First they went to Sioux City, Iowa, on August
15, to participate in ceremonies honoring the memory of Sergeant
Charles Floyd, as we have already discussed in Chapter XXII. They remained in Sioux City until August 25, when Coues and probably his wife
began a railroad journey, via the Elkhorn River route out of Omaha, to
the Black Hills of South Dakota. The "Book of Dates" tells of the extent
of his rambles in that region: "August 26, 7 a.m. Buffalo Gap [South
Dakota], 8 a.m. Hot Spr[ings], S.D. Sept. 4 Wind Cave. 6 Cascades
[Cascade].[47] 8 Onyx Cave.[48] Sept. 14 rail to Custer City, carriage to
Sylvan Lake and return to Custer. 16, addressed pupils of High School,
and went to Sylvan Lake Hotel. 29 on top of Harney's Peak on donkeys.
Oct. 14 left Sylvan Lake; rail from Custer via Englewood to Spearfish 6
p.m. 15 stayed."

His excursion to the Black Hills, which was not the scene of any of
the explorations he studied, seems to have been purely for pleasure
and a relaxed view of the animal life there. In a published communication
from Sylvan Lake ("a picturesque and romantic spot") he wrote: "I find
much to interest me ornithologically in the heart of the Black Hills of
South Dakota, where I am seeking respite from work and worry for a
few weeks."[49] In a letter to J. A. Allen on October 10, 1895, he gave his
observations on what he believed was a new subspecies of the "common
squirrel of this region," which he called "S[ciurus] hudsonius dakotensis."[50]

On October 16, from Englewood, he began his homeward trip via
Omaha, Sioux City, and Chicago. At Sioux City, on the 18th, he saw for
the first time a set of his edition of the Pike journals.[51]

Immediately after his arrival in Washington on October 24, he plunged again into the editing of the Henry journal. By this time he seems to have decided upon the format for presenting the Henry and Thompson materials in the same work: the main text was to be a paraphrase of Henry's original prose (much as Biddle had done for the Lewis and Clark journals); and the Thompson matter, supplementing Henry's narrative, was to be incorporated by means of footnotes (much as Coues had done with the original manuscripts in his reissue of the Biddle edition).

Harper agreed to the arrangement, and the contract between Harper and Coues for an edition of Henry's Mandan journal was superseded by a new contract, which Coues signed and returned on November 27. We know nothing of the details of the contract but assume that it was similar to that for the editing of the Pike journals. Coues' letters to Harper in November and December show that the editor was already feeding Henry-Thompson copy to the printer.

7

The thirteenth (1895) congress of the A.O.U. was held November 12-14 in the lecture hall of the U.S. National Museum, Washington, D.C. Coues, then serving as president for his third and last term, presided at all meetings.

This congress was notable—more so than most—on two scores. For one thing, on the evening of the third day a special memorial service was held for two illustrious honorary members who had died during the past year: George N. Lawrence (1806-95) and Thomas H. Huxley (1825-95). D. G. Elliot delivered the eulogy for Lawrence and Coues the one for Huxley. According to one writer, "The idea of a memorial meeting undoubtedly originated with Dr. Coues."[52] The other notable feature of the 1895 congress was Coues' exhibit of a portfolio of Louis Agassiz Fuertes's paintings.

Writing to Fuertes in October of that year, Coues had urged him to attend the A.O.U. meetings. Owing to scholastic demands, Fuertes could not be present, though he did accede to Coues' request for a number of his choicest paintings.

With the meetings concluded, Coues at once wrote Fuertes: "According to my promise I brought your name prominently before the American Ornithologists' Union by exhibiting about fifty of your best paintings and talking about them. You would have felt proud and pleased if you had been present to see how well they were received, and how highly they were praised by many besides myself. I hope you are persevering under competent instruction in certain points of technique, and that in the end the result will be that I can bring out for you a very handsome volume of colored plates, and thus secure for you a permanent reputation."[53]

Without exaggerating, Coues could have been even more enthusiastic about the way Fuertes's paintings had been received. According to one writer, a prominent bird portraitist, "The work of young Fuertes caused a furore at the A.O.U. meetings of 1895."[54] The results of the "furore" were far-reaching, as we shall see in pages to follow.

NOTES

1. The details of Coues' travels given in this chapter, unless otherwise noted, are taken from the "Book of Dates."
2. *Ibid.* (1893).
3. Coues to Harper, Sept. 12, 1893.
4. Pompey's Pillar is a rock around 200 feet high, twenty-eight miles down-river from Billings; named by William Clark, probably after Sacagawea's infant son. On it is the carved inscription: "Wm. Clark, July 25, 1806."
5. The news of Coues' presence here is given in the *Helena Independent*, Sept. 29, 1893, 4.
6. Judith Austin, research historian of the Idaho State Historical Society, wrote to us on Sept. 3, 1976: "The only logical stopping place after [Lemhi Pass] was originally known as Sharkey's—in the 1860s—and it's quite possible that by 1893 the lodgings there were run by someone named Sunderland. But so far as we know, there was never any community by that name." She further states that Coues must have hired a stage specially for this trip, since the usual stage route from Red Rock, Mont., to Salmon was through Bannock rather than Lemhi Pass.
7. The well-received lecture, on the subject of Lewis and Clark, was delivered before the Unity Club; see *Helena Independent*, Oct. 6, 1893, 5.
8. Fort Missoula was erected in 1877 on the right side of the Bitterroot River, about four miles southwest of the city of Missoula. Since the turn of the century it has been reactivated and discontinued many times.
9. Rex C. Myers, reference librarian of the Montana Historical Society, wrote to us on Sept. 3, 1976: "Given the location of Waugh's Creek and the nature of travel in that country in 1893, Waugh's House was probably some type of half-way house between Sula and the top of Lost Trail or Gibbon's passes."
10. Alvin William Krech (1858-1928), banker and officer of various railroad and insurance corporations in Minnesota and New York.
11. "Eleventh Congress of the American Ornithologists' Union," *Auk*, XI (Jan., 1894), 51-52.
12. Coues to Harper, Feb. 5, 7, and 14, 1894. It will be recalled that Harper had offered Coues $500 to $750 to prepare the reissue of Lewis and Clark.

13. Coues, ed., *The Expeditions of Zebulon Montgomery Pike* (1895), I, xii, xiv.

14. Coues to Harper, Feb. 5, 1894.

15. Jackson, ed., *The Journals of Zebulon Montgomery Pike* (1966), II, 191n.

16. *Ibid.,* I, 198n.

17. Coues to Harper, Oct. 18, 1895.

18. In an earlier letter to Harper, Feb. 17, 1894, Coues raised the possibility of a new edition of the Patrick Gass journal.

19. This Alexander Henry (d. 1814) was the nephew of another fur trader (1739-1824) of the same name, who also wrote his recollections: *Travels and Adventures in Canada and the Indian Countries between 1760 and 1776* (1809).

20. Edward Duffield Neill (1823-93), Presbyterian clergyman, historian, diplomat, and president of Macalester College (1874-84).

21. Coues-Biddle (1893), III, 1065n.

22. Coues to Neill, Mar. 11, 1893, Neill Mss., Minnesota Historical Society.

23. Coues, ed., *Henry-Thompson Journals* (1897), I, xxiv.

24. Coues to Harper, Jan. 7, 1894.

25. Charles Lindsey (1820-1909), journalist and author, was from 1867 until his death registrar of deeds for Toronto.

26. Coues to Harper, July 16, 1894; May 18, 1895.

27. Coues to Harper, July 31, 1894.

28. Coues, ed., *Henry-Thompson Journals,* I, xxiii.

29. *Ibid.,* 267n.

30. We have not succeeded in obtaining any biographical data on Frank Lytle.

31. Jacob Vradenberg Brower (1844-1905) was an archeologist and explorer. He charted the source of the Mississippi in 1889, and discovered mounds and the remains of an ancient village at Lake Itasca (1894-95).

32. Further details of the voyage are found in Coues, ed., *Expeditions of Pike,* I, 160-67n.

33. Coues, "Adventures of Government Explorers" (1897).

34. Coues, ed., *Expeditions of Pike,* I, 160n.

35. Ruby J. Shields, chief of reference, Manuscripts, Archives/Manuscripts Division, Minnesota Historical Society, to the authors, Sept. 8, 1975.

36. Coues, ed., *Expeditions of Pike,* I, 107n.

37. "Twelfth Congress of the American Ornithologists' Union," *Auk,* XII (Jan., 1895), 61, 63.

38. Charles Henrotin, nephew of Elliott Coues, remains an obscure figure. It is quite likely that he was the son of the man of the same name mentioned in Chapter XXI, note 14.

39. Boynton, ed., *Louis Agassiz Fuertes* (1956), 9.

40. *Ibid.*

41. *Ibid.,* 10.

42. Chapman, "In Memoriam: Louis Agassiz Fuertes" (1928), 7.

43. Coues' "Book of Dates" (1895).

44. *Ibid.* (1895).

45. Coues to Harper, July 28, 1895.

46. Coues to Harper, Aug. 17, 1895.

47. Intended to be a resort town since its founding in 1888, Cascade (or Cascade

Springs) was located in Fall River County and has been a ghost town for years, according to Janice Fleming, South Dakota Department of Education and Cultural Affairs, to the authors, Sept. 13, 1976.

48. Onyx Cave, Custer County, was regularly visited by tourists traveling in the Hot Springs area.

49. Coues, "Letter from Sylvan Lake, S. Dak." (1895), 14-15.

50. This subspecies is not recognized in the standard lists of North American mammals.

51. Coues' "Book of Dates" (1895).

52. T. S. Palmer, "A Brief History of the American Ornitholgists' Union," in Palmer and Chapman, eds., *Fifty Years' Progress of American Ornithology*, 21. Unfortunately Coues' tribute to Huxley seems never to have been published. All efforts to find it (published or unpublished) have failed.

53. Boynton, ed., *Fuertes*, 11.

54. George M. Sutton, "Fifty Years of Progress in American Bird-Art, 1883-1933," in Palmer and Chapman, eds., *Fifty Years' Progress of American Ornithology*, 188.

CHAPTER XXIV

Traders, Trappers, and Artists

Coues' reputation as an editor of western travel journals led several persons to bring to his attention a number of unpublished narratives in need of his talents. One who succeeded in persuading Coues to embark on another editing project was Reuben T. Durrett[1] of Louisville, president of the Filson Club, Kentucky's leading historical association.

The two men seem to have become acquainted while Coues was working on Lewis and Clark. Coues had thanked Durrett in the preface to those volumes for providing some sort of information. In May, 1896, he accepted Durrett's invitation to visit him for about a week at his Louisville home.[2] Durrett showed his guest various manuscripts in his possession, including a journal kept by Jacob Fowler (1765-1850), a Kentuckian who had been active in the early days of the Santa Fe trade. The manuscript of nearly 270 pages, which Durrett had acquired from one of Fowler's descendants, was Fowler's diary for 1821-22, when he and Hugh Glenn (1788-1833) led a trading party from Fort Smith, Arkansas, to Santa Fe.

Fowler's handwriting was unusually difficult to decipher—"modern hieroglyphics" according to Durrett, who had hoped that Coues' experience with handwritten documents would enable him to make sense of it. Durrett's optimism was well founded. Coues tackled the problem with his usual zeal and his usual success. His host gave a word-picture of Coues engaged in the work: " . . . with your constantly replenished pipe, you sat in my library, and smoked and puzzled over this manuscript . . . you smoked and read, and read and smoked, with manifest indication of successful or unsuccessful interpretation of the text, as your puffs were rapid or slow. It might be hard to say whether you smoked or read most, but you finally mastered the manuscript. . . ."[3]

Not only did Coues overcome Fowler's execrable penmanship, but he also transcribed much of the journal while in Durrett's home. Later his secretary, Mrs. Mary B. Anderson, completed the task of transcription.[4] By the time he bade good-bye to his Louisville friend and boarded the train for Washington on May 31, Coues was entertaining something more than idle thoughts about preparing Fowler's journal for publication.

Before he could immerse himself in this work, there were other matters that needed attention. In July he read proof for the index of the Henry-Thompson journals; on the 20th he finished reading proof for the *Papers Presented to the World's Congress on Ornithology* (which was published on November 8). On July 21 he set out for Cranberry, North Carolina. In the quiet of that place, which he enjoyed through most of September, he completed reading the page proofs of the text of the Henry-Thompson journals.[5] Shortly after his return to Washington on September 29 he turned to ornithological matters: the preparation of the fifth edition of the *Key to North American Birds*—the next to the last and the fullest version of that monumental work. By the winter of 1896-97 he was chiefly occupied with this task.[6]

Even these demanding commitments to his old profession could not keep him from his newer calling in the field of history. On November 26 he wrote to Harper, expressing his hope of persuading Durrett to allow him to edit the Fowler journal for publication by Harper rather than by the Filson Club. At the same time he was looking into other possibilities for the Coues-Harper combination. As he told Harper on November 20, 1896: "I am writing to Hartford about the Nathan Hale journal, to Philadelphia about the Sullivan journal, and to Louisville about the Santa Fé mss. It is 'dollars to doughnuts' that I get one or more of these for you!"[7]

2

Although Coues was unable to decide in the fall of 1896 upon which historical project to pursue, he was doing everything within his power to further the career of his friend and protégé, young Fuertes.

The fourteenth (1896) congress of the A.O.U. was held November 9-13 in Cambridge, Massachusetts, in the museum founded by Louis Agassiz, after whom Louis Aggasiz Fuertes had been named. It was fitting therefore, that young Louis, having gained a respite from his Cornell studies, should be attending his first A.O.U. congress in this museum.

Since the previous congress, when Coues had proudly exhibited Fuertes's paintings to A.O.U. members, word had rapidly spread that a new star had risen in the firmament of avian artists. One result was that in months immediately ahead Fuertes received inquiries from a number of writers who were seeking an illustrator for works soon to be published. The first of these seems to have been Florence Merriam, who in 1896 published *A-Birding on a Bronco* illustrated with several pen-and-ink sketches by Fuertes. In ensuing years Fuertes would illustrate many other books, but *A-Birding on a Bronco* was the first, and young Louis was understandably excited about it.

Then came news of an even more exciting proposition. Fuertes learned about it from Coues shortly before the A.O.U. meetings in Cambridge:

> You will no doubt soon receive from the Macmillan Company of New York a very important letter, in regard to making about one hundred drawings of birds for a work which they will publish, and of which I am one of the authors; and if you send me the letter, I shall be in a position to advise you how to reply to it. The publisers' choice lay between you and an artist of recognized ability and secure reputation; and I have such confidence in you that I have secured the offer for you. If this proposed arrangement can be made, and the results prove satisfactory, you will have been fairly started on the road to fame and fortune.[8]

An arrangement with the Macmillan Company was soon concluded whereby Fuertes would provide 111 drawings for a children's book about birds. The book bore the title *Citizen Bird* and its authors were Mabel Osgood Wright and Elliott Coues.

For a man just twenty-two years old and still an undergraduate student at Cornell, Louis Fuertes was indeed "fairly started on the road to fame and fortune," and his decision to attend the A.O.U. congress of 1896, a decision made at the insistence of Coues, proved to be one of far-reaching consequence. On October 10, one month in advance of the congress, Coues had written Fuertes: "I suppose you have received your notification of the next Ornithological Congress, at Cambridge, Nov. 9-12. Under existing circumstances this is an event of some importance to your affairs, and you should not fail to present yourself. Let nothing interfere with this. Better also bring with you about fifty of the best things you have in your portfolio, to show, and in all ways appear in your new role of an ornithological artist whose services have been secured by one of the great publishing houses of this country and England."[9]

Though attendance at the Cambridge meeting meant that Fuertes would have to miss a full week of classes, he did present himself, as he did at almost all future A.O.U. meetings as long as he lived. It is highly unlikely that any later meeting provided the exhilaration and overall

satisfaction of this first one. Coues had seen to it that Fuertes had a
place on the program, thus giving him the opportunity to show and
talk about his paintings, and, too, he introduced him to the other
A.O.U. members present, among them Abbott H. Thayer[10] and Frank
M. Chapman, who would figure prominently in his career in years
ahead.

Later Chapman recalled his impressions of Fuertes at this meeting:
"In bearing Fuertes was modest, and as became a new member, self-
effacing; but as the incarnation of Coues' mysterious protégé he could
not escape the limelight. Furthermore, he appeared not merely as a
potential artist. Already he was illustrating Dr. Coues' and Mrs. Mabel
Osgood Wright's *Citizen Bird,* and he had a number of drawings with
him. They were, indeed, the sensation of the meeting."[11]

Writing to Fuertes soon after the Cambridge meetings, Coues said:
"I think you have every reason to be gratified by recent events, and I
am sure you had a good time in Cambridge and N.Y. Don't let this
success turn your head, but just go ahead and work hard, remembering
that this is but the beginning of your career, in which final success can
only be achieved in the good old-fashioned way of hard work and plenty
of it; it remains with yourself to fill it, and prove that I have not said too
much about you. You did not say whether you had seen the article
which appeared in the *N.Y. Nation* of Nov. 12 regarding your work."[12]

The article in the *Nation* was actually a review of Florence Merriam's
A-Birding on a Bronco, and by Coues himself:

> About a year ago we had occasion to speak of some artistic work done
> by Mr. Louis Agassiz Fuertes, a student at Cornell University, whose
> paintings of birds were much admired when exhibited [in 1896] before the
> A.O.U. at its last meeting in Washington. He is self-taught, and his technique
> is still crude, he needs disciplining to keep him from straining for effect;
> but his power is unmistakable, and we miss our guess if he does not
> become a great artist in birds in due course, if he perseveres. Thus far his
> genius overreaches his talent, but his pictures are better than Audubon's
> were to begin with, and we suspect that the mantle has fallen upon Mr.
> Fuertes.[13]

The year had ended well for both men. Fuertes had achieved
recognition among American ornithologists far beyond his most sanguine dreams, and Coues had convinced his colleagues of Fuertes's
ripening genius. More than that, the relationship between the two,
already close, had grown even closer.

3

Innumerable times in this work we have cited Coues' "Book of Dates" and, less frequently, his "Miscellaneous Mementoes of the Coues' Family, 1784-1896," both unpublished but made available to us by Mr. William P. Coues, great-nephew of Elliott Coues. Of the two documents, the former is much more important. Its full title as it appears on the title page is:

BOOK OF DATES
in the life of
ELLIOTT COUES
and of the COUES family
together with many other dates
during the century
1800-1900
N.B.—All dates given are of incidents in the
life of Elliott Coues, unless otherwise stated.
[1896]

Since 1896 appears terminally in the titles of both of these records, we may reasonably assume that Coues did the work on them, at least most of it, in that year.

The main value of the "Book of Dates" lies in the fact that to Coues' biographers it is far and away the most important available source of information about his personal life. Its pages reveal a vast amount of material found nowhere else. For instance, only in the "Book of Dates" does one find complete day-to-day itineraries of Coues' travels, beginning with his Labrador trip of 1861 and ending with that to the Southwest in 1899. Without this record we would be unaware of many of his speaking engagements and, hence, of how much in demand he was as a public speaker, we would be ignorant of his election to membership in many learned societies, and we would be uninformed about specific extramarital affairs.

The "Book of Dates" discloses many other events, perhaps of lesser importance but of great interest. Particularly intriguing are those which reveal him as a boy sitting on the lap of Nathaniel Hawthorne; "body snatching" during his first year as a student at National Medical College; challenging Major Marcus A. Reno to a duel; excursions in the 1870s into poetry and music; his dining in London, on the Fourth of July, 1884, with Thomas Huxley.

Why did Coues in 1896, aged just fifty-four and busily engaged with the Henry-Thompson journals and a revision of his *Key*, suddenly decide to jot down the events, together with their dates, that grew into his "Book of Dates"? Explanations quite readily occur, though each may well be wide of the mark. Was the "Book of Dates" to serve as an outline for an autobiography he was thinking of writing? Was it possibly just a family record, urged on him by his wife, sister, or son? Or was it a document prompted by his unquestioned vanity to extoll the brilliance of his proud and significant past?

Whatever Coues' reason for writing the "Book of Dates," we have no quarrel with it. As a consequence, we have been able to present more fully a life of great diversity, animation, interest, and distinction.

4

In Coues' "Book of Dates" (1897) we read: "Feb.-Mar. working on Wright-Coues bird book." Coues was here alluding to *Citizen Bird*, the book that would soon bring the name of Fuertes to the forefront as a painter of birds.

It was on October 8, 1896, that Fuertes and the Macmillan Company had come to terms, with the former agreeing to furnish 111 paintings for *Citizen Bird* and to have them ready for the printer not later than the last of February. Perhaps young Louis did not realize until later that he had agreed to produce the 111 illustrations in some 150 days and that at the same time, if he were to graduate at the end of the school year, he had to keep up with his studies. He had other school obligations, too, as leader of the Glee Club and a member of the editorial staff of the *Widow*, Cornell's student magazine. In a moment of dejection he unburdened himself to Coues, stressing the difficulty he experienced in doing justice to both school work and painting. Coues charateristically wrote back, "Never mind your school work. What matters is what you are doing for me."[14]

That Fuertes's father continued unsympathetic to his son's bird painting is evident from his reaction to a check Louis received from Macmillan. It arrived as Louis was having lunch with his father and mother and Margaret Sumner, whom he would later marry. Louis opened the envelope, glanced at the check, and passed it to his mother. After looking at it, she handed it to his father, who without even a glance gave it to Miss Sumner. But curiosity later got the best of Louis's father. After lunch, when alone with Miss Sumner, he asked her the amount of the check. Annoyed by his refusal to acknowledge Louis's success, she replied, "Don't you wish you knew?"[15]

At about this same time, while Louis was still overburdened with school work and the drawings for Macmillan, Coues received a letter from Louis's mother. Unfortunately her letter has been lost, so we are only guessing when we say that her primary reason for writing was to thank Coues for all that he had done for Louis. Coues' reply, which was *not* lost, tends to support our guess:

I am naturally much pleased to receive your letter. "We understand."

I fully believe Louis is too sensitive and honest a character to be spoiled by what has been said, or I would have refrained from giving him in public his just dues. . . .

I am sure that real genius can never be stayed or thwarted—the most we can do is to guide it a little, in its modes of expression. . . .

If the present series of 111 pictures turn[s] out as I expect, I can probably secure him a contract worth several thousand dollars cash. Both fame and fortune seem to be within his grasp, if I can guide him along the way now opened. I have had the handling of a good many boys who wanted to do this or that in science, but had no means, and I have universally told them that the first thing was to secure a means of livelihood. . . . [16] With Louis it is different. If things turn out as I expect, the thousand dollars or so he will put in his pocket for this work [*Citizen Bird*] is very little in comparison with what he will be able to earn soon. He should be independent of the world from the start; if his work goes as it should, he could command more than a fair price for the productions of his pencil and brush. I have sometimes fancied his father not altogether pleased, or even satisfied, and imagined he had other plans for his son's future. But if Louis' gifts be what I believe them, he will never make anything of himself except along the lines of their exercise and development—never attain to more than "respectable mediocrity" (which for me means dead failure) in any other direction.

There was much more to this letter, with further expressions of praise for Fuertes such as, "This country has not before seen Louis' equal in the possibilities of zoological art."[17] Mrs. Fuertes must have been in ecstacy on reading the letter and, unless we measure her spirit incorrectly, showed it at once to her husband. Supporting our belief that she did so is the fact that we hear nothing further about the father's objections to his son's bent toward bird portraiture.

As the publication date for *Citizen Bird* drew nearer, Coues wrote Fuertes: "I have your letter and the 4 plates, which later go to Mr. Brett,[18] today. A couple more and you will have filled the bill. I am sure you have worked hard and faithfully, as well as successfully, and now hope you will soon take a good long rest and outing, which you need.

Don't undertake any more drawing for the present. I am pleased with what you say of Mr. Thayer. Nothing could be more agreeable or more desirable for you this summer, than to be in such relations with him. Let me know when you graduate. With regards to your parents."[19]

Citizen Bird, subtitled *Scenes from Bird-Life in Plain English for Beginners*, came from the press in mid-July. Coues soon (July 22) wrote to Fuertes and first congratulated him on his graduation from Cornell: "But that is not a circumstance to your accomplishment in *Citizen Bird*, through which you have made, at a single bound, a reputation that most artists struggle painfully for during many years of working and writing for recognition and mere livelihood. The book was out on the 14th, and is a phenomenal success at the start, with a sale averaging 500 copies a day."

Coues then went on: "This great hit is mainly due to your pictures, which I consider the finest series of bird portraits ever printed in black and white. The book sells on sight. . . . Now, what are you going to do next?" In conclusion, Coues answered his own question: "I want you to make for me five of the most perfect paintings of which you are capable, as specimens of what you can do in colors. With these under my arm, I can go to N.Y., and probably make the arrangements I have in mind—a plan which, if successful, will make you rich as well as famous."[20]

This letter requires at least two comments. In telling Fuertes that the success of *Citizen Bird* was "mainly due to your pictures," Coues did not exaggerate, nor did he mean to. Second, the "plan" Coues had in mind was, as mentioned in an earlier letter, a handsome volume of Fuertes's colored plates to be produced by a New York publisher.

Citizen Bird drew favorable notices. One reviewer wrote: "*Citizen Bird* is a unique contribution to the literature of ornithology. It addresses an audience which ornithologists had previously neglected and does it in so attractive a manner that the reader's attention is held from cover to cover. . . . The text is made more real by Mr. Fuertes's beautiful drawings, and their charm in turn is increased by the text."[21]

A notice in the *New York Times* stressed: "If the text of *Citizen Bird* gives the spirit of its subject with exceptional charm and veracity, the illustrations certainly do no less. Mr. Fuertes has caught the characteristic attitude, the poise of the body, the intelligence of the eye, and the gently modeled surfaces, with great skill and insight, he has made his birds live upon the page instead of presenting them with hopelessly stuffed and distorted bodies, after the manner of the average illustrator of bird books."[22] On spotting this notice, Coues immediately wrote Fuertes, "There is a chorus of applause in the newspaper notices. One of the very best of all has just appeared in N.Y. Times of the 7th inst [August 7]. I copy the part relating to you, as it is only your just due."[23]

For *Citizen Bird,* we must here explain, Mrs. Wright and Coues had created a cast of human characters including a knowledgeable naturalist and four youngsters, the latter birdlike, quarreling, chattering, and chirping from first to last among the innumerable questions propounded for the naturalist's responses. As a letter to a friend indicated, Coues was less enthusiastic about the youngsters than the published book: "I think you have *Citizen Bird* just about right. I could have swatted those children into the middle of next week, during the whole time I was working on the MS., but I knew the public Mrs. Wright was addressing, and consequently encouraged the young ones in their behavior. The result is the most popular and best selling bird book for children ever written."[24]

Only deep admiration and delight could have occasioned Coues' outbursts of praise in his above letters to Fuertes. By now an even closer relationship existed between the two, one akin in some respects to that which had earlier existed between Baird and Coues.

At the time *Citizen Bird* came from the press, Coues was at the Audubon home in Salem, New York, going over the journals of John James Audubon, which Maria Audubon[25] (with help from Coues) would soon publish, and Fuertes was in Dublin, New Hampshire, spending the summer with Abbott H. Thayer, a talented American artist who improved Fuertes's skill with brush and paints. A letter from Fuertes in late summer gave Coues concern about the health of his protégé. He replied at once:

> I see by your letter that you are nervous and overwrought, and not getting the rest and recreation you need during your vacation. . . . The great work I have in view for you can wait—in any event, even if all my plans should mature, it would be at least a year before we should come to the beginning of it. Meanwhile enjoy yourself, and take things perfectly easy; live as much as you can out of doors, letting your inspiration come as it pleases, not forcing it, and not studying art, or anything else. Make the most of your summer, in the way of ease, indolence and recreation, and you will feel all right soon.
>
> I go to Portland, Maine, soon, to be there some time, and when you get ready, or feel just like it, come there to see me, and we will talk things over quietly.[26]

Coues did not wait for Fuertes to visit him. Instead, soon after arriving in Portland, he went to Dublin. Apparently he was concerned not only about Fuertes's health but also about the influence, for good or bad, Thayer might be exerting on Louis. He need have had no concern in either direction. On his return to Portland Coues wrote Fuertes: "Besides being personally agreeable, my visit to Dublin, where you insisted on making me your guest, relieved my mind and I now have no fear about you. If our friend Thayer thought I 'wanted to pick you before you were ripe,' as he told me, I thought he wanted to fly away with you. But that is all right now, and I am more than satisfied with things as they are."[27]

The 1897 A.O.U. meetings were held November 8-11 in New York. Coues attended and showed more of Fuertes's paintings, although the artist himself was absent. Following the meetings Coues took the paintings to the Macmillan Company in an effort to have them published in resplendent color. But the publisher thought the cost prohibitive, and the whole plan, so enthusiastically suggested in Coues' earlier letters, had to be abandoned.[28]

5

At the very time that Coues was helping to launch Fuertes' career, he was doing much to perpetuate the memory of the man who still remains *the* artist of American wildlife, John James Audubon.

On behalf of Audubon's granddaughter, Maria R. Audubon, Coues exhibited at the 1896 meeting of the A.O.U. "some recently discovered manuscript journals of John James Audubon, including the one giving an account of his famous trip up the Missouri River." Miss Audubon, who was present at the meetings, was given a vote of thanks by the A.O.U.[29] With encouragement from Coues, Maria Audubon was editing these journals for publication. Coues publicized the forthcoming work in *The Osprey* and also announced that she was writing a biographical memoir of her grandfather, to accompany the edited journals, that would be superior to the previous accounts of the life of the "American Backwoodsman."[30]

Coues played an even more substantial role in the publication of the journals by agreeing to supply some of the annotation for them, chiefly zoological and geographical matter. To facilitate this work, Coues and his wife spent the month of July, 1897, at the home of Maria Audubon and her sister Florence in Salem, New York. While enjoying the Audubon sisters' "generous hospitality," Coues set about aiding Maria in preparing the journals for print.[31] The finished product was published in two volumes, later in 1897, with the title *Audubon and His Journals*. In her preface Miss Audubon described Coues' contributions and expressed her indebtedness to him: "Without the very material aid by both pen and advice, of Dr. Elliott Coues, these pages would have lost more than I care to contemplate. All the zoological notes are his, and many of the geographical, besides suggestions too numerous to mention; moreover, all this assistance was most liberally given at a time when he personally was more than busy; and yet my wishes and convenience have always been consulted."[32]

Probably most of his work in footnoting the journals was done during his one-month stay in Salem. The task was relatively easy for him, since it consisted largely of providing precise, up-to-date zoological definitions for "The European Journals. 1826-1829" and "The Labrador Journal. 1833" (pages 79-342 and 343-445 of volume I) and geographical and zoological notes for Audubon's account of his travels in an area with which Coues was thoroughly familiar—"The Missouri River Journals" (pages 453-532 of volume I and pages 3-195 of volume II).

As we have already noted, Coues left Salem on July 31 for a trip to New Hampshire, where he visited with Fuertes, who was, with Coues' blessing and help, emerging as a successor entirely worthy of the great Audubon.

At the 1897 A.O.U. meeting, held on November 8-11 in New York, Coues gave a talk entitled "Audubonia and Other Matters of Present Interest," in which he described the hitherto unpublished journals and letters of Audubon which his granddaughter would soon publish. To advertise the forthcoming volumes even more effectively, he held aloft a "worn old receptacle"—the portfolio in which in 1826 Audubon had carried to Europe the plates for the illustrations for his *Birds of America*. Coues later wrote that "the feeling with which the precious memento was greeted found expression in instant applause, and probably there was none present who did not share my own thrill."

Then Coues dramatically extracted from the portfolio other fabulous relics that Maria Audubon had entrusted to him: the original manuscript of most of the first volume of Audubon's *Ornithological Biography*; two original bird drawings by his son, John Woodhouse Audubon; and a photograph of a portrait by the son "representing his father as he appeared when just returned from his trip to the Yellow-stone in 1843, full-bearded, and rough as one of the grizzly bears he had encountered."[33]

A few years later Frank M. Chapman recalled the event vividly—particularly Coues' "keen enjoyment" in presenting the artifacts.[34] Making sure that he got the most out of the auspicious moment, Coues also displayed some of the latest work of Louis Agassiz Fuertes, Audubon's spiritual heir.[35]

6

On July 31, while still at the home of the Audubon sisters, Coues signed a contract with Harper for the publication of the Fowler jour-nal.[36] We do not know if the terms allowed for an honorarium, but they did provide for a royalty of 10 percent.[37] *The Journal of Jacob Fowler,* a single volume of 183 pages, was published sometime early in 1898 (Coues datelined the introduction "January 1, 1898"), and it was the first book in what Coues and Harper had dubbed the "American Explorers Series." Appropriately, Coues dedicated the volume to the "Nestor of Kentucky Historians," Reuben T. Durrett.

The book, which remains a valuable source for the history of the Santa Fe trade, represents a distinct departure from Coues' usual editorial procedures. He reproduced Fowler's prose *exactly* as he found it. He was able to overcome the temptation to tamper with original spelling, wording, grammar, and punctuation because, he explained, they were all "bad enough to preserve inviolate as a curiosity."[38] A second motive for presenting to the reading public such a faithful rendering of the original version was, as he frankly stated, to thumb his nose at his detractors: "I thought this would be a good way to show that awesome deference which I ought to feel for certain captious critics of former works with which my name is associated, whose green-eyed strabismus has seen me in the light of entirely too good an editor—that is to say, who have complimented me by their censure for making my authors too intelligible, too attractive, and altogether too readable, by the way I dressed them for the press."[39]

Just as he was getting the Fowler journal through the press, another narrative of western adventure came into his hands, this time from the distinguished anthropologist Washington Matthews.[40] Matthews was, as Coues had once been, an Army surgeon. While stationed at Fort Buford in 1872, he received from veteran fur-trader Charles Larpen-teur (1807-72) a letter stating that he had recently written his autobiography and asking if Matthews "could get it up in good shape for the print."

Coues described the subsequent history of Larpenteur's manuscript:

> After some further correspondence, the original manuscript of this "History of the Life of Charles Larpenteur," etc., making about two hundred closely written foolscap pages, was mailed to Dr. Matthews by its author, on June 14, 1872. A clerical copy was made, and the original returned to its owner. This copy was kindly placed in my hands by Dr. Matthews at Washington, D.C., on Oct. 17, 1897, for any use I might wish and be able to make of it. I soon afterward received the original from Mr. A. L. Larpenteur, of St. Paul, Minn., a nephew of the author. . . . [41]

Since Larpenteur, who by 1897 had been dead for twenty-five years, had given Matthews *carte blanche* in preparing the manuscript "for the print," Coues, who would be the editor in lieu of Matthews, assumed that Larpenteur wanted a practiced literary hand to improve upon his prose. Coues found that Larpenteur "was never on good terms with English orthography and syntax" and therefore he felt justified in making substantial stylistic changes: " . . . there was scarcely a sentence in it all that did not need to be recast to some extent in preparing the manuscript for publication. But this is a mere matter of grammar; I have simply helped the author to express himself; the sense and sentiment are his own, if the style is not."[42]

"Recasting" Larpenteur's autobiography probably took more of Coues' time than did the annotations for it. Once again he was on familiar ground—Larpenteur's activities had taken place in those areas of North America over which Lewis and Clark, Audubon, Henry, Thompson—and Coues himself—had traveled. The finished work, in two volumes, appeared in the latter part of 1898, with the title *Forty Years a Fur Trader on the Upper Missouri: The Personal Narrative of Charles Larpenteur, 1833-1872,* and as number two in the American Explorers Series. Once more the dedication was appropriately to a friend of Coues who had brought the account to light, in this case Washington Matthews.

Privately Coues expressed his opinion that neither the Fowler nor the Larpenteur journals were in the same category as his editions of Lewis and Clark, Pike, and Henry-Thompson.[43] There can be little argument on this score, yet this is not to say that the Fowler and Larpenteur narratives lack merit. Indeed, they are highly useful documents of nineteenth-century western history. If they are of secondary importance relative to Coues' earlier contributions to history, it is

simply because Fowler's and Larpenteur's travels did not have the
sweep and significance of those of Lewis, Clark, and Pike, and their
manuscripts did not have the bulk and detail found in those of Henry
and Thompson.

7

In the summer of 1898 Coues and his wife were once again
ranging through the West. We have only a few details of their itinerary.
The "Book of Dates" simply states that they went to Colorado, Utah,
and New Mexico. In one of Coues' letters written before he left for the
West, he told his correspondent that he intended to leave Washington
on June 15.[44] By June 29 he was in Denver, whence he, Governor Alva
Adams,[45] and a "party organized especially for the purpose" visited the
ruins of three early-day trading posts north of Denver on the South
Platte River: Forts Lupton, Vasquez, and St. Vrain.[46] Presumably the
Coueses soon thereafter went to Utah. By August they were in Santa
Fe, where they stayed until sometime in September. At some point in
their travels Mary Emily Coues broke a bone as a result of a railroad
accident. By early October they had returned to Washington.[47]

In the following month he attended the sixteenth congress of the
A.O.U., held that year in Washington. Although he presented no
paper himself, he commented upon at least four papers given by other
ornithologists.[48]

We do not know if his visit to Colorado related to any historical
project in particular, and we know nothing of the itinerary or motives
of his stay in Utah. His presence in Santa Fe, however, is no mystery.
He later wrote that he had been "overhauling the archives of New
Mexico."[49] Specifically, he was searching for documents relating to the
diary of the Franciscan missionary Francisco Garcés (1738-81), which
he was translating and editing. The project would prove to be Coues'
last contribution to the historical literature of the American West.

NOTES

1. Reuben Thomas Durrett (1824-1913) retired from a prosperous law practice
   to devote his time to the researching and writing of Kentucky history. He was
   one of the founders of the Filson Club.
2. Coues' "Book of Dates" (1896).
3. Coues, ed., *The Journal of Jacob Fowler* (1898), vii-ix.
4. *Ibid.*, xxiv. Other than the fact that Mrs. Anderson prepared indices for
   Coues' editions of Lewis and Clark, Pike, Henry-Thompson, Fowler, and

Larpenteur, and performed routine secretarial duties for him, we know virtually nothing else of her. Her transcription of the Fowler journal is housed in the Joseph Regenstein Library of the University of Chicago.

5. Coues' "Book of Dates" (1896).

6. *Ibid.* See also "Fourteenth Congress of the American Ornithologists' Union," *Auk*, XIV (Jan., 1897), 84.

7. Here Coues is referring to the manuscript diary of the Revolutionary martyr-spy Nathan Hale and to the journal (1775-78) of Thomas Sullivan, a sergeant in the British Army who served during the American Revolution. The diary of Hale is at the Connecticut Historical Society and the journal of Sullivan is housed at the American Philosophical Society. Coues edited neither of these journals for Harper.

8. Boynton, ed., *Fuertes*, 12.

9. *Ibid.*, 13.

10. Abbott Handerson Thayer (1849-1921), American artist, was born in Boston, Mass. He studied under Gérôme at the Ecole des Beaux Arts, Paris. Among naturalists he was especially well known for his theory of protective coloration, and for the publicity he received during a controversy with Theodore Roosevelt, who opposed his theories. Like Coues, Thayer was important in shaping Fuertes's career as an artist. After graduating from Cornell, Fuertes spent most of the next year with Thayer, who then and thereafter instructed him in ways to improve his techniques.

11. Chapman, *Autobiography of a Bird-Lover*, 77.

12. Boynton, ed., *Fuertes*, 15.

13. *Ibid.*, 15-16. See also *Nation*, LXIII (Nov. 12, 1896), 374.

14. Boynton, ed., *Fuertes*, 12.

15. *Ibid.*, 13.

16. Coues, as he says here, may have helped many young men. We recall, of course, his encouragement of A. C. Beals, hospital steward at Fort Macon.

17. Boynton, ed., *Fuertes*, 20-21.

18. George Platt Brett (1858-1936), president of the American branch of the Macmillan Company (1896-1931).

19. Boynton, ed., *Fuertes*, 24.

20. *Ibid.*, 28-29.

21. Frank M. Chapman review of *Citizen Bird* in *Auk*, XIV (Oct., 1897), 413-14.

22. Boynton, ed., *Fuertes*, 31. See also *New York Times*, Aug. 7, 1897, 7.

23. Boynton, ed., *Fuertes*, 30-31.

24. Coues to Julia Stockton (Mrs. Edward) Robins, Feb. 14, 1897. This letter is in Ms. Collections of the Library of the Academy of Natural Sciences of Philadelphia.

25. Maria Rebecca Audubon (1843-1925), granddaughter of John James Audubon, wrote several books and articles on natural history and art.

26. Boynton, ed., *Fuertes*, 29-30.

27. *Ibid.*, 30.

28. *Ibid.*, 32.

29. "Fourteenth Congress of the American Ornithologists' Union," *Auk*, XIV (Jan., 1897), 84.

30. "Dr. Coues' Column," *Osprey*, I (June, 1897), 135.

31. *Ibid.* (July-Aug., 1897), 150.

32. Maria R. Audubon, ed., *Audubon and His Journals, with Zoological and Other Notes by Elliott Coues*, 2 vols. (New York: Charles Scribner's Sons, 1897), I, vii.

33. "Dr. Coues' Column," *Osprey*, II (Dec., 1897), 54. See also John H. Sage, "The American Ornithologists' Union," *ibid.*, 51.

34. Chapman's editorial note to "Elliott Coues on Audubon" (a verbatim transcription of Coues' remarks taken down by a stenographer "chancing to be present"), *Bird-Lore*, III (Jan.-Feb., 1901), 9.

35. "Fifteenth Congress of the American Ornithologists' Union," *Auk*, XV (Jan., 1898), 45.

36. Coues' "Book of Dates" (1897).

37. Coues to Harper, July 22, 1897.

38. Coues, ed., *Forty Years a Fur Trader* (1898), I, xxv-xxvi.

39. Coues, ed., *Journal of Jacob Fowler*, xvii.

40. Matthews (1843-1905) wrote many important studies on American Indians, including *Grammar and Dictionary of the Hidatsa* (1873) and *The Night Chant* (1902).

41. Coues, ed., *Forty Years a Fur Trader*, I, xx-xxi.

42. *Ibid.*, xxiii, xxvi.

43. Coues to Harper, Oct. 16, 1897.

44. Coues to E. J. Nolan, June 6, 1898, Ms. Collections of the Library of the Academy of Natural Sciences of Philadelphia.

45. Alva Adams (1850-1922), Pueblo businessman, was thrice governor of Colorado (1887-89, 1897-99, and 1905).

46. *Rocky Mountain News* (Denver), June 30, 1898, 3.

47. Coues to Henry A. Boller, Oct. 7, 1898, Boller Mss., North Dakota Historical Society.

48. "Sixteenth Congress of the American Ornithologists' Union," *Auk*, XVI (Jan., 1899), 51-54.

49. Coues, ed., *On the Trail of a Spanish Pioneer* (1900), II, 471n.

CHAPTER XXV

Coues, Robins, and *The Osprey*

The practice of naming ornithological journals after birds has been popular ever since the British Ornithologists' Union in 1859 named its official organ *The Ibis*. In the years since, we have witnessed the advent of *The Emu* of Australia, *Alauda* (lark) of France, *El Hornero* (ovenbird) of Argentina, *Le Gerfaut* (falcon) of Belgium, and *The Auk, The Cardinal, The Loon, The Redstart*, and *The Ousel* of the United States.

The above is by way of introducing *The Osprey*, yet another bird magazine of the United States. It demands our attention because for a brief period Elliott Coues served as its editor. *The Osprey* owed its existence to a resident of Galesburg, Illinois, Walter A. Johnson,[1] who conceived it, gave it its name, and in November, 1896, brought out its first number.

Early in 1897 Johnson persuaded Coues to join the staff of *The Osprey* as an associate editor, and later that year he moved the magazine's publication office to New York City. Soon afterward, having become involved in other business enterprises, Johnson put *The Osprey* up for sale. The man who bought it was Theodore N. Gill, though seemingly not until he had gained Coues' consent to edit it for him. In all likelihood Coues jumped at the chance, never before having been handed the reins of editor-in-chief of any periodical. However, in a letter to Allen of November 7, 1898, he tried to play down his enthusiasm: "You wouldn't hesitate whether to congratulate or commiserate me on *The Osprey*. I don't want 'an organ,' and if I did, a magazine conducted by myself would not be one. . . . I took *The Osprey* at earnest solicitation . . . and don't feel about it anything except a sense of being d. f. [damn fool] enough to martyrize myself to duty. Besides, the arrangement with Gill isn't working worth a d—n as yet."

Theodore Gill, we need no reminding, had been one of Coues' science teachers at Columbian and since then had seen much of his former pupil, particularly when the two worked together on affairs of

the American Ornithologists' Union. At one time they had collaborated
on a treatise about mammals, but Gill's contributions to that work were
never completed on time; as Coues told a friend: "I will never write
another word in partnership with Gill to save his immortal soul."[2]
Having acquired *The Osprey*, Gill promptly moved it to Washington,
D.C. Here publication resumed at once, with Gill as owner and business
manager and Coues as editor.[3] Evidently Coues had conveniently forgotten his vow not to write anything in collaboration with Gill, even "to
save his immortal soul."

Available information about the Coues-Gill literary enterprise, a
brief one that terminated abruptly and unhappily, is derived almost
exclusively from two sources: the pages of *The Osprey* itself and a series
of remarkable letters that Coues, while editor of *The Osprey*, wrote to
Julia Stockton (Mrs. Edward) Robins of Philadelphia. Mrs. Robins, it
would appear, quite suddenly entered Coues' life and, after a brief
exchange of letters with him, just as suddenly dropped out of it.
During the period from late January to early May, 1899, Coues' letters
to Mrs. Robins averaged about one a week, and they reveal, as we assess
them, what a clever woman gifted in the use of cunning and flattery
can accomplish in eliciting confidences from a persuasible man.

From what Coues said in one of his letters to Mrs. Robins, we
gather that the two had earlier met, quite casually, at the Academy of
Natural Sciences of Philadelphia, where Mrs. Robins, then secretary of
the Pennsylvania Audubon Society,[4] had an office. We have the strong
feeling, too, that Coues had heard the "talk" about Mrs. Robins then
circulating through the ancient corridors of the academy, talk that
apparently had some foundation in fact and of a kind that surely would
have titillated Coues' restive, "nature-loving" mind. Otherwise, we find
it extremely difficult to understand Coues' ready responses to Mrs.
Robins's letters: his excessive compliment, lengthy replies, intermittent
coyness, and, beyond that, his willingness—if not eagerness—to entrust
her with confidences amounting in some instances to censure of fellow
naturalists so scathing that most men would hesitate to reveal them
even to their closest friends or relatives.

In pages immediately following we shall quote freely from Coues'
letters to Mrs. Robins and from his editorials in *The Osprey*, these
leaders appearing under two titles: "Editorial Eyrie" and "In the
Osprey's Claw." The letters disclose much pertinent information found
nowhere else, and the editorials throw considerable light on the quality
of Coues' editorship of *The Osprey*. Both letters and editorials were

often so surcharged with arrogance and animosity, and with unjusti-
fiable censure of colleagues, that we urge the reader—in the interests
of fairness—to keep in mind that Coues was then suffering from the
effects of illnesses that would prove fatal before the year ended.

2

Coues' first letter to Mrs. Julia Stockton Robins was dated January
31, 1899:

My dear Mrs. Robins:
   Your kind letter is to hand, and though I am as innocent of the
business of the Osprey as yourself, I take pleasure in saying that I have
personally attended to the enclosure, seen that your subscription is set
ahead, and now mail you the Osprey for Oct. & Nov. . . .
   There was much trouble with the mailing list, consequent upon the
transfer [of *The Osprey* from New York to Washington],[5] but I trust it is
now a thing of the past. I like to be "persecuted" with such letters as yours,
and hope to count upon you as a long friend of the Osprey, as well as of,
                                        Yours very sincerely,

                                        Elliott Coues[6]

As is evident, the correspondence began innocently enough: Mrs.
Robins inquiring why she, a subscriber to *The Osprey*, had failed to
receive the latest numbers of the journal, and Coues replying that he
had personally attended to the matter for her.
   Mrs. Robins promptly acknowledged receipt of the back numbers
of *The Osprey* and then inquired if Coues might be interested in an
article by her about Alexander Wilson. Coues answered on February 8:

   I am glad to hear that the Ospreys reached you and that you enjoyed
them. The magazine is not yet what I intend to make it . . . though I have
furnished the Osprey Company[7] with the best plates that could be made in
N.Y., and they ought to have come out as well as those beautiful ones Mr.
[Frank M.] Chapman is giving us in Bird-Lore.[8] I envy him the faultless
typography he has secured and . . . I hope [*Bird-Lore*] will receive all the
support it so well deserves.
   Shall be happy to have a good short article from your pen for the
Osprey, and why not let it be an Alexander Wilson article? Nothing would
please me more than to have you do up his love affair with Miss Annie
Bartram.[9] I have known a little about it, lo! these many years, since *Behind
the Veil*;[10] but (in answer to your question) I never came across any books
about Wilson, and know of none extant, excepting those fully accounted
for in my Bibliography of North American Ornithology. . . . Now if you
have any old letters or anything else relating to this love affair, do pray

make them up into an Osprey article for me. That would be delightful,
and I will give you a fine editorial "send off." If the poor man got crossed
in love with Miss Bartram, it would explain much of his moodiness,
melancholy, flute playing, and sad undertones of his ornithological work;
also, his close relation with Wm. Bartram.[11] I am full for February, but
shall be glad to run you in for March. You can trump my trick of "Behind
the Veil" with a charming "Behind the Wedding Veil," or "Where Were
the Orange Blossoms!"

Kindly let me hear from you at once.

Strange, is it not, that Coues should reply to Mrs. Robins, a comparative stranger, at such length, promise to publish her article sight
unseen, and ensure her of a "fine editorial 'send off'"? Odd, too, that in
this same letter he warmly complimented *Bird-Lore* when shortly, as we
shall see, he would belittle both the magazine and its editor.

Writing again to Mrs. Robins just a day or two later, Coues raised
and answered questions:

"*Why* I wanted to know?" Why, how can any man know even who he is
himself, or where he stands, nowadays, unless he knows how to sort out his
lady friends from their inextricable interrelations? Ask me something
hard, next time! The unpronounceable Neltje B. [Neltje Blanchan] is Mrs.
Doubleday,[12] whom I never met, but I corresponded with her when one of
her books was coming out, and reviewed it in several places. Then some of
my friends abused me for over praising it, and as I never heard from the
author after that, I suppose she thought I did not praise it enough—and
of such is the kingdom of the reviewer. And, by the way, how did you like
Citizen Bird? If you ever saw it. I shall be pleased to have your Wilson
article, as promised.

Mrs. Robins lost no time in replying to the above, and in for-
warding the Alexander Wilson piece. Judging by Coues' answer, he was
delighted with both letter and article—and perhaps even more so with
Mrs. Robins.

Permit me in turn to compliment you upon your knowledge of the
masculine gender, and of how to write to one of those superb creatures
called man—especially a letter which was to reach the favored recipient on
a Feb. 14. That sort of incense-burning would melt a stonier editorial heart
than that possessed by the innocent and inexperienced individual who
makes up the Osprey.

Your article [about Wilson] is all that I had been led by your letter to
expect, or could wish—altogether admirable and charming, and it shall go
into the next Osprey I make up—probably for March. There is only one
point; you say Wilson was his own engraver. I think not—Alexander

Lawson[13] was his engraver, unless I am much mistaken. Have you anything to support the statement, or shall I cross it out? . . .

I think, if you like, I will call your article "Behind the Wedding Veil," and perhaps make editorial reference to my old piece of like title—that is, if you approve . . . .

Tell me some more about what you think of people and their books. And if your pen runs away with you, let it run hitherward, where it will be perfectly safe. Isn't *Bird-Lore* a lovely magazine—and did you ever meet the cherub who edits it?

As Coues had indicated he might, he ran Mrs. Robins's article in *The Osprey* of March, and with the title he had suggested. More than that, he made it the lead article, an honor that may be questioned since it was next followed by another of superior merit.[14]

Mrs. Robins's "Behind the Wedding Veil" began with a brief sketch of the love affair between Ann Bartram and Alexander Wilson, a romance that ended unhappily when Miss Bartram's father forbade her marrying "a poor school teacher." She married instead, with paternal blessing, Colonel Robert Carr, a well-to-do Philadelphia printer. Then Mrs. Robins even more briefly summarized Wilson's life as an ornithologist and concluded with a poem by Wilson, "The Beechen Bower," obviously one he had written about Ann Bartram. Coues had described Mrs. Robins's article as "altogether admirable and charming"; we find it difficult to share in his enthusiasm.

The "cherub" Coues was referring to was Frank M. Chapman, editor of *Bird-Lore,* the first number of which appeared in February, 1899. In *The Osprey* of that month Coues commented on *Bird-Lore* and its editor:

The appearance of this magazine realized the expectations raised by the prospectus, which the Osprey cited last month. It is what the boys call a daisy—dainty, even exquisite, faultless in typographical full-dress. It might have been called Bird-Love instead of Bird-Lore. . . . The illustrations are the finest we have seen in any ornithological magazine. . . . Regarding the other contents of the magazine,[15] we are able to control our enthusiasm. The editor seems to be toying with ornithology in amateurish fashion, and will have to guard against dilettanteism, if he would not degenerate into mere prettiness or virtuosity. . . . Mr. Chapman's experience as a reviewer and critic may make this department of his magazine a strong one, if he will vow from the start never to be mealy-mouthed about killing a book that ought to be killed, like that silly one by Dekay[16] called "Bird Gods," which is very bad ornithology, and still worse philology and mythology. If Mr. Chapman or his anonymous reviewer had understood how to handle this book, it would not only have been damned with faint praise—it would have been skinned alive, and its hide hung on the fence to dry. . . . Bird-Lore sets forth bravely and handsomely. . . . If it continues to prosper, as we have no doubt will be its happy lot, Mr. Chapman will win with the camera and opera-glass a halo of radiant amateurishness which may fit him as well as that laurel wreath of the professional ornithologist already earned with the shot-gun, scalpel and eggdrill.

With the above quotation we begin the somewhat difficult task of attempting to mesh Coues *Osprey* editorials with his candid, handwritten revelations to Mrs. Robins. Earlier, in letters to Mrs. Robins, Coues had complimented *Bird-Lore;* now, in editorial, he had openly depreciated it. Of course, from the moment *Bird-Lore* opened its pages to ornithologists, it had become a rival of *The Osprey.* In appraising its worth to the reader, Coues had been able to "control his enthusiasm" for it and for its editor but was quite unable to harness his capricious judgment. It was regrettable, for a rift soon developed in the Coues-Gill relationship that seems to have had its origin in Coues' injudicious valuation of the first number of *Bird-Lore.*

In Coues' next (February 18) letter to Mrs. Robins we learn that she had asked Coues for a picture of himself, and that Coues, taking advantage of the request, tried to strike a bargain:

> Since you are interested in Rafinesque,[17] who was a most picturesque character, and since you do me the honor to request my photograph, I will tell you what I will do! I will lend you my private copy of the Biography and Bibliography of Raf[inesque] . . . and also send you my photo, if you will let me print the greater part of your last letter to me in the Osprey. It is simply delightful. . . . The trouble with most ornithological print is, it is so deadly dull, and I want, if possible, to make the Osprey bright, breezy, racy, pungent and trenchant. I propose to fly the bird on its two wings of fearlessness and truthfulness, with all the good fish in its claws it can catch and carry. . . .
>
> I remember you perfectly well at the last meeting of the A.O.U., of course—was only waiting for you to allude first to the incident.

As Coues' next (February 23) letter attests, Mrs. Robins did not succumb to the blandishments of *The Osprey* editor that he be allowed to publish certain passages from her latest communication:

> . . . As to printing portions of your former letter, perhaps you are right; truth is too precious to be squandered, and as you are on the "seraph staff of the cherub editor," you may have to be careful, or you may be disciplined by the lady[18] who conducts the Audubonian department of *Bird-Lore.* . . .

You are perfectly right about poor Keeler[19]—a boy who had original ideas, perhaps genius, & put his heart in his book, only to have it torn out and stamped on in the Auk. The book was crude, far from perfection of maturity, but it was cruelly & unjustly treated by Dr. Allen, just because he did not understand some of Keeler's ideas. The strange thing is, that Keeler was *right,* and A[llen] was wrong, in fact, on some points. Now I propose to right this wrong, if possible, in the Osprey, and do Keeler full justice, even thus tardily; and when I take up a man's cause, it is not dropped in a hurry. The Osprey shall fly, if it flies at all, on balanced wings of fearlessness and truthfulness. . . .

Keeler's book, *Evolution of the Colors of North American Land Birds,* had been published in 1893. Six years later, and almost certainly at the prompting of Mrs. Robins, Coues took up Keeler's cause in the April number of *The Osprey.* Coues' effort to validate the worth of Keeler's study began like a book review. In no time, however, it changed into an open, unrestrained attack against Allen in which he accused his long-time friend of everything from witlessness and incompetence to shifti-ness and dishonorable dealing:

> The Osprey is so full of matters of instant interest that it can seldom pause in current affairs to take up for review a book of past years. But this magazine is ever on the alert to see that justice is done where a wrong has been committed. . . .
>
> Early in 1893, when the present Director of the Museum of the California Academy of Sciences [Keeler] was younger than he is now, he published a remarkable book. . . . This work was not free from errors of fact . . . but it was set forth . . . with entire originality . . . in fine, with all the defects of its qualities, it bore the stamp of genius. . . .
>
> Why, then, has such a work been almost entirely ignored by American ornithologists?

The work had been ignored, Coues declared, because Allen had "killed" it with a derogatory review in *The Auk:*[20]

> We do not accuse "J.A.A." of dishonorable dealing with the book; we find that he simply abused it . . . meaning well, perhaps, but succeeding very badly, if he tried to be fair and candid. . . . "J.A.A." is well known to be the mildest-mannered man who ever cut an author's throat or scuttled a book. This will be obvious to any discerning reader of the way he under-took to demolish Mr. Keeler. The attack was covert, stealthy, shifty, evasive, with many a hum and a haw, a show of sorrow for his intended victim, and an appearance of that sort of fairness which consists of a pat on the head and a stab under the fifth rib in alternate paragraphs. . . . [21]

As is all too evident, Coues let Allen have both barrels, one charged—

as he would have it—with "fearlessness" and the other with "truthful-ness." Beyond question, this salvo was the straw that broke the back-bone of the already weakened Coues-Gill collaboration, for break it did, as we shall soon see. Even if Gill had been aware of Coues' illnesses—we cannot be sure that he was—he could hardly have con-doned Coues' callous broadside at Allen.

A few weeks earlier (March 8) Coues had written Allen: "I hold *readability* to be the prime requisite of a magazine soliciting public patronage. . . . *The Osprey* must be made *readable.*" Obviously Coues, in his role as editor, had gone beyond the acceptable limits of "readability."

3

In documenting Coues' letter of February 23 to Mrs. Robins—in which he rushed to the defense of Keeler—we have done harm to our chronology and must now return to February 27, when he wrote her next:

> Since you give me permission to appropriate your *mot,* I work it into an editorial. . . . Probably you are right, for your own peace of mind, to keep in the background with such scathing irony & satire, but I am long used to the clash of arms, and just such things as you send joggle my often jaded wits, and I can set them scintillating again on the pabulum you furnish. I will keep your secret piously, and shall always be glad to have anything bright "from the inside." So if you will play "dea ex machina" now and then, nobody will be any the wiser, and the Osprey will be brighter. . . . Better look out if you have sent anything to the "royal lady"[22] she don't like—I have been there myself! . . .

It was in his next letter to Mrs. Robins that he first said anything to her about his health. After asking her if anyone at the academy might copy for him a review that Edward D. Cope had done of Keeler's book, he wrote: "I am a mile and a half from the nearest file of the publi-cation, and my health is such that I can seldom leave the house." He finished his letter by complimenting Mrs. Robins on the way she had handled a mutual feminine acquaintance: "It is always better to do as you did with her; the machinery of life runs easiest for those who lubricate with an oil can, instead of going about with a sandblast to blow into the joints of the social fabric, as some of us do now and then."

By nature, it seems clear, Coues generally favored the sandblast to the oil can. On occasion, however, he could lubricate with the best of them. Consider, for instance, his next message to Mrs. Robins:

> Now I am going to write you a letter in strict confidence. . . . I don't

want to quietly appropriate your good things and pass them off as my own, and I *do* want them in the Osprey. Can we not come to some understanding by which you will furnish a letter, when you feel in the mood, over some pseudonym? I will carefully guard your secret. It might appear as "Our New York Letter"—or from any other place you please. . . . I will give you a column space any kind you like, if you will write just as you do in your letters, and submit just a touch of "sandpapering" if I think best. Be as bright and witty and humorous as you like—and especially be racy, pungent, trenchant. Name *names,* and hit off people and their books regardless, and give us the inside of things, as far as you can go without betraying your personality. . . . Your jewels shall sparkle in appropriate settings, if you but say the word.

It is easier to believe that Coues thought Mrs. Robins would accept his offer. How could she resist a column of her own, in a nationally circulated magazine, with liberty to "hit off people" in her own unique "racy, pungent, trenchant" style? Yet Mrs. Robins did not accept, thus leaving us with the disheartening assurance that her jewels would sparkle—if they did so at all—in other settings. Answering on March 16, Coues said: "No doubt you are right in declining my invitation . . . considering how you are situated in regard to the Audubon Society. . . . Pardon this seemingly curt letter—I am hurried, worried, and not feeling very well today."

Because of the nature of Coues' illness (a malignancy, of which more later), we must presume that he continued to feel increasingly unwell; yet, when addressing Mrs. Robins a few days later, he appeared to be in good spirits:

I suppose you have the March Osprey by this time, and hope the appearance of your charming article ["Behind the Wedding Veil"] is satisfactory. . . .

I shouldn't wonder if the cherub were angry with the Osprey on general principles, let alone your article. The *existence* of the Osprey makes the cherub's wings flutter, *i.e.,* green jealousy. He wrote me a queerly indirect letter, which I hardly understood, about declining to notice the Osprey in Bird-Lore, because, as he avers, of some criticism I passed on Dr. Allen in a matter of nomenclature! Which strikes me on the funnybone! I wrote to him asking him to explain himself, and telling him the Clever Kid[23] would catch him if he didn't watch out, but have heard nothing further. Do you remember what you once told me people would have to do who didn't like things I wrote?

Was Chapman, as Coues implied, smarting with jealousy because of *The Osprey?* Or was the shoe on the other foot? In either event, as

Coues' letter of March 31 to Mrs. Robins proves, Chapman continued
on Coues' mind:

> The cherub *told me* he could not notice the Osprey, because of my
> criticism of Dr. Allen. . . . and I asked him whose initials were on the collar
> he wore. So I suppose the stage is set for a very pretty serio-comedy.
>
> The Osprey seems to have stirred up a hornet's nest. Look where I
> will—except where you and some other sensible people are—I see the
> insects buzzing angrily. I perhaps have thought sometimes that I could
> write a little bit, but I never appreciated the power of the pen before. If Dr.
> Gill (who is the Osprey "Co.") doesn't kill the magazine with his curst
> penuriousness, pretty soon, I can make it a power for pure ornithology of
> the kind that Wilson, Nuttall, Audubon & Baird would understand. . . .
>
> Somehow I feel very much drawn toward you. Would you believe tnat,
> since I have been editing the magazine you and Miss Maria Audubon are
> the only women in America who have written to me about it without
> kicking and clawing me?

We may assume that Coues' incoming mail during the later months
of his editorship of *The Osprey* grew steadily in volume and in protest;
however, being "long used to the clash of arms" and endowed with
more self-assurance than most mortals, he was not easily shaken by
censure. He seems to have felt that if *The Osprey* should fold, the blame
would fall on Gill's shoulders, not his. Conversely, if it should continue,
he would make it a power that the great ornithologists of the past, if
still living, would belabor with praise. And Mrs. Robins, to whom he
felt "very much drawn," would *surely* understand and commend.

A longer interval than usual went by before Coues again (on April
22) addressed himself to Mrs. Robins. Possibly the pain inherent in his
illness had increased. Meanwhile Mrs. Robins had gained information
uncomplimentary to Robert W. Shufeldt:

> . . . Why don't I kill that cursed scoundrel [Shufeldt] who married and
> so shamefully treated poor Florence Audubon[24]—good God—I have been
> trying to do so for two years, and so have many other persons . . . . Two
> years ago Dr. Merriam and I prepared formal charges against him for
> almost unspeakable villainies—quite too indecent to write of to you—and
> he would have been expelled from the A.O.U. had not that coward [J. A.]
> Allen, and his echo, the cherub, basely betrayed me through fear, after
> promising & pledging full support. That was in Nov. 1897. Dr. Shufeldt is
> morally a cancer—the vilest & most depraved wretch I ever knew. His
> former wife committed suicide in an insane asylum to which his brutalities
> had consigned her. The horrors of poor Florence Audubon's situation I
> never saw surpassed.

Enlightening Mrs. Robins further, Coues described Shufeldt's present (third) wife, who at the time of Shufeldt's marriage to Florence Audubon had been their "cook, chambermaid and [Shufeldt's] mistress." As Coues told it, Shufeldt brought his third wife to the last A.O.U. meeting and introduced her to Allen and "a few other flaccid apologists for men."[25]

By the time Coues again (on April 25) wrote to Mrs. Robins, his "review" of Keeler's book had appeared in pages of *The Osprey:*

> . . . Since the April Osprey is so unconscionably delayed, as usual, by the failure, through the sheer penuriousness of the publisher (Dr. Gill) to provide for its publication—and since you are interested in poor Keeler's case, I send you my review of the situation. Please read it with care. It is severe, but not more so than the case requires, and I think its justice will be recognized by all the men—and women too—for whose opinion I care most.
>
> You have got Dr. A and the cherub down to fine dots. Allen is now called "Deacon Ephraim"—because he is wedded to his idols—and is so sanctimonious about it. He is not a bad man, but small and weak. . . . He makes a dogma & ritual of the A.O.U. Code, & constitutes himself the keeper of the seal of the same, to the extent of being personally grieved if any of the MEN choose to have ideas of their own on any canon of nomenclature. . . . An abortion or malformation of a name is sacred if it has been dipped in the drippings of the altar of the A.O.U. . . .

Happily or unhappily, depending on one's viewpoint, we find just one more letter from Coues to Mrs. Robins. It was dated May 6:

> I am glad you thought that review of Keeler's a strong one—certainly I will let you know what Mr. Keeler may say. I suppose the "Cherub & Co." will come gunning for me, but that is of no consequence. I have done my duty to the best of my ability, and they can take it or leave it. . . .
>
> Now talk back, my dear friend, as much and as fast as you please. I can stand it easily—send me some clever thing to work into my May editorial, or get up a parable for the Clever Kid. And in November [at the next A.O.U. congress] we will make things not only "go" but just *hum*—to the delight of our friends and, let us hope, the confusion of those who are not allowed to bask in your radiance.

"Cherub & Co." did not go gunning for Coues, but Gill did, with the result that Coues' days as editor of *The Osprey* were numbered, and so were those of his correspondence with his "dear friend," Mrs. Robins.

The May number of *The Osprey* included, as usual, Coues' two editorial columns, "Editorial Eyrie" and "In the Osprey's Claws," and its masthead displayed, as in the April number, the names of Elliott

Coues, editor; Walter A. Johnson, associate editor; and Louis Agassiz
Fuertes, art editor.

The June issue of *The Osprey*, however, differed conspicuously. It
contained neither the editorial columns nor the names of Coues, Johnson, and Fuertes. The number did carry a brief explanation: "Dr.
Coues has retired from the editorship of THE OSPREY, and Dr. Gill, who
had withdrawn his name from the April and May numbers, assumes
control. All communications of every nature and description—editorial
exchanges, books for review, and business generally—should be addressed hereafter *exclusively* to THE OSPREY CO., 321 and 323 4½ Street,
Washington, D.C."

All too plainly, Coues had been gunned down as editor of *The
Osprey*, little more than six months into the job. Whether Gill fired him
outright, or allowed him the face-saving benefit of resigning, does not
alter the result. In a letter soon afterward to Fuertes, Coues leaves the
impression that the decision to quit the job had been his own: "Last
May, my patience being utterly exhausted . . . I withdrew from the
Osprey, taking you and Johnson off also. I do not know whether there
has been a June number, but learn indirectly that G[ill] intends to start
up a new series of the magazine this month. I shall always be sorry that
I had anything to do with it, and would not touch it again under any
circumstances.[26]

Some years later a well-known scientist, one familiar in general with
the history of *The Osprey*, provided a fuller, more objective explanation
of the Coues-Gill fission: "It might have been expected that under such
able management 'The Osprey' would have prospered, but the combination proved disastrous. Coues who contributed most of the editorials
and supervised the makeup began to treat the magazine as a toy and
evidently soon tired of the routine work. The editorials at first in
humorous vein soon grew sarcastic and became so sharp that Gill,
thoroughly disgusted, withdrew his name from the numbers for April
and May, 1899."[27]

Perhaps the most regrettable feature of the entire Coues-Robins-
Osprey episode was Coues' injudicious and intemperate blast at Allen.
The two men had been friends for some thirty years and had at times
worked closely together, as in the production of *Monographs of North
American Rodentia* and in the formation of the American Ornithologists'
Union. More than once Coues had publicly acknowledged his indebt-
edness to Allen. For example, in his preface to the original (1872)
edition of *Key to North American Birds* he had declared: "I am par-

ticularly indebted to Mr. J. A. Allen, of Cambridge, Massachusetts, who has diligently revised nearly all the proofsheets, and whose critical suggestions have proved invaluable."[28] Also, in his letters to Allen we often find warm expressions of friendship. Writing from Whipple Barracks on May 15, 1881, he said: "Your letters are next best thing to yourself—and if you know the strength and straightforwardness of my friendship for you, you will know how much you are to me."

Why, then, at this stage of his life, did Coues, publicly in *The Osprey* and privately to Mrs. Robins, turn on his friend? The rift between the two probably had its origin in the 1883-85 sessions of the A.O.U. Committee on Classification and Nomenclature. In those meetings Allen's opinions often differed from Coues', particularly over the wording of Canon XL. The rift had widened after Allen had refused to go along with Coues' efforts to oust Shufeldt from the A.O.U. These matters, coupled with Allen's lukewarm review of Keeler's book, served as the perfect pretext for Coues to air his pent-up feelings about Allen.

That Mrs. Robins exerted some kind of captivating influence over Coues seems obvious. Indeed, if in one of her letters to Coues she had not alluded to Keeler, Coues might never have written the "review" so abusive of Allen. And would he, while editor of *The Osprey*, have written anything at all critical of Allen if his health had been sound?

Coues' editorship of *The Osprey* and his correspondence with Mrs. Robins seem to have ended almost simultaneously. Neither added luster to Coues' name. Even if Coues had enjoyed perfect health and had been in full command of his faculties, it is questionable if he would have made a success with *The Osprey*. He lacked such important qualifications as equable temperament and ordered mind, and the ability to contravene the lures of blunt speech and disputation.

NOTES

1. Walter Adam Johnson (1878-1935), publisher, was born in Galesburg, Ill. In addition to founding *The Osprey*, he was involved with such other publications as *Field Illustrated* and *The Garden Digest*.
2. *Dictionary of American Biography* (1931), VII, 286. The treatise on mammals was "Material for a Bibliography of North American Mammals" published in Coues and Allen, *Monographs of North American Rodentia* (1877), Appendix B, 951-1081.
3. For this early history of *The Osprey* see Palmer, "In Memoriam: Theodore Nicholas Gill," 399.
4. Mrs. Robins was also a member of the Academy of Natural Sciences of

Philadelphia, having been elected on Nov. 29, 1898, after Witmer Stone and Samuel Dixon had proposed her. She resigned her membership on Dec. 6, 1904. See *Procs. Acad. Nat. Scis. Phila.*, pt. III (Sept.-Dec., 1898), 481.

5. Coues blamed these troubles on Gill. Writing Jan. 24, 1899, to Witmer Stone, he said: "I have had a hard time of it, with a publisher who does nothing. . . . But I have put another person than our distinguished friend Gill in charge of the business, and hope things will go favorably hereafter."

6. The letters of Coues to Mrs. Robins (and to Witmer Stone) are to be found in the Ms. Collections of the Library of the Academy of Natural Sciences of Philadelphia.

7. The Osprey Company, founded by Gill, had its offices at 321 and 323 4 1/2 St. N.W., Washington, D.C.

8. *Bird-Lore*, an illustrated bimonthly magazine devoted to the study and protection of birds, edited by Frank M. Chapman, was the official organ of the Audubon Societies.

9. Annie Bartram was a granddaughter of John Bartram (1699-1777), celebrated early American botanist.

10. A reference to an article by Coues about Alexander Wilson which had appeared in *Bull. Nutt. Orn. Club*, V (Oct., 1880), 193-204.

11. William Bartram (1739-1823), naturalist, son of John Bartram, and author of *Travels through North & South Carolina, Georgia, East & West Florida* (1799).

12. Mrs. Nellie Blanchan (DeGraff) Doubleday (1865-1918), writer and naturalist, wrote under the pseudonym of Neltje Blanchan. Among her published works: *Birds That Hunt and Are Hunted* (1908) and *Bird Neighbors* (1911).

13. Alexander Lawson (1772-1845), Philadelphia engraver. His engravings of animals are today regarded as the best of those produced during his time.

14. An article by Witmer Stone called "An Old Case of Skins and Its Associations." Writing to Stone on Mar. 12, 1899, Coues said: "Your article on the old case of skins [formerly owned by Edward D. Cope] I read in type yesterday, and it goes in the March number [of *The Osprey*], following a charming one by our friend Mrs. Robins."

15. By "other contents" in this first number of *Bird-Lore*, Coues had in mind such articles as "In Warbler Time" by John Burroughs, "Bird Studies for Children" by Isabel Eaton, and "Our Doorstep Sparrow" by Florence A. Merriam.

16. Charles DeKay (1848-1935), writer and naturalist. His *Bird Gods* was published in 1898 by A. S. Barnes & Co. of New York City.

17. Constantine Samuel Rafinesque (1784-1842), naturalist, was born in Turkey. He came to Philadelphia in 1802. After a period as professor of botany at Transylvania College in Kentucky, he returned to Philadelphia and wrote extensively on many natural history topics.

18. The "lady" was Mabel Osgood Wright, editor of *Bird-Lore's* Audubon Department.

19. Charles Augustus Keeler (1871-1937), naturalist, became director of the California Academy of Sciences. He wrote *Evolution of the Colors of North American Land Birds* (1893) and *Bird Notes Afield, a Series of Essays on the Birds of California* (1899).

20. *Auk*, X (Apr., 1893), 189-95.

21. *Osprey*, III (Apr., 1899), 126-28.

22. Another reference to Mabel Osgood Wright.

23. In at least two or three issues of *The Osprey*, Coues added a sequel to his "Editorial Eyrie," calling it "Parable of the Clever Kid and His Aged Sire."

24. Florence Audubon was a granddaughter of John J. Audubon and a sister of Maria. Both were daughters of John Woodhouse Audubon and his second wife, Caroline Hall Audubon. As to Coues' charges against Shufeldt, they were essentially true; see "Shufeldt v. Shufeldt," 39 *Atlantic Reporter* (1898), 416-21. In his Apr. 25 letter to Mrs. Robins, Coues also told her that after Shufeldt and Florence were divorced, Shufeldt "began to write of her in published articles so vile that had they not been glossed over with a thin guise of medical literature they would have been debarred by statute from the U.S. mails." For one of the articles alluded to, see R. W. Shufeldt, "On the Medico-Legal Aspect of Impotency in Women," *Medico-Legal Journal* (1896), 189-206.

25. In a letter of Apr. 25 to Mrs. Robins, Coues further said of Shufeldt: "He is now under legal restraint, not allowed to leave the District of Columbia by order of the court; also, in the grip of the War Department, which will probably courtmartial & dismiss him for scandalous and outrageous conduct." The War Department, however, did not dismiss Shufeldt from the Army.

26. Boynton, ed., *Fuertes*, 53.

27. Palmer, "In Memoriam: Theodore Nicholas Gill," 399.

28. Coues, *Key to North American Birds*, 5th ed. (1903), I, xxv.

CHAPTER XXVI

Last Trails

In the brief period between 1893 and 1899 Coues had achieved a considerable reputation for historical scholarship, and his reputation has remained a brilliant one to this day. Yet in his own time and ever since, certain of Coues' practices in historical editing have been the target of criticism, some of it entirely justified.

The sin for which he is chiefly remembered is his handwritten interlineations of the texts of priceless manuscripts. The most notorious example of this unconscionable practice was his tampering with the original journals of Lewis and Clark. And he similarly damaged other important manuscript materials. Donald Jackson has noted that Coues' "distinctive, penciled comments . . . are to be found on some of the nation's most valuable documents."[1]

His changing of the prose of the original narratives has also been criticized. Yet Coues' revamping of the accounts of Henry and Larpenteur is at least partly justified. There can be little doubt that the published versions which Coues prepared are more readable than the prose of either of the original authors; Larpenteur himself wanted someone to overhaul his manuscript. Yet we are not certain that Coues was always able to change his author's wording without changing its meaning. And many will agree with the twentieth-century historian Milo Milton Quaife, who believed that Coues should have taken "the care to inform the reader what manner and degree of alterations he had introduced."[2]

Quaife also objected to Coues' "zeal for reconciling seeming discrepancies in the several journals of the [Lewis and Clark] expedition."[3] In their edition of Pike's *Arkansaw Journal* (1932) Archer B. Hulbert and Stephen H. Hart charged Coues with accusing Pike of being a bad geographer and of complicity in the Burr-Wilkinson plot because Coues was unable to square his map with Pike's account.[4]

Coues also censored the language of his authors—a practice that is understandable given the standards of his day. Although he knew the exact Anglo-Saxon words that William Clark had used to describe the sexual aspects of the Mandan buffalo dance, Coues left the passage exactly as Biddle had rendered it—in Latin.[5] In the preface to the Henry-Thompson journals he announced that he had "left the *risqué* passages much as they stand in copy, only Bowdlerizing some expressions that were doubtless currrent in the blunt speech of the trading-post, but would hardly bear print now."[6]

In Coues' own day the critics objected most to what they considered his over-long, often irrelevant footnotes. Frederick Jackson Turner, in reviewing the Henry-Thompson volumes, pronounced many of the notes "worthless."[7] A reviewer of the Pike journals, James Davies Butler, hinted that the frequency and length of Coues' notes for that work resulted from an attempt to make it as bulky and expensive as the edition of Lewis and Clark.[8] No doubt it was this review that caused Coues to tell Francis P. Harper in a letter of June 3, 1896, that he intended to present Butler with a black eye.[9]

Certainly many of Coues' comments in the footnotes were unnecessary. His repeated condemnation of Catholicism offended even Protestant readers.[10] His views on the treatment of the American Indian were ringing, poignant calls for toleration, understanding, and brotherhood with which most intelligent, feeling people will agree. Yet they do not contribute to the scholarly worth of the volumes in which they abound.

Coues used his footnotes to urge that certain western place-names be changed. For example, he insisted that Lemhi Pass be called "Lewis and Clark Pass" and that "the designation be officially enforced—if necessary by an Act of Congress."[11] He informed readers in a footnote in the Pike journals that in the 1890s Pike's Peak was "a convenient place [for tourists] to leave as soon as they have paid twenty-five cents for a cup of the worst coffee in the world."[12] Although he seldom expressed political opinions in any of his writings, he used footnotes in his historical works to announce his disagreement with the protective tariff[13] and to blast America's overseas imperialism.[14]

2

With all of these faults and shortcomings, is Coues entitled to respect as a historian of the American West? Emphatically, yes. After acknowledging that Coues had tampered with the spelling and grammar of the Biddle edition of Lewis and Clark and that he had shamefully mistreated the original journals, Donald Jackson put the case well when he answered his own rhetorical question, "What, then, makes Coues a good editor?"

> The amazing breadth of his information. His leisurely, almost gossipy, annotation is complete and generally accurate. His close attention to the rivers, creeks, and landmarks is partly the result of his personal knowledge of the area, partly the product of careful collating of maps. His attention to natural history arises from his lifelong dedication to the subject and from a boyish delight in flora and fauna that is evident in his notations. He is less at home with botany and ethnology than with zoology, but draws upon authoritative sources when his own knowledge wanes.[15]

Coues expressed his own opinion on his greatest asset as a researcher and writer: "If I could venture to agree even a little with some of my most partial friends, who think I have any genius, I should think that, if so, it is simply the genius of hard work—which I suppose amounts to holding down the chair at my desk for long periods and capacity for taking great pains with every detail of the work I have in hand."[16]

Two other persons, who were in positions to know, concur with this assessment. Francis P. Harper wrote that "he had a capacity for work that was almost beyond belief."[17] Mary Emily Coues told a correspondent that a characteristic remark by her husband was: "Now, I have finished that piece of writing. I have begun another."[18]

Other qualities noted by his contemporaries were his determination to discover historical truth and to expose falsity. One of the many admirers of his historical labors wrote that "he was human enough to love and hate—to love the true and to hate the sham."[19] His dedication to accuracy led him to point out his own errors. After mentioning in a footnote to the Henry-Thompson journals that he had misidentified someone in his edition of Lewis and Clark, he remarked, "My only consolation is that I have sinned in goodly and numerous company, and can now make amends, as no critic has found me out thus far."[20] In a footnote to the Larpenteur narrative identifying Sir William Stuart, he confessed that the title of a book written by Stuart was "one of a great many things I do not know."[21]

The pursuit of truth convinced him of the essentialness of first-hand materials: "Among my beliefs is that of the prime utility of contemporaneous documents for historical purposes. These are the great antiseptics to the ptomaines of tradition—the stocky facts so fatal to mythopoetic microbes."[22] The reverence expressed here for "contemporaneous documents" does not, at first glance, square with Coues' scribbling upon manuscripts. Yet there is no real contradiction. Coues obviously had little awe for them as physical objects; he valued them for the information they yielded.

Ironically, Coues did not consider himself a historian: "I wish to do my share as a curator of historical materials, even if I may not aspire to the office of historian."[23] His treatment of the documents gives added irony to the self-designation of "curator of historical materials."

Coues' strengths as a scholar of western American history were the same ones he possessed and used as a scientist, and his scientific background gave him a dimension most historians lack. As Frances F. Victor, a gifted contemporary of Coues, wrote: ". . . through his researches in natural history, which led him to explore wilderness regions, he became a historian of more than ordinary value, for he was never satisfied with work until he had gone to the very bottom of the subject."[24]

Another of Coues' admirers was the California editor and author Charles F. Lummis, who wrote in 1900: "There will be no other editions of Lewis and Clark, Zebulon Pike, Fowler, Larpenteur; and the monumental works of Coues are definitive. . . ."[25] Lummis's generous judgment was premature. As we have seen, the original journals of Lewis and Clark were published soon after Coues' death, and Jackson's edition of Pike, which has a far better claim to definitiveness than does the Coues version, appeared in 1966.

Another edition of Larpenteur's autobiography, prepared by Quaife, came out in 1933. Although the text was "an almost literal reprint" of the Coues edition, Quaife supplied his own "Historical Introduction," corrected a handful of Coues' errors, changed some of the capitalization, and substituted his own annotation for what he felt were Coues' "voluminous and frequently much-too-rambling foot-notes."[26] In 1965 John Galvin published his edition of another version of the Garcés diary which turned up after Coues' death.[27] In 1970 Raymond W. and Mary Lund Settle and Harry R. Stevens reissued Coues' edition of the Fowler journal, to which they supplied some additional annotation, a new index, and a few other minor changes.[28] A work which Lummis did not include in his list of Coues "definitive" works is, oddly enough, the only one which has not yet been re-edited, the Henry-Thompson journals.[29]

Despite the fact that most of Coues' historical works have been superseded or enlarged upon, the editors of the later, more complete

versions of these narratives are unanimous in their belief in the enduring value of the editorial skills of Elliott Coues. In his admirable one-
volume condensation of the Thwaites edition of Lewis and Clark,
Bernard De Voto stated: "We have no greater editor than Coues."[30]

3

In the course of his historical researches Coues sought help from a
number of knowledgeable persons. Among the many who gave him
valuable information and insights (and whom he gratefully thanked in
his prefaces) were Alfred J. Hill, John Wesley Powell, Charles Aldrich,
Reuben T. Durrett, Edward D. Neill, Frederick W. Hodge,[31] Jacob V.
Brower, Washington Matthews, and Henry A. Boller.[32]

Virtually all of these people were in turn aided by Coues. The
outstanding example of this sort of fruitful reciprocation was the
relationship between Coues and Hiram M. Chittenden (1858-1917). In
the early 1890s Chittenden, then a lieutenant in the Corps of Engineers,
became acquainted with Coues, who thanked the young officer in the
preface to the Pike journals for providing some sort of information.
The two men began corresponding regularly, resulting in Coues' encouragement of Chittenden's researches into western history.[33]

The first book from Chittenden's pen was *The Yellowstone National
Park* (1895). He later described Coues' role in bringing the book into
print: "I was quite astonished at his willingness to help me for he was
himself buried deep in his own historical work. His interest ran beyond
mere answers to my questions and seemed to extend to myself."[34]

Coues lent the same kind of support to the writing of Chittenden's
masterwork, *The American Fur Trade of the Far West* (1902). This monumental study was published by Francis P. Harper, who, as Chittenden
freely acknowledged, "may not so readily have taken over the publication of my work had it not been for the confidence of Dr. Coues."[35] In
his contract with Harper for the publication of *The Life, Letters and
Travels of Father Pierre-Jean de Smet* (1904), Chittenden agreed to
Harper's stipulation that the work be modeled after the Coues edition
of the Lewis and Clark journals.[36] As he matured as a scholar,
Chittenden was able to extend more valuable information and thoughts
to Coues. For example, he persuaded Coues to modify his harsh
evaluation of Washington Irving's *The Astorians*.[37]

4

Of the several possibilities available for Coues to bring out as number three of the American Explorers Series, he chose a manuscript entitled *Diario of Padre Fray Francisco Garcés*. The diary of the eighteenth-century Spanish Franciscan covered his missionary journey with the expedition of Juan Bautista de Anza[38] from Sonora through modern-day Arizona and California in 1775-76.

In Coues' day three variant forms of the Garcés diary were known to exist. The first was a handwritten copy, probably prepared for archival purposes and perhaps taken from Garcés's original holograph (which, if it exists, has never surfaced), which was donated to the Bureau of American Ethnology in 1897 by the Mexican historian Dr. Nicolas León.[39] This version, entrusted to Coues on April 30, 1898, 1898, by Frederick W. Hodge, distinguished ethnologist and a member of the bureau's staff, was the one that Coues translated and edited for publication.

After he had translated it, two other versions were made known to him: another manuscript copy, which was the property of Dr. León; and a published version, a badly done Mexican imprint of 1854. Coues decided to continue to work with the first version because he had already translated it and because it was "the most perfect one [of the three variant texts] besides being the official or archival one, and the one which nobody has hitherto utilized for any purpose."[40] The other two versions proved useful in Coues' annotation and for filling in a few gaps in the first version.[41]

Coues' other adventures in historical editing had involved the travel accounts of English-speaking, nineteenth-century figures. This time he was dealing with an eighteenth-century Spanish document. Coues scrupulously rendered Garcés's words into the closest nineteenth-century equivalents.[42] Although he was not particularly well versed in Spanish, his general facility with languages (so evident in his bibliographical works) allowed him to make an adequate translation of Garcés's words. His skills as a lexicographer were no doubt also useful to him in this endeavor.

Since the author of the narrative was a dedicated agent of an institution Coues detested, the Roman Catholic church, it is not surprising that he rarely passed up an opportunity to castigate and ridicule Catholicism in the footnotes of his edition of the Garcés diary. Yet he came to respect the courage and commitment of the doughty cleric.

In the course of editing his translation of the diary, the narrative of another priest traveling with the Anza expedition, Pedro Font (d. 1781), was brought to Coues' attention, probably by George Parker

Winship,[43] librarian of the John Carter Brown library at Providence, where the Font manuscript was housed. Coues believed Font to embody all of the worst elements of his religion; unlike Garcés, Font was totally unable to enlist Coues' sympathies. Yet he found Font's account useful for footnoting purposes (just as David Thompson's journal had been helpful for footnoting the Henry narrative). In fact, Coues found the data contained in Font's diary so illuminating that he had his secretary, Mary B. Anderson, prepare a typewritten copy[44] and announced that he would edit it for inclusion in the American Explorers Series. He also stated his intention of preparing an edition of the report of Fray Silvestre Veléz de Escalante for the same series.[45]

Since we have virtually no correspondence between Coues and Harper in this period, and only a couple of entries for 1898 and 1899 in the "Book of Dates," we have no clear notion of Coues' progress in bringing the Garcés diary into print. Yet there are a few records relating to what must have been the most remarkable phase of his research on Garcés.

Some time in early July, 1899, Coues, his wife, Hodge, Winship, Albert J. Bird, William H. Guilford,[46] and A. C. Vroman,[47] the noted California photographer, all converged in Santa Fe. According to the *Santa Fe New Mexican* of July 11, Coues and his wife were staying at the Palace Hotel. The group had gathered there in order to travel together through New Mexico, for purposes described in John Wesley Powell's annual report (1899-1900) as director of the Bureau of American Ethnology: "The journey was so planned as to touch the less known pueblos of the plateau country and vallies of New Mexico and Arizona and to obtain data relating to social organization, migrations, and customs, as well as typical photographs of individuals, habitations, etc. All of the existing pueblos of New Mexico were visited and many of the ruins. The trip yielded a large body of data for incorporation in the reports [of the bureau], especially in the Cyclopedia of Native tribes."[48]

The members of the group were each pursuing related but separate topics of research. According to Powell, Coues had been made a member of the party "by reason of his intimate acquaintance with the early records, and also in the hope that he might be able to discover unpublished manuscripts [relative to Garcés and his contemporaries] among the ancient archives of the missions. . . . Although no noteworthy discoveries of manuscripts were made, a considerable body of data essential to the discussion of social organization in the pueblo region was obtained." Powell further recorded that Coues "was brought in frequent touch with ethnologists and ethnologic problems, thereby acquiring extended and accurate knowledge of the aborigines."[49] Coues described his own objective as "a still hunt for old Spanish MSS."[50]

By the end of July the scholar-adventurers had traveled out of Santa Fe to the following pueblos and other localities of interest in the Rio Grande valley between Albuquerque and Taos: Santa Cruz, San Juan, Embudo, Taos, Cantonment Burgwin,[51] Picuris, Espanola, Santa Clara, San Ildefonso, Pojoaque, Nambe, and Tesuque.[52] According to the August 29, 1899, *Daily Evening Star* of Pasadena (Vroman's home town), "They found the ruins of Cibolitta [Cebolleta?] Valley and of the Santa Clara canyon the most interesting, being the best preserved." The trip into Santa Clara canyon took place in late July and lasted ten days.[53]

On August 6, when Coues, Hodge, and Winship were traveling by rail to Albuquerque, they were joined at Bernalillo by Charles F. Lummis. They arrived at Albuquerque in the evening and the men talked long into the night in the office of the European Hotel, while little Turbesé, Lummis's daughter, slept on the floor. In the early morning of August 7 they all boarded the train for the pueblo of Isleta (twelve miles south of Albuquerque), to visit Lummis's old friend Juan Rey Arbeita and his family.[54]

After arriving at Arbeita's home, they slept in the patio in their field bedding,[55] and the next morning they were treated to a splendid breakfast. Lummis later described the pleasant occasion:

> . . . we sat under rustling cottonwoods in the land we all loved and all had earned the right to love—Dr. Elliott Coues, the fresh-faced, gray-bearded dean; and Frederick Webb Hodge, the serious hero of the Enchanted Mesa and all it means,[56] and probably the logical successor to the dean's mantle as our foremost scientific editor; and George Parker Winship, the young giant of the MSS; and the Cowboy-who-Cares [Lummis]; and the little girl who was born to the care [Turbesé]. Comadre 'Pita[57] stood massive behind our chairs and waved away the flies, and urged us (who had no need of urging) to despoil her cherished chickens and Tuyo's [Arbeita's son] pet squabs and the golden-brown *supapillas* [*sopapillas*]; with that look on her face which would make any woman on earth fair to look upon. *All* was good—the delicious hospitality of the Indian friends whose faces beamed on all for the one's sake; and the New Mexican sky, unsullied as Truth; and the touch of men that had toiled for the same Truth's sake and now were met where it was best to meet.[58]

Vroman materialized from somewhere and took pictures of the gathering at Arbeita's, as well as of other scenes at Isleta. Hodge and Coues took the evening train, perhaps to Santa Fe, while the others remained for a time at Isleta.[59] Vroman took photographs of most of the pueblos and villages Coues and his colleagues visited during the summer of 1899, as well as Cochiti, Santo Domingo, Santa Ana, Acoma, and Zuni.[60] We assume that the other members of the party, Coues included, traveled to these points with Vroman.

By August 29, Coues was back in Santa Fe. Shortly thereafter he and Mrs. Coues (who had remained in the New Mexican capital while her husband had been making his visits to the pueblos) were among the guests at a reception given by Governor and Mrs. Miguel A. Otero.[61] Sometime before they left Santa Fe, Coues, Hodge, Winship, and Vroman posed with Amado Chaves for a group photograph.[62]

We can only imagine the discussions of the comrades as they sat about the campfires in the deserts and mountains of their beloved Southwest, but we can be certain that the exchanges of information and ideas were exhilarating indeed.

5

We hope that Coues in particular got every conceivable ounce of pleasure out of these stimulating conversations and New Mexico excursions because he was suffering great physical pain. He was, in fact, a dying man.

His suffering came from two sources. For the past seven years he had been increasingly troubled by a diverticulum (a pouch opening out of a tubular organ) in his esophagus, which made breathing and swallowing difficult and was also causing him to regurgitate around a pint and a half of material a day. In bed the condition became worse, so much so that he was forced to lie on his abdomen. The second source of pain was rectal, about which more later.[63]

As early as 1893 he had been told that he had not long to live. As he said in a letter of December 17 of that year to J. A. Allen, "There is no question that I am sick; specialist in Chicago told me I had but a few weeks to live, with stricture of the oesophagus—but I don't believe him, and propose to prove his diagnosis mistaken specifically—though unhappily there is a well marked 'subspecies' of trouble in my swallow, which has been developing for a couple of years as a result of the grippe." A few days later he wrote optimistically to Allen that he expected "to beat the Doctor yet!" Nevertheless the malady became aggravated over the years. And by 1899 there developed a second source of agony for Coues: difficulty in having bowel movements.

After what Allen later described as "a month of acute suffering in Santa Fe,"[64] Coues started homeward with his wife on October 5. The stopover in Chicago was perhaps made because Coues sensed that this was the last time he would be able to see his sister Lucy and her family. While in Chicago he was visited by D. G. Elliot, who later described the last talks with his old friend:

> He was greatly changed in appearance, but the old fire and enthusiasm, that I had so often admired and not infrequently contended with in friendly conflict during so many years, was not a whit abated, and he spoke with all his old time interest of the work he had himself in view and of that of others. But the voice was feeble and the frame was weak, and he was filled with a restlessness that was foreign to him. But when I bade him adieu, which was to be our last on earth, he was cheerful and spoke hopefully of meeting soon again.[65]

On December 4 he entered Johns Hopkins Hospital in Baltimore. Just before going there he began informing those closest to him of his grave condition. To Allen he wrote: "The friendship of half a lifetime cannot be killed at this late day, and I am sure you will be sorry to hear that my disease is desperate. I go to Johns Hopkins tomorrow, for the formidable surgical operation which seems to offer some hope of saving my life."[66] While in the hospital he steadfastly continued preparing the Garcés diary for publication—revising the last proofs and writing the introduction.[67] Fortunately, Hodge had agreed to supply much of the anthropological annotation, thus relieving Coues of work that would have further taxed his weakened body.

On December 5 he returned the corrected proof of one of his contributions to the *Nation*, to which he added a handwritten message: "I am to be knifed to-morrow A.M., and—I am unmoved."[68] His courage is better shown by something else he penned that day:

> The Last Will and Testament of Elliott Coues, executed in Johns Hopkins Hospital, at Baltimore Md., This fifth day of December, 1899.
> I, Elliott Coues, being of sound disposing mind and about to undergo a certain surgical operation, do hereby give and bequeath all my property, of whatever name and nature, unto my beloved wife, Mary Emily Coues, whom I hereby appoint my sole executrix.
>
> Elliott Coues[69]

Affixing their signatures to this document as witnesses were Harvey W. Cushing and William S. Baer. Cushing (1869-1930), who

later achieved fame as a neurosurgeon at Harvard, would on the
following day assist the hospital's chief surgeon, William Stewart
Halsted (1853-1922) in operating on Coues. Baer (1872-1931) was a
pioneer in the use of maggots for healing wounds and is best remembered for his work with crippled children. Thus Coues was receiving the attention of three of the most eminent medical men of that
day.

The hospital's records show that Coues had been admitted because
of the trouble with his bowels. Prior to his operation, an examination by
the attending surgeons had revealed that he had a large rectal car-
cinoma: cancer of the rectum. The surgery (an exploratory laparotomy)
was performed on schedule, December 6, by Halsted and Cushing.
After locating a number of metastases, they concluded that the
malignancy was inoperable. Yet they were able to lessen the discomfort
of their doomed patient by relieving (by means of a colostomy) the
bowel obstruction.

Now that he was fully aware that his condition was fatal, Coues
hoped for at least a brief reprieve in order to see the Garcés diary
through the press. Because Coues insisted and because his physical
condition was deteriorating from his inability to eat and sleep properly,
it was decided to attempt a second operation, to remove the esophageal
diverticulum.

From his own experience as a man of medicine, Coues knew that
his chances of surviving the ordeal were slim. Nevertheless, he was
determined to test the odds.[70] The operation was performed, again by
Halsted and Cushing, on December 24. The surgery resulted in pneumonia. Death came the following afternoon, on Christmas Day, 1899.
While dying, did he recall the words he had written several years
earlier? "Who is ever quite ready for the last? What pang is taken away
when the cry it extorts is drowned in a sea of like lamentation. We
theorize best before the Falcon's talon strikes."[71]

According to some obituaries, Coues' passing was dramatic: After
lying in a coma for several hours, he was reported to have "raised
himself in bed, and with all the old time vigor of voice exclaimed,
'Welcome! oh, welcome, beloved death.'"[72]

Following a complete autopsy, Coues' remains were transfered to a
receiving vault at Arlington National Cemetery, where on May 29, 1900,
his body was interred. The location of his grave was described as being
north of the main road, between the Fort Myer entrance and Arlington
(Custis) Mansion.[73]

NOTES

1. Jackson, ed., *Journals of Zebulon Montgomery Pike*, I, 136n.
2. Quaife, ed., *Forty Years a Fur Trader on the Upper Missouri: The Personal Narrative of Charles Larpenteur, 1833-1872* (Chicago: Lakeside Press, 1933), xx-xxi.
3. Quaife, ed., *The Journals of Captain Meriwether Lewis and Sergeant John Ordway* (Madison: State Historical Society of Wisconsin, 1916), 146-47n.
4. Hart and Hulbert, eds., *Zebulon Pike's Arkansaw Journal* (Denver: Denver Public Library, 1932), 137n. Supposedly General James Wilkinson and former vice-president Aaron Burr plotted either an invasion of Mexico or the detachment of the southwestern portion of the Louisiana Territory shortly after the latter was acquired from France.
5. Coues-Biddle (1893), I, 221-22.
6. Coues, ed., *Henry-Thompson Journals* (1897), I, xix.
7. Turner review of *Henry-Thompson Journals* in *American Historical Review*, III (Oct., 1897), 159.
8. Butler review of *The Expeditions of Zebulon Montgomery Pike* in *American Historical Review*, I (Jan., 1896), 363.
9. In another letter to Harper, Jan. 8, 1896, Coues called Butler a "driveling old idiot."
10. A. W. Greely review of *The Expeditions of Zebulon Montgomery Pike* in *Nation*, LXI (Nov. 28, 1895), 392.
11. Coues-Biddle, II, 550-51n.
12. Coues, ed., *The Expeditions of Zebulon Montgomery Pike* (1895), II, 456n.
13. *Ibid.*, I, 277n.
14. Coues, ed., *On the Trail of a Spanish Pioneer* (1900), II, 470n.
15. Jackson, ed., *Letters of the Lewis and Clark Expedition with Related Documents, 1783-1854* (Urbana: University of Illinois Press, 1962), 676.
16. Coues, ed., *On the Trail of a Spanish Pioneer*, I, xxvii-xxxix.
17. *Ibid.*, viii.
18. Victor, "Dr. Elliott Coues" (1900), 191.
19. Lummis, "Lost—A Man" (1900), 163-64.
20. Coues, ed., *Henry-Thompson Journals*, I, 425n.
21. Coues, ed., *Forty Years a Fur Trader* (1898), I, 17n.
22. *Ibid.*, xvi.
23. *Ibid.*
24. Victor, "Dr. Elliott Coues," 189.
25. Lummis, "Lost—A Man," 163. Charles Fletcher Lummis (1859-1928), author and editor, lived among the Pueblo Indians of New Mexico and wrote several books, including *Land of Poco Tiempo* (1893). He was founder and editor of *Land of Sunshine* (later changed to *Out West*), and he established the Southwest Museum in Los Angeles.
26. Quaife, ed., *Forty Years a Fur Trader*, xxiii.
27. Galvin, ed., *A Record of Travels in Arizona and California, 1775-1776* (San Francisco: John Howell Books, 1965).

28. This edition was published by the University of Nebraska Press.

29. This work was, however, reprinted in 1965 by Ross & Haines, Inc., of Minneapolis. That year the same firm reprinted Coues' edition of Pike.

30. De Voto, ed., *The Journals of Lewis and Clark* (Boston: Houghton Mifflin, 1953), ix.

31. Frederick Webb Hodge (1864-1956) was long one of the leading ethnologists of the United States. His major contribution was the *Handbook of American Indians North of Mexico* (1907-10). From 1931 to 1955 he was director of the Southwest Museum.

32. Henry A. Boller (1836-1902) graduated from the University of Pennsylvania in 1856. He worked as a clerk in the western fur trade (for a time with Larpenteur) and wrote *Among the Indians: Eight Years in the Far West, 1858-1866* (1867).

33. Gordon B. Dodds, *Hiram Martin Chittenden: His Public Career* (Lexington: University of Kentucky Press, 1973), 20, 74, 76, 77, 80, 93.

34. Bruce Le Roy, ed., *H. M. Chittenden: A Western Epic; Being Selections from His Unpublished Journals, Diaries and Reports* (Tacoma: Washington State Historical Society, 1961), 81.

35. *Ibid.*, 82-83.

36. Dodds, *Hiram Martin Chittenden*, 93.

37. Chittenden, *The American Fur Trade of the Far West*, 2 vols. (Stanford, Calif.: Academic Reprints, 1954), I, 246.

38. Juan Bautista de Anza (b. 1735) commanded a Spanish military expedition in 1774 to estabish an overland supply route from Sonora to Monterey. A second expedition in 1775-76, upon which he was accompanied by Garcés and Font, resulted in his selection of the site for a presidio and mission at San Francisco Bay.

39. León (1854-1927) wrote much on the history of Mexico and of medicine. At one time he was the director of the Museo Michoacano.

40. Coues, ed., *On the Trail of a Spanish Pioneer*, I, xiv-xv.

41. *Ibid.*, xvi-xx.

42. *Ibid.*, xx-xxi.

43. Winship (1871-1952) wrote several works on the history of Spanish exploration in North America, for example, *The Coronado Expedition* (1896), and on the history of printing. Later in his career he was the curator of the Widener Collection at Harvard.

44. At the Bancroft Library, University of California, Berkeley, we examined a 672-page typescript, copied in 1907 by Gertrude Redit from Mrs. Anderson's transcription of Font's diary. Font's diary was later translated and annotated by Herbert E. Bolton and makes up the fourth volume of Bolton's *Anza's California Expeditions* (1930).

45. Coues, ed., *On the Trail of a Spanish Pioneer*, I, 58n; II, 471n. Escalante (fl. 1768-79), a Spanish Franciscan, in 1776-77 explored the Great Basin in company with Fray Francisco Atanasio Dominquez, reaching Utah Lake. Herbert E. Bolton's *Pageant in the Wilderness* (1951) contains Escalante's "Diary and Itinerary" in translation. The most recent version is *The Dominquez-Escalante Journal: Their Expedition through Colorado, Utah, Arizona, and New*

Mexico in 1776, trans. Fray Angelico Chavez and ed. Ted J. Warner (Provo, Utah: Brigham Young University Press, 1976).

46. We have no information on either Bird or Guilford, except for the facts given in the *Santa Fe New Mexican,* July 28, 1899, that Bird was from Rochelle, Ill., and Guilford was from Oregon, Ill.

47. Adam Clark Vroman (1856-1916), book collector, bookseller, amateur archeologist, and photographer, performed some of the most significant work in photographing southwestern Indians, especially from 1895 to 1904.

48. *Twenty-first Annual Report of the Bureau of American Ethnology* . . .(Washington, D.C.: Government Printing Office, 1903), x-xi. The "Cyclopedia" is probably Hodge's *Handbook,* then in preparation.

49. *Ibid.,* xxii, xxxviii.

50. Elliot, "In Memoriam: Elliott Coues," 9.

51. Cantonment Burgwin, located ten miles south of Taos, was a regular Army post established in 1852 and abandoned in 1860.

52. *Santa Fe New Mexican,* July 28, 1899.

53. Mahood, ed., *Photographer of the Southwest* (1961), 24.

54. Entry for Aug. 6, 1899, Diary of Charles F. Lummis, Southwest Museum, Los Angeles. We are indebted to Keith Lummis for translating (from Spanish) the information from his father's diary and transmitting it to us.

55. Entry for Aug. 7, 1899, Lummis Diary.

56. In 1897 Hodge proved that, contrary to the assertion of another authority, there had been early human habitation of this famous New Mexico landmark.

57. Probably a member or friend of Arbeita's family. *Comadre* means both godmother and close female friend. 'Pita is a common designation for Lupita, a diminutive of Lupe, which in turn is derived from Guadalupe.

58. Lummis, "Lost—A Man," 159.

59. Entry for Aug. 7, 1899, Lummis Diary.

60. Mahood, ed., *Photographer of the Southwest,* 71-72, 111-13; William Webb and Robert A. Weinstein, *Dwellers at the Source: Southwestern Indian Photographs of A. C. Vroman* (New York: Grossman Publishers, 1973), 123-25, 144-46.

61. *Santa Fe New Mexican,* Aug. 29, Sept. 2, 1899.

62. Mahood, ed., *Photographer of the Southwest,* 113. Amado Chaves (1851-1930), lawyer, businessman, and legislator. In 1891 he became the territory's first superintendent of public instruction.

63. Except when otherwise noted, information on the medical history of Coues' last days has been kindly supplied to us in a letter of May 20, 1975, by Dr. Thomas B. Turner, Office of the Archives, the Johns Hopkins Medical Institutions, Baltimore.

64. [Allen], "Elliott Coues" (1900), 6.

65. Elliot, "In Memoriam: Elliott Coues," 9-10.

66. Quoted in Hellman, *Bankers, Bones and Beetles,* 107.

67. Coues, ed., *On the Trail of a Spanish Pioneer,* I, vii.

68. [Allen], "Elliott Coues," 7.

69. A Xerox copy of Coues' will was provided to us by the Office of the Register of Wills, Clerk of the Probate Court, U.S. District Court for the District of Columbia, Washington, D.C.

70. [Allen], "Elliott Coues," 7.

71. Coues, *Birds of the Northwest* (1874), 350.

72. Elliot, "In Memoriam: Elliott Coues," 10.

73. *Auk*, XXXVI (Oct., 1919), 633; *Osprey*, IV (June, 1900), 160. We are obliged to Colonel Terry E. Rowe for supplying the current designation of the location of Coues' grave at Arlington Cemetery: Section la, Grave no. 473.

POSTLUDE

Elliott Coues may well have had himself in mind when he wrote of William Clark's multifaceted career: "The world is slow to concede the greatness of any man in more than one thing."[1] Certainly Coues' brilliance and energy allowed him to achieve spectacularly in many callings; yet it was as an ornithologist that he was best known in his own day and is best remembered in later years.

His friend D. G. Elliot stated it well: "Although Coues gained a prominent position in various branches of natural science, and in literature as well, he was, above all, an ornithologist. From his earliest youth he loved birds, and delighted to talk about them and argue the various questions that a discussion of them gave rise to. His mind was always dwelling on them, and he never lost an opportunity to speak of his favorite subject."[2]

Coues was not one of those persons whose greatness was discovered long after his death. His contemporaries recognized it and readily acknowledged it. In recalling his visit to the United States in 1887-88, the distinguished British scientist Alfred Russel Wallace wrote: "Among my earliest acquaintances [in Washington] was Dr. Elliott Coues, a man of brilliant talents, wide culture, and delightful personality, with whose ideas I had much in common, and with whom I soon became intimate. He was not only a practical but highly philosophical biologist, and was equally interested with myself in psychical research." Wallace further described Coues as "a man of the mental calibre of Huxley with the charming personality of Mivart."[3]

In the assessments of his life and work, one of his attributes stands out particularly: "Dr. Coues's capacity for work," wrote J. A. Allen, "was enormous—indeed phenomenal if we consider his sedentary habits and disregard of the ordinary precautions of health—and the wonder is that he for so many years maintained a voluminous correspondence, writing with his own hand many letters of great length, in a style peculiarly brilliant and spicy—in short, *Couesian*."[4]

An anonymous obituary appearing in the British ornithological journal *The Ibis* gave a similar evaluation:

A perfect glutton for work, Coues never neglected an opportunity offered by his service on the coast or on the frontier; and after making every allowance for "devilling," with regard to the references in such books as "The Birds of the Northwest" and the various installments of "The Bibliography of Ornithology," even then his personal work must have been prodigious. Every successive edition of his "Key to North American Birds" marked epochs in ornithological progress, while the mere list of his contributions to science would fill at least a copy of our pages. And, be it remarked, all this work was solid, and not vamped up to swell the total, as is too often the case at the present day.[5]

His contemporaries regarded him highly not only as an able producer of monographs but also as an author of scientific works that were intelligible to laymen. Allen described him as "a writer of exceptional facility of expression and rare vivacity and readability."[6] According to William Hosea Ballou (writing in 1879), "The works of Dr. Coues have doubtless attracted more attention from the secular press than those of any other scientist who has written on natural history with the exception of Agassiz."[7] His staunch admirer Charles F. Lummis expressed the same sentiments in even more glowing terms: "Such a man never would have dried up to the proverbial scientific mummy. He humanized whatever he did without sacrifice of exactness. No one surpassed him in esoteric equipment; and as a 'readable' scientist he was easily unrivaled."[8]

Coues would have been pleased with such praise, because he was convinced that it was desirable for scientists to reach the widest possible audience. The popularizer, he wrote, was "an office of not less dignity than that of the systematist or monographer, one of practical importance and human interest, and one not so easy to fill creditably as those who have never tried to do so may imagine. The increase in knowledge is one thing, and its diffusion is another; but the latter is the real measure of the usefulness of the former."[9]

He was also remembered by his colleagues as a skilled and formidable critic. D. G. Elliot's assessment of Coues as a reviewer of scientific writings was doubtless shared by the great majority of ornithologists of the time:

As a critic in certain lines he was unrivaled and exhibited the highest practice of the art in his reviews, dwelling most upon what was meritorious in the treatment of the subject before him, for he believed true criticism was to seek that which was praiseworthy rather than something to condemn. But no one could be more caustic in his treatment, nor wield a sharper weapon, when he found that praise would be misapplied and it would be kinder to act as the skillful surgeon does, create wounds in order that the patient's recovery might be more sure and lasting.[10]

Allen expressed a similar view of Coues' critical writings but added a truth often avoided by his other obituarists: "As an antagonist he was sometimes bitter and unforgiving. . . . He was impulsive and sometimes indiscreet, having some of the failings that usually accompany genius."[11]

In spite of what Allen called "his sedentary habits," Coues was no "closet" ornithologist. His works sparkle largely because he was a skilled observer and collector of birds in the field. Donald Culross Peattie pointed out that although Coues "belonged to the moderns because he was a sound anatomist, systematist, critic, and self-critic . . . he partakes of Audubon's era because he too knew bird life in an almost primeval condition," especially in the Far West.[12] In partial testimony to his abilities as a field naturalist, the Smithsonian Institution reported in 1894 that through the years Coues had donated 2,383 specimens to the National Museum.[13]

2

The high esteem in which Coues' ornithological contributions were held by most of his contemporaries has continued among scientists of the twentieth century. Writing in 1931, Casey A. Wood stated flatly that Coues was "in many respects . . . the most brilliant writer on vertebrate zoology America has so far produced."[14]

Attesting to the value of Coues' more important ornithological publications, particularly his *Key to North American Birds,* "Ornithological Bibliography," and the second edition (1882) of the *Check List of North American Birds,* is the use of them by ornithologists today.

One scientist has written: "[The] *Key to North American Birds* is still regarded as a classic, one to which careful students refer when all other sources fail them."[15] Another has said: "I have referred to this book [the *Key*] frequently, and I recall that Dr. [Thomas Saddler] Roberts when writing his 'Birds of Minnesota' often spoke about finding material in the introductory section which he could find nowhere else."[16]

A third scientist has written:

> Dr. Coues has always been one of my favorite ornithologists, not just from the scientific viewpoint, but from the personal as well. I have used the 2d (1882) *Check List* extensively, as I am interested in the derivation and meaning of scientific names. I have received many pleasurable moments

from this volume. I have the 5th (1903) edition of the *Key to North American Birds* and I consider 'Part I, Field Ornithology' . . . one of the most delightful pieces of writing I have ever sampled, scientific or otherwise. I have also derived some interesting and astute natural history data from Coues' [other books], and have just recently cited one of his observations on the Western Meadowlark, contained in *Birds of the Northwest.*[17]

One of the country's leading bird artists has stated: "The work that I consult, almost every day, is not the fine Coues *Key*, but the *Coues Check List.* . . . That work I find truly indispensable, despite its being out of date. Coues' knowledge of etymology was truly vast, and his comments on scientific names of birds were unfailingly interesting—if not downright entertaining. . . . Coues' attitude toward ornithology (toward all things, in fact) has always intrigued me; at times it has inspired me."[18]

Yet another ornithologist, after taking a survey of several ornithologists at the Smithsonian Institution "as to the current value of the various Coues publications," found: "[The *Check List*] is still useful although inevitably some of the genera are no longer valid. The Bibliography is also still worthwhile, particularly if one is aiming at completeness in a history of a bird and distribution studies. [The *Key, Birds of the Northwest*, and *Birds of the Colorado Valley*] were very valuable in their day and as such were used by subsequent ornithologists to help erect the present noble edifice of Ornithology."[19]

In 1972 the compiler of an ambitious undertaking in ornithological bibliography dedicated his first volume "To the memory of Dr. Elliott Coues, nearly the first and certainly the greatest of ornithological bibliographers."[20]

A final tribute to Coues' greatness comes from the pen of a distinguished ornithologist, Dean Amadon:

> Elliott Coues, a gifted scientist and brilliant stylist, will always retain his rank as one of the greatest of ornithologists. This was reflected in 1972 when the American Ornithologists' Union established a citation of merit for innovative work in that science to be called the Coues Award. Three works in particular brought Coues eminence in ornithology: *Birds of the Northwest, Birds of the Colorado Valley*, and *Key to North American Birds*. The last named went through six editions altogether, with the fifth and sixth being illustrated by the great Louis Agassiz Fuertes, whose genius Coues had at once recognized and fostered. Coues' *Field Ornithology*, a companion piece to the *Key*, will always be treasured for its pithy advice to field men, in whatever branch of science.

Coues' erudition would suggest the cloistered scholar, but for years he was an army surgeon at lonely outposts on the western frontier. Back east, he would be found at his desk writing "as though his life depended upon it," to quote one visitor. In spare moments he compiled and saw through the press the four parts of his voluminous, scholarly, and valuable "Ornithological Bibliography."

Thus it comes as no surprise to learn that the ornithologist, indeed anyone with an interest in birds, still treasures the writings of Elliott Coues not only as science but also as literature.[21]

Copies of Coues' works offered for sale today by book dealers are snatched up quickly by collectors, though the prices are usually high. In the 1970s the Arno Press produced reprints of "American Ornithological Bibliography," the Coues-Gill "Material for a Bibliography of North American Mammals," *Birds of the Colorado Valley, Birds of the Northwest, Fur-Bearing Animals,* and the fifth edition of the *Key to North American Birds.* The appearance of a sixth edition of the *Key* in 1928, twenty-nine years after Coues' death, is a further indication of its enduring worth.

Thus it is apparent that ornithologists of the twentieth century agree with those of Coues' own time as to his monumental importance in the history of this branch of science. And certainly Coues himself would have agreed. Well aware of his own talents and worth as a scientist, he seldom missed an opportunity to publicize his contributions. He practiced what he called "self-congratulation," which was, he wrote, "a very different thing from self-laudation."[22]

To those who would charge that Coues' lack of modesty was unbecoming, we will simply reverse the Churchillian phrase and say that he had little to be modest about. His confidence in his own powers was tempered by the knowledge that even he had limitations: ". . . a man who thinks he knows it all has no business fooling around with printer's ink. I left 'Camp Omniscience' years ago, and since then haven't known more about everything than some other people."[23] Whatever his limitations, he most certainly measured up to his own definition of genius: "*Genius is that union of Passion and Patience which bears fruit unknown to Passion alone, to Patience alone impossible.*"[24]

In searching for appropriate closing words, we once more find that Coues himself supplied the most suitable ones. Again, he was evaluating someone else (in this case, William MacGillivray) and in so doing provided an epitaph for himself:

If he never hesitated to differ sharply with any one, or to express his own views pointedly—if he scarcely disguised his contempt for triflers, blockheads, pedants, compilers, and theorizers—if he was also fallible, even as the rest of us—he was nevertheless a lover of nature, an original thinker, a hard student, and, finally an ornithologist of large practical experience, who wrote down what he knew or believed to be true with great regard for accuracy of statement and in a very agreeable manner.[25]

NOTES

1. Coues-Biddle (1893), lxxxii.
2. Elliot, "Coues as a Young Man" (1902), 5.
3. Alfred Russel Wallace, *My Life: A Record of Events and Opinions*, 2 vols. (London: Chapman & Hall, 1905), II, 117, 123. St. George Jackson Mivart (1827-1900) was an English biologist who sought to reconcile evolutionary theory with religion.
4. Allen, "Biographical Memoir," 424.
5. *Ibis*, 7th ser., VI (Apr., 1900), 403.
6. [Allen], "Elliott Coues," 7.
7. Ballou, "The Literature of Dr. Elliott Coues" (1879), 726.
8. Lummis, "Lost—A Man," 163.
9. Coues, "Elliot's *Limicolae*" (1896), 64.
10. Elliot, "In Memoriam: Elliott Coues," 6.
11. Allen, "Biographical Memoir," 424.
12. Peattie, ed., *A Gathering of Birds*, 268.
13. *Annual Report of the Board of Regents of the Smithsonian Institution . . . 1894* (Washington, D.C.: Government Printing Office, 1896), 48.
14. Wood, comp. and ed., *An Introduction to the Literature of Vertebrate Zoology* (1931), 62.
15. Letter of Feb. 20, 1974, to the authors from Maurice G. Brooks, professor emeritus of wildlife management, West Virginia University, Morgantown.
16. Letter of Apr. 12, 1974, to the authors from Walter J. Breckenridge, Museum of Natural History, University of Minnesota, Minneapolis.
17. Letter of Mar. 4, 1977, to the authors from John Davis, research zoologist, Museum of Vertebrate Zoology, Hastings Natural History Reservation, Carmel Valley, Calif.
18. Letter of Jan. 19, 1977, to the authors from George Miksch Sutton, George Lynn Cross Research Professor Emeritus of Zoology, Stovall Museum of Science and History, University of Oklahoma, Norman.
19. Letter of Jan. 28, 1977, to the authors from Theodore S. Bober, museum specialist emeritus, Division of Birds, National Museum of Natural History, Smithsonian Institution, Washington, D.C.
20. Robert M. Mengel, comp., *A Catalogue of the Ellis Collection of Ornithological Books in the University of Kansas Libraries*, I (Lawrence: University of Kansas Libraries, 1972), v.
21. Letter of Oct. 14, 1977, to the authors from Dean Amadon, Lamont Curator

Emeritus of Ornithology, American Museum of Natural History, New York.

22. Coues to Allen, Nov. 13, 1878.
23. Coues to Alfred J. Hill, June 24, 1893, Hill Mss., Minnesota Historical Society.
24. Coues, "Behind the Veil" (1880), 195n. Italics in the original.
25. Coues, "Fourth Instalment of Ornithological Bibliography" (1880), 395.

APPENDIX A

New Birds Described by Elliott Coues

The number of new forms described by a naturalist has rarely been an index to his scientific contributions, and certainly was not with Elliott Coues. Still, as one aspect of his activity in the systematics of birds we list herewith the genera, species, and subspecies of North American birds described by Coues and included as valid in the latest (fifth) edition of the *Check-List of North American Birds* published by the American Ornithologists' Union in 1957. Although Coues was a pioneer in the recognition of subspecies, it will be noted that a number of birds described by him as full species are now regarded as subspecies of some other species. The vast majority of North American species of birds had, of course, been described before Coues' scientific career began.

In this list each scientific name—generic, subgeneric, specific, or subspecific—is followed by its vernacular name and the publication in which the original description appeared.

Genera

Aechmophorus Coues—WESTERN GREBE. *Procs. Acad. Nat. Scis. Phila.*, XIV, no. 5, Apr.-May (Aug. 1), 1862, 229.

Halocyptena Coues—STORM PETRELS in part. *Procs. Acad. Nat. Scis. Phila.*, Mar.-Apr. (June 30), 1864, 78.

Micrathene Coues—ELF OWLS. *Procs. Acad. Nat. Scis. Phila.*, 1866, 5i.

Asyndesmus Coues—LEWIS'S WOODPECKER. *Procs. Acad. Nat. Scis. Phila.*, XVII, no. 1, Jan.-Mar. (June 11), 1866, 55.

Iridoprocne Coues—TREE SWALLOWS and relatives. *Birds of the Colorado Valley* (1878), p. 412.

Amphispiza Coues—BLACK-THROATED AND SAGE SPARROWS. *Birds of the Northwest* (1874), p. 234.

Subgenera

Cymochorea Coues—STORM PETRELS in part. *Procs. Acad. Nat. Scis. Phila.*, Mar.-Apr. (June 30), 1864, 75.

Sieberocitta Coues—MEXICAN JAYS in part. *Key to North American Birds*, 5th ed., (1903), I, 497.

Species

The number in brackets is the A.O.U. *Check-List* number.

Puffinus creatopus Coues—PINK-FOOTED SHEARWATER [91]. *Procs. Acad. Nat. Scis. Phila.*, Mar.-Apr. (June 30), 1864, 131. San Nicholas Island, California.

Oceanodroma homochroa (Coues)—Ashy Petrel [108]. *Procs. Acad. Nat. Scis. Phila.*, Mar.-Apr. (June 30), 1864, 77. Farallone Islands, California.

Halocyptena microsoma Coues—Least Petrel [103]. *Procs. Acad. Nat. Scis. Phila.*, Mar.-Apr. (June 30), 1864, 79. Baja California.

Erolia ptilocnemis (Coues)—Rock Sandpiper [235b]. =*Tringa ptilocnemis* Coues. In Elliott, Rep. Seal Islands [in Affairs in Alaska] (1873) (not paged). St. George Island, Pribilof Islands.

Erolia bairdii (Coues)—Baird's Sandpiper [241]. =*Actodromas Bairdii* Coues. *Procs. Acad. Nat. Scis. Phila.*, XIII, June-Aug. (Dec. 28), 1861, sigs. 11-17, 194. Fort Resolution, Great Slave Lake, Mackenzie District.

Toxostoma bendirei (Coues)—Bendire's Thrasher [708]. =*Harporhynchus Bendirei* Coues. *Amer. Naturalist*, VII, no. 6, June, 1873, 330. Tucson, Arizona.

Vireo vicinior Coues—Gray Vireo [634]. *Procs. Acad. Nat. Scis. Phila.*, XVIII, no. 1, Jan.-Mar. (June 11), 1866, 75. Fort Whipple, Arizona.

Aimophila carpalis (Coues)—Rufous-winged Sparrow [579]. =*Peucaea carpalis* Coues. *Amer. Naturalist*, VII, no. 6, June, 1873, 322. Tucson, Arizona.

Subspecies

Puffinus puffinus opisthomelas Coues—Manx Shearwater [93]. =*Puffinus opisthomelas* Coues. *Procs. Acad. Nat. Scis. Phila.*, Mar.-Apr. (June 30), 1864, 139. Cape St. Lucas, Lower California.

Colinus virginianus floridanus (Coues)—Florida Bobwhite [289a]. =*Ortyx virginianus* var. *floridanus* Coues. *Key to North American Birds* (1872), p. 237. Enterprise, Volusia County, Florida.

Erolia alpina pacifica (Coues)—Dunlin [243a]. =*Pelidna pacifica* Coues. *Procs. Acad. Nat. Scis. Phila.*, XI, 1861, 189. Simiahmoo, Washington.

Larus argentatus smithsonianus Coues—Herring Gull [51a]. =*Larus Smithsonianus* Coues. *Procs. Acad. Nat. Scis. Phila.*, XIV, no. 6, June (Aug. 1), 1862, 296. Eastern and western coasts of North America.

Chodeiles minor sennetti Coues—Common Nighthawk [420c]. =*Chordiles* [sic] *popetue Sennetti* Coues. *Auk*, V, no. 1, Jan., 1888, 37. West of Pembina, North Dakota.

Chordeiles minor chapmani Coues—Common Nighthawk [420b]. =*Chordiles* [sic] *popetue Chapmani* Coues. *Auk*, V, no. 1, Jan., 1888, 37. Gainesville, Florida.

Empidonax fulvifrons pygmaeus Coues—Buff-breasted Flycatcher [470a]. =*Empidonax pygmaeus* Coues. *Ibis*, 2d ser., I, no. 4, Oct., 1865, 537. Fort Whipple (Prescott), Arizona.

Contopus sordidulus veliei Coues—Western Wood Peewee [462]. =*Contopus veliei* Coues. *Procs. Acad. Nat. Scis. Phila.*, Mar., 1866, 61. Fort Whipple, Arizona.

Eremophila alpestris leucolaema Coues—Horned Lark [474c]. *Birds of the Northwest* (1874), pp. 37-39. Fort Randall, South Dakota.

Corvus brachyrhynchos pascuus Coues—Common Crow [488a]. =*Corvus americanus pascuus* Coues. *Auk*, XVI, no. 1, Jan., 1899, 84. Southern Florida.

Toxostoma curvirostre palmeri (Coues)—Curve-billed Thrasher [707a]. =*Harporhynchus curvirostris* var. *palmeri* Coues. *Key to North American Birds* (1872), p. 351. Tucson, Arizona.

Vireo bellii pusillus Coues—BELL'S VIREO [633a]. =*Vireo pusillus* Coues. *Procs. Acad. Nat. Scis. Phila.,* XVIII, no. 1, Jan.-Mar. (June 11), 1866, 76. Cape St. Incas, Lower California.

Vireo solitarius plumbeus Coues—SOLITARY VIREO [629b]. =*Vireo plumbeus* Coues. *Procs. Acad. Nat. Scis. Phila.,* XVIII, no. 1, Jan.-Mar. (June 11), 1866, 74. Fort Whipple, Arizona.

Parula pitiayumi nigrilora Coues—OLIVE-BACKED WARBLER [649]. =*Parula nigrilora* Coues. *Bull. U.S. Geol. and Geogr. Surv. Terrs.,* IV, no. 1, Feb. 5, 1878, 11. Hidalgo, Texas.

Dendroica caerulescens cairnsi Coues—BLACK-THROATED BLUE WARBLER [654a]. *Auk,* XIV, no. 1, Jan., 1897, 96. Mountains of western North Carolina and eastern Tennessee.

Acanthis hornemanni exilipes (Coues)—HOARY REDPOLL [527a]. =*Aegiothus exilipes* Coues. *Procs. Acad. Nat. Scis. Phila.,* XIII, sigs. 26-36, Nov.-Dec., 1861 (Mar. 31, 1862), 378. Jakobshavn, Greenland.

Pipilo erythrophthalmus alleni Coues—RUFOUS-SIDED TOWHEE [587a]. =*Pipilo Alleni* Coues. *Amer. Naturalist,* V, no. 6, Aug., 1871, 366. Indian River, Florida.

Ammodramus savannarum perpallidus (Coues)—GRASSHOPPER SPARROW [546a]. = *Coturniculus passerinus* var. *perpallidus* Coues. *Key to North American Birds* (1872), p. 137. Antelope Island, Great Salt Lake, Utah.

Spizella passerina arizonae Coues—CHIPPING SPARROW [560a]. =*Spizella socialis* var. *arizonae* Coues. *Key to North American Birds* (1872), p. 143. Fort Whipple, Arizona.

Spizella atrogularis cana Coues—BLACK-CHINNED SPARROW [565a]. =*Spizella cana* Coues. *Procs. Acad. Nat. Scis. Phila.,* Jan.-Mar. (June 11), 1866, 88. Cape San Lucas, Lower California.

Coues was honored by having at least two birds (subspecies) named after him: *Erolia ptilocnemis couesi* (Ridgway), the ROCK SANDPIPER [235a], and *Campylorhynchus brunneicapillum couesi* Sharpe, the CACTUS WREN [713]. The former is sometimes called Coues' sandpiper and the latter Coues' northern cactus wren. Among other vernaculars paying tribute to Coues are Coues' shearwater (usually pink-footed shearwater) and Coues' flycatcher (*Contopus pertinax* Cabanis and Heine).

APPENDIX B

New Mammals Described by Elliott Coues

For nomenclature we have relied upon two sources: E. Raymond Hall and Keith R. Kelson, *The Mammals of North America*, 2 vols. (New York: Ronald Press, 1959), and Gerrit S. Miller, Jr., and Remington Kellogg, "List of North American Recent Mammals," *U.S. National Museum Bulletin*, no. 205 (Washington, D.C.: Smithsonian Institution, 1955). Hereafter the former will be abbreviated as H & K and the latter as M & K.

INSECTIVORA

Genera

Microsorex Coues—PYGMY SHREWS. *Bull. U.S. Geol. and Geogr. Surv. Terrs.*, III, May 15, 1877, 646. H & K, I, 50; M & K, 33.
Notiosorex Coues—DESERT SHREWS. *Bull. U.S. Geol. and Geogr. Surv. Terrs.*, III, May 15, 1877, 646. H & K, I, 64; M & K, 43.

Subspecies

Sorex vagrans pacificus Coues. =*Sorex pacificus pacificus* Coues—PACIFIC VAGRANT SHREW. *Bull. U.S. Geol. and Geogr. Surv. Terrs.*, III, May 15, 1877, 650. H & K, I, 33; M & K, 25.
Cryptotis mexicana mexicana Coues—MEXICAN SMALL-EARED SHREW. *Blarina (Soriciscus) mexicana* Coues. *Bull. U.S. Geol. and Geogr. Surv. Terrs.*, III, May 15, 1877, 652. H & K, I, 60; M & K, 40.
Notiosorex crawfordi crawfordi Coues—CRAWFORD'S DESERT SHREW. *Bull. U.S. Geol. and Geogr. Surv. Terrs.*, III, May 15, 1877, 651. H & K, I, 64; M & K, 43.
Notiosorex crawfordi evotis (Coues)—DESERT SHREW. *Sorex (Notiosorex) evotis* Coues. *Bull. U.S. Geol. and Geogr. Surv. Terrs.*, III, May 15, 1877, 652. H & K, I, 64; M & K, 43.

RODENTIA

Genus

Zapus Coues—JUMPING MICE. *Bull. U.S. Geol. and Geogr. Surv. Terrs.*, I, Jan. 8, 1876, 253. H & K, II, 771; M & K, 622.

Species

Microtus quasiater (Coues). =*Pitymys quasiater* (Coues)—JALAPAN PINE VOLE. *Arvicola (Pitymys) pinetorum* var. *quasiater* Coues. *Procs. Acad. Nat. Scis. Phila.*, XXVI, Dec. 15, 1874, 191. H & K, II, 751; M & K, 612.

Sciurus arizonensis Coues—ARIZONA GRAY SQUIRREL. *Amer. Naturalist*, I, Sept., 1867, 357. H & K, I, 393; M & K, 255.

Subspecies

Thomomys talpoides clusius Coues—NORTHERN POCKET GOPHER. *Thomomys clusius* Coues. *Procs. Acad. Nat. Scis. Phila.*, XXVII, June 15, 1875, 138. H & K, I, 437; M & K, 313.

Perognathus longimembris longimembris (Coues)—LITTLE POCKET MOUSE. *O[tognosis] longimembris* Coues. *Procs. Acad. Nat. Scis. Phila.*, XXVII, Aug. 31, 1875, 305. H & K, I, 484; M & K, 359.

Perognathus parvus mollipilosus Coues—GREAT BASIN POCKET MOUSE. *P[erognathus] mollipilosus* Coues. *Procs. Acad. Nat. Scis. Phila.*, XXII, Aug. 31, 1875, 296. H & K, I, 488; M & K, 367.

Liomys irroratus alleni (Coues)—MEXICAN SPINY POCKET MOUSE. *Heteromys alleni* Coues. *Bull. Mus. Comp. Zool.*, VIII, Mar., 1881, 187. H & K, I, 540; M & K, 422.

Peromyscus maniculatus nebrascensis (Coues)—NEBRASKA DEER MOUSE. *Hesperomys sonoriensis* var. *nebrascensis* Coues. In Coues and Allen, *Monographs of North American Rodentia* (1877), p. 79. H & K, II, 622; M & K, 482.

Peromyscus melanophrys melanophrys (Coues)—PLATEAU MOUSE. *Hesperomys (Vesperimus) melanophrys* Coues. *Procs. Acad. Nat. Scis. Phila.*, XXVI, Dec. 15, 1874, 181. H & K, II, 644; M & K, 502.

Onychomys torridus torridus (Coues)—SOUTHERN GRASSHOPPER MOUSE. *Hesperomys (Onychomys) torridus* Coues. *Procs. Acad. Nat. Scis. Phila.*, XXVI, Dec. 15, 1874, 183. H & K, II, 667; M & K, 517.

Synaptomys cooperi gossii (Coues)—BOG LEMMING. *Arvicola (Synaptomys) gossii* Coues. In Coues and Allen, *Monographs of North American Rodentia* (1877), p. 235. H & K, II, 762; M & K, 562.

CARNIVORA

Genus

Bassariscus Coues—RINGTAILS and CACOMISTLES. *Science*, IX, May 27, 1887, 516. H & K, II, 879; M & K, 712.

Coues was honored by having three mammalian subspecies named after him:

Oryzomys couesi couesi (Alston)—COUES' RICE RAT. *Hesperomys couesi* Alston. *Procs. Zool. Soc. London*, 1876, pt. 4, Apr., 1877, 756. H & K, II, 557; M & K, 430.

Erethizon dorsatum couesi Mearns—COUES' PORCUPINE. *Erethizon epixanthus couesi* Mearns. *Procs. U.S. Nat. Mus.*, XIX, July 30, 1897, 723. H & K, II, 781; M & K, 633.

Dama [Odocoileus] virginianus couesi (Coues and Yarrow)—COUES' WHITE-TAILED DEER. *Cariacus virginianus* var. *couesi*. Coues and Yarrow, "Report upon the Collections of Mammals," p. 111, in Rept. Geogr. Explor. and Surv. West of the One Hundredth Merid. (Wheeler), 5 (Zool.) (1875), 72. H & K, II, 1008; M & K, 803.

APPENDIX C

Elliott Coues' Memberships in Learned Societies

The fact that Coues held membership—active, foreign, corresponding, or honorary—in many learned societies may be attributed not only to his recognized abilities as an ornithologist but also to his versatility and general popularity. The list which follows is taken from handwritten entries in Coues' "Book of Dates":

1861, August 27—Named corresponding member of the Academy of Natural Sciences of Philadelphia. (At that date Coues was two weeks short of his nineteenth birthday.)

1863, December 21—Elected corresponding member of the New York Lyceum of Natural History.

1864, May 2—Elected corresponding member of the St. Louis Academy of Sciences.

1866, March 21—Elected corresponding member of the Boston Society of Natural History.

June 4—Elected corresponding member of Essex Institute, Salem, Massachusetts.

1871, September 18—Elected active member of the Maryland Academy of Sciences, Baltimore.

1872, June 5—Notified of election to foreign membership in the British Ornithologists' Union.

1873, August 13—Elected active member of the Minnesota Academy of Sciences.

1875, Fall—Elected active member of the Literary Society of Washington, D.C.

1876, May 18—Elected corresponding member of the Zoological Society of London.

1877, April 17—Elected active member of the National Academy of Sciences. (At that date, aged thirty-four, Coues was the youngest individual to have been elected to membership in that prestigious organization.)

April 27—Elected active member of Davenport (Iowa) Academy of Sciences.

1878, February 4—Elected honorary member of the Nuttall Ornithological Club, Cambridge, Massachusetts.

September—Elected active member of the American Philosophical Society, Philadelphia.

1879, May 8—Elected active member of the Anthropological Society of Washington, D.C.

1880, May 7—Named first honorary member of the Society of American Taxidermists.

1882, February 25—Elected corresponding member of the Boston Zoological Society.

437

1883, February 24—Elected honorary member of the Linnaean Society of New York.

May 12—Elected original member of the Society of Naturalists of the Eastern United States.

—Elected honorary member of the Newport (Rhode Island) Natural History Society.

September 26-28—Became charter member of the American Ornithologists' Union.

1884, April 3—Elected corresponding member of the Ridgway Ornithological Club, Chicago.

June 30—Elected associate member of the London Society for Psychical Research.

1887, June 17—Invited to become a fellow of the Society of Science, Letters and Art, London.

November 17—Elected honorary member of the Spencer F. Baird Naturalists' Association, Reading, Pennsylvania.

1888, January 3—Elected honorary member of the California Academy of Sciences.

1890—Elected active member of the American Anthropometric Society of Philadelphia.

December 2—Elected corresponding member of the Portland (Maine) Society of Natural History.

1891, May 17—Elected honorary member of the Second International Ornithological Congress, Budapest, Hungary.

September 17—Elected to the American Academy of Political and Social Sciences.

October 21—Notified of election as member of the University Marine Biological Association, Sea Isle, New Jersey.

1892, February 25—Elected perpetual honorary member of the Historical Society of Arizona, Tuscon.

April 29—Elected active member of the National Geographic Society, Washington, D.C.

1893, August 14—Elected honorary fellow of the Tacoma (Washington) Academy of Science.

—Elected honorary member of the Florida Society for Scientific Research.

1894, January 10—Elected corresponding member of the Medico-Legal Society, New York.

May 14—Elected honorary member of the Minnesota Historical Society, St. Paul.

1897, September 3—Elected honorary member of the Michigan Ornithological Club.

BIBLIOGRAPHY

General Literature

Allen, J. A. "On the Mammals and Winter Birds of East Florida." *Bull. Mus. Comp. Zoology*, II (1871), 161-450.

———. "History of the American Bison, *Bison americanus.*" In *Ninth Annual Report of the United States Geological and Geographical Survey of the Territories . . . 1875*. Washington, D.C.: Government Printing Office, 1877.

———. "Ridgway on the Nomenclature of North American Birds." *Bull. Nutt. Orn. Club*, V (July, 1880), 177-79.

———. "Zoological Nomenclature." *Auk*, I (Oct., 1884), 338-53.

———. "To What Extent Is It Profitable to Recognize Geographical Forms among North American Birds?" *Auk*, VII (Jan., 1890), 1-9.

———. "A Defense of Canon XL of the A.O.U. Code." *Auk*, XV (Oct., 1898), 298-303.

American Ornithologists' Union. *The Code of Nomenclature and Check-List of North American Birds*. New York: American Ornithologists' Union, 1886.

———. *Check-List of North American Birds*. 5th ed. Baltimore: American Ornithologists' Union, 1957.

———. "Proceedings of the Committee on Classification and Nomenclature, 1883-1885." Unpublished, and presently in A.O.U. files, National Museum of Natural History, Washington, D.C.

Baird, Spencer F. *Catalogue of North American Birds*. Washington, D.C.: Smithsonian Institution, 1858.

———, and Robert Ridgway. "On Some New Forms of American Birds." *Bull. Essex Inst.*, V (Dec., 1873), 197-201.

———, Thomas M. Brewer, and Robert Ridgway. *A History of North American Birds*. 3 vols. Boston: Little, Brown, 1874.

Baker, Marcus. "Survey of the Northwestern Boundary of the United States, 1857-1861." *Bull. U.S. Geol. Surv.*, no. 174 (1900).

Barrus, Clara. *The Life and Letters of John Burroughs*. 2 vols. Boston: Houghton Mifflin, 1925.

Batchelder, Charles Foster. "An Account of the Nuttall Ornithological Club, 1873 to 1919." *Mem. Nutt. Orn. Club*, no. 8 (1937).

Boynton, Mary Fuertes, ed. *Louis Agassiz Fuertes: His Life Briefly Told and His Correspondence*. New York: Oxford University Press, 1956.

Brewer, Thomas M. "The European House Sparrow." *Atlantic Monthly*, XXI (May, 1868), 583-88.

Cassin, John. *Illustrations of the Birds of California, Texas, Oregon, and British and Russian America*. Philadelphia: J. B. Lippincott, 1856.

Chapman, Frank M. *Handbook of Birds of Eastern North America*. 7th ed. New York: D. Appleton, 1906.

439

————. "In Memoriam: Louis Agassiz Fuertes." *Auk*, XLV (Jan., 1928), 7.

————. *Autobiography of a Bird-Lover*. New York: D. Appleton-Century, 1933.

Cohen, Daniel. *The Body Snatchers*. Philadelphia: J. B. Lippincott, 1975.

Coues, Samuel Elliott. *Outlines of a System of Mechanical Philosophy*. Boston: Charles C. Little and James Brown, 1851.

————. *Studies of the Earth*. Washington, D.C.: By the author, 1860.

Cutright, Paul Russell. *Lewis and Clark: Pioneering Naturalists*. Urbana: University of Illinois Press, 1969.

Dall, William Healey. *Spencer Fullerton Baird: A Biography*. Philadelphia: J. B. Lippincott, 1915.

Elliot, D. G. "Canon XL, A.O.U. Code." *Auk*, XV (Oct., 1898), 294-98.

————. "Truth *versus* Error." *Auk*, XVI (Jan., 1899), 38-46.

Faris, John T. *The Romance of the Boundaries*. New York: Harper & Brothers, 1926.

Frantz, J. H. "Columbia, S.C." In *A Report on the Hygiene of the United States Army, with Descriptions of Military Posts* (Circular No. 8, War Department, Surgeon General's Office), by John S. Billings, 126-28. Washington, D.C.: Government Printing Office, 1875.

Frazer, Robert W. *Forts of the West: Military Posts and Presidios and Posts Commonly Called Forts, West of the Mississippi River to 1898*. Norman: University of Oklahoma Press, 1965.

Gannett, Henry. "Boundaries of the United States and of the Several States and Territories, with a Historical Sketch of the Territorial Changes." *Bull. U.S. Geol. Surv.*, no. 13 (1885).

Goetzmann, William H. *Army Exploration in the American West, 1803-1863*. New Haven, Conn.: Yale University Press, 1959.

————. *Exploration and Empire: The Explorer and the Scientist in the Winning of the West*. New York: Vintage Books, 1972.

Goode, George Brown, ed. *The Smithsonian Institution, 1846-1896: The History of Its First Half Century*. Washington, D.C.: N.p., 1897.

Graustein, Jeannette E. "Collegians to Labrador and Greenland, 1860." *Explorers Journal*, XLVIII (Sept., 1970), 184-91.

Hall, E. Raymond, and Keith R. Kelson. *The Mammals of North America*. 2 vols. New York: Ronald Press Co., 1959.

Harris, Harry. "Robert Ridgway: With a Bibliography of His Published Writings and Fifty Illustrations." *Condor*, XXX (Jan.-Feb., 1928), 5-118.

Heitman, Francis B. *Historical Register and Dictionary of the United States Army, from Its Organization, September 29, 1789, to March 2, 1903*. 2 vols. Washington, D.C.: Government Printing Office, 1903.

Hellman, Geoffrey. *Bankers, Bones and Beetles: The First Century of the American Museum of Natural History*. Garden City, N.Y.: Natural History Press, 1969.

Jackson, Donald, ed. *The Journals of Zebulon Montgomery Pike, with Letters and Related Documents*. Norman: University of Oklahoma Press, 1966.

Jordan, David Starr, ed. *Leading American Men of Science*. New York: Henry Holt, 1910.

————. *Days of a Man*. 2 vols. Yonkers-on-Hudson, N.Y.: World Book, 1922.

McDermott, John Francis, ed. *Up the Missouri with Audubon: The Journal of Edward Harris*. Norman: University of Oklahoma Press, 1951.

Mearns, E. A. "Mammals of the Mexican Boundary of the United States: A Descriptive Catalogue of the Species of Mammals Occurring in That Region." *Bull. U.S. Nat. Mus.*, no. 56 (1907).

Miller, Gerrit S., and Remington Kellogg. "List of North American Recent Mammals." *Bull. U.S. Nat. Mus.*, no. 205 (1955).

Neff, Mark K., comp. *Personal Memoirs of H. P. Blavatsky*. Wheaton, Ill.: Theosophical Publishing House, 1967.

O'Shaughnessy, Edith (Coues). *A Diplomat's Wife in Mexico*. New York: Harper & Brothers, 1916.

———. *Diplomatic Days*. New York: Harper & Brothers, 1917.

———. *Other Ways and Other Flesh*. New York: Harcourt, Brace, 1929.

Otis, George A. *The Medical and Surgical History of the War of the Rebellion*, pt. II, vol. II, *Surgical History*. Washington, D.C.: Government Printing Office, 1876.

———, and D. L. Huntington. *The Medical and Surgical History of the War of the Rebellion*, pt. III, vol. II, *Surgical History*. Washington, D.C.: Government Printing Office, 1883.

Packard, Alpheus Spring, Jr. *The Labrador Coast: A Journal of Two Summer Cruises to That Region*. New York: N. D. C. Hodges, 1891.

Palmer, T. S. "In Memoriam: Theodore Nicholas Gill." *Auk*, XXXII (Oct., 1915), 391-405.

———. "A Brief History of the American Ornithologists' Union." In *Fifty Years' Progress of American Ornithology, 1883-1933*, ed. Frank M. Chapman and T. S. Palmer, 6-27. Lancaster, Pa.: American Ornitholgists' Union, 1933.

Parsons, John E. *West on the 49th Parallel: Red River to the Rockies, 1872-1876*. New York: William Morrow, 1963.

Prucha, Francis Paul. *A Guide to the Military Posts of the United States, 1789-1895*. Madison: State Historical Society of Wisconsin, 1964.

Ridgway, Robert. "On the Relation between Color and Geographical Distribution of Birds, as Exhibited in Melanism and Hyperchromism." *Amer. Jour. Science*, 3d ser., IV (Dec., 1872), 454-60; V (Jan., 1873), 39-44.

———. "The Relationship between the Color and the Geographical Distibution of Birds." *Amer. Naturalist*, VII (Sept., 1873), 548-55.

———. "A Catalogue of the Birds of North America." *Procs. U.S. Nat. Mus.*, III (Aug. 24–Sept. 4, 1880), 163-246.

———. "Nomenclature of North American Birds, Chiefly Contained in the U.S. National Museum." *Bull. U.S. Nat. Mus.*, no. 21 (1881), 3-94.

———. "Spencer Fullerton Baird." *Auk*, V (Jan., 1888), 1-14.

Sharpe, R. Bowdler. *A Review of Recent Attempts to Classify Birds; An Address Delivered before the Second International Ornithological Congress on the 18th of May, 1891*. Budapest: Office of the Congress, 1891.

Simpson, J., and D. Bache. "Fort McHenry, Baltimore, Maryland." In *A Report on the Hygiene of the United States Army, with Descriptions of Military Posts* (Circular No. 8, War Department, Surgeon General's Office), by John S.

Billings, 40-43. Washington, D.C.: Government Printing Office, 1875.

Smart, Charles. *The Medical and Surgical History of the War of the Rebellion,* pt. III, vol. I, *Medical History,* Washington, D.C.: Government Printing Office, 1888.

Stejneger, Leonhardt. "On the Use of Trinominals in American Ornithology." *Procs. U.S. Nat. Mus.,* VIII (1884), 70-81.

Sterling, Keir Brooks. *Last of the Naturalists: The Career of C. Hart Merriam.* New York: Arno Press, 1974.

Stresemann, Erwin. *Ornithology from Aristotle to the Present.* Cambridge, Mass.: Harvard University Press, 1975.

Way, Ethel J. "The Locations and Survey of the Northern International Boundary Line." *Colls. N. Dakota Hist. Soc.,* IV (1913), 179-234.

Weeds, J. F., and J. P. Kimball. "Fort Randall, Dakota Territory." In *A Report on the Hygiene of the United States Army, with Descriptions of Military Posts* (Circular No. 8, War Department, Surgeon General's Office), by John S. Billings, 417-21. Washington, D.C.: Government Printing Office, 1875.

Willard, Frances E., and Mary A. Livermore, eds. *A Woman of the Century . . . Leading American Women in All Walks of Life.* Buffalo: Charles Wells Moulton, 1893.

Wood, Casey A., comp. and ed. *An Introduction to the Literature of Vertebrate Zoology.* London: Oxford University Press, 1931.

Literature about Elliott Coues

Allen, J. A. "The Ornithology of the Century Dictionary." *Auk,* VIII (Apr., 1891), 222-24. [An appraisal of Coues' contributions to *The Century Dictionary.*]

———. "Elliott Coues." *Nation,* LXX (Jan. 4, 1900), 6-7.

———. "Elliott Coues." *Science,* n.s., XI (Feb. 2, 1900), 161-63.

———. "Biographical Memoir of Elliott Coues, 1842-1899." *Biographical Memoirs,* National Academy of Sciences, VI (June, 1909), 397-446.

Ballou, William Hosea. "The Literature of Dr. Elliott Coues." *Forest and Stream,* Oct. 16, 1879, 725-26.

———. "Bibliographical Manual of American Naturalists. Chapter II. Dr. Elliott Coues, U.S.A." *Chicago Field,* XIII (Mar. 20, 1880), 92; (Mar. 27, 1880), 103; (Apr. 3, 1880), 123; (Apr. 10, 1880), 141; (Apr. 17, 1880), 151; (May 1, 1880), 189; (May 8, 1880), 205; XIV (May 15, 1880), 221.

Barlow, Chester, "Dr. Elliott Coues." *Condor,* I (Jan., 1900), 23.

———. "The Last Portrait of Dr. Coues." *Condor,* II (May, 1900), 72.

Brewster, William, "Stearns and Coues's New England Bird Life, Part II." *Bull. Nutt. Orn. Club,* VIII (July, 1883), 164.

Brodhead, Michael J. "Dedication to the Memory of Elliott Coues, 1842-1899." *Arizona and the West,* XIII (Spring, 1971), 1-4.

———. "Elliott Coues and the Sparrow War." *New England Quart.,* XLIV (Sept., 1971), 420-32.

———. "Natural History along the Parallel of 49° North." *Io,* Earth Geography Booklet no. 2 (Spring, 1972), 270-84.

―――. *A Soldier-Scientist in the American Southwest*. Historical Monograph no. 1. Tucson: Arizona Historical Society, 1973.

―――. "Elliott Coues and the Apaches." *Jour. of Ariz. Hist.*, XIV (Summer, 1973), 87-94.

―――. "A Naturalist in the Colorado Rockies, 1876." *Colorado Magazine*, LII (Summer, 1975), 185-99.

Chickering, J. W. "Catalogue of Phaenogamous and Vascular Cryptogamous Plants Collected during the Summers of 1873 and 1874 in Dakota and Montana along the Forty-ninth Parallel, by Dr. Elliott Coues, U.S.A.; with which are incorporated those collected in the same region by Mr. George M. Dawson." *Bull. U.S. Geol. and Geogr. Surv. Terrs.*, IV, no. 4 (Dec. 11, 1878), 801-30.

Cope, Edward D. "On the Reptilia and Batrachia of the Sonoran Province of the Nearctic Region." *Procs. Acad. Nat. Scis. Phila.*, XVIII (Sept.-Nov., 1866), 300-311. [A description of more than fifty species of southwestern reptiles and amphibians collected by Coues.]

[Coues, Elliott]. *The Private Library of the Late Elliott Coues. To Be Sold at Auction Monday and Tuesday, December 3 and 4, 1906. The Anderson Auction Co., 5 West 29th Street, New York*. N.p., 1906?

Curtis, C. A. "Coues at His First Army Post." *Bird-Lore*, IV (Jan.-Feb., 1902), 5-7.

Cutright, Paul Russell. *A History of the Lewis and Clark Journals*. Norman: University of Oklahoma Press, 1976. [See Chapter VI, 73-103.]

[Darwin, Charles, *et al.*]. "Memorial to Elliott Coues." *Bull. Nutt. Orn. Club*, IV (July, 1879), 176-78.

"Dr. Coues' Colorado Expedition." *Forest and Stream*, Nov. 2, 1876, 200.

"Dr. Elliott Coues." *Nature* (London), LX (Jan. 18, 1900), 278-79. [Obituary notice.]

Edwards, W. H. "On the *Lepidoptera* Collected by Dr. Elliott Coues, U.S.A., in Montana, during 1874." *Bull. U.S. Geol. and Geogr. Surv. Terrs.*, IV, no. 2 (May 3, 1878), 513-17.

Elliot, D. G. "In Memoriam: Elliott Coues." *Auk*, XVIII (Jan., 1901), 1-11.

―――. "Coues as a Young Man." *Bird-Lore*, IV (Jan.-Feb., 1902), 3-5.

"Elliott Coues." *Ibis*, 7th ser., VI (Apr., 1900), 402-3. [Obituary notice.]

Gruson, Edward S. *Words for Birds*. New York: Quadrangle Books, 1972. [Contains, pp. 180-83, a short biographical sketch of Coues.]

Hallock, Charles. "Three Months in Labrador." *Harper's New Monthly Magazine*, XXII (Apr., 1861), 577-99; (May, 1861), 743-65.

Hanley, Wayne. *Natural History in America, from Mark Catesby to Rachel Carson*. New York: Quadrangle/New York Times Book Co., 1977. [Chapter XVII, 253-64, is about Coues.]

Hazard, R. G. "A Lay View of [Coues'] 'Ornithophilologicalities.'" *Auk*, I (July, 1884), 300-302.

Henshaw, Henry Wetherbee. "Autobiographical Notes." *Condor*, XXI (Nov., 1919), 220-21.

Howard, L. O. *Fighting the Insects: The Story of an Entomologist*. New York: Macmillan, 1933.

Hume, Edgar E. *Ornithologists of the U.S. Army Medical Corps.* Baltimore: Johns Hopkins University Press, 1942. [See pp. 52-89 for chapter on Coues.]

Jordan, David Starr. "Report on the Collection of Fishes Made by Dr. Elliott Coues, U.S.A., in Dakota and Montana, during the Seasons of 1873 and 1874." *Bull. U.S. Geol. and Geogr. Surv. Terrs.*, IV, no. 4 (Dec. 11, 1878), 777-99.

———. "The A.O.U. Code and Check-List of North American Birds." *Auk*, III (July, 1886), 393-97.

Kieran, John, ed. *Treasury of Great Nature Writing.* Garden City, N.Y.: Hanover House, 1957, 219-23.

Krutch, Joseph Wood, and Paul S. Eriksson, eds. *A Treasury of Birdlore.* Garden City, N.Y.: Doubleday, 1962, 57-60, 74-76.

Lawton, E. S. "Elliott Coues, Scientist." *Kansas City Scientist*, V (Aug., 1891), 119-24.

Lovejoy, B. G. *Francis Bacon (Lord Verulam), a Critical Review of His Life and Character.* Boston: Estes & Lauriat, 1883. [Dedicated by Lovejoy to his friend Elliott Coues.]

Lummis, Charles F. "Lost—A Man." *Land of Sunshine*, XII (Feb., 1900), 159-64.

McAtee, W. L. "Elliott Coues." *Nature Magazine*, XLVII (Oct., 1954), 431-32, 442.

———. *Elliott Coues as Represented in "The Nation," 1873-1900.* Chapel Hill, N.C.: Privately published, 1955.

McVaugh, Rogers. *Edward Palmer, Plant Explorer of the American West.* Norman: University of Oklahoma Press, 1956. [See pp. 25-26 for Coues.]

Mahood, Ruth I., ed. *Photographer of the Southwest: Adam Clark Vroman, 1856-1916.* Los Angeles: Ward Ritchie Press, 1961. [See, p. 113, photograph of Coues and others taken in Santa Fe in 1899.]

Marcham, Frederick George, ed. *Louis Agassiz Fuertes and the Singular Beauty of Birds.* New York: Harper & Row, 1971. [See Introduction by Dean Amadon, pp. vii, 5, 6.]

Mathiessen, Peter. *Wildlife in America.* New York: Viking Press, 1959.

Mengel, Robert M. "Bibliography and the Ornithologist." In *Bibliography & Natural History: Essays Presented at a Conference Convened in June 1964*, ed. Thomas R. Buckman, 121-30. Lawrence: University of Kansas Libraries, 1966. [Mengel, p. 121, praises Coues as "the greatest of ornithological bibliographers."]

Merriam, Augustus C. "The Coues Lexicon of North American Birds." *Auk*, I (Jan., 1884), 36-49.

Palmer, T. S. "Elliott Baird Coues." *Auk*, LX (Oct., 1943), 633.

———, et al. *Biographies of Members of the American Ornithologists' Union.* Reprinted from *The Auk*, 1884-1954. Washington, D.C.: N.p., 1954.

Peattie, Donald Culross, ed. *A Gathering of Birds: An Anthology of the Best Ornithological Prose.* New York: Dodd, Mead, 1939, 267-72.

Peterson, Roger Tory, ed. *The Bird Watcher's Anthology.* New York: Bonanza Books, 1957, 26-28.

"Recent Ornithological Publications." *Ibis*, IV (Jan., 1862), 84. [Re Coues' "Monograph of the *Tringeae* of North America."]

Seton, Ernest Thompson. *Trail of an Artist-Naturalist.* New York: Charles Scribner's Sons, 1940, 140, 166, 222, 224, 281.

Shufeldt, R. W. "The Couesian Period." *Forest and Stream,* May 22, 1884, 323; May 29, 1884, 343; June 5, 1884, 362-63.

Terrell, John Upton, and George Walton. *Faint the Trumpet Sounds: The Life and Trial of Major Reno.* New York: David McKay, 1966. [See pp. 86-87 for mention of Coues.]

Thomas, Cyrus. "On the *Orthoptera* Collected by Dr. Elliott Coues, U.S.A., in Dakota and Montana, during 1873-74." *Bull. U.S. Geol. and Geogr. Surv. Terrs.,* IV, no. 2 (May 3, 1878), 481-501.

Uhler, P. R. "On the *Hemiptera* Collected by Dr. Elliott Coues, U.S.A., in Dakota and Montana, during 1873-74." *Bull. U.S. Geol. and Geogr. Surv. Terrs.,* IV, no. 2 (May 3, 1878), 503-12.

Victor, Frances F. "Dr. Elliott Coues." *Oregon Hist. Quart.,* I (June, 1900), 189-92.

Wood, Casey A. "A Plea for the Continuation of Elliott Coues' Ornithological Bibliography." *Auk,* XLV (Apr., 1928), 148-54.

Yarrow, Henry Crècy. "Personal Recollections of Old Medical Officers: Major Elliott Coues." *Military Surgeon,* IX (May, 1927), 588-89.

Literature by Elliott Coues

In compiling this portion of the bibliography, we have made every effort to include all of Coues' writings, yet we realize that some minor items have undoubtedly eluded us. We found the following works especially valuable: Chapter II of William H. Ballou's "Bibliographical Manual of American Naturalists" (which contains a virtually complete list of Coues' works to 1880); the second edition (1882) of Coues' *Check List* (which includes, pp. 145-65, a "Catalogue of the Author's Ornithological Publications, 1861-1881"); "Materials for a Bibliography of North American Mammals," by Coues and Gill; and W. L. McAtee's *Elliott Coues as Represented in "The Nation," 1873-1900.* In those entries below which are anonymous or pseudonymous, or for which we have incomplete bibliographical information, we cite, in parentheses, one of the above authorities.

Within each year, the publications are listed in the following order: (1) books written by Coues; (2) books edited by Coues; (3) books compiled or largely written by others and containing contributions by Coues; (4) articles, notes, reviews, and articles written, edited, or annotated by Coues, with the periodicals arranged alphabetically and Coues' contributions to them arranged chronologically.

1861

"Ornithology." In *Philp's Washington Described. A Complete View of the American Capital, and the District of Columbia; with Many Notices, Historical, Topographical and Scientific, of the Seat of Government,* by William D. Haley, 24-27. Washington, D.C.: Philp & Solomons.

"A Monograph of the *Tringeae* of North America." *Procs. Acad. Nat. Scis. Phila.,* XIII (July), 170-205.

"Notes on the Ornithology of Labrador." *Procs. Acad. Nat. Scis. Phila.*, XIII (Aug.), 215-57.

"A Monograph of the Genus *Aegiothus*, with Descriptions of New Species." *Procs. Acad. Nat. Scis. Phila.*, XIII (Nov.), 373-90.

1862

[With D. Webster Prentiss.] "List of Birds Ascertained to Inhabit the District of Columbia, with the Times of Arrival and Departure of Such as Are Non-residents, and Brief Notices of Habits, Etc." *Annual Report of the Board of Regents of the Smithsonian Institution . . . 1861*, 399-421. Washington, D.C.: Government Printing Office.

"Report of Some Cases of Amputations and Resections, from Gunshot Wounds, Performed at the Mount Pleasant U.S. Hospital, by C. A. McCall, M.D., U.S.A." *Med. and Surg. Reporter*, IX (Nov. 22), 192-94; (Dec. 6), 229-32.

"Synopsis of the North American Forms of the *Colymbidae* and *Podicipidae*." *Procs. Acad. Nat. Scis. Phila.*, XIV (Apr.), 226-33.

"Revision of the Gulls [*Larinae*] of North America; Based upon Specimens in the Museum of the Smithsonian Institution." *Procs. Acad. Nat. Scis. Phila.*, XIV (June), 291-312.

"Supplementary Note to a 'Synopsis of the North American Forms of the *Colymbidae* and *Podicepidae* [*sic*]." *Procs. Acad. Nat. Scis. Phila.*, XIV (Sept.), 404.

"A Review of the Terns [*Sterninae*] of North America." *Procs. Acad. Nat. Scis. Phila.*, XIV (Dec.), 535-59.

1863

[On the specific validity of *Larus smithsonianus*.] *Ibis*, V (July), 367.

"Five Cases of Gun Shot Fracture of the Femur, Successfully Treated with 'Smith's Anterior.' by Charles A. McCall, M.D., U.S.A." *Med. and Surg. Reporter*, X (May 2), 3-5.

"Notes on the 'Soldiers' Chronic Diarrhoea.'" *Med. and Surg. Reporter*, X (Aug. 8), 207-9.

"Additional Remarks on the North American *Aegiothi*." *Procs. Acad. Nat. Scis. Phila.*, XV (Feb.), 40-41.

"On the *Lestris richardsoni* of Swainson; with a Critical Review of the Sub-family *Lestridinae*." *Procs. Acad. Nat. Scis. Phila.*, XV (May), 121-38.

1864

"Notes on Certain Central American *Laridae*, Collected by Mr. Osbert Salvin and Mr. F. Godman." *Ibis*, VI (July), 387-93.

"A Fatal Case of Traumatic Coxalgia." *Med. and Surg. Reporter*, XI (Jan. 30), 63-64.

"The Crania of *Colymbus torquatus* and *C. adamsii* Compared." *Procs. Acad. Nat. Scis. Phila.*, XVI (Feb.), 21-22.

"A Critical Review of the Family *Procellaridae*: Part I, Embracing the *Procellarieae*, or Stormy Petrels." *Procs. Acad. Nat. Scis. Phila.,* XVI (Mar.), 72-91.

"A Critical Review of the Family *Procellaridae:* Part II, Embracing the *Puffineae.*" *Procs. Acad. Nat. Scis. Phila.,* XVI (Apr.), 116-44.

1865

"Ornithology of a Prairie-Journey, and Notes on the Birds of Arizona." *Ibis,* 2d ser., I (Apr.), 157-65.

[Notes on various birds observed at Fort Whipple, Ariz.] *Ibis,* 2d ser., I (Oct.), 535-38.

1866

"Field Notes on *Lophortyx gambeli.*" *Ibis,* 2d ser., II (Jan.), 46-55.

"From Arizona to the Pacific." *Ibis,* 2d ser., II (July), 259-75.

"Some Notes on Arrow-Wounds." *Med. and Surg. Reporter,* XIV (Apr. 28), 321-24.

"On the Occurrence, in the Human Subject, of an Umbilical Coecum." *Med. and Surg. Reporter,* XV (Aug. 11), 142.

"The Osteology of the *Colymbus torquatus*; with Notes on Its Myology." *Mems. Bost. Soc. Nat. Hist.,* I, pt. II (Nov.), 131-72. Reissued as *On the Osteology and Myology of Colymbus torquatus* (Cambridge, Mass.: Riverside Press, 1866) (Coues, 147).

"List of the Birds of Fort Whipple, Arizona: with which are incorporated all other species ascertained to inhabit the Territory; with brief critical and field notes, descriptions of new species, etc." *Procs. Acad. Nat. Scis. Phila.,* XVIII (Mar.), 39-100. Reissued as *Prodrome of a Work on the Ornithology of Arizona Territory* (Philadelphia: Merrihew & Son, 1866) (Coues, 147).

"Critical Review of the Family *Procellariidae:* Part III, Embracing the *Fulmareae.*" *Procs. Acad. Nat. Scis. Phila.,* XVIII (Mar.), 25-33.

"Critical Review of the Family *Procellariidae:* Part IV, Embracing the *Aestrelateae* and *Prioneae.*" *Procs. Acad. Nat. Scis. Phila.,* XVIII (May), 134-72.

"Critical Review of the Family *Procellariidae:* Part V, Embracing the *Diomedeinae* and *Halodrominae.* With a General Supplement." *Procs. Acad. Nat. Scis. Phila.,* XVIII (May), 172-97.

[Notes to] "On the Reptilia and Batrachia of the Sonoran Province of the Nearctic Region," by Edward D. Cope. *Procs. Acad. Nat. Scis. Phila.,* XVIII (Sept.-Nov.), 300-311.

1867

"The Quadrupeds of Arizona." *Amer. Naturalist,* I (Aug.), 281-92; (Sept.), 351-63; (Oct.), 393-400; (Dec.), 531-41.

"Some Remarks on Delirium Tremens, with Cases." *Med. and Surg. Reporter,* XVI (Jan. 26), 61-64.

"A Method of Treating Phymosis." *Med. and Surg. Reporter,* XVI (Apr. 6), 273-74.

"A Case of Hernia of Large Size." *Med. and Surg. Reporter,* XVII (July 27), 69-70.

"Compound, Comminuted, Complicated Fracture of the Skull." *Med. and Surg. Reporter*, XVII (Nov. 23), 437-38.

"Notes on a Collection of Mammals from Arizona." *Procs. Acad. Nat. Scis. Phila.*, XIX (Nov.), 133-36.

[Anon.] "The Birds of New England." *Round Table*, VI (Sept. 28), 213-14. Review of E. A. Samuels's work (Coues, 147).

1868

"Instances of Albinism among Our Birds." *Amer. Naturalist*, II (May), 161-62.

"Bird's Eye Views." *Amer. Naturalist*, II (Dec.), 505-13; (Jan., 1869), 571-83.

"Antero-posterior Symmetry, with Special Reference to the Muscles of the Limbs." *New York Medical Record*, 149-52, 193-95, 222-24, 272-74, 297-99, 370-72, 390-91, 438-40.

"A Monograph of the *Alcidae*." *Procs. Acad. Nat. Scis. Phila.*, XX (Jan.), 2-81. Reprinted in *Zoologist*, 2d ser., V (1870), 2004-16, 2081-90, 2124-34, 2155-63, 2205-14, 2245-53, 2289-96, 2327-34, 2369-86 [?], 2396-2403 (Ballou, 92). Reissued as *A Monograph of the Alcidae* (Philadelphia: Merrihew & Son, 1868) (Coues, 147).

"List of Birds Collected in Southern Arizona by Dr. E. Palmer; with Remarks." *Procs. Acad. Nat. Scis. Phila.*, XX (Jan.), 81-85.

"Synopsis of the Birds of South Carolina." *Procs. Bost. Soc. Nat. Hist.*, XII (Oct.), 104-27.

"Catalogue of the Birds of North America Contained in the Museum of the Essex Institute; with Which Is Incorporated a List of the Birds of New England. With Brief Critical and Field Notes." *Procs. (Comms.) Essex Inst.*, V, 249-314. Reissued as *A List of the Birds of New England* (Salem, Mass.: Essex Institute Press, 1868) (Coues, 147-48).

[Anon.] "Acadian Geology." *Round Table*, VIII (Aug. 29), 137-38. Review of John William Dawson's work (Ballou, 92).

[Anon.] "Michael Faraday." *Round Table*, VIII (Sept. 19), 193-94. Review of John Tyndall's work (Ballou, 92).

"The Education of the Blacks." *Round Table*, VIII (Nov. 7), 308-9; (Nov. 14), 322-24.

[Anon.] "Elements of Physiology and Hygiene." *Round Table*, VIII (Dec. 26), 420-21. Review of J. C. Dalton's work (Ballou, 92).

1869

"Sea-Side Homes: And What Lives in Them." *Amer. Naturalist*, II (Sept.), 337-49.

[Pseud., "P.H.D."] "The Sick Call." *Army and Navy Journal*, July 31 (Ballou, 92).

[Pseud., "A Wayfaring Man."] "Of Doves and Thorns." *Liberal Christian*, July 24 (Coues, 148).

[Anon.] "On the Cacti, Great and Small." *Liberal Christian*, July 31 (Ballou, 103).

[Pseud., "A Wayfaring Man."] "Of Growing Inside and Out." *Liberal Christian*, Aug. 7 (Ballou, 103).

"Rain and Prairie." *Liberal Christian*, Aug. 7.

[Pseud., "A Wayfaring Man."] "Of a 'Fast' Bird." *Liberal Christian*, Aug. 14 (Coues, 148).

"Caging the Sun." *Liberal Christian*, Aug. 28.

"A Possible Process." *Liberal Christian*, Sept. 4.

[Anon.] "A Skeleton in the House." *Liberal Christian*, Sept. 11 (Coues, 148).

[Anon.] "Structure of Feathers." *Liberal Christian*, Oct. 9 (Coues, 148).

[Anon.] "The Serpent's Tooth." *Liberal Christian*, Oct. 16 (Ballou, 103).

[Anon.] "Fascination." *Liberal Christian*, Nov. 27 (Ballou, 103).

"Slovenly Prescriptions." *Med. and Surg. Reporter*, XXI (Aug. 28), 188-89.

"Umbilical Coecum." *Med. and Surg. Reporter*, XXI (Nov. 13), 305. Letter to the editor.

[Anon.] "Malbone: An Old Port Romance." *New York Citizen*, July 10. Review of T. W. Higginson's novel (Ballou, 103).

[Anon.] "The Elements of Theoretical and Descriptive Astronomy." *New York Citizen*, July 17. Review of C. J. Wheeler's work (Ballou, 103).

[Anon.] "The Mississippi Valley." *New York Citizen*, Aug. 7. Review of J. W. Foster's work (Ballou, 103).

"Nine Bones in the Cranium." *New York Medical Record*, Aug. 16. Letter to the editor.

[Anon.] "The Principles of Psychology." *New York Times*, Oct. 14. Review of John Bascom's book (Ballou, 103).

"On the Variations in the Genus *Aegiothus*." *Procs. Acad. Nat. Scis. Phila.*, XXI (Oct.), 180-89.

"On the Classification of Water Birds." *Procs. Acad. Nat. Scis. Phila.*, XXI (Dec.), 193-218.

"On a Chick with Supernumerary Legs." *Procs. Bost. Soc. Nat. Hist.*, XIII, 78-82.

"Observations on the Marsh Hare." *Procs. Bost. Soc. Nat. Hist.*, XIII, 86-93.

"Notice of a Cyclopean Pig." *Procs. Bost. Soc. Nat. Hist.*, XIII, 93-101.

[Anon.] "The Gates Ajar." *Round Table*, IX (Jan. 2), 9-10. Review of Elizabeth Stuart Phelps's novel (Ballou, 92).

[Anon.] "Moral Uses of Dark Things." *Round Table*, IX (Jan. 16), 41-42. Review of Horace Bushnell's book (Ballou, 92).

[Anon.] "Gloverson and His Silent Partner." *Round Table*, IX (Jan. 23), 58. Review of Ralph Keeler's novel (Ballou, 92).

[Anon.] "John Carter." *Round Table*, IX (Feb. 13), 105-6. Review of Frederick James Mills's book (Ballou, 92).

[Anon.] "Adventures in Apache Country." *Round Table*, IX (Feb. 27), 138-39. Review of J. Ross Browne's work (Ballou, 92).

[Anon.] "Greater Britain." *Round Table*, IX (Apr. 3), 217-18. Review of Sir Charles Dilke's work (Ballou, 92).

[Anon.] "Juvenile Delinquents." *Round Table*, IX (Apr. 24), 264-65. Review of B. K. Peirce's book (Ballou, 92).

[Anon.] "Winslow's System of Energetics." *Round Table*, IX (June 5), 361-62; "Second Notice," *ibid.* (June 12), 377-78. Reviews of C. F. Winslow's *Force and Nature* (Ballou, 92).

[Anon.] "Hilt to Hilt." *Round Table*, IX (June 5), 362-63. Review of Esten Cooke's novel (Ballou, 92).

[Anon.] "Warwick." *Round Table*, IX (June 19), 393. Review of Mansfield Tracy Walworth's novel (Ballou, 103).

1870

"Fort Macon, North Carolina." In *A Report on Barracks and Hospitals, with Descriptions of Military Posts* (Circular No. 4, War Department, Surgeon General's Office), 83-91. Washington, D.C.: Government Printing Office.
"The Clapper Rail." *Amer. Naturalist*, IV (Jan.), 600-607.
"Disposal of the Placenta." *Amer. Naturalist*, IV (Mar.), 56.
"The Great Auk." *Amer. Naturalist*, IV (Mar.), 57.
"The Cow Bird." *Amer. Naturalist*, IV (Mar.), 58.
"Foot-notes from a Page of Sand." *Amer. Naturalist*, IV (July), 297-303.
"Ornithological Results of the Exploration of the Northwest." *Amer. Naturalist*, IV (Aug.), 367-71. Review.
"The Natural History of *Quiscalus major*." *Ibis*, VI (July), 367-68.
"Those Worms." *Med. and Surg. Reporter*, XIII (Sept.), 253-54.
[Pseud., "An Old Fogy."] "The Obsolete in Journalism." *Newark* (N.J.) *Daily Journal*, Jan. 15 (Ballou, 123).
"Osteological Notes." *Procs. Bost. Soc. Nat. Hist.*, XIV (1870-71), 251-53.
"Om Tornskadernes Vane at spidde Insekter fortaeller den amerikanske Ornithologo Elliot[t] Coues følgende." *Tidssk. for Populaere Fremst. of Naturvidensk.*, 4th ser., II, 480. Danish translation of *Procs. Bost. Soc. Nat. Hist.*, II (1868), 112-13 (Coues, 598).

1871

Catalogue of the Ornithological Collection in the Museum of the Society. I. Spheniscidae, by Alpheus Hyatt. With a note on the osteology of the family, by Elliott Coues, 15-17. Boston: Boston Society of Natural History. Reprinted from *Procs. Bost. Soc. Nat. Hist.* (1871).
"The Yellow-headed Blackbird." *Amer. Naturalist*, V (June), 195-200.
"Recent Ornithological Publications." *Amer. Naturalist*, V (June), 234-38. Review.
"Progress of American Ornithology." *Amer. Naturalist*, V (Aug.), 364-73. Review of J. A. Allen's "On the Mammals and Winter Birds of East Florida."
[Note appended to "Two Ornithological Items," by B.Walker.] *Amer. Naturalist*, V (Sept.), 437-38.
"Bullock's Oriole." *Amer. Naturalist*, V (Nov.), 678-82.
"Former Eastward Range of the Buffalo." *Amer. Naturalist*, V (Nov.), 719-20.
"A Singular Albino." *Amer. Naturalist*, V (Dec.), 733.
"The Long-crested Jay." *Amer. Naturalist*, V (Dec.), 770-75.
"Gray's Hand List of Birds." *Amer. Naturalist*, V (Dec.), 775-79. Review.
"Aneurism of Aorta, Innominate and Carotid Arteries." *New York Medical Record*, VI, 459-60.
"Notes on the Natural History of Fort Macon, N.C., and Vicinity." (No. 1.) [Vertebrates, except fishes.] *Procs. Acad. Nat. Scis. Phila.*, XXIII (May), 12-49.

"Notes on the Natural History of Fort Macon." (No. 2.) [Invertebrates.] *Procs. Acad. Nat. Scis. Phila.*, XXIII (July), 120-48.

"Mechanism of Flexion and Extension in Birds' Wings." *Procs. Amer. Assn. Adv. Sci.*, XX, 278-84. Abstracted in *Amer. Naturalist*, V (Sept., 1871), 513-14.

["On the Susceptibility to Variation in Numerical Composition of the Bones of the Digits, etc."] *Procs. Bost. Soc. Nat. Hist.*, XIV, 251-53 (Ballou, 123).

"On the Myology of the *Ornithorhynchus*." *Procs. (Comms.) Essex Inst.*, VI, 128-73.

1872

Key to North American Birds: Containing a Concise Account of Every Species of Living and Fossil Bird at Present Known from the Continent North of the Mexican and United States Boundary. Salem, Mass.: Naturalists' Agency.

[Contributions to] *A History of the Birds of Europe, including All the Species Inhabiting the Western Palaearctic Region*, by Henry Eeles Dresser and R. Bowdler Sharpe, pts. XI, XII, XV. London: By the authors.

"Ornithological Query." *Amer. Naturalist*, VI (Jan.), 47.

"Note on *Hemirhamphus (Richardi?).*" *Amer. Naturalist*, VI (Jan.), 49.

"Two Late American Papers on Ornithology." *Amer. Naturalist*, VI (Mar.), 165-66. Review.

[Anon.] "An Ornithological Blunder." *Amer. Naturalist*, VI (Mar.), 172-73 (Coues, 150).

"More about Singing Mice." *Amer. Naturalist*, VI (May), 309-10.

"Newton's Ornithological Register." *Amer. Naturalist*, VI (June), 360-61. Review.

"Geographical Distribution of *Bassaris astuta.*" *Amer. Naturalist*, VI (June), 364.

"A New Bird to the United States." *Amer. Naturalist*, VI (June), 370.

"The Nest, Eggs, and Breeding Habits of *Harporhynchus crissalis.*" *Amer. Naturalist*, VI (June), 370-71.

"Scientific Record." *Amer. Naturalist*, VI (Aug.), 471-74. Review.

"The Boston Society's Ornithological Catalogue." *Amer. Naturalist*, VI (Aug.), 472-73. Review.

"Nests and Eggs of *Helminthophaga luciae.*" *Amer. Naturalist*, VI (Aug.), 493.

"Occurrence of Couch's Flycatcher in the United States." *Amer. Naturalist*, VI (Aug.), 493.

"Giebel's Thesaurus." *Amer. Naturalist*, VI (Sept.), 549-51. Review.

"Recent Discoveries in Ornithotomy." *Amer. Naturalist*, VI (Oct.), 631-35. Review.

"Observations on *Picicorvus columbianus.*" *Ibis*, 3d ser., II (Jan.), 52-59.

"Contribution to the History of the Blue Crow of America." *Ibis*, 3d ser., II (Apr.), 152-58.

"The Osteology and Myology of *Didelphys virginiana*. With an Appendix on the Brain by Jeffries Wyman." *Mems. Bost. Soc. Nat. Hist.*, II, pt. I, no. 3, 41-154.

"Studies of the *Tyrannidae*. Part I: Revision of the Species of *Myiarchus.*" *Procs. Acad. Nat. Scis. Phila.*, XXIV (June 25–July 16), 56-81.

"Material for a Monograph of the *Spheniscidae.*" *Procs. Acad. Nat. Scis. Phila.*, XXIV (Sept.), 170-212.

"Osteological Notes." *Procs. Bost. Soc. Nat. Hist.*, XIV, 251-53.

1873

A Check List of North American Birds. Salem, Mass.: Naturalists' Agency.

[Contributions to] *A History of the Birds of Europe, including All the Species Inhabiting the Western Palaearctic Region,* by Henry Eeles Dresser and R. Bowdler Sharpe, pts. XVI, XX, XXI. London: By the authors.

"Ornithology of the Prybilov Islands." In *Report on the Prybilov Group, or Seal Islands of Alaska,* by Henry W. Elliott; not paged but Coues' contribution occupies 36 pages. Washington, D.C.: Government Printing Office.

[Anon.] "Dubois' Conspectus." *Amer. Naturalist,* VII (Jan.), 40-42. Review (Coues, 151).

"New England Ornithology." *Amer. Naturalist,* VII (Jan.), 42-43. Review.

"Handbook of British Birds." *Amer. Naturalist,* VII (Mar.), 163-65. Review.

"Ornithology of the West." *Amer. Naturalist,* VII (Apr.), 220-23. Review.

"Intermembral Homologies." *Amer. Naturalist,* VII (Apr.), 223-24. Review.

"African Ornithology." *Amer. Naturalist,* VII (Apr.), 226-27. Review.

"Some United States Birds, New to Science and Other Things Ornithological." *Amer. Naturalist,* VII (June), 321-31.

"New Avian Subclass." *Amer. Naturalist,* VII (June), 364.

"The Prairie Wolf, or Coyoté: *Canis latrans.*" *Amer. Naturalist,* VII (July), 385-89.

"Color-variation in Birds Dependent upon Climatic Influences." *Amer. Naturalist,* VII (July), 415-18. Review.

"Late Local Lists." *Amer. Naturalist,* VII (July), 418-21. Review.

"Variation in Dentition." *Amer. Naturalist,* VII (Aug.), 495-96.

"Notes on Two Little-known Birds of the United States." *Amer. Naturalist,* VII (Nov.), 695-97.

"Range of the Eared Grebe." *Amer. Naturalist,* VII (Dec.), 745.

"Notice of a Rare Bird." *Amer. Naturalist,* VII (Dec.), 748-49.

"Range of the *Geococcyx californianus.*" *Amer. Naturalist,* VII (Dec.), 751.

"Use of Small Shot." *Amer. Sportsman,* Nov. 22, 117.

"Specimens of Bird Architecture [Icteridae]." *Amer. Sportsman,* Nov. 29, 129.

"Birds Walking under Water." *Forest and Stream,* Oct. 16, 149-50.

[Circular relating to *Birds of the Northwest.*] *Headquarters Department of Dakota,* Feb. 14 (Coues, 151).

[Anon.] "Love's Meine: Lectures on Greek and English Birds." *Nation,* XVII (Dec. 11), 391-92. Review of John Ruskin's book (McAtee, 3).

1874

Birds of the Northwest: A Hand-book of the Ornithology of the Region Drained by the Missouri River and Its Tributaries. U.S. Geological Survey of the Territories, Miscellaneous Publications, no. 3. Washington, D.C.: Government Printing Office.

Field Ornithology, Comprising a Manual of Instruction for Procuring, Preparing and Preserving Birds, and a Check List of North American Birds. Salem, Mass.: Naturalists' Agency.

["On the Classification of Birds, with Characters of the Higher Groups, and Analytical Tables of North American Families."] In *A History of North*

American Birds, by Spencer F. Baird, Thomas M. Brewer, and Robert Ridgway, I, xiv-xxviii. Boston: Little, Brown.

"Glossary of Technical Terms used in Descriptive Ornithology." In *A History of North American Birds*, by Spencer F. Baird, Thomas M. Brewer, and Robert Ridgway, III, 535-60. Boston: Little, Brown.

"Monograph of the North American *Laridae*." In *Birds of the Northwest*, 589-717.

"Avifauna of Colorado and Wyoming." *Amer. Naturalist*, VIII (Apr.), 240. Review.

"Habits and Characteristics of Swainson's Buzzard." *Amer. Naturalist*. VIII (May), 282-87.

"Surveys West of the 100th Meridian." *Amer. Naturalist*, VIII (May), 302-3. Review.

"English Sparrows." *Amer. Naturalist*, VIII (July), 436.

"New Species of North American Bird."*Amer. Naturalist*, VIII (Aug.), 500-501.

"Recent Publications on Ornithology." *Amer. Naturalist*, VIII (Sept.), 541-46. Review.

"New Variety of the Blue Grosbeak." *Amer. Naturalist*, VIII (Sept.), 563.

"On the Nesting of Certain Hawks, Etc." *Amer. Naturalist*, VIII (Oct.), 596-603.

"Dr. Coues on Shot for Squirrels." *Amer. Sportsman* (Ballou, 141).

"Specimens of Bird Architecture [*Cinclus mexicanus*]." *Amer. Sportsman*, Jan. 17, 245.

"Specimen of a Cougar." *Amer. Sportsman*, Jan. 24, 260.

"Specimens of Bird Architecture [*Chaetura pelasgica*]." *Amer. Sportsman*, Feb. 14, 313.

"Pet Owls." *Amer. Sportsman*, Mar. 7, 354.

"The New Work on Birds." *Amer. Sportsman*, Mar. 28, 412. Review.

"A Useful Hint." *Amer. Sportsman*, Apr. 4, 3-4.

"Specimens of Bird Architecture [hole-breeders]." *Amer. Sportsman*, Apr. 11, 19-20.

"Compliments of Mr. & Mrs. Robert White." *Amer. Sportsman*, May 2, 65.

"The Pine Mouse—*Arvicola pinetorum*." *Amer. Sportsman*, May 9, 81.

"The Mule-deer, *Cervus (Cariacus) macrotis*, Say." *Amer. Sportsman*, May 30, 129.

"Small Shot. Reply to 'Arrow.'" *Amer. Sportsman*, May 30, 140.

"The Californian Vulture." *Amer. Sportsman*, June 13, 161.

"Shooting the Wood Ibis." *Amer. Sportsman*, July 11, 225.

"A Short Chapter on American Rabbits, or Hares." *Amer. Sportsman*, Aug. 29, 387.

"The Rails—Family *Rallidae*." *Amer. Sportsman*, Oct. 31, 65.

"The Sparrow War." *Amer. Sportsman*, Nov. 21, 113.

"Wanted!" *Amer. Sportsman*, Nov. 28, 129.

"From the Headwaters of the Saskatchewan." *Amer. Sportsman*, Dec. 26, 193.

"The Snow-bird as a Sparrow." *Field and Stream*, Apr. 4.

"Birds of Illinois." *Field and Stream*, May 2. Review.

"Wild Turkeys." *Field and Stream*, June 13.

"Dusky Grouse; Blue Grouse; Pine Grouse." *Field and Stream*, June 27, 154; July 11, 170.

"Plumed Quail." *Field and Stream*, July 25, 187; Aug. 8, 203; Aug. 22, 224.

"The Blue Quail." *Field and Stream*, Aug. 29.

"How to Shoot." *Field and Stream*, Sept. 26.

[Anon.] "A History of North American Birds." *Field and Stream*, Oct. 31. Review (Coues, 154).

"Hybrid Ducks [*Anas boscas x Hyonetta moschata*]." *Forest and Stream*, Feb. 19, 22.

"Hybrid Ducks [*Anas boscas x Dafila acuta*]." *Forest and Stream*, Mar. 5, 54.

"Powder-down." *Forest and Stream*, Apr. 9, 134.

[Anon.] "History of North American Birds." *Forest and Stream*, Apr. 30, 179. Review (Coues, 153).

"The Cranes of America." *Forest and Stream*, Aug. 20, 20-21.

"Shells—Paper or Brass?" *Forest and Stream*, Dec. 24, 316.

[Anon.] "The Birds of North America." *Nation*, XVIII (Jan. 22), 65. Review (McAtee, 3).

[Anon.] "North American Ornithology." *Nation*, XVIII (Apr. 23), 270. Review (McAtee, 3).

"Synopsis of the *Muridae* of North America." *Procs. Acad. Nat. Scis. Phila.*, XXVI (Dec.), 173-96. Reissued with additions as U.S. Northern Boundary Commission: Archibald Campbell, Esq., Commissioner. Maj. W. J. Twining, U.S. Engrs., Chief Astronomer. Natural History. No. 1. *On the Muridae*. Philadelphia: Collins, Printer.

1875

"Abstract of Results of a Study of the Genera *Geomys* and *Thomomys*." In *Exploration of the Colorado River of the West, 1869-1872*, by John Wesley Powell, 217-85. Washington, D.C.: Government Printing Office. Separately published as *Abstract of Results of a Study of the Genera Geomys and Thomomys: with Addenda on the Osteology of Geomyidae, and on the Habits of Geomys tuza*. (Washington, D.C.: Government Printing Office, 1875).

"Ornithology of the Prybilov Islands." In *A Report upon the Condition of Affairs in the Territory of Alaska*, by Henry W. Elliott, 168-212. Washington, D.C.: Government Printing Office. An abridged version, with the title "The Fauna of the Prybilov Islands," was published in London in 1875, by J. E. Harting, "reprinted from the Natural History columns of 'The Field' for private circulation" (Coues, 155).

[With H. C. Yarrow.] "Report upon the Collections of Mammals Made in Portions of Nevada, Utah, California, Colorado, New Mexico, and Arizona during the Years 1871, 1872, 1873, and 1874." In *Report upon Geographical and Geological Explorations and Surveys West of the One Hundredth Meridian, in Charge of First Lieutenant George W. Wheeler . . .*, V, 35-129. Washington, D.C.: Government Printing Office.

"Synopsis of the Reptiles and Batrachians of Arizona, with Critical and Field Notes, and an Extensive Synonymy." In *Report upon Geographical and Geological Explorations and Surveys West of the One Hundredth Meridian . . .*, V, 585-633. Washington, D.C.: Government Printing Office.

[*Peucedramus*, Coues, nov. gen., MS.] In *Report upon Geographical and Geological Explorations and Surveys West of the One Hundredth Meridian . . .*, V, 201-2. Washington, D.C.: Government Printing Office.

"On the Breeding of Certain Birds." *Amer. Naturalist*, IX (Feb.), 75-78.

"The Prairie Gopher." *Amer. Naturalist*, IX (Mar.), 147-56, and *Rod and Gun*, Mar. 27. "Reprinted in a great many papers under various editorial modifications" (Coues and Gill, 1068).

"A Late Paper on Birds." *Amer. Naturalist*, IX (Nov.), 570-71.

"The Sparrows." *Amer. Sportsman*, Jan. 23, 264.

"Synonymy, Description, History, Distribution and Habits of the Prairie Hare (*Lepus campestris*)." *Bull. Essex. Inst.*, VII (May), 73-85.

"The Cranial and Dental Characters of *Mephitinae*, with Description of *Mephitis frontata*, n. sp. foss." *Bull. U.S. Geol. and Geogr. Surv. Terrs.*, 2d ser., no. 1, 7-15.

"The Cranial and Dental Characters of *Geomyidae*." *Bull. U.S. Geol. and Geogr. Surv. Terrs.*, 2d ser., no. 2, 83-90.

"Some Account, Critical, Descriptive, and Historical, of *Zapus hudsonius*." *Bull. U.S. Geol. and Geogr. Surv. Terrs.*, 2d ser., no. 5, 253-62.

[Ed.] "Contributions to the Natural History of Kerguelen Island, Made in Connection with the American Transit-of-Venus Expedition, 1874-1875. I. Ornithology," by J. H. Kidder. *Bull. U.S. Nat. Mus.*, no. 2, i-ix, 1-51.

"Salutatory." *Field and Forest*, I (June), 1-2.

"Chips from the Buffalo's Workshop." *Forest and Stream* extra, "printed for special distribution, April 1, 1875" (Coues and Gill, 1032).

"Ornithology of the Transit-of-Venus 'Centennial.'" *Forest and Stream*, Aug. 19, 20.

[Anon.] "First Book of Zoology." *Forest and Stream*, Oct. 21, 167. Review (Ballou, 141).

["On the Nest and Eggs of *Gymnocitta cyanocephala*."] *Ibis*, 3d ser., V (Apr.), 270-71.

[Anon.] "First Book of Zoology." *Nation*, XXI (Nov. 11), 315-16. Review (McAtee, 3).

[Anon. Notice of Thomas M. Brewer's *Catalogue of the Birds of New England*.] *New York Independent*, Oct. 7. Review (Coues, 155).

"Recent Text-Books of Zoology." *New York Independent*, Dec. 2, 7.

"Winged Quadrupeds." *Penn Monthly*, VI (May), 341-53.

"Synopsis of *Geomyidae*." *Procs. Acad. Nat. Scis. Phila.*, XXVI (June), 130-38.

"A Critical Review of the North American *Saccomyidae*." *Procs. Acad. Nat. Scis. Phila.*, XXVI (Aug.), 272-327.

"Fasti Ornithologiae Redivivi.—No. 1. Bartram's 'Travels.'" *Procs. Acad. Nat. Scis. Phila.*, XXVI (Sept.-Oct.), 338-58.

"Albino Black-bird." *Rod and Gun*, Apr. 10, 24.

"Duck Shooting *à Cheval*." *Rod and Gun*, Apr. 24, 49-50.

"The Silvery Mole." *Rod and Gun*, May 22, 113.

"Concerning 'Pocket Gophers.'" *Rod and Gun*, June 5, 146.

"Sparrows—More Evidence." *Rod and Gun*, July 17, 249.

[Anon.] "First Book of Zoology." *Rod and Gun*, Oct. 22. Review (Ballou, 141).

1876

[Reports on cases at Mount Pleasant Hospital, Washington, D.C., 1863.] In *The*

Medical and Surgical History of the War of the Rebellion, pt. II, vol. II, *Surgical History*, by George A. Otis, 580, 762, 785. Washington, D.C.: Government Printing Office.

"Bewick's Wren, *Thryothorus bewicki*." *Amer. Naturalist*, X (Jan.), 48.

"Range of the Bay Ibis." *Amer. Naturalist*, X (Jan.), 48.

"Reply to Mr. J. A. Allen's 'Availability of Certain Bartramian Names in Ornithology.'" *Amer. Naturalist*, X (Feb.), 98-102.

"Breeding Range of the Snow-Bird." *Amer. Naturalist*, X (Feb.), 114-15.

"Unusual Nesting Sites of the Night Hawk and Towhee Bunting." *Amer. Naturalist*, X (Apr.), 239.

"The Labrador Duck." *Amer. Naturalist*, X (May), 303.

"The European Woodcock Shot in Virginia." *Amer. Naturalist*, X (June), 372.

"Notable Changes of Habit of the Bank Swallow." *Amer. Naturalist*, X (June), 372-73.

"The Destruction of Birds by Telegraph Wire." *Amer. Naturalist*, X (Dec.), 734-36.

"Tarsal Envelope in *Campylorhynchus* and Allied Genera." *Bull. Nutt. Orn. Club*, I (July), 50-51.

"On the Number of Primaries in *Oscines*." *Bull. Nutt. Orn. Club*, I (Sept.), 60-63.

"Peculiar Nesting-Site of the Bank-Swallow." *Bull. Nutt. Orn. Club*, I (Nov.), 96.

"On the Breeding-Habits, Nest, and Eggs, of the White-tailed Ptarmigan *(Lagopus leucurus)*." *Bull. U.S. Geol. and Geogr. Surv. Terrs.*, 2d ser., no. 5, 263-66.

"An Account of the Various Publications Relating to the Travels of Lewis and Clarke [*sic*], with a Commentary on the Zoological Results of Their Expedition." *Bull. U.S. Geol. and Geogr. Surv. Terrs.*, 2d ser., no. 6, 417-44.

[With J. H. Kidder.] "Oology, etc." In "Contributions to the Natural History of Kerguelen Island, Made in Connection with the United States Transit-of-Venus Expedition, 1874-75." *Bull. U.S. Nat. Mus.*, no. 3, 7-20.

[With J. H. Kidder.] "A Study of *Chionis minor* with Reference to Its Structure and Systematic Position." In "Contributions to the Natural History of Kerguelen Island, Made in Connection with the United States Transit-of-Venus Expedition, 1874-75." *Bull. U.S. Nat. Mus.*, no. 3, 85-116.

"Letters on Ornithology. No. 1.—The Oregon Robin." *Chicago Field*, June 24.

"Letters on Ornithology. No. 2.—The American Tree-Creeper." *Chicago Field*, Aug. 12.

"Letters on Ornithology. No. 3.—The Blue-gray Gnatcatcher." *Chicago Field*, Aug. 26.

"Letters on Ornithology. No. 4.—The Horned or Shore Lark." *Chicago Field*, Oct. 7.

"Letters on Ornithology. No. 5.—Marsh Wrens." *Chicago Field*, Nov. 18.

"Letters on Ornithology. No. 6.—The Shrike, or Butcher Bird." *Chicago Field*, Dec. 2.

"Letters on Ornithology. No. 7.—The Catbird." *Chicago Field*, Dec. 9.

"Letters on Ornithology. No. 8.—Nuthatches." *Chicago Field*, Dec. 16.

"Letters on Ornithology. No. 9.—The Red-tailed Buzzard." *Chicago Field*, Dec. 23.

"Letters on Ornithology. No. 10.—Titmice, Tomtits, or Chickadees." *Chicago Field*, Dec. 30.

"A Correction." *Forest and Stream*, Feb. 24, 36.

"A Letter of Promise." *Forest and Stream*, Mar. 2, 52.

"Reversion of the Dog to the Feral State." *Forest and Stream*, Nov. 9, 213.

[Covering note to] "Melanism in *Cynomys ludovicianus*," by Julia S. Gilliss. *Forest and Stream*, Nov. 23, 245.

"Musical Mice." *Musician and Artist*, I (Mar.), 76-82.

[Anon.] "Life Histories of the Birds of Eastern Pennsylvania." *Nation*, XXII (May 4), 296-97. Review (McAtee, 3).

[Anon. Notice of the first issue of the *Bulletin of the Nuttall Ornithological Club.*] *Nation*, XXII (May 25), 335 (McAtee, 3).

[Anon.] "Life Histories of Animals, including Man." *Nation*, XXII (May 25), 340. Review (McAtee, 3).

[Anon. Notice of J. A. Allen's *The American Bison.*] *Nation*, XXIII (Dec. 7), 341. (McAtee, 3).

[Anon. Notice of George M. Dawson's paper on the locust invasion.] *Nation*, XXIII (Dec. 14), 357 (McAtee, 3).

[Anon. Notice of publications of the U.S. Geological and Geographical Survey of the Territories.] *Nation*, XXIII (Dec. 21), 369-70 (McAtee, 3).

[Anon.] "The Land-Birds and Game-Birds of New England." *Nation*, XXIII (Dec. 28), 388. Review (McAtee, 3).

[Anon.] "Anecdote of a Crow's Intelligence." *New York Independent*, Nov. 23 (Coues, 157).

[Anon.] "Recent Text-books of Zoology." *New York Independent*, Dec. 2. Review (Coues, 157).

"Coues to 'Boone.'" *Rod and Gun*, Jan. 15, 248.

"Dr. Coues on Brant, etc." *Rod and Gun*. Apr. 1, 8-9.

"Dr. Coues upon Quail, etc." *Rod and Gun*, Apr. 1, 9.

"Mr. Gentry's Book about Birds." *Rod and Gun*, Apr. 29, 71. Review.

"Brant Once More." *Rod and Gun*, July 8, 234.

"This Brant Business." *Rod and Gun*, July 22, 266.

"Au Revoir(?)." *Rod and Gun*, Aug. 5, 299.

[Introduction to] "Prairie Dogs as Pets," by Julia S. Gilliss. *Rod and Gun*, Sept. 2, 362.

"Dr. Coues on 'Partridge', 'Quail', etc." *Rod and Gun*, Nov. 11, 88-89.

[Anon.] "Art of Work." *Washington Capitol*, Feb. 13 (Ballou, 151).

[Pseud., "S. O. T."] "A Married Man's Meditation on How and Why People Go to the Springs." *Washington Capitol*, Sept. 26 (Ballou, 151).

1877

Birds of the North-West: A Hand-book of American Ornithology, Containing Accounts of All the Birds Inhabiting the Great Missouri Valley, and Many Others, together Representing a Large Majority of Birds of North America, with Copious Biographical Details from Personal Observation, and an Extensive Synonymy. Boston: Estes and Lauriat; Salem, Mass.: Naturalists' Agency. "This is simply 214 copies of the original *Birds of the North-West*, 1874, . . . reissued, rebound with publisher's new title-leaf as above" (Coues, *Birds of the Colorado Valley* (1878), 730).

Fur-Bearing Animals: A Monograph of North American Mustelidae, in Which an Account of the Wolverene, the Martens or Sables, the Ermine, the Mink and Various Other Kinds of Weasels, Several Species of Skunks, the Badger, the Land and Sea Otters, and Numerous Exotic Allies of These Animals, Is Contributed to the History of North American Animals. U.S. Geological Survey of the Territories, Miscellaneous Publications, no. 8. Washington, D.C.: Government Printing Office. A trade edition of this work was published in Boston by Estes and Lauriat, also in 1877.

[With J. A. Allen.] *Monographs of North American Rodentia.* Report of the U.S. Geological Survey of the Territories, XI. Washington, D.C: Government Printing Office.

[With Theodore Gill.] "Material for a Bibliography of North American Mammals." Appendix B of *Monographs of North American Rodentia*, by Coues and Allen, 951-1081. Washington, D.C.: Government Printing Office.

"O Breathe It under Thy Breath Love!" Song, with words by Coues and music by J. P. Caulfield. Boston: Oliver Ditson.

[Ed.] "History of the American Bison, *Bison americanus*," by J. A. Allen, 443-587. In *Ninth Annual Report of the United States Geological and Geographical Survey of the Territories, Embracing Colorado and Parts of Adjacent Territories: Being a Report of Progress of the Exploration for the Year 1875.* Washington, D.C.: Government Printing Office.

"Notes on the Deformed Antler of a Deer." *Amer. Naturalist*, XI (Apr.), 242.

"Caton's Deer of America." *Amer. Naturalist*, XI (June), 354-58. Review.

"Mammals New to the United States Fauna." *Amer. Naturalist*, XI (Aug.), 492-93.

"Notes on the Mexican *Spermophilus*." *Amer. Naturalist*, XI (Nov.), 688.

"Birds." (Baltimore) *Mirror*, June 1, July 1, Aug. 1, Sept. 1, Oct. 1, Nov. 1, Dec. 1. From *Birds of the Northwest* (Coues, 159).

"Notes on *Podiceps dominicus*." *Bull. Nutt. Orn. Club*, II (Jan.), 26.

"Eastward Range of the Ferruginous Buzzard." *Bull. Nutt. Orn. Club*, II (Jan.), 26.

"Corrections of Nomenclature in the Genus *Siurus*." *Bull. Nutt. Orn. Club*, II (Apr.), 29-33.

"Minot's 'Birds of New England.'" *Bull. Nutt. Orn. Club*, II (Apr.), 49-50. Review.

"Western Range of *Conurus carolinensis*." *Bull. Nutt. Orn. Club*, II (Apr.), 50.

"Note on the Cinnamon Teal (*Querquedula cyanoptera*)." *Bull. Nutt. Orn. Club*, II (Apr.), 51.

"*Leptoptila albifrons*, a Pigeon New to the United States Fauna." *Bull. Nutt. Orn. Club*, II (July), 82-83.

"*Melopelia leucoptera* in Colorado." *Bull. Nutt. Orn. Club*, II (July), 83.

[Annotations for] "Notes on the Ornithology of the Region about the Source of the Red River of Texas, from Observations Made during the Explorations Conducted by Lieut. E. H. Ruffner, Corps of Engineers, U.S.A.," by C. A. H. McCauley. *Bull. U.S. Geol. and Geogr. Surv. Terrs.*, III, no. 3, 655-95.

"Precursory Notes on American Insectivorous Mammals." *Bull. U.S. Geol. and Geogr. Surv. Terrs.*, III, no. 3, 631-53.

"To the Swallow." *Chicago Field*, Jan. 6. Reprinted in *Rod and Gun*, Feb. 3, 1877.

"Letters on Ornithology. No. 11.—Swallows." *Chicago Field*, Jan. 6.

"Letters on Ornithology. No. 12.—Woodpeckers." *Chicago Field*, Jan. 13.

"Letters on Ornithology. No. 13.—The Harrier." *Chicago Field*, Feb. 3.

"Letters on Ornithology. No. 13 [bis=14].—Grasshoppers." *Chicago Field*, Mar. 17.

"Letters on Ornithology. No. 15.—Curious Crows." *Chicago Field*, July 14.

"Letters on Ornithology. No. 16.—The English Sparrows." *Chicago Field*, July 21.

"Letters on Ornithology. No. 16 [bis=17].—The American Warblers.—Family *Sylvicolidae*." *Chicago Field*, Dec. 15.

"A 'Stand-off' between Snake and Frog." *Field and Forest*, II (Jan.), 123.

[With D. Webster Prentiss.] "Remarks on Birds of the District of Columbia." *Field and Forest*, II (May), 191-93. Reprinted in *Catalogue of the Birds of the District of Columbia*, by Pierre Louis Jouy, 9-11 (Washington, D.C.: Columbia Press, 1877).

"History and Habits of the Wolverene *(Gulo luscus)*." *Forest and Stream*, Jan. 4, 337-39.

"The Mammals of Wyoming." *Forest and Stream*, Jan. 18, 373.

[Anon.] "The Land Birds and Game Birds of New England." *Forest and Stream*, Jan. 25, 391. Review (Coues, 158).

"Our Washington Letter. Zoology and Comparative Anatomy—Lectures by Dr. Elliott Coues." *Forest and Stream*, June 21, 327-28.

"Quail at Sea." *Forest and Stream*, Nov. 29, 327.

"The Song That the Bluebird Sings." *Harper's New Monthly Magazine*, LIV (May), 891.

[Anon.] "Life-history of Our Planet." *Nation*, XXIV (Jan. 25), 62-63. Review (McAtee, 4).

[Anon. Reference to a circular from the Surgeon General's Office requesting medical officers to cooperate for Coues' projected "History of North American Mammals."] *Nation*, XXIV (Apr. 5), 206-7 (McAtee, 4).

[Anon.] "Our Birds of Prey." *Nation*, XXIV (June 7), 341-42. Review (McAtee, 4).

[Anon.] "The Antelope and Deer of America." *Nation*, XXV (Aug. 9), 94. Review (McAtee, 4).

[Anon. Notice of the new (1877) edition of J. A. Allen's monograph on the American bison.] *Nation*, XXV (Aug. 16), 105-6 (McAtee, 4).

"Imagination." *Popular Science Monthly*, XI (Aug.), 455-61.

[Anon.] "Land Birds and Game Birds of New England." *Rod and Gun*, Jan. 27, 263. Review (Coues, 158).

"Communion with Birds." (Terrell, Tex.) *Temperance Vidette*, Aug. 11. Extract from *Birds of the Northwest*, by "Massena" (Ballou, 200).

[Circular about "History of North American Mammals," War Department, Surgeon General's Office, Washington, D.C., Mar. 31.] "Reprinted in many periodicals" (Ballou, 200).

"The Sparrow Once More.—Dr. Coues Replies to Dr. Brewer." (Washington) *Gazette*, July 8.

1878

Birds of the Colorado Valley: A Repository of Scientific and Popular Information concerning North American Ornithology. Part first. Passeres to Laniidae. U.S. Geological Survey of the Territories, Miscellaneous Publications, no. 11. Washington, D.C.: Government Printing Office.

"List of Faunal Publications relating to North American Ornithology." Bibliographical appendix to *Birds of the Colorado Valley*, 567-784. This constitutes the first installment of Coues' "Ornithological Bibliography"; for the second, third, and fourth installments, see 1879 and 1880.

"Peculiar Feather of the Young Ruddy Duck." *Amer. Naturalist*, XII (Feb.), 123-24.

"*Bassaris astuta* in Oregon." *Amer. Naturalist*, XII (Apr.), 253.

"The Ineligibility of the European House Sparrow in America." *Amer. Naturalist*, XII (Aug.), 499-505.

"Note on *Passerculus bairdi* and *P. princeps*." *Bull. Nutt. Orn. Club*, III (Jan.), 1-3.

"The Northern Phalarope in North Carolina." *Bull. Nutt. Orn. Club.* III (Jan.), 40-41.

"The Willow Grouse in New York." *Bull. Nutt. Orn. Club*, III (Jan.), 41.

"*Pipilo erythrophthalmus* with Spotted Scapulars." *Bull. Nutt. Orn. Club*, III (Jan.), 41-42.

"Melanism in *Turdus migratorius*." *Bull. Nutt. Orn. Club*, III (Jan.), 47-48.

"On the Moult of the Bill and Palpebral Ornaments in *Fratercula arctica*." *Bull. Nutt. Orn. Club*, III (Apr.), 87-91.

"Habits of the Kingfisher." *Bull. Nutt. Orn. Club*, III (Apr.), 92.

"Nesting of *Vireo olivaceus*." *Bull. Nutt. Orn. Club*, III (Apr.), 95.

"Nests and Eggs of *Selasphorus platycercus*." *Bull. Nutt. Orn. Club*, III (Apr.), 95.

"Meaning of the Word 'Anhinga.'" *Bull. Nutt. Orn. Club*, III (Apr.), 101.

"The Eave, Cliff, or Crescent Swallow *(Petrochelidon lunifrons)*." *Bull. Nutt. Orn. Club*, III (July), 105-12.

"Mr. H. Saunders on the *Sterninae*." *Bull. Nutt. Orn. Club*, III (July), 140-44. Review.

"Swallow-tailed Kite in Dakota in Winter." *Bull. Nutt. Orn. Club*, III (July), 147.

"A Hint to Egg-Collectors." *Bull. Nutt. Orn. Club*, III (Oct.), 191.

"Nest and Eggs of *Helminthophaga pinus*." *Bull. Nutt. Orn. Club*, III (Oct.), 194.

[Ed.] "Notes on the Ornithology of the Lower Rio Grande of Texas, from Observations Made during the Season of 1877," by George B. Sennett. *Bull. U.S. Geol. and Geogr. Surv. Terrs.*, IV, no. 1, 1-66.

[Annotations to] "Notes on the Mammals of Fort Sisseton, Dakota," by C. E. McChesney. *Bull. U.S. Geol. and Geogr. Surv. Terrs.*, IV, no. 1, 201-18.

[With H. C. Yarrow.] "Notes on the Herpetology of Dakota and Montana." *Bull. U.S. Geol. and Geogr. Surv. Terrs.*, IV, no. 1, 259-91.

"On the Consolidation of the Hoofs in the Virginian Deer." *Bull. U.S. Geol. and Geogr. Surv. Terrs.*, IV, no. 1, 293-94.

"On a Breed of Solid-Hoofed Pigs Apparently Established in Texas." *Bull. U.S. Geol. and Geogr. Surv. Terrs.*, IV, no. 1, 295-97.

"Field-notes on Birds Observed in Dakota and Montana along the Forty-ninth Parallel during the Seasons of 1873 and 1874." *Bull. U.S. Geol. and Geogr. Surv. Terrs.*, V, no. 3, 545-661.

"Letters on Ornithology. No. 17.—The Aquatic Wood-Wagtail, or New York Water Thrush. (*Siurus naevius*)." *Chicago Field*, Feb. 2.

"Letters on Ornithology. No. 18.—The Yellow-breasted Chat." *Chicago Field*, June 29.

"The Sparrow Pest." *Country*, Jan. 19.

"Justice to the English Sparrow." *Country*, Feb. 16.

"A Book on Bird-Architecture." *Country*, Mar. 6. Review.

"New Birds for the United States Fauna." *Country*, July 13.

[A note to a French translation of "Jim Crow," by A. R. Warnwright.] *Literary World*, VIII (Feb.), 169.

[Anon.] "Wilson's and Bonaparte's American Ornithology." *Nation*, XXVII (Nov. 7), 289-90. Review (McAtee, 4).

[With H. C. Yarrow.] "Notes on the Natural History of Fort Macon, N.C. and Vicinity." (No. 4.) [Vertebrates, supplement to No. 1.] *Procs. Acad. Nat. Scis. Phila.*, XXX (Mar.-Apr.), 21-28.

[With H. C. Yarrow.] "Notes on the Natural History of Fort Macon, N.C. and Vicinity." (No. 5.) [*Crustacea.*] *Procs. Acad. Nat. Scis. Phila.*, XXX (Nov., 1878–Jan., 1879), 297-330.

1879

"Notice of Mrs. Maxwell's Exhibit of Colorado Mammals." In *On the Plains, and among the Peaks; or, How Mrs. Maxwell Made Her Natural History Collection*, by Mary Dartt, 217-25. Philadelphia: Claxton, Remsen & Haffelfinger.

"Special Report on Cases of Acute Dysentery Occurring in the Detachment of Troops Stationed at Columbia, South Carolina . . . November 30, 1868." In *The Medical and Surgical History of the War of the Rebellion*, pt. II, vol. I, *Medical History*, 2d issue, by Joseph Janvier Woodward, 62-65. Washington, D.C.: Government Printing Office.

"The Outer Ear of *Blarina brevicauda*." *Amer. Journal of Otology*, I (July), 161-62. Reissued as *The Outer Ear of Blarina brevicauda* (New York: William Wood, 1879).

"Note on the Hairy-tailed Mole, *Scalops breweri* of Authors." *Amer. Naturalist*, XIII (Mar.), 189-90.

"To Prevent Grease from Injuring the Plumage of Birds." *Amer. Naturalist*, XIII (July), 456.

"Ingersoll's Nests and Eggs of American Birds." *Amer. Naturalist*, XIII (Aug.), 515-16. Review.

"Texan Ornithology." *Amer. Naturalist*, XIII (Aug.), 516-19. Review.

"Destructiveness of English Sparrows." *Amer. Naturalist*, XIII (Nov.), 706.

"Habits of *Spermophilus richardsoni*." *Amer. Naturalist*, XIII (Nov.), 709.

"Notes on the Nomenclature of *Hesperomys americanus* Coues and Yarrow." *Amer. Naturalist*, XIII (Dec.), 784.

"Jones and Shulze's Illustrations of the Nest and Eggs of the Birds of Ohio." *Bull. Nutt. Orn. Club*, IV (Jan.), 52. Review.

[Note on *Dendroeca chrysoparia*.] *Bull. Nutt. Orn. Club*, IV (Jan.), 60n.

"History of the Evening Grosbeak." *Bull. Nutt. Orn. Club*, IV (Apr.), 65-75.

"Langdon's Revised List of Cincinnati Birds." *Bull. Nutt. Orn. Club*, IV (Apr.), 112-13. Review.

"Note on *Dendroeca townsendi*." *Bull. Nutt. Orn. Club*, IV (Apr.), 117.

"Note on *Bucephala islandica*." *Bull. Nutt. Orn. Club*, IV (Apr.), 126-27.

["On the Use of Trinomials in Zoological Nomenclature."] *Bull. Nutt. Orn. Club*, IV (July), 171.

"Note on the Black-capped Greenlet, *Vireo atricapillus* of Woodhouse." *Bull. Nutt. Orn. Club*, IV (Oct.), 193-94.

"Obituary [of Genevieve E. Jones]." *Bull. Nutt. Orn. Club*, IV (Oct.), 228.

"Southward Range of *Centrophanes lapponica*." *Bull. Nutt. Orn. Club*, IV (Oct.), 238.

"A Correction." *Bull. Nutt. Orn. Club*, IV (Oct.), 242.

"Note on *Alle nigricans*, Link." *Bull. Nutt. Orn. Club*, IV (Oct.), 244.

"On the Present Status of *Passer domesticus* in America, with Special Reference to the Western States and Territories." *Bull. U.S. Geol. and Geogr. Surv. Terrs.*, V, no. 2, 175-93.

"Second Instalment of American Ornithological Bibliography." *Bull. U.S. Geol. and Geogr. Surv. Terrs.*, V, no. 2, 239-330.

[Ed.] "Further Notes on the Ornithology of the Lower Rio Grande of Texas, from Observations Made during the Spring of 1878," by George B. Sennett. *Bull. U.S. Geol. and Geogr. Surv. Terrs.*, V, no. 3, 371-440.

"Third Instalment of American Ornithological Bibliography." *Bull. U.S. Geol. and Geogr. Surv. Terrs.*, V, no. 4, 521-1066.

"Letters on Ornithology. No. 19.—The Curlews." *Chicago Field*, Apr. 26.

"Letters on Ornithology. No. 20.—The American Bittern." *Chicago Field*, May 10.

"Letters on Ornithology. No. 21.—History of the Red-breasted, or Cinnamon Teal." *Chicago Field*, May 17.

"Letters on Ornithology. No. 22.—The Snow Goose, or White Brant." *Chicago Field*, May 24.

"Letters on Ornithology. No. 23.—The American Coot." *Chicago Field*, June 9.

"Letters on Ornithology. No. 24.—The Wood Ibis." *Chicago Field*, June 14.

"Letters on Ornithology. No. 25.—The Solitary Tattler; Wood Tattler." *Chicago Field*, June 21.

"Letters on Ornithology. No. 26.—Semipalmated Tattler, Willet, Stone Snipe." *Chicago Field*, June 28.

"Letters on Ornithology. No. 27.—Bartramian Sandpiper or Tattler; Upland Plover." *Chicago Field*, July 5.

"Letters on Ornithology. No. 28.—The Buff-breasted Sandpiper." *Chicago Field*, July 12.

"Letters on Ornithology. No. 29.—Green Marbled Godwit." *Chicago Field*, July 19.

"Letters on Ornithology. No. 30.—The Great White Egret." *Chicago Field*, July 26.

"Nesting of the Great Blue Heron in the West." *Chicago Field*, Aug. 2.

"Dr. Elliott Coues Makes a Grave Charge against Archer." *Chicago Field*, Nov. 29.

"The Sea Lion." *Chicago Field*, Dec. 27.

"Caton's Antelope and Deer of North America." *Chicago Field*, Dec. 27.

"Latest from the Seat of War in Sparrowland." *Forest and Stream*, Feb. 27, 66.

"Two Fragments." *Forest and Stream*, May 8, 264.

[Anon.] "Manuel du Voyageur." *Nation*, XXVIII (Mar. 27), 220-21. Review (McAtee, 4).

[Anon.] "The Evolution of Man." *Nation*, XXIX (Dec. 18), 429-30. Review (McAtee, 4).

"Nest and Eggs of the Clay-colored Bunting." *Oologist*, IV (Feb.), 50.

"Coues on the Nest and Eggs of the Water Thrush." *Oologist*, IV (Mar.), 57.

"Le Conte's Thrasher." *Oologist*, IV (July), 99-100.

"The Western Sphynx, an Analysis of Indian Traits and Tendencies." *Penn Monthly*, X (Mar.), 180-93.

"Private Letters of Wilson, Ord and Bonaparte." *Penn Monthly*, X (June), 443-55.

"The Sparrow Nuisance." *Washington World*, Mar. 17.

1880

[American editor's preface to] *Rural Bird Life: Being Essays on Ornithology, with Instructions for Preserving Objects relating to That Science*, by Charles Dixon, iii-viii. Boston: Estes and Lauriat.

"Sketch of North American Ornithology in 1879." *Amer. Naturalist*, XIV (Jan.), 20-25.

"Differences in the Habits of *Scalops aquaticus* and *Scaranus americanus*." *Amer. Naturalist*, XIV (Jan.), 52-53.

"Depredations of the European Sparrow." *Amer. Naturalist*, XIV (Feb.), 130.

"Sketch of Progress in Mammalogy in the United States in 1879." *Amer. Naturalist*, XIV (Mar.), 161-66.

"Advent of *Passer domesticus* in North Carolina." *Amer. Naturalist*, XIV (Mar.), 213.

"On the Nesting in Missouri of *Empidonax acadicus* and *E. trailii*." *Bull. Nutt. Orn. Club*, V (Jan.), 20-25.

"Ingersoll's Nests and Eggs of American Birds." *Bull. Nutt. Orn. Club*, V (Jan.), 38-39. Review.

"The Misses Jones and Shulze's Nests and Eggs of Ohio Birds." *Bull. Nutt. Orn. Club*, V (Jan.), 39-40. Review.

"Description of the Female *Dendroeca kirtlandi*." *Bull. Nutt. Orn. Club*, V (Jan.), 49-50.

"Note on *Limosa haemastica*." *Bull. Nutt. Orn. Club*, V (Jan.), 59-60.

"Capture of *Phaethon flavirostris* in Western New York." *Bull. Nutt. Orn. Club*, V (Jan.), 63.

"Notes and Queries concerning the Nomenclature of North America Birds." *Bull. Nutt. Orn. Club*, V (Apr.), 95-102.

"Further Light on the Moult of the Bill in Certain *Mormonidae*." *Bull Nutt. Orn. Club*, V (Apr.), 127-28.

"Shufeldt's Memoir on the Osteology of *Speotyto cunicularia hypogaea*." *Bull. Orn. Club*, V (July), 129-30.

"Gentry's Nests and Eggs of the Birds of Pennsylvania." *Bull. Nutt. Orn. Club*, V (July), 179. Review.

"Ober's Camps in the Caribees." *Bull. Nutt. Orn. Club*, V (July), 179. Review.

"Nests and Eggs of *Catherpes mexicanus conspersus*." *Bull. Nutt. Orn. Club*, V (July), 181-82.

"Number of Eggs of *Ardea herodias*." *Bull. Nutt. Orn. Club*, V (July), 187.

"Note of *Grus fraterculus* of Cassin." *Bull. Nutt. Orn. Club*, V (July), 188.

"Behind the Veil." *Bull. Nutt. Orn. Club*, V (Oct.), 193-204.

"Marsh's Palaeornithology." *Bull. Nutt. Orn. Club*, V (Oct.), 234-36. Review.

"The Origin of the Turkey." *Forest and Stream*, Jan. 1, 947-48.

[Letters on *Passer domesticus* in America and Australia.] *Forest and Stream*, Apr. 15, 204.

[Anon. Notice of Joseph Leidy's *Fresh-water Rhizopods of North America*.] Nation, XXX (Feb. 12), 117 (McAtee, 4).

[Anon. Announcement of plans for the publication of a "History of North American Mammals" and comments on the printing of the third and fourth installments of the bibliography of ornithology.] *Nation*, XXX (Apr. 29), 327 (McAtee, 4).

[Anon. News of the Apr. 20-23 meeting of the National Academy of Sciences.] *Nation*, XXX (Apr. 29), 327 (McAtee, 4).

[Anon. Notice of a delay in the publication of the third installment of the bibliography of ornithology and an announcement of the publication of the fourth installment.] *Nation*, XXXI (Aug. 5), 96 (McAtee, 4).

"Fourth Instalment of Ornithological Bibliography: Being a List of Faunal Publications relating to British Birds." *Procs. U.S. Nat. Mus.*, II, 359-482.

1881

[Ed.] *New England Bird Life, Being a Manual of New England Ornithology, Revised and Edited from the Manuscript of Winfrid A. Stearns, Member of the Nuttall Ornithological Club etc. Part I.—Oscines*. Boston: Lee and Shepard.

"A Curious *Colaptes*." *Bull. Nutt. Orn. Club*, VI (July), 183.

"A Correction." *Bull. Nutt. Orn. Club*, VI (July), 188.

"Probable Occurrence of *Sarcorhamphus papa* in Arizona." *Bull. Nutt. Orn. Club*, VI (Oct.), 248.

[Trans., with notes, of] "Revision of the Genus *Sciurus*," by E. L. Trouessart. *Bull. U.S. Geol. and Geogr. Surv. Terrs.*, VI, no. 2, 301-7.

"Names of the 'Blue-Water' Indians." *Nation*, XXXIII (July 28), 73.

1882

Biogen: A Speculation on the Origin and Nature of Life. Washington, D.C.: Judd & Detweiler.

The Coues Check List of North American Birds. Second Edition, Revised to Date, and Entirely Rewritten, under Direction of the Author, with a Dictionary of the Etymology, Orthography, and Orthoepy of the Scientific Names, the Concordance of Previous Lists, and a Catalogue of His Ornithological Publications. Boston: Estes and Lauriat.

"The Nature of the Human Temporal Bone." *Amer. Journal of Otology*, IV, 17-36.

"The Sparrow Pest in Australia." *Amer. Naturalist*, XVI (Feb.), 140-41.

"Occurrence of the Opossum in Central New York." *Amer. Naturalist*, XVI (Feb.), 141.

"Habits of the English Sparrow." *Amer. Naturalist*, XVI (Dec.), 1009.

"Memorial Volume of Garrod's Scientific Papers." *Bull. Nutt. Orn. Club*, VII (Jan.), 43-44. Review.

"Illustrations of Ohio Nests and Eggs." *Bull. Nutt. Orn. Club*, VII (Jan.), 45-46. Review.

"Papers on Minnesota Birds." *Bull. Nutt. Orn. Club*, VII (Jan.), 47. Review.

"Nesting of the White-bellied Wren *(Thryothorus bewicki leucogaster)*." *Bull. Nutt. Orn. Club*, VII (Jan.), 52-53.

"Note on *Mitrephanes*, a New Generic Name." *Bull. Nutt. Orn. Club*, VII (Jan.), 55.

"Wilson's Plover *(Aegialites wilsonius)* in New England." *Bull. Nutt. Orn. Club*, VII (Jan.), 59-60.

"The Snake-bird in Kansas." *Bull. Nutt. Orn. Club*, VII (Jan.), 61.

"Nests and Eggs of Ohio Birds." *Bull. Nutt. Orn. Club*, VII (Apr.), 112-13. Review.

"Prof. Macoun's Report of Exploration." *Bull. Nutt. Orn. Club*, VII (Apr.), 113. Review.

"Bailey's Index to Forest and Stream." *Bull. Nutt. Orn. Club*, VII (July), 175-76. Review.

"Stejneger's Nomenclatural Innovations." *Bull. Nutt. Orn. Club*, VII (July), 178-79. Review.

"A 'Tidal Wave' of Birds in Washington." *Bull. Nutt. Orn. Club*, VII (July), 185-86.

"The Evening Grosbeak in New York." *Bull. Nutt. Orn. Club*, VII (Oct.), 250.

"The New Check List." *Forest and Stream*, Mar. 30, 166-67.

"The Pine Grosbeak." *Forest and Stream*, Nov. 2, 264-65.

[Introductory note to] "The Boston Anti-Sparrow Crusade," by Wilson Flagg. *Forest and Stream*, Nov. 30, 345.

"The Pine Siskin." *Forest and Stream*, Dec. 7, 364.

[Anon.] "The Twit-Twats." *Nation*, XXXIV (Jan. 19), 62. Review (McAtee, 5).

[Anon.] "Bird-Nesting." *Nation*, XXXIV (May 4), 387-88. Review (McAtee, 5).

[Anon.] "Natural History and Sport in Moray." *Nation*, XXXV (Dec. 14), 515-16. Review (McAtee, 5).

1883

The Harmony of Scientific Knowledge and Religious Faith. Washington, D.C.: Judd & Detweiler.

[Ed.] *New England Bird Life, Being a Manual of New England Ornithology, Revised and Edited from the Manuscript of Winfrid A. Stearns, Member of the Nuttall Ornithological Club etc. Part II.—Non-Oscine Passeres, Birds of Prey, Game and Water Birds.* Boston: Lee and Shepard.

"Compliments of the Season." *Bull. Nutt. Orn. Club*, VIII (Jan.), 1-6.

"Canadian Birds." *Bull. Nutt. Orn. Club*, VIII (Jan.), 55. Review.

"Note on 'Passerculus caboti.'" *Bull. Nutt. Orn. Club*, VIII (Jan.), 58.

"The Burrowing Owl in Florida." *Bull. Nutt. Orn. Club*, VIII (Jan.), 61.

"Note on the Mississippi Kite." *Bull. Nutt. Orn. Club*, VIII (Jan.), 61.

"Occurrence of the Swallow-tailed Kite in Massachusetts." *Bull. Nutt. Orn. Club*, VIII (Jan.), 61.

"Caspian Tern in Ohio." *Bull. Nutt. Orn. Club*, VIII (Jan.), 62-63.

"Polygamy among Oscines." *Bull. Nutt. Orn. Club*, VIII (Jan.), 63.

"Birds and Insects." *Bull. Nutt. Orn. Club*, VIII (Apr.), 105-7. Review.

"Economic Relations of Birds Again." *Bull. Nutt. Orn. Club*, VIII (Apr.), 107-10. Review.

"Report on the Birds of Ohio." *Bull. Nutt. Orn. Club*, VIII (Apr.), 110-12. Review.

"Illustrations of the Nests and Eggs of the Birds of Ohio." *Bull. Nutt. Orn. Club*, VIII (Apr.), 112. Review.

"Brown's Birds of Portland." *Bull. Nutt. Orn. Club*, VIII (Apr.), 112-13. Review.

"The Barn Owl in Canada West." *Bull. Nutt. Orn. Club*, VIII (Apr.), 122.

"Wintering of Sora Rail at the North." *Bull. Nutt. Orn. Club*, VIII (Apr.), 124.

"Nests and Eggs of the Birds of Ohio." *Bull. Nutt. Orn. Club*, VIII (July), 166. Review.

"Contributions to the Anatomy of Birds." *Bull. Nutt. Orn. Club*, VIII (July), 166-68. Review.

"Birds of Pennsylvania." *Bull. Nutt. Orn. Club*, VIII (July), 171. Review.

"Susceptibility of a Bird to Color." *Bull. Nutt. Orn. Club*, VIII (July), 181.

"Breeding of the Mallard in New England." *Bull. Nutt. Orn. Club*, VIII (July), 186.

"Nest and Eggs of *Myiadestes townsendi.*" *Bull. Nutt. Orn. Club*, VIII (Oct.), 239.

"Nest and Eggs of *Parus montanus.*" *Bull. Nutt. Orn. Club*, VIII (Oct.), 240.

[With D. Webster Prentiss.] "Avifauna Columbiana: Being a List of Birds Ascertained to Inhabit the District of Columbia, with the Times of Arrival and Departure of Such as Are Non-Residents, and Brief Notices of Habits, etc." 2d ed. *Bull. U.S. Nat. Mus.*, no. 26, 1-133.

"The Purple Finch and His Cousins. I. *Carpodacus purpureus.*" *Forest and Stream*, Dec. 13, 385-86.

"The Purple Finch and His Cousins. II. *Carpodacus cassini.*" *Forest and Stream*, Dec. 27, 435.

[Anon.] "Knocking round the Rockies." *Nation*, XXXVI (Jan. 4), 22. Review (McAtee, 5).

[Anon.] "Frontier Army Sketches." *Nation*, XXXVI (Jan. 11), 43. Review (McAtee, 5).

[Anon. Notice of the formation of the American Ornithologists' Union and its first meeting.] *Nation*, XXXVII (Oct. 11), 311 (McAtee, 5).

"Concerning Public Documents." *Nation*, XXXVII (Oct. 18), 332-33.

[Anon.] "Animal Life." *Nation*, XXXVII (Oct. 25), 359-60. Review (McAtee, 5).

"The Sparrow Nuisance." *New York Times*, July 8, 6.

"A Hearing of Birds' Ears." *Science*, II (Sept. 28), 422-24; (Oct. 26), 552-54; (Nov. 2), 586-89.

"On the Application of Trinomial Nomenclature to Zoology." *Zoologist*, 3d ser., VIII (July), 241-47.

1884

Biogen: A Speculation on the Origin and Nature of Life. 2d ed. Biogen Series, no. 1. Boston: Estes and Lauriat.

Biogen: A Speculation on the Origin and Nature of Life. 3d ed. Boston: Estes and Lauriat.

Key to North American Birds. Containing a Concise Account of Every Species of Living and Fossil Bird at Present Known from the Continent North of the Mexican and United States Boundary, Inclusive of Greenland. Second Edition, Revised to Date and Entirely Rewritten: with Which are Incorporated General Ornithology: An Outline of the Structure and Classification of Birds; and Field Ornithology: A Manual of Collecting, Preparing, and Preserving Birds. Boston: Estes and Lauriat.

"Rodentia." In *The Standard Natural History*, ed. John Sterling Kingsley, V, 68-133. Boston: S. E. Cassino.

"Renumeration of the Spinal Nerves and Reconstruction of the Plexuses in the Human Subject." *Amer. Naturalist*, XVIII (Apr.), 379-85.

"*Thomasomys*, a New Subgeneric Type of *Hesperomys*." *Amer. Naturalist*, XVIII (Dec.), 1275.

"Ornithophilologicalities." *Auk*, I (Jan.), 49-58; (Apr.), 140-44.

"Nelson's Birds of Bering Sea and the Arctic Ocean." *Auk*, I (Jan.), 76-81. Review.

"Trinomials Are Necessary." *Auk*, I (Apr.), 197-98.

"Egg of the Cowbird in Nest of the Carolina Dove." *Auk*, I (July), 293.

"On Some New Terms Recommended for Use in Zoological Nomenclature." *Auk*, I (Oct.), 320-22.

"Strickland as an Advocate of 'Linnaeus at '58.'" *Auk*, I (Oct.), 400.

"The Purple Finch and His Cousins. III. *Carpodacus frontalis*." *Forest and Stream*, Jan. 3, 451.

"Application of Trinomial Nomenclature to Zoology." *Forest and Stream*, May 1, 264.

"Swainson's Warbler Rediscovered (*Helmintherus swainsoni*)." *Forest and Stream*, Nov. 6, 285-86.

[Anon. Notice of the second annual meeting of the American Ornithologists' Union.] *Nation*, XXXIX (Oct. 16), 334 (McAtee, 5).

[Anon.] "Country Cousins." *Nation*, XXXIX (Nov. 13), 425-26. Review (McAtee, 5).

"Can Ghosts Be Investigated?" *Nation*, XXXIX (Dec. 25), 543.

"The American Ornithologists' Union." *Science Record*, II, 13-14.

1885

Biogen: A Speculation on the Origin and Nature of Life. 4th ed. Boston: Estes and Lauriat.

The Daemon of Darwin. Biogen Series, no. 2. Boston: Estes and Lauriat.

[Ed.] *A Buddhist Catechism, according to the Canon of the Southern Church,* by Henry S. Olcott. Biogen Series, no. 3. Boston: Estes and Lauriat.

"The Meaning of the Human Body." In *Addresses Delivered at the Sixty-third Annual Commencement of the National Medical College,* 3-12. Washington, D.C.: W. H. Moore.

"On the Present Status of *Passer domesticus* in America, with Special Reference to the Western States and Territories." In *The House Sparrow: by an Ornithologist, J. H. Gurney, Junr.; by a Friend of the Farmers, Colonel C. Russell; and The English Sparrow in America, by Dr. Elliott Coues,* 50-59. London: William Wesley and Son.

"Shufeldt on the Avian Patella." *Auk*, II (Jan.), 96. Review.

"Nests and Eggs of the Birds of Ohio." *Auk*, II (July), 289. Review.

"Probable Occurrence of *Diomedea exulans* in Florida." *Auk*, II (Oct.), 387.

[Anon.] "The Water Birds of North America." *Nation*, XL (Jan. 1), 17. Review (McAtee, 5).

"An Explanation of Telepathy." *Nation*, XL (Jan. 15), 54.

[Anon.] "Our Birds in Their Haunts." *Nation*, XLI (July 2), 19. Review (McAtee, 5).

[Pseud., "F. T. S."] "What Is Theosophy?" *Nation*, XLI (Aug. 6), 113.

1886

[Ed.] *Can Matter Think? A Problem in Psychics,* by F. T. S. [Fellow of the Theosophical Society]. Biogen Series, no. 4. Boston: Estes and Lauriat.

Kuthumi: The True and Complete Oeconomy of Life, Based on the System of Theosophical Ethics. Biogen Series, no. 5. Boston: Estes and Lauriat.

"Nests and Eggs of the Birds of Ohio." *Auk*, III (July), 400.

"The Collapse of the Theosophists." *Science*, VII (Jan. 24), 102.

"Is the Dodo an Extinct Bird?" *Science*, VII (Feb. 19), 168.

"Feline Telepathy." *Science*, VIII (Aug. 6), 123-24.

1887

Key to North American Birds. Containing a Concise Account of Every Species of Living and Fossil Bird at Present Known from the Continent North of the Mexican and United States Boundary, Inclusive of Greenland and Lower California, with Which are Incorporated General Ornithology: An Outline of the Structure and Classification of Birds; and Field Ornithology, a Manual of Collecting, Preparing, and

Preserving Birds. The Third Edition, Exhibiting the New Nomenclature of the American Ornithologists' Union, and Including Descriptions of Additional Species, etc. Boston: Estes and Lauriat.

"*A Woman in the Case.*" An Address, Delivered at the Annual Commencement of the National Medical College, in the Congregational Church of Washington, March 16, *1887.* Washington, D.C.: Brentano's.

[Ed.] *New England Bird Life, Being a Manual of New England Ornithology, Revised and Edited from the Manuscript of Winfrid A. Stearns, Member of the Nuttall Ornithological Club etc.* 2 vols. 2d ed. Boston: Lee and Shepard.

"Conclusion of the Great Work on the Nests and Eggs of the Birds of Ohio." *Auk*, IV (Apr.), 150-52. Review.

"The New Canadian Ornithology." *Auk*, IV (July), 245-46. Review.

"Ridgway Ornithological Club." *Auk*, IV (July), 251. Review.

[With D. K. Shute.] "Neuro-Myology: Classification of the Muscles of the Human Body with Reference to Their Innervation, and New Nomenclature of the Muscles." *Medical Record*, XXXII (July 23), 93-98; (July 30), 121-26.

[Anon.] "A Nomenclature of Colors for Naturalists." *Nation*, XLIV (Mar. 10), 216. Review (McAtee, 5).

"The Mechanism of the Flight of Birds." *Science*, X (Dec. 30), 321-22.

1888

[Contributions to] *The Medical and Surgical History of the War of the Rebellion*, pt. III, vol. I, *Medical History*, by Charles Smart, 410, 920. Washington, D.C.: Government Printing Office.

[Contributions to] *Supplement to Encyclopaedia Britannica. (Ninth Edition.) A Dictionary of Arts, Sciences, and General Literature*, vol. I. New York: Henry G. Allen.

"Abiogenesis," 17.

"Accentor," 25.

"Accipitres," 26-27.

"Acromyodi," 34.

"Aetiology," 57-58.

"Aetomorphae," 58.

"Agelaeinae," 72.

"Agouti," 73-74.

"Alaudidae," 180.

"Albatross," 184.

"Albino," 185.

"Alcedinidae," 186.

"Alcidae," 186-88.

"Alectorides," 193.

"Alecyoromorphae," 193.

"Alectoropodes," 193-94.

"Allantois," 204-5.

"Aluconidae," 216.

"Amnion," 239-40.
"Amoeba," 240-41.
"Ampelidae," 241-42.
"Amphibia," 242.
"Amphimorphae," 242.
"Anatidae," 247.
"Anatinae," 247-48.
"Anhinga," 260.
"Ani," 260.
"Anseres," 265.
"Anserinae," 265.
"Antelope, American, or Prong-horn," 266-72.
"Anthinae," 272.
"Aphrizinae," 295.
"Aramidae," 312.
"Archaeopteryx," 324.
"Ardeidae," 350.
"Armadillo," 364.
"Artiodactyles," 390.
"Arvicolinae," 391-93.
"Assapan," 402.
"Auk," 419.
"Aurochs," 421.
"Avocet," 434.
"Aye-Aye," 435.
"Badger, American," 450-51.
"Barnacle," 512.
"Beaver," 543-44.
"Bill or Beak of Birds," 600-601.
"Birds (North American)," 604-13.
"Biscacha, Biscacho, or Viscacha," 614.
"Bison, American, living and extinct," 622-24.
"Bluebird," 647.
"Bobolink," 650.
"Bob-white," 650-51.
"Bovidae," 678.

[With "Old Dominion" and "Picus."] "The English Sparrow." *Amer. Field*, June 9.

"Albatrosses on Puget Sound." *Amer. Field*, June 9.

"New Forms of North American *Chordiles*." *Auk*, V (Jan.), 37.

"Shufeldt's Contributions to Avisection." *Auk*, V (Jan.), 104-5. Review.

"A New *Ornithichnite*." *Auk*, V (Jan.), 105. Review.

"Chamberlain's Canadian Birds." *Auk*, V (Apr.), 189. Review.

"Note on *Rostratulinae*." *Auk*, V (Apr.), 204.

"*Corydomorphae*." *Auk*, V (Apr.), 207.

"Vernacular Ornithology." *Auk*, (Oct.), 414-18. Review.

"Allen on the Emargination of the Primaries." *Auk*, V (Oct.), 418-21. Review.

"Notes on the Nomenclature of the Muscles of Volation in Birds' Wings." *Auk*, V (Oct.), 435-37.

"The Study of Backboned Animals." *Dial*, IX (Dec.), 201-3. Review.

[Anon.] "A Manual of North American Birds." *Nation*, XLVI (Apr. 5), 287-88. Review (McAtee, 6).

[Anon.] "Names and Portraits of Birds Which Interest Gunners." *Nation*, XLVII (Aug. 2), 97. Review (McAtee, 6).

[Anon.] "Birds in Nature." *Nation*, XLVII (Nov. 1), 362-63. Review (McAtee, 6).

[Anon.] "Song Birds and Seasons." *Nation*, XLVII (Nov. 1), 362-63. Review (McAtee, 6).

[Anon.] "Tales of Birds." *Nation*, XLVII (Nov. 22), 423. Review (McAtee, 6).

1889

The Signs of the Times: From the Standpoint of a Scientist. An Address Delivered at the First Methodist Church [Chicago], *April 26, 1888, under the Auspices of the Western Society for Psychical Research.* Chicago: Religio-Philosophical Publishing House.

[Contributions to] *Supplement to Encyclopaedia Britannica (Ninth Edition.) A Dictionary of Arts, Sciences, and General Literature*, vol. II. New York: Henry G. Allen.

"Bullfinch," 26.

"Bunting," 32.

"Burion," 34.

"Buzzard," 45.

"Cañon Wren," 70-71.

"Canvas-back," 73-74.

"Capybara," 80.

"Caracara," 80-81.

"Cardinal, or Cardinal Grosbeak," 81.

"Carinatae," 85.

"Castoridae," 109-10.

"Cat-bird," 111.

"Cathartidae," 112-13.

"Cavy," 122.

"Certhidae," 137-38.

"Chat," 171-72.

"Chickadee," 198.

"Chinchilla," 213.

"Chipmunk," 213-14.

"Chuck-wills-widow," 231.

"Clavicle," 269.

"Coerebidae," 439.

"Coot," 579-80.

"Coracoid," 587.

"Cormorant," 592-93.

"Corvidae," 601.

"Cotton Rat," 615-16.
"Courlan," 618.
"Cow-bird," 629-30.
"Coypu, Couia, or Racoonda," 633.
"Crake," 634.
"Crane," 634-35.
"Creeper," 636.
"Cross-bill," 661-62.
"Crow," 662-63.
"Cuckoo," 673.
"Curlew," 679-80.

[Contributions to] *Supplement to Encyclopaedia Britannica. (Ninth Edition.) A Dictionary of Arts, Sciences, and General Literature*, vol. IV. New York: Henry G. Allen.

"Night-hawk," 536.
"Night-heron," 536.
"Partridge," 639-40.

"A New Generic Name for the Elf Owl." *Auk*, VI (Jan.), 71.

[Anon.] "Gould's Ornithological Works." *Nation*, XLIX (July 25), 77-78. Review (McAtee, 6).

1889-93

[An estimated 40,000 entries on natural history for] *The Century Dictionary, an Encyclopaedic Lexicon of the English Language*, 6 vols. New York: Century Co.

1890

Handbook of Field and General Ornithology, a Manual of the Structure and Classification of Birds, with Instructions for Collecting and Preserving Specimens. London: Macmillan.

Key to North American Birds. Containing a Concise Account of Every Species of Living and Fossil Bird at Present Known from the Continent North of the Mexican and United States Boundary, Inclusive of Greenland and Lower California, with Which are Incorporated General Ornithology: An Outline of the Structure and Classification of Birds; and Field Ornithology, a Manual of Collecting, Preparing, and Preserving Birds. The Fourth Edition, Exhibiting the New Nomenclature of the American Ornithologists' Union, and Including Descriptions of Additional Species, etc. Boston: Estes and Lauriat.

"A Woman in the Case." An Address, Delivered at the Annual Commencement of the National Medical College, in the Congregational Church of Washington, March 16, 1887. 2d ed. Biogen Series, no. 6. Boston: Occult Publishing Co.

"Nehrling's Bird Biographies." *Auk*, VII (Jan.), 78-79. Review.

"Blavatsky Unveiled!" *New York Sun*, July 20.

1891

"Scenopoeetes dentirostris." Auk, VIII (Jan.), 115.

1892

"Major Bourke's Book 'On the Border with Crook.'" *Arizona Journal-Miner*, Feb. 10. Review.

"Wintering of the Canvasback in Arizona." *Auk*, IX (Apr.), 198.

"Nesting of the Golden Eagle in Arizona." *Auk*, IX (Apr.), 201.

"Original Description of Lewis's Woodpecker." *Auk*, IX (Oct.), 394.

"Theosophy: What It Is Not." *Californian*, I (Feb.), 133-37.

"Can Ghosts Be Photographed?" *Californian*, II (Sept.), 467-83.

"Psychical Science at the World's Fair in 1893." *Nation*, LIV (Apr. 14), 282.

[Anon.] "Little Brothers of the Air." *Nation*, LIV (May 26), 403-4. Review (McAtee, 6).

[Anon.] "Wood Notes Wild." *Nation*, LIV (May 26), 403-4. Review (McAtee, 6).

[Anon.] "A Popular Handbook of the Ornithology of the United States and Canada." *Nation*, LIV (June 16), 453. Review (McAtee, 6).

"William Clark (not Clarke)." *Nation*, LV (Dec. 8), 431.

"Sgt. Patrick Gass." *St. Joseph* (Mo.) *News*, Nov. 29.

"On Biological Nomenclature." *Science*, XX (Oct. 14), 219-20.

1893

[Ed.] *History of the Expedition under the Command of Lewis and Clark, to the Sources of the Missouri River, Thence across the Rocky Mountains and down the Columbia River to the Pacific Ocean, Performed during the Years 1804-5-6, by Order of the Government of the United States.* 4 vols. New York: Francis P. Harper.

"'Snibar.'" *Nation*, LVI (Jan. 19), 50.

"Description of the Original Manuscript Journals and Field Notebooks of Lewis and Clark, on Which Was Based Biddle's History of the Expedition of 1804-6, and Which Are Now in the Possession of the American Philosophical Society in Philadelphia." *Procs. Amer. Phil. Soc.*, XXXI, 17-33.

1894

"Nehrling's Birds." *Auk*, XI (Apr.), 166-67. Review.

[Remarks on wild rice.] In "The Wild Rice of Minnesota," by Frederick V. Coville. *Botanical Gazette*, XIX (Dec.), 504-6.

"Two Rare Editions of Gass." *Nation*, LVIII (Jan. 11), 29.

[Anon. Notice of *A Bird-Lover in the West*, by Olive Thorne Miller.] *Nation*, LVIII (May 10), 347 (McAtee, 6).

1895

[Ed.] *The Expeditions of Zebulon Montgomery Pike, to Headwaters of the Mississippi River, through Louisiana Territory, and in New Spain, during the Years 1805-6-7.* 3 vols. New York: Francis P. Harper.

[American editor's preface to] *Rural Bird Life of England, Being Essays on Ornithology, with Instructions for Preserving Objects relating to That Science*, by Charles Dixon, iii-vi. [2d ed.] Chicago and New York: Werner Co.

"Introduction." In *Doty Dontcare: A Story of the Garden of the Antilles*, by Mary Farrington Foster, v-x. Boston: Estes and Lauriat.

"Letters of William Clark and Nathaniel Pryor." *Annals of Iowa*, 3d ser., I (Jan.), 613-20.

"Historico-Geographical Notes on the Mississippi River, from Cass Lake to Lake Itasca." *Annals of Iowa*, 3d ser., II (Apr.), 20-31.

"*Diomedea exulans* on the Columbia in 1813." *Auk*, XII (Apr.), 178-79.

"Gätke's Heligoland." *Auk*, XII (Oct.), 322-46. Review.

"The Telekinetic Theory of Levitation." *Metaphysical Magazine*, I (Jan.), 1-11.

[Anon. Announcement of Coues' edition of the Pike journals.] *Nation*, LX (May 16), 382 (McAtee, 6).

"A Monument to Sergeant Floyd." *Nation*, LX (May 30), 421.

[Anon.] "Birdcraft." *Nation*, LX (May 30), 428-29. Review (McAtee, 7).

[Anon.] "Pocket Guide to the Common Land-Birds of New England." *Nation*, LX (May 30), 428-29. Review (McAtee, 7).

[Anon.] "Summer Studies of Birds and Books." *Nation*, LX (May 30), 428-29. Review (McAtee, 7).

[Anon.] "Handbook of Birds of Eastern North America." *Nation*, LX (June 27), 504-5. Review (McAtee, 7).

[Anon.] "Bird-Lore at Heligoland." *Nation*, LXI (Aug. 8), 99-100. Review (McAtee, 7).

[Anon.] "British Birds." *Nation*, LXI (Nov. 21), 369-70. Review (McAtee, 7).

[Anon.] "Wild England of To-day and the Wild Life in It." *Nation*, LXI (Nov. 21), 369-70. Review (McAtee, 7).

[Anon.] "North American Shore Birds." *Nation*, LXI (Dec. 12), 435. Review (McAtee, 7).

"Letter from Sylvan Lake, S. Dak." *Nidologist*, III (Oct.), 14-15.

"Prof. Coues' Letter [on a monument to Sergeant Charles Floyd]." *Sioux City* (Iowa) *Journal*, May 26.

"In Memory of Sergt. Floyd." *Washington Post*, June 13.

1896

"The Presidential Address." In *Papers Presented to the World's Congress on Ornithology*, ed. E. Irene Rood, "under the direction of Dr. Elliott Coues," 15-30. Chicago: Charles H. Sergel.

"Elliot's *Limicolae*." *Auk*, XIII (Jan.), 64-67. Review.

"An Early Description of *Phalacrocorax dilophus*." *Auk*, XIII (Jan.), 78.

"Name of the Large-billed Puffin." *Auk*, XIII (July), 255.

"Merrem's Work." *Auk*, XIII (July), 265-66.

"Mandt's Inaugural Dissertation." *Auk*, XIII (July), 266.

"*Thriothorus* or *Thryothorus?*" *Auk*, XIII (Oct.), 344.

[Anon.] "Shaler's Domesticated Animals." *Nation*, LXII (Jan. 9), 39-40. Review (McAtee, 7).

[Anon.] "English's Conquest of the Northwest." *Nation*, LXII (Jan. 30), 102-4. Review (McAtee, 7).

"'Carry' as a Noun." *Nation*, LXII (Mar. 5), 197.

[Anon.] "The Yellowstone Park." *Nation*, LXII (Mar. 12), 219-20. Review (McAtee, 7).

[Anon.] "The Structure and Life of Birds." *Nation*, LXII (Apr. 23), 332. Review (McAtee, 7).

[Anon.]"Marcou's Agassiz." *Nation*, LXII (May 7), 362-64. Review (McAtee, 7).

[Anon.] "Hunting and Fishing in Florida." *Nation*, LXII (May 21), 404-5. Review (McAtee, 7).

"John Sparks, of Pike's Expedition." *Nation*, LXIII (July 2), 9-10.

[Anon.] "A Fauna of the Moray Basin." *Nation*, LXIII (July 2), 16. Review (McAtee, 7).

[Anon.] "My Literary Zoo." *Nation*, LXIII (July 23), 72-73. Review (McAtee, 7).

[Anon.] "Four-handed Folk." *Nation*, LXIII (July 23), 72-73. Review (McAtee, 8).

[Anon.] "The Evolution of Bird Song." *Nation*, LXIII (July 23), 72-73. Review (McAtee, 8).

[Anon.] "Artistic and Scientific Taxidermy and Modelling." *Nation*, LXIII (July 23), 72-73. Review (McAtee, 8).

[Anon.] "On Snow-shoes to the Barren Grounds." *Nation*, LXIII (Aug. 6), 110-11. Review (McAtee, 8).

[Anon. Notice of *Life Histories of North American Birds*, by Charles Bendire.] *Nation*, LXIII (Oct. 22), 312 (McAtee, 8).

[Anon.] "Pioneers of Science in America." *Nation*, LXIII (Oct. 22), 317. Review (McAtee, 8).

[Anon.] "Through the Subarctic Forest." *Nation*, LXIII (Nov. 5), 352-53. Review (McAtee, 8).

"A-birding on a Bronco." *Nation*, LXIII (Nov. 12), 374.

"Three Subcutaneous Glandular Areas of *Blarina brevicauda*." *Science*, new ser., II (May 22), 779-80.

"Miscellaneous Mementoes of the Coues' Family, 1784-1896." Unpublished document in the possession of William P. Coues, Boston, Mass.

"Book of Dates in the Life of Elliott Coues and of the Coues family, together with many other dates during the century 1800-1900." Unpublished manuscript in the possession of William P. Coues, Boston, Mass.

1897

[With Mabel Osgood Wright.] *Citizen Bird: Scenes from Bird-Life in Plain English for Beginners.* New York: Macmillan.

In Memoriam. Sergeant Charles Floyd: Report of the Floyd Memorial Association, Prepared on Behalf of the Committee on Publications by Elliott Coues. Sioux City, Iowa: Press of Perkins Bros.

[Ed.] *New Light on the Early History of the Greater Northwest: The Manuscript Journals of Alexander Henry, Fur Trader of the Northwest Company, and of David Thompson, Official Geographer and Explorer of the Same Company, 1799-1814. Exploration and Adventure among the Indians on the Red, Saskatchewan, Missouri, and Columbia Rivers.* 2 vols. New York: Francis P. Harper.

[Notes to] *Audubon and His Journals*, ed. Maria R. Audubon. 2 vols. New York: Charles Scribner's Sons.

"*Zamelodia* against *Habia*." *Auk*, XIV (Jan.), 39-42.

"*Asarcia spinosa*." *Auk*, XIV (Jan.), 88.

"The *Cuculidae* of the A.O.U. List." *Auk*, XIV (Jan.), 90-91.

"Authority for the Name *Myiarchus mexicanus*." *Auk*, XIV (Jan.), 92.

"*Ammodramus (Passerculus) sanctorum*." *Auk*, XIV (Jan.), 92-93.

"Rectifications of Synonymy in the Genus *Junco*." *Auk*, XIV (Jan.), 94-95.

"Characters of *Dendroica caerulescens cairnsi*." *Auk*, XIV (Jan.), 96-97.

"Note on the Genus *Lucar* of Bartram." *Auk*, XIV (Jan.), 97.

"*Uria lomvia* in South Carolina." *Auk*, XIV (Apr.), 203.

"Type Locality of *Fuligula collaris*." *Auk*, XIV (Apr.), 206-7.

"*Dafilula*, a New Subgenus." *Auk*, XIV (Apr.), 207.

"*Branta bernicula glaucogastra*." *Auk*, XIV (Apr.), 207-8.

"A North American Snipe New to the A.O.U. List." *Auk*, XIV (Apr.), 209.

"Status of *Helodromas ochropus* in the A.O.U. List." *Auk*, XIV (Apr.), 210-11.

"Status of the Redshank as a North American Bird." *Auk*, XIV (Apr.), 211-12.

"Validity of the Genus *Lophortyx*." *Auk*, XIV (Apr.), 214-15.

"Notes on the Mexican Ground Dove." *Auk*, XIV (Apr.), 215.

"Note on *Elanus glaucus*." *Auk*, XIV (Apr.), 216.

"How the Chimney Swift Secures Twigs for Its Nest." *Auk*, XIV (Apr.), 217-18.

"Probable First Description of *Empidonax flaviventris*." *Auk*, XIV (Apr.), 218.

"How about the Genus *Pipilo* Now?" *Auk*, XIV (Apr.), 221.

"Untenability of the Genus *Sylvania* Nutt." *Auk*, XIV (Apr.), 223-24.

"The Most General Fault of the A.O.U. Check-List." *Auk*, XIV (Apr.), 229-31.

"Newton's Dictionary of Birds: Part IV." *Auk*, XIV (Apr.), 234-44. Review.

"The Turkey Question." *Auk*, XIV (July), 272-75.

"Note on *Pagophila alba*." *Auk*, XIV (July), 313.

"*Onychoprion*, not *Haliplana*." *Auk*, XIV (July), 314.

"Remarks on Certain *Procellariidae*." *Auk*, XIV (July), 314-15.

"Rectrices of Cormorants." *Auk*, XIV (July), 316.

"Concordance of *Merganser americanus*." *Auk*, XIV (July), 316.

"Bibliographical Note." *Auk*, XIV (July), 327-29.

"Nehrling's Birds: Vol. II." *Auk*, XIV (July), 335-36. Review.

"Early Notice of *Gavia adamsi*." *Auk*, XIV (Oct.), 402.

[Anon.] "Bird Land Echoes." *Nation*, LXIV (Jan. 7), 18. Review (McAtee, 8).

[Anon.] "Letters to Young Shooters." *Nation*, LXIV (Feb. 11), 113. Review (McAtee, 8).

[Anon.] "Fifty Years' Reminiscences of India." *Nation*, LXIV (Mar. 25), 231. Review (McAtee, 8).

[Anon.] "Upon the Tree-Tops." *Nation*, LXIV (Apr. 8), 271. Review (McAtee, 8).

[Anon.] "The Story of the Birds." *Nation*, LXIV (Apr. 8), 271. Review (McAtee, 8).

[Anon. Notice of *The Ghost Dance Religion*, by James Mooney.] *Nation*, LXV (July 1), 13 (McAtee, 8).

[Anon.] "Bird-Life." *Nation*, LXV (July 15), 52-53. Review (McAtee, 8).

[Anon.] "Wild Norway." *Nation*, LXV (July 15), 52-53. Review (McAtee, 8).

[Anon. Notice of *Wild Neighbors*, by Ernest Ingersoll.] *Nation*, LXV (Nov. 4), 355-56 (McAtee, 8).

[Anon.] "Natural History." *Nation*, LXV (Nov. 25), 422-23. Review (McAtee, 8).

[Anon.] "Song Birds and Water Fowl." *Nation*, LXV (Dec. 2), 440-41. Review (McAtee, 8).

[Anon.] "Bird Neighbors." *Nation*, LXV (Dec. 2), 440-41. Review (McAtee, 8).

[Anon.] "How to Know the Shore Birds." *Nation*, LXV (Dec. 2), 440-41. Review (McAtee, 9).

[Anon.] "How to Know the Ducks, Geese, and Swans." *Nation*, LXV (Dec. 2), 440-41. Review (McAtee, 9).

[Anon.] "The Gallinaceous Game Birds of North America." *Nation*, LXV (Dec. 2), 440-41. Review (McAtee, 9).

[Anon.] "The Old Santa Fe Trail." *Nation*, LXV (Dec. 9), 463. Review (McAtee, 9).

[Anon.] "Irving's Astoria." *Nation*, LXV (Dec. 29), 499-501. Review (McAtee, 9).

[Letter to the editor "regarding the exact manner in which the Chimney Swift breaks off the bits of twigs which it uses in the construction of its nest."] *Nidologist*, IV (Jan.), 53.

"Louis Agassiz Fuertes, the Painter of Birds." *Osprey*, I (Mar.), 91.

"Dr. Coues' Column." *Osprey*, I (Apr.), 113.

"Important—If True." *Osprey*, I (Apr.), 114.

"Dr. Coues' Column." *Osprey*, I (May), 124.

"Dr. Coues' Column." *Osprey*, I (June), 134.

"Dr. Coues' Column." *Osprey*, I (July-Aug.), 150.

"Dr. Coues' Column." *Osprey*, II (Sept.), 11.

"The Documents in the Bendire Business." *Osprey*, II (Oct.), 22-23.

[Review of *How to Know the Shore Birds (Limicolae) of North America*, by Charles B. Cory.] *Osprey*, II (Nov.), 39.

"Dr. Coues' Column." *Osprey*, II (Nov.), 39-40.

[Response to questions regarding *Citizen Bird*.] *Osprey*, II (Nov.), 41.

"Dr. Coues' Column." *Osprey*, II (Dec.), 54.

[Review of *Dictionary of Birds*, by Alfred Newton.] *Science*, new ser., V (Apr. 2), 553-56.

[With J. A. Allen.] "The Merton Rules." *Science*, new ser., VI (July 2), 9-19.

"Adventures of Government Explorers. Chapters from the Experience of Scientific Men in Our Government Service as Told by Themselves, Especially for 'The Voice.' III.—An Adventure with Apaches—'Covering' the Mississippi River—The Northern Boundary Survey." *Voice* (New York), Dec. 9.

1898

[Ed.] *Forty Years a Fur Trader on the Upper Missouri: The Personal Narrative of Charles Larpenteur, 1833-1872*. 2 vols. New York: Francis P. Harper.

[Ed.] *The Journal of Jacob Fowler: Narrating an Adventure from Arkansas through the Indian Territory, Oklahoma, Kansas, Colorado, and New Mexico, to the Sources of Rio Grande del Norte, 1821-22*. New York: Francis P. Harper.

"William Swainson to John James Audubon. (A hitherto unpublished letter.)" *Auk*, XV (Jan.), 11-13.

"Elliot's Shore Birds, 2d Ed." *Auk*, XV (Jan.), 63. Review.

"Elliot's Gallinaceous Game Birds of North America." *Auk*, XV (Jan.), 63-65. Review.

"Notes on Generic Names of Certain Swallows." *Auk*, XV (July), 271-72.

"My Only Indian Massacre." *Forest and Stream*, June 25, 1898, 505.

[Anon. Notice of *Afloat on the Ohio*, by Reuben Gold Thwaites.] *Nation*, LXVI (Feb. 10), 108 (McAtee, 9).

[Anon.] "Two Bird Books." *Nation*, LXVI (June 23), 483-84. Review (McAtee, 9).

[Anon.] "Across the Sub-Arctics of Canada." *Nation*, LXVI (June 30), 504-5. Review (McAtee, 9).

[Anon.] "The Smithsonian Institution." *Nation*, LXVII (July 7), 16-17. Review (McAtee, 9).

[Anon.] "Filson Club Publications, No. 13." *Nation*, LXVII (July 21), 59. Review (McAtee, 9).

[Anon.] "The Art of Taxidermy." *Nation*, LXVII (Nov. 10), 357-58. Review (McAtee, 9).

[Coues?] "Editorial Eyrie." *Osprey*, III (Oct.), 26.

[Review of *Wild Animals I Have Known*, by Ernest Seton Thompson.] *Osprey*, III (Oct.), 32.

[Review of *Birds of Washington and Vicinity*, by Mrs. L. W. Maynard.] *Osprey*, III (Oct.), 32.

[Coues?] "Editorial Eyrie." *Osprey*, III (Nov.), 44.

[Review of "A Revision of the Wrens of the Genus *Thryomanes* Sclater," by Harry C. Oberholser.] *Osprey*, III (Nov.), 47.

[Coues?] "Editorial Eyrie" ["Parable of the Clever Kid and His Aged Sire"]. *Osprey*, III (Dec.), 58.

[Review of *Catalogue of Birds in the British Museum*, vol. XXVI, by R. Bowdler Sharpe.] *Osprey*, III (Dec.), 63.

"Notes on Mr. Thomas Meehan's Paper on the Plants of Lewis and Clark's Expedition across the Continent, 1804-06." *Procs. Acad. Nat. Scis. Phila.*, L (Apr.-Sept.), 291-315.

1899

"Note on *Meleagris gallopavo fera*." *Auk*, XVI (Jan.), 77.

"The Finishing Stroke to Bartram." *Auk*, XVI (Jan.), 83-84.

"Very Early Record of the Cliff Swallow." *Auk*, XVI (Oct.), 359.

[Anon.] "The Wild Fowl of the United States and British Possessions." *Nation*, LXVIII (Jan. 19), 54. Review (McAtee, 9).

[Anon.] "The Great Salt Lake Trail." *Nation*, LXVIII (Jan. 26), 74. Review (McAtee, 9).

[Anon.] "The Last Link." *Nation*, LXVIII (Mar. 16), 211-12. Review (McAtee, 9).

[Anon.] "The Structure and Classification of Birds." *Nation*, LXVIII (Apr. 6), 264-65. Review (McAtee, 9).

[Anon.] "The Dawn of Reason, or Mental Traits in the Lower Animals." *Nation*, LXVIII (May 25), 403-4. Review (McAtee, 9).

[Coues?] "Editorial Eyrie." *Osprey*, III (Jan.), 74.

[Review of the Jan., 1899, issue of *The Auk*.] *Osprey*, III (Jan.), 79-80.

[Coues?] "Editorial Eyrie." *Osprey*, III (Feb.), 87.

[Review of the first issue of *Bird-Lore*.] *Osprey*, III (Feb.), 94-95.

[Coues?] "Editorial Eyrie." *Osprey*, III (Mar.), 106.

[Review of the *Bulletin of the Michigan Ornithological Club*, II, nos. 3-4 (July-Dec., 1899).] *Osprey*, III (Mar.), 111.

[Review of *In Brush, Sedge, and Stubble*, by Dwight W. Huntington.] *Osprey*, III (Mar.), 111-12.

"Charles Hallock." *Osprey*, III (Apr.), 117-18.

[Coues?] "Editorial Eyrie." *Osprey*, III (Apr.), 123-24.

"Nest and Eggs of the Alder Flycatcher." *Osprey*, III (Apr.), 126.

"The University of Nebraska." *Osprey*, III (Apr.), 126. Review.

"Bulletin of the Cooper Ornithological Club." *Osprey*, III (Apr.), 126. Review.

[Review of *Evolution of the Colors of North American Land Birds*, by Charles A. Keeler.] *Osprey*, III (Apr.), 126-28.

[Coues?] "Editorial Eyrie." *Osprey*, III (May), 136.

[Review of the Apr., 1899, issue of *The Auk*.] *Osprey*, III (May), 143-44.

"On Certain Generic and Subgeneric Names in the A.O.U. Check-List." *Osprey*, III (May), 144.

1900

[Ed. and trans.] *On the Trail of a Spanish Pioneer. The Diary and Itinerary of Francisco Garcés (Missionary Priest) in His Travels through Sonora, Arizona, and California, 1775-1776*. 2 vols. New York: Francis P. Harper.

"*Pipile vs. Pipilo*." *Auk*, XVII (Jan.), 65.

"*Strix vs. Aluco*." *Auk*, XVII (Jan.), 65-66.

"The 'Churca' (*Geococcyx californianus*)." *Auk*, XVII (Jan.), 66.

"Date of Discovery and Type Locality of the Mountain Mockingbird." *Auk*, XVII (Jan.), 68-69.

"Coues' Ideas on Ghosts." *Current Literature*, XXVII (Mar.), 246-47.

"San Gabriel in 1776." *Land of Sunshine*, XIII (June), 46-49.

1901

"Elliott Coues on Audubon." *Bird-Lore*, III (Jan.-Feb.), 9-13.

1902

"Extract from Journal of Elliott Coues' First Journey to the West." *Bird-Lore*, IV (Jan.-Feb.), 8-9.

"A Letter from Dr. Coues to Dr. [James G.] Cooper." *Condor*, IV (Sept.-Oct.),

106-7. Also found in *Biographical Sketch of the Late James G. Cooper, M.D., of Hayward, Alameda Co., California,* 22-25 (N.p., 1902).

1903

Key to North American Birds. Containing a Concise Account of Every Species of Living and Fossil Bird at Present Known from the Continent North of the Mexican and United States Boundary, Inclusive of Greenland and Lower California, with Which are Incorporated General Ornithology: An Outline of the Structure and Classification of Birds; and Field Ornithology, a Manual of Collecting, Preparing, and Preserving Birds. The Fifth Edition, (Entirely Revised) Exhibiting the Nomenclature of the American Ornithologists' Union, and Including Descriptions of Additional Species. 2 vols. Boston: Page Co.

1927

Key to North American Birds. Containing a Concise Account of Every Species of Living and Fossil Bird at Present Known from the Continent North of the Mexican and United States Boundary, Inclusive of Greenland and Lower California, with Which are Incorporated General Ornithology: An Outline of the Structure and Classification of Birds; and Field Ornithology, a Manual of Collecting, Preparing, and Preserving Birds. The Fifth Edition, (Entirely Revised) [i.e., 6th ed.] *Exhibiting the Nomenclature of the American Ornithologists' Union, and Including Descriptions of Additional Species.* 2 vols. Boston: Page Co.

INDEX

The following abbreviations are used in this index: AOU, American Ornithologists' Union; EC, Elliott Coues.